BEGINNING
SHAREPOINT® 2010 ADMINISTRATION™

W9-ACQ-989

BEGINNING

SharePoint® 2010 Administration™

MICROSOFT® SHAREPOINT® FOUNDATION 2010 AND MICROSOFT® SHAREPOINT® SERVER 2010

Göran Husman
Christian Ståhl

WILEY

Wiley Publishing, Inc.

EDGAR H. RHODE
TECHNICAL LIBRARY
91012 Station Avenue
Fort Hood, TX 76544-5068

Beginning SharePoint® 2010 Administration™: Microsoft® SharePoint® Foundation 2010 and Microsoft® SharePoint® Server 2010

Published by
Wiley Publishing, Inc.
10475 Crosspoint Boulevard
Indianapolis, IN 46256
www.wiley.com

Copyright © 2010 by Wiley Publishing, Inc., Indianapolis, Indiana

Published simultaneously in Canada

ISBN: 978-0-470-59712-5

ISBN: 9780470398661 (ebk)

ISBN: 9780470901670 (ebk)

Manufactured in the United States of America

10 9 8 7 6 5 4 3 2 1

No part of this publication may be reproduced, stored in a retrieval system or transmitted in any form or by any means, electronic, mechanical, photocopying, recording, scanning or otherwise, except as permitted under Sections 107 or 108 of the 1976 United States Copyright Act, without either the prior written permission of the Publisher, or authorization through payment of the appropriate per-copy fee to the Copyright Clearance Center, 222 Rosewood Drive, Danvers, MA 01923, (978) 750-8400, fax (978) 646-8600. Requests to the Publisher for permission should be addressed to the Permissions Department, John Wiley & Sons, Inc., 111 River Street, Hoboken, NJ 07030, (201) 748-6011, fax (201) 748-6008, or online at http://www.wiley.com/go/permissions.

Limit of Liability/Disclaimer of Warranty: The publisher and the author make no representations or warranties with respect to the accuracy or completeness of the contents of this work and specifically disclaim all warranties, including without limitation warranties of fitness for a particular purpose. No warranty may be created or extended by sales or promotional materials. The advice and strategies contained herein may not be suitable for every situation. This work is sold with the understanding that the publisher is not engaged in rendering legal, accounting, or other professional services. If professional assistance is required, the services of a competent professional person should be sought. Neither the publisher nor the author shall be liable for damages arising herefrom. The fact that an organization or website is referred to in this work as a citation and/or a potential source of further information does not mean that the author or the publisher endorses the information the organization or website may provide or recommendations it may make. Further, readers should be aware that Internet websites listed in this work may have changed or disappeared between when this work was written and when it is read.

For general information on our other products and services please contact our Customer Care Department within the United States at (877) 762-2974, outside the United States at (317) 572-3993 or fax (317) 572-4002.

Wiley also publishes its books in a variety of electronic formats. Some content that appears in print may not be available in electronic books.

Library of Congress Control Number: 2010926598

Trademarks: Wiley, the Wiley logo, Wrox, the Wrox logo, Wrox Programmer to Programmer, and related trade dress are trademarks or registered trademarks of John Wiley & Sons, Inc. and/or its affiliates, in the United States and other countries, and may not be used without written permission. Microsoft and SharePoint are registered trademarks of Microsoft Corporation in the United States and/or other countries. All other trademarks are the property of their respective owners. Wiley Publishing, Inc. is not associated with any product or vendor mentioned in this book.

I dedicate this book to my beloved father who passed away much too soon.

—GÖRAN HUSMAN

To my family.

—CHRISTIAN STÅHL

12 - 12   25 Oct 12   39 22 (B+T)

CREDITS

ACQUISITIONS EDITOR
Paul Reese

PROJECT EDITOR
Kelly Talbot

TECHNICAL EDITOR
Martin Reid

PRODUCTION EDITOR
Rebecca Anderson

COPY EDITOR
Paula Lowell

EDITORIAL DIRECTOR
Robyn B. Siesky

EDITORIAL MANAGER
Mary Beth Wakefield

PRODUCTION MANAGER
Tim Tate

VICE PRESIDENT AND EXECUTIVE GROUP PUBLISHER
Richard Swadley

VICE PRESIDENT AND EXECUTIVE PUBLISHER
Barry Pruett

ASSOCIATE PUBLISHER
Jim Minatel

PROJECT COORDINATOR, COVER
Lynsey Stanford

COVER DESIGNER
Michael E. Trent

COVER PHOTO
© George Peters/istockphoto

PROOFREADERS
Kathi Duggan
Beth Prouty, Word One New York

INDEXER
Robert Swanson

ABOUT THE AUTHORS

GÖRAN HUSMAN is a computer geek and proud of it. He has been in the computer business since 1978. He started as a software developer and switched to consulting in 1989. For more than a decade he focused on e-mail systems, especially Microsoft Mail and then Microsoft Exchange. In 2003 he switched focus again, this time to Microsoft SharePoint. Göran has also worked as a computer trainer since 1981, and he achieved the status of a Microsoft Certified Trainer in 1993, which he still is today. He is mainly doing consulting as a SharePoint solution architect and is engaged by all kinds of organizations, including the Swedish Government. Göran has written one book about Microsoft Exchange, and this book is his third about SharePoint administration. Göran was awarded his first Microsoft Most Valuable Professional (MVP) status for Exchange in 2004, and SharePoint Server MVP every year since 2006 up to today.

CHRISTIAN STÅHL is a SharePoint nerd who has worked with various kinds of web design and web development for more than 10 years, specializing in SharePoint for the past five years. Christian works at Human Data as an Senior SharePoint trainer and consultant, MCT & MCTS, with a focus on branding and no-code solutions with SharePoint Designer and InfoPath. He has been a speaker at Swedish conferences related to SharePoint. Christian also enjoys jQuery, Silverlight and the world of .NET, among other cool technologies. Christian is the founder of the community SharePointDesigners.net (http://www.sharepointdesigners.net/). His blog can be found at http://chrisstahl.wordpress.com and he tweets on Twitter under the name @Cstahl.

ACKNOWLEDGMENTS

THIS IS MY THIRD BOOK about my absolute favorite software application: SharePoint! I am very grateful that Paul Reese at Wiley offered me a chance to once again write a book about SharePoint. A special thanks goes to my favorite editor, Kelly Talbot. He is an incredible editor, the best I have ever had. I also want to thank my two other editors Martin Reid and Paula Lowell, who did an amazing job correcting and helping me write this book. You are really professional editors! As in my previous books, my agent and friend Neil Salkind did a really great job, and without him and his team at Studio B, I would not have written this book. There are two groups I really want to thank: First is my colleagues and dear friends at my company Human Data, who supported me and inspired me during this book project, and among them I especially want to thank Christian Ståhl, who accepted with very short notice the offer to help me with two chapters in this book. You are among the best SharePoint Designer specialists in the world! The other group who helped and inspired me is the SharePoint MVP Team. They are an incredible group of men and women who share my passion for SharePoint, especially Todd O. Klindt. Finally I want to thank my beloved wife Marina who actually put up with me writing another book, although she did not see much of me for four months. Then all my kids: Johan, Beatrice, Alex, Marielle, Thomas, and Anna. You are the true joy of my life! Without you I would be nothing. I love you all.

— Göran Husman

THANKS TO GÖRAN HUSMAN, all my colleagues, Kelly and the Wrox crew, Microsoft, the SharePoint community, and my family.

— Christian Ståhl

CONTENTS

INTRODUCTION

BECAUSE YOU ARE READING THIS, I assume that you share my interest for Microsoft SharePoint. In my case it is more than an interest, it is a passion! For more than 30 years, I have been working with computers, from assembler programming to complex software solutions. For more than 10 years my whole world was e-mail (my personal car plate is "SMTP" still today), but in 2001 I stumbled on a product that was called SharePoint Portal Server. I was amazed! Its objective was to help end users be more productive by making it easy to share and find information, typically Office documents.

When SharePoint 2003 was released, I decided to focus on SharePoint 100 percent (or 150 percent, as my wife likes to put it) and no one at my consulting company objected (after all, I am their boss). Today I can admit that SharePoint 2003 was a bit of a disappointment, since it lacked a number of features that were in SharePoint 2001, so I really looked forward to the next release. Then, in 2007 MS Office SharePoint Server 2007 (MOSS) was released; it was a lot better, really a good collaboration platform with fantastic integration features and excellent performance. However, after implementing a large number of MOSS installations at all kinds of organizations, it was clear that there were also some weak areas in this fine product, especially web content management features and search functionality.

The moment of truth is here: SharePoint 2010 is now released. Does it fix the weaknesses of MOSS 2007? Yes! Does it offer a world-class solution for both public facing Internet portals as well as any kind of intranet? Absolutely! Does it come with other new or enhanced features compared to SharePoint 2007? You bet! I know it may sound as if I am paid by Microsoft to say this, but I am not: SharePoint is the most incredible piece of software I have seen for sharing, searching, collaborating, and enhancing the typical end users everyday life. I know that the SharePoint team at Microsoft is already on its way to design and build the next version of SharePoint. It must be very hard for them to come up with new and even more enhanced features for that release, but I know I will be here waiting for it!

Will your professional life be better if you implement SharePoint in your organization? Yes, if you do it right and avoid the pitfalls on the way. This book is written to give you the knowledge and background to help you do it right. SharePoint 2010 is a really large product, especially SharePoint Server 2010 Enterprise edition. There is no universal solution that I can give you. Your implementation all depends on the needs and requirements of your organization, and all organizations have their special objectives.

One of the biggest challenges when implementing SharePoint is to decide what to use SharePoint for and then stick to that plan. I have seen over and over again how one organization decides to implement SharePoint for one or two specific features, for example to build an intranet. Then, during the progress of the project, the project team realizes how powerful SharePoint's other features are, so they decided to add them as well. The problem is that the project planning and budget is based on the original objective, but now SharePoint will be used for 10 different other things as well, still within the same time and budget. You don't have to be Einstein to figure out that this is an impossible equation! Instead, you should plan your implementation exactly like how you should eat an elephant — one slice at a time. I don't mean that you should avoid using SharePoint for many things, just that you must make a plan that consists of multiple projects, instead of one giant monster project. For example, you could divide your SharePoint implementation project into multiple phases:

1. Implement SharePoint as an intranet.

    a. Decide what features to implement, together with both stakeholders and end users.

    b. Implement and evaluate that it works as expected.

    c. Correct any issues.

    d. Publish the intranet to all users.

    e. Educate users how the intranet works.

    f. When the intranet is accepted, then you are ready to go on with the next SharePoint feature.

2. Implement the collaboration platform, for example for project workspaces.

    a. Repeat steps a – f in the first project phase.

3. Implement SharePoint for business intelligence.

    a. Repeat steps a – f in the first project phase.

You get the idea. This may sound simple and easy, but in reality it is so tempting to stretch the original objectives, to include "just some small extra features." You must never forget that you are building a solution for your end users. They have no idea what SharePoint is, and they probably have no clue about the project objectives. So you work for some time, build what you think is a fantastic solution, throw it at their feet, and expect them to at least faint from excitement, if not nominate you for a Nobel price. This will not happen: You are in fact changing their everyday procedures and expecting them to be happy. The truth is that no one is happy when someone else changes their familiar environment. Think about it: Would you be happy if someone one day changed they way you work and you didn't understand why they did it? Everyone dislikes change, unless there is some really obvious benefit to them that they can believe in.

A good strategy is to find out what procedures, activities, or things people dislike and then try to find out a solution to that, based on the rich set of features SharePoint offers. This requires that you talk with a lot of users to find out what they dislike, that you engage end users from different parts of your organization very early in the project, or that you possibly do both. If your project does not include end users as team members, there is a great risk that it will be much harder for you to get acceptance for the solution. Remember that the end users are your customers: If they don't buy your solution, you have just wasted time and money building something that will not be used as intended.

Another tip I want to give you is to try and stay out of custom solutions for SharePoint. If you have a strong background in software development, this might be frustrating to hear. But from the customer's perspective, every custom solution will increase the total cost of ownership. So what is the problem with custom code? The most obvious issue is that the solution is built by a small group of people, very often just one single developer. And if there is a need to adjust the custom solution after some time (which is very common), you need this developer again, since he or she is the one who knows the solution best. If you want to bring in another developer to adjust the custom solution, he or she will probably say that it is easiest to rebuild the solution from scratch. That is not the best way to build a good long-term professional reputation.

In reality, it is very hard to stay out of custom solutions, especially if the requirements cannot be met by SharePoint's standard features. That is why I have several colleagues who are SharePoint developers. But before you decide to build a custom solution, think hard about the requirements: Can it be met in another way? Is there a good third-party product on the market that you can add to SharePoint? If the answers are no, then by all means build your custom solutions, since you have done an analysis of the need and ways to solve it. If you hire someone to build that custom solution for you, make them guarantee that it will also work after you add service packs and hotfixes for SharePoint. However, it is impossible to guarantee that the custom solution should also work for a future SharePoint release, since no one today knows what that release will contain.

Okay, those were a few of the tips I wanted to give you up front before you even start reading this book. I just want to help you plan and implement SharePoint 2010 and then build that fantastic solution you have in mind! It can be done. Just make sure to plan ahead, engage your end users early, and remember how to eat an elephant!

WHO THIS BOOK IS FOR

This book is written for several audiences. One audience is consultants and IT professionals who need to understand how to plan, implement, and configure SharePoint. Another audience is administrators and the support team that must know how to manage SharePoint, both the more advanced administration of service applications and site collections, as well as managing sites and workspaces. A third audience is the reader who wants to understand how SharePoint works and what to expect from it; this is typically IT managers and project leaders.

This book assumes no previous knowledge of SharePoint, but if you do have experience with SharePoint you will learn how SharePoint 2010 differs from previous releases. If you intend to read and try all the exercises in this book, you will need some basic understanding of network applications such as Windows Servers, Microsoft SQL, Active Directory, DNS and IIS, as well as experience with Microsoft Office. If you don't intend to install SharePoint yourself, then it is not necessary to have that network understanding.

If you are a power user who wants to understand how to manage team sites, project sites, web content management, and document management, then this book will give you lots of tips and background information. You can safely skip the chapters that do not appeal to you, although it might be good to skim them over, just in case there are some tips you actually have use for.

WHAT THIS BOOK COVERS

This book consists of 10 chapters and 4 appendixes. If you want to learn how to install and configure SharePoint Foundation, you should start reading Appendixes A and B. If you will install SharePoint Server 2010, you should still quickly read Appendixes A and B, since they cover the basic functionality also valid for SharePoint Server; then you should continue reading carefully Appendixes C and D. All these appendixes are very technical and detailed, but you need to understand all this in order to install a SharePoint 2010 environment that follows Microsoft's Best Practice to match the requirements of your organization.

If you don't plan to install SharePoint yourself, then you can start reading Chapter 1 and all the other chapters. If some of them are less interesting to you, you should still read them quickly to get an understanding of what they cover. Later you might need that information, and then it will be valuable to know where to find it.

The main part of this book is divided into 10 chapters. Some of these chapters focus more on SharePoint Foundation (SPF), some on SharePoint Server (SPS):

➤ Chapter 1, Introduction to Microsoft SharePoint 2010: This chapter gives you an overview of SharePoint and most of its important features. If you want to understand what SharePoint 2010 can do for you, then read this chapter.

➤ Chapter 2, Building SPF Sites: This chapter focuses on the fundamental features of SharePoint 2010; if you plan to build an SharePoint Foundation-based solution, read this. If you plan to build an SharePoint Server solution, this chapter covers the basic functionality you also need to know.

➤ Chapter 3, Office Integration: This chapter describes how SharePoint 2010 integrates with MS Office. If you are interested in document management features in SharePoint, then you should read this chapter.

➤ Chapter 4, Content Management in SharePoint 2010: This chapter focus on managing content, especially web content management using wiki pages, but also social computing features, integration with offline solutions like Microsoft Outlook and SharePoint Workspace, and managing multilanguage sites.

➤ Chapter 5, Managing My Sites: This chapter focus on features only available in SharePoint Server, not SharePoint Foundation. It describes how to manage and and take advantage of the user's personal My Site, both for personal use and for collaboration and information sharing.

➤ Chapter 6, SharePoint Administration: This chapter is a deep dive into many important features in SharePoint, such as permissions, templates, search and indexing, and how to manage SharePoint 2010 with PowerShell and STSADM. Readers only interested in SharePoint Foundation should read the parts that covers SharePoint Foundation features, while the SharePoint Server administrator and IT pro should read the complete chapter.

➤ Chapter 7, Building Intranets and Internet Portals: This chapter focuses on features related to intranets and public-facing Internet sites. It explains what features will be of interest and how to use them. You will get a number of tips in this chapter, such as how to display Twitter content on a SharePoint site.

➤ Chapter 8, Customizing SharePoint 2010: This chapter explains how to customize both SharePoint Foundation and SharePoint Server sites. You will learn how to use SharePoint Designer 2010 as well as how to customize web parts, including Silverlight-based media web parts.

➤ Chapter 9, Using SharePoint Designer 2010: This chapter focus on what you can do with the free tool SharePoint Designer 2010. If you need to know how to configure and design web pages in SharePoint, this chapter is for you.

➤ Chapter 10, Backup and Restore: This chapter describes how to backup and then restore documents, lists, sites, site collections, and complete SharePoint farms, using SharePoint Central Administration, PowerShell, and STSADM. If you are a SharePoint administrator, you should read this chapter.

➤ Appendix A, Installing SharePoint Foundation 2010: This appendix describes how to plan and implement SharePoint Foundation 2010. It also covers how to upgrade from WSS 3.0.

➤ Appendix B, Configuring SharePoint Foundation 2010: This appendix describes how to configure and manage a newly installed SharePoint Foundation environment. It covers many important and general concepts in SharePoint that are also valid for SharePoint Server, so both SharePoint Foundation and SharePoint Server administrators and IT professionals should read this appendix.

➤ Appendix C, Installing SharePoint Server 2010: This appendix describes how to plan and implement SharePoint Server 2010, including how to upgrade and migrate from MOSS 2007.

➤ Appendix D, Configuring SharePoint Server 2010: This appendix describes how to configure and manage a newly created SharePoint Server 2010 environment. Before you read this appendix you should read Appendix B.

WHAT YOU NEED TO USE THIS BOOK

If you want to follow the Try It Outs in this book, you will need to build a SharePoint 2010 environment. Appendixes A and C describe the software and hardware requirements and where to find evaluation versions of SharePoint 2010. You will need Windows Server 2008 or later, configured to run within an Active Directory domain. If you follow the Try It Out exercises describe in Appendixes A and B (for SharePoint Foundation) or Appendixes C and D (for SharePoint Server), you will have the SharePoint environment required. You also need some demo user accounts created in Active Directory. If you want to use other server names, Active Directory domains, and site names that better match your requirements, then just replace the example names.

You will need a Microsoft Office 2010 and SharePoint Designer 2010 to complete all the Try It Outs. To complete the e-mail-related Try It Outs, you will need an SMTP-based mail server, and for a few cases you will need Microsoft Exchange. With Office 2007, you will be able to do most of the document management exercises, but not all of them. In addition, some of the Try It Outs in this book require setting up specific servers or user accounts before starting them. In these instances, instructions for the setup are given at the beginning of the chapter and the Try It Out includes an explanation of what is needed. Again, if you want to use other server names, Active Directory domains, and site names that better match your requirements, then just replace the example names.

CONVENTIONS

To help you get the most from the text and keep track of what's happening, we've used a number of conventions throughout the book.

TRY IT OUT

The *Try It Out* is an exercise you should work through, following the text in the book. Some of the Try It Outs in this book require setting up specific servers or user accounts before starting them. In these instances, instructions for the setup are given at the beginning of the chapter and the Try It Out includes an explanation of what is needed.

1. They usually consist of a set of steps.

2. Each step has a number.

3. Follow the steps through.

How It Works

After each *Try It Out*, there will be a brief explanation.

> **WARNING** *Boxes with a warning icon like this one hold important, not-to-be-forgotten information that is directly relevant to the surrounding text.*

> **NOTE** *The pencil icon indicates notes, tips, hints, tricks, and/or asides to the current discussion.*

As for styles in the text:

➤ We *highlight* new terms and important words when we introduce them.

➤ We show keyboard strokes like this: Ctrl+A.

➤ We show file names, URLs, and code within the text like so: `persistence.properties`.

➤ We present code like this:

```
We use a monofont type with no highlighting for most code examples.
```

ERRATA

We make every effort to ensure that there are no errors in the text or in the code. However, no one is perfect, and mistakes do occur. If you find an error in one of our books, like a spelling mistake or faulty piece of code, we would be very grateful for your feedback. By sending in errata, you may save another reader hours of frustration, and at the same time, you will be helping us provide even higher quality information.

To find the errata page for this book, go to `http://www.wrox.com` and locate the title using the Search box or one of the title lists. Then, on the book details page, click the Book Errata link. On this page, you can view all errata that has been submitted for this book and posted by Wrox editors. A complete book list, including links to each book's errata, is also available at `www.wrox.com/misc-pages/booklist.shtml`.

If you don't spot "your" error on the Book Errata page, go to `www.wrox.com/contact/techsupport.shtml` and complete the form there to send us the error you have found. We'll check the information and, if appropriate, post a message to the book's errata page and fix the problem in subsequent editions of the book.

P2P.WROX.COM

For author and peer discussion, join the P2P forums at `p2p.wrox.com`. The forums are a Web-based system for you to post messages relating to Wrox books and related technologies and interact with other readers and technology users. The forums offer a subscription feature to e-mail you topics of interest of your choosing when new posts are made to the forums. Wrox authors, editors, other industry experts, and your fellow readers are present on these forums.

At `http://p2p.wrox.com`, you will find a number of different forums that will help you, not only as you read this book, but also as you develop your own applications. To join the forums, just follow these steps:

1. Go to `p2p.wrox.com` and click the Register link.

2. Read the terms of use and click Agree.

3. Complete the required information to join, as well as any optional information you wish to provide, and click Submit.

4. You will receive an e-mail with information describing how to verify your account and complete the joining process.

> **NOTE** *You can read messages in the forums without joining P2P, but in order to post your own messages, you must join.*

Once you join, you can post new messages and respond to messages other users post. You can read messages at any time on the Web. If you would like to have new messages from a particular forum e-mailed to you, click the Subscribe to this Forum icon by the forum name in the forum listing.

For more information about how to use the Wrox P2P, be sure to read the P2P FAQs for answers to questions about how the forum software works, as well as many common questions specific to P2P and Wrox books. To read the FAQs, click the FAQ link on any P2P page.

1

Introduction to Microsoft SharePoint 2010

WHAT YOU WILL LEARN IN THIS CHAPTER:

➤   Understanding SharePoint 2010

➤   Planning for Requirements

➤   Exploring SharePoint Features

In 2008, I was hired by an organization with several thousand users who needed to get a better way of managing their documents. The challenges were several: The number of documents was more than 10 million; they had offices in a large number of locations; a large number of documents had multiple authors, some as many as 100 authors; and many documents had to be reviewed and commented by sometimes more than 50 people, in different locations and time zones. A typical scenario would look like this: Anna created a 50-page report in Microsoft Word, and she needed 25 people to review and possibly update the document, but only the sections that affected them. Anna sent the document by e-mail to each of these 25 people, and asked them to review and if needed update a specific section of the document. After about two weeks, and several reminders, she got 25 new versions back by e-mail. Now Anna had to consolidate all those versions into her original document. The easiest way to do this was to print out all 26 versions, find a really large table, put up the first page from all versions, compare them, continue with the next page, and so forth. Sometimes multiple reviewers had different opinions about the same section, so Anna had to send a new e-mail and ask these people if they could agree on a specific version of that particular section. Finalizing the document usually took several weeks using this method. With Microsoft SharePoint 2010 and Office 2010, Anna can instead share the document in real-time, using the new co-authoring feature in SharePoint 2010 (see Chapter 3 for more information on co-authoring). This fantastic feature enables Anna to invite her 25 reviewers to different sections in the document. These people can read and update the document simultaneously as others work with the same document, or they can do their reviews and updates at a time that suits them best. Anna can directly see whether someone has changed the document, regardless of whether or not it is done in real-time.

Similar to the scenario described above, practically all people need a system that will help them store, share, and find information, regardless of its type, origin, and geographic location. Such a system should also allow secure access to this information using different kinds of devices and applications. SharePoint is such a system! It is designed with these objectives in mind. It is important to understand that SharePoint is a system for managing data, often created by other systems, such as Microsoft Office.

So welcome to this book! It is about how to install, configure, and especially how to use SharePoint 2010. Because it is the fourth generation of SharePoint, you likely have experience with previous versions; however, the book does not require any previous knowledge of SharePoint. I have been working with SharePoint since its first release in 2001, and in my experience a lot of planning and design is required. A successful SharePoint installation requires a lot more than simply putting the CD in a drive and installing it. Sometimes I see organizations that fail to understand their users' needs, and therefore how to take advantage of SharePoint. They simply believe that the mere fact that SharePoint is installed will by magic make things easier. This will not happen, believe me! A good implementation helps an organization do their work easier, faster, and sometimes even in a way that's more fun, whereas a bad implementation keeps an organization from working efficiently and irritates their end users. The main objective for this book is to give you the information you need to do a good implementation. This book offers lots of best practices, advice, and tips and tricks, based on a large number of SharePoint implementations, in all kinds of organizations, both small (with just a few users) and large (with many thousands of users).

A Microsoft representative once told me about how the company builds a new software application: "First we do a lot of planning, analysis, and of course, guessing what the customer wants in such a product; this results in version 1.0. Of course, we quickly realize that we missed a number of things, so we learn from that, rebuild the product, and then release version 2.0. This version will most likely also miss some important features, which our dear customers tell us in a very frank and honest way, so we sit down again, add the missing features, plus a lot more, and fix weaknesses, then we release version 3.0 — and this time we usually get it right!" This is the fourth generation of SharePoint, and it brings a lot of new and enhanced features compared to its predecessors. One of the important lessons learned from the three previous versions is that SharePoint needs to be feature rich, but at the same time flexible, so that building a SharePoint solution that will satisfy any type of need is easy.

WHAT IS SHAREPOINT?

One of the major strengths of SharePoint is that it helps you collect, manage, and work with information, regardless of what type it is. It may be Microsoft Office documents, PDF documents, pictures, or any other type of file. But it may also be information that you usually store in other types of applications, such as contact lists, team calendars, product databases, project planning, and a news list. SharePoint helps you find information, even when you don't know where it is stored, based on its content or properties. It also helps you keep track of changes; for example, when a document you work with gets updated by another user. In other words, SharePoint does not invent any new information types; instead, it helps you get the right information when you need it, without spending time looking for it. Even more importantly, all this information is easily shared between users, such as project teams, departments, or even entire organizations.

Microsoft has, over the years, performed a thorough analysis of how people, in all types of organizations, use their computers. How is that possible, you ask? Do you remember the last time you installed Microsoft Office? When you completed the installation, you were asked whether you wanted to participate anonymously in the Microsoft user experience analysis. Most people accept the default, which is to say no, but several million users have actually accepted. Their computer regularly sends a log file to Microsoft, stating what type of features they use in Microsoft Office. For example, Microsoft knows that

➤ The average use of the Copy and Paste features is about 300 times per month, which is about 20 percent of all your clicks.

➤ The most common command that immediately follows Paste is Undo.

➤ The average Microsoft Word document has 16 different styles; the most common is Bold, and then Font Size, but only a few use ALL CAPS.

➤ Sixty percent of all users print more than 60 times per month.

➤ Insert Picture is the fourth most used command, and 95 percent of all documents have fewer than 20 pictures inside.

➤ The typical Outlook user reads about 1,800 e-mails per month, and deletes about 1,500 of them.

Microsoft uses all of these statistics to understand how you work, and this information affects the look and feel of the user interface of Office clients. The user interface of SharePoint 2007 clearly needed a facelift, so in SharePoint 2010, you will find the same type of toolbar introduced in Office 2007, also known as the "Ribbon" or the "Office Fluent" user interface, which will make it easy for Office 2007 users to understand how to work in SharePoint 2010.

Self-Service, a new feature introduced in SharePoint 2007, was to empower end users, giving them a simple but powerful means to adjust the layout and color of their sites, and add and modify lists and document libraries, without the assistance of an administrator or software developer. This power is increased even more in SharePoint 2010. Self-service is a rather new trend in the computer business. Besides having the ability to create and design their own SharePoint sites, users can also find third-party applications that allow them to control systems outside SharePoint; for example, to reset an account password, change properties in the Active Directory (AD), and so on.

SharePoint is built around this concept of self-service; the main idea is to allow the ordinary user to create websites for projects and other activities without any support from the server administrator or Help Desk. The SharePoint user requires some training, but SharePoint is straightforward and easy to learn. However, don't underestimate this training, because it is crucial for a succesful SharePoint implementation. Your role, as the SharePoint Server administrator, is to install, maintain, and configure SharePoint. You are also the person that people will contact when they need help understanding how do things in SharePoint, such as creating sites and managing lists of information. That's why this book tells you how to do these things and gives you tips and hints to make things easier for you and your users. I am sure you will like it for your own personal use, too — SharePoint is simply a fantastic application with enormous potential, if you know how to use it correctly!

Describing what SharePoint is, in just a few words, is actually hard, but I can give it a try. Using this application, you can build a web-based environment for things like these:

➤ An intranet portal for the organization, and each department

➤ A public Internet site

➤ An extranet portal for your customers and partners

➤ A team site, for your sales department

➤ A project site, for the development team

➤ A document management system that is compliant with Sarbanes-Oxley (SOX) and ISO-9000

➤ A personal site for each user, where they can store personal data, plus find links to their team sites

➤ A digital dashboard for storing business intelligence data, such as key performance indicators

➤ A place to search and locate any type of information, regardless of where it is stored

➤ A record management system, for storing legal information in a secure way

> **NOTE** *SOX (a U.S. law) and ISO-9000 (an ISO standard) define a number of rules on how to manage documents and information in an organization.*

Many other features in addition to those listed will be described throughout this book. Because SharePoint is such a flexible and powerful application, what you can do with it is limited almost only by your imagination. Some features may require third-party products or custom development, but the list of features that comes out of the box is amazing, especially for the SharePoint Server Enteprise edition. It is also very fun to work with, because it is so easy to build an impressive solution with it. Microsoft has most certainly created a killer application — again! Figure 1-1 shows a simple SharePoint 2010 team site, just to give you an idea of how it looks. If you don't like the design, changing it without software development tools is easy.

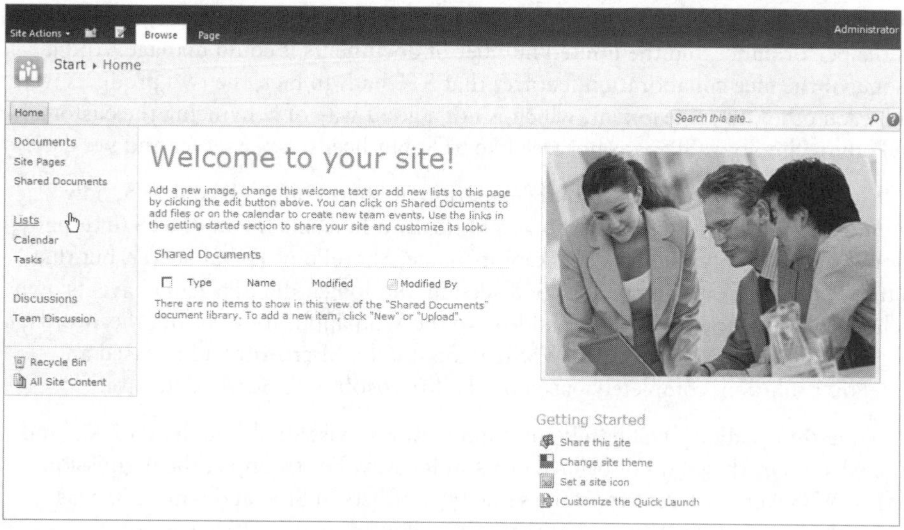

FIGURE 1-1

The History of SharePoint

To understand how to install and manage SharePoint, it helps to know this history. Knowing this not only helps you understand where SharePoint comes from, but it also helps you understand some abbreviations that are used even in SharePoint 2010.

Around 2000, Microsoft unveiled an application called a *digital dashboard*. This web-based application used a new concept called *web parts,* which are rectangular areas on a web page that display some type of information, such as a list of contacts, links, or documents. This was innovative, because the user could now arrange the web parts on the web page herself, without any help from an HTML programmer.

In 2001, Microsoft released its first two SharePoint products. One was *SharePoint Team Services (STS),* and the other was *SharePoint Portal Server (SPS) 2001.* Only a few organizations implemented these products, which was a pity, because they offered a good value. STS was a free web-based product used for creating collaboration sites. You could use it to share contacts, calendar events, and documents within teams and small departments. The information was stored in an Microsoft SQL database. It was a nice application, but it did not have any document-management features, nor was it built for creating intranet solutions.

SPS 2001 was a separate product, initially developed as an Microsoft Exchange 2000 public folder application (under the beta name Tahoe). However, during the beta phase of Tahoe, Microsoft got a loud and clear message from the customers: "Do not mess with our Exchange systems!" So Microsoft finally released the SPS 2001 using a built-in Microsoft Exchange 2000 server database hidden beneath, which made more than one SharePoint administrator wonder why on earth the SharePoint server event log contained messages from the Exchange Information Store! The SPS 2001 application had built-in document-management features, such as document versioning, checkout/check-in, and support for document workflows. It also had a good search engine that enabled the user to find information, regardless of where it was stored. One serious problem with SPS 2001 was the performance and the limited number of documents it could manage. And it did not have some of the nice collaboration features that STS had. In fact, the two products were competing with each other, to some extent, which is not a good way of convincing the customer to invest in SharePoint technology. SPS was not free like STS, but licensed per server and per user.

In October 2003, Microsoft released its second generation of SharePoint. The old STS, now renamed *Windows SharePoint Services (WSS)*, was basically a fancier version of STS (internally, Microsoft referred to it as STS version 2). SPS kept its name, SharePoint Portal Server, but that was about all that was kept from the previous SPS version. No longer did SPS 2003 have its own Microsoft Exchange database; now it was an add-on to the WSS application, or in other words, when installing SPS 2003, you also installed WSS 2.0. So finally, Microsoft had released an integrated SharePoint solution, completely based on the Microsoft SQL Server database.

Still, some annoying things about the SharePoint 2003 editions existed; although SPS 2003 and WSS 2 now looked similar, they did not behave in a similar way. For example, the permission settings for lists in WSS were different from the same type of lists in SPS, and while SPS was security trimmed (that is, users only saw what they were allowed to see), WSS was not.

At the end of 2006, Microsoft released the third generation of SharePoint. WSS kept its name, but changed the version number to 3.0. WSS was still a free add-on for Windows 2003 Server, and as before, it used a Microsoft SQL database to store its content. Its bigger brother, SPS, was renamed to *Microsoft Office SharePoint Server (MOSS) 2007*, but contrary to the 2003 version, MOSS just put extra features on top of WSS 3.0, and was using the same Microsoft SQL database. The MOSS package was available in two editions: *MOSS 2007 Standard* and *MOSS 2007 Enterprise*. They differed only in the number of features available and the price for the *client access licenses*, or CAL.

Finally, in April 2010, Microsoft released its fourth generation of SharePoint. It resembles the 2007 architecture a lot, but the names for both WSS and MOSS were changed. The new name for WSS is *SharePoint Foundation*, and the new name for MOSS is *SharePoint Server*. As before, SharePoint Foundation is the base package that offers all the basic functionality, although greatly improved compared to WSS 3, and Microsoft SharePoint Server 2010 consists of two levels of feature packages on top of SharePoint Foundation.

The important things you should remember from this section are

➤ STS is the old name for WSS, and this abbreviation is still used even in SharePoint 2010 in some places, such as the *sts* folder that stores the site definition for SharePoint Foundation sites.

➤ SharePoint Server has replaced MOSS 2007.

➤ SharePoint Server comes in *Standard* and *Enterprise* editions.

➤ Microsoft SQL Server is used by SharePoint Foundation and therefore by SharePoint Server.

> **NOTE** *This book describes the features and functionality of both SharePoint Foundation and SharePoint Server — they are often referred to as the* SharePoint Products and Technology (SPPT) 2010 *package.*

DIFFERENCES BETWEEN SHAREPOINT FOUNDATION AND SHAREPOINT SERVER

When you think of SharePoint Foundation and SharePoint Server 2010, the important thing to understand is that SharePoint Foundation is the foundation, and SharePoint Server is simply an optional add-on package of more advanced features. In fact, you cannot install SharePoint Server by itself, because installing it automatically also installs SharePoint Foundation.

So the question is: What differs between SharePoint Foundation and SharePoint Server? What version do you need? The answer depends on your requirements, and not so much on the size of your organization. For example, if you want a good platform for a basic intranet plus collaboration and project management, then SharePoint Foundation may be just what you need. If you need the best web content management, more advanced document management, or tight integration with Excel, Access, and Visio, then SharePoint Server is what you need. The following sections about SharePoint Foundation and SharePoint Server give you a short overview of the features in each version, and you will find much more in the following chapters.

SharePoint Foundation

Here are some of the more frequently used features and characteristics of SharePoint Foundation:

➤ It's a web-based application running on top of Internet Information Services (IIS).

➤ It's a free 64-bit only add-on to any edition of Microsoft Windows 2008 Server or Windows 2008 R2.

➤ It requires a 64-bit Windows Server operating system.

➤ It stores all its data and information in one or more Microsoft SQL Server databases.

➤ It displays information using a web page file, usually containing one or more web parts.

➤ It has very good document-management features, such as version history, custom metadata, and Microsoft Office integration.

➤ It has a number of list types that you can use for storing different types of information, such as documents, contacts and calendar items.

➤ It enables you to build workflow solutions; for example, sending an e-mail to a given user when a document is changed or a list column is set to a specific value.

➤ It's perfect for building basic, but effective, intranet solutions, with its built-in web content management features.

➤ It's ideal for collaboration on project data, meetings, social events, blogs, and such.

In other words, SharePoint Foundation is the perfect place to collect and share information about your projects, your customers, and your meetings. Before you can take advantage of all the powerful document management features in SharePoint Foundation, you must first move your files into a *document library*; that is, a kind of root folder in a SharePoint site. Luckily, SharePoint Foundation comes with a file upload feature that makes copying or moving files and folders directly into a particular SharePoint document library easy. SharePoint Foundation is also a very good solution when you need local intranets for teams or departments. And all this is free when you run Windows 2008 Server!

But there are also important features that SharePoint Foundation does not offer. Here are just a few examples:

➤ No built-in advanced search functionality. SharePoint Foundation offers limited search functionality, but still it will only allow users to search within the current site and sites below it.

➤ No advanced web content management features, such as publishing control, targeted information, and multilingual support.

➤ No advanced document management features, such as global document IDs, document sets, and document policies.

➤ No record management of legal and other important documents.

➤ No support for displaying InfoPath forms in a web browser.

➤ No support for displaying MS Excel spreadsheets as web parts.

➤ No support for displaying MS Visio 2010 diagrams as a web part.

➤ No support for *key performance indicators (KPIs)*.

This is where SharePoint Server 2010 comes in.

SharePoint Server 2010

SharePoint Server 2010 uses the same types of web sites and features as SharePoint Foundation but adds a lot of functionality. In addition to the previous list, SharePoint Server 2010 also provides the following features, which will be described further throughout the book:

➤ Use the global search functionality to find any type of information, regardless of type and location, based on content or metadata properties.

➤ Use Social Search to find people based on their typical activities and interests.

➤ Target displayed information to one or more user groups.

➤ Import user properties from AD, and make them searchable.

➤ Use advanced content management features for public Internet sites or portal intranet sites.

➤ Allow globally unique document IDs and document sets.

➤ Display and use InfoPath forms with a web client, using the Forms Service.

➤ Display Microsoft Excel spreadsheets and charts in a web part, using Excel Services.

➤ Display Microsoft Visio 2010 diagrams directly on a web page, using the Visio web part.

➤ Search, display, and edit content in external databases, such as SAP, Oracle, and Microsoft SQL, using the Business Connectivity Service.

➤ Give each SharePoint user a personal website, for both private and public use.

➤ Create dashboards with scorecards and key performance indicators.

These characteristics make SharePoint Server 2010 a very good solution for building any kind of website, including public-facing Internet sites, extranets, or intranets that are smart enough to show the right information to the right people. SharePoint Server is also a good solution when you want to build web pages with dashboards for displaying scorecards and business data, such as Microsoft Excel spreadsheets, electronic forms, and key performance indicators with built-in drill-down functionality.

WHAT YOU NEED TO RUN SHAREPOINT 2010

This section provides general information about what you need to install and run both SharePoint Foundation and SharePoint Server. It also has general guidelines on the hardware configuration and some tips for building a test environment. Appendix A provides the exact steps on how to do the actual installation of a SharePoint Foundation–only environment; Appendix C provides the installation steps for a SharePoint Server 2010 environment.

Software Requirements

Because SharePoint is a web application, you need to have a web server. The only version supporting SharePoint 2010 as of this writing is Internet Information Service version 7 (IIS 7), which runs on Windows 2008 Server and Windows 2008 R2 Server — note that it will not work on a Windows 2003 Server! You can use any edition of Windows 2008 Server, including the cheaper Web Edition. One important change from previous versions of SharePoint is that SharePoint Foundation and SharePoint Server are 64-bit only, and thus the Windows operating system they run on must also be 64-bit. Microsoft's reason for this requirement is that the 32-bit environment is limited to a maximum of 4GB of memory, whereas the 64-bit limit is approximately 17.2 billion GB, or 16.8 million TB — that is, about 10 trillion times larger than the address space of the 32-bit, which hopefully will be enough for a long time. This change also has implications on the test and development environment. In previous versions of SharePoint, building 32-bit environments for these types of installations, and running them on a desktop or even laptop computer, using a virtual server technology such as Microsoft Virtual PC (VPC), was common. This is no longer possible because, as of this writing, VPC does not support 64-bit guest operating systems. So the only options today are to use the Hyper-V feature of Windows 2008 Server or a VMware product. If you want to run a virtual environment on top of your Windows 7 computer, you may use the 64-bit version of VMware Workstation, or set up a dual-boot on your computer with Windows Server 2008 and Hyper-V as the second boot option.

The Windows 2008 server needs to be properly prepared before you install SharePoint. Luckily, this task is taken care of by the installation wizard, which not only detects whether something needs to be done, it actually does it as well. If you want SharePoint to act as a mail server, thus allowing users to send mail to SharePoint lists, you must also install and configure the IIS component SMTP.

The last, but not least, component you need is an Microsoft SQL Server. You have these choices:

➤   Microsoft SQL Server 2008 Express, which comes free with SharePoint 2010

➤   The full MS SQL Server product — either MS SQL 2005 Server with SP2 or MS SQL 2008 Server

Once again, you must use only the 64-bit versions of each of the preceding options. Actually, SharePoint 2010 will also work on a remote 32-bit SQL Server, but it will not be supported by Microsoft! These two choices give you different features, as listed in the following table.

FEATURE	EMBEDDED SQL SERVER 2008 EXPRESS 64-BIT	MS SQL 2005/2008 SERVER 64-BIT
Limited database size	Server: 4GB max (see the discussion following this table)	No
Can run on a separate server	No	Yes
Includes management tools	No	Yes
License type	Free	Per CPU or per user

The limited database size of SQL Server Express mentioned in the preceding table is interesting! If you install a pure SharePoint Foundation server, you will get a special version of SQL Server Express referred to as *Embedded SQL Server Express*. This version is limited to 4GB per database, which means that only small installations of SharePoint Foundation can use this embedded database edition in a production environment, without any extra cost besides the Windows 2008 Server license.

> **NOTE** *You can install the free management tool pack for SQL Express 2008 from Microsoft:* `http://tinyurl.com/SQLExp-Mgmt-tools`

The same is true also SharePoint Server 2010: you will get the 4GB size-limited version of SQL Server Express! Most SharePoint Server installations require much more database capacity, so in reality this means that you cannot use SharePoint Server with the SQL Server Express in a production environment due to the limitation; rather, you must use the MS SQL 2008 Server.

> **NOTE** *You can download and install the standard version of SQL Server 2008 Express (64-bit) on the server, before installing SharePoint. This will give you an unlimited database size for free that supports a few hundred users. Download it from Microsoft:* `http://TinyURL.com/sqlexp2008-withtools`

There is one more important difference regarding SQL Server Express and the full SQL Server: The former must be installed on the same server as SharePoint (SharePoint Foundation or SharePoint Server), whereas Microsoft SQL Server gives you an option of choosing what server to use for storing all the data. Only by using the full SQL 2008 Server can you keep SharePoint and the database on separate servers, which will provide improved performance and scalability. This type of setup is known in SharePoint terms as a *small server farm*, whereas the option of running both the SharePoint server and SQL 2008 Server on the same hardware is known as a *single-server* installation.

Hardware Requirements

In addition to all the software requirements, the server hardware must also be configured properly. For a reasonable test environment with a single-server configuration (that is, both SharePoint and SQL Server), you can get by with 4GB of memory and at least 30GB of free disk space. In a production environment, you need at least 4GB for the SharePoint server alone, and then at least 2GB for the SQL Server — this configuration is okay for an organization with about 100 users. For better performance, you should consider running SharePoint and SQL Server on separate servers, with 8GB and 4GB of memory, respectively. The CPU is also an important factor, especially when using SharePoint Server, because the indexing feature requires a lot of CPU resources. The network performance is crucial, because it directly affects the client's perception of the performance. SharePoint depends on several supporting systems to do its job, such as the SQL Server, AD, DNS, and the mail server. You learn more about these supporting systems in Appendixes B and D.

Building a Test Environment

To build a fully functional test environment with SharePoint 2010, you need access to a number of servers and services. This type of requirement is easily met by using virtual server software, such as a 64-bit version of VMware Workstation, running on 64-bit Windows 7. The CPU type is not that important in a test environment, although a dual CPU will also increase the performance in a virtual environment. Here are two common types of setup for a test environment:

➤ Install SharePoint 2010 on a server that belongs to your production environment.

➤ Build a complete virtual world, with SharePoint 2010, active domain controllers, DNS servers, and mail servers.

The first option is easiest to build, because you will use the existing infrastructure; the only thing to install is the SharePoint 2010 server, whether it is SharePoint Foundation or SharePoint Server 2010. Here are the pros and cons for this type of test environment:

Pros:

➤ **Easy:** You just install the SharePoint server, using existing SQL Servers, user accounts, and mail servers. You just create the extra accounts that SharePoint requires.

➤ **Realistic:** When testing SharePoint, you will clearly see how it works in your network environment, and with properly configured hardware, you will also get a realistic performance indication.

Cons:

➤ **Pollution:** This option creates test data and user accounts only used by the test environment that you will need to clean up after the test is over. Reduce this problem by using a specific SQL server for the test environment that you can uninstall later.

➤ **Transformation:** A test environment that is available on the production infrastructure has a remarkable way of transforming into a production environment. People tend to use the test for real-world activities and will not allow you to uninstall the test server.

The other installation option is to use a complete virtual world, where all the servers and systems are unreachable from the production environment. It, too, has both pros and cons, as described here:

Pros:

➤ **Control:** You are in control of all systems engaged in the test environment, and its users.

➤ **Safe:** You can test different scenarios and stop and restart systems without worrying about anything outside the test environment getting affected. If you use a virtual environment, such as Hyper-V or VMware, you can even roll back changes.

Con:

➤ **Unrealistic:** If you want to perform a realistic test, you need a full replica of all servers in your IT infrastructure that are related to SharePoint. So you must create a virtual replica of such servers as the AD, the DNS, the mail server, and possibly even the firewall, if you want to test external access. Often this task is too complicated, so you will settle for a simpler model; that is, your virtual world will not be a 100 percent replica of your production environment, and therefore you cannot fully trust the results from the virtual test.

The primary benefit of using a virtual environment is that it makes testing and playing with different configurations and scenarios possible. And if (or, more likely, when) things go wrong, you can simply use the undo feature of the virtual application. Another nice option with virtual servers is to make a copy of the virtual server environment at any time and, if necessary, restore that copy later in case your test environment is messed up beyond repair!

I recommend that you use a virtual server for testing everything detailed in this book. Doing so will make things much easier for you to recover if something goes wrong. You can also be bold and try things other than what's described in the exercises. After you know how SharePoint works, you can then go on to use your own production environment.

INTEGRATING WITH MICROSOFT OFFICE

Given that you are reading this book, the chance that you use Microsoft Office for creating documents, spreadsheets, and presentations is rather high. Therefore, this section is important for you. SharePoint will not change the way you work with Office documents, but it will enhance its functionality, making many tasks a lot easier than doing them without using SharePoint, such as setting document properties and comparing different document versions. The number of features depends on what Office version you use. It's best to use Microsoft Office 2010 with SharePoint 2010 — they are simply made for each other.

Here's the story: Microsoft Office 2010 was released together with SharePoint 2010 — this is no coincidence. Microsoft invested a lot of time and energy to make sure that the Office 2010 client applications could leverage all the new and enhanced features of SharePoint 2010. If you use Office 2003 or Office 2007 along with SharePoint 2010, you will get access to a lot of the functionality in SharePoint 2010, but not everything. Using older Microsoft Office versions, such as 2000 or XP, will allow you to read and save documents to SharePoint 2010, but nothing more. The reason is that these older versions of Microsoft Office do not know about SharePoint, so they lack this integration capability. Do not expect Microsoft to release an update for older Office versions, allowing them the same functionality as Office 2010. Frankly, when you see what Office 2010 can do, you will want to upgrade — it is both much easier to work with, and has a lot of new features.

The following gives you an idea about what to expect when running Office 2000/XP versions with SharePoint 2010:

➤ **File save integration:** Microsoft Office 2000 integrates with Windows SharePoint Services. Users can open and save files stored on SharePoint sites. They can also receive alerts in Outlook 2000.

➤ **Basic data integration:** Microsoft Office XP provides for data integration with SharePoint sites. Users can view properties and metadata for files stored on SharePoint sites. They can also export list data to Microsoft Excel 2002.

➤ **Contextual integration:** SharePoint integrates fully into the business tasks that users perform every day with Microsoft Office 2003 Editions.

Microsoft has produced a white paper describing the Office integration with SharePoint 2010 called "Fair, Good, Better, Best." *Fair* is what you get with Office 2002/XP; *Good* refers to the functionality achieved by Microsoft Office 2003; *Better* is what you get with Microsoft Office 2007; and *Best* requires you to run Microsoft Office 2010. Note that no technical problem exists in using SharePoint in a mixed Microsoft Office environment, but it will place an extra burden on the Help Desk and the support team, because each version will support different SharePoint 2007 features. For example, in Office 2003 the user is presented with a separate dialog window that shows up after you save a document, asking for document properties (also known as "metadata"), whereas Office 2010 and 2007 show the Document Information Panel (DIP) on the same page as the document itself, allowing the user to enter both metadata and text simultaneously. The following table presents a more detailed comparison between the four latest Microsoft Office versions.

FEATURE	OFFICE VERSION
Save and open files from SharePoint sites	Office XP: Yes Office 2003: Enhanced Office 2007: Like 2003 plus automatic links to your sites Office 2010: Like 2007, plus better browsing in the site tree
Create new documents in the web browser	Office XP: Yes Office 2003: Yes, including SharePoint content types Office 2007: Like Office 2003 Office 2010: Like Office 2003
Collect documents	Office XP: No Office 2003: Yes Office 2007: Yes Office 2010: Yes

continues

(continued)

FEATURE	OFFICE VERSION
Change document columns in both Office and the web browser	Office XP: No Office 2003: Sort of, using a dialog box after saving the document Office 2007: Yes, using the DIP Office 2010: Like Office 2007
Track document versions	Office XP: No; use the web browser to view and manage document versions Office 2003: Yes (Excel, PowerPoint, Visio, and Word) Office 2007: Yes, and can also compare different versions easily Office 2010: Like Office 2007
Check out and check in documents	Office XP: No; use the web browser to manually check out and check in documents Office 2003: Yes, with Excel, PowerPoint, Visio, and Word; use the web browser to manually check out and check in other types of documents Office 2007: Yes; like Office 2003, but more intuitive Office 2010: Like Office 2007
Upload multiple documents	Office XP: No Office 2003: Yes Office 2007: Yes Office 2010: Yes
Use inline discussions	Office XP: Yes Office 2003: Yes Office 2007: Yes, using Notes for comments Office 2010: Yes, using Notes for comments
Create Document Workspace	Office XP: No Office 2003: Yes Office 2007: Yes Office 2010: Yes
Create Meeting Workspace	Office XP: No Office 2003: Yes, with Outlook 2003 Office 2007: Yes, with Outlook 2007 Office 2010: Yes, with Outlook 2010

FEATURE	OFFICE VERSION
Synchronize calendar, tasks, and contact list in SharePoint sites	Office XP: No Office 2003: Yes, but only one-way from SharePoint to Outlook 2003 Office 2007: Yes, two-way synchronization with Outlook 2007 Office 2010: Yes, two-way synchronization with Outlook 2010
Alert integration with Outlook	Office XP: No Office 2003: Yes Office 2007: Yes Office 2010: Yes
Display lists as RSS information	Office XP: No Office 2003: No Office 2007: Yes, with Outlook 2007 Office 2010: Yes, with Outlook 2010
Use Excel Services	Office XP: No Office 2003: Yes; can publish to SharePoint site from Excel Office 2007: Yes; same as Office 2003 Office 2010: Yes; same as Office 2007
Access to Business Connectivity Service	Office XP: No Office 2003: No Office 2007: Yes; allows Office 2007 documents to display content in external data sources, using SharePoint 2007 lists Office 2010: Yes; same as Office 2007
Publish forms to InfoPath forms services	Office XP: No Office 2003: No Office 2007: Yes Office 2010: Yes
InfoPath forms in Office clients	Office XP: No Office 2003: No Office 2007: Yes Office 2010: Yes
Access to DIP	Office XP: No Office 2003: No Office 2007: Yes Office 2010: Yes

continues

(continued)

FEATURE	OFFICE VERSION
Access to workflows	Office XP: No Office 2003: No Office 2007: Yes; can start and complete workflow tasks from within the Office 2007 client Office 2010: Yes; like Office 2007
PowerPoint slide libraries	Office XP: No Office 2003: No Office 2007: Yes Office 2010: Yes
Use record management	Office XP: No Office 2003: No Office 2007: Yes; allows Office 2007 documents to be stored in a record repository Office 2010: Yes; allows Office 2010 documents to be marked as records while stored in a standard document library
Compose and publish wikis and blogs using Word	Office XP: No Office 2003: No Office 2007: Yes Office 2010: Yes
Allow multiple authors in the same Office document at the same time (also known as co-authoring)	Office XP: No Office 2003: No Office 2007: No Office 2010: Yes
Offline usage of Office documents	Office XP: No Office 2003: No Office 2007: Yes, with Outlook 2007 Office 2010: Yes, with SharePoint Workspace
Store a central copy of OneNote documents in SharePoint	Office XP: No Office 2003: No Office 2007: No Office 2010: Yes

BUILT-IN FEATURES OF SHAREPOINT

So what features can you expect in SharePoint 2010? The answer depends on what version you implement: SharePoint Server or SharePoint Foundation. The following sections address everyday scenarios and show you examples of how SharePoint can make things easier for you and your users. Chapters 9 and 10 provide more detailed steps on how to create a SharePoint environment that solves these problems.

Alerts

One feature that both SharePoint Foundation and SharePoint Server offer is something Microsoft refers to as alerts. An *alert* is a request you create in SharePoint to be notified by e-mail or by text message (SMS) when SharePoint content changes (for example, when a document is updated, a contact is deleted, or news items are created). Using alerts, you can be sure to keep yourself updated about changes to information that is important to you! SharePoint will send you an e-mail or a text message (SMS) to your phone, to notify you what has happened. The following information types are examples of what can be monitored by alerts:

➤ A document library or a single document

➤ A picture library or a single picture

➤ A contact list or a single contact

➤ A link list or a single link

➤ A news list or a single news item

➤ An event list or a single event

> **NOTE** *You need to subscribe to an SMS before text messages can be sent by SharePoint; see Appendix B for more information.*

Alerts can watch a lot more places and types of information, as you will see in Chapters 9 and 10. This feature is extremely useful — you will no longer miss any important updates; instead you can concentrate on doing your job!

RSS (Really Simple Syndication)

A very handy feature introduced in SharePoint 2007 that also is supported in SharePoint 2010 is support for the *Really Simple Syndication* (RSS) technique. Using this feature, a user can be notified when new items are added to any type of SharePoint list, such as document libraries, contacts, news, and tasks lists. This is similar to alerts mentioned earlier, but the main difference between them is that alerts send e-mail that will be stored in your inbox along with other e-mail, whereas all RSS notifications will be collected in one folder, thus giving you a much better overview of all the notifications, as shown in Figure 1-2.

FIGURE 1-2

File and Document Management

You organize your files by using a folder structure and giving your files descriptive names so that they are easy to find. But you also know that after some time, finding the file when you need it gets harder and harder. And even worse, you may have several copies of the same file stored in different locations, probably also in different versions. How can you be sure you found the right version? If you are looking for a file that somebody else created, the task gets even harder, because the folder structure may not be as intuitive as you would like it to be, and the filenames may not be as descriptive as they should be.

This is where SharePoint comes in. All files and documents in SharePoint are stored in document libraries. This is very similar to a folder in the file system, but on steroids! The document library in SharePoint 2010 has many new features compared to previous SharePoint versions that will help you organize, compose, and find the file you are looking for. The key features are as follows:

> **Document columns:** Also known as *metadata*. Instead of building a folder structure, you can add your own columns to describe and categorize the files and documents stored in a document library. Common examples of such columns are Document Type, Customer Name, Project Name, and Status. These columns can be local for a specific document library, or they can be shared between libraries, using a feature called *site columns*.

> **Document views:** Create public and private views of how the files in the document library should be presented, based on the document's column values. For example, you could create a view that shows only documents where the column *Customer* equals *Volvo*, sorted by its column *Status*.

> **Document IDs:** A new feature in SharePoint Server 2010 allows you to set a unique document ID, which works as an absolute reference to the document. For example, assume

that one document links to a second document — this link will work even if the second document is moved to a new location, thanks to this absolute reference.

➤ **Document versions:** SharePoint 2010 has the same type of version history as its predecessor — *No history*, *Major only*, or *Major and Minor versions*. A version history offers several advantages. One is that you don't have to name the files with your own version name standard (for example, `Qote-version_5.doc`); you just overwrite the file with the updated version — you can always revert to a previous version. Also, you never have to be unsure whether a file is the latest version or not; the version history ensures that you always gets the latest version when opening an existing document. Another advantage is that the version history can save you a lot of trouble. Here's a story from real life: A user edits an existing Excel spreadsheet, used by multiple users. By mistake she removes a macro in that spreadsheet and stores the files. Then she realizes her mistake. Without a version history, she must rely on a backup that will probably take hours, if not days, to recover. With version history, she could have reverted to the previous version herself, in just a minute.

➤ **Document workflows:** Adding, deleting, or modifying a document or its metadata can trigger a workflow to start. For example, one workflow could send an e-mail to all members in your team when a document is updated to collect feedback or to get an approval by your manager, before the document gets published.

➤ **Content types:** This is a definition of a list item — its columns, default content, workflows, and policies. For example, you can use content types to define multiple Office templates for a specific document library, so when a user creates a new document for that library, she will be able to choose between these Office templates. A content type can also inherit properties from a parent content type; any change to the parent will be replicated to its children (this can also be prohibited).

➤ **Individual permissions:** You can set a specific permission for each document, if necessary. For example, you may allow the Managers group full access, while another group only has contributing permissions. A group or user deprived of the read permission for a specific document will not see it at all.

➤ **Check-out/check-in:** You can force a user to check out, that is, lock a document, before editing a document. Only when this document is checked back in, that is, unlocked, will the updated version be visible to all users.

All these features make managing and controlling your documents easier. You no longer need to create files with names like `Contract-Volvo-version3.doc`; instead, you create metadata columns and views to organize all files. And more importantly, you can force the writers of documents to enter information in these columns when saving these files, and that will automatically trigger the workflow you have defined. All the features listed earlier, except document ID and check-out/check-in, also apply to any kind of list, such as Contacts, Links, and Calendar lists; you will learn more about that later in this book. SharePoint offers even more interesting features related to document management. In this book, you will learn about all of these important features.

Project Management

Think about how you work with projects. What type of information is related to a standard project? Although it depends on the project, you will still find that most projects share the following types of information:

➤ **Gantt schema:** A list of project tasks, including start and due dates and allocated resources, displayed in a graphical calendar view.

➤ **Documents:** Typical file types include Microsoft Word documents, Excel spreadsheets, text files, and PowerPoint presentations.

➤ **Members:** A list of all the members in the project.

➤ **Calendar:** A list of events, such as meetings, conferences, and project milestones.

➤ **Contacts:** A list of external contacts, such as vendors, partners, consultants, and other resources.

➤ **Tasks:** A list of things to do, assigned to project members.

➤ **E-mail:** Questions, status, and comments regarding the project.

The problem (if you're not using SharePoint and other specific project management tools) is that this information is stored in several places. Documents and files are stored in a file share; members exist in an e-mail distribution list; calendar events, contacts, and tasks are stored in an Outlook public folder; and e-mail is, of course, stored in each member's personal inbox. Another way to describe this is organized chaos. Each project member needs to know and remember exactly where each type of information is stored. If they do not do so, valuable time is wasted searching for the information. To make things worse, if a new member joins the project, you must explain to her where everything is stored and how it is organized. To make sure the new member understands what has been going on before she joined the team, you must forward a copy of all mail related to this project — if you can find it. The new member then faces the challenging task of reading all this e-mail and understanding what it contains.

I am sure you recognize this situation! To solve this problem, you need something that can store all this information in a single place — or at least make all the information available through a single place. This is exactly what SharePoint does! Here is how you do it:

1. Create a SharePoint website for the project.

2. Add the members to the site. SharePoint will offer to send each member an e-mail with an invitation and a link to the site. SharePoint may also create a mailing list for this project team, making sharing e-mail easy for you.

3. Create a document library to store all files and documents, and copy any related file to this document library.

4. Create another document library to store all e-mail, and copy all project-related e-mail to this document library. Give this document library an e-mail address, and make that address a member of the project team mailing list.

5. Create a calendar, a link list, and a contact list, and use these lists for keeping track of project information and activities.

6. Create a project task list; add tasks, dates, and resources to it; and display it as a Gantt chart.

Such a project site could look similar to Figure 1-3. Chapter 2 includes detailed steps on how to create this type of website and all its lists and fill it with data. You will also learn to design the page to make it easy to use.

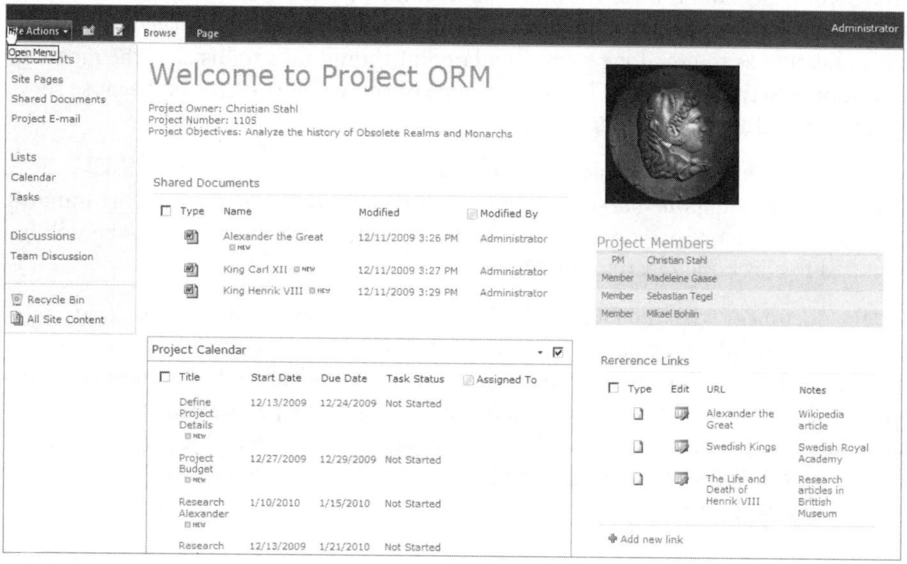

FIGURE 1-3

Managing Meetings

If there's one thing that almost all employees agree on, it is that most meetings are a huge pain! Why? The usual complaints are that they are a waste of time, boring, and too long; that meeting participants are unprepared; and that following up on tasks and activities after the meeting is hard. All of this indicates that even a small step forward to make meetings more effective is important. SharePoint enables you to change many tasks related to meetings into something more positive.

Before a typical meeting, the meeting organizer uses Microsoft Outlook to invite participants, as well as to book resources such as the conference room. Take a closer look at a meeting to understand how you can enhance this type of activity. A meeting is an event where the following steps typically occur:

1. A number of people are invited.

2. The invitees come together, usually in a meeting room.

3. While together, they discuss a number of topics defined in an agenda.

4. The discussion results in a number of actions and decisions, documented in meeting minutes.

Understanding the Typical Meeting Process

In this example, the meeting organizer creates an agenda and describes the meeting objective. (By the way, have you noticed how many meetings don't have a clear objective?) The meeting organizer then estimates the length of the meeting and sends an invitation to all participants. Sometimes documents with information that will be discussed during the meeting are attached to the invitation.

Later, the actual meeting takes place. Each participant has his own copy of the agenda and the attached documents. Well, actually, some participants forgot their copy of the agenda and need to print a copy, and some others did not see the attached document, so they also need to print a copy. About 15 minutes after the meeting should have started, everyone is ready to proceed. Because there is no clear indication as to how long each agenda point should take to discuss, the meeting takes 30 minutes longer than estimated. This makes some of the attendees stressed because they have other appointments after this meeting.

During the meeting, someone is responsible for taking notes about all the decisions, tasks assigned, and activities agreed upon. These notes will be used later to create the meeting minutes. At important meetings, one more person also takes notes because, after this meeting, she will be the person appointed to check the meeting minutes.

One week later, the document with the meeting minutes is created, reviewed by the second note taker, and then sent to all participants by e-mail. A few of these participants actually read the meeting minutes carefully, some just take a quick glance at them, and some do not have time to even open the document. The next time this team has a meeting, only a few participants have read the previous minutes, and many have missed that they were assigned tasks, so the new meeting must start with a summary of the previous meetings, and therefore this meeting will also take longer than estimated, and the story goes on.

Using SharePoint for Effective Meetings

The preceding story might not be true for every organization, of course, but I am sure you are familiar with the ways meetings can go wrong. So what can SharePoint do to make this process both more effective and more interesting? Thanks to the integration of Outlook and SharePoint, you can now simultaneously create the meeting invitation, book a conference room, and create a *Meeting Workspace*, which is a specially designed website in SharePoint where all the information regarding the meeting will be stored, including the following:

➤ **Agenda:** A list of all the items you will discuss during the meeting, including who is responsible for each one, how long it will take, and any comments regarding the items.

➤ **Participants:** SharePoint automatically creates a list of all invited participants and displays it on the Meeting Workspace. This list is automatically updated with the reply status of each participant so that everyone can see who will come or why someone declined the invitation.

➤ **Tasks:** A list of all the tasks agreed upon during the meeting, including who is assigned to each task, its priority, and a due date.

➤ **Decisions:** A list of all the decisions agreed upon during the meeting.

➤ **Document library:** Contains any document with information that relates to this meeting instance, as well as documents created as a result of the meeting.

All this information is available to all participants directly when they receive their meeting invitation, thanks to a link to the Meeting Workspace that is included in the invitation. This means that the participant can see the agenda before the meeting takes place, maybe add some extra items to it, and get access to any document with information related to the meeting. If needed, the participant can add her own documents.

When the actual meeting takes place, the organizer uses a video projector that displays the meeting workspace so everyone can see it. No one needs a printed copy of the meeting agenda, because it is listed on the Meeting Workspace for everyone to see. All documents are listed in the document library — if there is a discussion about what a specific document contains, the organizer can quickly open the document to display its contents on the screen.

Any activities, tasks, or decisions that are agreed upon during the meeting are directly entered into the list. Everyone can see this, so there is no need for anyone to review the meeting minutes afterwards. The result is that everyone will be involved in whatever decision is made. This makes the meeting more interesting and engaging. Because the agenda clearly states the amount of time it should take to discuss each item, the participants can focus on that subject and try to stay within the estimated time.

Because everything agreed upon is entered directly into the tasks and decision lists during the meeting, you don't need any meeting minutes at all! If a participant needs to see what was discussed in the meeting, she can simply open the calendar meeting in her Outlook and click the link inside to open the Meeting Workspace again.

This meeting procedure may not work for all kinds of meetings; for example, meetings that for legal reasons require meeting minutes to be printed out and signed. But if you just need a printout of the meeting minutes, you can add a separate web page to the meeting site that displays the current meeting details arranged as typical meeting minutes.

Chapters 2 and 3 explore how to create a Meeting Workspace, configure its lists, and fill it with data. It also shows you how to link repeated meetings to the same Meeting Workspace, giving you one web page for each meeting instance and making it very simple to go back and see what you discussed in a previous meeting.

KEEPING YOUR ORGANIZATION UPDATED

For many years now, organizations have used an intranet to make sure that everyone has access to general information, such as company news, information from the Human Resources department, or a list of all employees and their contact information. SharePoint is a great tool to help you create an intranet. With SharePoint, you often refer to the intranet as "the portal site," or simply "the portal."

Benefits of a SharePoint Intranet

Using SharePoint for your intranet has many advantages. It is fast, it can support any size of organization up to millions of users, and it has several powerful features, such as the following:

➤ **Content management:** SharePoint Server has greatly improved the content management features introduced in previous versions of SharePoint Server. These enhanced features are based on the wiki functionality and allow you to edit web content much easier than before, while still having full control over the content. For example, you may use content management for intranet home pages and news, with features like check-out/check-in, approval procedures, version history, and workflows. Many of these features are available in SharePoint Foundation, but only SharePoint Server offers full content management functionality.

➤ **News:** This is a special site in SharePoint Server where all users with the proper permissions can create news articles, typically about the company and its customers and partners. This news site is based on the content management features mentioned previously. Regardless of where this news site is located, its content can be displayed on any site in the SharePoint farm. For example, you may want each department to create its own news articles, and show them all on the intranet start page.

➤ **Targeting:** This very handy feature is available in SharePoint Server, but not in SharePoint Foundation. It allows you to filter the content so it is visible only to a specific group of people. Targeting can be used to filter both web parts and list content. For example, you can use it to make sure only IT employees can see the IT news, while the sales team will only see sales information — on the same page! The people who will see the information are referred to as an *audience*; they may be an AD group, both security and distribution groups, a SharePoint group, and a special type of group that SharePoint calls an Audience group.

➤ **User Profile Synchronization:** This is a feature in SharePoint Server that makes it possible to collect user information that is stored in AD and other external databases, such as their full name, e-mail addresses, department, manager, phone numbers, picture, description, and so on. SharePoint stores this information in its user profile database.

➤ **Document Center:** This SharePoint Server feature solves a common problem — how to make specific files available to a large group of users without giving them access to other files. For example, in a project site with 100 files, one of these files is a final report and should be made available to all other users. Instead of modifying the permissions for this final report, and forcing each user to enter the project site to read it, SharePoint can make a copy of the file and store a read-only copy of it in a public document archive; that is, the Document Center. If the original document is later modified, the author can see that a copy exists in the Document Center and choose to update that copy.

➤ **Report Center:** This is a site in SharePoint Server where you can create, distribute, and manage important business data. For example, you can use it to display diagrams in Excel spreadsheets, reports based on data stored in an external SQL database, and Key Performance Indicators (KPI) that show how your organization meets the expected sales goals. Some of these features take advantage of a new component in SharePoint Server, previously known as a separate server product named PerformancePoint Server.

➤ **Site Directory:** This SharePoint Server site displays a list of existing websites, including their names, descriptions, owners, and other properties. This list makes finding a specific website quick and easy for a user. For example, you could use it to group project sites belonging to specific departments, or list archived sites. This directory can also take advantage of the filtering technique in SharePoint Server, so users only see sites that are available to them.

> ➤ **My Site:** This is a personal site type that comes with SharePoint Server. It allows users to have a personal site that they can design to match their own needs. It is typically used to store local files, pictures, and other personal information; that is, it replaces their previous Home directory. It can also list the team sites that this user is a member of, and the documents and tasks that relate to the users on those sites. My Site allows the user to enter personal properties, such as a picture, description, interests, expertise areas, education, and more. SharePoint Server 2010 also enables the use of features similar to micro-blogs like Twitter and Facebook wall chatting, but focused to enhance team collaboration.

In addition, you will find that the News pages allow you to define when to display and remove the news from the list. News is not automatically deleted; instead, it is archived, and can still be found using the search feature in SharePoint, or by browsing the news archive. In SharePoint 2010, adding and working with pictures is much easier compared to its predecessor. Even SharePoint Foundation now allows you to add pictures more easily, as well as resize and move pictures between different parts of the web page. These pictures are typically stored in a Site Asset Library or a Picture Library and may be linked to news articles, start pages, and other types of lists that allow pictures as content.

Understanding a Typical Intranet

An intranet based on SharePoint Server will automatically add links to the websites you create for your projects, meetings, and other shared team sites. These links may have categories assigned to them that will show up on the *Site Directory* page, thus making locating and opening a specific site easy for the user. The categories used in the site directory are created and managed by the SharePoint administrator, and their values are entered by the person who creates the site. The intranet also allows you to create any type of list, including document libraries, contacts, and events. If you decide to go with SharePoint Server 2010 as the platform for your intranet, it is hard to find a good reason why you should use another web server product for your Internet Portal site. Doing this will not only make things harder for you to support and manage (including backup and restore), but it will also force your organization to pay for two server licenses rather than one.

That is the reason why many organizations choose to use SharePoint as a platform for their public-facing Internet sites. This trend started with Microsoft Office SharePoint Server 2007 (MOSS), and SharePoint Server 2010 is a really great platform for this type of public site, due to its much enhanced web content management and richness of built-in features and functionality. Chapter 7 covers more about building both intranet- and Internet-facing portals.

But let's go back to a typical intranet scenario. Suppose your organization has three departments: Sales, IT, and Human Resources. You also have some special groups: the executive team, a project team, and an external sales force. Your task is to make sure each of them gets the right information in an easy and intuitive way. Your CEO requires a common intranet where all important information regarding the company, its customers, and its employees are presented. Each department requires its own intranet. The IT folks tell you they are sick and tired of all the sales info, and the sales guys ask you politely whether a way exists to filter out everything except the sales-related information. And all of them say they want a fast and easy way to find the right website where all the information is stored for the projects, meetings, customers, and so on. And by the way, the executive group wants an easy way of finding all contracts, regardless of where they are stored. How do you solve all these issues?

One simple solution for this small organization could look like this:

1. Install SharePoint Server 2010.

2. Create a common intranet portal site for the organization.

3. Create a separate site on the intranet for each department, with its own news listing, document libraries, and contact lists. These pages are

   ➤ Sales

   ➤ IT

   ➤ HR

4. Create the following SharePoint groups, make AD groups and users members of these groups, and use them for permission settings and audience targeting:

   ➤ Sales Team

   ➤ IT Team

   ➤ HR Team

   ➤ Executive Team

   ➤ Project Team

   ➤ External Sales Team

5. Instruct the authors responsible for creating general news to target their news items to all audience groups, so each user in the organization will be able to see this information.

6. Instruct local news authors in each department to create news items that are displayed only on each department's local intranet site.

7. Use the Site Directory as the parent site, and create new websites for each project, team site, and so on, under this parent. This ensures that all websites are listed in the site directory and are therefore easy to find. Make sure to set the permission correctly so only the intended users will have access to the sites.

8. Create a document library named Contract on the Document Center site. Tell the salespeople that whenever they create a new contract in their team sites to make sure it gets copied to the Contract library in the Document Center. Set the permission to the Contract library so only the Executive Team will have read access.

9. Make sure every user has updated information in the AD, such as phone numbers, department, company name, and e-mail address. Then synchronize the AD with SharePoint once every night. Make sure each user profile in SharePoint links to a photo of the user. Instruct your users that whenever they see a name listed in a SharePoint site, they can simply click it to get more information about that user.

The preceding solution and structure are typical for many small organizations, but there is one flaw: To be fully updated about the organization, a user must read the intranet start page, as well as the local department page that the user belongs to. This may be harder for the average user than one might think. Let's face it — the typical user is more interested in her daily activities, such as working with documents, creating reports, and participating in projects. News is something a user reads occasionally, and if the intranet structure displays news and other general information in multiple locations, the risk is high that the user will miss important information. Chapter 7 offers strategies to use when building intranet portals.

FINDING YOUR INFORMATION FASTER IN SHAREPOINT SERVER

How often do you search for information? I would guess at least once every day. Assume the average user spends 10 minutes every day searching for information. If you have 200 users, this would be about 2000 minutes, or 33 hours per day. You could also put it this way: Your organization pays for 200 employees, but it only gets the efficiency of 196 (4 people × 8 working hours = 32 hours total per day). What this means is that even small improvements in efficiency may lead to big results. And not just for the owners of the company — the employees will be happy, too, because they can concentrate on doing their jobs instead of searching for information.

Since its first release in 2001, SharePoint Server has had a very advanced search and index feature. For each generation, this feature has been enhanced, and this is also true in SharePoint Server 2010. In 2008, Microsoft bought a very advanced search engine named FAST from a Norwegian company — this product is included in the enterprise version of SharePoint Server and greatly enhances the search experience for users. SharePoint Foundation also has a basic search feature, but this is a far cry from the feature that comes with SharePoint Server. Luckily, Microsoft offers the free product Search Server Express 2010, which can be integrated with SharePoint Foundation. These products together offer users a very good search experience that is close to but not the same as what SharePoint Server offers.

A number of Internet search tools are available, such as Microsoft Bing and Google Search. So why not use these tools instead of the SharePoint built-in search engine? The answer is that they rank the search result in different ways. For example, if you use Google and search for "Volvo," you will probably be satisfied by several of the search results; but when searching in SharePoint, you most likely are looking for a specific document, not just any document that contains the word "Volvo." Chapter 6 and Appendix D show you how to configure and manage the search feature in SharePoint, including how to extend the search feature built into MS Vista, Windows 7, and Internet Explorer so they will also show search results from SharePoint. One of many great features in SharePoint search is that you can index information stored outside SharePoint and by that make it searchable. The following are examples of content sources that SharePoint can index:

➤   Every website in the SharePoint environment (including all SharePoint Server and SharePoint Foundation sites)

➤   Any file server in your IT environment, including Windows, UNIX, and Linux servers

➤   Your Microsoft Exchange database (including all public folders or role-based mailboxes such as Help Desk)

➤   External business and production databases, such as SAP and Oracle

➤   Any Lotus Notes database you may have

➤   Other internal websites (such as your old intranet and your public website)

➤   External websites (such as your partner's website; and why not your competitor's?)

What File Types Can You Search?

Before SharePoint allows you to search, it must index the content sources. So the question in the preceding heading should really be, "What file types can SharePoint index?" And the answer is, "Practically anything stored in a computer!" Indexing is the process where sources of content, like SharePoint sites and file servers, are crawled by a small program that opens files, documents, and other types of information and looks for words and numbers. This information is stored in an index file, including a pointer to that specific information source. By default, SharePoint allows you to index Microsoft Office file formats, such as Microsoft Word and Microsoft Excel, plus all standard file formats, such as HTML, RTF, and TXT files.

What about other common file types, such as PDF, ZIP, and CAD files? To explain this, I have to tell you a little more about the indexing process. The process is more complicated than this list indicates, but the basic steps are as follow:

1.   A scheduled task starts the index process. The index engine looks into every location you have instructed it to look into — these locations are also known as content sources.

2.   When it finds a file, it looks at its file type; for example, DOCX.

3.   It checks a list in SharePoint where the administrator has specified what file types you want indexed — DOCX is in this list and will be indexed.

4.   The index process now needs a small application that understands how to read DOCX files. Such applications are referred to as Index Filters, or IFilters, for short. Every file type needs its own IFilter, including DOCX files.

5.   The IFilter opens the file and starts to crawl it. Whenever it finds some text or numbers, it sends this information through a filter that removes words that should not be indexed, such as yes, no, 1, and 2. The resulting stream of words is then stored in an index file along with information about the name and location of this file, plus the security settings for the file and its language. This information will be used later on when a user searches for content that will match this file.

6.   When all the text in the file is read, the IFilter closes the file, and the process starts again with step 2, looking for the next file, until all the files and information in this content source have been indexed. Then the next content source, if any, will be opened and indexed in the same way.

So if you want to make file types like PDF searchable, you need to do two things: configure the SharePoint index engine to look for PDF files, and install an IFilter for the PDF file type. The index engine does not include this IFilter by default. You may wonder why Microsoft has not added a common file type such as PDF. The answer is simple: Adobe owns the PDF format, so Microsoft is not allowed to include an IFilter for legal reasons. So Adobe is making the IFilter for the PDF — and the good news is that Adobe is giving it away for free to encourage people to use the PDF format for storing all kinds of content. Chapter 6 shows you how to find and install common IFilters, including the PDF version.

What Types of Search Can You Perform?

The default configuration of the SharePoint search engine allows you to search for whole words and their stemmers only. For example, if you search for "write," you will also find files with "writing" and "wrote," thanks to the stemming support.

You can also search for document properties, often referred to as metadata or tags, such as author, title, and file size. The list of properties is different for different types of documents. The following Try It Out helps you see what properties a standard Microsoft Word document has available.

TRY IT OUT Viewing a Document's Properties

1. Open a SharePoint site that contains a document library.

2. Open any DOCX file in this library, with Microsoft Word 2010.

3. Click the Office Button, and the Backstage page opens.

4. On the right side of this page, you can see all the standard properties for this document, such as Author and Title. Click on Properties to open its drop-down list, and then select Show Document Panel.

How It Works

These steps reopen the document page, including the *Document Information Panel* or DIP, just above the text body, where you will also see all custom columns in the document library where this document is stored, because Word and SharePoint automatically synchronize, or propagate, custom columns between them.

All standard properties of a document are automatically indexed and therefore searchable in SharePoint. You can also search for combinations, such as documents containing the word "Viking" with the standard attribute "Author" equal to "Göran Husman." Although this method is satisfactory for most search scenarios, you may also want to search for a document that matches your own custom column value. You may recall that you can add any number of columns to a document library; for example, "Doc Type" or "Status." As explained in Chapter 6, even these custom columns can be searchable if you configure the SharePoint index engine properly.

If you know that the information you are searching for is stored in a specific location, you can limit the search results to that location by using *search scopes*. For example, you can create one search scope per content source, such as one for SharePoint content only, and one for file server; or you can create a search scope for metadata, such as Customer=Volvo. These search scopes must be defined by the administrator before they can be used by the users.

You can also define keyword best bets. This feature helps your users find frequently requested information. For example, suppose that when you talk with the sales manager, she tells you that members in her team often need access to the product specifications. The problem is that these products have several names. The best-selling product is article X2025A, but most customers refer to this as the "Super Gadget"; to add to the problem, the internal name used by the sales team is the

"Money Maker." She wants her team to be able to search for any of these terms and still find the product specification for the X2025A. The keyword best bet feature in SharePoint is an easy fix for this type of search. You simply need to create a list of each alias for the keyword X2025A and then link this keyword to the proper document for that specification. When someone later searches for any of these words, that person will find the X2025A specification at the top of the search results. Below it, all other documents that match this search criterion will be listed.

ACCESSING SHAREPOINT OVER THE INTERNET

Very soon after you start working with SharePoint, you find that it contains more and more of your business-critical data. You also become aware of the fact that you need online access to the SharePoint server in order to work with the documents, projects, and everything else stored in the SharePoint database. So you start thinking, "How do I access this information when I am not at the office?" One way is to use the integration between SharePoint and Microsoft Outlook 2010, which allows a user to make a copy of a document library and store it in an Outlook folder, thus making it possible to read while offline. You can also use the SharePoint Workspace client, and select almost any type of list in a SharePoint site for offline access; any changes made while you're offline is replicated back to the original list when you're online again. Another way to solve the need to work with SharePoint content is to make your SharePoint environment accessible over the Internet, in a secure way, while still getting good performance.

> **NOTE** *SharePoint 2010 allows a mobile phone to connect to a SharePoint list, using a special view that only shows text, if the SharePoint server is accessible over the Internet. In Windows Mobile 6.5 and Windows Phone 7, you will even find a specific SharePoint application that allows access to rich content, such as documents and images. The iPhone and iPod Touch devices also offer applications that allow the reading and writing of rich SharePoint content.*

How You Do It

Because SharePoint is a web application running on top of Windows Server's IIS 7, making SharePoint accessible from outside your organization is very easy. You simply configure your firewall to allow connections to the SharePoint server from the Internet. But this solution is not good from a security perspective. It exposes your SharePoint server to the world, and it would probably take just hours before this server is hacked or taken down by people with more time than conscience. Another big problem with this simple solution is that your password and user account may be transferred over the Internet unencrypted, depending on what type of authentication method you use. Someone listening in on your communication could learn your password and be able to log on as you!

A better solution is to install a *Secure Socket Layer* (SSL) certificate on your IIS 7 and force every access to the SharePoint server to use SSL-encrypted connections. That is, the user must enter the *Uniform Resource Locator (URL)* address to the SharePoint server starting with `https://`. The effect of this is that your logon credentials are protected. There is no longer any risk that someone will see your password.

The best solution is to prohibit the external users from accessing the SharePoint server directly from the outside, combined with the SSL-encrypted connection. Instead, your users would access something that looks like the SharePoint server but in reality is a replica. This type of replica is known as an application proxy server. Microsoft has a great product for this: the *Forefront Threat Management Gateway*, or TMG, which replaced the *Internet Security and Acceleration Server*, also known as the *MS ISA* server. With this solution, things work like so:

1. The external user connects to the SharePoint web address over the Internet, using an SSL connection such as `https://intranet.filobit.com`. This could be the exact same address for users on the inside, except for the `https://` part (internally, you would use `http://` instead).

2. The user connection passes through the firewall, but is directed to the TMG server instead of the real SharePoint server.

3. The TMG server looks at the requested URL address, checks its rules, and if everything is okay, it connects to that URL and retrieves the SharePoint page. This page is then sent back to the user.

4. The user sees the requested URL, and believes he is connected to the real SharePoint server. He clicks a link on that page, and, once again, the TMG server gets a request for the new URL, repeating step 3.

> **NOTE** The TMG, server is by itself an excellent firewall that meets the highest security standards. A common practice is that organizations use a TMG server both as the primary firewall and a proxy server, thus no extra firewall is needed.

The nice thing with this solution is that the user never gets access to anything more than the TMG server, which normally is installed on the *demilitarized zone (DMZ)* segment of the network. This segment is where you put all your publicly available servers, such as your public website. You can use the rules in the TMG server to control exactly what the user can see and do. For example, in some organizations, users have different levels of access, depending on where they are situated at the moment. Inside the network, they have full access; on the Internet, they have access to only some part of SharePoint. This is something that only a solution like the TMG server can help you deploy, because SharePoint itself cannot distinguish access to its information in this way. Another bonus effect is that frequently requested web pages are cached on the TMG server, meaning that these pages will be displayed more quickly for the users.

Allowing External Partners Access

Now you know the general steps in configuring the SharePoint environment for access over the Internet. But how do you manage partners and other users outside your organization? If there is a need to give them limited access to your SharePoint server, it can be done! Before you do this, you must understand how SharePoint controls what the user can do with its access control feature.

Every user who wants to access any part of SharePoint must be granted permissions, either directly, as a member of an AD group, or as a member of a *SharePoint group*. There are a number of default *permission levels* in SharePoint that define the exact type of access a user or group may be granted. Here are the most common levels (see Appendix B for more information):

➤ **Read:** Allows the user to open and read information, including documents, pictures, and list content. The user will not be able to create, modify, or delete information in SharePoint.

➤ **Contribute:** Allows the user to do everything a Reader can do, plus create, modify, and delete information, including news, documents, contacts, and so on.

➤ **Designer:** Allows the user to do everything a Contributor can do, plus create new document libraries, lists, document columns, and document views, as well as change the layout of the website by adding or moving web parts.

➤ **Full Control:** The user has full access to the site and can do everything, including adding and deleting members and changing their access.

> **NOTE** *A SharePoint group is a special type of group only available in SharePoint. Its purpose is to allow collections of AD groups and users, and other security identities, and grant them access to SharePoint sites and objects.*

Creating Local User Accounts for External Users

Take a look at how you can control access for internal users: Assume that you have an employee named Anna. She needs access to the intranet, and she will only read information. You solve this by adding Anna's user account to the SharePoint group *Visitors* on the intranet portal site. For a while, Anna is satisfied, but later, Anna comes back to you and says that she needs both read and write access to a given project site. So you add Anna's user account to the site group *Members* for this particular project site. Anna now belongs to different SharePoint groups in different parts of the SharePoint environment. Whenever she accesses SharePoint, IIS will validate her user account and check that she belongs to a SharePoint group with the proper permissions.

If you want to allow access to a user outside your organization, authenticating that user must be possible. In other words, the external user needs to log on so that IIS can see what access he is granted in SharePoint. This will be a problem with external users, because they don't have a local user account in your AD domain. One simple way to solve this problem is to create a local user account for each of these external users. Now you can assign these users membership in any SharePoint group. To extend the security, you can create rules in the TMG server to control exactly what part of SharePoint users can access. The external user must remember to log on with the local account you created. So everyone is happy now, at least for a while.

> *NOTE SharePoint 2010 allows other authentication methods to be installed. For example, using a separate SQL database for storing the user names and passwords for external users (frequently referred to as Forms-Based Authentication, FBA) is possible. You can also grant access to users with Windows Live ID accounts. Both of these methods require some coding, so they are outside the scope of this book.*

But this solution is far from perfect. It works, this is true, but what happens if this external person moves to another company? For example, suppose that Michael works for the company ABC. Michael is involved in a project in your organization, Filobit, Inc., and needs access to the SharePoint site where all the project information is stored. You create a local user account for Michael, grant him the proper access, and tell him the URL for the project site and that his logon name is Filobit\Michael. He starts working with the project, and everything works as expected. One month later, Michael leaves ABC, and starts working for its competitor, XYZ. You don't have a business relation with XYZ, so its employees are not allowed access to your project site. Now you must disable the account Filobit\Michael. But how will you know that Michael has left his old company, ABC? There is no automatic process that will inform you about this situation. Hopefully, someone at ABC tells you, or somebody in the project team gets this information and tells you. Clearly, this situation will be very hard to handle if you have 10 or more external partners. But at the moment, this is how this solution works.

Active Directory Federation Service (ADFS)

There is some light at the end of the tunnel with regard to allowing external users access to your environment. Windows Server 2008 has an interesting feature that Microsoft calls *Active Directory Federation Service* (ADFS). The objective of ADFS is to resolve precisely this type situation (that is, letting two completely separate organizations share access to web applications like SharePoint without the need to create local accounts for the remote organization). The idea is rather simple and easy to understand, but the technique beneath is advanced and worth its own book.

The basic idea of ADFS is to make it possible for an organization to use its own user accounts to get access on a remote web application. For example, assume that you have two companies, A and B. User Bob works for B, and he needs access to a SharePoint site in A. Bob talks to the administrator for the site in A, who then grants the B\Bob account access to the requested site.

You manage the magic in this scenario by adding extra servers to your AD domain, one in each organization. The primary ADFS server is referred to as the *federation server* and hosts the federation service component. Its primary task is to route incoming requests from the Internet to the website a user is trying to access. It is also responsible for creating a security token that will be passed on to the web application. The process that validates the external user is the ADFS Web Agent, which runs on the web server (in this case, the SharePoint server).

Most organizations do not want their federation server exposed to the Internet. You can protect it by installing an optional federation proxy server. This proxy relays federation requests from the outside world to your internal federation server, meaning that your federation server is no longer exposed directly to the outside world.

NOTE *ADFS is based on the standard Security Assertion Markup Language (SAML), which means that the external company need not be running the Microsoft Windows.*

SharePoint Workspace 2010

Microsoft Office 2010 Pro Plus offers a new solution for sharing documents and any type of SharePoint information with users both inside and outside your organization, without the need for ADFS or local AD user accounts. Thanks to its simplicity, it is a very attractive solution for teams with up to 15 members. All that is needed is that all team members install the SharePoint Workspace 2010 client and accept an invitation from the team leader. SharePoint Workspace then automatically synchronizes any updates of these lists and libraries between all members as soon as they get connected to the Internet. This client application is an enhanced version of what previously was called Groove. This application uses its own user database, so there is no requirement that all members have user accounts in the same Windows domain.

NOTE *For more information about Microsoft SharePoint Workspace, go to* `www.microsoft.com/office/2010/en/sharepoint-workspace/`.

▶ WHAT YOU LEARNED IN THIS CHAPTER

TOPIC	KEY CONCEPTS
SharePoint Functionality	A web-based application that helps users share and collaborate on any type of data and information. Allows the ordinary user to create sites and document libraries in a secure and controlled manner.
Typical usage of SharePoint	Intranet, extranet, and Internet sites Project sites, document archives Business Intelligence solutions
History of SharePoint	The previous versions of SharePoint were SharePoint 2001, SharePoint 2003, and SharePoint 2007. SharePoint 2010 is the fourth generation and comes in two versions: *SharePoint Foundation*, which replaces WSS 3.0, and *Microsoft SharePoint Server 2010*, which replaces MOSS 2007.
SharePoint 2010 editions	SharePoint Foundation 2010 SharePoint Server 2010 Standard SharePoint Server 2010 Enterprise
SharePoint Foundation	This is the base module of SharePoint. It is used to create sites for managing and sharing information, such as projects, customer data, meetings, and workspace areas.
SharePoint Server	This is an add-on package on top of SharePoint Foundation. It enhances SharePoint Foundation with a large number of features, such as Search, Excel Services, Visio Services, Access Service, and Forms Server, plus new site templates such as an Internet Site, Intranet Portal, and Document Centers site.
Hardware requirements	Minimum requirements: 64-bit CPU, 4GB RAM, 30GB Disk
Software requirements	Windows Server 2008 / 2008 R2, 64-bit IIS, ASP.NET, PowerShell 2.0 SQL Server 2008 64-bit (Express or the full product)
SharePoint Index Engine	Index almost any content source beside SharePoint itself, such as Exchange, File Servers, Lotus Notes, Web Applications, and external databases. Can also index the User Profile database in SharePoint Server, to support people search.

TOPIC	KEY CONCEPTS
External Access to SharePoint	Configure firewalls to grant external users access to SharePoint.
	All users must have an account, including external users.
	Microsoft Forefront TMG comes with wizards for easy and fast configurations to enable access to SharePoint from the Internet.
Offline Access to SharePoint Content	Microsoft Outlook 2007/2010
	Microsoft Access
	Microsoft SharePoint Workspace

2

Building SharePoint Foundation Sites

WHAT YOU WILL LEARN IN THIS CHAPTER:

➤ Differences Between SharePoint Foundation Sites and SharePoint Server Sites

➤ Understanding Site Templates

➤ Managing Permissions for Sites, Lists, and Items

➤ Changing Site Layouts Using a Web Browser

➤ Managing Blog Sites

➤ Working with Site Content

Chapter 1 offered an overview of SharePoint and its features. You learned that there are basically two editions: SharePoint Foundation and SharePoint Server. SharePoint Foundation is the base edition that offers an excellent platform for collaboration and sharing information. SharePoint Server extends this platform with a lot of new and enhanced functionality, which makes SharePoint Server a great choice for building any type of web-based solution; for example intranet, extranet, and Internet sites, plus advanced document management, content management, business intelligence solutions, and more.

This chapter discusses the basic structure and building blocks of SharePoint 2010. It focuses on what you can do with a standard SharePoint Foundation server. Keep in mind that even if you run your environment based on SharePoint Server, everything described in this chapter will also be true for this SharePoint Server environment, so make sure to read this chapter carefully.

Before you read this chapter and try out the steps described, there are a few things you need. You will need to have two demo user accounts set up in the Active Directory (AD) for Anna and Malin, who also both have a Microsoft Exchange e-mail account. You need to grant these users Contribute permission to an intranet at `http://srv1` before proceeding with the Try It Outs in this chapter. You will also need to set up an intranet at `http://srv1`, with two subsites at `http://srv1/test` and `http://srv1/honey` (both based on the Team Site site template).

If you follow the instructions in Appendixes A and B for SharePoint Foundation, or Appendixes C and D for SharePoint Server, you will have a site collection to test the Try It Out instructions in this chapter; Appendix B covers the details of how to grant user access to SharePoint sites. If you need to create a new subsite in this site collection, follow the steps in the following Try It Out.

TRY IT OUT **Building a Subsite**

In this example, you already have a site collection created with the URL address of `http://srv1`. (If you don't have a site collection and need to make one, see this book's appendixes for appropriate instructions.) Follow these steps to create a subsite named "Test" based on the Team Site site template; its URL will be `http://srv1/test`:

1. Log on as a site collection administrator. Start a web browser and open the URL address `http://srv1` (note that in your environment, you may have another URL for this top site).

2. In the page that appears, click Site Actions ➪ New Site, enter the following values in the new form, and accept the other default settings:

   a. Title: Test

   b. URL name: http://srv1/test

   c. Select a template: Team Site

   d. Use the top link bar from the parent site: Yes

3. Verify that the new subsite opens, and that the URL is correct; that is, `http://srv1/test` (see the following note).

> **NOTE** The URL listed for the new subsite will actually be `http://srv1/test/SitePages/Home.aspx`. Later in this chapter, you will learn that SitePages is a system list for page files, and Home.aspx is the page file currently displayed. But the actual URL address to this site is still `http://srv1/test` — you don't have to enter the rest of the URL, because SharePoint will automatically add it.

How It Works

Creating a subsite in an existing site collection gives you a test environment for the step-by-step instructions in this chapter.

DEFINING SHAREPOINT WEBSITES

All SharePoint solutions are based on websites, regardless of how simple or complex the solutions are. As described in Appendix B, these websites are grouped into one or more site collections that consist of one top site and any number and levels of subsites, also known as *webs* or sometimes *subwebs*. These site collections exist inside a web application, which is an extended version of Internet Information Services (IIS) websites.

All content in a site collection is stored in the SQL database that is associated with each web application; these databases are often referred to as *content databases*. One web application can host multiple site collections. The default maximum number is 15,000, and a warning is generated when the number exceeds 9000, but these are configurable values that you can set using the steps in the following Try It Out. Every site collection must be managed individually, so keeping the number of site collections down to a minimum will reduce the amount of administrative work.

 NOTE *The term* sites *in the following instructions means* site collections.

TRY IT OUT **Managing the Maximum Number of Site Collections for a Web Application**

In this example, you — the farm administrator — change the default value of 15,000 site collections to a maximum of 10 for the WSS_Content database, which is associated with the SharePoint – 80 web application.

1. Log on as a farm administrator to the SharePoint server, and open the SharePoint Central Administration tool: Click Start ➪ All Programs ➪ Microsoft SharePoint 2010 Products ➪ SharePoint 2010 Central Administration.

2. Click Application Management ➪ Manage Content Database.

3. In the configuration page that appears, check that the correct web application (at the top right) is listed, and you can see its content database(s). If it's not correct, click the web application and change it.

4. Click the database you want to configure; in this example, WSS_Content, to open its configuration page.

5. In the Database Capacity Settings section, you can see that the "Number of sites before a warning events is generated" is 9000, and the "Maximum number of sites that can be generated in this database" is 15,000. Change the warning level to 9 and the maximum number to 10.

6. Click OK to save and close the new settings.

7. In the page that appears, verify that this database has the new values listed.

How It Works

By configuring the maximum number of site collections for a content database, you can ensure that this database cannot host any more site collections than you planned for.

Comparing SharePoint Foundation and SharePoint Server Sites

All types of sites you can generate in a SharePoint Foundation environment are also available in SharePoint Server. In fact, in most SharePoint Server installations you will find that the majority of all sites are SharePoint Foundation sites. So what differs between the SharePoint Foundation sites and the SharePoint Server sites? The answer is *functionality*. Appendixes B and D describe this functionality in technical depth, but this chapter explains these differences in plain English.

SharePoint Foundation comes with a basic functionality, and SharePoint Server adds a lot more to each feature, plus a large number of new features. See Table 2-1 for a comparison.

TABLE 2-1: Differences Between SharePoint Foundation and SharePoint Server (Enterprise Edition)

TYPE OF FUNCTIONALITY	# IN SHAREPOINT FOUNDATION	# IN SHAREPOINT SERVER
Web parts	10	63
Service applications	1	12
Site features	2	18
List types	12	17
Site templates	9	19

So it should not come as a surprise that SharePoint Server is a richer environment for building SharePoint sites. This is also the reason for the difference in price: Whereas SharePoint Foundation comes free with Windows Server 2008, SharePoint Server requires both a server license and a client license. The question is, of course, whether you can settle for SharePoint Foundation, or you must use SharePoint Server. Appendixes A and C give you more information about how to find out what version you need.

What Is a SharePoint Site?

A good and reasonable question is, "What is a website?" This question can be answered in different ways; for example, by explaining how the IIS operates, or by explaining a website from a developer perspective. Because this book is for IT professionals, it focuses on how a website works.

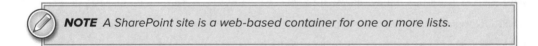 **NOTE** *A SharePoint site is a web-based container for one or more lists.*

Each SharePoint site contains one or more lists; these lists contain information, such as contacts, calendar bookings, and tasks. Some lists are called *discussion boards*, others are called *surveys*, and some are called *libraries* (for example, document libraries and picture libraries). These libraries differ from ordinary lists by functionality. For example:

➤ A *document library* allows the user to check out a document; this operation is not possible with list items.

➤ A *picture library* contains a slideshow feature, which is not possible with list items.

➤ A *site asset library* allows a preview of its pictures, audio, and video files, which is not possible with list items.

SharePoint organizes everything around the list concept. All content stored in SharePoint is stored in a list, which in turn is stored in an SQL Server database. The easiest way of checking this organization is to open a site to reveal its content, as demonstrated in the following Try It Out.

TRY IT OUT   Displaying All Site Content

In this example, you open a site to see its content. To make sure you see everything, log on as a site owner.

1. Log on as a site owner and open any SharePoint site; for example, `http://srv1/test`.

2. In the web page that appears, click Site Actions ➪ View All Site Content. All the lists and libraries displayed on this page are stored inside this particular site. See Figure 2-1 for an example of the content inside a standard team site.

FIGURE 2-1

How It Works

The content in lists and libraries is stored within tables in a database. SharePoint's list concept makes it very easy to manage these lists and their content.

Lists and Libraries

To master SharePoint, you must understand what lists are available, what they do, and how to manage them. Some of these list types are only available in an SharePoint Server environment, as Table 2-2 shows.

TABLE 2-2: List Types in SharePoint 2010

LIST TYPE	DESCRIPTION	SHAREPOINT FOUNDATION	SHAREPOINT SERVER
Document Library	Stores any type of files and documents allowed in SharePoint. Supports check out/in, version history, metadata, and more. Supports two-way synchronization with Microsoft Outlook.	Yes	Yes
Form Library	Stores XML-based forms; for example, Microsoft InfoPath forms.	Yes	Yes
Wiki Page Library	Stores Wiki pages, used in Wiki-based sites.	Yes	Yes
Picture Library	Stores pictures and image files. Supports check out/in, version history, metadata, and slideshows.	Yes	Yes
Asset Library (this is an automatically created System List)	Stores image, audio, and video files. Supports preview, plus check out/in, version history, metadata, and more.	Yes	Yes
Data Connection Library	Stores files that contain information about external data connections.	No	Yes
Translation Management Library	Stores documents written in multiple languages. Supports translation tasks, including workflows for the translation process, and check out/in, version history, and metadata.	No	Yes
Report Library	Stores web pages and documents used with Key Performance Indicators (KPIs) for tracking metrics, goals, and Business Intelligence (BI) information.	No	Yes
Slide Library	Stores individual slides from Microsoft PowerPoint presentations. Supports managing, finding, and reusing sides, including check out/in, version history, and metadata.	No	Yes

LIST TYPE	DESCRIPTION	SHAREPOINT FOUNDATION	SHAREPOINT SERVER
Announcements	Stores short messages and news, including rich text formatting (RTF), pictures, links, and tables. Supports version history and metadata.	Yes	Yes
Contact	Stores contact information about people. Includes version history and metadata. Supports two-way synchronization with Microsoft Outlook.	Yes	Yes
Discussion Board	Stores threaded discussion postings. Supports version history, metadata, and two-way synchronization with Microsoft Outlook.	Yes	Yes
Links	Stores links to any destination. Supports HTTP, HTTPS, FTP, FILE, and MAILTO types of URL.	Yes	Yes
Calendar	Stores time-based calendar events, like meetings, reservations, and deadlines. Supports version history, metadata, and two-way synchronization with Microsoft Outlook.	Yes	Yes
Tasks	Stores tasks events, like things to do, actions to complete before a given date, and so on. Supports version history, metadata, and two-way synchronization with Microsoft Outlook.	Yes	Yes
Project Tasks	Stores team and personal tasks that typically relate to each other. Supports version history and metadata, plus a Gantt Chart that can also be opened by Microsoft Project.	Yes	Yes
Issue Tracking	Stores issues and problems; for example, in a project. Supports relationships between issues and comments/solutions to an issue, plus version history and metadata.	Yes	Yes
Survey	Stores lists of questions, including nested questions. Supports graphical presentation of the results, including export of data to Microsoft Access and Microsoft Excel for further analysis.	Yes	Yes

continues

TABLE 2-2 *(continued)*

LIST TYPE	DESCRIPTION	SHAREPOINT FOUNDATION	SHAREPOINT SERVER
Custom Lists	A list with only the Title metadata column. Typically used when you want to add all metadata from scratch.	Yes	Yes
Custom List in Datasheet View	Like Custom List but displayed as a spreadsheet, to make entering values easy. Note that this type of list requires a local ActiveX component that comes with Microsoft Office 2007 and later.	Yes	Yes
External List	A list that is connected to an external content type. This list supports two-way communication with the external data source. No metadata or version history is available.	Yes	Yes
Language and Translators	Creates a list of languages for which the Translation Management workflow will assign translation tasks.	No	Yes
Status List	Stores KPI values that enable the user to track and display a set of goals, using colored icons as indicators.	No	Yes
Import Spreadsheet	Creates a Custom List from an Excel spreadsheet; column names will be used as the list column names; all data in the spreadsheet will also be imported.	Yes	Yes

This book shows numerous examples of how to use list types. The majority of these lists existed in the previous SharePoint version, but note that some of them have extended functionality in SharePoint 2010; for example, now almost all lists support version history.

The best way to understand how and when to use these lists is to actually use them. Take some time and add all the lists that you are interested in to a test site, and then and enter data in these lists and see how they behave. Due to the large number of list types, this book describes only some of them in detail.

In the following Try It Out you learn how to add lists to a SharePoint site, and then change the default settings of this list.

> **NOTE** *If you install Microsoft Silverlight, then SharePoint will take advantage of this fact in several configuration forms; for example, when creating a new list as described in the following Try It Out. You can download Silverlight from* `www.microsoft.com/Silverlight`.

TRY IT OUT Creating a New List and Configuring It

In this example, you add a contact list named Customers to your test site and then enter some list items. Then you will change the list columns; that is, the metadata that this list stores by default.

1. Log on as the site owner and open `http://srv1/test`. (You need to be a site owner to add new lists.)

2. Click Site Actions ⇨ More Options. A new form opens that displays all the lists and library types available (plus the options to create pages and subsites, discussed later).

If Silverlight is installed, you will see a form with nicer graphics, where you can easily select a list and enter its name directly (see Figure 2-2). Steps 3 and 4 assume you don't have Silverlight installed.

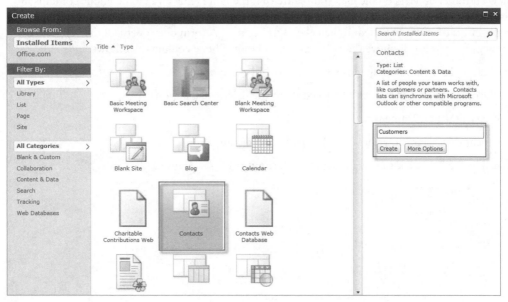

FIGURE 2-2

3. Select Contacts in the Communications section.

4. A new form for this contact list appears. Enter the following values:

a. **Name:** Customers

b. **Description:** This list contains all our customers

c. **Display this list on the Quick Launch:** Yes

Click OK to save and close this form.

5. The contact list now appears. A ribbon for this type of list is also displayed, containing several buttons. Take a look at each button, and hover the mouse over it to see a short description of what it does. If a button is greyed out, that means the button is not currently available for use.

To add a customer name to this list, either click the Add New Item link, or switch to the Items tab and click New Item on the ribbon. A new form opens. Fill in these values:

a.   **Last Name:** Gates

b.   **First Name:** Bill

c.   **E-mail Address:** billg@microsoft.com

d.   **Company:** Microsoft

e.   **Business Phone:** 555-1000

Click Save, either on the toolbar or at the end of this form.

6.   The new customer appears on the list. You realize that the Full Name and Home Phone columns in this list are not used, so you want to delete them. To do this, you must customize the list settings. Open the List tab on the ribbon, and then click List Settings. A form opens with all the properties and settings for this list. Remove the Full Name and Home Phone columns as follows:

a.   Click on Full Name to open the settings for this metadata.

b.   Click Delete, and then click OK to confirm the delete instruction.

c.   Verify that Full Name is removed.

d.   Repeat these steps to remove the Home Phone metadata.

7.   To return to the list, click the Customers breadcrumb trail (see Figure 2-3).

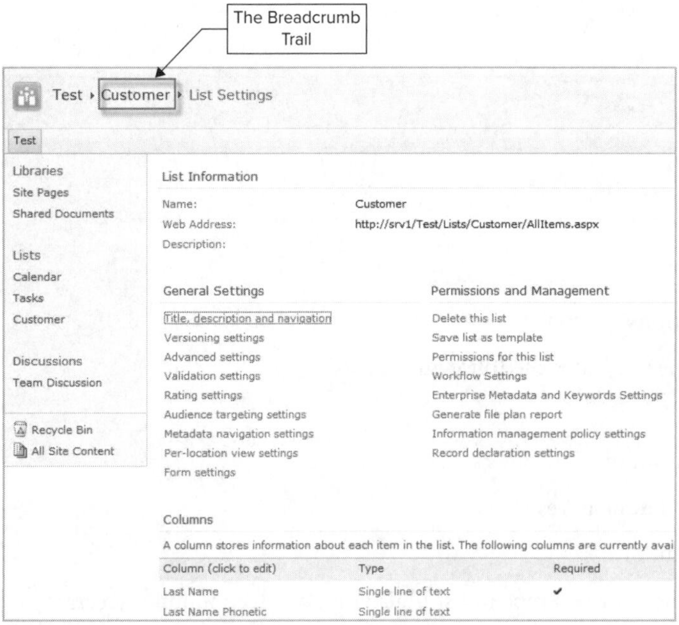

FIGURE 2-3

8.   Click Add New Item and add a second contact; for example, Steve Jobs, Apple, steve@apple.com, 555-2000. Note that the Full Name and Home Phone metadata is now gone.

How It Works

By adding new lists to a site, you extend the content this site contains. Many different types of lists are available, so make sure you create the right type. Whatever list you choose, you can customize it to meet your needs.

MANAGING SITE TEMPLATES

When designing SharePoint, Microsoft had two options: either give the user a completely empty site and force the user to add everything from scratch, such as a web page layout, lists, and libraries or create a number of typical sites with the basic content, and let the user start using these lists and libraries immediately. Then if needed, let the user easily customize the site; for example, add new lists or modify existing lists.

Some web products on the market selected the first option; Microsoft selected the second. These pre-defined sites are known as *site templates*. These templates are one important reason why getting started with SharePoint is so easy. Table 2-3 lists the default site templates for a SharePoint Foundation environment.

> **NOTE** The term standard site *means a site with the same layout as in WSS 3.0; that is, a web page with a larger (70 percent) web part zone on the left and a smaller (30 percent) web part zone on the right. These types of sites are not based on the Wiki template.*

TABLE 2-3: Default Site Templates in SharePoint Foundation

SITE TEMPLATE NAME	DESCRIPTION	TYPICAL USE
Team Site	A Wiki-based site that contains the lists and libraries commonly used for sharing information within a small- or medium-size group.	Department intranet site, a project site, and a general collaboration site.
Blank Site	This template creates a standard site with no lists or libraries. This site is not based on the Wiki type.	Used when you want to create all lists and libraries from scratch.
Document Workspace	A standard site typically used to collaborate on a specific document. It contains multiple lists (for example, Announcements and a Calendar) and a document library.	This type of site is usually created from a document's quick menu, as described later in this chapter.

continues

TABLE 2-3 *(continued)*

SITE TEMPLATE NAME	DESCRIPTION	TYPICAL USE
Blog	A site designed for managing blog posts. Contains lists for posts, categories, comments, and links. Also contains a picture library.	The preferred site template when you need a blog site.
Group Work Site	A standard site with a document library, plus multiple lists typically used in a group that shares information.	Used when a group needs a common site to share documents, a calendar for all group members, resources, a list for storing phone call memos, and so on.
Basic Meeting Workspace	A standard site for meeting items. Contains typical lists like agenda, attendees, and objectives. Also contains a document library.	The default site type for typical meetings. Can also be created when inviting people to a meeting using a Microsoft Outlook calendar.
Blank Meeting Workspace	A blank meeting site that only contains a list for attendees, but no lists or libraries.	Used when you need a meeting site, but you want to create all lists manually.
Decision Meeting Workspace	A standard site for decision meetings. Contains lists like agenda, attendees, tasks, and decisions.	Use this type of site for decision meetings. This site template is very similar to a basic meeting workspace.
Social Meeting Workspace	A standard site for social meetings. Contains lists like attendees, directions, things to bring, and discussions.	Use this type of site when planning a social event, like a company celebration party, birthday party, and so on.
Multipage Meeting Workspace	A standard site for meetings. This site is similar to a basic meeting workspace, but with multiple web pages to allow management of more content.	Use this type of site when you need to work with more lists and libraries than the basic meeting workspace allows.

These site templates are used when you create a new site with your web browser; for example, a project site on the intranet. Some of these templates are also available when creating sites from within other Microsoft Office clients. For example, say you are creating a meeting invitation for a group of people, using your Microsoft Outlook calendar. With these site templates, you can create a meeting workspace simultaneously as you create the meeting invitation.

Another example is when you open an existing Microsoft Word document in a document library, and you realize that you and two colleagues need to collaborate on this particular document for several weeks, and you need a private place for this collaboration. Simply create a new site using the Document Workspace template, and invite your colleagues to that site. These examples and more are described in detail later in this chapter and in Chapter 3.

There is actually one more site type you can choose to create: < Select template later. . . >. This one is rather special and only available when you're creating the top site in a new site collection. Sometimes you need to create a new site collection without applying a template to its top site. This will actually make the top site impossible to use; if you open such a site SharePoint will ask you what site template to apply.

For example, a user may ask for your assistance to create a site collection, but they have not decided what template to apply for the top site. In a case like this, you create the site collection, choose to select a template later, and then enter the user as the site collection administrator. Now this user can open this site, and choose whatever site template is required. See the following Try It Out.

> **NOTE** *As discussed at the beginning of this chapter, you need to set up an intranet at* `http://srv1` *with subsites at* `http://srv1/test` *and* `http://srv1/honey` *(both based on the Team Site site template) and user accounts for Anna and Malin in order to follow along with the Try It Outs.*

TRY IT OUT   Creating a Site Collection Without a Site Template

In this example, you create a new site collection named Finance with the URL `http://srv1/sites/finance`, without applying a site template. The user Anna will be listed as a site collection administrator. Then Anna will be able to open this site and select the site template.

1.   Log on as a farm administrator and start SharePoint Central Administration.

2.   Choose Application Management ➪ Create Site collections. A new web form opens. Enter the following values:

    a.   Verify that the web application (listed in yellow) is where the new site collection should belong; if it's not, click on the web application name and change it.

    b.   Title: Finance

    c.   Description: (leave this blank)

    d.   URL: http://srv1/sites/finance

    e.   Select a template: Click the Custom tab and select *<Select template later>*

    f.   Primary Site Collection Administrator: Filobit\Anna

    g.   Secondary Site Collection Administrator: Filobit\Administrator

    h.   Select a quota template: No Quota (which means there are no size limitations for this site collection).

    Click OK to close this page and create the site collection.

3.   Verify that the site collection was successfully created.

4. Log on as Anna, and then open the URL `http://srv1/sites/finance`; she will now see a form that lists all available site templates (see Figure 2-4). Tell Anna to do the following:

  a. Choose a template, and then click OK. A new form opens where Anna can define the three standard SharePoint groups for readers, contributors, and owners of this site.

  b. Click OK. The new top site opens, and Anna now has full access to this site collection.

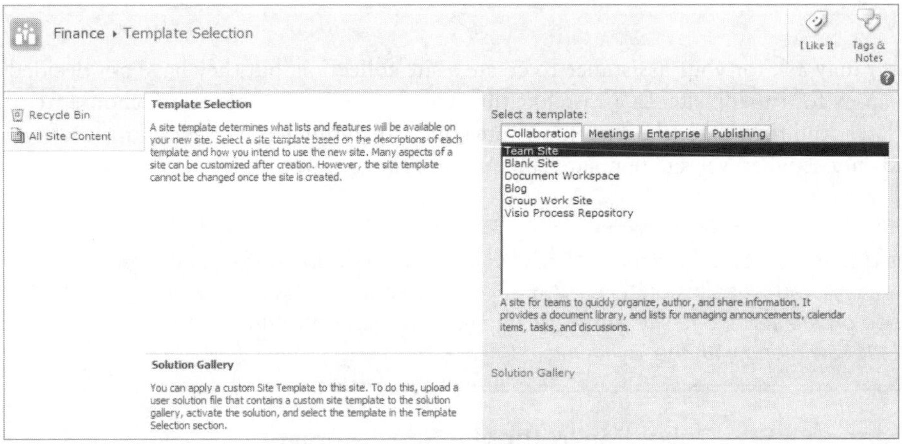

FIGURE 2-4

How It Works

Creating a site collection without a site template enables the administrator to prepare a new site collection for a user who later can choose the site template needed.

Creating Customized Site Templates

All the site templates that come with SharePoint Foundation give you a good start when building sites, but what if you want to create a new site template? For example, say that the Team Site template is close but not exactly what you want to use for project sites. This section shows you how to create customized site templates.

Go ahead and create a new site template, and then read the discussion about how it works. Start with any subsite based on the Team Site template; for example, `http://srv1/test` (see the steps for creating subsites earlier in this chapter). Continue by customizing it the way you want the project sites to look, and then create a template of this site using the steps in the following Try It Out.

TRY IT OUT Creating a Customized Site Template

In this example, you start with an existing site, built on the Team Site template. You want to add two lists, remove the default picture, and then save it as a custom site template. To do this, you need to be a Site Collection Administrator.

1. Log on as a Site Collection Administrator and open the team site.

2. Click Site Actions ⇨ More Options. In this example, you have Silverlight installed, so the Silverlight-based form opens.

3. Click List in the left pane, and select Project Tasks. Enter the name **Project Planning**, and then click Create. The new list opens.

4. Repeat steps 2 and 3 and add the list **Issue Tracking**. This list opens.

5. Verify that the two new lists appear in the left navigation pane; that is, the Quick Launch pane. Navigate back to the start page for this site by using the navigation button on the ribbon (see Figure 2-5).

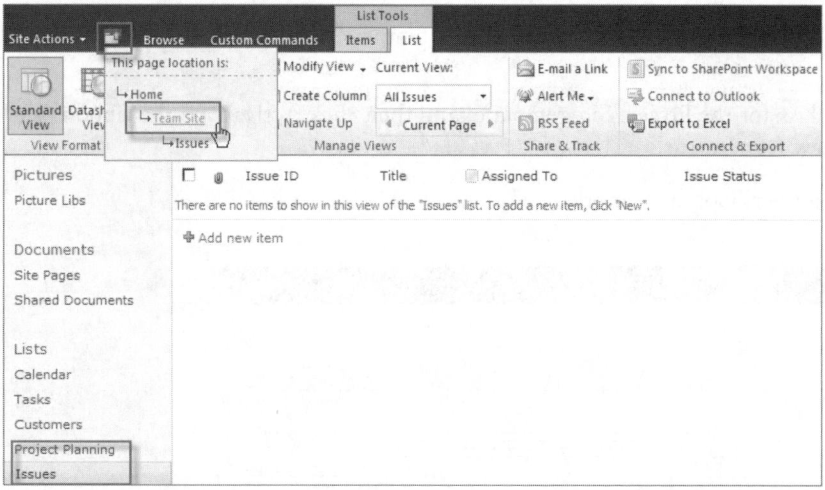

FIGURE 2-5

6. To remove the default picture:

    a. Click the Edit button on the ribbon (or click Site Actions ⇨ Edit Page).

    b. Select the picture (you will see small square handles around the picture), and then press the Delete button on the keyboard.

    c. Click Save on the ribbon. The new layout is now ready to be used.

7. Now that you have the look and feel you want for the future project sites, continue by saving this site as a site template like this:

    a. Click Site Actions ⇨ Site Settings.

    b. Click Save Site As Template (in the Site Actions section).

c. Enter these values:

Filename: Project Site

Template name: Project Site Template

Template description: Use this template when creating project sites

d. Click OK to save and close.

e. After a few seconds, you should see a page that says, "Operation Completed Successfully." Click OK. This template is now created and stored in a specific gallery on the top site in this site collection.

f. Before you can use this site template, you must activate it. Click Site Actions ⇨ Site Settings ⇨ Go To Top Level Site Settings. The Site Settings for the top site open.

g. Click Solutions in the Galleries section to list all site templates and other custom solutions in this farm.

h. Select the check box for the Project Site template, and then click Activate on the ribbon (see Figure 2-6). A new form opens.

i. Click Activate on the ribbon once more.

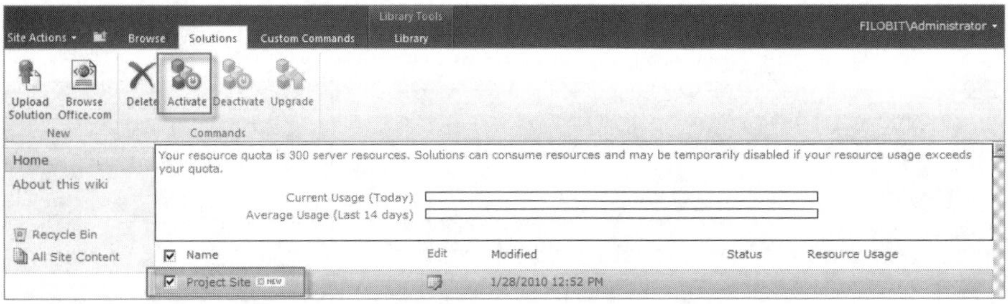

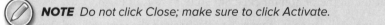

FIGURE 2-6

> *✎* **NOTE** *Do not click Close; make sure to click Activate.*

8. Now it is time to test this site template. Open a site that will be the parent for the new subsite; for example, `http://srv1`.

9. Click Site Actions ⇨ New Site.

10. Locate the Project Site template. The easiest way is to click Blank & Custom in the left pane to filter the site templates.

11. Select Project Site, and enter the title **Test Project** and the URL name **testproject** (without spaces). Click Create.

The new site opens. Verify that it is exactly like the template site; that is, it has the same extra lists and no picture.

How It Works

By saving an existing site as a site template, creating the templates needed without doing any coding or special customizing is very easy. If you need to do more advanced customizing you can use SharePoint Designer (see Chapter 9), or build special site definitions (for example, in Visual Studio 2010).

Making a site template based on an existing site is very easy, as you can see. There is also an option in step 7c of the preceding procedure that lets you save all current documents with the template. This could be used if you want each new site to contain a set of base documents from the beginning (for example, a project site template that contains document templates for project description, project planning, and project tasks).

There are some "gotchas" related to these site templates that you must be aware of before you start using them in a production environment. They are as follows:

➤ No relationship exists between the site and the site template after the site is created. For example, changing the site you used for creating the template does not affect the template itself, or any sites that were built upon this template.

➤ A site template cannot be modified after it is created. The only way to change it is to delete the template and create a new one from scratch. For example, open the original site you saved as a template before, do the modifications needed, and then save the site as a template once again.

➤ Site templates are local for a site collection. For example, say you have three site collections, and you want the same customized site templates available in all site collections. You need to either create the same site template in each site collection, or export it from one site collection and import it to the other two site collections.

Because of these shortcomings, you may want to build site definitions instead.

Site Definitions

All site templates are actually based on a number of configuration files in the SharePoint server. For example, the Blank Site template is defined in the following folder (assuming that SharePoint is installed in disk C):

```
C:\Program Files\Common Files\Microsoft Shared\14\TEMPLATE\SiteTemplates\sts
```

These files are known as *site definitions*; that is, each site template builds upon a site definition (some templates are built upon the same site definition). You may recall from earlier in this chapter that sites built on the Blank Site template had one left web part zone that is given 70 percent of the page, and a right zone that is given 30 percent. Create one or more such sites and use the following Try It Out to test whether existing sites can be updated.

> **WARNING** *You must never complete the following Try It Out in a production environment, because it will affect all existing sites based on this site definition! Make sure to use a test server.*

TRY IT OUT **Modifying a Site Definition**

In this example, you modify the size for the two web part zones from 70/30 percent to 50/50 percent for the standard site, such as Blank Site (but not Team Site, because that is built upon a Wiki definition).

1. Log on to the SharePoint Server as a farm administrator.

2. Open Windows Explorer (not Internet Explorer), and navigate to `C:\Program Files\Common Files\Microsoft Shared\14\TEMPLATE\SiteTemplates\sts`.

3. Right-click on the `Default.aspx` file and select Edit. The file opens in Notepad.

4. Locate the text string `<td valign="top" width="70%">` (at the end of the file).

5. Change `"70%"` to `"50%"`.

6. Then a few lines below, change `"30%"` to `"50%"`.

7. Save the file.

8. Open any site based on the Blank Site template, and refresh the page. Verify that the zones are now equal in size.

9. Open the `Default.aspx` file again, restore the web part settings to `"70%"` and `"30%"`, and save the file. Open the site and verify that it has the default size settings again.

How It Works

Modifying a site definition file affects all existing and future sites based on that site definition.

> **WARNING** *Although changing the default site definitions is easy, you should avoid it. Microsoft does not support modified site definitions, and there is no guarantee that a future service pack or update will not overwrite your modifications. Instead, you should create new site definitions; for example, based on a standard site definition.*

So, how do site templates relate to site definitions? The answer is that a site template defines customizations of site definitions. For example, the site definition may not contain a document library. But you can create a site template that adds the document library. In other words, a site template contains only the features and configurations that differ from its site definition.

To build your own site definition, you must understand exactly how its files are constructed and how these files relate to each other. The following Try It Out walks you through the general steps for creating a site definition.

TRY IT OUT Creating a Custom Site Definition

These steps are just a simple example of what to do when creating a site definition. For more information and examples, search the Internet; for example, see Todd Baginsi's excellent blog at http://tinyurl.com/sp2010-sitedef.

1. Open the following folder on the SharePoint 2010 server:

```
C:\Program Files\Common Files\Microsoft Shared\web server extensions\14\TEMPLATE\
SiteTemplates
```

2. Copy an existing site definition folder, such as sts and save it under the same parent, but with a new name — for example, MYDEF.

3. Open C:\Program Files\Common Files\Microsoft Shared\web server extensions\14\ TEMPLATE\1033\XML (1033 is the U.S. English language ID; make sure to use your language ID if it is not English).

4. Create an XML file named WEBTEMP*xxx*, where *xxx* is your new site definition folder; for example, WEBTEMPMYDEF.XML.

5. Edit the content of this WEBTEMPMYDEF.XML file to define and register the following site definition:

```
<?xml version="1.0" encoding="utf-8"?>
<!-- _lcid="1033" _version="14.0.4536" _dal="1" -->
<!-- _LocalBinding -->
<Templates xmlns:ows="Microsoft SharePoint">
<Template Name="MYSITE" ID="10001">
<Configuration ID="0"
Title="My Custom Site Definition"
Hidden="FALSE"
ImageUrl="/_layouts/images/stts.png"
Description="My Custom Site Def"
DisplayCategory="Blank & Custom" >
    </Configuration>
  </Template>
</Templates>
```

6. Run IISRESET by choosing Start ⇨ Run, typing **IISRESET**, and pressing Enter. Wait for the command to complete, and then open a SharePoint site (it needs to be refreshed).

7. Create a new site, using the new site definition, by clicking Site Actions ⇨ New Site in the form that is displayed. Select the Blank & Custom section in the left pane; your new site definition will be listed here. Select it, give it a name and URL, and click Create.

How It Works

Creating custom site definitions is a safe way to ensure that you have a site definition that Microsoft service packs, or updates, will not touch. If you later change that site definition, all existing sites based on that site definition will also update immediately.

> **NOTE** *You can also create new site definitions using Visual Studio 2010. This is, in fact, easier than manually customizing each file that belongs to a site definition, and it gives you more control, but it also requires knowledge in how to work with Visual Studio.*

GRANTING SITE PERMISSIONS

SharePoint is a very secure environment, but at the same time, adjusting the access permissions to match the need of any organization is very easy. When you create a site collection (using SharePoint Central Administration), it will automatically get three SharePoint groups in a SharePoint Foundation environment. If you do the same thing in a SharePoint Server environment, that top site will get eight different SharePoint groups, because SharePoint Server contains a lot more features and therefore requires more types of groups.

The following sections provide more details about these SharePoint groups, and how you can use them for granting permissions to lists and list items, such as individual documents in a document library.

SharePoint Groups

Why do you need SharePoint groups? The answer is because they are convenient. As described in more detail in Appendix B, a user must be granted at least read access to open a SharePoint site and its content. This access can be granted either to the user directly, or to a SharePoint group that the user belongs to. You can also grant a security group access directly to SharePoint, and all members of that security group will inherit these permissions. A security group can also be a member of a SharePoint group.

The following types of objects can be granted access to SharePoint:

➤ User accounts in AD

➤ User accounts in the local server

➤ Security groups in AD

➤ Security groups in the local server

But SharePoint's accessibility options do not stop here. What about external users, such as partners and customers? If this type of user needs access, then most organizations want to avoid to creating user accounts in AD for each of them. Granting access to external users can be solved in the following two ways:

➤ Create a database (for example, in Microsoft SQL) that stores users and their passwords, and then configure what is known as *forms-based authentication* (FBA) to enable SharePoint to authenticate these users by checking this database.

➤ Use *claims-based authentication*, which enables you to grant SharePoint permissions to user accounts in external data sources, including corporate account database systems beside AD.

So why use SharePoint groups if all the objects listed earlier can be granted access? Because most times, you want to treat a number of users as a group, instead of individual user accounts.

An example explains this better. Organization Alfa has three departments: Sales, Marketing, and IT. Each department has a corresponding security group in AD. A new project will start next week, and the project team will consist of two users from each department. You quickly realize there is no matching security group in AD. Should you create one? Probably not, because when this project is completed, there will no longer be a need for this group. Instead, you can solve this problem by creating a SharePoint group for this project team, and then adding the two users from each department.

Typically in larger organizations, different people administrate AD and SharePoint, which makes it very convenient for the SharePoint administrator to be able to create the groups needed in SharePoint without asking the AD administrator for assistance.

Table 2-4 compares the default SharePoint groups for SharePoint Server and SharePoint Foundation.

TABLE 2-4: Default SharePoint Groups in SharePoint Server and SharePoint Foundation

SHAREPOINT GROUP	SHAREPOINT FOUNDATION	SHAREPOINT SERVER	DEFAULT PERMISSIONS
Visitors	Yes	Yes	Can read and copy information.
Members	Yes	Yes	Can create and modify list items.
Owners	Yes	Yes	Full control of the site and its content.
Viewers	Yes	No	Can view pages and list items, but not download documents.
Approvers	No	Yes	Can edit and approve pages, list items, and documents.
Designers	No	Yes	Can edit lists, libraries, and pages. Can create master pages and page layouts, and the look and feel of the site, including CSS files.
Hierarchy Managers	No	Yes	Can create sites, lists, list items, and documents.
Quick Deploy Users	No	Yes	Can schedule Quick Deploy jobs.
Restricted Readers	No	Yes	Can view pages and documents, but not previous versions or review user rights.

Permissions for Lists and Items

The general rule regarding permissions is that all content in a site will inherit the permission settings from the site itself. For example, if you grant Anna read permission to the site `http://srv1/test`, then she will have read permissions to all the lists and libraries in this site.

This is also true for the items in the lists and libraries. For example, if Anna has read access to a document library, then she also has read access to all the documents in that library.

This rule is known as *permission inheritance*. However, you can break this inheritance whenever needed. For example, if a site has two document libraries, you can let one of them inherit its permissions from the site, while letting the other have unique permissions, which also are inherited by its documents.

Or you can let the libraries inherit permissions from the site, but have a single document configured to use a unique permission. Here are the objects in a site that can have unique permissions:

➤ A list or library

➤ A folder in a list or library

➤ A list item; for example, a document in a library

By using this technique, you can design sites with the exact permissions needed. Note that only the site owner can set the permissions; that is, a standard user, such as a contributor, cannot modify permissions. The following Try It Out describes how to break the permission inheritance and set unique permissions for different objects in a SharePoint site.

TRY IT OUT Managing Permissions for Lists and Items

In this example, you change the permissions for lists and items in the `http://srv1/test` site. This is a subsite that inherits its permissions from the top site; that is, `http://srv1`.

1. Log on as the site owner, and open the intranet site `http://srv1` with a web browser.

2. Check the permission for this top site by choosing Site Actions ⇨ Site Settings and then clicking Site Permissions. A form opens, displaying the current permission settings for this top site. Typically, you will see three SharePoint groups that are named after the site they belong to; for example if the site name is Start, then these three groups are named Start Members, Start Owners, and Start Visitors. Note that the permission levels for these three groups are Contribute, Full Control, and Read, respectively.

3. Open the Test subsite; that is, `http://srv1/test`.

4. Check this subsite's permissions by clicking Site Actions ⇨ Site Settings and then clicking Site Permissions. Note that the subsite also has the same groups with the same permissions as the parent site (refer to step 2). Clearly these settings are inherited from the top site.

5. Open the start page for the Test site again and verify the permission settings for the document library as follows:

a. Click Shared Documents to open this library.

b. Switch to the Library tab on the ribbon, and then click the Library Permissions button (a small button to the far right on the ribbon).

c. Note that the library also inherits these permission settings, not from the top site, but instead from its own site. You can also see a yellow status line stating that "This library inherits permissions from its parent. (Start)." This indicates that all permissions originate from the Start site, which is `http://srv1`.

6. Now break the inheritance. Click Stop inheriting Permissions on the ribbon. A message appears informing you that you are about to create unique permissions for this document library. Click OK. Note that the yellow status line now says, "This library has unique permissions."

7. Change the permissions this list inherited. Select Start Visitors and then click Remove User Permissions. Click OK to confirm your action in the message form that opens. Now change the permission level for one of the remaining groups. Select Start Members and click Edit User Permissions. Change the permissions from Contribute to Design, and click OK (see Figure 2-7). The permissions now looks like this:

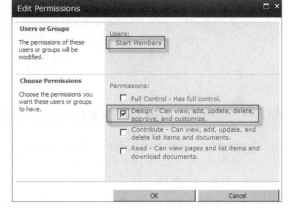

➤ Start Members - Design

➤ Start Owners - Full Control

FIGURE 2-7

8. Use the navigation button on the ribbon and open Shared Documents again to check that these customized permission settings are inherited by the documents in this library. Click Add New Document, and then click Browse to add a document (the type is not important).

9. Select the check box for the new document, and then click the Document Permissions button on the ribbon (a small button). Note that the yellow status line says, "This document inherits permissions from its parent (Shared Documents)."

10. Navigate back to Shared Documents, and click the Library Permissions button again (on the Library tab). This time, revert to the original inheritance as follows:

a. Click Inherit Permissions. A message appears, stating that you are about to inherit permissions from the parent website and lose all custom permissions.

b. Click OK to confirm. Note that the yellow status line now says, "This library inherits permissions from its parent" again.

c. Check the permissions settings. You will see that all groups and permission levels are back again. But you can also see that the Start Members group now has an extra permission level: Limited Access. This depends on the special permission level you granted this group earlier in step 7. SharePoint remembers this setting, but it will not have any effect.

11. Open Shared Documents again, and check the document permissions for the same document you investigated in step 9. Note that it now lists the same permissions as the document library.

How It Works

SharePoint allows you to mix inherited permissions and unique permissions. All permissions for a site will be inherited by its lists and libraries. You can break the inheritance any time, and then revert to the original inheritance.

> **NOTE** *Instead of setting unique permissions for multiple documents or list items, you can create a list folder and configure the required permission there; then all documents or list items stored in this folder will inherit their permissions from the folder.*

MANAGING MEETING WORKSPACES

Chapter 1 discussed how SharePoint can be used to manage meetings in a smarter way. Instead of traditional meetings with an agenda and meeting minutes, SharePoint has a special site template for meeting workspaces. There are many benefits to using a meeting workspace, including the following:

➤ It is Integrated with Microsoft Outlook 2007 and 2010. You can create a meeting invitation and at the same time create a meeting workspace in SharePoint.

➤ The meeting workspace contains a list for typical meeting details, such as the agenda, tasks, decisions, and document library.

➤ No separate agenda needs to be sent out. All invited users can access the meeting workspace where the agenda is listed.

➤ Repetitive meetings can be linked together, which makes it very easy to jump between different meeting instances.

➤ No meeting minutes need to be created, because all details about the meeting are listed in the meeting workspace. All attendees can go back to a previous meeting to see its content.

In the following sections, you will learn how to create and manage meeting workspaces.

Creating a Meeting Workspace

There are three ways to create a meeting workspace as follows:

➤ Create a site based on any of the site templates for meeting workspaces (see Chapter 1 for more details).

➤ Create a SharePoint calendar event, and connect it to a meeting workspace.

➤ Create a meeting invitation in Outlook and create a meeting workspace for this meeting.

Of these three options, the last one is the most natural for organizations that use Outlook as a mail client, because it integrates with the typical meeting invitations that Outlook users are familiar with.

The second option is also common, and if the organization doesn't use Outlook, then this is the best way to create meeting workspaces. Both methods are described below.

> **NOTE** As discussed at the beginning of this chapter, you need to set up an intranet at `http://srv1` with subsites at `http://srv1/test` and `http://srv1/honey` (both based on the Team Site site template) and user accounts for Anna and Malin in order to follow along with the Try It Outs.

TRY IT OUT　Creating a Meeting Workspace Using a SharePoint Calendar

In this example, you have a team site named IT that contains a calendar. You want to use it to create meeting workspaces connected to some calendar events.

1. Log on as a site owner, and open the IT site.

2. Open the calendar list, switch to the Events tab on the ribbon, and then click New Event.

3. When the new form opens, enter these values:

　a. Title: Project Zimmer

　b. Location: Room 5

　c. Start Time and End Time: Enter a valid date and times (your choice)

　d. Description: Follow up project meeting

　e. Workspace: Select this option

　Click Save.

4. Since you opted to create a meeting workspace, you now get a new web page where you can define its settings. Note that the workspace will be created as a subsite under the current site. Accept all the default settings, and click OK.

5. A new web page opens where you define the type of workspace you want to create. Accept the default Basic Meeting Workspace, and click OK.

6. The meeting workspace opens. Enter the following values:

　a. Click Add New Item in the Agenda list web part, enter some text in the Subject, Owner, Time, and Notes field, and then click Save.

　b. Click Add New Item in the Objectives web part, enter some text in the Objective field, and then click Save.

　c. Click Manage Attendees in the Attendees web part. Switch to the Items tab on the ribbon, and then click New Item. Enter an existing user account, for example Filobit\anna, and then click Save.

7. Click the Navigate Up button on the ribbon, and go back to the start page for this meeting workspace. Verify that it contains the values you entered.

8. Open the team site with the calendar you used in step 2, and verify that the meeting event is listed. Click on the event to open a form with its details. In this form, click the link in the section Workspace to open the connected meeting workspace.

How It Works

A meeting event in a SharePoint calendar can be connected to a meeting workspace. By default, the meeting workspace is created as a subsite to the current site; that is, the site with the calendar list.

The only issue with this method is that you need to open the meeting event in order to find the link to the meeting workspace. However, you can manually add a link directly to that meeting workspace; for example, to a SharePoint link list.

Another method (the third option in the list at the beginning of this section) is to use the fact that Outlook is integrated with SharePoint. Before you do this, you need to add a button in Outlook 2010 for creating meeting workspaces, as described in the next Try It Out.

TRY IT OUT   **Enabling the Meeting Workspace Button in Outlook 2010**

In Office 2010, the Meeting Workspace button is hidden by default. You want to add it to the ribbon.

1. Start your Outlook 2010 client, and log on.

2. Switch to the Outlook Calendar.

3. Click New Meeting in the ribbon.

4. In the form that's displayed, click File ➪ Options and then select Quick Access Toolbar.

5. In the form that's displayed, click Meeting Workspace in the left pane and then click the Add >> button. Then click OK.

6. Verify that the Meeting Workspace is displayed in the quick access toolbar.

7. The configuration is now complete. Cancel this meeting invitation.

How It Works

Outlook 2010 does not show the "Meeting Workspace" button by default. You can add it to the quick access toolbar or to a custom section in the ribbon.

When the Meeting Workspace button is enabled, you can easily create a meeting invitation in Outlook plus create a meeting workspace for that meeting instance, as the following Try It Out demonstrates.

> **NOTE** *As discussed at the beginning of this chapter, you need to set up an intranet at* http://srv1 *with subsites at* http://srv1/test *and* http://srv1/honey *(both based on the Team Site site template) and user accounts for Anna and Malin in order to follow along with the Try It Outs.*

TRY IT OUT Creating a Meeting in Outlook 2010 with a Meeting Workspace

In this example, you have a team site created on http://srv1/honey that you are using as a project site. You want to invite Anna and Malin to a startup meeting next Monday for your new Honey project. This meeting will also have a meeting workspace.

1. Log on as a site owner to the project site http://srv1/honey.

2. Start Outlook 2010, and open its calendar.

3. Click New Meeting on the ribbon, and then enter the following values:

   a. To: Anna; Malin

   b. Subject: Meeting Honey

   c. Location: Room 9

   d. Start Time and End Time: Set these for next Monday between 9a.m. - 10a.m.

4. All of the above is standard behavior when inviting people to a meeting in Outlook. Next you will add a meeting workspace for this meeting:

   a. Click the Meeting Workspace button on the quick access toolbar at the top of the page. A new pane named Meeting Workspace will be displayed at the right of the form.

   b. In the new form, click the Change Settings link. The form changes to enable you to define the settings for the meeting workspace.

   c. In the Select a location section, open its menu and select Other.

   d. A dialog box opens. Enter the URL to the site that will be the parent site for the meeting workspace. In this example you want to create it directly under the project site, so enter its URL: http://srv1/honey.

   e. Below the new location, note the default settings for creating a new workspace based on English and the Basic Meeting Workspace template. Click OK.

   f. The location and template you selected are displayed in the Create A Workspace section of the Meeting Workspace page. Click the Create button, and the workspace will be created.

   g. When completed, you will see a link in the mail body (to the left of the Meeting Workspace pane) that points to the new workspace. You can now add more text in the mail body, for example a welcome message. When ready, click the Send button to send this meeting invitation to Anna and Malin.

5. Since you are the meeting owner, your Outlook calendar will automatically be updated with this meeting event. When Anna and Malin accept their meeting invitation, they will also get this meeting added to their Outlook calendar. Now open the new meeting event in the Outlook calendar, then click its link to open the meeting workspace.

How It Works

When creating meeting events in the Outlook 2010 calendar, you can also create a meeting workspace in SharePoint for that specific event.

Managing Repetitive Meetings

Meetings are very often related to each other; for example, an organization may have internal meetings every Monday morning. When creating a new meeting workspace in SharePoint, you can link it to a previous meeting, thus collecting all such meetings in a series. Then, when viewing any one of the meeting instances, you can switch to a previous meeting by just selecting another meeting date.

> **NOTE** *As discussed at the beginning of this chapter, you need to set up an intranet at* `http://srv1` *with subsites at* `http://srv1/test` *and* `http://srv1/honey` *(both based on the Team Site site template) and user accounts for Anna and Malin in order to follow along with the Try It Outs.*

TRY IT OUT   **Linking Meeting Workspaces**

In this example, you will invite Anna and Malin to a second meeting regarding the Honey project (from the previous section of this chapter). You want the meeting workspace for this second meeting to be linked to the first workspace.

1. Start Outlook 2010 and open its calendar.

2. Click New Meeting on the ribbon, and then enter:

    a. **To**: Anna; Malin

    b. **Subject**: Follow up meeting for Honey

    c. **Location**: Room 5

    d. **Start Time** and **End Time**: Set for three days after the first meeting

3. Now create a new meeting workspace that will be linked to the first:

    a. Click the Meeting Workspace button on the quick access toolbar at the top of this page. The Meeting Workspace pane will be displayed at the right of the form.

b. At the end of this pane, you will see a tip: "You can also link to an existing workspace." Click this link.

c. The pane now displays the last used location (Honey), which is just the location you want to use in this example. In the Select A Workspace section, make sure the option "Link to an existing workspace" is selected, and open the Select A Workspace menu, and select the name of your first meeting workspace (Meeting for Honey). Click OK.

d. Still in this pane, click Link. The result will be that this meeting workspace is added as a new meeting instance in the first meeting workspace.

e. When finished, you will see a link to this meeting workspace in the mail body, just like with the first meeting. Click the Send button to send this second meeting invitation to Anna and Malin.

4. This meeting event is saved in the Outlook calendar. Open it, and click the link to the meeting workspace to open that site. Note that this meeting workspace site now has a left pane with the dates of the two meeting instances; click on either of them to view the settings for that particular instance.

How It Works

You can link new meeting workspace instances to existing workspaces, thus creating a series of meetings in SharePoint.

Meeting Workspace Security

Here are some things to remember regarding security when you're working with meeting workspaces:

➤ You must have permission to create a subsite in order to create a meeting workspace under that particular site. That is the reason you needed to log on as a site owner to the site http://srv1/honey in the previous two examples.

➤ All invited meeting participants in an Outlook meeting event will be granted member permissions by default, meaning they will be able to read, write, and delete information in the meeting workspace.

➤ If you have a series of linked meeting workspaces, users will get the same permissions to all instances in that series.

➤ You can grant any user access to the meeting workspace, not only meeting participants. Follow the same steps as when granting users access to any site; see Appendix B for more information about managing site access.

WORKING WITH BLOG SITES

SharePoint Foundation comes with a site template for creating blog sites. The term *blog* is an abbreviation of the phrase *Web Log*, and was from the beginning a website where a user published a log about something he or she worked with. The first known blog site in the world was created by

Justin Hall in 1994, but around the year 2000, blogs as we know them started to be popular. Today, blogs are among the Internet's most popular information sources, and during 2009, more than 190,000 blog posts were published per day according to Wikipedia.

Public blogs on the Internet are interesting, because setting up a new blog site is easy, they are usually free, and everyone on the Internet can read your blog posts. What makes public blogs extra interesting is that in most blog sites, a reader can comment on blog posts or other comments. This encourages two-way communications, which is an important concept in social computing.

Although most blog sites on the Internet are more or less unorganized (everyone can create blog posts about everything), companies and organizations also realize they need this kind of two-way communication to engage their users and get feedback and comments on things that relate to the organization. This kind of internal blog site often requires more structure and control. For example, it must be possible to do the following:

➤ Control who can create blog sites and where

➤ Enable and disable comments

➤ Configure approval of blog posts

➤ Configure approval of comments

All of these control mechanisms are possible with blog sites in SharePoint Foundation, and therefore also in SharePoint Server 2010.

Creating a Blog Site

Creating a blog site is no different from creating any other type of SharePoint Foundation site. You need the permission to create a subsite, and that is all. In SharePoint Server, all users with a personal My Site will be able to create a local blog site, which all users can view and comment on. SharePoint Foundation does not have the My Site feature, so the blog sites need to be integrated with the other sites; for example, as a subsite in the intranet, which requires some planning. Here are some typical users of blog sites:

➤ A CEO who wants to inform everyone about what is happening with the organization

➤ Local team leaders who need to keep their teams updated

➤ Interest groups; for example, the Golf Club in the organization, or Frank Zappa lovers

Remember that in SharePoint, you must be a site owner to create a subsite. This is also true if you want to create a new blog site (see the following Try It Out). If you don't want to make people site owners just because they need to create blog sites (and other site types), you can instead grant the Create Subsites permission to SharePoint groups, user accounts, or security groups, as described in Appendix B.

TRY IT OUT Creating a Blog Site

In this example, you create a blog site as a subsite directly under the top site at `http://srv1`. These steps assume you have Silverlight installed.

1. Log on as a site owner to `http://srv1`, and open that site.

2. Click Site Actions ⇨ New Site.

3. Select the Blog site template, and enter the name **My Blog** and the URL name **myblog**. Click Create.

4. The new blog site opens (see Figure 2-8).

FIGURE 2-8

How It Works

When creating a blog site, you create a new site that uses the Blog site template.

One of the first things you probably want to do with a new blog is to update the picture of the blog owner and the text for "About this blog." You can use a picture that is stored in another location; for example, a shared library with pictures of all employees in the organization. Or you can upload a picture from the file system, and store it in the local Photos library. To make these changes, you edit the start page for the blog site, as described in the following Try It Out.

TRY IT OUT   Updating the Blog Picture and Description

In this example, you upload a picture from the local disk and use it as the blog owner picture. Then you update the description in the "About this blog" text.

1. Log on as the site owner and open the blog.

2. Click Site Actions ⇨ Edit Page to open this page in edit mode.

3. Select the blog owner image, and switch to the Picture Tools - Design tab on the ribbon.

4. Click on the *text* Change Picture on the ribbon to open the menu for this button, and select From Computer. A new form opens where you upload the blog author picture, as described below:

    a. Click Browse next to the Name field, and then locate the picture you want to add.

    b. Accept the default Photos as the upload destination.

    c. Click OK to save and close this form.

    d. Because the picture is uploaded to the Photos picture library, you will get a preview of the picture, as well as the options for adding properties such as a title, date the picture was taken, description, and keywords. Click Save to continue. The picture is auto-resized to fit the blog.

5. Next you must update the "About this blog" description. The blog page is still in edit mode. Select the default text under the picture, and replace it with the text you want.

6. When ready, click Stop Editing on the ribbon (on the Page tab).

7. Verify that the picture and "About" text now look good.

How It Works

The picture and "About this blog" text both belong to the same web part. Edit the page to update these settings.

The blog site supports two easy ways for a user to follow updates on this blog: RSS feeds and alerts. They are both available below the blog posts and work like any RSS feed or alert in SharePoint; that is, if the reader of this blog wants an e-mail whenever a new post is published, he can click Alert Me. In the form that appears he can define how often SharePoint checks this list for changes (the default is every 5 minutes), whether he wants an e-mail or an SMS text message to his mobile phone (Appendix B describes how to enable SMS Text messages), and what type of update triggers an alert.

The blog site supports other blog programs; for example, you can configure the blog to accept posts created with Microsoft Word 2010. Click the "Launch blog program to post" link in the Blog Tools to enable Microsoft Word as an alternative blog post program.

Managing a Blog Site

The default blog site contains the typical lists and layout for a blog site. You can add more lists if needed, and you'll need to configure some of the default lists. You should avoid removing the default lists, because the functionality of the blog site depends on these lists:

➤ **Posts:** Stores blog posts

➤ **Photos:** Stores a picture library for photos displayed on blog posts

➤ **Categories:** Defines the categories you can apply to blog posts

➤ **Comments:** Stores readers' comments

➤ **Links:** Contains links to other blogs and resources

The following sections provide more details about how to work with these lists.

Blog List: Posts

Posts is the main list; it contains all blog posts. You can add rich format text to the post, plus links, tables, and pictures. In other words, the post editor is similar to a basic word processor. To add a blog post, use the steps in the following Try It Out.

TRY IT OUT   Creating a Blog Post

In this exercise you will add a new blog post to your blog site.

1. Open the blog site you created earlier.

2. Click "Create a post" in the right pane on the blog site page, and enter these values:

a. Title: My first blog post

b. Body: This is the body of the post. Make sure to test what you can do with this editor. For example, to change the format, click the Font button on the ribbon and try bold, italic, and different fonts and sizes. Then select a single word and click Styles to test the predefined styles (that is, pre-configured fonts, sizes, and colors). Finally, place the cursor anywhere on a line with text and click Markup Styles; hover the mouse arrow over the different alternatives in this menu, and see how the text looks. Note that although you did not select anything on the line, Markup Styles will affect the complete sentence.

c. In the Category section, accept the default Category 1, and click Add. You will learn more about categories later.

d. In the Published section, you can enter the date and time this post will be published; by default it will be the current date. This setting can be very handy if you want to create a blog now but publish it another day. For example, if you enter a publishing day that is two days from now, and then select Publish (see the next step), this post will not show up until then.

e. At the bottom of this form are three buttons. Use them as follows:

Save As Draft: Select this button if you want to save but not publish; for example, the post is not complete and you want to continue later, or you simply want to publish this post later.

Publish: Select this button if you want to publish this post now.

Cancel: Select this button if you want to cancel and delete this post now.

For this example, click Publish.

3. Verify that the post is visible. If it's not, check that the publishing date is not in the future, and that you selected to Publish the post. If you need to change any post, click Manage Posts in the right pane of the blog home page.

Blog List: Photos

Blog posts often contain one or more pictures and images. These pictures may be stored in the Photos list if you want to display the image on the post. You can also add links to pictures and images in other locations, but you have to manually enter the URL to these files. Any picture you add may be resized in the post, but be careful with adding high-resolution pictures, because these files use resources to resize them and require a lot of space in the Photos list.

TRY IT OUT   **Adding Pictures to a Blog Post**

In this example, you add a picture by adding it to the Photos list, and then by linking to an image file stored in another location.

1.   Open your blog site.

2.   Click Create A Post.

3.   Enter a title; for example, **This post contains pictures**.

4.   Edit the body as follows:

    a.   Enter a headline, such as **These are my pictures**, and then select the Colored Heading 1 option in the Markup Style menu. Press Enter to create a new line, where the picture will be inserted.

    b.   Switch to the Insert tab, and click the Picture button. A new form named Select Picture opens.

    c.   Click Browse, and select an image you like (for example, from your hard drive). Then click OK.

    d.   The Select Picture form reappears. Note that the Upload To field is preset to Photos, which is the default list for pictures and images. Click OK to import your picture to the Photos list. A new form opens where you can set the properties for this picture; that is, name, title, date, and description. Click Save when you are done.

    e.   The new picture now appears in the post. Note the small white handles around the picture; use them to resize it (the aspect ratio will be retained automatically by default). You can also drag the picture to a new position.

    f.   Now add a picture stored in another location (in this example, in another SharePoint image library). In the next step, you must enter the URL to the new picture, so copying this URL first is smart. Open a new browser window, navigate to the new picture you want to add, right-click the picture, and select the link Copy Shortcut.

    g.   Make sure the blog post body is still open, and that the previous picture is not selected (because then it will be replaced by the new picture added in the following steps). Switch to the Insert tab. Click the small arrow under the Picture button to open its menu, and select From Address, which is a form similar to the one you saw previously in step 4b. Now either manually enter the URL to that picture, or use the URL you copied in the previous step.

Enter text in the Alternative text field. It will display when a user later hovers over this picture. Click OK.

h. The second picture now appears on the blog post. Resize it if necessary, and click Publish.

5. Verify that the new blog post appears and that it contains two pictures, similar to what's shown in Figure 2-9.

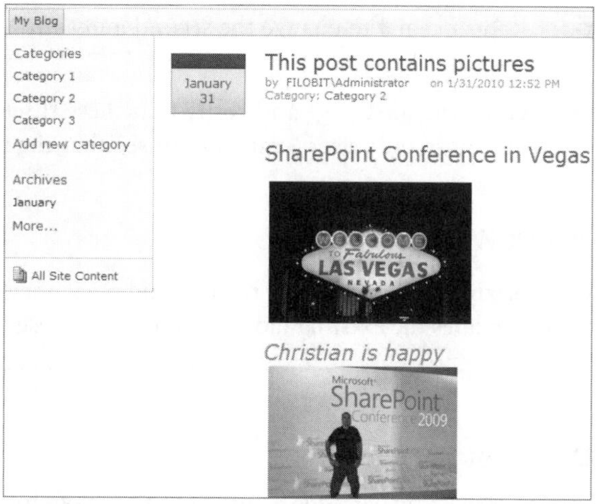

How It Works

Blog posts can display pictures stored in a local image library or images stored in external locations, such as other SharePoint sites or sites on the Internet.

FIGURE 2-9

Blog List: Categories

This list contains all the categories you will use for the blog posts. A user can later use these categories as a quick way to list all posts of a certain category. By default, this list contains three examples named Category 1, Category 2, and Category 3. You are supposed to change these to something more meaningful before you start adding blog posts you want others to see.

In the previous examples, you added two blog posts, categorized as Category 1 and Category 2. Open the start page for your blog, and click on these categories. You can see that they work as a filter — that is, only posts with the selected category appear, including a headline that states what category you are looking at now.

In the following Try It Out, you delete the default categories and create three new ones: Business, Personal, and Travel. You then see what happens to the first two posts and their categories.

TRY IT OUT Managing Blog Categories

1. Open the start page for your blog site.

2. Click the header Categories in the left pane. The Categories list opens.

3. Click the edit button to the right of Category 1, and then change the title to **Business**. The new title appears in the list.

4. In a previous Try It Out, you created a blog post as Category 1. Now open the start page for the blog site, and click the Business category in the left pane. Note that it still displays the same post. In other words, changing an existing category also updates all blog posts classified as this category.

5. Repeat step 3 to change the second and third default categories to **Personal** and **Travel**, respectively.

6. Open the start page and verify that these three new categories appear in the left pane. Also add a new post and select a category to see that the new categories work.

How It Works

Categorizing blog posts helps readers find posts they are interested in. You can modify these categories, which updates the existing blog posts that use these categories. You can have as many categories you like.

Blog List: Comments

Any time a reader adds a comment to a blog post, it is stored in the Comments list. By default, all SharePoint users will be granted Contribute access to this particular list, which gives them permission to add comments. Any comment will be published directly, by default. In some scenarios, you want these comments to be approved before published. The "Managing Blog Permissions" section later in this chapter describes setting up this feature.

The owner of the blog site has the permission to manage comments, including modifying and deleting them. In the following Try It Out, you first add a comment to a blog as user Anna so you can then log on as the blog owner to manage this comment.

> **NOTE** As discussed at the beginning of this chapter, you need to set up an intranet at `http://srv1` with subsites at `http://srv1/test` and `http://srv1/honey` (both based on the Team Site site template) and user accounts for Anna and Malin in order to follow along with the Try It Outs.

TRY IT OUT   Adding a Blog Comment

In this example, you log on as user Anna to add a comment to a blog, and then log on as the blog owner to change this comment.

1. Open the blog owned by you, the administrator. Change the user to Anna by clicking the user name (top-right corner), selecting Sign In As Different User, and entering Anna's logon credentials.

2. Open any of the blog posts, and then click Comment(s) below the post. This adds the fields Title and Body to the page. Enter the following text:

a. Title: This is a comment from Anna.

b. Body: I like this posting!

3. Click Submit Comment to save the comment. Anna's comment is immediately published, and is visible to anyone with access to this blog. Note that the number of comments is updated.

4. Now open the same blog, but change to your administrative account.

5. Verify that you can see Anna's comment. Now delete this comment as follows:

    a. Open the post.

    b. Scroll down to Anna's comment and click the Edit link to the right of the comment title.

    c. Click Delete Item (or modify the comment and save it, if needed).

    d. Click OK to accept the delete operation.

6. Verify that Anna's comment is now deleted.

How It Works

All authenticated users with access to SharePoint can read and comment on blog posts. The owner of the blog site may change or delete these comments when necessary.

> **NOTE** *You can configure the Comments list to send alerts when new comments are added or modified. Just open the list, click Alert Me ⇨ Set alert on this list on the ribbon, and define when and what to alert.*

Blog List: Links

Blog sites commonly list a number of links, often to other blog sites in the organization or on the Internet. SharePoint's blog contains a list just for this purpose. By default, it contains only one link, Pictures, which links to the picture library in this blog site. The blog owner can add new links by clicking Add New Link and entering the URL for this link, including a description (which will be displayed on the blog page) and a note about this link.

The blog owner can manage the Links list, by clicking the Links headline to open the list. It contains the same type of buttons on its ribbon as other lists in SharePoint. Use them to edit or delete these links, and to change the item order.

> **NOTE** *You can set unique permissions to links to control who can see them. Open the list with links, select the link to be modified, click Item Permission, click Stop Inheriting Permissions, and set the permissions you need for this link.*

Managing Blog Permissions

When you add new blog posts, you must publish them so they become visible to other users. In the section "Blog List: Posts" earlier in this chapter, you learned how to add new posts, and you also saw that there are two buttons named Save As Draft and Publish. If you select Publish, then the post immediately becomes visible to all users. If you instead select Save As Draft, only you will be able to see it. This can be handy if you start to write a blog, but you need to get more information before it can be published.

In some situations, you need to approve the blog post before it goes public. For example, say that you have a blog with multiple authors — a common practice for official blogs, like company blogs. To make sure the information is correct in these posts, one user will be responsible for approving them. By default, the blog site owner will have the permission to approve any postings, including their own. If you need this type of permission, make sure to create a blog site where the blog authors are granted Contributors permissions to the Posts list, as described in the following Try It Out.

> **NOTE** As discussed at the beginning of this chapter, you need to set up an intranet at http://srv1 *with subsites at* http://srv1/test *and* http://srv1/honey *(both based on the Team Site site template) and user accounts for Anna and Malin in order to follow along with the Try It Outs.*

TRY IT OUT   Configuring Posts to Be Approved Before Published

In this example, your blog postings need to be approved by Anna before they are published. As the site owner, you can always approve, so you have to grant Anna the permission to approve blog posts.

1. Log on as the blog site owner, and open the blog site.

2. Click Manage Posts in the right pane of the blog home page.

3. Switch to the List tab on the ribbon.

4. Click the Lists Permissions button (a small button at the right on the ribbon), and a new page will open where you configure permission settings.

5. Click Stop Inheriting Permissions. Click OK in the dialog box that appears to confirm that you want to create unique permissions.

6. Click Grant Permissions to add the blog authors and grant them Contribute permissions. Either enter each user account, or use an existing SharePoint group for this purpose. To learn how to create these groups, see Appendix B. Click OK to save and close this form.

7. Verify that the permissions work as expected by asking a blog author to add a post. They should now only see Save As Draft and Cancel buttons. The Publish button is no longer visible (see Figure 2-10).

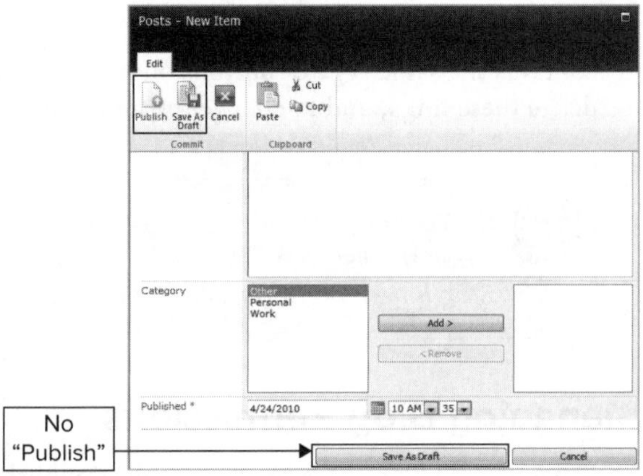

FIGURE 2-10

8. The new post must be approved. Switch the user to the site owner, and open the blog home page.

9. Click Manage posts in the right pane.

10. Note that the new post is listed, but the Approval Status is Pending. Select the check box for this post, and click the Approve/Reject button on the ribbon (see Figure 2-11).

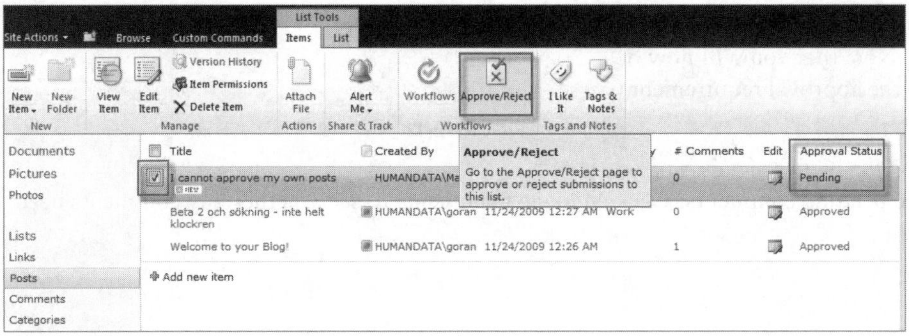

FIGURE 2-11

11. On the Approval form that appears, select Approve and click OK.

12. Verify that this new post is now published.

How It Works

By changing the list permissions for posts, you can prevent blog authors from approving their own posts.

Another blog permission often required is to approve blog comments before they go public. You do this by enabling approval of new comments, as described in the following Try It Out.

TRY IT OUT   Configuring Approval of Blog Comments

In this exercise, you activate the approval process for blog comments to view and approve them before they get published.

1. Open the blog home page as the site owner.

2. Click Manage Comments in the right pane.

3. Switch to the List tab on the ribbon.

4. Click List Settings.

5. Click Versioning Settings.

6. Set the "Require content approval for submitted items" option to Yes, and verify that the "Who should see draft items in this list" option is set to "Only users who can approve items (and the author of the item)."

7. Click OK to save and close this form.

8. Log on as another user, and add a comment to a blog post. Note that you will now be notified about the approval requirement (see Figure 2-12).

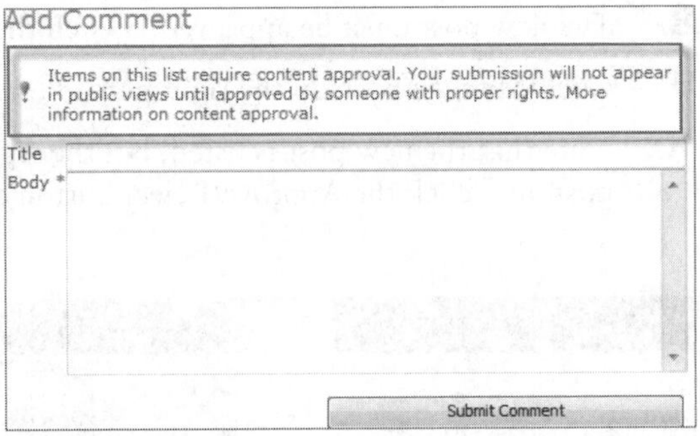

Add Comment

> Items on this list require content approval. Your submission will not appear in public views until approved by someone with proper rights. More information on content approval.

Title

Body *

Submit Comment

FIGURE 2-12

9. By default, only the owner of this blog site is able to approve pending comments. Click Manage Comments to see whether any comments need to be approved.

How It Works

By enabling the approval option for the Comments list, all comments must be approved, typically by the blog owner, before getting published.

▶ **WHAT YOU LEARNED IN THIS CHAPTER**

TOPIC	KEY CONCEPTS
Site templates	A site template is a predefined site configuration that defines the default layout, the lists and libraries for this site, and the web parts displayed.
	SharePoint Foundation comes with 9 default site templates, and SharePoint Server comes with 19 templates.
	All site templates are based on a *site definition*.
	You can create a site template from an existing site.
	There are no live relationships between a site and the site template it was based on.
SharePoint site	A SharePoint site is a container for lists.
	It always belongs to a specific site collection.
	A subsite is sometimes referred to as a *web* or a *subweb*.
	Some sites are named *workspaces*, like Meeting Workspace and Document Workspace.
SharePoint lists	A SharePoint list contains the data that belongs to a site, such as a document, a calendar booking, and a contact.
	Lists are sometimes called a *library*; for example, a document library.
Silverlight	Silverlight is a web-application framework for creating graphical objects, including animated icons, sliding menus, and so on.
	SharePoint takes advantage of Silverlight if it is installed; for example, when you create a site or a list.
Permissions	A site can inherit its parent's permissions, or it can have unique permissions.
	Inherited permissions can be converted to unique permissions.
	Unique permissions can be converted to inherited permissions.
	Lists of any kind always inherit their permissions from their site.
	Each folder in a list inherits permissions from that list.
	List items, such as a document or calendar booking, inherit their permissions from their folder. If there are no folders, then they inherit directly from their list.
	Lists, folders, and list items can break and retake inheritance of permissions.

continues

(continued)

TOPIC	KEY CONCEPTS
Blog sites	Blogs encourage interaction with their readers; that is, blog readers can enter comments.
	Blog posts support a rich set of formatting options, including images, tables, and predefined styles.
	Images on a blog post can be resized.
	Word 2010 can be used as a blog editor that stores the posts directly to the blog site.
	Blog posts are, by default, configured for content approval. Only the blog owner can add posts that are approved and published directly.
	You can activate approval of blog comments by enabling "Require content approval for submitted items" for the Comments list.

3

Office Integration

WHAT YOU WILL LEARN IN THIS CHAPTER:

➤ Understanding Lists and Libraries

➤ Using Version History

➤ The Problem with Traditional File Systems

➤ Managing Custom Columns, Tags, and Metadata

➤ Datasheet Views and List Views

➤ Managing Site Columns and Content Types

➤ Understanding Information Policies

➤ Enabling Document ID

➤ Managing In-Place Records and Document Sets

In Chapter 2, you learned how easy the process is for a user to create sites for collaboration and blogs, without assistance from a developer or administrator. You also learned that SharePoint stores all information in different types of lists, depending on what type of information it is. The real magic in SharePoint shows up when you integrate other applications with these lists — for example, to read and write documents in a document library.

Multiple products from different vendors can use SharePoint's document libraries directly for storing files and documents, but one product family really shines when it comes to SharePoint integration: Microsoft Office — that is, Microsoft Word, Microsoft Excel, and so on. Other Microsoft applications also have excellent integration with SharePoint, especially Microsoft Outlook, Microsoft OneNote, Microsoft Access, and Microsoft InfoPath. In fact, one can safely say that today, finding any program from Microsoft that does not have some sort of integration with SharePoint 2010 is hard.

This chapter describes how this integration works, and what differs between the current Microsoft Office 2010 and previous versions of Microsoft Office. This chapter contains a lot of examples and step-by-step instructions on how to use a number of applications with SharePoint 2010. The features described in this chapter are valid for both SharePoint Foundation and SharePoint Server, unless stated otherwise.

COMPARING OFFICE EDITIONS

The Microsoft Office suite has grown since its beginning in 1989, and it contains tools for almost any kind of work that organizations do today. Several of the products in the Microsoft Office 2010 suite are more or less made for SharePoint, whereas others may take advantage of SharePoint if it is available. The following is the complete list of products in Microsoft Office 2010 Professional Plus:

➤ Microsoft Word 2010

➤ Microsoft Excel 2010

➤ Microsoft PowerPoint 2010

➤ Microsoft Access 2010

➤ Microsoft OneNote 2010

➤ Microsoft Publisher 2010

➤ Microsoft InfoPath 2010

➤ Microsoft SharePoint Workspace 2010

➤ Microsoft Communicator

➤ Microsoft Outlook 2010

➤ Microsoft Office Web Apps

Microsoft Office Web Apps is a bit special, because it includes web-based editions of some of the most popular Office products: Word, Excel, PowerPoint, and OneNote. When you purchase Microsoft Office Professional Plus, you also get a client access license (CAL) for using Microsoft Office Web Apps. In addition to the products in the preceding list, several other SharePoint-aware desktop applications are distributed as separate products. Two of these, especially, are commonly used in many organizations:

➤ Microsoft Visio 2010

➤ Microsoft Project 2010

Microsoft Office 2010 comes in different packages, called Office Suites, so you can purchase the only the products you will use. However, some of these packages lack one or more products that are tightly integrated with SharePoint 2010. In other words, to get the most out of a SharePoint 2010 installation, you should select the *Office 2010 Professional Plus* edition, because it contains everything you need when using SharePoint as a place to collaborate and share information. Table 3-1 lists the different Office suites, and comments regarding how they relate to SharePoint. The next section presents more details about the differences between these Office suites.

TABLE 3-1: Office 2010 Suites

OFFICE SUITE	COMMENT
Office Professional Plus	The complete set of products. If you want to take full advantage of SharePoint, you should definitely select this package.
Office Professional	Lacks Microsoft Communicator, Microsoft InfoPath, and Microsoft SharePoint Workspace — all of these are commonly used in a SharePoint environment. This suite also lacks user licenses for using Office Web App. No support exists for Microsoft Rights Management Service (RMS). Think carefully before you select this package in a SharePoint environment — you may have to upgrade sooner than you expect!
Office Standard	This suite is only available via Microsoft volume licensing. It contains the same products as Office Professional, except Microsoft Access, but it also contains the Office Web App user licenses.
Office Home & Business	Contains only the typical Office products, such as Microsoft Word, Microsoft Excel, Microsoft PowerPoint, Microsoft Outlook, and Microsoft OneNote. This basic package only contains the fundamental integrations with SharePoint.

Many organizations have older versions of Office, like Office 2007 and Office 2003. They are able to work with SharePoint, but only Office 2010 offers full functionality. Do not expect upgrade packages from Microsoft that will allow Office 2003 or Office 2007 users to get the same functionality as Office 2010. This will not happen! The reason is not only that Microsoft wants to give you a good reason for upgrading Office (they do, of course!), but also because these new features are deeply integrated in the code and design of Office 2010. The following sections present more about how these different Office versions integrate with SharePoint 2010.

> **NOTE** *Office 2003 does not support the new* Open XML *file format introduced in SharePoint 2007. A free add-on called* Microsoft Office Compatibility Pack *enables users to both read and write documents using the Open XML format, thus making the sharing of documents with Office 2007 and Office 2010 users possible. Use the following link to download this add-on:*
> `http://tinyurl.com/compatibilitypack.`

Office 2010 Integration

SharePoint 2010 is a platform on which you share and collaborate. The most common desktop client in today's organizations is Microsoft Office. Many of the new features in SharePoint 2010 will only be available for users with Office 2010. But not just any Office 2010 suite — you need the Office 2010 Professional Plus edition to take full advantage of all these new features. If you don't get this edition, you will have less functionality.

Office 2010 Professional Plus

The following bulleted list presents an overview of what Office 2010 Professional Plus allows the user to do in a SharePoint 2010 environment. Note that features and operations are available directly from within the Office client.

➤ *Open, edit, and save* Office documents in document libraries. Office 2010 has a special navigation feature that makes seeing your latest SharePoint sites easy. The SharePoint administrator can also push out quick links to Office 2010 users to make sure the most common sites will be listed in Office.

➤ Open, edit, and save documents using *Office Web Apps*. If you need more features than the Office Web App client can provide, you can use a button that opens the current document in the full Office client.

➤ *Check out and check in* documents. When you check out documents stored in SharePoint, the document is locked by you, and no other user can edit it until you check in the document.

➤ View and update *standard Office document properties*, such as Title and Comments.

➤ View and update *SharePoint columns* associated with the content type used by the current document. These columns are often referred to as the document's *metadata*.

➤ View and update SharePoint's new feature: *managed keywords and tags*. This includes managed taxonomies and folksonomies that are defined for the current document.

➤ *Display SharePoint properties*, including SharePoint columns, managed keywords, and tags within the actual document.

➤ To open an existing document, *navigate by managed keywords and tags* when browsing large document libraries, as an alternative to the default browse method.

➤ View, recover, and compare *document versions* stored in SharePoint. This requires that version history be activated on the document library.

➤ *Protect documents*, using Microsoft Rights Management Service (RMS). For example, the user can define who can read and who can edit a document, regardless of how and where the document is stored, including on USB sticks. To the uninvited user, the document is encrypted and therefore unusable.

➤ Add *digital signatures* with Microsoft RMS. Other users can verify that this document was signed by a particular user, and that the content has not been changed.

➤ *Restrict editing* per user with Microsoft RMS. This feature allows an author to place different types of restrictions on a document. For example, everyone may be allowed to read a document, but only Anna may be allowed to edit its first paragraph. Another example is that Anna asks five different users to comment on a specific document; to prohibit anyone of these five from modifying the content, Anna defines restricted editing for everyone, except herself, that only allows any one of these five users to add comments, but not anything else.

➤ Publish Word 2010 documents as *blog posts* in SharePoint, as an alternative to creating posts inside the actual blog site.

➤ Start SharePoint *workflows* that are associated with the current document — for example, to ask a manager for approval to send a contact to a customer.

➤ Allow *co-authoring* of an Office document in real-time. This works with Word, Excel, PowerPoint, and OneNote documents.

➤ Publish Excel spreadsheets to SharePoint's *Excel Services*, which makes sharing a complete workbook or all or part of a specific spreadsheet easy. This Excel data can be displayed directly on a SharePoint site, and users can be granted permission to enter values and calculate, without having a local Excel (or Office Web App) client installed.

➤ *Share OneNote* documents in SharePoint. By storing a OneNote notebook, multiple users can both see and update the same notes. This feature is perfect for use in a brainstorm meeting where users are working in different locations.

➤ Get offline access to SharePoint content with *SharePoint Workspace*. Previously, this client was called Groove, but Office 2010 gave it a new name. This offline tool replicates almost all types of SharePoint lists, including their settings, for example document libraries along with their custom columns and content types.

➤ Create and work with *intelligent forms* in SharePoint, such as forms for travel expenses and tax calculations, using Microsoft InfoPath. With SharePoint Forms Service, these forms can be converted to web-based forms, so the user doesn't need a local InfoPath client installed.

➤ Integrate *Microsoft Access applications* in SharePoint. You can build an Access database, including relations, joins, and forms for entering and presenting the data, and then publish it to a SharePoint website for users to utilize. This feature provides an excellent way of sharing Microsoft Access applications without having to distribute the actual database to each user.

➤ Get *two-way synchronization* of contacts, calendar, tasks, discussions, and documents with Outlook. This kind of sync was introduced with SharePoint and Outlook 2007. It still uses the same type of synchronization mechanism, and it is very handy for managing list content offline. To some extent, this feature competes with the functionality that comes with SharePoint Workspace, but while synchronization of offline modifications is automatic in SharePoint Workspace, documents modified offline in Outlook need to be replicated manually by the user.

➤ Show *presence status* of SharePoint users and quick links for communicating with these users — via instant messaging, mail, a live meeting, or phone — using Microsoft Communicator and its server component, Microsoft Office Communication Server (OCS).

➤ Browse *multimedia asset libraries* in SharePoint when adding pictures and video to PowerPoint and Word.

This is only a summary, but it is still an impressive list of functions that shows how important SharePoint 2010 is to Microsoft Office 2010.

Comparing Other Office 2010 Suites

What happens if you choose another Office 2010 suite — for example, Professional or Standard? Table 3-2 lists the features included in each of these Office suites. For more details about each feature, see the earlier bulleted list.

TABLE 3-2: Comparing Office 2010 Suites

FEATURE	PRO PLUS	PROFESSIONAL	STANDARD	HOME & STUDENT
Target audience	Business	Small Business	Business	Personal
Open, edit, and save documents	Yes	Yes	Yes	Yes
Office Web Apps license	Yes	No	Yes	No
Check out/in	Yes	Yes	Yes	Yes
Update standard document properties	Yes	Yes	Yes	Yes
Update SharePoint columns	Yes	No	No	No
Update managed keywords	Yes	No	No	No
Display SharePoint metadata in documents	Yes	No	No	No
Navigate by metadata	Yes	No	No	No
Manage document versions	Yes	No	Yes	No
Protect by Microsoft RMS	Yes	No	No	No
Digital signatures	Yes	No	No	No
Restrict editing	Yes	No	Yes	No
Publish blogs	Yes	No	Yes	No
Start workflows	Yes	No	Yes	No
Co-authoring	Yes	No	Yes	No
Publish to Excel Services	Yes	No	No	No
Share OneNote documents	Yes	No	Yes	No
Manage intelligent forms	Yes	No	No	No
Integrate Microsoft Access	Yes	No	No	No
Two-way sync with Outlook	Yes	Yes	Yes	Yes
Presence status	Yes	No	No	No
Browse media asset libraries	Yes	No	No	No

Table 3-2 shows that big differences exist among these Office 2010 suites. In a SharePoint environment, only two suites offer good integration: Professional Plus and Standard. But for full access to all SharePoint 2010 features, you must have Office 2010 Professional Plus.

Office Web Apps is interesting, because it is completely web-based and works with web browsers such as Internet Explorer 7 or later, Firefox, and Safari. Note that Office Web App is not a replacement for the full Office 2010 clients, because for one thing, you need a license to run Office Web App, even though they are web clients. Also, they only have the basic features for editing documents. For example, with Excel Office Web App, you can view existing diagrams, but you cannot create a new one. Note that only two Office 2010 suites come with the client access licenses to run Office Web App in a SharePoint 2010 environment: Office Professional Plus and Office Standard.

> **NOTE** *Office Web Apps will be available for free when users access documents stored in some of Microsoft's cloud solutions, such as Microsoft SkyDrive. Using Office Web App and SkyDrive is an excellent way of sharing documents, including co-authoring abilities, with people outside your organization who cannot access your internal SharePoint environment.*

Office 2007 Integration

Using SharePoint 2010 with Office 2007 is almost as good as using Office 2010, but not quite. All features that Office 2007 offers when users work with SharePoint 2007 are still available when they use SharePoint 2010. The big question is, of course, what features you and your users will miss out on by not using SharePoint 2010 and how much they matter. The following list describes what features Office 2007 users will NOT have:

➤ Open, edit, and save documents using Office Web Apps

➤ View and update SharePoint's managed keywords and tags

➤ Display SharePoint's managed keywords and tags within the actual document

➤ Navigate by keywords when browsing existing Office documents

➤ Reduced protection of documents using Microsoft Information Rights Management (IRM)

➤ Reduced ability to add digital signatures with Microsoft IMS

➤ Restrict editing per user with Microsoft IMS

➤ Allow co-authoring of an Office document in real-time

➤ Offline access to SharePoint content with SharePoint Workspace

➤ Integrate Microsoft Access applications in SharePoint

Do you need any of these features? Because they are new to Office 2007 users, answering this question without performing a serious test can be hard. Note that such a test must be done together with users, absolutely not by IT professionals only. This decision is about the tools that your users use every day, so it is a very important one to make.

A good test involves a number of people with different responsibilities who get trained by someone who understands how the preceding list of features could add value to users and their daily activities. Such a test may take a month or more and require thorough planning. Then again, the decision is really important, so taking the time to weigh the options will be worth it.

Maybe the result of this test will conclude that 50 percent of the users need Office 2010 Professional Plus, while the other 50 percent will do fine with Office 2010 Standard. Think twice before selecting a mixed solution. Most organizations want a single Office edition to make the helpdesk team's job easier and for support and maintenance reasons. The extra work required to maintain a mixed Office solution may quickly be more expensive than the cost of giving all users the full Office edition.

Office 2003 Integration

Even today, a number of organizations still rely on Office 2003, which is easy to understand. It is an excellent product, as long as you are happy with the features it provides. But when you implement SharePoint 2010, you expect a number of new features to be available to all users that will help them be more productive and remove tedious and repetitive procedures. Now you must think very hard whether Office 2003 is the right desktop client for your SharePoint users. Here is a list of what these users will NOT get:

➤ Open, edit, and save documents using Office Web Apps

➤ View and update SharePoint managed keywords and tags

➤ Display SharePoint properties, including keywords and tags within the actual document

➤ Navigate by keywords when opening an existing Office document

➤ Protection of documents using Microsoft Information Rights Management (IMS)

➤ Add digital signatures with Microsoft IMS

➤ Restrict editing per user with Microsoft IMS

➤ Publish Word 2010 documents as blog posts in SharePoint

➤ Start SharePoint workflows that are associated with the current document

➤ Allow co-authoring of an Office document in real-time

➤ Publish Excel spreadsheets to SharePoint

➤ Share OneNote documents in SharePoint

➤ Offline access to SharePoint content with SharePoint Workspace

➤ Create and work with intelligent forms in SharePoint using Microsoft InfoPath

➤ Integrate Microsoft Access applications in SharePoint

➤ Two-way synchronization of contacts, calendar, tasks, discussions, and documents with Outlook

➤ Show presence status of SharePoint users and quick links for communicating with these users — via instant messaging, mail, a live meeting, or phone — using Microsoft Communicator

Again this is a list of things that Office 2003 users cannot do! Clearly, Office 2003 gives SharePoint 2010 users a very poor environment, and one can debate whether SharePoint 2010 is really worth the investment in time and money unless the organization will upgrade to a newer version of Microsoft Office. You should think about it like this: Office is the client, and SharePoint is the server. Most organizations would never plan to run the old Outlook 2003 with the new Exchange 2010, because so many e-mail features would not be available. My tip to you is to make sure that your Office version matches SharePoint's version; that is, that both are 2010 versions.

Older Office and Non-Microsoft Desktop Applications

What happens if an organization runs an Office version previous to 2003? These users will have the same experience as users running non-Microsoft desktop packages, such as Star Office or OpenOffice. These users will be able to work with documents as if SharePoint is an enhanced file server. For example, standard features for document libraries will still be available, like check out/in, version history, and metadata, but not from within the desktop client. This may be satisfying for some special scenarios, although most organizations cannot accept the shortcomings of this environment.

Non-Microsoft desktop applications must support read and write operations to a URL address in order to open and save files to a SharePoint document library. Several popular applications don't support this feature, such as Acrobat Reader and several computer-aided design (CAD) applications. You can, however, make these types of applications believe that SharePoint is a standard file server by setting up a Uniform Naming Convention (UNC) path, such as G:, as described in the following Try It Out.

> **NOTE** The following steps require that the Windows client is running the Web Client *Windows service. By default, this service runs on Windows XP, Vista and Windows 7 clients, but not on Windows Server.*

TRY IT OUT **Create an UNC Path to SharePoint**

In this example, you create an UNC path named X: on your Windows 7 or Vista based client computer that points to the top site at `http://srv1`. From this node, you can navigate to any library and subsite. Note that you will see all lists and folders in the site, including locations you cannot use for storing documents!

1. Log on to your client computer as a local administrator.

2. Verify that you can open the website on `http://srv1`.

3. Open a command shell prompt by choosing Start ⇨ All Programs ⇨ Accessories ⇨ Command Prompt. A command prompt window opens.

4. Enter the following text and press Enter: `Net Use X: \\SRV1`

5. Still in the command prompt window, type `x:` and press Enter; then type `DIR` and press Enter. You should now see all the lists, libraries, and subsites in this SharePoint site.

6. Open Windows Explorer and verify that X: is listed. Its name will be `DavWWWRoot(\\srv1) (X:)` in Windows 7.

7. Test that you can save a file to a document library. For example, open an Adobe PDF file, and save it to X:. Make sure to navigate to a document library. Then open this library using a web browser, and verify that the file is listed.

How It Works

Windows XP, Vista, and Windows 7 allow you to create an UNC path to URL addresses, using a protocol called *WebDAV*.

MANAGING DOCUMENT LIBRARIES

Documents are, without question, the most common items that users work with in a typical SharePoint environment. In fact, many organizations completely replace their traditional file servers with document libraries. Here are some of the reasons (of which there are many):

➤ Document libraries provide automatic version history, including draft versions.

➤ Document metadata and tags can be used for categorizing and organizing.

➤ Alerts are sent out when documents are updated, created, or deleted.

➤ Workflows can be used to automate processes.

➤ Users can rate documents.

➤ Office Web Apps allow web-based clients access, plus co-authoring of Word, PowerPoint, Excel, and OneNote files.

➤ Document libraries include a check out/in feature.

➤ You can audit document usage.

None of these features are available for documents stored in a file server, except Windows Server 2008 R2 (see the following Note regarding File Classification Infrastructure). Although a document library can store any type of file, some files need more functionality than the document library offers. For example, when storing images and video files, having a preview feature would be nice — such as a feature to help a user who is looking for a specific image to add to a web page. That is why there are different libraries, as described in the following section.

> **NOTE** *Windows Server 2008 R2 has a new feature called* File Classification Infrastructure *(FCI), which makes adding metadata to files stored in a file server possible. If these files later are imported into SharePoint, the associated metadata will also be imported. See* `http://tinyurl.com/Win2008R2-FCI` *for more information about the FCI feature.*

Different Types of Libraries

Some files — such as multimedia files, forms, and PowerPoint slides — need to be treated in a special way to make using them easier for users. That is why SharePoint supports different libraries, as presented in Table 3-3.

TABLE 3-3 Different Types of Libraries

LIBRARY	PRIMARY USAGE	SPECIAL FEATURES
Document Library	All types of documents and files	Standard features
Asset Library	Multimedia files, such as image, audio, and video files	Preview of images, audio, and video
Connection Library	Stores files that define external connections	Accessible when configuring external connections
Form Library	XML-based forms, such as InfoPath forms	Stores XML forms as content types; synchronizes fields in the form with library columns
Picture Library	Images and picture files	Automatic presentation of images in this library
Record Library	Business records	
Report Library	Key performance indicators (KPIs), business intelligence (BI) information, and goals	Connects to web parts presenting KPI status, statistics, and graphics
Slide Library	Individual PowerPoint slides	Create new presentations by selecting PowerPoint slides
Translation Management	For managing documents in multiple languages	Contains workflows for managing the translation of documents
Wiki Pages	Enables easy editing of rich content, such as text, images, and Wiki links	Standard page for team sites and publishing pages; supports web parts.

This list shows all the library types in SharePoint Server 2010 Enterprise edition. A SharePoint Foundation installation will only contain these libraries: Document Library, Picture Library, Form Library, and Wiki Pages.

Version History for List Items

By default, document libraries in SharePoint do not store previous versions of any document. However, it is possible to activate the version history feature for most types of lists and document libraries, XML libraries, and picture libraries. The reason version history is disabled by default is that it requires disk and CPU resources.

SharePoint 2010 offers two types of version history: one that only stores public versions (1, 2, and 3); and another type that keeps track of both draft versions (1.1 and 1.2) and major versions (1.0 and 2.0). Choose the one that best suits your needs, as demonstrated in the following Try It Out.

TRY IT OUT   **Enable Version History**

1.   Log on as a site owner.

2.   Click on the document library (for example, Shared Documents) to view its content.

3.   Click Library Settings (Library tab) on the ribbon, to open the Document Library Settings page. If you do not see the Library Settings option, then your account does not have permission to change the settings for this library!

4.   Click the Version settings link, and the Versioning Settings page opens. In the Document Version History section, you can choose the following types of version history for this library:

➤   No versioning

➤   Create major versions

➤   Create major and minor (draft) versions

Note that you can also set the number of versions to be stored here. Another related setting is in Draft Item Security: If you earlier selected "Create major and minor (draft) versions," you can define who will see the draft's versions as follows:

➤   **Any users who can read items:** Choose this option if all users should be able to read draft versions.

➤   **Only users who can edit items:** Choose this option to limit the groups of users who will see draft versions to authors only; that is, not users with only read access.

➤   **Only users who can approve items (and the author of the item):** Choose this option when nobody except the author and the user with approve permission should be able to see the draft version. Note that this option is only available if you set the "Require content approval for submitted items" option to Yes at the top of this web form!

5.   Click OK, and then click Shared Documents in the left pane.

How It Works

Version history works for almost all types of lists and libraries. By default, no version history is saved. The two types of version history are Major only (1, 2, and 3) and Major plus draft (1.1, 1.2, 1.3, and so on).

Regardless of the type of version history you selected, it is now active, but only for this current library! If you have more document libraries and want a version history of them all, you must enable this feature for all of these libraries. Now test out the version history as described in the following Try It Out.

TRY IT OUT   Use Version History

The version history is now activated if you performed the preceding Try It Out. In this example you test how it works for documents.

1.   Edit any Microsoft Office document in this document library, and then save and close this file.

2.   Use the file's quick menu and select Version History (or click Version History on the ribbon) to open the Version History page. Depending on the type of version history you selected in step 4 of the previous Try It Out, you will now see the following version history:

> ➤   **Only Major Versions:** The list shows that the current version is 2.0.

> ➤   **Major and Draft Versions:** The list shows that this is version 1.1; that is, it is a draft version, not a major (published) version. To make it the published version, click the X button on this window to close it and go back to the document library, and open the quick menu for this file again. This time, select Publish A Major Version, enter a version comment in the Publish Major Version dialog box that appears, and then click OK. Open the version history again, and the current version now appears as 2.0.

3.   If you changed an existing file once, you should now see a list of two files, but with different version numbers, times, and dates, plus the name of the user who modified the file. You can also see information about what was changed in a specific version. These versions also have a quick menu. You can use it to view, restore, or delete any of the previous versions. If you choose to restore a previous version, the current version will be changed to be the second newest version.

How It Works

Using major version history is very simple; the user works as before, and nothing is changed. Using major plus draft versions requires that users manually switch from the draft version to the major version to publish the document.

> **NOTE** *SharePoint 2010 stores complete versions only; that is, if you save a document of 2MB three times, the version history will take up 6GB.*

Using Document Metadata and Tagging

Without SharePoint, users must rely on folders and filenames to categorize and organize files. This method works fine, at least as long as the numbers of files are not too many. The issues with this method are as follows:

> ➤   It requires that all users understand the folder structure and will follow the name standard for files.

> ➤   The existing folder structure is rigid; changing it without making users confused is hard.

> ➤   Most organizations have multiple folder structures, not just one, which makes understanding which one to use hard for users.

Every user is managing files and documents every day. Finding the file they need quickly and ensuring it is the correct version is an important and often frustrating task. Every step you can take to make this task easier will be received with standing applause from your users. If you can also make it just a bit more fun, they will cheer. File and document management is this important!

SharePoint can help you make this happen. The key to the solution is to work with document metadata and tagging — that is, keywords.

Traditional File Chaos

To understand what SharePoint can do requires that you analyze how things work traditionally. The following are the typical tasks a user performs with files and documents every day, and the inherent challenges and questions related to those tasks:

➤ **Creating a file:** Where should I save this file so my colleagues and I can later find it? What name should I give this file so it is clear what it contains?

➤ **Opening a file:** How do I find the file? How can I be sure it is the latest version? How can I contact the most recent author if necessary?

➤ **Updating a file:** How do I find the file to be updated? How can I save the new version without overwriting the old file? How can I update a public file over a period of days and avoid someone seeing the document before it is fully updated? How can several people cooperate when updating a file?

➤ **Deleting a file:** How can I be sure no other copy of this file still exists?

Your users deal with these challenges with every time they work with a file or document. Let's face it: Every user solves these challenges in her own way, and the consequence is that you soon will have file chaos. No one is sure where all the files are stored, no one is sure that the file they found are the latest version, and all these file copies make the backup and restore procedures unnecessarily complicated and time consuming.

What Users Really Need

You need a new method to organize and group files without relying on folders — something that will be easy to change, or even adjust itself automatically for each user looking at these files. For example, a project manager might want to see project documents presented in one way, but each project member may need to organize this information in another way, maybe even hiding everything except the files that he or she works with.

All these problems with filenames could be solved if you were allowed to create your own properties for a file or document, such as *Document Type*, *Year*, and *Period*. Then you could store this information in the properties instead of building it into the actual filename. If the system also could keep track of versions automatically, you would not have this mess anymore either, right?

The Solution

Every list and library in SharePoint allows you to create any (well, almost any) number of columns. These columns are known as *metadata*, and are used to store properties about list items. You can also use these columns to create different views of the data, that is, to sort and filter the list items — for example, documents in a document library. There are two types of columns in SharePoint Foundation, plus two more in SharePoint Server 2010 (both Standard and Enterprise), as presented in Table 3-4.

TABLE 3-4: Column Types in SharePoint

COLUMN TYPE	SHAREPOINT FOUNDATION?	SHAREPOINT SERVER?	COMMENTS
System Column	Yes	Yes	For example, Title, Created By, Size
Custom Column	Yes	Yes	User-created columns for properties; for example, Security Class and DocType
Enterprise Keywords	No	Yes	Tags entered by users to categorize items
Managed Metadata	No	Yes	Hierarchical taxonomy created by the administrator

The system columns match the standard properties typically found for Office documents stored in a file system; for example, file name, created by, and modified by. SharePoint will automatically keep track of these system columns for all file types in a document library, not only Office documents.

The Enterprise Keywords column is special, because it is not created. Instead, it is a built-in feature in SharePoint Server that you enable for the list. Then you make it visible in a list view to enable users to see all tags. The same goes for the Managed Metadata column. It is a SharePoint Server feature you enable for the list. Then you connect it to a hierarchical metadata tree that is created using the site settings page.

In the Try It Out steps in the following section, you learn how to manage these four types of metadata columns in a document library. This metadata description works for any type of list or library, but only SharePoint Server supports enterprise keywords and managed metadata.

Managing Custom Columns

Custom columns are typically used to store properties about list items. They are easy to create and manage. All you need is the web browser. They work very similarly to how custom columns worked in previous versions of SharePoint, but there are important enhancements. For example:

➤ Lookup columns can now fetch more than one property from another list. In previous versions, only one property was fetched.

➤ External data fetches its values from an external data source, and populates a choice list.

➤ Managed Metadata columns fetch values from a hierarchical metadata tree, and populate a choice list.

Start by creating some basic custom columns as described in the following Try It Out, and then continue with lookup fields.

Create List Columns

In this example, you add two custom columns named Product and Price.

1. Log on as a site owner and open any site; for example, a team site.

2. Open a document library; for example, Shared Documents.

3. Add the first column: Switch to the Library tab on the ribbon, and then click Create Column. In the Create Column form that appears, enter the following values, and accept the other default values:

   a. **Column Name:** Product

   b. **Column Type:** Choice

   c. **Description:** Our Fruit Products

   d. Type each choice on a separate line: **Apple, Orange,** and **Banana**

   e. **Default Value:** Apple

   Click OK to save and close this form.

4. Add the second column: Click Create Column, and in the Create Column form that appears, enter these values, and accept the other default values:

   a. **Column Name:** Price

   b. **Column Type:** Number

   c. **Min:** 0 and **Max:** 100

   d. **Number of Decimal Places:** 0

   Click OK to save and close this form.

5. Verify that these two custom columns are listed (at the far right).

6. On the ribbon, click Upload Document, browse to an existing document, and click OK. In the form that appears, you will see the two custom columns. Select Product=Banana and Price=5, and then click Save.

7. Verify that the new document is listed, including the custom columns.

How It Works

Properties for list and library items, such as documents, are stored in columns, sometimes referred to as metadata. A user with the proper permission can add more columns, usually referred to as custom columns. You can add different types of custom columns, such as choice, text, numeric, and user account names.

Managing Lookup Columns

Columns can also integrate with other lists. For example, suppose that you have a list of your customers, plus a document library. You want to define what customer belongs to a specific document. You can easily do this by creating a *lookup column* in the document library that fetches its values from the customer list.

TRY IT OUT   **Work with Lookup Columns**

In this example, you first create a list for Customers, and then you create a lookup column in the document library that gets its values from the Company field in the Customers list.

1.   Open a team site as a list owner.

2.   Create the Customer list based on the Contacts list template, as follows:

   a.   Click Site Actions ➪ More Options ➪ Contacts.

   b.   Enter **Customers** in the Name field, and click Create.

   c.   Click Add New Item and fill in values for the fields Last Name, First Name, E-mail Address, and Company (for example, Gates, Bill, billg@microsoft.com, Microsoft). Then click Save.

   d.   Enter at least two more customers (for example, Steve Jobs, Apple and Larry Ellison, Oracle).

   e.   Verify that you have at least three items in this list, with different Customer names.

3.   Now create a lookup column in the document library. To begin, open the Shared Documents library, and switch to the List tab on the ribbon.

4.   Click Create Column, enter the following values in the form, and then click OK:

   a.   **Column Name:** Customer

   b.   **Column Type:** Lookup

   c.   **Get Information From:** Customers

   d.   **In This Column:** Company

   e.   Select the Last Name check box.

5.   Verify that Shared Documents now has a column named Customer.

6.   Test that it works: Click Upload Document on the ribbon, click Browse, select any type of file, and click OK. Then do the following:

   a.   In the form that appears, open the Customer value, and verify that you can see all the companies listed in the Customers list. Select any one of them.

   b.   Click Save.

   c.   Verify that this list item displays the company name.

d. Click on the company name. Note that you will see the complete list of properties for that particular customer, without moving away from the document library. There is also an Edit Item button, in case you need to modify that customer. Click Close (or the X) button to close this form.

7. This lookup column is a really handy feature. But you can do more! For example, make sure Shared Documents is open, and then click Library Settings on the Library tab.

8. Scroll down to the Columns section and do the following:

a. Click on Customer (the lookup field) to open a form with the column settings.

b. Locate the section "Add a column to show each of these additional fields." Then select Last Name, First Name, and E-mail Address.

c. Click OK.

9. Open Shared Documents again. Note that the list now displays not only the company name, but also the customer's first and last name and e-mail address.

How It Works

Lookup columns fetch values from other lists in the same site and are very easy to set up and manage. Using SharePoint Designer or code, you can also fetch values from lists in other sites or site collections.

Working with Enterprise Keywords Columns

This type of keyword property is often called a *tag*. Users add tags to any type of object to classify and categorize it. Tags are important features in social computing; that is, in IT-based systems where users tag, comment, and grade information created by themselves or others. Note that users can enter any kind of keyword, so the administrator needs to know how to manage them. Keywords are global, thus the name *enterprise keywords*. Here are some of the great advantages of enterprise keywords:

➤ Users will recognize keywords as "tags," which they are familiar with from Internet sites such as Facebook and blogs.

➤ A user can add tags to documents to show team members how he or she categorizes documents.

➤ Users will see a list of all their tags, that is keywords, on their My Site. Click on a tag to see all documents with this tag. This is a very easy way to find documents a specific user is working with.

➤ Users have a personal *tag cloud* that gives them and other users a good overview of their most popular tags.

➤ A special web part displays a tag cloud that lists all tags for all users. This shows what tags that are most popular for your organization.

A keyword entered by a user in one library will be available in any other library, regardless of whether it is in another site or site collection. For example, if user Malin adds the word *Aero* as a keyword for one of her files, then user Alex will see *Aero* as a suggestion when he types **A** in the Keyword field for one of his files.

Some organizations might be afraid to enable enterprise keywords, because they fear that it will create chaos if every user can create any keyword. Tagging is a very valuable feature for all users, and the only way to understand its value to your organization is to start using it. If you, for some reason, do not want this feature, disabling it is easy. I am sure your users will love it! However, there are ways to minimize the risk of "keyword chaos":

➤ An administrator can manage enterprise keywords; for example, to add, delete, or correct spelling errors.

➤ Users will see existing keywords when adding their keywords, which encourages users to pick an existing keyword instead of creating a new synonym or similar keyword.

➤ You can teach and train users how enterprise keywords work and how to get the most out of this feature.

Enterprise keywords are also indexed, and therefore searchable. As mentioned earlier, this kind of column is a built-in feature of any list in SharePoint Server 2010, but not in SharePoint Foundation. In the following example, you learn how to activate the keyword column, and how to manage keywords.

> **NOTE** *The Managed Metadata Service in SharePoint Server 2010 must be configured in order to enable enterprise keywords. See Appendix D for more information on how to configure this service.*

TRY IT OUT Enable Enterprise Keywords

In this example, you first enable the keyword field in the default list view. Then you learn how to manage all the keywords that users enter.

1. Log on as a site owner and open the same site as in the preceding Try It Out.

2. Open Shared Documents, and switch to the Library tab on the ribbon.

3. Click Library Settings to open the configuration page for this library.

4. Click Enterprise Metadata And Keyword Settings in the Permissions And Management section.

5. Check Enterprise Keywords and click OK.

6. Scroll down to the Columns section. Verify that Enterprise Keywords is listed. This column has no special settings.

7. Check that the enterprise keywords work: Open Shared Documents, and edit the properties for an existing document to verify that you now have the Enterprise Keywords column (see Figure 3-1). Enable Enterprise Keywords in other lists and sites, and enter tags for multiple documents. (You learn later how to manage these keywords.) Note that you get suggestions when entering a new tag that starts with the same letters as existing tags.

8. Open the start page of any site. Click on Tags And Notes in the top-right corner of the page. Enter any tag, and then click Save and close this form.

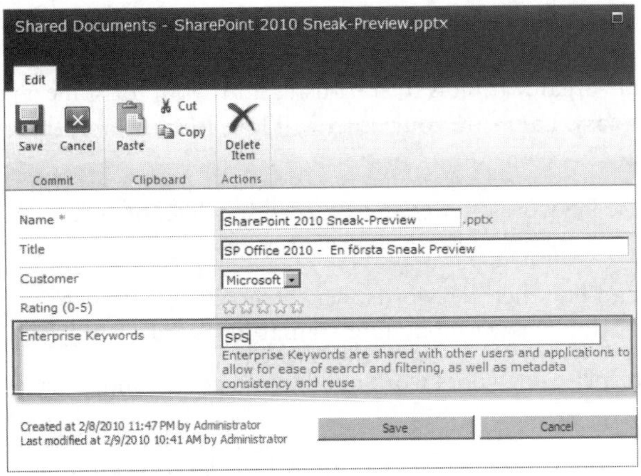

FIGURE 3-1

How It Works

To enable users to add tags to list items, you must first enable the Enterprise Keywords feature for the list.

> **NOTE** *If you want to add multiple tags as keywords, separate them with a semicolon — for example,* **Volvo; Car; Vehicle**.

By now you should have created multiple keywords, and it is time to see how to manage them. Remember that keywords are global; that is, all keywords are stored in a single database, regardless of what site or library they are created in. As described in the following Try It Out, you must first define the *term store administrator*; after that, you learn how an administrator can manage keywords.

TRY IT OUT Add a Term Store Administrator

To manage keywords, you need to be a *term store administrator*. By default, no such administrator exists. To add this account, follow these steps:

1. Log on as a farm administrator to a site; for example, `http://srv1`.

2. Open a top site and click Site Actions ⇨ Site Settings ⇨ Term Store Management to open the Term Store Management Service page.

3. Click Managed Metadata Service in the left pane.

4. Enter your account in the Term Store Administrator field in the right pane, and click Save.

How It Works

The term store is a global repository for all keywords and managed metadata. The term store has its own management page that you can reach from all sites as well as from SharePoint Central Administration.

This makes having term store administrators who are not necessarily farm administrators easy. You can also add a security group as a term store administrator.

TRY IT OUT **Manage the Term Store**

1. Log on as a Term Store Administrator, and open any site.

2. Click Site Actions ⇨ Site Settings to open the Site Settings page.

3. In the Site Administration section, click Term Store Management. The Term Store Management Service page opens. Do the following to manage the keywords:

 a. Click the triangle next to System to expand this node, and then expand Keywords. This lists all known user defined tags, also known as *terms*.

 b. Hover the mouse over a tag that you created, and then click its little black arrow to open a menu that contains two options: Move Keyword and Delete Keyword (see Figure 3-2). Use the first option if you want to move a tag to another term set. Select to delete this keyword, but make sure to remember where this tag was used so you can see what happens with it when you delete it from the term store.

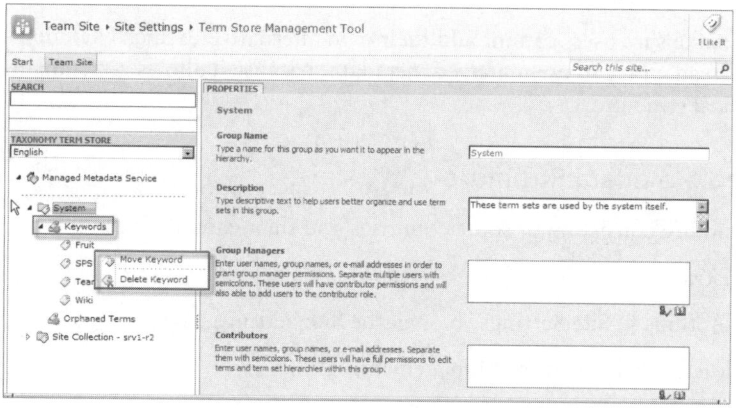

FIGURE 3-2

 c. Pick another tag, click twice on its name, type in another name for this tag, and press Enter.

 d. Select a tag. Note that you can disable this tag by deselecting Available For Tagging. If you do this, then this term will still be visible for list items that are tagged, but you cannot add it to new items.

4. What happened with the tag that you deleted? To find out, open the properties for a document where this tag was used. Note that the tag will still be listed, but it's marked as Not Valid. You can now enter it again, thus creating it again, or delete it.

5. What happened with the tag you renamed? Open the properties for a document where this tag was used. Depending on how fast you are, you will at first see the old name, and then within one hour, it will be replaced with the new name.

How It Works

The Term Store Management Service page is used to view and manage all tags entered by users as enterprise keywords in lists and libraries. The term store administrator can create, remove, and rename any tag on this page. These tags are visible in all sites that use the same Managed Metadata Service application (see Appendix D).

Working with Managed Metadata

Another special column type is *Managed Metadata*, which has a lot in common with enterprise keywords. The differences are that managed metadata consists of a predefined list of keywords, and you can use it to create a metadata hierarchy. For example, suppose that you need to tag a list of documents with capital cities for some countries. You could then create the following hierarchical structure:

```
Country
    USA
            Washington DC
    France
            Paris
    Sweden
            Stockholm
```

In this example, you also need to make sure users cannot add their own alternatives, which excludes the use of enterprise keywords. Instead, you can use managed metadata, because it allows a metadata administrator to create a hierarchical structure.

TRY IT OUT   **Create Managed Metadata Structure**

In this example, you create a tree structure consisting of some countries and their capital cities.

1.   Log on as a Term Store Administrator.

2.   Open any site, and choose Site Actions ⇨ Site Settings to open the Site Settings page.

3.   In the Site Administration section, click Term Store Management.

4.   In the left pane, open the menu for the Managed Metadata Service (click its little arrow to expand the node), and then select New Group. This creates a new node, referred to as a *group*.

5.   The new group is selected automatically. Enter **Customer Locations** in the Name field, and press Enter. A number of configuration settings show up to the right; use them to enter a description. Also notice the two security settings: *Contributors* can edit the values for this group; *Group Managers* are like Contributors, plus they can add and remove users to the Contributors group. In this example, you don't need to change any of these security settings.

6.   Hover over the new Customer Locations group, and click the arrow to open its menu; then select New Term Set.

7.   A sublevel node is created. Enter **Countries**, and press Enter in the Name field. Again, a configuration pane shows up to the right. Most of these settings are self-explanatory, but Submission Policy is interesting: If it is "open," then users can add their own terms; that is, new countries. If it is "closed," then only the term store administrator can change the terms.

8. Hover over the Countries term set and open its menu. Select Create Term and enter **USA**; then open its menu and enter the term **Washington DC**.

9. Repeat steps 7–8 two times to create the terms **France** and **Sweden**, including their sublevel terms; that is, the capital cities **Paris** and **Stockholm**. You should now have a hierarchical tree similar to the one shown in Figure 3-3.

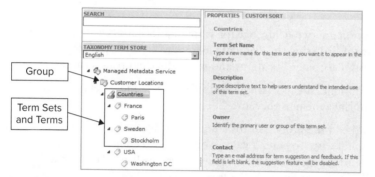

FIGURE 3-3

How It Works

You create and configure managed metadata on the same Term Store Management page as enterprise keywords. Use managed metadata when you need structured metadata. The root begins with a *group* that consists of *term sets*, which in turn consist of *terms*, which also can contain sublevel terms, and so on. You can have as many groups, term sets, and terms as you need.

After this managed metadata structure is created, you need to test it to see how it operates. Remember that this metadata structure is global; that is, it will be visible for all libraries that enable the keyword feature, as described in the following Try It Out.

TRY IT OUT **Use Managed Metadata Structures**

In this example, you enable managed metadata for a document library, and then create a column that shows all countries (that is, term sets) for the Countries group.

1. Log on as a Term Store Administrator, and open the same site you used in the previous Try It Out.

2. Open the Shared Documents document library.

3. Click Library Settings on the ribbon (on the Library tab) to open the Document Library Settings page.

4. Click Enterprise Metadata And Keyword Settings.

5. Select the "Save metadata on this list as a social tag" option, and click OK.

6. Scroll down to the Columns section, click Create Column, and enter the following values in the Create Column form that appears:

   a. **Column name:** Capital City

    b. **Column Type:** Managed Metadata. This displays a warning indicating that Office versions older than 2010 will not support this kind of metadata. Because you are running Office Professional Plus 2010, you are not affected by this warning.

    c. Accept the default "Display term label in the field" option. This ensures that only the term (that is, the selected capital city) will be displayed. If you want the complete path (for example, *France/Paris*) choose the option "Display the entire path to the term in the field" instead.

    d. In the Term Set Settings section are two fields: one for searching for term sets (when there are many of them), and one for browsing the metadata hierarchy. In this example, choose Managed Metadata Service ⇨ Customer Locations and select the Countries term set.

    e. There are other interesting options, such as "Allow 'Fill-in' choices" and "Default value," but in this example, you can leave them as they are. Click OK.

7. Go back to Shared Documents and edit the properties for a document. Note that the library now shows a new field named Capital City. To enter a value, you have two choices. You can either enter it manually — for example, start typing **Pa** and a list of suggestions such as "Paris" appears — then you click this suggestion to choose it (see Figure 3-4). Or you can click the tag icon at the end of the Capital City field to browse all countries and their capital cities, as shown in Figure 3-5. Click Save to close this property page.

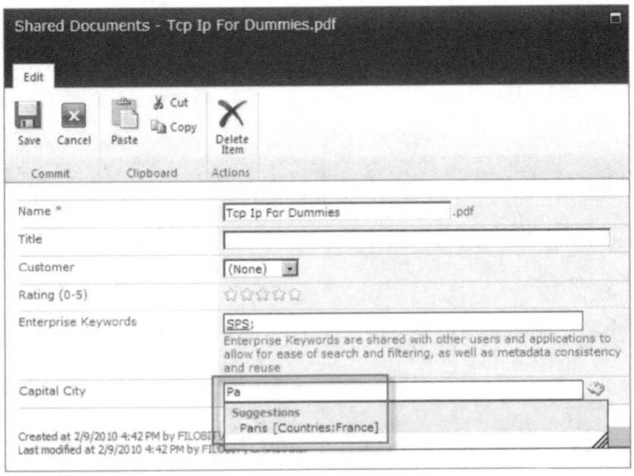

FIGURE 3-4

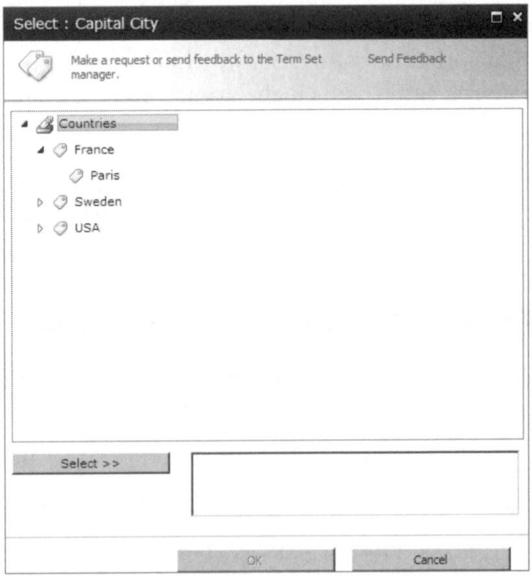

FIGURE 3-5

8. Verify that the Capital City is listed for this document library. If you don't see it, then you may have to change the list view to display this column. Click Modify View (on the Library tab), select Capital City, and click OK.

How It Works

To enable managed metadata for a list or library, you must create a Managed Metadata column and select a specific term set. You can go down deeper in the tree; for example, selecting the term *Sweden*, makes Stockholm the only possible choice for the capital city.

Managing the Rating Column

There is one more special column, another typical feature in social computing that is found in most community sites such as Facebook and blogs. It is the rating column that allows the users to grade a list item; for example, a document in a document library. The rating column is available for SharePoint Server, but not for SharePoint Foundation.

The rating setting is simple; it is a six-graded star rating, where 0 is the lowest (that is, no rating) and 5 stars is the highest rating. When this feature is enabled in a list or library, you see the following two columns:

➤ **Ratings (0–5):** Shows the average ratings given this list item.

➤ **Number of Ratings:** Shows how many times this list item has been rated.

The number of ratings is an important figure, because it gives an indication of how trustworthy this rating is. For example, a document that has an average rating of 4 from just two users is very different from a document rated as 4 from 200 users.

The rating feature is activated per list or library and is available for all items in that list. In other words, you cannot enable rating for just a subset of documents in a library; it's either all or none. But you don't have to rate items just because the rating column is enabled.

Ratings also have another interesting characteristic — items with higher rating averages get a higher ranking in the search results. For example, if you have five documents that all contain the word *Bollibompa*, and a user searches for that word, then the document with the highest ratings will be at the top, if all other properties for these documents are equal.

TRY IT OUT   Enable the Rating Setting

In this example, you enable the rating setting and then test it.

1. Log on as a site owner, and open a site with a document library.

2. Open the library, and then click Library Settings on the ribbon to open the Document Library Settings page.

3. Click Rating Settings in the General Settings section.

4. Enable "Allow items in this list to be rated" and click OK.

5. Scroll down to the Columns section and verify that you have two new columns: Ratings (0–5) and Number of Ratings.

6. Click on the document library name to close the Document Library Settings page, and then open this document library and add a new document. When entering the document properties, you will see a new column named Rating (0–5). Click on five stars, and then click Save.

7. The document is listed, but it will take some time before you see the average rating of 5 stars. Meanwhile, you can change the list view to also display the number of ratings, as follows:

    a. Switch to the Library tab, and click Modify View.

    b. Check the Number of Ratings (at the end of this list), and click OK.

    c. Verify that you now see both the Ratings (0–5) and Number of Ratings columns. They will still be empty, because SharePoint must run a timer job in order to update the rating values. Just wait a while, and you will see it.

8. You can also rate a list item directly in the list, without editing the item's properties. Open the document library so you can see the existing files; then click directly on the rating stars, and your rating will be saved (see Figure 3-6). Note that it may take some time before the new rating appears, but you can hover the mouse over your rating to see it.

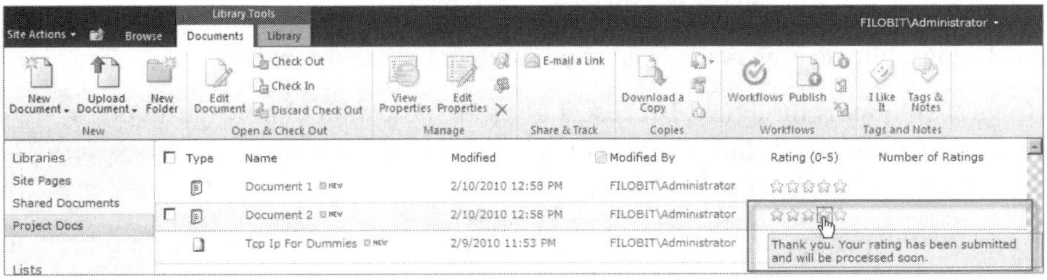

FIGURE 3-6

How It Works

Rating is a feature in SharePoint Server that allows users to grade any type of list item in SharePoint. This is an important signal to other users that can help them find documents and other items of good quality.

Managing List Views

One of the great advantages of using columns for storing metadata about list and library items is the possibility of using the metadata to create multiple views; that is, to sort and organize information, such as documents and files, in a document library. It is an excellent replacement for the traditional folder structures in a file server. All lists, including document libraries, have the following two types of list views:

➤ **Public views:** These are visible for every user who has at least read access to the list. To create a public view you must have the Manage Lists permission, which by default is only granted to the site owner, Designer, and Manage Hierarchy permission levels, but not for example Read or Contribute levels.

➤ **Personal views:** These are private views, only visible to the user who created them. All users with at least Contributor permissions can create personal views.

A list can have as many views as required, but when you have more than 50 views, getting an overview of them all may be hard. All views are stored as files in a hidden folder in the list, so all views have a specific URL that you can use to build your own navigation solution, if required.

List views are based on all kinds of metadata, both default system columns such as Creator and Title, as well as custom columns you have created. All lists have at least one view; for example, a document library comes with a preconfigured view named *All Documents*. The easiest way to learn about views, as always, is to try them out and see how they work, as you do in the Try It Out in the following section.

Creating Lists and Library Views

Before you create new views, you need to see what columns you can use when creating a view. Table 3-5 shows what columns you can use and for what purpose.

TABLE 3-5: What Columns Can Be Used in a View

COLUMN TYPE	DISPLAY	SORT	FILTER	GROUP
Standard columns	Yes	Yes	Yes	Yes
Ratings	Yes	Yes	Yes	Yes
Enterprise keywords	Yes	No	Yes	No
Managed metadata	Yes	Yes	Yes	Yes
Custom columns	Yes	Yes	Yes	Yes

TRY IT OUT Create List Views

In this example, you have a document library with just the default columns, and the default view All Documents. You need a new view that sorts so the last modified file is at the top, thus making it easier to see the latest documents.

1. Log on as the site owner, and then open a team site and its default document library, Shared Documents. Populate it with a number of different file types so you can see how the views operate.

2. On the ribbon, switch to the Library tab, and verify that it lists the current view as All Documents.

3. Note that it now displays all files in alphabetic order, based on the column Name. You can change the sort order by clicking on the column names (for example, Type and Modified) and selecting descending order or a specific sort type. But the next time you open this library, it will use the default view again.

4. To create a new view based on descending modification dates, click Create View on the ribbon and select the Standard view format. This opens the Create View form. Make the following selections:

   a. Title: Last Modified

   b. Accept the default view audience, Create a Public View.

c. Accept the default columns to be displayed.

d. In the Sort section, change the "First sort by the column" to Modified, and then select the option "Show items in descending order."

e. Scroll to the end (or beginning) of the form and click OK.

f. Verify that the new view is created and works as expected.

In the next few steps, you add two custom columns, *Security* and *DocType*, and set them both to use choice lists. Then you will create a new view that sorts by primarily by DocType, and secondarily by Security.

5. Switch to the Library tab, and then click Create Column (this button may be displayed as an icon only, if the space on the ribbon is small). On the Create Column form that appears, enter these values:

a. **Column name:** Security

b. Set the column type to Choice.

c. Go down to "Type each choice on a separate line" and type (one per line) **Public, Internal,** and **Secret.**

d. Scroll down to Default value and enter **Internal.**

e. Click OK.

6. Repeat *a* through *e* in step 5, create a second column named DocType of the Choice type, and enter these values (one per line): **Quote, Order, Contract.** Click OK.

7. Look at the library now. It should show the All Documents view, and the two new columns should appear at the far right side.

8. It's time to do a new view that sorts as described in steps 1 through 4 of this Try It Out. Click Create View and select the Standard view format. This opens a new Create View form. Make the following changes:

a. **Title:** Document Types

b. Accept the default view audience — Create a Public View.

c. Verify that the two custom columns are selected to be displayed by default. The display order is listed at the right of the column names; change them so DocType is 3 and Security is 4. Note that the other numbers are automatically reordered.

d. In the Sort section, change "Name (for use in forms)" to sort by filenames.

e. Expand the Group By section, and set "First group by the column" to DocType and "Then group by the column" to Security.

f. Scroll to the end (or beginning) of the form and click OK.

g. This new view shows no documents initially, because the documents have no values for these new columns. It's time to give those values. On the Library tab, change back to the All Documents view.

h. Select the check box in front of the first document, and click Edit Properties; then set Security to Public and DocType to Quote. Click Save.

i. Repeat these steps and set different combinations for at least five documents.

j. Switch to the Document Types view. Verify that you see a folder-like structure based on DocType. Expand one of these DocTypes with two or more documents. Verify that the files within a given DocType are grouped based on security level.

How It Works

List views are dynamic presentations of content in a list. You create a view by selecting what columns to display, in what order, whether or not they should be grouped by a column, and more.

If you want to replace the folder structure with something similar in SharePoint, you need to analyze the existing folder structure. For example, is it organized by customers? Or document types? Or projects? When you know this, you also know what columns you need to create in order to set up list views that offer the same type of navigation. But the big difference is that you don't have to stop with just a single view, as in a file system. A list can contain as many views you need, satisfying different needs for different users.

If you need to modify or delete the current view, use the Modify View button on the Lists tab to open the configuration settings for this view. This form also contains a button for deleting the current view.

> **WARNING** *Deleted list views are not stored in the recycle bin; if you deleted a view by mistake you have to re-create it from scratch!*

Performing Inline Editing

A new feature in SharePoint 2010 is *inline editing*. This is simply a configuration of an ordinary list view. It allows users to edit properties for a list item, without requiring that them to open the properties for this item. Note that you can only change one item at a time. If you need to do a bulk update of multiple files, see the Try It Out "Work with Datasheet Views" in the following section. To enable inline editing, use the steps in the following Try It Out.

TRY IT OUT   **Enable Inline Editing**

In this example, you enable inline editing for a document library, then test how it works.

1. Log on as a site owner, and open a site with a document library that contains files and at least one custom property (described earlier in this chapter).

2. Click on the document library to open it.

3. Click Modify View in the ribbon to open the Edit View page.

4. Scroll down this page and expand the Inline Editing section.

5. Enable "Allow inline editing" and click OK to save and close.

6. Now test the feature as follows:

   a. In the document library, hover the mouse to the left of a document icon. An edit icon appears. Click this icon.

   b. All fields that are editable for this document now switch to edit mode. Edit one or more metadata field, and then click the blue disk icon to save (see Figure 3-7).

   c. Verify that the new properties are saved for this file.

FIGURE 3-7

How It Works

Inline editing is a feature that is built into the list view. It enables users to add and edit item properties directly. This is not a Microsoft ActiveX component. It works for all web browsers that SharePoint supports, such as Firefox, Safari, and so on.

Working with Datasheet Views

Editing properties for a single file is easy, but what if you need to do a bulk update of multiple files in a document library? This is what Datasheet views are used for. This feature requires Microsoft Office 2007 or later installed on the client computer, because it's based on Microsoft's technique of using ActiveX to allow SharePoint to "borrow" features from the local Microsoft Office installation. If the client does not have Office installed, a message appears that says that Datasheet view is not available (see Figure 3-8). Both SharePoint Foundation and SharePoint Server 2010 support the Datasheet view.

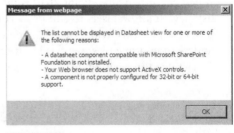

FIGURE 3-8

For a client computer with Microsoft Office installed, you activate this feature as described in the following Try It Out.

TRY IT OUT Work with Datasheet Views

In this example, you are using a client computer with Microsoft Office 2010 installed. You want to change the custom column, called Security, to Internal for all documents.

1. Log on as a user with at least Contributor permissions, and open a document library that contains a custom column named Security.

2. Switch to the Library tab, and click Datasheet View. Note that the view changes to something that looks very similar to Microsoft Excel or Microsoft Access. This is the ActiveX component that SharePoint now borrows from Microsoft Office (see Figure 3-9).

FIGURE 3-9

3. Select the Security column for the first document, and then select Internal.

4. To copy this value to all other documents, you need to do a little trick: Click on another cell, and then click again on the cell with *Internal*. A little black square appears in the right corner; use the mouse and drag this black square down to all documents below it. Now all documents have Internal as the Security setting.

5. To switch back to the normal list view, click Standard View on the ribbon, or reopen this document library to open the default list view.

How It Works

SharePoint uses an ActiveX component that comes with Microsoft Office to open a list in a Datasheet view, much like that of an Excel spreadsheet. In this view, you can copy cells and edit any document property visible in this view.

> **NOTE** *ActiveX components are not supported by default in Firefox, Safari, and many other web clients. Use Microsoft Internet Explorer if you want to use this feature.*

Learning the basic features of Datasheet view is just the beginning; you can do much more with it. For example, you can print this list using Microsoft Exchange, or create a report using Microsoft Access. This feature is particularly important, because the print capabilities in any web application, including SharePoint, are not too impressive.

A cleverly hidden button is located at the far right side of the Datasheet view. It looks like a part of the right frame. Click on it, and a task pane appears (see Figure 3-10). Another way of displaying this pane is to click the Show Task Pane button in the ribbon. Note that the Datasheet view must be displayed before this button is enabled.

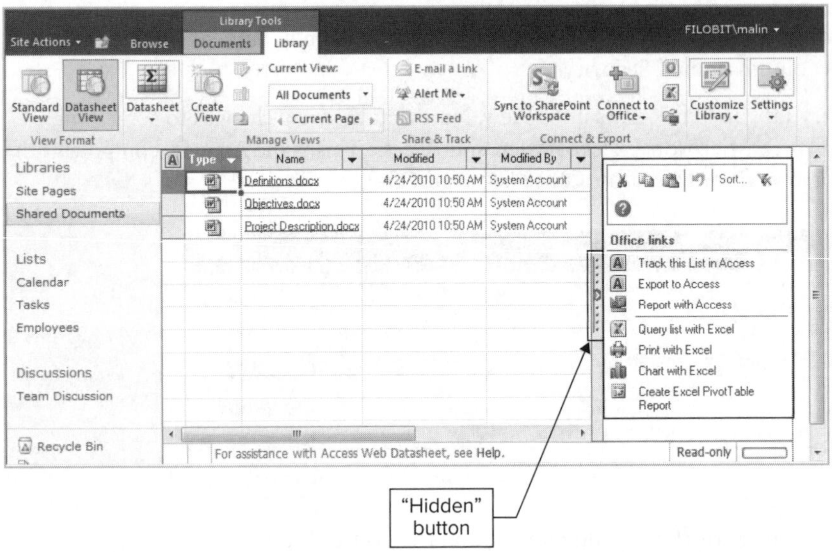

FIGURE 3-10

Using this task pane, a user can activate the following features:

➤ **Track this List in Access:** You can link this list into an Access database, and use it to create reports, or work with its data using all the features of Microsoft Access. If the content in this list is modified, then the Access database will automatically get updated; if you modify a value in the Access database, then the content of this list in SharePoint will be updated. This is also a way to take this list offline, because all the actual content of the list is copied to the Access database, not only the columns displayed in the current view. You can use one Access database for several lists, or you can create a separate database for each list, whatever suits your needs.

➤ **Export to Access:** This is simply a way to copy all the content of the current list to an Access database table. It will not have the two-way synchronization feature that the previous option has. Use this option when you simply want to take a snapshot of the current values in this list, possibly for calculating or reporting purposes.

➤ **Report with Access:** The content of this SharePoint list is copied to Access, and a default report is created. You can then modify this report; for example, remove columns, change the order of columns, change the logotype, and use the Access AutoFormat feature to create a better-looking report.

➤ **Query list with Excel:** Use this option to copy the list content to an Excel spreadsheet. By default, Excel warns about opening this data connection. To continue, you must select Enable. The result is a formatted table in Excel. You can now use this content with all the features of Excel, such as calculating, sorting, building a diagram, and printing. Note that this option does not replicate any local modifications in the spreadsheet back to the SharePoint list, as it did in SharePoint 2003. To modify list content outside SharePoint, use the option Track this List in Access.

➤ **Print with Excel:** Because SharePoint is a web application, it has poor printing functionality. Use Microsoft Excel if you want more control of the print process for this list content, such as the formatting, fonts, and colors. By default, Excel warns you about opening this data connection; you must click Enable to continue.

➤ **Chart with Excel:** If you have columns with numerical or date formatting, you can use these values in Microsoft Excel to create charts, such as histograms and pie charts. By deault, Excel warns you about opening and data connection. Select Enable to continue, and then select the columns to be used for the diagram and the type of diagram. The resulting diagram is displayed.

➤ **Create Excel Pivot Table Report:** Use the column properties to create a dynamic summary of these cell values, typically for pivot tables. Excel also warns here about the data connection; click Enable to continue.

At the top of this task pane you also find buttons for actions like sort, cut, copy, and paste documents or columns.

Site Columns and Content Types

You have now seen how to use columns to store almost any type of metadata for a list or library. Sometimes you need the same columns in multiple lists and libraries. The technique described so far requires you to create the same column manually for all lists that need it. Is there a way to create a column once and then use it in multiple lists? Yes! You can create a column that is globally available for a specific site collection and all its sites with their lists and libraries — this is known as a *site column*.

Would it not be great if you could configure all documents of a certain kind, such as Contracts, to contain a specific column? This is what you do with *content types*. These two features, site columns and content types, are described next.

Managing Site Columns

Site columns are global columns available in every site and in every list and library. You need to be a site collection administrator to manage these site columns, because changes made affect a complete site collection.

For example, suppose you want to classify all documents in all document libraries with the column *Security*. This column contains three options: Internal, Public, and Secret. Now assume you have manually created this column in all document libraries, and then you need to add a fourth option named *Top Secret*. How can you add this new option to all existing copies of the Security column? Well, either you do it manually and edit each of these libraries, or you could write code that updates this column for all libraries.

With site columns, this task is much simpler! The basic idea is that a site collection administrator creates global columns in the top site, and then site owners can add these columns to their lists and libraries, as described in the following Try It Out.

TRY IT OUT Create a Site Column

In this example, you create a site column named Security, and make it a Choice type column. Then you add this site column to existing lists.

1. Log on as a site collection administrator, and open the top site; in this example, `http://srv1`.

2. Click Site Actions ⇨ Site Settings to open the Site Settings page.

3. In the Galleries section, click Site columns and make the following changes:

   a. Click Create at the top (below the ribbon).

   b. **Column name:** Security

   c. **Column type:** Choice

   d. **Put this site column into:** Select New Group, and enter the name **Demo Columns**.

   e. Type each choice on a separate line: **Internal, Public,** and **Secret**

   f. **Default value:** Internal

   g. Click OK.

4. Verify that the new Security column is listed under the section Demo Columns.

   This column is now created and ready to be used. Next, you'll add it to two lists.

5. Open a site where you are the site owner.

6. Click on a list; for example, Tasks.

7. Click List Settings on the ribbon, and then do the following:

   a. Below the Columns section, click "Add from existing site columns."

   b. Change "Select site columns from" to Demo Columns.

   c. One column will be listed: **Security.** Click Add and then OK.

8. Open the Task list, and add a new item. Note that it asks for the Security metadata, and that it offers the same three options you defined for this site column. Add any values and click Save.

9. Now open another list in this or another site, and add the same site column using the settings in step 7. The same three options are available for this column.

   Now you have this site column added to two lists in this site collection. Next, you'll add a fourth option to the Security column.

10. Open the top site again, as a site collection administrator.

11. Click Site Actions ⇨ Site Settings ⇨ Site Columns.

12. Locate and click on the Security column in the Demo Columns section.

13. Add Top Secret as the fourth option in the "Type each choice on a separate line" field, and then click OK.

14. Open the properties for the same list item as in step 8. Note that the Security metadata now has four options instead of three.

How It Works

Use site columns to create columns that are global for a site collection. If you modify a site column, its new settings will be applied to all copies of this site column.

Managing Content Types

When you create a new document in a document library, you will only have one type of document template; for example, an empty Microsoft Word document. But for most organizations, this is not enough — they need multiple templates to choose between; for example, a blank Word file, a Contract template, a Quote template, and so on. Another common request is to have the document library contain templates for different applications, typically a blank Word file, plus an Excel spreadsheet, and a PowerPoint presentation.

Microsoft's solution was to design a feature it called *content types* in SharePoint that offers more than just a standard document template. Why? Because Microsoft knows users will request it, although they do not think about it at first. Another reason was that content types could be used for much more than just Office templates. For example, all standard lists in SharePoint contain one default item type; this type is based on a content type.

For example, suppose you need two Office templates in a document library: one for Sales Quotes, and one for Contracts. These templates are both based on Word files, but will look different, of course. Each template will probably need different properties, or metadata. For example, the Sales Quote needs to keep track of the due date for the quote, while the Contract should store the period for when it is valid (the start and end dates). The Sales Quote also needs a special workflow, so every time a new quote is created, the sales manager will get an e-mail. The Contract needs another workflow that will send an alert by e-mail to inform the manager one month before the contract period ends.

Even more differences may exist among these types of documents, and if you have more than two templates, the differences may be even greater. All of these properties and more can be defined for a content type. This is why Microsoft did not just call its solution a "document template," but instead a "content type."

Content types can be local for a specific site, or global for a site collection. New in SharePoint 2010 is the ability to create content types that are available in several site collections; for example, for every site in a large SharePoint farm.

TRY IT OUT Manage Content Types

In this example, you create two content types: one for a simple Microsoft Word template with just a headline that says *Contract*, and one for a blank PowerPoint presentation.

1. Log on as a site collection administrator.

2. Create a document that you later will use as a template for a content type, as follows:

   a. Open Microsoft Word.

   b. Enter the headline **Contract** at the top of this document.

   c. Save it as **Contract Template.DOCX**.

3. Create a blank PowerPoint presentation, as follows:

    a. Open Microsoft PowerPoint.

    b. Create a new blank presentation.

    c. Save it as **PPT Template.PPTX**.

4. Open the top site in your site collection.

5. Click Site Actions ⇨ Site Settings to open the Site Settings page, and then click Site Content Types in the Galleries section.

6. To create the first content type, do the following:

    a. Click Create.

    b. Enter **Contract** in the Name field.

    c. Enter **Standard Template for Contracts** in the Description field.

    d. Change "Select parent content type from" to Document Content Types.

    e. Change Parent Content Type to Document.

    f. Select New Group and enter **Demo Content Types**.

    g. Click OK.

7. The Contracts content type is now created, and its configuration page opens, but this content type just contains an empty document at this point. Now add the Word template created in step 2 like this:

    a. Click Advanced Settings, and select "Upload a new document template."

    b. Click Browse, and select the Contract Template file.

    c. Click Open.

    d. Click OK to save and close.

8. To create the second content type, do this:

    a. Click Create.

    b. Enter **Presentation** in the Name field.

    c. Enter **Blank PPTX Presentation** in the Description field.

    d. Change "Select parent content type from" to Document Content Types.

    e. Change Parent Content Type to Document.

    f. Change Existing group to Demo Content Types.

    g. Click OK.

9. The Presentation content type is now created, and its configuration page opens. At this moment, this content type is just an empty document. Now add the PowerPoint template you created in step 3 like this:

a. Click Advanced Settings, and select "Upload a new document template."

b. Click Browse, and select the PPT Template file.

c. Click Open.

d. Click OK to save and close.

Now you have two new content types. Next, you'll add them to one or more document libraries.

10. Open a document library in a site.

11. Click Library Settings on the ribbon to open the Document Library Settings page.

12. Click the Advanced Settings link to open the Advanced Settings page.

13. Select "Allow management of content types," and then click OK. This activates a new section named Content Types in the Library Settings page.

14. Scroll down to the Content Type section. Note that it now contains a single content type named *Document*; this is the one that you will activate when creating a new document in this library.

15. Click "Add from existing site content types," and then do the following:

a. Change "Select site content types from" to Demo Content Types. It should list both new content types you just created.

b. Select both of these content types and click Add.

c. Click OK.

16. Verify that you now see three content types listed, and that Documents is set as the Default Content Type. This is the type that users will get when they click the New button for this library.

17. Now you'll check that this feature works. Begin by opening this document library.

18. Switch to the Documents tab on the ribbon.

19. Click the text *New Document* (not the icon), and a drop-down menu with the three content types appears (see Figure 3-11). Select one of the new ones you just created. A new document based on this template appears. Verify that it looks exactly like the one this template is based on.

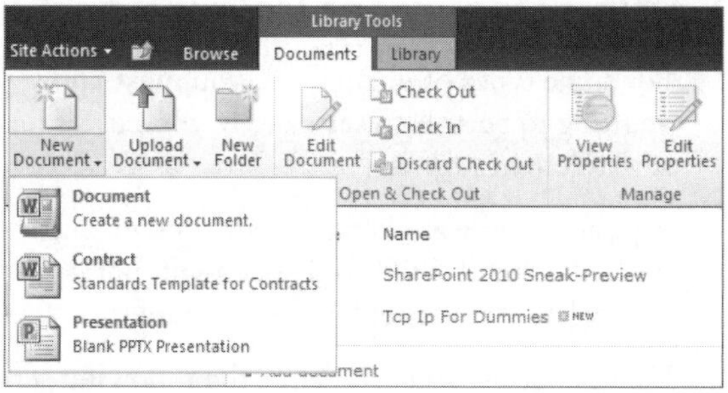

FIGURE 3-11

So far, you have created something very similar to ordinary Office templates. Next, you add your previously created *Security* site column to the Contract template; that is, you will add global metadata, which only is possible in a content type.

20. Open the top site, and click Site Actions ⇨ Site Settings ⇨ Site Content Types.

21. In the Demo Content Types section, click on the Contracts content type and then do the following:

    a. In the Columns section, click "Add from existing site columns."

    b. Change "Select columns from" to Demo Columns.

    c. Add Security and click OK.

22. Open the document library where you previously added the content types.

23. Open the New Document menu and select Contract. Microsoft Word starts and opens a new document based on this template. Click File, open the Properties menu in the right pane, and click Show Document Panel. You can now see the Security property and all the other columns for this content type. Enter some text in the document, and then select Top Secret as the Security level. Then save and close this document. Verify that this document is created, and that its Security property is set to Top Secret.

24. Now create a new document based on the Presentation template. Note that it does not have a Security property associated with it. In other words, these two content types are stored in the same document library, but they have different properties associated with them.

How It Works

All list items in SharePoint are based on a content type, regardless of what kind of list or library the items are contained in. A content type is a definition of an object stored in a list; for example, a document in a library or a contact in a list. You can create new content types, and define their content, columns, and workflows. New content types can also inherit all settings from a parent content type. In SharePoint Server, you can also define policies for a content type.

Setting Document Policies and Auditing

For some types of documents, you must apply actions that should start on a certain date, or perform auditing to be able to see exactly what users have accessed a specific file. These types of setting are referred to as *policies*.

A policy can be applied to all the documents in a document library or to a content type. Policies can be applied to all kinds of list content, not only documents. For example, you can define a policy that will delete all tasks older than six months.

Using policies, you can define the following settings:

➤ Policy statement

➤ Retention

➤ Auditing

➤ Barcodes

➤ Labels

These settings are described in more detail a little later; but first, the following Try It Out demonstrates how to manage policies.

TRY IT OUT Manage Policies

In this example, you open the policy for a document library. These steps also work for any kind of list.

1. Log on as a site owner, and open a document library.

2. Click Library Settings on the ribbon (or List Settings if it is a list) to open the Document Library Settings page.

3. Click "Information management policy settings."

4. Select Document to manage the policies for the default content type. You can also select another content type that exists in this library, if needed.

5. The Edit Policy form appears, where you can define the following five types of policies (you'll learn more about each type of policy after this Try It Out):

    a. **Policy Statement:** Text that is displayed to the end user when they open items subject to this policy.

    b. **Retention:** Schedule when and how items in this list are retained.

    c. **Auditing:** Specify what events will be audited.

    d. **Barcodes:** Assign barcodes to documents.

    e. **Labels:** Add a label to a document to ensure that important information about the document will be included when printed.

How It Works

All content types, including the default content type associated with a document library, can be configured to follow policies. If you set a policy for a specific site content type on the top site, this policy will be applied wherever this site content type is used.

NOTE *Only SharePoint Server supports policies; SharePoint Foundation does not.*

The following sections present more information about each part of a policy. To see these policy parts, follow the instructions in the preceding Try It Out, "Manage Policies."

Policy Statements

A *policy statement* is text that's displayed when a user opens a document or list item. This is a good way to inform users that there is a policy applied, which otherwise may be hard or even impossible to detect.

Retention

Retention is a definition of what will happen to a list item (such as a document) after a given time. SharePoint 2010 introduces the possibility of multiple retention stages. For example, you can define a retention that deletes files two years after they were created (see Figure 3-12). Another example is that files can be moved to another location six months after they are last modified. Retention is a very powerful feature for managing information, especially if you need to follow SOX, ISO 9000, and similar standards.

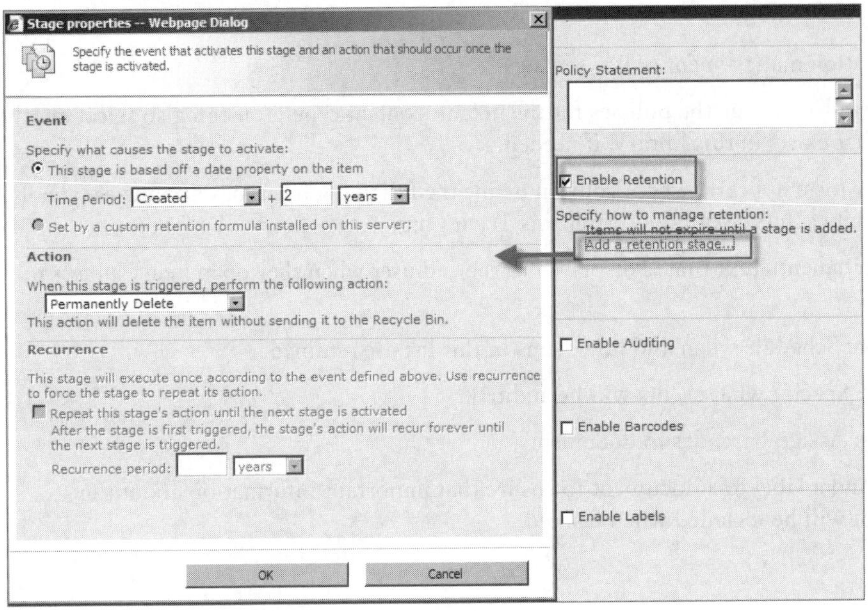

FIGURE 3-12

Auditing

Some organizations, such as hospitals and financial institutions, must adhere to strict rules for information management. This type of organization must log every activity regarding specific objects. For example, logging every user who reads a document may be necessary. Activate auditing in policies to log one or more of the following actions:

➤ Opening or downloading documents

➤ Viewing items in a list, or viewing properties for a list item

➤ Editing items and documents

➤ Checking out or checking in items or documents

➤ Moving or copying items or documents

➤ Deleting or restoring items or documents

All auditing actions are compiled and stored in an XML file, in a location defined by the farm administrator. To define the audit log, use the steps in the following Try It Out.

`TRY IT OUT`   **Manage the Policy Usage Reports**

SharePoint Central Administration is used to manage audit logs and policy reports. In this example, you save these reports to a document library named PolicyReports in `http://srv1`.

1. Log on as a farm administrator to the SharePoint Server.

2. Start the SharePoint Central Administration tool.

3. Select Monitoring in the left pane.

4. Click Information Management Policy Usage Reports. In the page that appears, enter information to schedule a report every day at 6:00 a.m. and store it in the `http://srv1/PolicyReports` document library, as follows:

    a. Select "Enable recurring policy usage reports."

    b. Select Daily and set the time to 6.00 a.m.

    c. Under "Report file location," enter **http://srv1/PolicyReports**.

    d. Click OK.

5. If you cannot wait until 6:00 a.m. the next day, click the Create Reports Now button, and then open `http://srv1/PolicyReports` to view the report.

How It Works

Use the settings in this Try It Out to create policy reports based on the audit logs. The file format for these reports is based on XML, which Microsoft Excel can open.

Barcodes

If you need to print documents and store them as physical paper, then printing a barcode on these documents may be very handy. This feature makes it easy to locate and identify paper documents stored in a physical archive.

Enable barcodes in policies to ensure that all printed copies of a document will be assigned a barcode and that the barcode will also be printed. You can also configure Microsoft Office to prompt the user for a barcode before saving or printing the document.

Labels

SharePoint can add a text label to documents to ensure that important information will follow the document, even as a printed copy. You can define the text, font, and location of a policy label for printed documents.

Instead of predefined text for this label, you can request that the policy prompt the user for the label text when printing the document.

Managing Document IDs and Document Sets

SharePoint Server 2010 introduces several features that many organizations have been asking for, particularly companies that want to move away from a traditional document management system such as Documentum to SharePoint. One of these new features is a global document identity, or DocID, that is assigned automatically to all new documents and that will follow the document during its lifetime. Another feature is the document set, described later in this chapter.

Document Identities

Without document identities (DocIDs), a document is only unique within a given folder; that is, you can have two documents named Budget.XLS that are stored in different document libraries or in different folders in the same library. This can be very confusing for users, because they need to know both the name and the location to be sure about what document they are referring to.

DocID is only available for SharePoint Server, not for SharePoint Foundation installations. It is a feature that is enabled per site collection, and then all documents in this collection, both existing documents and new documents, will be assigned a unique DocID.

Every site collection defines a prefix for the DocID, such as *Finance*, and then two index numbers are assigned: one for the library and one for the document. For example, a document assigned *Finance-1-5* can be identified as belonging to the site collection that uses the DocID prefix *Finance*, and that it is stored in the first library in this site collection, and it was the fifth document stored in that library.

If you have multiple site collections, then using the DocID prefix as an indication of where the document is stored is a good idea. For example, if there are three site collections — one for each department Alpha, Beta, and Gamma — you can use these names as the prefix.

A special web part exists where you can enter the DocID for the document you are looking for. If you enter a DocID for a Microsoft Word document, then Word opens and displays this particular document. If the DocID points to a file that cannot be opened directly, a property page with a link to that file appears.

The following Try It Out describes how to enable and use DocID for a site collection.

TRY IT OUT   **Manage Document Identities**

In this example, you enable the DocID feature for a site collection, and then configure it to use "Alpha" as the prefix.

1. Log on as the site collection administrator, and open the top site for your site collection.

2. Click Site Actions ⇨ Site Settings.

3. In the Site Collection Administration section, click Site Collection Features to open the Features page.

4. Click the Activate button for Document ID Service, wait until it is listed as Active, and then go back to the Site Settings page (for example, click the Site Collection Administration link at the top).

5. Look at the Site Collection Administration section again; note that it now has a new link named Document ID settings. Click this link, and then do the following:

a. Enable Assign Document ID.

b. Enter the prefix **Alpha** in the field "Begin ID with the following characters." If another prefix already exists for this document ID, and you want to replace it with the new prefix, select the check box "Reset all Document IDs in this Site Collection to begin with these characters".

c. Accept the default setting for the Search Scope; that is, All Sites.

d. Click OK.

6. It will take some time before the DocID will be visible for documents, because this is managed by two scheduled timer jobs that run once every day: "Document ID assignment job" and "Document enable/disable job." When these jobs are completed, you can see the DocID in the document properties. To display the DocID in a library, go to the site and do the following:

a. Open its document library.

b. Click Modify View on the ribbon.

c. Enable the Document ID column.

d. Click OK to save and close.

How It Works

DocID is a feature that is activated per site collection. It assigns a unique identity to each document, both existing and new. Two timer jobs are associated with the DocID feature, and both run once per day.

You can retrieve documents that have been assigned a DocID in the following ways:

➤ **Insert the Find by Document ID web part to a web page:** Use this web part to locate a document with a specific identity.

➤ **Search for it:** Use the document's DocID property; for example, to search for "Alpha-3-13," enter the search string **DocID=Alpha-3-13** in the standard search field.

➤ **Link to this document:** To find the absolute URL link to a specific DocID, open the properties for this document, right-click on the identity, and select Copy Shortcut. Paste this link wherever you need it; for example, in another document or as an item in a link list.

Document Sets

Another new feature in SharePoint Server 2010 (but not in SharePoint Foundation) is the *document set*. It works much like a ZIP file in that a number of files, possibly of different types, are grouped together under a common name. Document sets are very handy when you need to work with a group of files, but treat them as one.

For example, suppose you are planning to buy a new house. You have multiple pictures of the house, both inside and outside, plus a blueprint. You also have calculations in Excel spreadsheets, and Word documents with more information about this house. All of these files are related, so you want to treat them as a complete package. You could create a folder for all of these files in a document library, but you would also like to enter some custom properties just for this group. This is what document sets are used for: grouping a number of files while treating them as one package.

SharePoint 2010 implements document sets as a kind of super-folder that is stored in a typical document library. Each document set can have unique properties that are different from the ordinary files in the document library. The reason for this is that document sets are implemented as a content type, so you can add to and modify any of its columns. By default, a document set has the following characteristics:

➤ Two default properties, Name and Description, with the potential to add more columns

➤ A special icon for document sets

➤ Version history (if version history is enabled for the document library)

➤ DocID (if this is enabled for this site collection)

➤ Workflows (if this is defined for this library)

The following Try It Out describes how to enable and manage document sets.

TRY IT OUT   **Manage Document Sets**

In this example, you enable document sets for a site collection, and then activate this feature in a document library.

1. Log on as a site collection administrator, and open the top site in your site collection.

2. Click Site Action ➪ Site Settings ➪ Site Collection Features.

3. Activate Document Sets. Now any document library in this site collection can activate document sets.

4. Open a document library where you have full permissions.

5. To activate document sets for this document library, you must add the Document Set content type as described here:

    a. Click Library Settings on the ribbon to open the Document Library Settings page, and then click the Advanced Settings link to open a page with the same name.

    b. Enable "Allow management of content types."

    c. Click OK. This will reopen the Document Library Settings page.

    d. In the Content Types section, click "Add from existing site content types."

    e. Select Document Set in the Available Site Content Types field, and click Add.

    f. Click OK.

6. Open the document library.

7. Create a document set like this:

 a. Switch to the Documents tab on the ribbon.

 b. Click on the text *New Document* (not the icon), and select Document Set (see Figure 3-13).

 c. Enter **Spring Vacation** in the Name field.

 d. Enter **Travel documents, Pictures and Calculations** in the Description field.

 e. Click OK.

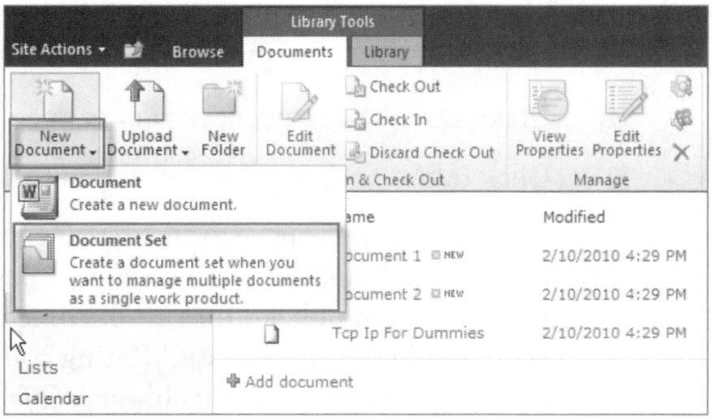

FIGURE 3-13

8. Add files and documents to this document set like this:

 a. Click Upload Document on the ribbon (the Document tab), browse for a document, and add it to the document set.

 b. Repeat step 8a to add at least four documents and files of different types to the Spring Vacation document set (see Figure 3-14).

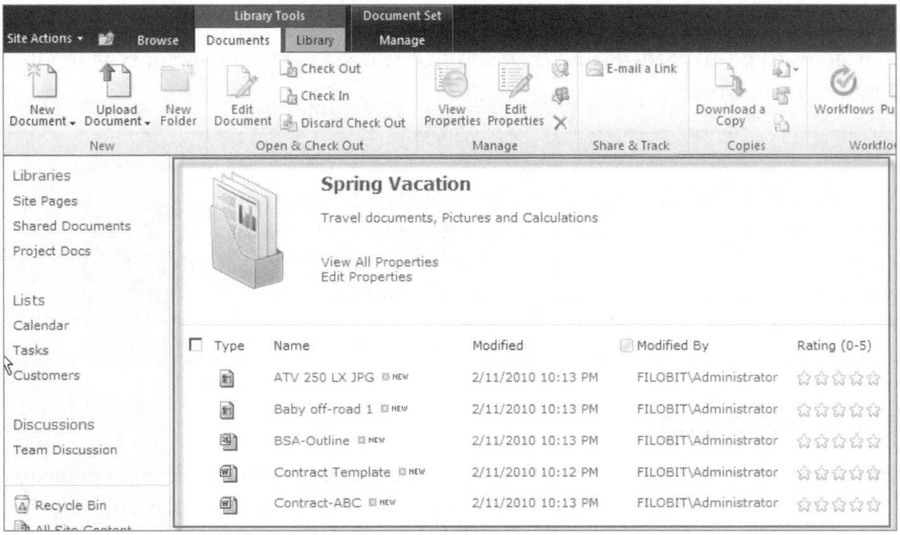

FIGURE 3-14

 c. To go up to the document library, click the Browse tab, and then click the document library name in the breadcrumb trail. As you can see, a document set looks much like a folder. In fact, it is a kind of folder.

9. Locate the Spring Vacation document set, and note that it has a special icon. Also note that it does not have any custom properties, ratings, or metadata like the other files. The reason is that a document set is a content type. To add columns and metadata to it, you add them to the content type as follows:

a. Make sure the document library is open.

b. Click Library Settings on the ribbon to open the Document Library Settings page.

c. In the Content Types section, click Document Set. The management page for this content type opens. Using the settings on this page, you can make document sets read-only, define workflows and policies for this document set, and create columns. In this example, you want to add the Security and Rating columns, plus the enterprise keywords that are used for the other documents in this library. Click "Add from existing site or list columns," and then add Rating (0–5) and Security. Then change "Select columns from" to Enterprise Keyword Group and add the Enterprise Keywords column.

d. Click OK to save and close.

10. Open the document library and select the check box for the Spring Vacation document set, and then click Edit Properties on the ribbon. Note that this document set now contains new properties for Security, Enterprise Keywords, and Rating (0–5).

11. Switch to the Document Set tab on the ribbon. Take a moment to inspect the buttons on this ribbon tab; for example, you can send a link to a document set.

How It Works

Enable document sets by activating this feature, and then adding the document set content type to all document libraries that need this feature.

> **NOTE** If you cannot see existing document sets, but instead, you see its files mixed with other documents in this library, then this list view is probably configured to ignore folders. To correct this, either switch to a list view that shows folders, or modify the current view by choosing Modify View ⇨ Folders ⇨ Show Items Inside Folders.

Managing In-Place Records

Some documents are more important than others; for example, contracts and other legal documents. These documents are usually referred to as *records*, and need to adhere to strict regulation; for example, they must exist for 10 years as a write-protected document. In previous versions of SharePoint (MOSS 2007), these records were moved into a specific site, known as a record center, usually created in a separate site collection and using a separate SQL content database or SQL server. Think of a record center as a secure document vault, much like a safe.

> **NOTE** SharePoint Foundation does not support a record center or in-place records management.

Moving records to a record center can sometimes create an issue. For example, assume that your team needs to create an important document, such as a contract for a big customer. Before you can create this contract, you need to do calculations in Excel, describe risks in a Word file, and present the contract to the team using a PowerPoint presentation. So you have multiple documents that served as background information to the final contract. Your team probably used a team site in SharePoint for managing all information for this contract. Now assume that the final contract is moved into the record center to be protected from tampering and stored for 10 years. Now you have a "hole" in the document list in the team site; that is, all the background documents are there, but not the result. You don't want to save a copy of the contract, because doing so creates a risk of confusion.

Activating In-Place Record Management

SharePoint Server 2010 comes with an alternative solution: in-place records. With this feature, the document adheres to the policies and regulations for this type of record, even though it stays in the original document library. This solves the issue described earlier. However, some organizations need the records center, so SharePoint Server 2010 also supports that type of site. You can mix these two methods as you like for managing records in SharePoint Server 2010.

TRY IT OUT   **Manage In-Place Records**

In this example, you learn how to enable the in-place records feature, and how to work with in-place records in a document library.

1. Log on as a site collection administrator, and open the top site in your site collection.

2. Enable the in-place record feature for this site collection by clicking Site Actions ➪ Site Settings. On the Site Settings page that appears, do the following:

    a. Click "Site collection features" in the Site Collection Administration section.

    b. Click the Activate button for In Place Records Management.

3. Activate this feature for a document library as follows:

    a. Open the document library where you want to activate in-place records management.

    b. Click Library Settings on the ribbon to open the Document Library Settings page.

    c. Click "Record declaration settings."

    d. In the new Library Record Declaration Settings page, select the "Always allow the manual declaration of records" option.

    e. Click OK.

4. This feature is now ready to be used. You must be a site owner to declare documents as in-place records. Open the document library you just configured.

5. Select an existing document by clicking its check box, and then click Declare Record (see Figure 3-15). Click OK to confirm that you want to declare this document as a record.

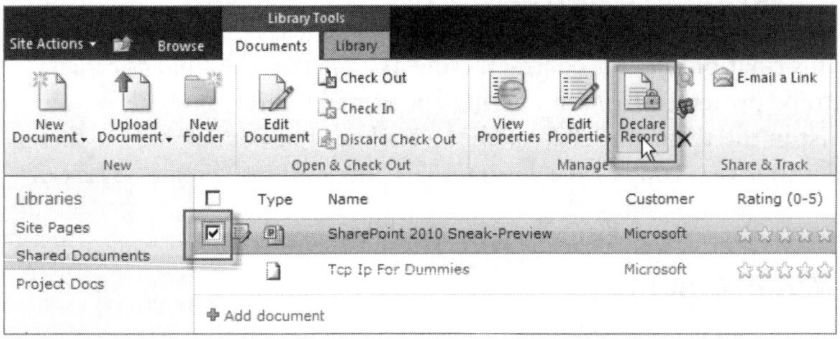

FIGURE 3-15

6. Verify that the icon for this document now has a yellow padlock symbol (if it does not, refresh this page).

How It Works

In-place records allow a document to be classified and therefore treated as a record, although it is still stored in a document library.

Setting Permissions and Policies for In-Place Records

Two important questions regarding in-place records is about permissions: Who can declare a document to be an in-place record? Who can undeclare it, that is, convert it back to a standard document? This permission is defined per site collection, on the site settings page for the top site as described in the following Try It Out.

TRY IT OUT   Manage Permissions Policies for In-Place Records

In this example, you view the permissions and restriction policies for in-place records for a specific site collection.

1. Log on as a site collection administrator, and open the top site.

2. Click Site Actions ⇨ Site Settings and then click "Record declaration settings" in the Site Collection Administration section to open the Record Declaration Settings page (see Figure 3-16).

3. In the Record Restrictions section, you define the restriction that will be enforced for documents that are declared records. The default is Block Edit and Delete.

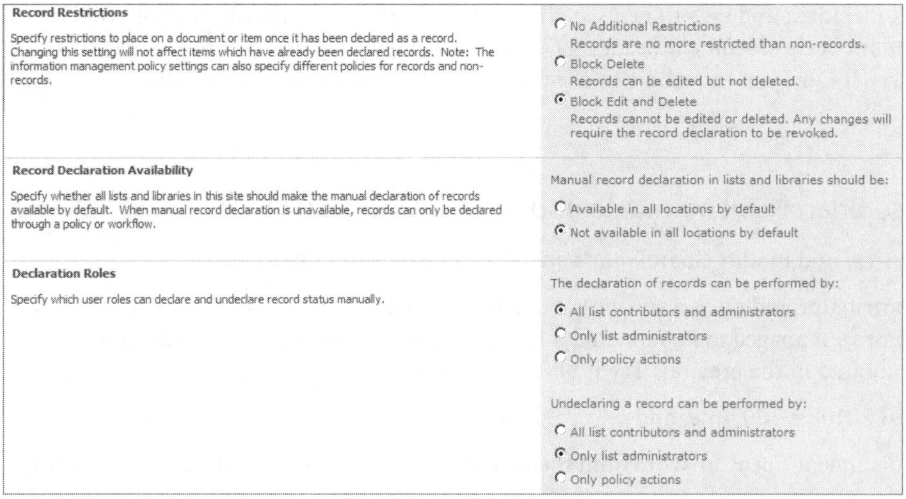

Record Restrictions	

Specify restrictions to place on a document or item once it has been declared as a record. Changing this setting will not affect items which have already been declared records. Note: The information management policy settings can also specify different policies for records and non-records.	○ No Additional Restrictions
	   Records are no more restricted than non-records.
	○ Block Delete
	   Records can be edited but not deleted.
	◉ Block Edit and Delete
	   Records cannot be edited or deleted. Any changes will
	   require the record declaration to be revoked.

Record Declaration Availability	
Specify whether all lists and libraries in this site should make the manual declaration of records available by default. When manual record declaration is unavailable, records can only be declared through a policy or workflow.	Manual record declaration in lists and libraries should be: ○ Available in all locations by default ◉ Not available in all locations by default
Declaration Roles	
Specify which user roles can declare and undeclare record status manually.	The declaration of records can be performed by: ◉ All list contributors and administrators ○ Only list administrators ○ Only policy actions Undeclaring a record can be performed by: ○ All list contributors and administrators ◉ Only list administrators ○ Only policy actions

FIGURE 3-16

4. In the Record Declaration Availability section, you define whether in-place records should be available in all libraries. The default is No, which means you need to activate this feature individually for each library that needs in-place records.

5. In the Declaration Roles section, you define who can declare a record. The default is "All list contributors and administrators," but you can change that to either "Only list administrators" or "Only policy actions." The latter option means that you need to define a policy that declares a document as a record; for example, for the Contracts content type.

6. Also in the Declaration Rules section, you can define the corresponding permissions for undeclared records; the default is "Only list administrators."

DOCUMENT MANAGEMENT WITH OFFICE 2010

All the features mentioned in this chapter — custom columns, enterprise keywords, and managed metadata — are integrated with Office 2010. There is also integration between the new Office Web Apps feature and the full Office 2010 client. The following sections present more about these features.

Metadata and Tagging in Office 2010

When users apply tags and metadata to documents, they also expect to view and use these values from within Microsoft Office. The integration between Office 2010 and SharePoint 2010 is very similar to the integration between the previous Office 2007 and SharePoint 2007. However, some new features in SharePoint 2010 require Office 2010; for example, managed metadata and rating.

Office also allows metadata and tags to be used within the actual document; for example, adding the Security metadata in the document header, or using the Customer name within the text body. In the following Try It Out, you learn how to use these SharePoint features within Office 2010.

TRY IT OUT   Use SharePoint Metadata and Tags in Office 2010

In this example, you view and modify SharePoint's metadata in Microsoft Word 2010.

1. Log on as a Contributor and open a site with a document library that contains custom columns, enterprise keywords, managed metadata, and a rating column — for example, the document library you configured in the previous Try It Out, "Create Managed Metadata Structure."

2. Click on a Word 2010 or 2007 file, and select Edit This File.

3. Wait until the document opens in Word, and then click File to open the Backstage part of Word 2010 and its Info section.

4. At the right, some document properties are listed — in the bottom of the right pane, click Show All Properties. Note that all document properties now appear, including properties stored in SharePoint such as custom columns, enterprise keywords, and managed metadata. Figure 3-17 shows the Security property displayed.

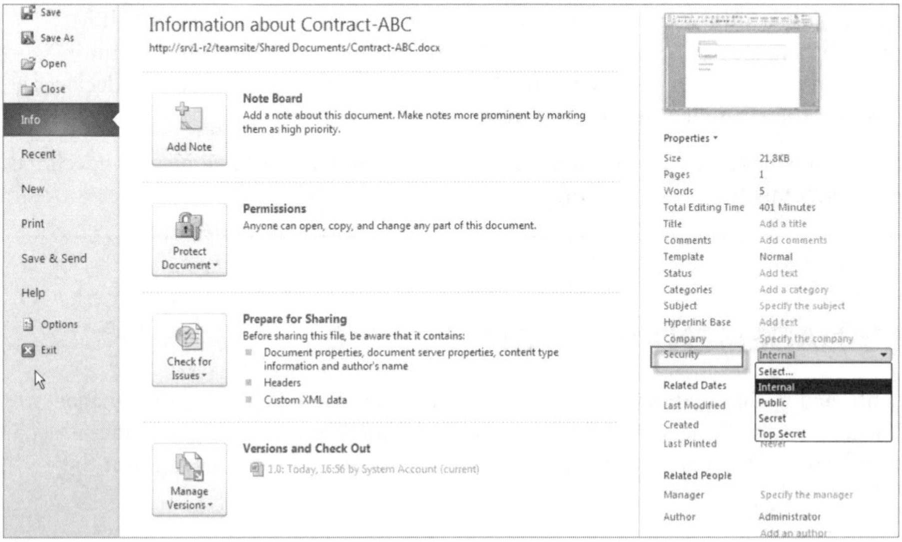

FIGURE 3-17

5. To add a SharePoint property such as Security into the document, do the following:

    a. Open a document that contains SharePoint properties.

    b. Place the curser at the position in the document where the property should appear.

c. Switch to the Insert tab on the Office ribbon, and then click Quick Parts ⇨ Document Property ⇨ Security. The value for this property appears on the document (see Figure 3-18).

d. Click on the property value in the document (Internal in this example), and you will see the same options as in SharePoint's document library.

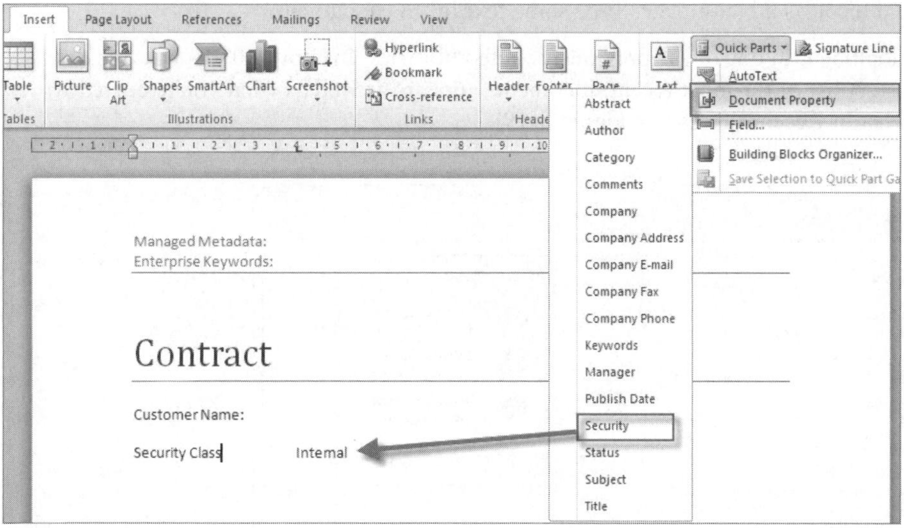

FIGURE 3-18

How It Works

Office 2010 is tightly integrated with SharePoint 2010. Properties created as list columns in a document library will be visible in Office 2010, and users can set these properties and use them in the document.

Adding Paths to SharePoint Libraries

One of the challenges in previous versions of SharePoint was that users needed to change their behavior when saving new documents. They had to go to the destination library, and then click New on the document library. This method still works in SharePoint 2010, but now there are other ways to locate a destination library. They are as follows:

➤ **Recent Places:** Office 2010 remembers the URL to the libraries you have used.

➤ **Connect to Office:** Use a button on the ribbon to add the current library to Recent Places in Office 2010.

➤ **Pushing URLs:** A farm administrator can push URLs to common libraries so they will show up in Open and Save dialog boxes in Microsoft Office 2010.

These three new methods will make navigating to a document library much more natural for the user. The following Try It Out describes how to push URLs to document libraries.

TRY IT OUT   Push the URL to Document Libraries in Office 2010

In this example, you are running Office 2010. You have previously worked with several documents in different SharePoint libraries. This example shows you how to find them again.

1. Log on as a Contributor and start Microsoft Word 2010.

2. Word starts, and displays a blank page. Type some text in this document.

3. Now save the document in one of the previously visited libraries: In Word 2010, click File and switch to Recent. A list of the most recent documents appears as well as what you're currently interested in: a list of Recent Places (see Figure 3-19).

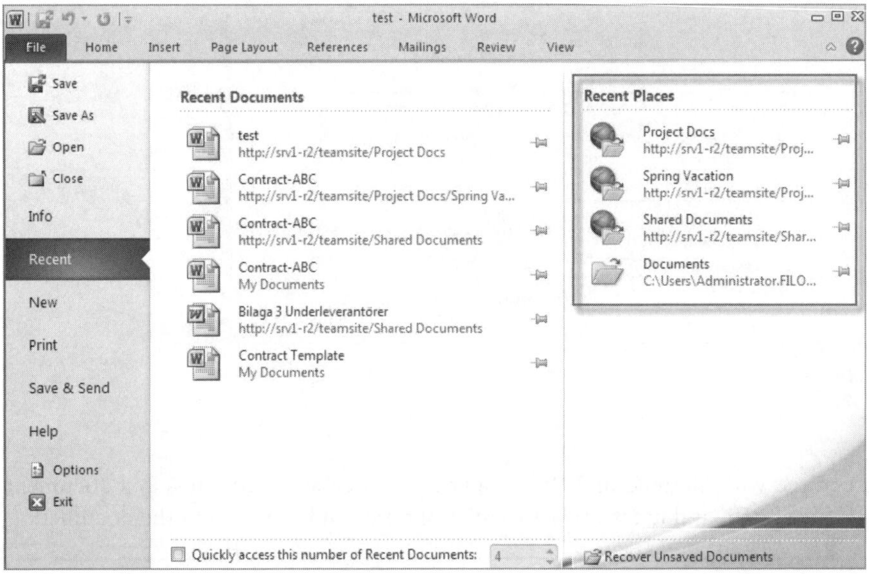

FIGURE 3-19

4. Select one of the document libraries in Recent Places, enter a name, and save this document.

5. Another way to make navigating to SharePoint sites and libraries easier for users is to push out common URL links to Office clients, like this:

    a.   Log on as a farm administrator to the SharePoint server.

    b.   Start the SharePoint Central Administration tool.

    c.   Select Application Management in the left pane.

    d.   Click Manage Service Applications ➪ User Profile Service Application to open its configuration page.

    e.   In the My Site Settings section, click Publish Links To Office Client Applications to open a page with the same name.

    f.   Click New Link to open the Add Published Link page.

g. In the Properties page, enter the URL (for example, `http://srv1/teamsite/`) and that a Description the users will see. Then set the Type to match what the URL points to — for example, Team Site. Use the Target Audience option if you need to control who will see this URL link, or leave it blank if everyone should see it.

h. Click OK.

These links will be pushed using a scheduled timer job; so typically they will show up the next day, when Office users open or save documents.

How It Works

Office "learns" about what SharePoint locations you are using for document management. A SharePoint administrator can also publish URL links for common locations to Office 2010 users.

> **NOTE** Only SharePoint Server supports the feature to publish URLs to Office users; SharePoint Foundation does not.

A third way to navigate from Office 2010 to SharePoint sites is this: The user opens a library in SharePoint, and then clicks the Connect To Office button on the ribbon, and a link to this library will be added to Office, as explained in the following Try It Out.

TRY IT OUT Add a Link to a Document Library

In this example, you want Office 2010 to remember the URL to a document library.

1. Log on as a Contributor, and open a document library you want Office to remember.

2. Click Connect To Office in the ribbon and this link will be added to Office. Note that if you click the *text* "Connect to Office," a menu appears with options to add (the default option), remove, and manage these links.

3. Start Word 2010 and open the Backstage page by clicking the File button.

4. Open Save & Send.

5. Click Save To SharePoint and a list with all locations appears in the right pane.

How It Works

In SharePoint Server and SharePoint Foundation, a user can ask SharePoint to store a link in Office 2010 to a given document library.

▶ **WHAT YOU LEARNED IN THIS CHAPTER**

TOPIC	KEY CONCEPTS
Office 2010	Comes in multiple editions. Office 2010 Professional Plus is the ultimate edition for SharePoint users.
Office 2007	Most SharePoint features will work, including custom columns.
Office 2003	Supports basic SharePoint features.
Older Office and non-Microsoft desktop applications	Will use SharePoint as a file server.
SharePoint libraries	There are nine different libraries in SharePoint Server Enterprise; SharePoint Foundation only comes with four types of libraries.
Version history	Same functionality as in MOSS 2007: Choose between no version history (default), major version only, and major plus draft editions. List items support version history, but this is not activated by default.
Columns, keywords, and metadata	SharePoint 2010 supports the same type of custom columns as for MOSS 2007. Enterprise keywords are used for social tagging; that is, users can enter anything they like. Managed metadata is a structured set of metadata, where users normally cannot add their own options.
Rating	This is an important feature in social computing. It gives a user a good idea of what other members think about a specific document, page, or list item.
Term store	A central database where all the tags and managed metadata is stored. Can be reachable from any site in the farm, but only its term store administrator can change any of its settings,
List views	These views are used to sort, group, and filter large lists. There are views for all types of lists, including document libraries and standard lists.

TOPIC	KEY CONCEPTS
Datasheet views	Excellent for bulk-updating properties for list items.
	Requires that the user have a locally installed Microsoft Office 2007 or later.
Site columns	Global columns that can be used anywhere in a site collection.
Site content types	Global content types that can be used anywhere in a site collection.
	SharePoint Server 2010 supports truly global content types, which means they also work in any site collection or in other farms.
Information policy	Defines what will happen with documents after a given time.
	Can log all activities for a list item; for example, a document.
Document ID	The DocID feature creates globally unique identities for all files in document libraries.
Document set	A package of multiple files, like a ZIP file.
	Supports custom columns, tags, metadata, and rating.
	Version history for the document set is supported.
In-place records	Protect important and legal documents even if they stay in a non-protected document library.
Office 2010 integration	Supports SharePoint's custom columns, enterprise keywords, managed metadata, and ratings.
	Learns the URL to sites visited by the user.

4

Content Management in SharePoint 2010

WHAT YOU WILL LEARN IN THIS CHAPTER:

➤ New and Enhanced Content Management Features

➤ Important CM Differences Between SharePoint Foundation and SharePoint Server

➤ How Web Content Management Works in SharePoint 2010

➤ Using Social Computing Features

➤ Integrating Content Management with Outlook

➤ Using Microsoft Communicator with SharePoint Content

➤ Managing Content Offline with SharePoint Workspace

➤ Managing Content with Wiki Pages

➤ Working with Multilingual Sites

In Chapter 3, you learned about file and document management, and how to configure columns, views, and many other related features. In this chapter, you learn about managing web content, for example, building intranets, publishing sites, and news sites. This is often referred to as *content management*. Document management and content management share many common features, so to get the details about these features, make sure to read Chapter 3 before this chapter.

> **NOTE** *This chapter is very focused on features in SharePoint Server 2010. If you are running SharePoint Foundation, read this chapter to understand what you are missing.*

WHAT IS CONTENT MANAGEMENT?

In a SharePoint environment, content management is all about managing files, documents, and web content. The objective is to make the content easy to use and manage in a secure way. Dividing content management into *web content management (WCM)* and *enterprise content management (ECM)* is a common practice. The difference is that WCM mainly focuses on web content, that is, public Internet portals, intranets, and collaboration portals, whereas ECM is a much broader term that covers just about every type of content that an organization works with, including document and web content.

The term *content management (CM)* means different things to different people, but in general, it is a technical process that supports the management of digital information during its lifecycle. Very often, when people talk about content management they typically mean either or both of these areas: document management and web content management; this is also what this chapter focuses on. The type of digital information that is the target for content management is anything that requires some management during its lifespan; that is, any information that you want to keep for a while. For example:

➤ **Standard files:** Text files, configuration files, source code, and files created with any type of applications, including non-Microsoft applications, such as desktop publishing files, and computer aided design (CAD) files

➤ **Multimedia files:** Music and audio files (MP3, WAV), image files (JPEG, GIF, PNG), and video files (AVI, MPEG)

➤ **Document files:** Files created by Microsoft Word, Microsoft Excel, Microsoft OneNote, Microsoft InfoPath, and similar applications

➤ **Web content files:** Files, or pages, displayed on a web page, typically an intranet or public website

One important goal with content management is to make adding, updating, and deleting these files easier for users; this in turn makes organizing, finding, and controlling how these files are used during the file's lifecycle easier for the users. The management process can be divided into the following steps:

➤ **Create:** Such as creating a new Microsoft Word file

➤ **Update:** When editing the Microsoft Word file

➤ **Publish:** Making this file available to other users

➤ **Archive:** When replacing a published file by a newer version, but keeping it in case of possible future need

➤ **Retire:** Removing or deleting the file

Exactly who will be responsible for what process step depends on the type of file content, and on the organization. In small companies, the same person may be responsible for all steps, but for larger organizations different people may be responsible for different steps. The roles for the content management process are usually described as follows:

➤ **Content author:** The user who creates and edits the file; for example, the Microsoft Word document

➤ **Editor:** The user who is responsible for the content itself; for example, a user who approves the content and its look, and possibly also localizations and translations

➤ **Publisher:** The user who will be responsible for making this file available to other users; for example, a news item presented on the intranet

➤ **Administrator:** The user who is responsible for managing permissions for the content; for example, to the Microsoft Word files, and the folders they are stored in

➤ **Consumer:** The user who consumes (views) and possibly copies the content

These roles relate directly to what SharePoint groups can do, so implementing a role-based content management process will be easy. SharePoint also supports the technical requirements necessary to implement the content management process. The rest of this chapter describes how to manage content in SharePoint 2010.

Why Content Management?

Why manage content? The simple answer is to have control over it. A more elaborate answer is that content management helps organizations keep track of all their digital information, such as documents, files, and web content. The more people who will consume this digital information, the more important content management becomes. If you are working alone, the chances are that you will do fine without content management, although it will help you organize your files in smarter ways.

Here are some of the more common issues when working with digital information without a content management system:

➤ **No version control:** Being 100 percent sure that the file you are using is the latest version is often very hard; to be sure, you may have to look in multiple locations to see whether any other versions of this file exist.

➤ **No check out/check in:** When you need to update a publicly available document or web content, you will most likely copy that information to your local computer, then update its content, and then republish it again. This process cannot prevent another user, unaware of your activity, from also updating the same content, so a conflict can occur about what update should be published.

➤ **No approval:** When the author is satisfied with the content, he will publish it directly. No support exists for demanding that another person approve the update before it gets published.

➤ **No workflows:** You cannot define a process that triggers on new or updated content; for example, when a document status is changed from *Preliminary* to *Completed* you may want to copy this document to the intranet.

➤ **No policies:** No way exists to determine what will happen with a web page or Microsoft Word file during its lifetime. For example, you cannot define a process that will delete a specific document after five years.

Still, large numbers of organizations today have not implemented any form of content management, so obviously people can do without it! Or can we? If you work in such an organization you can answer this question yourself — just look at how the digital information is managed in such an organization. Users spend a lot of time finding the right document and the latest version of it. They manually copy documents to a shared location to make them publicly available, when necessary. If they need approval, they use e-mail to send the files back and forth. Clearly all these steps take time, and make it easier to make mistakes, such as using the wrong version of a document. Of course these companies need content management; we all do!

Important CM Features

The previous list about what you will miss without content management is at the same time a list of what must be included in a content management system. The following is a wish list of features and concepts that a good content management system should provide:

➤ **Metadata:** Filenames and folders are the only ways to describe and organize files and documents in a traditional file server. A content management system must allow the user to add properties and information about the content, also known as *metadata*, to files and other types of content. The metadata should also be searchable and be used to sort and organize this content.

➤ **Version history:** Whenever content such as a web page, or a Microsoft Word document is updated, the previous version may need to be preserved. This ensures that you can revert to a previous version, if necessary. You can also see how this content has evolved over time, and which users have updated this content.

➤ **Check out/check in:** Being able to update publicly available content without needing to copy its content to another location must be possible. To allow a user to update content without affecting what the consumers (that is, the users with read access) can see, the system must create two copies of the same content: one for the consumers (the latest published version), and one for the content author. The system must also prohibit another content author from editing the same content, to avoid conflicting content versions. This is exactly what the check out process does. When the content author finishes updating the content, this new version replaces the public content, which is what the check-in process does.

➤ **Approval:** Before updated content goes public, it sometimes must be approved by a person other than the content author. For example, in some organizations, when you add a news item to the intranet, the manager must approve its content before it goes public. The system must notify the approver that there is something to approve; for example, by e-mail.

➤ **Workflows:** When content or its metadata is updated, you sometimes need to start an activity, or a process. For example, every time a new customer is added to a customer list, the sales team should be informed. Another example is when the "In Stock" metadata for a product list falls below a specific value, a purchase order should automatically be sent to the vendor of that product. These are typical tasks you can do with workflows; they can trigger a preconfigured process when something happens, such as when a new document is added, or when the document or any of its metadata is updated. A workflow must also be able to start manually; a typical example is when a content author wants to send an e-mail about an updated document to her colleagues, with a request for comments.

➤ **Localizations:** For web content on intranet and public Internet sites, it is sometimes very important that the content be localized, depending on the person looking at the web page; that is, a German user should see the information in German, whereas a Swedish user should see it in Swedish.

➤ **Policies:** You can use policies to define what will happen to content, such as a web page or a document, during its lifetime. For example, every time a document is printed, it will automatically have the text "Only for internal use!" added to it. Another policy example is to have all actions regarding a document audited, such as when somebody reads, copies, or modifies it. A third policy example may be that after a specific time something will happen to the content, such as its being archived or deleted, or having a metadata change.

Having a system to support these features can help your organization to better manage content. SharePoint Server 2010 has support for all of these features, and more, as follows:

➤ **Tagging:** This feature allows each user to enter a tag, or a keyword, to any type of content. Usually this helps both the user and her colleagues understand what type of information this is. It is also a great way to navigate back to the content, because SharePoint Server 2010 allows users to view all objects they have tagged.

➤ **Managed metadata:** This allows the organization to define hierarchical metadata tree structures, which ensures that users only add authorized metadata terms.

➤ **Comments:** These allow the user to enter comments about content; for example, a website or a document.

➤ **Ratings:** This feature allows users to rate content such as a web page, a file, or a blog post.

The preceding list describes features that typically are associated with Web 2.0. Even more features that relate to content management are available in SharePoint Server 2010, as you will see later, so it is safe to say that SharePoint Server 2010 is one of the absolute best solutions for content management on the market today.

Web Content Management

Web content management (WCM) is similar to document management, except the content is different. For example, document management describes how to manage files and documents, whereas web content management describes how to manage web-based content, such as web pages and their content.

Because SharePoint 2010 is a web application, web content management is definitely something you need to learn about. This chapter describes how to manage web pages and their content, such as news articles, pictures, video, and sound. It also describes how a web page can interact with other applications and content sources, such as external databases.

The History of WCM in SharePoint

The web content management features for SharePoint Portal Server 2003 were close to nonexistent; it had support for approval, but that's about it. This deficiency required content editors of the intranet, extranet, or a public Internet site, to edit, test, and get the approval of new content on a server other than the production SharePoint Server 2003 server. This method was clearly not the ideal way to work with web-based content for an organization with high standards. This lack of content-management features in SharePoint Server 2003 was at the same time a great business opportunity for other vendors that developed smart add-on products that enhanced the content-management features of SharePoint Server 2003.

Microsoft was fully aware of these shortcomings in SharePoint Server 2003, and its solution was that customers should add Microsoft Content Management Server (Microsoft CMS), which had all the standard content-management features asked for. There was, to some extent, an integration between Microsoft CMS and SharePoint Server 2003; for example, content in SharePoint Server 2003 could be published to the Microsoft CSM website, but the two products still worked in very different ways, and managing both of them was hard for the IT department.

With the release of Microsoft Office SharePoint Server 2007 (MOSS), Microsoft actually integrated the Microsoft CMS product into MOSS, and added many new features, such as support for workflows. The result was an advanced, yet easy-to-use web content management system. It worked a lot better than the previous SharePoint Server 2003 with Microsoft CMS solution, although the web content management in MOSS was not as easy to work with as many competing products.

During the design of SharePoint 2010, Microsoft invested a lot of time in understanding the shortcomings of MOSS 2007. For example, it tested and analyzed all the popular CMS products on the market to see how they worked. The result was the new CMS features in SharePoint Server 2010. One can easily see that Microsoft has greatly enhanced these content management features, and this release of SharePoint has outstanding support for both document management and web content management, especially when integrated with Microsoft Office Pro Plus 2010.

Note that to get all these features, you must deploy SharePoint Server 2010 Enterprise edition; with SharePoint Server 2010 Standard edition you will get most of them, but not all — for example, not Excel Services and Access Service. If you choose to deploy SharePoint Foundation 2010, you only get a very limited set of these content management features. If web content management is important for your organization, you should consider SharePoint Server 2010.

Enterprise Content Management

Enterprise Content Management (ECM) is also a common topic when discussing different forms of content management. It usually describes the total management of content for an enterprise, and includes document management and web content management.

If you want to know more about document management, then read Chapter 3, which covers all the details about managing documents in SharePoint 2010, such as document libraries, metadata, ratings, and version history, and how SharePoint Server 2010 integrates with Microsoft Office 2010.

Social Computing and Web 2.0

Today's users use social communities such as Facebook, LinkedIn, and MySpace. These users appreciate features such as tags, comments, and ratings, because they give users a chance to tell others what they think, and to see what other users say and like. These features are sometimes referred to as Web 2.0, and the basic idea is to encourage two-way communication.

People are social. It is important to us what other people do and think. For example, a while ago I wanted to buy a new Blu-ray player; I started by searching for products, and found some interesting sites, where I found technical info, prices, and ratings. The product with the highest rankings was the one I looked at first, and finally also purchased.

Is social computing also interesting for an organization such as a company? The answer is a loud and clear, "Yes! Definitely!" People are no different when at work than at home — we not only get formal feedback such as comments, ratings, and meeting information by e-mail, but also make informal contacts during lunch discussions and coffee breaks. The main difference between social computing on a public Web site like Facebook and social computing in a company is that these comments and ratings are not necessarily shared with other users who would likely be interested to learn about them.

SharePoint Server 2010 is the first version of SharePoint that has social computing features built-in. And it is available almost anywhere and for any type of object. It also affects other features; for example, high-rated documents will be listed higher in the search results, and users can navigate back to objects by their tags. The following sections offer more details about these features.

Tags, Ratings, and Comments

Chapter 3 covered a lot of details regarding these social computing features, but this chapter focuses on how to use them in a content management perspective. Here are the three main features discussed in this chapter:

➤ **Tagging:** Also known as *Enterprise Keywords*; often used by users to flag or categorize objects, such as documents and web pages.

➤ **Comments:** Allows the user to add public or private comments. Public comments are used when you want others to see your comments, whereas private comments tend to be remarks to help the user remember something about an object; for example, that she needs to fix something later on.

➤ **Ratings:** Use the six-level grading feature (0–5) to tell others what you think about a specific object; for example, a web page or a document.

All three features are important for users because they give them the tools they need to communicate with others. In the following examples, you see how two users, Anna and Malin, can use the features to interact and share thoughts and ideas with each other. The example uses a document library in a team site that has activated the *Enterprise Keyword*, *Ratings*, and *Tagging* features; the *Inline* editing feature is enabled in the default list view for this library. Chapter 3 describes these features.

Tagging Objects

In this example, Anna cooperates with her colleague Malin; they share documents and Malin needs to know what Anna thinks about these documents. Anna is working with customized Volvo trucks, and has tagged both contact names and web links with "Volvo" before this example begins. Anna will use several ways to add tags and comments to files and web pages.

1. Log on as Anna, and open the team site; for example `http://srv1/teamsite`.

2. Open the Shared Documents document library.

3. Anna is interested in three documents; she reads the first of them and decides to add the tags "Volvo" and "Truck" directly from within Microsoft Word 2010:

    a. While reading this document in Word, Anna clicks on Edit Document in order to be able to enter the tags.

    b. She clicks on the File button in Word to open the Backstage page.

    c. In the right pane, Properties (on the Info page), Anna selects the Enterprise Keywords field and enters **Volvo; Truck**.

    d. Anna saves and closes the document.

    e. She verifies that these tags are now listed in the Enterprise Keyword column.

4. Anna has already read the second document and knows what tags she wants to give it: "Volvo; Custom." She also wants to comment on this document, so instead of opening this document in Word, she sets the tags and comments for this document directly in the document library:

    a. Anna selects the checkbox for the second document and clicks Tags and Notes on the ribbon. A new window opens.

    b. In the My Tags field, Anna enters the first characters **Vo**; immediately a menu appears that suggests the keyword "Volvo." She clicks on the suggestion and this word is copied to the field.

    c. Anna then enters the second keyword in this field, **Custom**, and clicks Save.

    d. She then switches to the Note Board tab, enters her comment **More details are needed**, and clicks Post to save it.

    e. She closes this window by clicking the "X" button.

5. Anna has also read the third document before, so she does not need to open it; she just wants to tag it "Volvo; Description." This time she chooses to do it by using the inline editing feature:

    a. Anna locates the third document in the library and clicks the edit icon in front of the document.

    b. She types **Vo** and the suggestion shows up immediately, just like when editing the document properties. She selects the suggestion "Volvo" and then adds **Description**.

    c. She clicks on the save icon in the front of this document name.

    d. Anna verifies that this document has the correct tags.

6. Anna realizes she needs a special team site for managing all the details about customized Volvo trucks, so she creates a new subsite named **Custom Trucks**. Then she tags this site like this:

   a. Anna opens the start page for Custom Trucks.

   b. She clicks on the Tags and Notes icon at the top right of the page, and a new window opens.

   c. She fills in the tags she wants for this site: **Volvo, Custom, 4x4**, and **Trucks**, and then clicks Save and closes this window (see Figure 4-1).

7. Anna now tells Malin she is done with the tagging of these three documents.

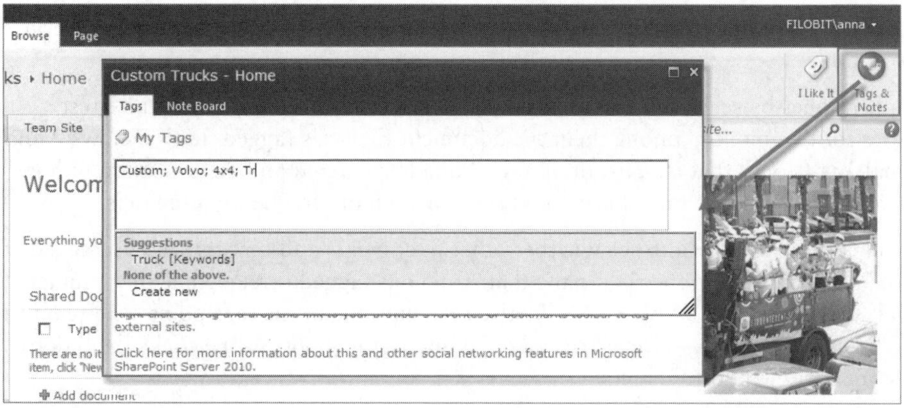

FIGURE 4-1

Tagging an Microsoft Office document can be done in multiple ways. In the preceding example, the tags were entered directly in Word, then by using the inline editing feature, and then by using Tags and Notes, which also allows the entering of comments into a file. Adding tags by editing the document properties is also possible. Web pages in SharePoint can also be tagged and commented using the Tags and Notes icon.

> **NOTE** When adding tags using the Tags and Notes feature, note that these tags do not appear in the Enterprise Keywords column, but they are recognized and presented in SharePoint like other tags. Another difference is that Tags and Notes allow a user to classify tags as public or private.

Anna does not actually have to tell Malin she is done tagging, because Malin previously created an alert that informed her via e-mail about all modifications in this document library. Still, Malin would like to see what tags Anna has entered; maybe there are other tags that might be interesting to see. Malin decides to use Anna's public profile page to check, as described next.

> **NOTE** *It will take up to an hour before Anna's latest tags will show up in her public My Site, because this is a scheduled job in SharePoint. Appendix D contains more information about scheduled timer jobs.*

Checking Other Users' Tags

In this example, Malin checks all the tags that Anna has created in this intranet.

1. Malin logs on and opens the intranet start page.

2. She opens her personal site by clicking her name at the top right of this page, and selects My Site in the menu.

3. She clicks on the Colleagues tab, and then on the name Anna to open her public My Site in a new window.

4. Malin continues by selecting Anna's Tags and Notes tab. This page shows the latest activities for this month, among them the document that was tagged. It also shows Anna's personal Tag Cloud; that is, a list of all tags Anna has entered and an indication of how frequently she uses these tags. Larger text sizes mean more frequently used tags.

5. Malin clicks the Volvo tag to see whether other documents and objects are also tagged with "Volvo"; she now sees in the right pane that Anna has tagged three people in a contact list and some links with "Volvo." Malin also sees that one of the tags points to a team site about "Custom Trucks — Home" that she did not know about, so she clicks the link to open it in a new window.

> **NOTE** *If you want to follow a specific tag, you can open the Tags and Notes window where this tag is listed and click on the tag. Select Go to tag profile for [tag name], and then click "Follow this tag in My Newsfeed." From now on, any new object tagged with this keyword will be listed in your My Site page.*

Malin just learned about Anna's new site Custom Trucks from the tags. She opens the site and looks at the information stored in this site. Malin thinks this site is great, but that the text on the start page for this site needs to be completed by adding more text, and possibly some video and sound as well. Instead of sending Anna this suggestion by e-mail, Malin wants to add her comments to the actual page; this makes it easier for others to see and comment on her comments. In the following steps, Malin adds both her comments and a tag that she likes the site.

Tagging "I Like It" and Commenting on a Web Page

In this example, Malin adds comments, also known as Notes, to a web page. She also adds a tag.

1. Malin continues with the current session (from the previous section of this chapter) and opens Anna's new Custom Trucks site.

2. She wants to tag that she likes this site, so she clicks the I Like It icon at the top right part of this page. This tag will be stored as a standard tag, and will be listed in Malin's My Site and as a tag for this page.

3. Malin wants to suggest some changes to the page. She clicks on the Tags and Notes button at top right of the page. This opens a new window with all existing tags; for example, one can now see all the tags for this page in the Suggested Tags section, including the ones that Anna entered earlier.

To enter the comments and suggestions Malin now does the following:

    a. Switches to Note Board in the new window.

    b. Enters comments and suggestions in the text field.

    c. Clicks Post to save and then close this page (see Figure 4-2).

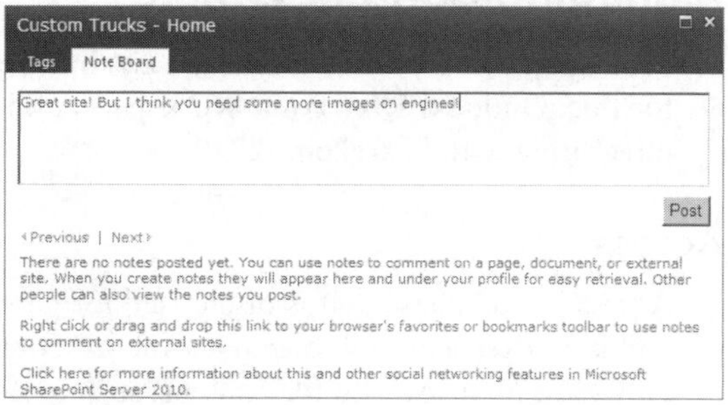

FIGURE 4-2

The next time Anna looks at the Custom Trucks site, she can click the Tags and Notes button to view all the tags and notes added by her and everybody else.

The preceding scenario shows just a few ways to use social computing features in content management, but it should give you an idea how these features work. The challenge is to explain to users how the social computing features work, but after they see them in action, they will most likely love it.

Keeping Updated with Microsoft Communicator

Content management in SharePoint 2010 is also integrated with several other Microsoft applications, such as Microsoft Office Communication Server (Microsoft OCS), with its client Microsoft Communicator. This application adds an important feature to SharePoint, especially when managing content. For example, with Microsoft Communicator a user can find out the following information by just pointing to a user name in a list or on a web page:

➤ **Real-time status information:** Is the author of this document online and active right now?

➤ **Current calendar status:** Is this author in a meeting now? When will he be free?

➤ **Communication options:** Create an instant-messaging chat with the author, start a video meeting, or send an e-mail, with just a click.

Look at Figure 4-3. By just pointing the mouse to the author's name you can immediately see what he is doing and when he will be free, and you have several options to communicate with this user.

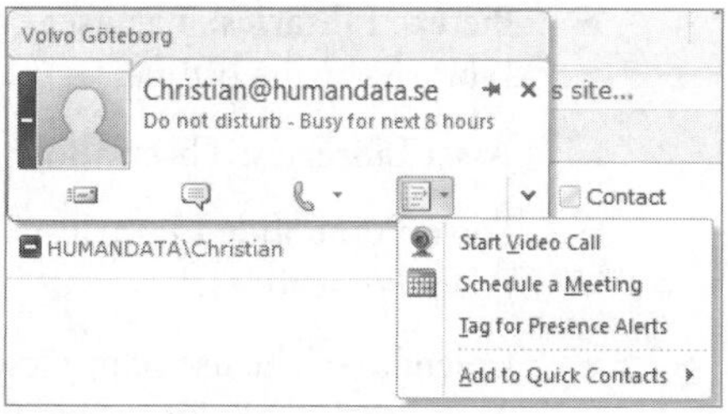

FIGURE 4-3

With this information so easily available, users working with content can collaborate or get answers instantly, when they need it. This is a great advantage, compared to how it's done today; that is, when you need to talk to somebody you first have to find out her e-mail address or phone number, and then contact her. Using Microsoft Communicator, and its server counterpart, Microsoft OCS, users can focus on working with content instead of looking for contact information.

Managing Content Offline

Managing content while online is easy, but what if you are offline? Microsoft has three solutions for this: Outlook, SharePoint Workspace, and Access. All three of them have great features for integrating with SharePoint 2010.

Access

Access is a database that is often used for personal use. Access comes with Microsoft Office 2010 and is an excellent tool for replicating list content in SharePoint, such as contacts, tasks, and links. However, libraries with file content, such as document libraries, are not able to replicate to Access. This tool will integrate with SharePoint 2010 in several ways, for example:

➤   It can copy a complete SharePoint list to a Access database; for example, for creating reports and for print-outs.

➤   It can create a two-way replica in Access of a SharePoint list; any changes you make in Access will automatically be replicated back to the SharePoint list.

The last point or bulletpoint above can be used to create an offline copy of a SharePoint list. But you can also do more with Access. For example, in Chapter 10 you will learn more on how to use Access to copy and move complete lists between sites and site collections.

Outlook 2010

Outlook comes with Microsoft Office 2010 and is a great tool for content management. Besides its ordinary features like e-mail, calendar, and contacts, it also helps the user work more effectively with content, especially when offline. For example, Outlook 2010 offers two-way synchronization and offline management of the following SharePoint lists:

➤   **Document Libraries:** These allow the user to read and update documents and their SharePoint metadata while offline.

➤   **Picture Libraries:** The user can view, copy, and update pictures and images with Picture Libraries while offline.

➤   **Asset Libraries:** These allow the user to view, play, and copy multimedia files.

➤   **PowerPoint Slide Libraries:** These allow the user to view, copy, and update single PowerPoint slides.

➤   **Calendars:** The user can view and update calendars stored in SharePoint. They can also compare SharePoint calendars with their Outlook calendars.

➤   **Task Lists:** The user can view and update tasks stored in SharePoint; these will be listed in Outlook as a separate task list.

➤ **Project Tasks:** These allow the user to view and update project tasks from Outlook. These project tasks will be listed as Outlook tasks.

➤ **Contacts:** The user can view, update, and send e-mail to contacts stored in SharePoint. These contacts will be listed as Outlook contacts.

➤ **Discussion Lists:** The user can view and update posts in the SharePoint discussing list. Using Outlook is a great way to work with discussions.

This two-way synchronization feature is especially handy when working with contacts, calendars, tasks, and discussion lists in SharePoint, because Outlook is designed to work with these types of objects.

> **NOTE** *Think twice before synchronizing libraries with many thousands of documents and files. All this information will be stored on the client in this local file:* `SharePoint Lists.pst`.

In the following example, you learn how to create two-way synchronization between SharePoint lists and Outlook 2010. Several of these lists also synchronize with Outlook 2007, but not all of them.

TRY IT OUT Synchronize SharePoint Lists to Outlook 2010

In the following examples, you find out how to synchronize a document library, a contact list, and a calendar from SharePoint 2010 with Outlook 2010. You also test how modifications in Outlook are replicated back to SharePoint.

1. Log on as a user and open a team site with a document library, a contact list, and a calendar.

2. Start Outlook 2010.

3. Synchronize a SharePoint document library:

    a. Open a document library; for example, Shared Documents.

    b. Switch to the Library tab on the ribbon.

    c. Click Connect to Outlook (a square with an "O" inside).

    d. A dialog box prompts you with the following: "Do you want to allow this website to open a program on your computer?" Click Allow.

    e. If you get a warning that says, "A website wants to open web content using this program on your computer," click Allow.

    f. A third (and final) prompt appears: "Connect this SharePoint Document Library to Outlook?" Click Yes. However, if you want to change the name of this folder in Outlook, then click Advanced first. You can also change this name afterwards, by right-clicking the new folder and selecting Rename Folder.

g. A new folder in Outlook is created under the headline SharePoint Lists. The document library now starts to synchronize with Outlook; after just a short time the documents show up in this new folder. Select any synchronized Office file in this folder, and it appears in the Outlook reading pane.

h. Try to edit a synchronized file. Double-click on a Word file, which starts Word in read-only mode.

i. Click Edit Offline.

j. The dialog box Edit Offline that appears tells you that Outlook needs to copy this document to a temporary file folder on this client: SharePoint Drafts, which was automatically created in your My Documents. This drafts folder contains all the documents you started to edit, but have not yet completed. Click OK to switch to edit mode.

k. Change whatever content you need, including metadata stored in SharePoint. Save and close Word when done.

l. If you are online, a dialog box named "Edit Offline" appears asking whether you want to update the server now. Click Update to replicate immediately. Verify that the preview in the Outlook reading pane now shows the new version. If you are not online, or choose to click "Do not update server," you only get a local copy of this modified file. This file then gets a special icon (see Figure 4-4). When you are online next time, open this document and click Update directly under the ribbon to get this document in sync again.

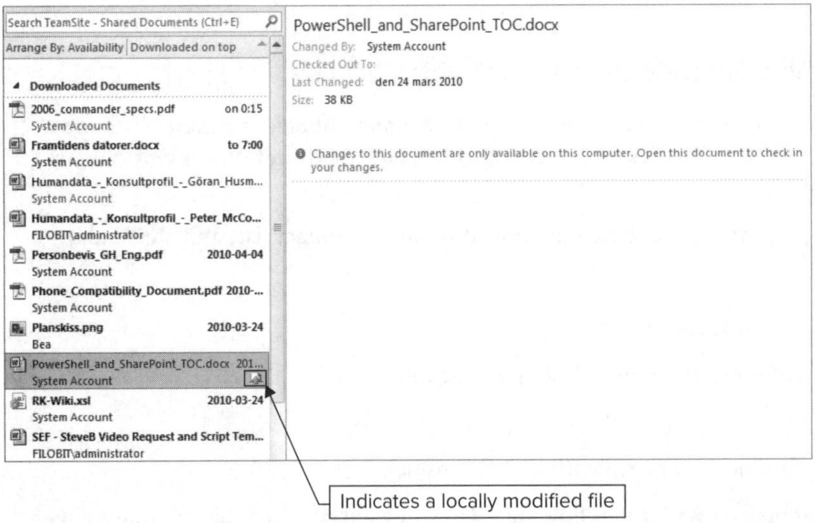

Indicates a locally modified file

FIGURE 4-4

> **NOTE** There are things to remember about document synchronization in Outlook. Locally modified documents will not be synchronized automatically. You must open the document and choose Update. Documents cannot be deleted in Outlook to prevent a user from accidentally deleting shared documents in SharePoint. Enable Version History in SharePoint to protect users from overwriting other users' documents.

4. Now synchronize a Contact list:

    a. In the team site, open a contact list.

    b. Switch to the Library tab on the ribbon.

    c. Click Connect to Outlook on the ribbon.

    d. A dialog prompts you with the following: "Do you want to allow this website to open a program on your computer?" Click Allow.

    e. If you get a warning that says, "A website wants to open web content using this program on your computer," click Allow.

    f. A third (and final) prompt appears: "Connect this SharePoint Contact List to Outlook?" Click Yes.

    g. To see the new contact list, open Outlooks Contacts; it is listed under the Other Contacts headline.

    h. Verify that you can see all contacts stored in this SharePoint list.

    i. Test out changing a contact: Double-click an existing contact, change some settings, and then click Save & Close. Then switch to SharePoint, open this contact list, and verify that the modification is replicated.

> **NOTE** *Contacts lists replicated to Outlook offer the same functionality as for standard Outlook contacts; that is, you can add, delete, and modify contacts and the changes are replicated to SharePoint. You can also copy contacts between other contact lists, and send e-mail, do a mail merge, and send meeting invitations to contacts.*

5. Now replicate a SharePoint calendar to Outlook:

    a. In the team site, open a calendar.

    b. Switch to the Library tab on the ribbon.

    c. Click Connect to Outlook on the ribbon.

    d. A dialog box prompts you with the following: "Do you want to allow this website to open a program on your computer?" Click Allow.

    e. If you get a warning that says, "A website wants to open web content using this program on your computer," click Allow.

    f. A third (and final) prompt appears: "Connect this SharePoint Calendar List to Outlook?" Click Yes.

    g. To see the new contact list, open the Outlook Calendar. It appears under the Other Calendar heading.

h. Verify that you can see all meeting events stored in this SharePoint list.

i. Test out changing a meeting. Double-click an existing meeting, change some settings, and then click Save & Close. Then switch to SharePoint, refresh the page, and open this calendar list. Verify that the modification is replicated.

> **NOTE** *Calendar lists replicated to Outlook offer the same functionality as standard Outlook calendars; that is, you can add, delete, and modify meeting items, and the changes will be replicated to SharePoint. You can also copy meetings between other calendar lists, and view multiple calendars in overlay mode, just like with standard Outlook calendars.*

How It Works

Most lists in SharePoint can be replicated to Outlook 2010. Modifications in Outlook will be replicated back to SharePoint, next time you are online, except for documents. You have to reopen these documents when online to start the replication.

SharePoint Workspace 2010

If you need a richer offline client than Outlook 2010, then look at SharePoint Workspace. This product replaces Microsoft Groove, which was included in Microsoft Office 2007, and comes with many improvements related to SharePoint 2010. For example, SharePoint Workspace allows the user to work offline with all the defined features for a given content type, such as custom metadata and workflows. All local modifications are replicated automatically to SharePoint when you are next online. The lists and libraries that can be replicated to SharePoint Workspace are as follows:

➤ **Document Libraries:** Allow you to read, create, delete, and update documents and SharePoint metadata, including check out/in and version history, as well as work with content types and workflows.

➤ **Picture Libraries:** Allow you to view, create, delete, and update images and SharePoint metadata, including check out/in, as well as work with content types and workflows.

➤ **Asset Library:** Allows you to add, delete, and edit the content and properties of multimedia files stored in this library. Supports check out/in and workflows.

➤ **Slide Library:** Allows you to view, create, delete, and update PowerPoint slides, including SharePoint metadata and check out/in, as well as work with content types and workflows.

➤ **Tasks Lists:** Allows you to view, add, delete, and modify tasks, including all SharePoint metadata.

➤ **Project Tasks:** Allow you to view, add, delete, and modify project tasks, including SharePoint metadata.

➤ **Contact Lists:** Allow you to view, add, delete, and modify contacts, including SharePoint metadata.

➤ **Issue Tracking:** Allows you to view, add, delete, and update issues, including all SharePoint metadata.

➤ **Announcements:** Allow you to view, add, delete, and modify Announcement posts. This has very similar formatting features as the web client, but does not allow you to add pictures and links.

➤ **Discussion Lists:** Allow you to view, add, delete, and modify discussion threads, including SharePoint metadata for this list.

➤ **Links:** Allow you to open, add, delete, and modify links, including SharePoint metadata.

An impressive number of lists and libraries can be replicated to SharePoint Workspace. A common question is whether one would have any use for the replication feature in Outlook 2010, besides SharePoint Workspace — the answer is definitely, "Yes!" You may have noticed that SharePoint Workspace does not support calendars; that is a very good reason for using Outlook 2010 for this type of list. Follow these recommendations to get the best replication environment with SharePoint 2010:

➤ Use SharePoint Workspace for all kinds of libraries, such as document libraries, image libraries, and so on. It fully supports all metadata, check out/in, and content types that are stored in the corresponding SharePoint library. It also supports automatic replication of any changes performed while you're offline.

➤ Use SharePoint Workspace for Issue Tracking lists, Announcements, and Links, because Outlook does not support these types of lists.

➤ Use Outlook 2010 to replicate Tasks, Project Tasks, Contacts, Calendars, and Discussion Lists. All of these lists have corresponding functionality built into Outlook 2010, and can be utilized in the same way. Outlook also replicates any changes back to SharePoint automatically.

> **NOTE** *SharePoint Workspace supports drag-and-drop to libraries. For example, when you drag files and documents from Windows Explorer and drop them into a library in SharePoint Workspace, this change is automatically replicated to SharePoint.*

Users who prefer to work with SharePoint documents and files as if they were stored in a shared file server should definitely look at SharePoint Workspace. With this tool, users also have full access when offline, as well as the usual drag-and-drop features, including copy and paste.

> **NOTE** *The first time you start a SharePoint Workspace, you will be asked to create an account. Just accept the default to set up this account.*

In the following example, you see how to create a connection between SharePoint lists and SharePoint Workspace, how to add and modify the content locally, and then how to verify that it was replicated back to SharePoint.

TRY IT OUT   Synchronize Lists to a SharePoint Workspace

In this example, you synchronize a document library, and then modify its content locally.

1.   Open a team site as a Contributor.

2.   Open a document library — if possible with multiple content types and with custom columns to see how they work in SharePoint Workspace.

3.   Switch to the Library tab on the ribbon.

4.   Click Sync to SharePoint Workspace (see Figure 4-5).

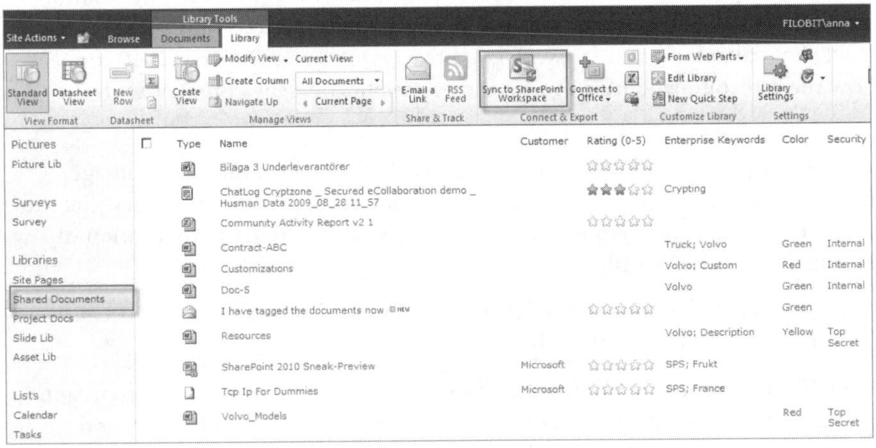

FIGURE 4-5

5.   A dialog window appears with the following: "Sync the list 'Shared Documents' to your computer?" Click OK.

6.   A summary window appears when the Initialization is completed, and if you selected to replicate all items, then all documents properties, that is, filename, author, company, and so on, will start to synchronize with SharePoint. Click Open Workspace to see what lists it contains and whether the lists are replicated or not.

7.   Verify that you see all the documents in SharePoint Workspace. To edit a document, do this:

     a.   Double-click on the file to download it from the SharePoint server.

     b.   Double-click it again to open the document.

     c.   Edit its content.

     d.   Modify its SharePoint properties: Click File to open the Backstage page, then click "Show all properties" in the lower-right corner. All SharePoint metadata — that is, its properties — is listed just before the Related Dates heading in the right pane. Change any of its values. For a choice list column, click on it to see all choices; for an Enterprise Keyword, you will get suggestions when you begin typing, just like when you work directly in SharePoint lists.

     e.   Save and close the modified document. After a short period, the document on the SharePoint server will also be updated automatically.

8. If this library has multiple content types, then they are also replicated to SharePoint Workspace. To create a new document based on any of these content types, do this:

    a. Switch to SharePoint Workspace.

    b. Select the document library that you synchronized earlier in step 5.

    c. If it contains multiple folders, then select the folder you want to store the new file in.

    d. Click the *text* New Document on the ribbon, and all available content types appear. Select one of them, and the corresponding application starts; for example, if the content type contains a Word file, then Word starts (see Figure 4-6).

    e. Enter some content, and set the SharePoint metadata in the panel, also known as the *Document Information Panel (DIP)*, that appears at the top of the document. Save the document.

    f. Open this document library in SharePoint (that is, with a web browser), and verify that the new document is listed and that it contains the correct content and metadata.

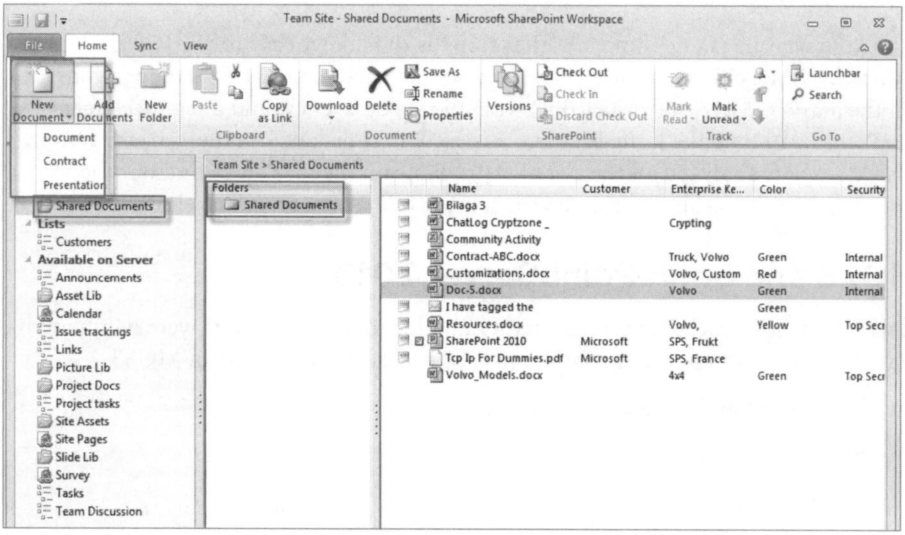

FIGURE 4-6

How It Works

SharePoint Workspace allows the user to take most SharePoint content offline and work with it. Any modifications will be automatically replicated back to SharePoint. If the original file in SharePoint has been modified while offline, you will be notified that there is a conflict and be given options on how to solve it.

ENHANCEMENTS IN WEB CONTENT MANAGEMENT

Web Content Management (WCM) is a big market with lots of products specifically designed to build and manage intranets, public-facing Internet sites, and extranets. Microsoft initially had a product called Microsoft Content Management Service 2002 (CMS) that later got integrated with Microsoft Office SharePoint Server 2007 (MOSS). To be honest, MOSS was not the best WCM product on the market, so organizations tended to choose other solutions, especially for Internet-facing portals, or to purchase third-party add-on products to extend the WCM feature in MOSS. Still, many really good public MOSS sites exist; for example:

➤ http://www.volvocars.com

➤ http://www.ferrari.com

➤ http://www.hawaiianair.com

➤ http://www.sabo.se

Sites like these have been more or less heavily extended by custom code. But they show that MOSS sites can be as good as any other WCM product on the market. In fact, SharePoint is now one of the fastest-growing solutions for public-facing Internet sites.

Creating a good-looking website is one thing; another thing is to make it easy to work with — that is, to manage its content. Maybe this was one of the biggest weaknesses of MOSS, compared to other products on the market. Microsoft was fully aware of this deficiency, and a big investment was made in SharePoint 2010 to make it the best and easiest WCM product on the market. The SharePoint team at Microsoft analyzed all the popular products on the market to find out their advantages and weaknesses; the result is the new web content management in SharePoint 2010.

Comparing MOSS and SharePoint Server 2010

MOSS had good web content management functionality and lots of organizations were happy with it. Other organizations were less happy and complained about features like these in MOSS:

➤ Too many clicks to add and update news articles

➤ Too many clicks to add images

➤ Limited rich text formatting

➤ Limited support for accessibility

If you compare MOSS to other WCM products, understanding why some people were unhappy is easy. At the same time, MOSS offers really nice features that often are missing in other products, for example:

➤ Support for approval of new and updated content before publishing

➤ Support for workflows on web content

➤ Integration with other features in SharePoint, such as metadata, and content types

➤ An advanced search engine

➤ Support for integration with Microsoft Office; for example, you can write news articles in Word

➤ Content deployment; that is, can replicate content from one site to another such as from an internal site to a public site.

➤ Support for variations; for example, web pages in different languages, or adjustments for mobile devices.

So what is better in SharePoint 2010? A lot! Microsoft has kept all the good features in MOSS 2007 and totally rebuilt the way users manage web content. This will make the content authors and editors happy. The following lists describe the new and enhanced features in SharePoint Server 2010:

New:

➤ **Wiki pages:** Make editing web pages very easy; for example, when adding text, images, and web parts, as well as multimedia content

➤ **Multimedia web parts:** Make publishing and playing pictures, music, and video on a web page easy

➤ **Digital Asset Library:** Allows you to store picture, audio, and video files

➤ **Tagging, ratings, and comments:** Allows users to describe what they think about a given web page

➤ **Ribbon:** Enables easy access to all buttons and features that apply to the currently active object on the web page; for example, text, images, and tables

➤ **Resize pictures:** Allows users to resize pictures that appear on the web page

➤ **Tag Clouds:** Display the most popular tags via a tag cloud web part

➤ **Silverlight Web Parts:** Display Silverlight applications on the web page; for example, animated diagrams or games

Enhanced:

➤ **Picture Management:** Makes uploading and displaying picture files in one step easy.

➤ **Web Parts gallery:** Makes adding and managing web parts easier than in SharePoint 2007.

➤ **Picture control:** Allows you to drag pictures to any position.

➤ **Page Layout:** Allows you to change the layout for the web page; for example, from two columns to three columns.

➤ **HTML formatting:** Supports the use of the new *Markup Styles* to apply predefined styles, edit HTML source, or convert to XHTML.

You can find more information about these features in the following sections, and see examples on how to use them in Chapter 7.

Differences Between SharePoint Foundation and SharePoint Server

What if you deployed SharePoint Foundation? Does it also offer better and easier-to-use web content management? Absolutely! Of course, SharePoint Foundation features are not as complete as SharePoint Server features, but they are a giant leap forward compared to the previous version, that is, WSS 3.0. Here are the main enhancements compared to WSS:

New:

➤ **Wiki pages:** SharePoint Foundation Team Sites are based on the new Wiki site template, which makes them as easy to manage as the new SharePoint Server publishing sites.

➤ **Version History and Check out/in:** Makes editing a public web page, without displaying it until it is completed, possible. You can also view and go back to previous versions of this web page.

➤ **Ribbon:** Enables easy access to all buttons and features that apply to the currently active object on the web page; for example, text, images, and tables.

➤ **Resize pictures:** Allows users to resize pictures that appear on the web page.

➤ **Silverlight Web Parts:** Display Silverlight applications on the web page; for example, animated diagrams or games.

Enhanced:

➤ **Picture management:** Makes uploading and displaying picture files in one step easy.

➤ **Multiple Wiki pages:** Make adding and displaying multiple web pages to a team site easier.

➤ **Web Parts gallery:** Makes adding and managing web parts easier.

➤ **Picture control:** Allows you to drag pictures to any position.

➤ **Page layout:** Allows you to change the layout for the web page; for example, from two columns to three columns.

➤ **HTML formatting:** Supports the use of the new *Markup Styles* to apply predefined styles, edit HTML source, or convert to XHTML.

The result is that portal sites based on SharePoint Foundation also have very good web content management, especially compared to the SharePoint Foundation predecessor, WSS 3.0.

Building Blocks for a Portal

Whether you are building a team site, an intranet portal, or a public-facing Internet site, you need an environment that is very easy to set up and configure, and to manage. The previous sections have described all the new and enhanced features in SharePoint Server 2010 and SharePoint Foundation 2010, which will be your building blocks when building web portals.

One of the main enhancements regarding WCM is that SharePoint now uses Wiki pages as the default site template for publishing sites and team sites. These Wiki sites are greatly enhanced compared to the Wiki sites introduced in SharePoint 2007, so they are very easy to work with both as a content author and a site administrator.

Here is a summary of the most required building blocks when building team sites and publishing portals:

➤ **Web pages that are easy to edit, manage, and control:** Wiki sites are perfect for these tasks, and SharePoint implementation also allows version history and check out/in of any Wiki page.

➤ **Ease in changing the layout of the web page:** Typically an organization uses several page layouts, depending on the content and the location in the site map. SharePoint allows you to define multiple layouts and to change the current layout for existing pages.

➤ **Ease in adding pictures, video, and audio to a web page:** SharePoint Server 2010, especially, makes these additions very easy, but SharePoint Foundation is also good at managing pictures, although not video or audio.

➤ **Support for Silverlight applications:** Microsoft is promoting Silverlight as its preferred method for displaying animated and graphical presentations on web pages. Both SharePoint Server and SharePoint Foundation come with a web part for displaying Silverlight applications.

➤ **A rich set of web parts:** This set makes creating interesting web pages possible; SharePoint Foundation comes with a basic set, whereas SharePoint Server comes with a large number of web parts. You can also create new web parts using Visual Studio, or purchase them from third-party vendors.

➤ **Filtering features:** These features make it possible to create a web page that adjusts its content to show only information that is relevant to the current user. SharePoint uses audience targeting and security trim to achieve this task.

➤ **Security:** Being able to easily define what content a given user or group is allowed to view, edit, and manage is a necessity. SharePoint has a rich security model that allows predefined security settings to users and groups for any type of object; for example, web pages, documents, and pictures.

Wiki Pages

Both SharePoint Server and SharePoint Foundation support Wiki-based sites. The main advantage of Wiki pages is that creating and editing them is so simple. These pages also accept all types of content. Try editing a Wiki page to see how easy it is.

> **NOTE** *Silverlight is a generic add-on from Microsoft for web clients for supporting animated and multimedia content. Download Silverlight for free from* `www.microsoft.com/silverlight`.

TRY IT OUT **Edit a Wiki Site**

In this example, you edit an existing intranet portal based on a Wiki site template. The following steps are the same for an enterprise Wiki in SharePoint Server as for a team site in SharePoint Foundation, except for the procedure to change the page layout. The following instructions are for team sites. You must also have installed Silverlight in your client computer.

1. Open any site based on a Wiki site template.

2. Click the edit button (see Figure 4-7), or click Site Actions ⇨ Edit Page.

3. The page switches to edit mode; that is, you can place the cursor anywhere on that page and start editing text. Try this:

    a. Switch to the Format Text tab on the ribbon.

FIGURE 4-7

    b. Select some existing text.

    c. Open the drop-down menu for fonts, and hover the mouse over different fonts. Notice that the selected text shows a preview so you can see how it looks.

    d. Also test other formatting controls, like colors, size, and bulleted and numbered lists.

    e. Test applying different Styles and Markup Styles to the selected text.

4. Add a picture to the web page. This picture will be stored by default in a local list in this site; in publishing sites this list is usually named Asset Library:

    a. Place the cursor where you want the picture to appear. Note that the cursor must be placed in an editable wiki part of this page, and not inside a web part on this page.

    b. Switch to the Insert tab on the ribbon.

    c. Click the arrow under the Picture icon, then select From Computer in the menu. The "Select Picture" dialog box opens.

    d. Use the Browse button to add a picture in your file system. In this example, select the default library, where this picture will be stored. Then click OK.

    e. A new dialog box opens, allowing you to enter some properties. Click Save. The picture uploads to the library, and also appears on the web page.

    f. Drag the picture to another location.

    g. Use the square handles that surround the picture to resize it. Note that it retains its aspect ratio. On the Picture Tools Design tab, deselect the Lock Aspect Ratio option and then resize the picture again. Press Ctrl+Z to undo.

    h. Select any Image Style to see how it looks, then test Position.

    i. Enter **My first picture** in the Alt Text field on the ribbon.

    j. Click the Save & Close icon (a blue diskette).

    k. Check out the result.

5. Change the page layout — a team site has a two-column layout by default, so use these steps to change it to a three-column layout:

a. Make sure the page is in edit mode (see step 2 earlier).

b. Notice the page has two columns. Click on Text Layout and select Three columns.

c. A third column appears at the right of this page. It is small, because it does not contain any content. Drag the picture you added in step 4 into this third column, and resize it. Type some text under the picture.

d. To see what happens if you decrease the number of columns, click Text Layout and change back to two columns. Notice that the picture and text are moved to the bottom of the second column — in other words, no content is lost.

6. Add a web part, such as the web part that lists the users and groups that can access this site as members; that is, Contributors:

a. Make sure the page is in edit mode.

b. Place the cursor in a text area (but not within an existing web part or list) in the second column.

c. Switch to the Insert tab on the ribbon.

d. Click Web Part, which opens a categorized list of available web parts.

e. Select the People category, and then select the Site Users web part (in SharePoint Server, select the Social Collaboration category to find this web part). Then click Add.

f. The Site Users web part appears, with default settings. Change these settings by either setting the check box for this web part and clicking Web Part Properties on the ribbon, or opening the menu for this web part and selecting Edit Web Part (see Figure 4-8). Either method opens a configuration panel at the left of the page.

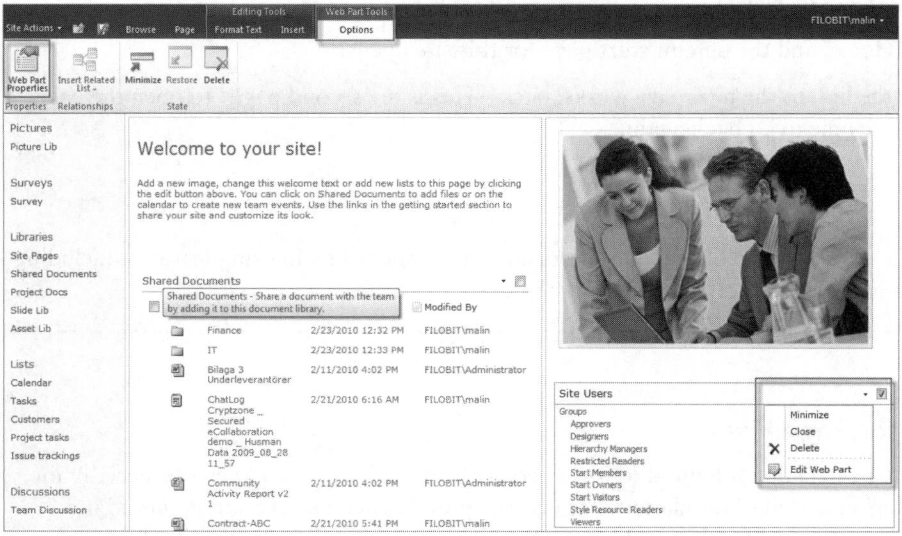

FIGURE 4-8

    g.   Change the Display Type to "Show people in this site's member group."

    h.   Expand the Appearance section, and change the Title to **Site Members**.

    i.   Click OK to save and close this configuration pane.

    j.   Verify that the web part shows the new settings.

7.   Add a new Wiki page, such as one that shows a news article. To make opening the new page easy, create a link to it on the start page. Because this is a Wiki site, use the Wiki method to create this new Wiki page and link:

    a.   Make sure the page is in edit mode.

    b.   Place the cursor where you want the link to the new page.

    c.   Then type the following exactly: [[**This is my second page**]]. Notice that SharePoint tries to find an existing page or list with this name, but it will fail because you are creating a new page.

    d.   Click Save & Close on the ribbon.

    e.   Note that your new link has a dotted line under it. This indicates that the link is pointing to a non-existing Wiki page. Click on the link, and a question appears, asking whether you want to create a new page; click Create. The new page then appears in edit mode.

    f.   Change the text layout, then add text and any other content you like.

    g.   You may want to give the user a quick link back to the first page, for example, at the top of the page, as follows: Set the cursor where you want the link back, then type just [[. You will then see a list of all available pages; select Home and press Enter on the keyboard. The complete Wiki link [[Home]] will be automatically created.

    h.   Click Save & Close. The new page appears, including the Home link — that is, the square brackets are not displayed.

    i.   Click on Home, and the default start page for this site opens.

    j.   Test that the link to the new page works; click "This is my second page" to open the page. Then click Home to go back again.

How It Works

Editing Wiki pages is very easy, and SharePoint offers a great number of formatting features, including adding pictures, web parts, and more, in just a few steps.

Version History for Page Files

All Wiki pages are by default configured to use a version history. This is good news, especially for organizations using SharePoint Foundation, because the previous version of SharePoint did not support version history or any kind of undo features. A content author who will edit a Wiki page for a longer time, maybe days or even weeks, can force a persistent checkout that will both prohibit others from editing this page, and give the content author a private copy to work with, for as long as it takes. When ready, she will check in the modified Wiki page, which will make it public.

The version history for Wiki pages is exactly like it is for any other type of library; for example, document libraries and picture libraries. It allows the user (with at least Contribute permissions) to

> ➤ View a previous version

> ➤ Restore a previous version

You must understand that when restoring a previous version, the current version is not overwritten; that is, if you want to undo the restore operation, you can simple restore the second newest version. For example, if the current version is 5.0, and you restore version 2.0, then version 6.0 will be created, which will be an exact copy of 2.0. So, if you want to undo this operation, then restore version 5.0 (which will be version 7.0). Understanding this convention is easy when you use the steps in the following example.

TRY IT OUT Manage Version History for Wiki Pages

In this example, you restore a previous version of a Wiki page, then undo this restore operation by doing a new restore.

1. In the previous exercise, you edited Wiki pages. In this example, you continue with the same Wiki pages. You made several changes to this Wiki page. What if you want to cancel all of them and revert to the original version? Doing so is simple, because all Wiki pages by default have a version history activated:

 a. Switch to the Page tab on the ribbon.

 b. Click View All Pages on the ribbon. This lists all existing Wiki pages for this site, including the one you did in step 7 in the previous exercise.

 c. Select the Home check box, which is the default start page.

 d. Click Version History on the ribbon.

 e. All versions of the Home page are listed, including what was changed. Scroll down to version 1.0, open its menu (see Figure 4-9), and select Restore. Click OK to confirm you want to restore this version.

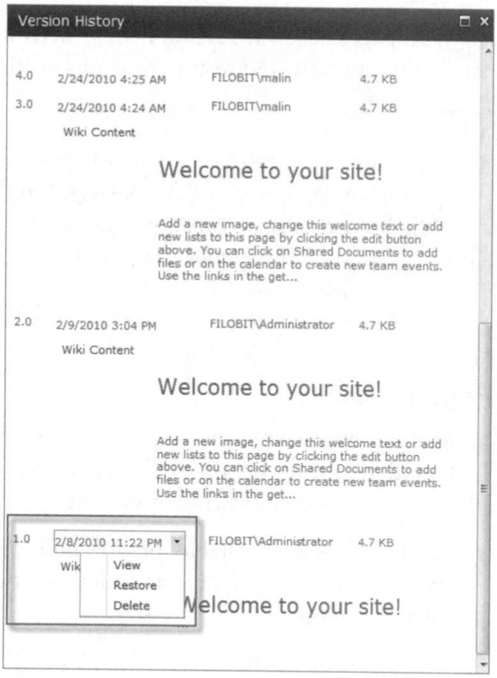

FIGURE 4-9

     f.   Close the version history page (click on the X at the top right).

     g.   Open the start page; for example, switch to the Browse tab, and then click on the link to this site. Verify that the first version of this Wiki page appears.

2. Now you change your mind. You really did not want to restore version 1.0, so you want to undo the restore operation. The easiest way to do so is to:

     a.   Switch to the Pages tab on the ribbon.

     b.   Click View All Pages on the ribbon.

     c.   Select the Home check box.

     d.   Click Version History on the ribbon.

     e.   Notice that the current version is identical to version 1.0; that is, same size and same content. Locate the second newest version, open its menu, and select Restore. Click OK to confirm you want to restore this version.

     f.   Close the version history page (click on the X at the top right).

     g.   Open the start page; for example, switch to the Browse tab, and then click on the link to this site. Verify that the modified Wiki page is now restored.

How It Works

All Wiki pages have the version history activated by default. It allows the user, with at least Contribute permission, to view and restore previous versions of any Wiki page.

> **NOTE** *If a status line displays the message "The current page has been customized from its template," then click Revert to template, which ensures that the page layout is based on the default layout. To do this, you must be a site owner!*

Page Layouts

Multiple page layouts come with SharePoint; they differ depending on whether it is an SharePoint Foundation team site or an SharePoint Server Enterprise Wiki page. You can also create new page layouts or modify existing ones with SharePoint Designer 2010. Chapter 9 describes how to do this.

The page layouts available for sites built on the Team Site template come with the following text layouts. These text layouts are built into the site definition, and customizing them using the web client is not possible.

➤   One column

➤   One column with sidebar

➤   Two columns (the default layout)

➤   Two columns with header

➤ Two columns with header and footer

➤ Three columns

➤ Three columns with header

➤ Three columns with header and footer

SharePoint Server comes with the Enterprise Wiki site template; it is a more advanced Wiki site that is used more for publishing sites such as intranets. The Enterprise Wiki comes with the following page layouts:

➤ Basic Page (the default layout)

➤ Basic Project Page

➤ Redirect

These page layouts are stored in a local gallery named "Master pages and page layouts" inside SharePoint Server. The names in the galley for these three page layouts are `EnterpriseWiki.aspx`, `ProjectPage.aspx`, and `RedirectPageLayout.aspx`. The following exercise shows you how to manage the settings for these layouts.

TRY IT OUT **View the Enterprise Wiki Page Layouts**

In this example, you view the current settings for the default Enterprise Wiki page layout. Note that this only works in an SharePoint Server installation.

1. Log on as a site collection administrator, and open the top site.

2. Click Site Actions ➪ Site Settings and then "Master pages and page layouts" in the Galleries section to open the "All Masters Pages" page.

3. Select the `EnterpriseWiki.aspx` file, and click Edit Properties on the ribbon. You are choosing edit instead of view properties, even though you will not edit any settings, because you will see much more of what you can do with this page layout. A message asks whether you want to check out; click Yes.

4. Scroll down and inspect the different settings and options. Note the option to hide a page layout. This can be of value if you need to ensure users do not use a specific page layout, but you do not want to delete it.

5. When done, click Cancel to close without saving.

6. The file is still checked out. Select the `EnterpriseWiki.aspx` file once more, and select Discard Check Out on the ribbon (a small icon with a green arrow pointing down). Click OK to accept the discarding of the check out.

How It Works

SharePoint Server 2010 uses publishing features for sites typically used as intranet, extranet, and Internet-facing portals. These publishing sites are based on Wiki pages, and the page layouts for these Wiki pages are stored in the "Master pages and page layouts" gallery that is stored in the top site.

Approval of New Content

In a small organization, it is common for the content author to also have permission to publish new content; for example, a news article. But often in larger organizations, dedicated people review the content before it gets approved and then published. SharePoint 2010 supports both of these working processes, and also a mix of them:

> ➤ **No Approval required:** Content authors can publish new and modified content at will.

> ➤ **No Approval required, but content authors can ask for an approval when it is necessary:** This is the same configuration setting as the preceding, but used in another way.

> ➤ **Approval Required:** All new and modified content must be approved, even if the content author has the permission to approve. In this case you always have two steps: first new content is created, and then it gets approved.

The approval settings for web content are identical to those for any list or library content; that is, if you know how approval of documents works, then you also know how to use approval for web content. The following exercise shows how it works.

TRY IT OUT **Manage Approval of Web Content**

In this example, there are three users: you are the Site Owner, Malin is granted site permission as a Contributor, and Anna is granted site permission as an Approver and will approve any modification. First, you configure the Wiki pages to require approval. Then Malin will change the web content, and finally, Anna will approve the modifications.

1. Log on as a site owner and open a top site based on the Enterprise Wiki site template.

2. Click Site Actions ➪ View All Site Content to open the page "All Site Content."

3. Click on Pages to view its contents. This library contains all Wiki pages for this site.

4. Switch to the Library tab, then click Library Settings.

5. Click Versioning Settings, and then:

    a. Set "Require content approval for submitted items" to Yes.

    b. Click OK to save and close.

6. Now test this new setting: Log on as Malin, the content author, who only has Contributor permissions to this site.

7. Open the Wiki site (still as Malin).

8. Edit the Wiki page, as described in an earlier Try It Out, and then save the page.

9. The modified page is not publicly available; it must be approved first:

    a. Log on as Anna, the site owner.

b. Open the Wiki page, and notice that a yellow status message says "Waiting for approval" (see Figure 4-10).

c. Switch to the Publish tab on the ribbon.

d. Click on Approve, and then you can add a comment. Click Continue. The yellow status message disappears, and the updated page becomes visible to everyone with at least read access.

How It Works

Configure the Page library to require approval if you want control over new and modified web content. The approver must manually check this page to discover that there is something to approve.

FIGURE 4-10

The preceding procedure is acceptable if the content author notifies the approver that there is new content to approve. This may be inconvenient if there are many approvers, or different approvers for different content. The easiest way to solve this issue is to use an approval workflow. SharePoint Server 2010 comes with a predefined workflow that does exactly this, whereas installations built upon SharePoint Foundation must build their own workflow.

In the following example, you activate the predefined approval workflow that comes with SharePoint Server 2010; then Malin, the content author, edits the web page, and Anna is expected to view and approve the new content.

TRY IT OUT Approve Web Content by A Workflow

You use the same website and same three users as in the previous example: You are the site owner, Malin is the contributor, and Anna is the approver, but this time you enable and configure the approval workflow in SharePoint Server 2010.

1. Log on as the site owner, and open the top site.

2. Switch to the Pages tab on the ribbon, then click View All Pages, to open "All Documents"; note that this is the same page library as in step 3 in the preceding Try It Out.

3. Switch to the Library tab on the ribbon, then click Library Settings.

4. Click Workflow Settings to open the "Add a Workflow" page, and then:

a. Set the Workflow field to **Approval - SharePoint 2010**.

b. Set the Name field to **Approval of new web content**.

c. Select the Start Options: "Start this workflow when a new item is created" and "Start this workflow when an item is changed."

d. Click Next; a page named "Approving" opens.

e. Set the Assigned To option to **Anna**.

f. Enter this comment in the Request field: **Please review and approve this new content.**

g. Select the Enable Content Approval option.

h. Click Save.

i. Verify that the new workflow "Approval of new web content" is listed.

5. Now test how it works: Log on as Malin (the content author) and open the same site.

6. Edit the same page as before, then save the page. The modified content is not published, due to the approval requirement.

7. Log on as Anna, and open her e-mail client; she has received an e-mail where she is assigned a task to approve the new content (see Figure 4-11). Now do the following:

a. Click the *home* link (that is, the site name) from step 1 at the bottom of this e-mail; a new page opens displaying the new content.

b. When the page opens you can, as in the previous Try It Out, see a yellow status line saying "Waiting for approval."

c. Anna reviews the content and decides it is okay; she clicks the Open this Task button in the e-mail.

d. The "Workflow Task" dialog window opens: Anna enters the comment **Nice job, Malin!**, and then clicks Approve. Then she closes this e-mail. The new content is now approved.

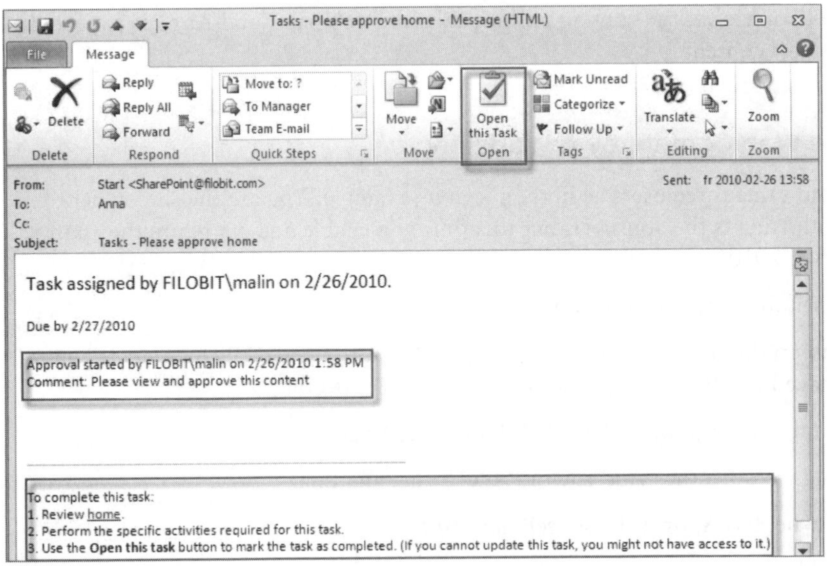

FIGURE 4-11

How It Works

Using an approval workflow eases the approval process; instead of relying on manual procedures, an e-mail notice will be sent out to approvers. This workflow allows one or multiple approvers who approve the new content in parallel or serial fashion.

Support for Multilingual Sites

In the previous version of SharePoint, Microsoft added support for multilingual sites with a feature named *variations*. The basic idea of variations is that you have one master site, for example, in English, and then replicas of that site in other languages, implemented as subsites. When new content was added to the master site, it was replicated to the subsites, but not automatically translated. So a content editor had to translate the new content in each subsite before it was published.

SharePoint Server 2010 also supports variations, in the same way, but has enhanced the replication between the master site and its subsites, that is, variations, to make it more robust. This technique is rather advanced and is beyond the scope in this book.

A new feature that supports multilingual sites is introduced in SharePoint Server 2010 — *Multilingual User Interface* (MUI). This feature makes it possible to offer ribbon controls, menus, and site navigations in different languages. Before you can use this feature you must install the corresponding SharePoint 2010 language pack, which you can download for free from www.microsoft.com/download (search for *SharePoint 2010 Language Pack)*. Separate language packs exist for SharePoint Foundation and SharePoint Server, so make sure to install the correct package.

After you have installed multiple language packs, you must activate the multilingual user interface feature for each site that requires support for multiple MUI. This displays a new option in the menu that opens when the user clicks his name at the top-right position of the web page. This new option allows the user to choose any of the languages enabled for this site, which affects the following settings:

➤   The heading for each standard column in lists and libraries

➤   The ribbon, including its buttons and menus

➤   All standard texts, headings, and other user interface elements

➤   The navigation menus

SharePoint remembers the user's preferred language the next time he opens the same site. This MUI support is a great feature for organizations working with different languages. Note that nothing more than the language packs are needed; in other words, no variations have to be installed.

In the following example, you see how to enable the MUI feature and how it works. It assumes you have at least one language pack installed on the SharePoint server.

TRY IT OUT   **Manage Multiuser Language Support**

In this example, you have installed an English version of SharePoint, and then added a German language pack. Now you want to enable the MUI support for the top site at `http://srv1`.

1. Log on as a site collection owner and open the site where MUI will be activated — `http://srv1` in this example.

2. Click Site Actions ⇨ Site Settings and then click Language Settings, in the Site Administration section. A new page named "Language Settings" lists all installed language packs.

3. Enable the alternate language German, then click OK (see Figure 4-12).

Start ▸ Site Settings ▸ Language Settings
Use this page to configure language settings for this site.

I Like It   Tags & Notes

| Start | Custom Trucks | Publishing Site | Team Site |

About this wiki

Recycle Bin
All Site Content

Default Language

The default language of the site is specified when the site is first created.

Default Language:
English

Alternate language(s)

Specify the alternate language(s) that this site will support. Users navigating to this site will be able to change the display language of the site to any one of these languages.

Alternate language(s):
☑ German

Overwrite Translations

User-specified text, such as Title and Description of the site, can be translated into the alternate language(s) supported by the site. Specify whether the changes made to user-specified text in the default language should automatically overwrite the existing translations made in all alternate languages.

Overwrite Translations:
○ Yes   ● No

FIGURE 4-12

4. Open `http://srv1` again.

5. Click on your name at the top-right corner of the page to open the menu, click Select Display Language, and select Deutsch (see Figure 4-13).

6. The page reloads; now all standard strings are in German. Open any list or library and look at the ribbon to verify that everything, except the page content and custom columns, are in German (see Figure 4-14).

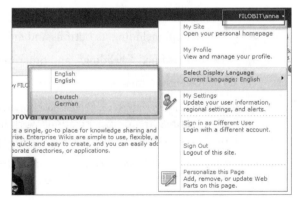

FIGURE 4-13

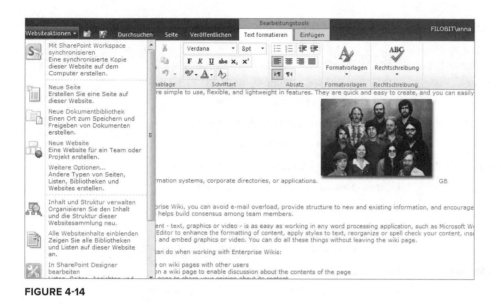

FIGURE 4-14

7. To change back to English again, click the username to open the menu, click Anzeigesprache auswählen, select English, and then click OK to confirm.

How It Works

When adding language packs to SharePoint, you can enable support for multiuser languages. Each user selects his or her preferred language, which affects all standard text strings in the site, including the ribbon, navigation, and site settings.

▶ **WHAT YOU LEARNED IN THIS CHAPTER**

TOPIC	KEY CONCEPTS
Common terms	CM — Content Management WCM — Web Content Management ECM — Enterprise Content Management MUI — Multilingual User Interface
Typical user roles in CM	Content Author — Creates and edits content Editor — Reviews and approves content Publisher — Publishes content Administrator — Manages permissions Consumer — The user who consumes the content
Important CM features	Metadata — To categorize and classify data Version history — Keep track of previous versions Check Out/In — Lock editing to one user Approval — Ensure that content is correct Workflows — Automate processes Localizations — Support MUI Policies — Define rules for content
Social computing features	Tagging — User-defined tags Comments — User-defined comments Ratings — User-defined ratings Managed metadata — Predefined metadata
Enterprise keywords	Refers to user-defined tags, sometimes known as Folksonomy
Taxonomy	Refers to predefined managed metadata
Wiki pages	Used in both SharePoint Foundation and SharePoint Server by several site templates; for example, Enterprise Wiki in SharePoint Server and Team Sites in SharePoint Foundation
Approval of content	Can be enforced on any type of list and library, including Wiki page libraries
Approval workflows	Automates the notification of approvers
Multilingual support	Requires separate installation of language packs from the Microsoft website at no cost Can be enabled per server Each user can set his or her own language preference

TOPIC	KEY CONCEPTS
Variations	Another way to support multilingual environments, based on separate sites for each language
Content Management	Procedures that enable content editors and content owners to manage any type of content, such as Web pages, Microsoft Office, documents and images
	Web content management is greatly enhanced in both SharePoint Foundation and SharePoint Server 2010
	Content management in SharePoint Server 2010 is much more advanced than in SharePoint Foundation 2010
Offline Management	Upload Center allows offline access to Office documents stored in SharePoint 2010
	Outlook 2010 supports two-way synchronization with several list types in SharePoint, such as Contacts, Calendars, and Tasks. Also, Document Libraries are supported but will not automatically replicate modified documents back to SharePoint
	SharePoint Workspace comes with Office 2010 Professional Plus, supports two-way synchronization of most list and library types in SharePoint, and automatically updates SharePoint with any offline modifications
	Access supports two-way synchronization of most list types in SharePoint, but not Document Libraries and other library types
Multilingual Support	Any site can be displayed in all languages that have been installed on the SharePoint server. These languages are available from free language packs that can be downloaded from www.microsoft.com
	Every user can choose their preferred language setting for a site, and SharePoint will remember this the next time the site opens
	Content entered by users will not be translated, but all standard text, buttons, menus, navigation objects, and list columns are translated

5

Managing My Sites

WHAT YOU WILL LEARN IN THIS CHAPTER:

➤ Understanding What My Site Is

➤ Discovering the Personal and Private Parts of My Site

➤ Getting to Know the New and Enhanced Features Compared to MOSS 2007

➤ Learning How to Create and Manage My Site

➤ Customizing My Site

➤ Adding Rollups and Web Parts

➤ Managing User Profiles

➤ Discovering How Social Computing Is Integrated in My Site

Previous chapters show you how to create different types of sites, how to use social computing features such as tagging and rating, and how to create links from sites and libraries to Microsoft Office. This chapter gives you more details about how managing sites connects to that information and explains how to get an overview of the content you work with; for example, the tags and notes you have created. In this chapter, you will learn about some important administrative aspects of My Site. You will also learn about some common features of My Site that users will be working with. This foundation of information will better help you manage the use of My Site.

For this chapter, you will need to have four demo user accounts set up in the Active Directory (AD) for Johan, Alex, Anna, and Malin. You need to grant these users Contribute permission to an intranet at `http://srv1` before proceeding with the Try It Outs in this chapter. You will also need to set up an intranet at `http://srv1`. Creating a site collection to be used as an SPS 2010 intranet is covered in Appendix D. Granting user accounts access to SharePoint sites is covered in Appendix B.

GETTING TO KNOW MY SITE

My Site is a special type of site that only comes with SharePoint Server Standard and Enterprise editions; that is, SharePoint Foundation does not support it. The basic idea is to offer each user a personal site that contains information relevant to them. It is also tightly related with a public part of My Site known as *My Profile*, which displays information about the user; for example, their name, e-mail address, department, skills, responsibilities, and interests. Some of this information is retrieved from external data sources, typically AD, and some is added manually by the user herself.

My Site was introduced in SharePoint Portal Server (SPS) 2003 and stayed basically the same in Microsoft Office SharePoint Server (MOSS) 2007, but in SharePoint Server 2010, it has been completely rebuilt to match the rich set of new features in SPS 2010.

Understanding the Purpose of Personal Sites

Although My Site is in its third generation, many organizations have hesitated to implement it, at least for all users. The main reason is that the very concept of offering a personal site to each user is sometimes hard to accept, especially for the IT department who is responsible for managing the SharePoint environment, including backup and restore.

Another common reason not to implement My Site is that the people responsible for deploying SharePoint in the organization don't understand how it works, so they decide not to implement it without testing it. This is a big mistake! My Site is a very important complement to the SharePoint environment that helps the users keep track of their personal content as well as find out information about other users. For example, the following list describes some of the more common uses of My Site in SharePoint Server 2010:

- ➤ **Store personal documents, files, and images,** instead of storing them in the traditional Home directory, which has been around for several decades.

- ➤ **Share documents and files** with other users; for example, files you want to share but that do not belong to a specific site, or documents that are not yet completed but that you still need to share with other users without sending them as e-mail attachments.

- ➤ **List all the tags and notes** you have created, and find the objects they connect to.

- ➤ **List all your member sites;** that is, team sites, project sites, and so on where you are a member. For each of these sites, you can list the documents you have been working with, as well as the tasks you have been assigned.

- ➤ **View your Mailbox and Calendar,** which requires that users have their mailboxes on Microsoft Exchange Server version 2003 or later.

- ➤ **Manage your personal blog site,** that is, add new postings and read notes to previous posts. By default, your blog is visible to all other SharePoint users.

- ➤ **View the status of your colleagues;** for example, see whether someone has created a new blog post, or whether someone has a birthday, has changed departments, and so on.

- ➤ **Update your personal profile;** for example, if you have a new responsibility or have changed your mobile phone number.

These are just some of the features that you enable when implementing My Site in your organization. Maybe explaining the consequence of *not* implementing My Site would be easier. Not implementing My Site leads to the following:

➤ A home directory on the file server must be retained.

➤ People must use e-mail when collaborating on documents that cannot be stored in a standard team site.

➤ Users will not get a global overview of their tags and notes, and therefore will not be able to open the objects that are tagged.

➤ Information about each user must be stored in another location, maybe even another system.

➤ Users will not be automatically updated about new information regarding their colleagues.

➤ Personal blogs must be created elsewhere in the SharePoint site environment.

➤ Users will not get an overview of the sites where they are members, which forces users to manually navigate to these sites.

➤ Users will not have access to an organizational chart, unless it is implemented as a special feature on the intranet, typically by purchasing a third-party product.

➤ Users will not be able to create a personal content page; for example, with RSS feeds from their favorite news sites and weather sites.

You get the idea, right? Deciding not to implement My Site is unwise, and it creates extra burden for all users, including the administrators. So please, please make sure to implement it. If you are really worried, then implement it in a smaller scale, explain to the users how it works, and let them run it for at least three months. Make sure to enter the personal properties for the users, so they can see how valuable it is to find out information about people by looking at their personal profiles in My Site. Then analyze the result. You will most likely find it a very valuable feature, and wonder how you could have survived without it before.

> **NOTE** *You'll learn more about managing My Site site collections later in this chapter and in Appendix D.*

Introducing New and Enhanced Features of My Site

When you compare My Site in MOSS 2007 with My Site in SharePoint Server 2010, you see a lot of differences. To start, the graphical layout and presentation is completely rebuilt. For example, now you have an interactive organizational chart, which is especially good-looking if you have implemented Microsoft Silverlight. Other new or enhanced features in the new version of My Site are as follows:

➤ **Ask Me About:** You can define topics that other people can ask you about. For example, you can define "WCM" as a topic you can answer questions about.

➤ **Recent Activities:** List recent activities performed by the user.

➤ **Note Board:** Use this feature to enter notes and comments that other users will see when they visit your personal site. This is similar to the Wall in Facebook.

➤ **What's Happening?:** Enter a short description of what you are doing right now. This field is typically updated very frequently, sometimes several times a day. Other users will see this description.

➤ **Organizational Chart:** Now much more interactive and graphically intuitive, this feature lets you view your colleagues and their position in the organization and traverse up and down the organizational hierarchy.

➤ **Tags and Notes:** Lists all the tags and comments or notes you have added, month per month; click a tag to open the object that was tagged (which is a quick way to find a specific document).

➤ **Memberships:** This page lists all sites where you are a member; click a site link to open that site.

➤ **Colleagues:** This page lists all of your colleagues, and you can configure how this list is displayed to other users.

➤ **My Newsfeed:** This page lists all activities related to your colleagues; your interests; and a newsfeed that lists all tags, status updates, and notes you are following.

WORKING WITH MY SITE

You must activate and configure My Site using SharePoint Central Administration before users can access it. Appendix D provides details on how to configure My Sites, which is part of the User Profile service application in SharePoint Server 2010. In this chapter, you learn how each user's My Site is created, and how to manage and use it in an effective way.

My Site really consists of two sites: one that is personal for each user, and one that is shared among all users with a personal site. The shared site displays profile information about a user; for example, the user's name, picture, and responsibility. Users don't have to know that two sites exist, but if you look carefully at the URL address, it is clear that there are two different sites, which also explains why some differences exist between some web pages. For example, sometimes the user sees the Site Action link, and sometimes not. The reason is that each user is the owner of their personal site, and therefore has access to all settings and configurations through the Site Actions menu, whereas users only have read access to the shared profile site.

Creating My Site

The first time a user accesses their personal site, it will be created automatically, which takes a few seconds, and then is ready to be used. The reason why you can view profile information about users who have not yet created their personal site is that the shared site was created when you used SharePoint Central Administration to configure the User Profile service application and its My Site.

Before your users start creating their personal sites, you should configure the navigation so users can go from My Site back to the intranet again. This navigation is not added by default, because users' personal sites are separate site collections, and therefore do not inherit navigation to other site collections in the farm. Most users expect to be able to navigate back, although it is not necessary for using My Site. The following Try It Out shows you how to configure the navigation; this capability will then be inherited by all new My Sites created after that. Any My Site that exists before this configuration will not be affected, and you will have to configure this navigation manually.

TRY IT OUT   Configuring Navigation from My Site

In this example, you are the farm administrator, and therefore have full access to the shared site used together with My Site. This procedure only has to be performed once!

1.   Log on as the farm administrator.

2.   Open the top site in the intranet; for example, `http://srv1`.

3.   Click your name in the top-right corner, and select My Profile to open the My Profile page.

4.   Click Site Actions ⇨ Site Settings to open the Site Settings page.

> **NOTE** *If you do not see the Site Actions menu, then you are not logged on as a full farm administrator — the account used to install SharePoint Server.*

5.   Click the Portal Site Connection link in the Site Collection Administration section.

6.   Select the Connect To Portal Site option and then do the following:

a.   In the Portal Web Address field, enter the URL to the intranet; for example, `http://srv1`.

b.   In the Portal Name field, enter the name of the intranet, as shown in Figure 5-1.

c.   Click OK.

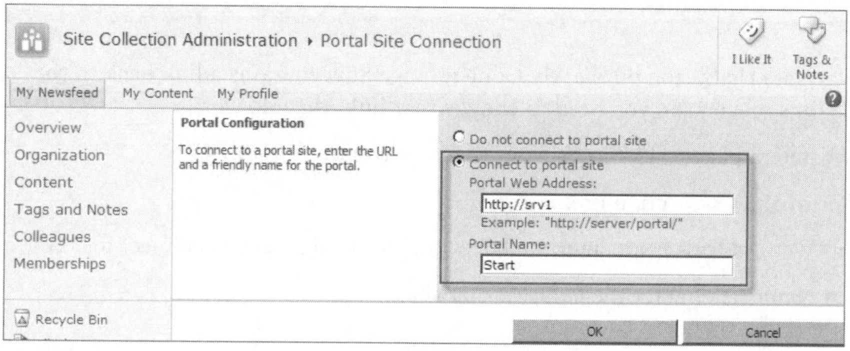

FIGURE 5-1

7.   Click the Navigate Up button on the ribbon, and verify that it now starts with the portal name you entered in step 6b (which is Start in the figure example).

How It Works

Configuring the portal site connection feature for the shared site used with My Site makes navigating back from My Site possible. This setting will also be inherited by all future personal My Sites.

After configuring the default portal site connection, users can start creating My Sites, and inherit this portal site connection automatically. Each user must create their own My Site in order to be the owner of that site. The following Try It Out shows how to create a My Site as a user.

> **NOTE** As discussed at the beginning of this chapter, you must set up an intranet at http://srv1 and user accounts for Johan, Alex, Anna, and Malin in order to follow along with the Try It Outs.

TRY IT OUT   **Creating a My Site**

In this example, you log on as the user Alex and create a personal My Site. (You will delete Alex's My Site as the site administrator in the next Try It Out.)

1. Log on as Alex, and open the intranet; for example, http://srv1.

2. Click the name Alex at the top-right corner of the web page, and select My Site. The site opens; some parts are available directly because they belong to the shared part of My Site.

3. Click My Content, and the personal part of My Site is created in a few seconds.

> **NOTE** The first time a user accesses their new My Site, they will be asked whether they want to add a link to their My Site in their Microsoft Office. This is very convenient for storing documents in My Site libraries.

4. Verify that the Navigate Up button on the My Content page now contains a link back to the intranet portal. If for some reason you need to change that link, then do this:

    a. On the My Content page, click Site Actions ➪ Site Settings.

    b. Click the Portal Site Connection link.

    c. In the Portal Web Address field, enter the URL to the site you want to connect to.

    d. In the Portal Name field, enter the name of that site.

    e. Click OK.

How It Works

A user's personal site is created when they select the My Content page for the first time. It will automatically be integrated with the shared site.

Now that you have both a personal site and the shared site, you can take a closer look at their structures. Start by opening the My Content page in My Site. Take a close look at the URL; for a user with the logon identity "alex" and an intranet that starts on `http://srv1` it will be as follows:

    http://srv1/my/personal/alex/default.aspx

Now open the My Profile page in My Site; its URL will be as follows:

    http://srv1/my/person.aspx

Finally, look at the URL for the My Newsfeed page, which is identical to the My Site page; that is, these two links show the same page:

    http://srv1/my/default.aspx

The `my` part of the URL is actually a separate site collection, which in this case was created in the same web application as the intranet portal. (See Appendix D for more information about how to configure My Sites.)

> **NOTE** You do not have to create a My Site using the same web application as the intranet portal. In fact, in medium-size and larger organizations you may want to create My Sites in a separate web application.

The `personal` part of the URL is a managed path; that is, a string delimiter that separates the `my` site collection from each user's personal site collection — in this case `alex`.

The `person.aspx` part of the URL is a page on the top page for the site collection `my`.

The `default.aspx` is also a page in the `my` site collection.

Figure 5-2 shows how these pages relate to each other.

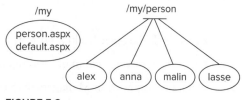

FIGURE 5-2

You need to know this site structure in order to manage individual My Sites. For example, maybe you want to back up or restore a specific user's My Site, or you want to delete the personal site for a user who left the organization — the latter example is described in the following exercise.

TRY IT OUT **Deleting a User's Personal My Site**

In this example, the user Alex has left the company, so you want to delete his personal My Site (which you created in the previous Try It Out). Note that there is no undo for this operation, so you do a backup of this site first, in case you need to restore it!

1. Log on as a farm administrator to the SharePoint server, and start the SharePoint Central Administration tool by choosing Start ➪ All Programs ➪ Microsoft SharePoint 2010 Products ➪ SharePoint 2010 Central Administration.

2. Make a backup of Alex's My Site as follows:

    a. Click Backup in the left pane of the SharePoint Central Administration tool.

    b. Click the "Perform a site collection backup" link.

    c. Click the site collection, and change it to **/srv1/my/personal/alex**.

    d. Enter the filename for the backup; for example, **\\srv1\bkup\alex_sitecollection.bak** (see Figure 5-3).

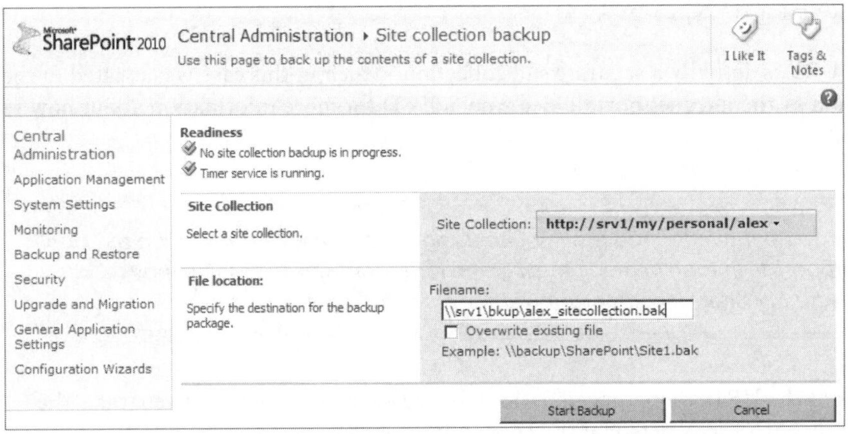

FIGURE 5-3

    e. Click the Start Backup button.

    f. Wait for the backup process to complete.

3. Open the Application Management page and click the "Delete a site collection" link. Then do the following:

    a. Click "No selection," change the site collection to **/my/personal/alex**, and click OK.

    b. Ensure that this is the correct site collection, and then click Delete.

    c. A dialog box appears that asks, "Are you sure you want to permanently delete this Web site and all its content?" Click OK to confirm this deletion.

The personal My Site for Alex is now deleted.

How It Works

The steps for deleting personal My Sites are exactly the same as for deleting any other site collection. You must be a farm administrator to delete site collections.

Table 5-1 answers some common questions related to My Sites.

TABLE 5-1: Common Questions About My Sites

QUESTION	ANSWER
Will a user still have access to SharePoint sites even if their My Site is deleted?	Yes. My Site has nothing to do with access to the rest of the SharePoint environment, only with users' personal My Sites.
If a personal site is deleted, can users re-create it?	Yes. They can do exactly what they did the first time, and the personal site will be created, but it will be empty.
Can I prohibit a user from creating a personal site?	Yes. To create a personal My Site, the user must have the proper permission, as described after this table.
Can I move a personal My Site to another farm; for example, if the user wants to take it with them to a new organization?	Yes, if the new organization also runs SharePoint Server 2010, and supports the same language. You simply take a site collection backup of the personal site, and then restore it in the new SharePoint farm.
Can users select their preferred language on their personal My Site?	Yes, if the required language pack is installed on the server. Users need to enable language support (see Chapter 4) for their personal My Site. The farm administrator must also enable language support for the shared part of My Site. If these conditions are true, then the language that the user selects for any site (for example, the intranet) will also be selected for all pages of My Site.

One of the questions in the preceding table asks about permission to create My Site. This question is important and needs to be answered in detail. By default, all authenticated users and users with read-only access can create a personal My Site. This permission is regulated by a configuration setting in the User Profile service application. Note that there is no Deny permission to exclude a single user; instead, you must create a security group in AD that doesn't include the user you want to prohibit from creating the personal My Site, as described in the following Try It Out. However, even if users don't have a personal site, they can still view other users' shared My Site part; that is, the part that shows user profile information.

> **NOTE** *As discussed at the beginning of this chapter, you must set up an intranet at* `http://srv1` *and grant Contribute access to the user accounts for Johan, Alex, Anna, and Malin in order to follow along with the Try It Outs.*

TRY IT OUT Prohibiting a User from Creating a Personal My Site

In this example, you're going to prohibit Alex from creating a personal My Site. To complete this exercise, you must have permission to create a new security group in AD.

1. Log on as a Domain Administrator on any Domain Controller.

2. Start the Active Directory Users and Computers (ADUC) by choosing Start ➪ Administrative Tools ➪ Active Directory Users and Computers. Continue as follows:

   a. Open the organizational unit container where the new security group will be created; for example, Users.

   b. Click the "Create a new group in the current container" button.

   c. Enter a group name; for example, **My Site Users,** and ensure that the Group type is set as Security. Click Next.

   d. If you get an option to create an Exchange e-mail address, skip it. Click Next.

   e. The last page that appears is a summary. Verify that the name and container are correct, and then click Finish.

3. Populate this new group with the users that you want to be able to create a personal My Site, like this:

   a. Locate the new group name.

   b. Double-click the group name, and select the Members tab.

   c. Click Add and add all users who can create personal My Sites.

   d. Click OK.

4. Now you have the security group with users who can create a personal My Site. The next step is to grant that group the corresponding permissions in SharePoint. Log on to the SharePoint server as a farm administrator.

5. Start the SharePoint Central Administration tool, as described earlier in this chapter.

6. Open the Application Management page.

7. Click Manage Service Applications.

8. Click User Profile Service Application.

9. Click Manage User Permissions in the People section to open the Permissions for User Profile Service Application page, and then do the following:

    a. Select and remove all existing security groups in the middle field.

    b. In the top field, enter the name of the security group that you created in step 3, and click Add.

    c. Set all three options for your group: User Personal Features, Create Personal Sites, and User Social Features.

    d. Click OK.

10. Test this new setting. Make sure people log off and then on again to update their group membership, and then try to create a personal site for a user who is not a member of the new security group. When you click that user's name to open the menu, it will no longer contain any links to My Site.

How It Works

The permission to create My Sites, Social Features, and Personal Features is regulated by settings in the User Profile Service Application.

Understanding the Basic Features of My Site

My Site comes with a number of basic features that make it a valuable tool for users. These features are divided into different pages to make My Site easier to work with, because they later will display a lot of information. My Site has the following three pages:

➤ **My Newsfeed:** Displays a summary of activities

➤ **My Content:** Contains personal lists and libraries

➤ **My Profile:** Provides information about the user's content

There is also one more tab, My Site, but it opens the same page as My Newsfeed. More details about these pages follow.

My Newsfeed

This page displays an update about information and actions related to a user's colleagues, their interests, and their newsfeeds. The idea behind this page is to give the user a page to get a quick overview of what is happening; for example, if a colleague has changed their phone number, or if a new note exists for a web page. Table 5-2 describes how to manage these three areas.

TABLE 5-2: The Newsfeed Areas

AREA NAME	DESCRIPTION	COMMENTS
My Colleagues	Displays a list of your colleagues	Click this link to open the Colleagues tab on the My Profile page, where you can add new colleagues or accept suggested colleagues.
My Interests	Defines what information you are interested in; for example, a user profile update, a new blog post, or that someone is leaving a note on My Site	Click this link to open the page with your profile settings. You can also open this page by choosing My Profile ⇨ Edit My Profile.
My Newsfeed	Defines what activities you want to see in this newsfeed	Click this link to open the same page as for My Interests and define the activities you are interested in.

My Content

My Content is your personal content. If you used My Sites in MOSS 2007, you will recognize this page; it shows your personal lists and libraries, both for private information and for that which you share with others. By default, it contains the following lists and libraries:

➤ **Personal Documents:** A document library that only the user has access to. This library corresponds to the traditional Home directory (H:) on a file server. It has the same features as any other SharePoint library; for example, you can create custom columns, enable Version History, and run workflows.

➤ **Shared Documents:** A document library that is configured so every user in the organization is granted read access to its content; that is, users can read and copy but not update files in this library. This place is very good for storing documents you want to share with others, instead of sending them by e-mail.

➤ **Shared Pictures:** An image library to which all users in the organization have read access. Use it to share your pictures with other users.

If you have created a blog site or any other subsite in your My Site, the My Content page lists a link to these sites. You can also create new list, as described in the following Try It Out.

> **NOTE** *The default permission for all new lists and libraries in My Site is to allow read access to all users. Make sure to change that setting if you want to store personal information.*

> **NOTE** *As discussed at the beginning of this chapter, you must set up an intranet at* http://srv1 *and user accounts for Johan, Alex, Anna, and Malin in order to follow along with the Try It Outs.*

TRY IT OUT   Adding New Lists to My Site

In this example, you're going create a calendar for golf as user Anna, to be shared with Malin and Alex only.

1.   Log on as Anna, and open Anna's My Site.

2.   Switch to the My Content page.

3.   Click Site Actions ➪ More Options to display all the different types of lists, libraries, and sites you (as Anna) can create. Then do the following to add a golf calendar to share with Malin and Alex:

    a.   Click on Calendar.

    b.   Enter the name **Golf**.

    c.   Click Create. The calendar appears.

    d.   Click List Permissions on the ribbon to change the default access.

    e.   Click Stop Inheriting Permissions on the ribbon, and click OK to confirm.

    f.   Select the NT Authority\Authenticated Users and Viewers check box, and click Remove User Permissions on the ribbon. Click OK to confirm.

    g.   Click Grant Permission, enter **Malin; Alex** in the Users/Groups field, and then click Check Names.

    h.   Set the Read permission for Malin and Alex.

    i.   Enter a personal message that will be sent to these users as e-mail.

    j.   Click OK.

The new Golf calendar list is ready to be used. Everything you type here is readable for Malin and Alex. If they want to make reading this calendar easy, they can synchronize it with their Outlook clients.

How It Works

The steps for adding lists, libraries, and subsites to My Site are exactly the same as for adding this type of content to any standard SharePoint site.

Because each user is the site owner of their My Content page, they can change its content whenever needed. They can also change the web parts and layouts of this page. You learn more about that later in this chapter.

My Profile

The My Profile page appears when you click on another user's name. For example, if Anna is listed as the author of a document, and you click her name, then her My Profile page appears. This page contains a lot of information, so to make using the information easy, it is divided into the following six tabs:

    ➤   **Overview:** This is the default tab for My Profile. It shows recent activities, Ask me about, the organization chart, the note board, and In common with You; that is, when you look at another user's Overview page, you will see what you two have in common, such as being members in the same team site.

➤ **Organization:** An interactive presentation of the user's position in the organization, based on properties about who they report to, and who reports to them. This information is usually retrieved from AD. Use this chart to traverse up and down the organization to view information about any user.

➤ **Content:** This page lists all content that this user shares with you, including their latest blog posts.

➤ **Tags and Notes:** Shows the tags and notes created by this user. You can select a specific month, and filter on the type (tag or note), sorted alphabetically or by size. This page also shows a tag cloud that indicates how frequently a tag is used. You can click a tag to view all objects associated with this tag, click a document that is tagged, or click View Related Activities to view all tags and notes linked to this object (see Figure 5-4).

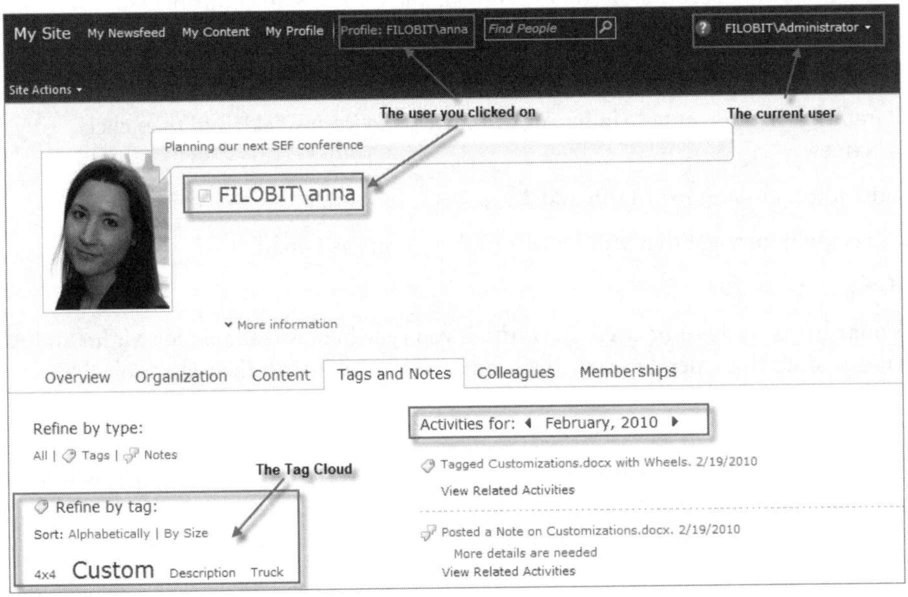

FIGURE 5-4

➤ **Colleagues:** This page lists all colleagues for a user. If you need to find out more about these colleagues, just click their names (see Figure 5-5).

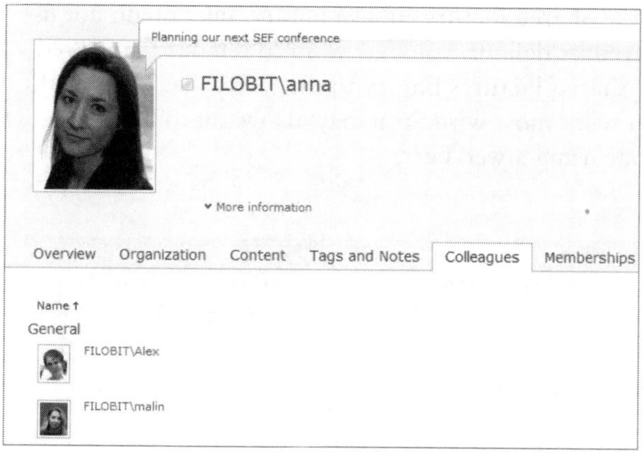

FIGURE 5-5

➤ **Memberships:** This page lists all sites where this user is listed as a member of the Member SharePoint group. For example, if the Phantom site has unique permissions, it will have three default SharePoint groups: Phantom Visitors, Phantom Members, and Phantom Owners; only users in Phantom Members will see the Phantom site listed on the Membership page (see Figure 5-6).

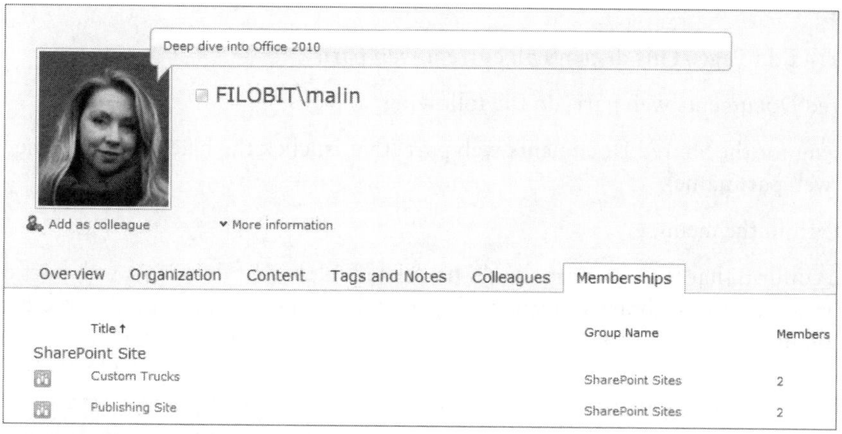

FIGURE 5-6

Extending and Personalizing My Site

A user with a personal My Site can customize it to meet their needs. For example, they can add web parts to the My Content page that lists their personal document library and images. However, they cannot change the layout of the shared part of My Site, because that is a separate site. But they can edit their personal profile; for example, their picture, mobile phone, and assistant.

The personal My Site part, that is, My Content, is fully owned by the user, which means that they can add and delete new lists, libraries, and web parts to this site. They can also add navigation links and change the site theme to make it more personal.

For example, if you are working a lot with the Shared Pictures image library, but you do not use the Shared Documents library that is displayed by default, you may want to remove the Shared Documents from the web page and add the Shared Pictures library to the web page. This would make it easier for you to see the content you work most with. You may also want to display an RSS feed on your personal page; this is easily done using a web part.

> **NOTE** *As discussed at the beginning of this chapter, you must set up an intranet at* http://srv1 *and user accounts for Johan, Alex, Anna, and Malin in order to follow along with the Try It Outs.*

TRY IT OUT **Displaying Libraries and RSS Web Parts on the My Content Page**

In this example, you're going to display Shared Pictures and Personal Documents only on My Content.

1. Log on as a user with a newly created My Site; in this example, you are the user Johan.

2. Open Johan's My Site.

3. Click My Content.

4. Click Site Actions ⇨ Edit Page. This displays all current web parts.

5. To delete the Shared Documents web part, do the following:

   a. Open the menu for the Shared Documents web part (that is, click the black arrow to the right of the web part name).

   b. Select Delete from the menu.

   c. Click OK to confirm that the web part should be deleted. Note that deleting a web part does not affect the actual list or library it displays. If you make a mistake, just add the web part for this list again.

> **NOTE** *Another way to manage web parts is to select the check box to the right of the web part name, and switch to the Web Part Tools tab on the ribbon.*

6. Now you're going to add the Shared Picture library. Click the Add a Web Part in the Middle Left Zone link at the top of the Middle Left Zone, and then do the following:

   a. Select Lists And Libraries in the Categories pane.

   b. Select Shared Pictures.

   c. Click Add.

d. The new web part for Shared Pictures now appears at the top of the Middle Left Zone. But you want Shared Documents to be at the top. Simply use the mouse to drag the Shared Documents web part to the top, and then release the mouse button.

7. Click the Stop Editing button on the ribbon (on the Page tab for this web page).

8. Add some files to these two libraries to see how they look on the web page.

9. Add an RSS web part that shows the RSS feed from a public Internet site, such as www.microsoft.com/presspass, as follows:

a. Open this site's page in edit mode (choose Site Actions ⇨ Edit Page).

b. In the Middle Right Zone, click Add A Web Part.

c. Select the Recommended Items category and select RSS Viewer in the right pane.

d. Click Add.

e. In the new web part, click the "Open the tool pane" link.

f. In the RSS Feed URL field, enter the URL to the RSS source; in this example, **http://www.microsoft.com/presspass/rss/TopStory.xml**.

g. Change the Feed refresh time to 60 minutes to check for updates once per hour, and then select the "Show feed title and description" option.

h. Click OK.

i. Click Stop Editing on the ribbon.

j. Verify that the RSS feed shows information. If you get an error, you may need to configure your web proxy settings.

How It Works

As on any other site, web parts can be added to and deleted from the My Content page. However, a user can only do this for their own My Content page on their personal My Site.

Another popular customization is to change the colors for this site. Note that this change only affects the personal site, not the shared part of My Site. The easiest way to change colors is to change the site theme, as described in the next Try It Out.

> **NOTE** As discussed at the beginning of this chapter, you must set up an intranet at http://srv1 and user accounts for Johan, Alex, Anna, and Malin in order to follow along with the Try It Outs.

TRY IT OUT   **Displaying the Site Theme**

In this example, you, as user Johan, are going to change the theme (that is, the colors and fonts) for your personal site to make it easier to distinguish when you're on the personal site versus the shared part of My Site.

1. Log on as Johan and open Johan's My Site.

2. Click Site Actions ⇨ Site Settings to open the Site Settings page.

3. Click Site theme in the Look and Feel section, and then do the following:

     a. Select another theme you like; for example, Azure.

     b. Click Apply.

4. Verify that the new site theme is what you want. If it's not, change the theme. To go back to the first theme, select Default Theme.

How It Works

Themes are preconfigured settings of the colors used on a website. When applying a new theme, you are, in fact, applying a new Cascading Style Sheet (CSS) setting to this web page.

A common request is the ability to modify the navigation parts of My Content, such as to add links to other web pages in SharePoint or on an external site. You have two options: You can either add links to a top bar on your personal site, or add them to the quick launch bar to the left of the page.

TRY IT OUT   **Adding a Link for the Intranet**

In this exercise, you add one link at the top that points to the start page for the intranet `http://srv1`. Then you add a link to `www.microsoft.com` on the quick launch bar.

1. Log on as Johan and open the My Content page in Johan's My Site.

2. Choose Site Actions ⇨ Site Settings to open the Site Settings page.

3. Add a link to the top link bar as follows:

     a. Click Top Link Bar in the Look and Feel section.

     b. Click New Navigation Link.

     c. In the Type The Web Address field, enter **`http://srv1`**.

     d. In the Description field, enter **Intranet**.

     e. Click OK to save and close.

     f. Verify that the new Intranet link is visible and opens the right site.

4. Now add a link to the quick launch bar to `www.microsoft.com` as follows:

     a. Choose Site Actions ⇨ Site Settings.

    b.   Click Quick Launch.

    c.   To make finding the new link easy, create a heading for it: **Click New Heading.**

    d.   You must also enter a URL to a heading, even if you don't intend to use it, so enter the URL to your current site, which is in this example is `http://srv1/my/personal/johan`.

    e.   Enter the description **External Sites,** and then click OK.

    f.   Now add the actual link: **Click New Navigation Link.**

    g.   Enter the web address: `http://www.microsoft.com`.

    h.   Enter the description: **MS Home.**

    i.   Select the External Sites heading.

    j.   Click OK.

5.   Open the My Content page and verify that both of these new links are visible and work as expected.

How It Works

Navigation links enable you to quickly reach sites that users work with. Note that you don't have to add links to SharePoint sites where you are a member, because these sites will be listed automatically on the Memberships page (on My Profile).

Creating Rollups for Documents and Sites

A *rollup* is a web part that shows information stored in other sites and systems. For example, if you want to see all the sites where you are a member, then you would use a rollup web part. SharePoint Server comes with the following rollup web parts, which are all listed under the Content Rollups web part category:

➤   **Memberships:** Lists all sites and distribution groups of which you are a member.

➤   **SharePoint Documents:** Lists all documents authored by you but only in sites of which you are a member.

➤   **My SharePoint Sites:** Lists all documents authored by you in sites where you are a member. You can also add other sites to this list.

➤   **My Inbox:** Lists the content in your Exchange main inbox.

➤   **My Calendar:** Lists the content in your Exchange calendar.

➤   **My Contact:** Lists all contacts in your Exchange contact folder.

➤   **My Mail Folder:** Lists all content in any given Exchange folder that you have at least read access to.

➤   **My Tasks:** Lists all task items in your Exchange task folder.

The Outlook-related web parts are a nice way to view the new content in your Microsoft Outlook folders. Notice that because these web parts require a mailbox name, they can only be used on personal My Site and not on a public page. However, you can use another neat trick if you want to display public folders in a SharePoint page, and it does not require that you add them to My Site. It will work on any site, as long as the readers of that site also have at least read access to the public folder.

For example, suppose that you have a public folder named Project-Calendar under All Public Folders; to display that calendar on a web site, you add a Page Viewer web part, which is configured to show the following URL link. See also the next Try It Out.

```
http://<exchange>/public/<folderpath>/?cmd=contents&part=1
```

If the Exchange server runs on server DC1, then this link would be as follows:

```
http://DC1/public/Project-Calendar/?cmd=contents&part=1
```

In the following exercise, you see how public folder web parts work.

> **NOTE** *As discussed at the beginning of this chapter, you must set up an intranet at* http://srv1 *and user accounts for Johan, Alex, Anna, and Malin in order to follow along with the Try It Outs.*

TRY IT OUT **Displaying a Public Folder Calendar in SharePoint**

In this example, you'll display the Project-Calendar public folder on the My Content page. The Exchange Server is running on DC1.

1. Log on as Johan, and open Johan's My Content page. Remember that this trick also works in other SharePoint sites.

2. Choose Site Actions ⇨ Edit Page to open this page in edit mode.

3. Click Add A Web Part in the Top Zone.

4. Select the Media and Content web part category.

5. Select Page Viewer.

6. Click Add.

7. In the web part, click Open The Tool Pane.

8. In the tool pane (at the right), do the following:

    a. Select to display a Web Page (the default).

    b. In the link field, enter **http://DC1/public/Project-Calendar/?cmd=contents&part=1**.

    c. Expand the Appearance section.

d. Set the title as **Project Calendar**.

e. Click OK. The new calendar should appear immediately.

9. Click Stop Editing on the ribbon (on the Page tab).

10. Verify that you can see the calendar (Figure 5-7).

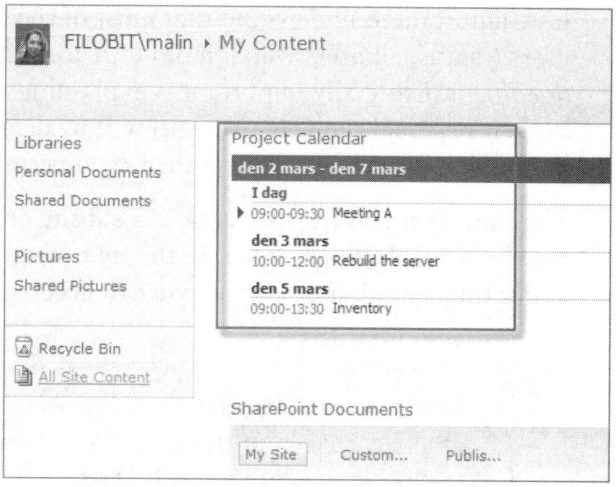

How It Works

You can use the Page View web part to display public folders. You need to know the URL path to that folder, and add a command that will control how the public folder will be displayed.

FIGURE 5-7

NOTE *You can also use the command* `?cmd=contents&view=Weekly` *(or* `Daily` *or* `Monthly`*) with this URL path.*

Managing Access Control to My Sites

The default access for My Sites depends on what pages and objects you are looking at. Typically everyone has read access to the public parts, whereas the personal site is partly open, partly locked down, as described in Table 5-3.

TABLE 5-3: Default Permissions in My Site

OBJECT	DEFAULT PERMISSION
My Newsfeed	All authenticated users have read access. Farm administrator has full control.
My Content — Site Permissions	All authenticated users have read access. The Viewers SharePoint group has view-only access. Each user has full control over his or her site.
My Content — Personal Documents	Unique permissions — no one except the owner has access.
My Profile — Site Permissions	All authenticated users have read access. Each user has full control over his or her site content; that is, lists and libraries.

It is important to understand that most of the content in My Site is open for all authenticated users (that is, all users who log on) to read and copy content, except a single object: the *personal document*. Especially important is explaining to users that all new lists and libraries they create in their personal site (My Content) will by default be readable by all users, unless they break the permission inheritance and set their own permissions.

The same is true if the user creates a subsite and accepts to inherit permissions — then that site will also be readable by everyone. In the following Try It Out, you create a new list, and then a subsite, and set the permission so only you can access that information.

> **NOTE** *As discussed at the beginning of this chapter, you must set up an intranet at* `http://srv1` *and user accounts for Johan, Alex, Anna, and Malin in order to follow along with the Try It Outs.*

TRY IT OUT Creating Personal Lists and Subsites in My Site

In this example, you'll create a personal contact list as user Johan and then add a personal subsite for a special interest, guitars.

1. Log on as Johan and open Johan's My Content page.

2. Create the personal contact list, as follows:

   a. Choose Site Actions ⇨ More Options to open the Create page.

   b. Select Contact, enter **Geek Friends** in the Name field, and then click Create.

   c. By default this list can be read by anyone. To change this to a personal list, click List Permissions on the ribbon to open the Permission page that displays all groups and users with access to this list.

   d. Click Stop Inheriting Permissions, and then click OK to confirm.

   e. Select the two names NT AUTHORITY\Authenticated Users and Viewers, and then click Remove User Permissions. Click OK to confirm. The list is now exclusively yours (as Johan).

3. Create a personal subsite as follows:

   a. Open My Content again.

   b. Choose Site Actions ⇨ New Site.

   c. Select Team Site and click the More Options button.

   d. Set the Title to **Guitars**, the Description to **All you want to know about guitars**, and the URL name to **guitars**.

   e. Change the User Permissions to Use Unique Permissions. This is the key to creating a private subsite!

   f. Click Create.

g. Because you requested unique permissions, you must define the access to this site. By default you (as Johan, the creator) will be listed both as a member and an owner. Because no other user in this example will have access, this is what you need now. Click OK to create the subsite.

h. This site is now ready to be used. Verify that Guitar is listed as a link on the top navigation bar. Only you (as Johan) can see its name and access its content.

How It Works

Be aware that the default permission for all sites in My Site is set to allow every authenticated user read access. If you want a private list or site, you have to change the permission for that object.

DISCOVERING THE HUB FOR INTERACTING WITH PEOPLE

In SharePoint Server 2010, My Site is a very important module for managing social computing features, such as tags, notes and comments, and ratings. These features help the user to not only get an overview of the content that is interesting to them, but also to tell other users what they think and like. My Site is also used to show user properties — referred to as *user profiles* in SharePoint. This section describes how to manage both social computing features and user profiles.

Managing Personal Profiles

A very common situation is this: You need someone who can answer a specific question, but you don't know who to ask. So you contact another person you believe may be able to help you, but they just refer you to a third person. This person has no clue, so you are back to square one again. After some more hunting, you finally find someone who could help you, but what you didn't know is that you actually had an expert just 10 yards from your desk. This is irritating to you (and to the people you disturb), because finding the answer takes time, and it forces you to focus on things other than what you really need to work on. There must be a better way.

Rest assured — there is a better way! In SharePoint Server, every user can define their own responsibilities, skills, and interests. This information is stored in a special database table called User Profile.

Configuring User Profiles

Before you can start using user profiles, you must configure the User Profile service application using SharePoint Central Administration. Appendix D provides details about how to do this. This chapter focuses more on managing the user profile properties.

There are three ways to input data to the User Profile database:

➤ You can import from external sources, for example AD.

➤ An administrator manages the user profile properties.

➤ Each user enters values into their own user profile.

The two first options require that you manage the user profiles with the SharePoint Central Administration tool or by running PowerShell. The third option is to use My Site. By default, My Site allows users to change the following user profile properties:

➤ **About Me:** Enter a personal description of yourself; for example, who you are and what you like to work with.

➤ **Picture:** Upload and display a picture of yourself.

➤ **Ask Me About:** Enter keywords that describe topics you know well, and that you are prepared to answer questions about.

➤ **Mobile Phone:** Enter your cell phone number.

➤ **Fax:** Enter your fax number.

➤ **Home Phone:** Enter your home phone number.

➤ **Time Zone:** Enter the time zone where you live.

➤ **Assistant:** Enter the name of your assistant.

➤ **Past Projects:** Enter the names of recent projects you believe other users may be interested in.

➤ **Skills:** Enter your skills, separated by a comma (for example "SharePoint, Exchange")

➤ **Schools:** Enter what schools you have attended.

➤ **Birthday:** Enter your birth date (not the year); for example, May 16.

➤ **Interests:** Enter your personal and business interests.

➤ **Email Notifications:** Select the events you want to be notified about. By default, all actions are selected.

➤ **Activities I Am Following:** Select the activities you want to follow. By default, all options are selected.

Most of these fields are integrated with managed metadata. This means that if a previous user has added a certain keyword or tag, and you begin typing a word that starts with the same letters, a list of matching suggestions appears. In the following Try It Out, you add a picture and enter *SharePoint* as a keyword in Skills.

> **NOTE** *As discussed at the beginning of this chapter, you must set up an intranet at* `http://srv1` *and grant Contribute access to the user accounts for Johan, Alex, Anna, and Malin in order to follow along with the Try It Outs.*

TRY IT OUT Managing My Profile

In this example you, as user Johan, will add a picture to your user profile, and enter the keyword *SharePoint* as a skill. You will also enter a home phone number, but only make it visible to his manager.

1. Log on as Johan, and open Johan's My Profile page on My Site.

2. Click Edit My Profile.

3. To add a picture, click Choose Picture, and browse for a picture you want other users to see. Avoid using a picture that is larger than 300 pixels, because it requires disk space to store it and CPU resources to resize it in real time, every time this picture is displayed.

4. Enter a home phone number in the Home Phone field, and then select My Manager from the As Seen By menu.

5. Scroll down to Skills, and enter **SharePoint**. Note that if someone has already created this keyword or tag, then you will see a list of suggestions as soon as you type the first few characters (for example, `Sha`).

6. At the top or bottom of this long page, click Save and Close.

7. Now you see the new picture, but not the skills; click More Information to see that property (Figure 5-8). If another user does a people search and enters `SharePoint`, Johan will be listed in the result.

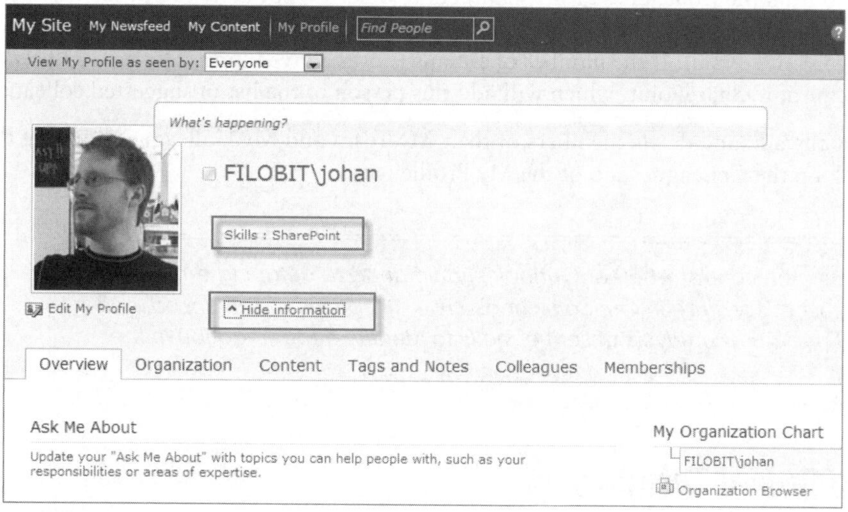

FIGURE 5-8

How It Works

The user can edit some, but not all, properties that are stored in the User Profile database, using the Edit My Profile link in My Site. There are more properties for each user, but they are either set by the farm administrator in the User Profile service application in SharePoint Central Administration, or they are copied from an external data source, typically AD.

Managing Visibility for User Profile Properties

Most, but not all, of the properties in a user profile are visible to all users in the organization. Every property is indexed so a user can search for a person with a specific property; for example, people working in the Finance department, or users with a specific skill. However, sometimes storing more personal properties in the user profile, without making them available to all users, is necessary. This is why SharePoint allows you to define the visibility, also known as the *privacy level*, for each property.

You can use the following five groups for targeting the visibility for user properties:

➤   **Only Me:** As it says, information only you can see

➤   **My Manager:** The person you report to, according to the organization chart

➤   **My Team:** A group that you define

➤   **My Colleagues:** The group you have defined as colleagues

➤   **Everyone**

Two of these visibility groups are defined by the user: My Team and My Colleagues. The other three are computed automatically by SharePoint. Colleagues are added manually by the user, and team members are selected from the Colleagues group. SharePoint looks at your activities to see whether someone should be suggested as a colleague. For example, Outlook 2010 has a special feature that analyzes to whom you send e-mail. If the number of e-mails is over a given limit, Outlook will send the name of this recipient to SharePoint, which will add this person to the list of suggested colleagues.

Each user can manually add and delete members of their My Team and My Colleagues by using the Add Colleagues link on the Colleagues tab of the My Profile page.

> **NOTE** *A user can control whether Outlook should analyze outgoing e-mail or not. To enable this feature in Outlook, choose File ➪ Options ➪ Advanced, and then select the "Allow analysis of sent e-mails to identify people" option in the Other section.*

Understanding Social Tagging

Chapter 4 describes social computing in detail, so this section just provides a quick summary. This feature is new in SharePoint Server 2010; it is not available in SharePoint Foundation 2010. It allows users to add their own tags, notes, and comments to objects, and also rank any kind of object in SharePoint, such as web pages, documents, and pictures.

Adding tags and notes to documents and other objects helps the user categorize and remember the content. It is also an excellent way to find these objects later on; that is, the user does not have to search or remember where that objects where stored.

Seeing what tags, notes, and ratings a specific user has added is also very interesting for other users. For example, if Malin is a Microsoft Office expert, and she rates two documents about Microsoft Office development as 5 stars, then Johan will certainly be more interested in these two documents if he needs to read about Microsoft Office development.

My Site in SharePoint Server 2010 is designed to help users keep track of tags and notes, both their own as well as what other users have created. This section describes how that works.

Viewing Status Updates and Activities

Every time you add a tag, a keyword, or a note for an object, it appears on the Tags And Notes tab of your My Profile page. This tab shows the following information about tags and notes:

➤ A tag cloud appears, in which frequently used tags appear in a larger font.

➤ A summary of activities lists all tags and notes for a specific month.

➤ Click a tag to see a list of all activities for that tag.

➤ Click a tagged object (for example, a document or a site) to open it.

➤ Click the View Related Activities link for a tagged object to open that tag page and see what other tags this object has, who added them, and when.

➤ Users can delete a tag or note, or change it to a private tag so that other people will not be able to view or search for it.

These are very powerful features that users will love, but because they are new in SharePoint Server 2010, you may have to train your users before they truly appreciate the benefits of these status updates and activity lists.

Working with Bookmarks

You can tag more than just objects inside SharePoint. SharePoint Server 2010 comes with a special *bookmark tool* that makes it possible for users to tag any external site or page. This tool works with all the supported web browsers, such as Internet Explorer, Firefox, and Safari. The following Try It Out shows you how to work with this bookmark tool.

> **NOTE** *As discussed at the beginning of this chapter, you must set up an intranet at* `http://srv1` *and grant Contribute permissions to the user accounts for Johan, Alex, Anna, and Malin in order to follow along with the Try It Outs.*

TRY IT OUT   **Working with Bookmarks**

In this example, you, as user Anna, will enable the bookmark tool in Internet Explorer in order to add tags and notes to external content related to your job.

1. Log on as Anna, open Anna's My Profile, and switch to the Tags And Notes tab.

2. At the bottom of the page, right-click the link that says "Right-click or drag and drop this link to your browser's favorites or bookmarks toolbar to tag external sites," and select Add To Favorites.

3. You will be presented with a security alert box that says "You are adding a favorite that might not be safe. Do you want to continue?" Click Yes. Select in what Favorite folder you want to add this **Tags And Note Board** link.

4. Time to test this bookmark tool: Open a new browser tab, and then navigate to an external site; for example, `http://sharepoint.microsoft.com`.

5. Open the Favorites menu and select Tags And Notes Board. The Tags And Notes page opens.

6. Add **SharePoint** as a tag, and then click Save.

7. Open the Tags And Notes tab on Anna's My Profile. The latest activity says "Tagged Microsoft Office SharePoint . . . with SharePoint." Click this link and verify that it opens the external site.

How It Works

The *bookmark tool* allows a user to add tags and notes to any web page on the Internet. This makes it very easy to go back to important resources. For example, tagging all documents, sites, and external websites you are working with in a project with the same tag provides a very easy way to find them all, regardless of where they are located.

Using the Note Board

My Site offers one more cool feature: the Note Board. If you have worked with the Wall in Facebook and other social media, you know how this works. The idea is that users can post questions and notes to a specific person, and then this person can reply. Others can see this conversation, which may help them in their daily work.

The Note Board is a replacement for e-mail conversations. Its biggest advantage is that any user can check this conversation, even if they were not involved from the beginning. A typical scenario is when someone is looking at your Tags And Notes page, and suddenly realizes that the Note Board conversation contains information they're also interested in. They may even decide to jump into the conversation, and comment or add new questions.

▶ **WHAT YOU LEARNED IN THIS CHAPTER**

TOPIC	KEY CONCEPTS
My Site	My Sites are based on two different site collections: one personal and one shared.
	The user is the owner of their own personal site.
	My Sites are managed by the User Profile service application.
Usage of My Site	My Sites are used to store personal and shared information, such as documents and pictures.
	My Site lists all tags and notes entered by a user.
	My Site can be used to display personal web parts, like Inbox.
	My Site shows the status of colleagues.
	My Site displays your organizational structure.
	My Site lists documents and sites where you are a member.
	Use My Site to manage your user profile.
New and enhanced features in My Site	Tags and notes.
	The Ask Me About feature.
	Your recent activities.
	Note Board, which is like FaceBook's Wall.
	A graphical organizational chart.
	What's Happening, which describes what you are doing right now.
	My Newsfeed, a summary page with all new activities for colleagues and My Team members.
My Site permissions	By default, every authenticated user can create a My Site.
	By default, every list and library is readable by any user, except personal documents.
	All subsites created in My Site will be readable by all users, unless the Use Unique Permissions option is selected
Basic structure of My Site	My Site consists of three main pages:
	My Newsfeed: A public page
	My Content: The personal site
	My Profile: A public page
My Profile	The properties listed in My Profile are defined in the User Profile service application.
	Some user properties are copied from an external system, typically AD.
	Farm administrators can edit user properties.
	End users can edit some properties, but not all.

TOPIC	KEY CONCEPTS
Customizing My Site	Add new lists and libraries.
	Add web parts, including RSS and My Inbox.
	Change the site theme.
	Display public folder calendars with the Page Viewer web part.
Social computing features	My Site lists tags and notes.
	A tag cloud indicates the most popular tags for this user.
	Click on tags and notes to open that object.
	Add a bookmark tool to add tags and notes to any website on the Internet.
	Use the Note Board for public dialogues.

6

SharePoint Administration

WHAT YOU WILL LEARN IN THIS CHAPTER:

➤ Understand SharePoint Permissions

➤ Learn to Configure Custom Permission Levels

➤ Manage SharePoint Groups

➤ Work with List, Library, and Site Templates

➤ Manage Search and Indexing Features

➤ Learn How to Index PDF Files

➤ Customize Search Web Parts

➤ Learn About Antivirus Solutions

➤ Work with STSADM and PowerShell

In previous chapters, you have seen many examples of how to configure and manage different SharePoint features. Appendixes B and D also contain many detailed configuration settings. This chapter summarizes the typical tasks and settings that a SharePoint 2010 administrator will deal with.

SETTING UP FOR ADMINISTRATION

This chapter is going to use a simple setup of a test environment for administration. If you duplicate this setup, you can easily follow along with the Try It Outs in this chapter. Or if you have an existing setup, you can substitute existing users, document libraries, and groups that you already have. Follow these steps to set up the core essentials for this chapter:

1. Create a site collection with the URL http://srv1 with the title "Start." If you are running SharePoint Foundation, then follow the instructions in Appendix A; if you are running SharePoint Server, then follow the instructions in Appendix C.

Installing this Start site will automatically create three SharePoint groups: Start Members, Start Visitors and Start Owners.

2. Create these domain accounts: Johan, Anna, Beatrice, and Malin. You will grant these users different permissions to see how they affect these users and what features they can use.

3. Create a subsite named Team Site based on the site template Team Site. Enter the URL = `http://srv1/teamsite`.

WARNING *Whenever learning new processes, it is better to not work in real systems that are being used by existing businesses. It is safer to set up a separate test environment to experiment with.*

CONTROLLING WHAT USERS CAN DO IN SHAREPOINT

SharePoint 2010 is a web application, and therefore relies on the Internet Information Services module in Windows Server 2008 for authentication of users; that is, it requires that the password and user account match. In other words, SharePoint does not authenticate users; instead it contains definitions of what permissions users and groups have to SharePoint objects, like sites and documents, to ensure that intended users can do what they are allowed to do.

SharePoint 2010 has a rich set of security features, which are basically the same as those of its predecessor MOSS 2007. One important difference is that you can now more easily delegate administrative permissions to the new service applications, and to the managed metadata store. Larger organizations often need to delegate different tasks to different subject matter experts. This was rather hard in MOSS 2007, but in SharePoint 2010 it will be much easier.

Permissions rule both what users can do, and what objects and features an administrator can manage. This section describes the different scenarios that you must understand as a SharePoint administrator, so you can inform your local site owners and users how permissions work in SharePoint 2010. Most of the following information is valid for both SharePoint Foundation and SharePoint Server 2010, unless otherwise indicated.

The Different Types of Administrators

An administrator is a person who can configure and manage one or more objects in SharePoint; for example, a site collection, a site, or a document library. Note that no relationship exists between a SharePoint administrator and a Windows Domain administrator. Having high permissions in SharePoint without being a network administrator is perfectly okay. This is important, because many organizations need to delegate administrative permissions to users without requiring them to have administrative permissions to the Windows Domain. In smaller organizations, a common occurrence is that the same person is both a domain administrator and a full SharePoint administrator. Deciding what is best for your organization is up to you.

There are three main levels of administrators:

➤ Farm administrator

➤ Site collection administrator

➤ Site owners

Being an administrator is kind of like ruling a country. If we compare these three administrative levels to a political hierarchy, one could say that a site owner is a mayor of a small town, a site collection administrator is a regional governor, and the farm administrator is like a president or prime minister.

Farm Administrator

A farm administrator can do everything! You should be very careful with granting users membership in the farm administrative group. In a newly installed SharePoint farm, three user accounts are listed as members of the farm administrative group:

➤ The user account that you defined as the IIS application pool identity for *SharePoint Central Administration v4*, often referred to as the *Central Administration account*.

➤ The local administrators group in the server running SharePoint. This means that if you add members to that local admin group, they will also become farm administrators.

➤ The user account used when installing SharePoint.

TRY IT OUT   Manage the Farm Administrator Group

In this example, you, as the farm administrator, want to add a new user as another farm administrator.

1. Log on as a farm administrator to the SharePoint server.

2. Open the SharePoint Central Administration tool. Click Start ➪ All Programs ➪ Microsoft SharePoint 2010 Products ➪ SharePoint 2010 Central Administration.

3. Click on Security in the left pane.

4. Click "Manage the farm administrators group" in the Users section.

5. Click New to open the "Grant Permissions" form, then enter the user account you want to add to the farm administrators group in the "Users/Groups" field, and then click OK. You can also add security groups in this field.

6. This user is now a farm administrator and has full administrative access to this SharePoint farm.

How It Works

Members of the farm administrator group have full access to any part of SharePoint. You can add users and security groups either from Active Directory or local accounts/groups from the SharePoint Server.

Site Collection Administrator

Members of this group have full access to the site collection, including all sites and their lists and libraries. Every site collection has its own set of administrators; that is, if you have two site collections you can be the site collection administrator for one of them but have no access to the other.

There are two ways to manage members of the site collection administrative group: either from within the site collection itself that all site collection administrators can use, or from a configuration page in SharePoint Central Administration that only farm administrators can use.

> **NOTE** *The farm administrator account that creates a new site collection will also be its first site collection administrator.*

In the following example, you add a new user as a member to the site collection administrative group from within the site collection.

> **NOTE** *As discussed at the beginning of this chapter, you should set up an intranet at* http://srv1, *a subsite named "Team Site," and user accounts for Johan, Anna, Beatrice, and Malin to be able to follow along with the Try It Outs.*

TRY IT OUT   **Manage Site Collection Administrators**

In this example, you grant the user Beatrice permission as a site collection administrator.

1. Log on as a site collection administrator to an existing site collection.
2. Open the top site in the site collection.
3. Click Site Actions ⇨ Site Settings to open the Site Settings page.
4. Click Site Collection Administrators in the Users and Permissions section.
5. Add the user account, in this example Beatrice, and click OK.
6. The user Beatrice now has full access to all settings and sites in this site collection.

How It Works

Existing site collection administrators can add new administrators and remove existing ones from within the top site of the site collection.

> **NOTE** *You can only add user accounts as site collection administrators; adding groups is not possible.*

Site Owner

The highest level of permission in a specific site is the site owner, who is granted the permission level Full Control. The user who creates a new site will be its default site owner, if the site is configured to use unique permissions. This site owner can then add new user or group accounts as owners or remove them, including removing his or her own user account.

When creating a new site, you have two permissions options: either inherit all permissions from its parent site, or create unique permissions. The default is to inherit, in which case the owner of the parent site will also be the owner of the new site. Only if you choose to create unique site permissions will you be the owner of the new site.

Special Administrative Roles

Besides these three basic levels, you also have administrators who are dedicated to specific tasks or features. For example, you can grant a user administrative permission to:

➤ **A list item:** For example, a document, or a calendar item

➤ **A folder:** For example, inside a document library

➤ **A list or library:** For example, a task list or a document library

➤ **A term store:** For example, a metadata tree with all states in the U.S.

➤ **A service application:** For example, to manage the Business Data Connectivity service application

One thing to avoid is granting user accounts direct access, if possible. For example, suppose you need to grant Anna and Thomas administrative permissions to a service application. After one year, Anna leaves the company, and her account is locked. Will you still remember that Anna is granted permissions to this service account? Now imagine that Anna has been granted administrative permissions to sites, several libraries, and three service applications. A new employee will take over Anna's responsibilities — what is the easiest way to replace all her permissions with the new administrator's?

There is one way to avoid situations like this: create a group, grant that group administrative permissions, and make Anna a member of that group. Now replacing her account with a new administrator is very easy. The follow-up question is, "Where should you create this group?" You have two options:

➤ A standard **security group** in an Active Directory (or a local server group). This solution is good, but it may result in a great number of security groups, which may cause the AD to be hard to manage.

➤ A **SharePoint group.** This solution is also good, and it does not require you to create new security groups in the AD. However, the scope for SharePoint groups is only within a specific site collection; that is, if you have 100 site collections you must create and maintain 100 copies of the same SharePoint group. This task is easy if you use PowerShell, but it is hard if you manage these groups using the graphical user interface. There are also third party products that will ease the management of security settings for sites.

These rules do not only apply to administrative permissions; they are definitely also true when granting ordinary users access to sites and content, for example, contributors and readers. Always think twice before granting permissions to users instead of groups. This method is very easy at first, but after some time, maintaining control over the permissions given to all users will become very hard.

Setting Permission Levels

Each user or group account must be granted some level of permission to get any access to SharePoint and its content. Basically, you do this in one of two ways: make the user a member of a SharePoint group, or add the user or security group account directly to the permission list for the SharePoint object the user needs to access. The level of access is controlled by the *permission level*, which you can think of as a security role.

Appendix B describes the details regarding permission levels and the underlying list, site, and personal permissions these levels consist of. It also describes how to create new permission levels. The following sections summarize the default levels for SharePoint Foundation, and then for SharePoint Server 2010.

Permission Levels in SharePoint Foundation

SharePoint Server 2010 has more default permission levels than SharePoint Foundation, but all SharePoint Foundation levels also exist in SharePoint Server (which is only logical because SharePoint Server is built upon SharePoint Foundation). By default all SharePoint Foundation sites have the following permission levels defined:

➤ **Limited Access:** This is a special type of security role that a user or group is granted when getting access to a specific list, library, or item, but not the site itself. For example, if the user Anna is granted Read access to a specific document library, but not the site it belongs to, then Anna would get Limited Access to the site. The reason is that Anna must be able to open objects in the site, such as this document library. She will not have any other access, though; for example, she will not be able to see anything else on this site, including its home page.

➤ **Read:** Users with this permission level can read, copy, and print documents, files, and list content in a user website, and can create alerts for lists, libraries, and their content, but cannot create subsites.

➤ **Contribute:** This option is the same as Read, but users can also create, modify, and delete documents, files, and list content. They can add personal views of lists and libraries and do a personal customization of the site's home page.

➤ **Design:** This option is the same as Contribute, with the addition that these users can customize the design of the home page, such as change the color of the page, add and modify shared web parts, and create new document libraries and lists.

➤ **Full Control:** The user has full access to everything, including security settings and local management of the website. By default, this is the only permission level that can create subsites.

Permission Levels in SharePoint Server

As mentioned in the preceding section, all the permission levels for SharePoint Foundation are also available in SharePoint Server, as well as these:

➤ **Approve:** This level has the same permissions as Contribute, and users can approve documents and items awaiting approval, and override check out; for example, if Anna checks out a document and then leaves the company for a vacation, then an approver can either discard the check out or check in the document to make it available for others.

➤ **Manage Hierarchy:** This level offers almost Full Control, including creating subsites, but users cannot approve documents, change design or style sheets, or create SharePoint groups.

➤ **Restricted Read:** This level is similar to Read, but users cannot view the version history and user permissions for lists and items.

➤ **View Only:** Users can view web pages, lists, and list items.

Defining local permission levels in every site is possible, but doing that can be very confusing; for example, imagine that the Contribute level has one set of permissions in one site, and another set of permissions in another site. If you want to change permission levels, be sure to do so on the top site, and the change will automatically be applied to all subsites in this site collection. To view and manage permission levels, see the following Try It Out.

TRY IT OUT   Manage Permission Levels for a Site Collection

In this example, you check the existing permission levels for a site collection.

1. Log on as a site collection owner.

2. Open the top site in the site collection.

3. Click Site Actions ⇨ Site Settings to open the Site Settings page.

4. Click Site Permissions to open the Permissions page.

5. Click Permission Levels in the ribbon; the Permission Level page opens.

6. You can now click on any existing permission level on this page to view or change its detailed permission settings. For example, click Read to view its detailed permissions (see Appendix B for more details about each type of permission). Click Cancel to close this page. In the Try It Out "Create New SharePoint Groups" later in this chapter, you will learn how to create new permission levels.

How It Works

Each site collection has its own set of default permission levels; you can change or add new levels when required, and these new settings will be automatically replicated down to all subsites in the site collection.

> **NOTE** *Even though it is possible to change the detailed permissions for any of the standard permission levels, such as Contributor, you should avoid that in order to prevent confusion in the future. Instead, copy an existing permission level, and grant it the detailed permission needed, as in step 7 in the previous Try It Out.*

Assigning Permissions to Users and Groups

When adding permissions to users, you either grant them directly to the user account, to a security group to which the user belongs, or to a SharePoint group to which the user belongs. As stated earlier, managing permissions is easier when you use groups instead of individual user accounts, so try to use SharePoint groups (see the following sections and Appendix A) or security groups in the AD.

In the following example, you want to grant a user Read access to the intranet, and then Contribute access to a document library in a subsite.

> **NOTE** *As discussed at the beginning of this chapter, you should set up an intranet at* `http://srv1`, *a subsite named "Team Site," and user accounts for Johan, Anna, Beatrice, and Malin to be able to follow along with the Try It Outs.*

TRY IT OUT **Assign Permissions to a User**

In this example, you will grant the user Johan Read access to `http://srv1` by making him a member of the SharePoint group Start Members, and then granting him Contribute access to the Shared Documents document library in `http://srv1/teamsite`.

1. Log on as a site collection owner.

2. Open the top site `http://srv1`, which is given the name Start.

3. Click Site Actions ⇨ Site Permissions to open the Permissions page.

4. Click on the Start Visitors group to open its configuration page. This auto-created SharePoint group is assigned the Read permission level. Continue as follows:

   a. Click New to open the Grant Permissions form.

   b. Add Johan's name to the Users/Groups field.

   c. Click Check Name; that is, the little icon at the right of the User/Groups field, to verify this account is recognized.

   d. Write a short personal message to welcome Johan as a reader.

   e. Click OK to save and close. Johan now has Read access to the intranet and all sites that inherit its settings from this top site.

5. Now assign Johan Contribute permission to the Shared Documents document library in `http://srv1/teamsite`. Open this team site.

6. Click on Shared Documents to open this library. Then continue as follows:

    a. Switch to the Library tab on the ribbon.

    b. Click on the Library Permissions button (to the far right on the ribbon; note that if there is little space you will only see its icon and no text).

    c. To make Johan a contributor to this library only, you must break the inherited permissions and switch to unique permissions. Click Stop Inheriting Permissions, and then click OK to confirm.

    d. Click Grant Permissions.

    e. Enter Johan in the Users/Groups field, and click Check Names.

    f. Select the "Grant users permission directly" option, and select Contribute.

    g. Again, fill in a personal welcome message, which will be sent to Johan, including a link to this library.

    h. Click OK to save and close. Johan now has Contribute permissions to this document library and all its content.

7. Log on as Johan and verify that he has received these two welcome messages by e-mail, and that he has the intended access to the intranet and to this document library.

How It Works

You grant permissions to a user by adding him as a member of a SharePoint group that has the requested permission level and thereby the user will inherit the permissions of this group. You can also grant a user access to a direct permission level without making him a member of any group.

Working with SharePoint Groups

A SharePoint group is very similar to an Active Directory security group; it is used to grant permissions to objects. One difference is that AD groups can be used with many types of objects, such as files, Exchange mailboxes, and SharePoint sites. However, a SharePoint group can only be used to grant permissions to SharePoint objects. Another difference is that AD groups can only be created and managed by domain administrators, whereas SharePoint groups are created and managed by site collection administrators, who do not need any special permissions in the domain.

> **NOTE** *SharePoint groups are only visible within the site collection they were created in. Using a SharePoint group outside its home site collection is not possible; that is, there are no global farm SharePoint groups.*

The easiest way to grant a user permissions is to use any of the three SharePoint groups that are automatically created for each new SharePoint site configured to use its own security settings; that is, a site that does not inherit its permissions from a parent site. The name for these SharePoint groups will start with the name of the site they belong to, as a prefix. For example, if the site is named "ABC," the three default SharePoint groups will start with "ABC."

➤ **ABC Visitors:** This SharePoint group is associated with the Read permission level. Any member of this group can view, copy, and print content in lists and libraries, including previous versions, if any.

➤ **ABC Members:** This SharePoint group is associated with the Contribute permission level. Members of this group can also add, modify, and delete lists and library content.

➤ **ABC Owners:** This SharePoint group is associated with the Full Control permission level. Members of this group have full access to this site and all its content.

> **NOTE** *Not only are these SharePoint groups convenient for granting users access, the Member group also has some magic functionality when used in SharePoint Server 2010 and its My Site feature. More about that feature appears in Chapter 5.*

When necessary, you can create new SharePoint groups; for example, if you need a group of users who can create content and also create subsites, none of the three default groups will allow that. The following exercise describes how to create such a SharePoint group.

TRY IT OUT **Create New SharePoint Groups**

In this example, you need a new SharePoint group that allows its members to both add and manage content like a contributor and also create subsites. This requires that you create a new permission level. You want this group to be available everywhere in this site collection, so you create the SharePoint group at the top site level.

1. Log on as a site collection owner, and open the top site.

2. Click Site Actions ⇨ Site Permissions to open the Permissions page.

3. Create the new permission level required: Click Permission Levels.

4. Click Contribute, because it is most like the permission level you need, then continue as follows:

    a. Scroll down to the bottom of this long form.

    b. Click Copy Permission Level.

    c. Enter the name **Super Contributor Permissions**.

    d. Enter the description **Like a contributor, but can also create subsites**.

    e. Locate and select the Create Subsites site permission.

    f. Click Create. The new permission level is created and will be listed among the default levels.

5. Click Site Actions ⇨ Site Permissions again.

6. Click Create Group on the ribbon, and then continue as follows:

   a. Set Name to **Enhanced Contributors**.

   b. Set About me to **Contributor + Site Creator**.

   c. Accept your account as the group owner.

   d. Accept the default settings about viewing membership, and how to handle requests to join and leave this group.

   e. Select the Super Contributor Permissions permission level.

   f. Click Create; the configuration page for this new SharePoint group will open.

7. Click Groups in the left pane to open the All Groups page. This displays all SharePoint groups in this site collection; verify that Enhanced Contributors is listed. This group is now ready to be used anywhere in this site collection — for example, the Shared Documents document library in `http://srv1/teamsite` that you earlier broke the inheritance for:

   a. Open `http://srv1/teamsite`.

   b. Open the Shared Documents library.

   c. Click Library Permissions on the ribbon.

   d. Click Grant Permissions.

   e. Enter **Enhanced Contributors** and click Check Names.

   f. Select the Super Contributor Permissions permission level.

   g. Deselect the "Send welcome E-mail to the new users" option.

   h. Click OK.

How It Works

You can create new SharePoint groups in any site, but to make them available everywhere in the site collection you create them in the top site. Every time this SharePoint group is added to a site or an object, you must also define what permission level it will get. That is, the permission level it has in the top site will not follow the SharePoint group when used elsewhere.

Viewing Existing Permissions

In previous versions of SharePoint, getting an overview of the permissions granted to a specific user was almost impossible; the only way to find out was to open all the sites and see whether the user was granted permissions, and you also needed to check what security groups and SharePoint groups this user was a member of. Some smart developers created software tools to do this job; for example, Access Checker (which can be found at `http://www.codeplex.com/AccessChecker`), and several third-party products. Without such tools, larger organizations would find this task gigantic.

SharePoint 2010, both SharePoint Foundation and SharePoint Server, comes with a new feature known as *Check Permission* that can ease the challenge of finding out about all permissions granted to a specific user; see the following Try It Out.

> **NOTE** *As discussed at the beginning of this chapter, you should set up an intranet at* `http://srv1`, *a subsite named "Team Site," and user accounts for Johan, Anna, Beatrice, and Malin to be able to follow along with the Try It Outs.*

TRY IT OUT **Check Permissions for a User**

In this example, you want to know what permission is granted to Johan to the top site in `http://srv1`.

1. Log on as a site owner and open `http://srv1`.

2. Click Site Actions ⇨ Site Permissions to open the Permissions page.

3. Click Check Permissions in the ribbon to open the "Check Permissions" form.

4. Enter Johan's account in the Users/Groups field, and click Check Names.

5. View the list of permissions granted to Johan; see Figure 6-1.

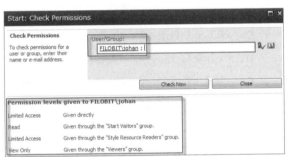

FIGURE 6-1

How It Works

You can use the built-in feature Check Permissions to view the permissions for a given user in the current site and all subsites that inherits from the current site.

Note that this new feature has its flaws that you need to be aware of:

➤ It only shows the permissions for the current site, not for subsites with unique permissions.

➤ It cannot expand AD security groups. For example, if Johan is a member of the A-Team security group, and that group is granted Contribute permissions, then Check Permissions will not show it.

To summarize the Check Permission feature, it is a good start, and it can be a really good help to find out permissions to a specific site, as long as you don't use AD security groups. However, finding out permissions of AD groups is exactly what a lot of organizations want to do, so in this case the Check Permissions feature is less useful. In that case, you may want to look for commercial tools, such as DeliverPoint, which is available from `www.lightningtools.com`.

MANAGING TEMPLATES, LISTS, AND LIBRARIES

Throughout the book, you have seen numerous examples of SharePoint storing content in lists and libraries, so you know that they are very important. As a SharePoint administrator, you need to know how to manage these lists; for example, how to create a list template that you can use in other site collections and how to copy document libraries. The following sections describe these tasks in more detail.

Creating a List Template

Creating a list or library template is very easy: simply save an existing list as a template, with or without its content, as described in the next exercise. You will soon realize that this template is only visible within the site collection in which it is created. So what do you do if you need the same template in your other site collections? The answer is that you export the list template, and then import it into other site collections, as shown in the following Try It Out.

TRY IT OUT   Create a Library Template

In this example, you save an existing library as a template: it will contain all settings and custom columns, but no content. Note that the following procedure is also valid for any type of list, not only libraries. Only site collection administrators can create templates, because these templates will be stored in a global template gallery on the top site.

1. Log on as a site collection administrator, and open your site; for example, `http://srv1/teamsite`.

2. Open an existing document library that you want to save as a template.

3. Click Library Settings on the ribbon (on the Library tab), and then:

    a. Click "Save document library as template" (if you don't see this link, you don't have enough permissions — log on as a user with higher permissions). See Figure 6-2.

    b. Enter a File name for this template; for example, **Project DocLib**.

    c. Enter a Template name; for example, **Project Document Library**. Note that this text will be visible to all users who can create lists, so think of a descriptive name.

    d. Enter a Template description; for example, **This document library contains columns for keyword metadata, security, and country.** Also, this text will be visible to other users.

    e. Leave the Include Content option deselected. If you select it, then all current content, that is, documents, will also be stored with the template.

f. Click OK to save the template. Then click OK to confirm that the operation completed successfully.

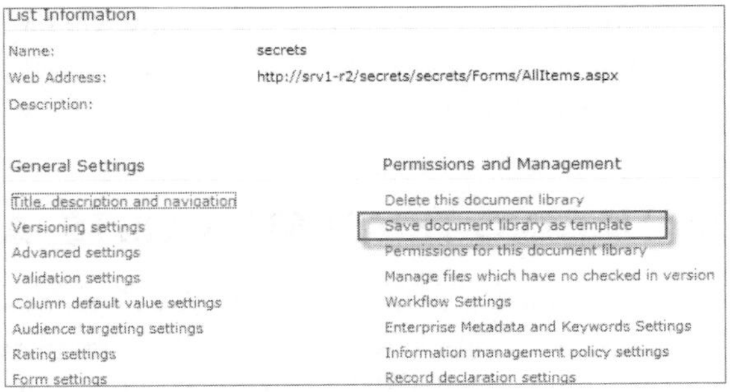

4. Verify that the template is created and available:

a. Open another site in this site collection, where you are the site owner.

b. Click Site Actions ⇨ More Options to open the Create form. Note that the layout of this form depends on whether you have Silverlight installed, as described in Chapter 4. The steps below assume that Silverlight is installed on your computer.

List Information	
Name:	secrets
Web Address:	http://srv1-r2/secrets/secrets/Forms/AllItems.aspx
Description:	

General Settings	Permissions and Management
Title, description and navigation	Delete this document library
Versioning settings	Save document library as template
Advanced settings	Permissions for this document library
Validation settings	Manage files which have no checked in version
Column default value settings	Workflow Settings
Audience targeting settings	Enterprise Metadata and Keywords Settings
Rating settings	Information management policy settings
Form settings	Record declaration settings

FIGURE 6-2

c. Select Library, then Content in the left pane. You will now see your Project Document Library library template.

d. Click on your template; notice the description in the right pane.

e. Enter a name; for example, **Project Documents**, and click Create (see Figure 6-3). The new document opens.

f. Verify that the document contains the same settings — for example, version history settings, custom columns, and so on — as the library you saved as a template.

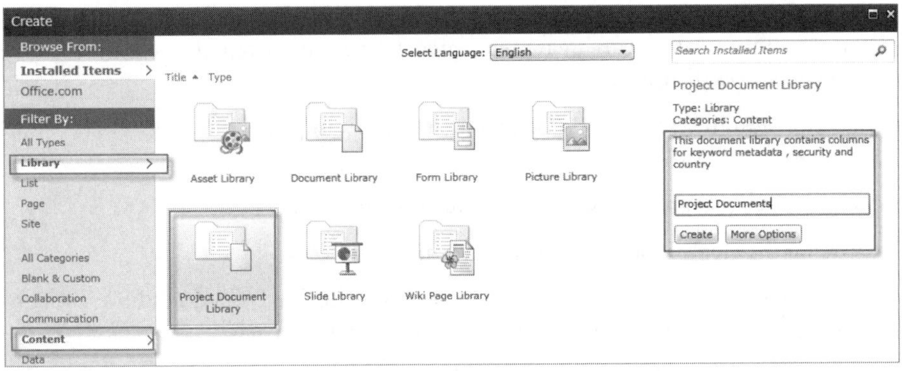

FIGURE 6-3

How It Works

You can save lists and libraries as templates that can be used anywhere in the site collection they were created in.

Making list and library templates like this one is very easy. But there are some drawbacks with these templates you need to be aware of:

➤ They only work within the site collection they were created in.

➤ You cannot update an existing template. Instead, you have to delete the existing template and create a new one based on an updated list or library.

➤ There is no relationship between the library or list and the template; for example, you can delete the original list without affecting the corresponding template.

➤ Templates are language dependent. For example, you cannot use English templates in a site built on a Swedish site template.

A developer can also create list and library templates; such templates are more complicated to develop, but they can be modified afterwards, and these modifications will immediately apply to both new and existing libraries based on this template.

Copying List and Library Templates

If you need to copy a list or library template from one site collection to another, you must first export and then import the template file. Note that these templates are stored inside a SQL Server database that SharePoint creates; that is, you cannot copy the template file like an ordinary file. That is why you must export the template from the SQL Server, and then import it into another site collection, as the following Try It Out describes.

TRY IT OUT **Copy List Templates to Other Site Collections**

In this example, you export a library template from one site collection and import it into another. To complete this exercise, you need two site collections and one library template that you created earlier.

1. Log on as a site collection administrator and open the top site, for example `http://srv1`, where you have at least one existing library template (see the previous Try It Out "Create a Library Template").

2. Click Site Actions ➪ Site Settings.

3. Navigate to the template gallery by clicking List Templates in the Galleries section; this will open the "All Templates" page that lists all existing list and library templates. Continue as follows:

  a. Click on the template name you created in the earlier Try It Out. A dialog window appears.

  b. Select Save, and save the file to your local file system.

  c. Click Close on the download dialog that appears.

4. The template is now exported. Using this file in another SharePoint 2010 environment — for example, a production environment — is possible. Now import this file to a new site collection:

  a. Open another site collection where you want to import the template file; make sure you are a site collection administrator.

   b.   Click Site Actions ⇨ Site Settings ⇨ List Templates.

   c.   Switch to the Documents tab on the ribbon, and then click Upload document.

   d.   Click Browse and select the template file you saved in step 3. If this template already exists, you can choose to overwrite it with the template you are about to upload. Then click OK to upload this file to the template gallery.

   e.   You can change the title and description if needed; click Save. This template is now available to all sites in this site collection.

5.   Verify that the imported template works as expected. Open any site in this site collection, and then click Site Actions ⇨ More Options and create a new document library based on the imported template. The new document library will have the same settings and columns as the original library the template is based on.

How It Works

To copy a template, you must first export it from SharePoint to a file, and then you can import it into any site collection in this or another SharePoint 2010 farm.

Using a Site Template

Sometimes you want to save a complete site as a template, so you can later create new sites with the exact same configuration, including lists, libraries, and site templates. This is actually as easy as creating a list template: you design one site as you want the template to be, then save the site as a template, and after that you can create new sites based on this template.

Site templates have the same limitations as list templates, that is:

➤   They only work within the site collection they were created in.

➤   You cannot update an existing template. Instead, you have to delete the existing template and create a new one.

➤   No relationship exists between the original site and the template; for example, if you change the original site, nothing will happen with the template.

➤   Templates are language dependent. For example, you cannot use an English site template to create a site in a Swedish SharePoint installation, unless you have installed an English language pack first.

A developer can create another type of site template, known as *site definitions*. These are sets of XML files and other file types that describe exactly what the site template will contain and look like. If the site definition is changed afterward, then these modifications will immediately apply to both new and existing sites based on this template. Creating site definitions goes beyond the scope of this book, but there are many advanced books about SharePoint 2010 development with more information about this interesting topic.

Copying Lists and Libraries

Sometimes you need to copy a complete list or library, which may be harder than one first anticipates, especially in SharePoint Foundation. In SharePoint Server 2010, you have a special tool for managing sites and lists, and it includes a move and copy feature that works with both sites and lists, including libraries. But in SharePoint Foundation you need to export the site, and then import it, and this method has some important drawbacks.

In the following Try It Out, you learn how to copy a list or library using both of the aforementioned methods.

> **NOTE** As discussed at the beginning of this chapter, you should set up an intranet at http://srv1, a subsite named "Team Site," and user accounts for Johan, Anna, Beatrice, and Malin to be able to follow along with the Try It Outs.

TRY IT OUT   Copy a Library with SharePoint Server

In this example, you have a library named Shared Documents that you want to move to another site in an SharePoint Server 2010 environment.

1.   Log on as a site collection administrator and open the site collection that contains the site with the library you want to copy.

2.   Click Site Actions ⇨ Manage Content and Structure to open the "Site Content and Structure" page.

3.   Select the site in the left pane where the source document library is located, and then:

   a.   In the right pane, select the Shared Documents checkbox.

   b.   Open the Actions menu, then select Copy (see Figure 6-4).

   c.   In the tree view that opens, select the destination site, and click OK. The library gets copied to that site.

4.   Open the destination site and verify that it contains a copy of the document library.

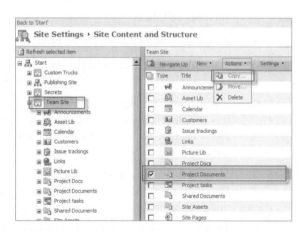

FIGURE 6-4

How It Works

Using the *Manage Content and Structure* SharePoint Server feature, you can move and copy lists, libraries, and sites, but only within the same site collection.

But what do you do if you run SharePoint Foundation, or if you need to copy a list to another site collection? Then you have the following options:

➤ Save the list as a template, including its content.

➤ Copy the list to Microsoft Access, and then copy it back to another destination.

However, limitations exist with both of these options, and you must be aware of them before you start copying or moving lists this way. The following list describes these limitations:

➤ If you need to copy or move a library — for example, a document library or a picture library — you can only use the first method; that is, save as a template including its content.

➤ Copying and moving lists and libraries always resets all dates to today and "Created By" to your account — that is, the user who performed the copy process.

➤ All version history is lost when copying or moving lists and libraries.

You learned in a previous exercise how to save a library as a template, so the following exercise describes how to copy a list using Microsoft Access.

TRY IT OUT   Copy a List Using Microsoft Access

In this example, you have a team site with a tasks list that you want to copy to another site; this procedure works the same regardless of whether the destination is the same site collection, or whether it is another site collection. This exercise requires that Microsoft Access is installed on the client computer, and that the task list contains at least one task.

1. Log on as a site collection administrator, and open the site that contains the tasks list.

2. Open this list, and then:

a. Switch to the List tab on the ribbon.

b. Click Open with Access (if the space on the ribbon is small, then only an icon with an "A" is visible). The question "Would you like to link or export this list?" appears.

c. If you choose the option "Link to data on the SharePoint site," then you will create a two-way synchronization copy of this tasks list in Microsoft Access. This is not necessary if you just want to copy this list to another site; in that case, select the option "Export a copy of the data" and click OK.

d. Microsoft Access will start and open a newly created table with the same name as the SharePoint list. Double-click on this table to view its content. If you want to change anything in this list, then do it now. You can also add new tasks to this table, if needed.

e. To copy that table into a new SharePoint list, right-click on the table, select Export, and select SharePoint List (see Figure 6-5). A new form named "Export data to SharePoint list" opens.

f. Enter the Site Address to the destination site in the top field, and then accept the default name for this site. Note that if there already exists a list with this name, a number will be appended to the new list. You can also enter a description for this new list. When ready, click OK.

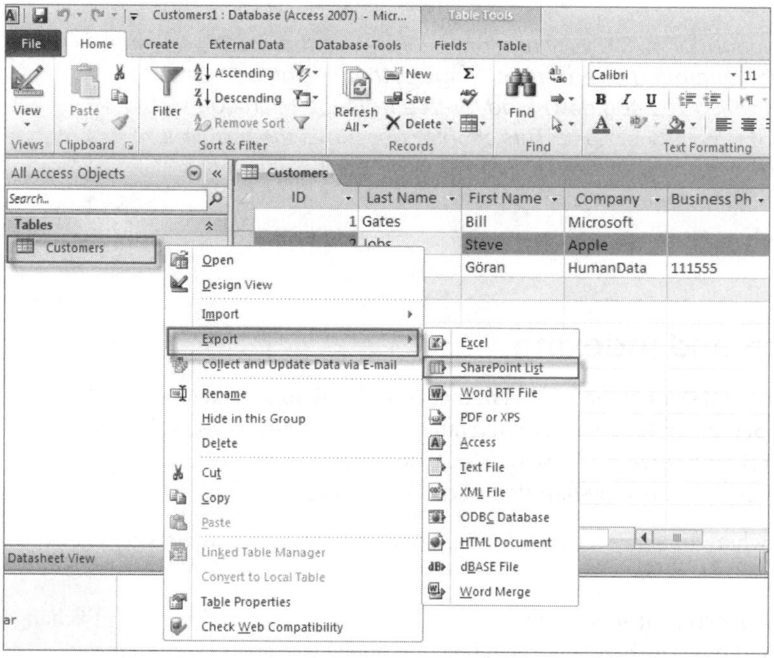

FIGURE 6-5

3. Verify that the new list is created and contains the same content as the original contact list, including any changes or new entries you added to the Microsoft Access table before exporting it.

How It Works

Microsoft Access is a good choice if you need to copy SharePoint lists from one site to another, including other site collections or even other SharePoint farms. However, copying libraries with file content using this method is not possible.

SEARCHING AND INDEXING WITH SHAREPOINT SERVER

One of the most important and fundamental features of SharePoint has always been the search and index system. For each version of SharePoint since its first version in 2001, it has steadily become better and easier to use. SharePoint Server 2010 is no exception. It contains a smarter ranking system for search results, better service architecture to enable resilient design, and a rebuilt user interface, all of which make it much easier for end users to search and find what they are looking for.

Appendixes C and D contain more details about installing and managing the search and index service roles and describe their architecture. This chapter focuses more on configuring and managing the search and index features.

> **NOTE** *SharePoint Foundation has a very fundamental search feature. If you run SharePoint Foundation and need a real search engine, then install Search Server Express 2010, which you can download for free from the Microsoft web page at* www.microsoft.com/download. *This chapter describes the features in SharePoint Server 2010, but Search Server Express 2010 offers almost the same features, except for people search.*

Understanding Search and Indexing

SharePoint Server 2010 has its own search and index engine, completely independent of the Full-Text indexing service in SQL Server. In fact, you can activate them both, but it would be a waste of resources, because the SharePoint Server 2010 search and indexing feature works in any type of website. A summary of the search features in SharePoint Server are as follow:

> ➤ You can search everywhere in SharePoint — for example, any Wiki site, team site, and workspace site.

> ➤ You can search almost any content source outside SharePoint — file servers, Microsoft Exchange servers, Lotus Notes, and other web servers, including any public website on the Internet.

> ➤ With SharePoint Server 2010 Enterprise edition, you can also search in external databases and applications, such as Oracle, SAP, and Navision.

> ➤ You can search all Microsoft Office file types by default, as well as all standard file formats, such as TXT, HTML, and so on.

> ➤ You can extend the search to crawl any file type — all you need is an *index filter* (IFilter) for each file type.

> ➤ You can control what file types to index, even if an IFilter is installed for it.

> ➤ The user profile properties will be indexed; that is, you can search for a user with a specific property.

> ➤ All social tags and notes are also indexed, and therefore searchable.

This search and indexing feature is activated by default for all information stored in SharePoint. Because this feature is advanced, you as a farm administrator must understand how it works in SharePoint Server and what you can do to optimize it. This is especially true when some problem arises, such as when the search results are not as expected, or when a content source fails to be indexed. The following section tells you all you need to know for everyday work as an administrator, and how to extend and adjust this very important feature.

The search and indexing feature in SharePoint Server 2010 is implemented as a specific search service application, which you manage via the SharePoint Central Administration tool or PowerShell scripts.

NOTE *The STSADM command tool also offers several operations that relate to search and indexing, but because that tool is no longer the preferred script tool, you should instead use PowerShell.*

NOTE *For an in-depth description of the search and indexing feature, see the Microsoft SharePoint Product and Technology 2010 Resource Kit.*

Getting the Basics Down

Two MOSS services are engaged in the search and indexing feature:

➤ **Indexing:** Responsible for crawling content sources and building index files

➤ **Search:** Responsible for finding all information matching the search query by searching the index files

This is important: all searching is performed against the index files; if they don't contain what the user is looking for, no match will be found. The index files are critical to the success of the search feature of MOSS. In fact, practically all configuration and management is related to the indexing service. The search functionality may be described in its simplest form as a web page where the user defines a search query.

You can configure the index role either to run on its own SharePoint Server server or to run together with all the other roles, such as the Web Service, Excel Services, and Forms Services. It performs its indexing tasks following this general workflow:

1. SharePoint stores all configuration settings about the indexing in its database.

2. When activated, indexing looks in the SharePoint databases to see what content sources to index, and what type, such as a full or incremental indexing.

3. The index service starts a program called the *crawler* — a program that will try opening the content that should be indexed.

4. For each information type, the crawler will need an *index filter*, or IFilter, that knows how to read text inside this particular type of information. For example, to read an Microsoft Word file, an IFilter for .DOCX is needed.

5. The crawler receives a stream of Unicode characters from the IFilter. It now uses a small program called a *word breaker*; its job is to convert the stream of Unicode characters into words.

6. However, some words may not be interesting to store in the index, such as *the*, *a*, and *if*; the *gatherer* program now compares each word found against a list of *noise words*. This text file contains all words to be removed from the stream of words.

7. The remaining words are stored in an index file, together with a link to the source. If that word already exists, only the source will be added; so one word can point to multiple sources.

8. If the source was information stored in SharePoint, or a file in the file system, the index will also store the security settings for this source; this prevents a user from getting search results that she is not allowed to open.

This process is straightforward, if you think about it. But the underlying process is a bit more complex; fortunately, you do not need to dive into these details unless you have a very good reason. By default, SharePoint creates several single index files. Some of these index files are stored in the SQL database, whereas others are stored in the file system on the server configured to run the Index role in the SharePoint farm. These index files are stored in a folder structure in the following location:

```
<Drive:>\Program Files\Microsoft Office Servers\14.0\DATA\Office Server\
Applications\<Application GUID>
```

The *Application GUID* is a unique hexadecimal string that identifies a specific SharePoint Server instance, such as ae0cd4fe-ed29-418f-aa0f-eecfd7956b4f; if you have more than one Search service application instance created on the same server, you can check the following registry key to see exactly to which portal each Application GUID is pointing:

```
HKEY_Local_Machine/Software/Microsoft/Office Server/14.0/Search/Applications/
<GUID>/CatalogNames
```

The property `DisplayName` tells you what Search service application instance this is. The number of files and folders stored in each index folder may surprise you, but indexing is a complex process, which shows in these folders. You do not need to configure these files, because everything is managed by the SharePoint administration pages, or by PowerShell.

The crawler process keeps a log, known as the *gatherer log*, of all its activities; these log files are also stored in this folder structure, but the easiest way to view these log entries is to use the SharePoint administrative web pages.

Setting the Crawler Schedule

To make searching for objects such as documents, tasks, and web pages possible, they must first be indexed, which is done with a crawler process. A default configuration of the Search service application indexes every object in every site collection in SharePoint. When new sites are created they will automatically be added to the list of objects to be indexed — so far, so good. But the index schedule in a default configured search service application is not defined. In other words, the index service will never try to crawl any of its preconfigured locations and their objects. So the first thing you need to do is to define this index schedule, as described in the following Try It Out.

TRY IT OUT   Configure the Index Crawler Schedule

In this example, you set the index schedule to crawl once every ten minutes; that is, users must wait up to ten minutes before they can find newly added content. This exercise assumes the Search service application is created and configured. See Appendix C for more information about managing the Search Service Application.

1. Log on as a farm administrator to the SharePoint server and start SharePoint Central Administration.

2. Click Manage Service Applications in the Application Management section.

3. Click Search Service Application. The start page for managing search and index settings opens. Look at this page: it shows the current system status regarding search and indexing. If the "Searchable items" is 0; then the index schedule is not configured in which case:

   a. Click Content Sources in the left pane. The "Manage Content Sources" page opens.

   b. Click "Local SharePoint sites."

   c. Note that the field Start Addresses contains a link to all existing web applications (see Appendix A), plus a link to sps3://srv1 (assuming your server is srv1). These links point to all content sources in SharePoint that will be indexed, such as ordinary site collections, people search, and My Sites. Do *not* add or delete anything in this field, unless Microsoft Support tells you to. This field is automatically updated by SharePoint and you don't have to touch it. In fact, if you do, the risk is that the index will not work properly!

   d. Scroll down to Crawl Schedules. It contains two settings: Full and Incremental Crawl. Click "Edit schedule" for Incremental Crawl to open the Manage Schedules form, select the option "Repeat within the day," and set Every to 10 minutes. Click OK (see Figure 6-6). The Manage Content Souces page reappears.

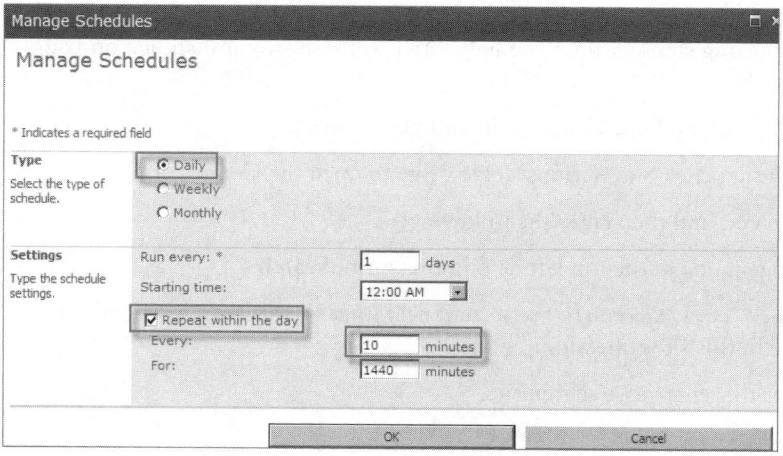

FIGURE 6-6

> **NOTE** The best practice is to configure incremental crawl only! Why not full? When you have many hundreds of gigabytes, the crawl will take days, or even weeks, to complete. It will not simply complete before the next schedule is scheduled to run. If you need to force a full index, then open the menu for the Local SharePoint sites content source, and select Start Full Crawl.

e. In order to make sure all content will be indexed from start, select the "Start full crawl of this content source" option, and then click OK.

4. The index crawler starts, and will run every 10 minutes.

How It Works

You must configure the index crawler schedule to activate the indexing of SharePoint objects. Typically you only configure a scheduled incremental crawl, never full crawl. Click Search Administration in the left pane of the "Manage Content Sources" page to reopen the Search Administration page.

Creating a Search Site

Before users can start searching in SharePoint Server, you need to have a search site. Other sites, like the start page for the intranet, need to connect to that search site to make searching in all indexed information possible for users. If you don't do this, only objects in the current site will appear in the search results.

TRY IT OUT Create a Search Site

In this example, you create a search site that also will be configured to be the default search center for all searches in this farm. The following steps assume you have Microsoft Silverlight installed on your computer.

1. Log on as a site collection owner, and open the top site in `http://srv1`.

2. Start by creating the search site: click Site Actions ⇨ New Site to open the Create form.

3. Select Enterprise Search Center, and then enter the following:

   a. Enter the following site name in the top left field in this form: **Search**.

   b. Enter the URL: **http://srv1/search** in the second field (that is, this search site will be a subsite to the top site in this site collection).

   c. Click Create to create this enterprise search site.

4. Open the top site in `http://srv1`.

5. Add the search site as the default search center for this site collection:

   a. Click Site Actions ⇨ Site Settings to open the Site Settings page.

   b. Click "Search Settings" in the Site Collection Administration section.

   c. Select the Enable Custom Scope option, and then enter the URL: **/search/pages** (that is, the relative URL path to the search site. Avoid absolute URL paths like "`http://srv1/search/pages`" because they may not work for users accessing the intranet from the Internet). Do not leave out /pages, because it is required when you search later on.

    d.   Change the Site Collection Search Dropdown Mode to Show Scopes Dropdown. This ensures that users can change search scope when necessary.

    e.   Click OK.

6.   Open the start page for the `http://srv1` intranet. Verify that you now have a search scope to the left of the search field at the top of the page.

How It Works

To activate the search you must create a search site. If you want search to be available in all sites in a site collection, you must also define the search site as the default search center.

Indexing New Content Sources

Most organizations have a lot of information stored in their file servers. Some, but most likely not all, of this information will be moved into SharePoint, which makes searching that content easy. What should you do with the other files? You probably don't want to delete them; after all, that information may be needed someday. An elegant solution to make this information available to users is to add this content to the SharePoint index file. This enables users to search for both old and new information, without requiring them to know exactly where this information is stored.

To add external information to the SharePoint index file, you create new content sources. As mentioned earlier in this chapter, SharePoint can index almost any type of data source and location, such as the SharePoint database, any fileserver, Microsoft Exchange folders, Lotus Notes databases, other web applications, and external web applications. The way to make that information searchable is to define a content source that points to that location. This action enables the index engine to crawl that content.

For example, suppose you want to index a specific file share in your network environment. Let's assume it is: `\\dc1\projects`. You can replace it with your own file share in the following Try It Out. The following Try It Out shows you how.

<code>TRY IT OUT</code>   **Add New Content Sources**

In this example, you add a new content source that points to the file share `\\dc1\projects`. (You can replace it with your own file share if you want to.) The result will be that the content of this file share will be indexed by SharePoint and is therefore searchable.

1.   Log on to the SharePoint server as a farm administrator, and start SharePoint Central Administration.

2.   Click Manage Service Applications in the Application Management section.

3.   Click Search Service Application. The start page for managing search and index settings opens.

4. Click Content Sources, then continue as follows:

    a. Click New Content Source.

    b. Enter the Name: **Project Files**.

    c. Select the type: File Share.

    d. In the Start Address field, type **\\dc1\projects**.

    e. Accept the default of "Crawl the folder and all subfolders of each start address."

    f. Configure the Incremental Crawl schedule to run once every day at 5:00 a.m. (The previous exercise described how to do this.)

    g. Select the "Start full crawl of this content source" option to ensure that all content in this file share is fully indexed before the scheduled incremental index process starts the first time.

    h. Click OK to save and close this content source definition.

5. Verify that the new Projects content source is listed on the Manage Content Sources page, and that the status shows that a full crawl has started (you may have to click Refresh to update the status).

6. Click Search Administration in the left pane of the Manage Content Sources page to go back to the Search Administration page for search and index management.

7. Wait until the Crawl status shows Online for crawling; that is, that the crawler process has completed. Open the intranet and search for something you know exists in the indexed file share.

How It Works

Add a content source to index information outside SharePoint, such as a file server — Exchange or another web server in your organization.

> **NOTE** *Before you can add a content source to Lotus Notes, you must first install a Lotus Notes client on the SharePoint server. The crawler will use this client to read the Notes database. Unless this client is installed, there will be no option to install Lotus Notes content sources.*

Indexing PDF and Other File Formats

Besides the default file types indexed, you can add almost any other well-known file type. In fact, you can add your own type, if necessary, but this will require that you write some code to do it. There are two things that must be in place in order to enable to indexer to crawl a new file type:

➤ The file type must be listed in the File types list, discussed earlier.

➤ There must be a 64-bit IFilter installed that can read this type of file.

The trick, of course, is to find the IFilter. The good news is that many sources are on the Internet. These IFilters are not specific to the SharePoint index engine, but most will also work for the SQL Server full-text indexing and other Microsoft Search–based engines. The same type of IFilters used for MOSS 2007 will also work fine with the SharePoint Server 2010 search engine. Table 6-1 presents a list of the most common IFilters and at least one source. Some are free, others are commercial, but these most often have a low price.

TABLE 6-1: Some 64-bit IFilters for the Indexer

FILE TYPE	DOWNLOAD SOURCE	PRICE/SERVER
PDF	www.adobe.com/support/downloads/detail.jsp?ftpID=4025	Free
	www.foxitsoftware.com/pdf/ifilter/ (This iFilter is faster than Adobe.)	$6.99 USD
docx, .docm, .pptx, .pptm, .xlsx, .xlsm, .xlsb, .zip, .one, .vdx, .vsd, .vss, .vst, .vdx, .vsx, and .vtx	http://tinyurl.com/MS-IFilterpack. This package is released by Microsoft.	Free
MindManager files	www.ifiltershop.com	$2.99 USD
CHP (Help files)	www.ifiltershop.com	$2.99 USD
MSG (Outlook mail)	www.ifiltershop.com	$2.99 USD
DWG (AutoCad)	www.ifiltershop.com	$2.99 USD

This list is growing constantly. Remember that each new file type indexed will increase the CPU load and the size of the index files; be sure you really need to search files, such as MP3, before you add an iFilter, even if it is cool!

> **NOTE** Go to www.citeknet.com *for a very nice (and free) 64-bit version of the IFilter Explorer tool. Use it to see all the IFilters installed on the server.*

If you need to remove an IFilter, just uninstall it like any other program, using the Add/Remove Programs applet in the Control Panel.

So, let's practice by adding a new file type to be indexed. In the following example, you will add PDF as an indexed file. The download link to the IFilter is listed in the preceding table, and you know how to add PDF as a file type to be indexed. But in this case, and some others, too, one thing is missing: users will not see the familiar PDF icon next to PDF files in the SharePoint document libraries. You must also download this icon and install it in a proper way, as shown in the following Try It Out.

TRY IT OUT **Index PDF Files**

In this example, you install an IFilter for PDF from Adobe, and then configure the indexer to crawl PDF files.

1. Download the IFilter for the PDF format as listed in Table 6-1. Install the IFilter on the SharePoint server. If you are running a SharePoint farm, it must be installed on the SharePoint server running the Index role!

2. Open the SharePoint Central Administration tool, and click Manage Service Applications ➪ Search Service Application to open the Search Administration page, then continue as follows:

    a. Click File Types. A table appears with all the file types that the crawler will open.

    b. Add the PDF file type: click New file Type, and enter **PDF**. Then click OK to save.

    c. Verify that PDF is now listed in this table.

3. The preceding two steps are really all that are needed to index PDF files. However, your users will wonder why PDF files in SharePoint do not show the typical PDF file icon. So, the next step is purely for cosmetic reasons:

    a. Download the PDF icon from the Internet; for example, from `www.adobe.com/misc/linking.html`, and save the icon file as **pdficon.gif** in the following location on the SharePoint Server: `C:\Program Files\Common Files\Microsoft Shared\web server extensions\14\TEMPLATE\IMAGES`.

    b. You next must teach SharePoint to display this icon for PDF files. Open the following file with Notepad: `C:\Program Files\Common Files\Microsoft Shared\web server extensions\14\TEMPLATE\XML\DOCICON.XML`.

> **NOTE** *Make a backup of the original* DOCICON.XLM *just to be safe.*

    c. Add this line: `<Mapping Key="pdf" Value="pdficon.gif"/>` within the section that starts with `<ByExtensions>`; the exact location is not important, but why not add it at the end so you can easily remember that you added it? See Figure 6-7.

    d. Save and close `DOCICON.XML`.

    e. Open a command prompt, and run `iisreset`. This is necessary to make sure SharePoint reads the new settings in the `DOCICON.XML` file.

    f. Open the SharePoint File types administrative page again. You should now see that the PDF file type has its well-known icon next to it! If not, you did something wrong.

```
DOCICON - Notepad                                                          _□X
File  Edit  Format  View  Help
      <Mapping Key="webpart" Value="icdwp.gif" OpenControl=""/>
      <Mapping Key="wm" Value="icwm.gif" OpenControl=""/>
      <Mapping Key="wma" Value="icwma.gif" OpenControl=""/>
      <Mapping Key="wmd" Value="icwmd.gif" OpenControl=""/>
      <Mapping Key="wmp" Value="icwmp.gif" OpenControl=""/>
      <Mapping Key="wms" Value="icwms.gif" OpenControl=""/>
      <Mapping Key="wmv" Value="icwmv.gif" OpenControl=""/>
      <Mapping Key="wmx" Value="icwmx.gif" OpenControl=""/>
      <Mapping Key="wmz" Value="icwmz.gif" OpenControl=""/>
      <Mapping Key="wsf" Value="icwsf.gif" OpenControl=""/>
      <Mapping Key="xla" Value="icxla.png" EditText="Microsoft Excel" OpenControl="SharePoint.
      <Mapping Key="xlam" Value="icxlam.png" EditText="Microsoft Excel" OpenControl="SharePoin
      <Mapping Key="xls" Value="icxls.png" EditText="Microsoft Excel" OpenControl="SharePoint.
      <Mapping Key="xlsb" Value="icxlsb.png" EditText="Microsoft Excel" OpenControl="SharePoin
      <Mapping Key="xlsm" Value="icxlsm.png" EditText="Microsoft Excel" OpenControl="SharePoin
      <Mapping Key="xlsx" Value="icxlsx.png" EditText="Microsoft Excel" OpenControl="SharePoin
      <Mapping Key="xlt" Value="icxlt.png" EditText="Microsoft Excel" OpenControl="SharePoint.
      <Mapping Key="xltb" Value="icxltx.gif" EditText="Microsoft Excel" OpenControl="SharePoin
      <Mapping Key="xltm" Value="icxltm.png" EditText="Microsoft Excel" OpenControl="SharePoin
      <Mapping Key="xltx" Value="icxltx.png" EditText="Microsoft Excel" OpenControl="SharePoin
      <Mapping Key="xml" Value="icxml.gif"/>
      <Mapping Key="xps" Value="icxps.gif" OpenControl=""/>
      <Mapping Key="xsd" Value="icxsd.gif"/>
      <Mapping Key="xsl" Value="icxsl.gif"/>
      <Mapping Key="xsn" Value="icxsn.gif" EditText="Microsoft InfoPath" OpenControl="SharePoi
      <Mapping Key="xslt" Value="icxslt.gif"/>
      <Mapping Key="zip" Value="iczip.gif" OpenControl=""/>
      ┌─────────────────────────────────────────────┐
      │ <Mapping Key="pdf" Value="pdficon.gif"/>     │
      └─────────────────────────────────────────────┘
  </ByExtension>
  <Default>
      <Mapping Value="icgen.gif"/>
```

FIGURE 6-7

4. To get all existing PDF files indexed, you need to force a full indexing:

    a. Open the Search Service Application page, as described earlier in step 2.

    b. Click Content Sources.

    c. Click Start all crawls. Wait for the crawl to complete, then search for text you know is stored within a PDF file to confirm that the index now also crawls PDF files.

How It Works

When adding new file types to be indexed you do two things: install an IFilter, and add the file type to the list of crawled files. You also have the option to add the file icon so it shows up when these files are listed in document libraries and in search results.

Managing Search Scopes

SharePoint allows you to limit the search scope to make finding the information users are searching for easier. This feature is especially handy when the index file contains information from several content sources. For example, if the user knows that the document she is looking for is stored somewhere in the file system, she can set the search scope to the file system only. This makes the search faster and more focused, and generates less CPU load on the SharePoint server.

By default there is a single search scope: *All Sites*. To define new search scopes is a two-step process: first you create the search scope in the Central Administration tool, and then you enable this search scope in a site collection. Depending on what scope you want to use, these steps are easy or may require some planning. For example, suppose that you want to create a search scope that only matches information in the Sales team site, but no other site. The following Try It Out shows you how you would do it:

TRY IT OUT **Add a New Search Scope**

In this example, you add two new search scopes named File System and Team Sites Only.

1. Log on as a farm administrator to the SharePoint server, and then start SharePoint Central Administration.

2. Click Manage Service Applications in the Application Management section.

3. Click Search Service Application. The start page for managing search and index settings opens.

4. Click Scopes under Queries and Results to open the "View Scopes" page. Note that this page by default contains two scopes that were created when the Search Service Application was created: People and All Sites. Create the following two new scopes:

   a. Click New Scope.

   b. Set Title to **File System**.

   c. Accept the other default settings, and then click OK.

   d. Click New Scope.

   e. Set Title to **Team Site Only**.

   f. Accept the other default settings, and then click OK.

5. Now you have two new scopes (see Figure 6-8), but they are not configured yet. Note that the Items column shows Empty, which indicates that no matching items are in the index. Configure these scopes as follows:

   a. Click Add rules for the File System scope.

   b. Set the Scope Rule Type to Content Source.

   c. Set the Content Source to Project Files; that is, the content source you created in an earlier exercise.

   d. Accept the other default settings, and click OK.

   e. Now configure the next scope: click Add rule for the Team Site Only scope.

   f. Set the Scope Rule Type to Web Address.

   g. In the Folder field, enter `http://srv1/teamsite` (that is, the URL path to the subsite).

   h. Accept the other defaults, and then click OK.

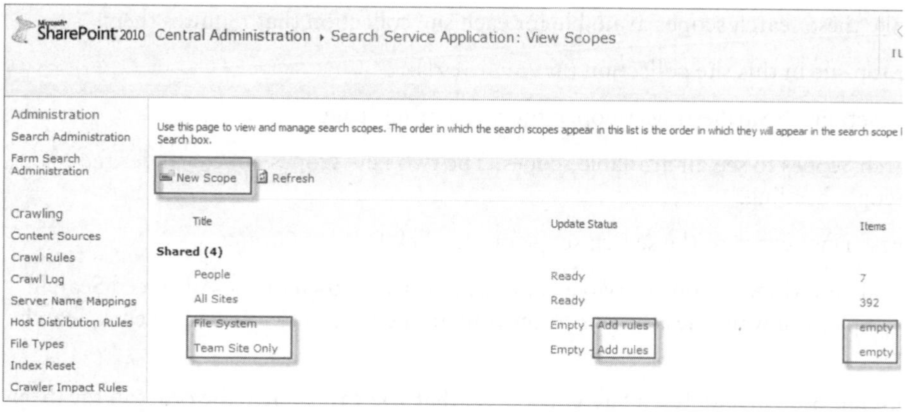

FIGURE 6-8

6. All four scopes now have rules defined; it will take some time before the number of matching items will appear, due to a scheduled process that compiles the scope rules. You can force the compilation of the scopes like this:

a. Click Search Administration in the left pane of the View Scopes page to open the Search Administration page for search and index management.

b. Locate the "Search needing update" row in the System Status section and click Start Update Now (see Figure 6-9).

c. Click Scopes and verify that the two new scopes also have items that match their rules. If they do not, either the rule is wrong, or no information yet matches these rules.

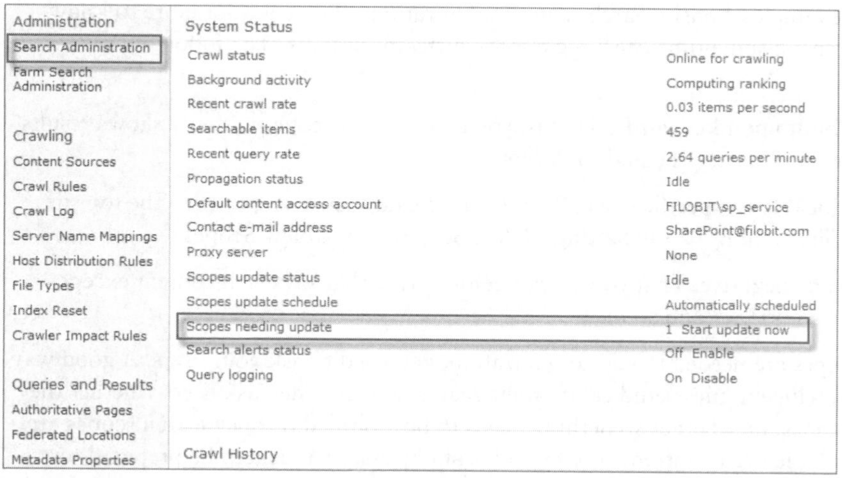

FIGURE 6-9

7. You need to make these search scopes available for each site collection that requires them:

    a. Open the top site in this site collection (`http://srv1`).

    b. Click Site Actions ➪ Site Settings to open the Site Settings page.

    c. Click Search Scopes to see all available scopes. The two new scopes appear under the Unused Scopes heading.

    d. To add these new scopes to the search scope menu, click Display Groups.

    e. You can add new scopes to one of two groups: Search Dropdown or the Advanced Search. In this example, you want these scopes to show up in the drop-down menu, so click Search Dropdown.

    f. Select both File System and Team Site Only. Note that you can change the order in the drop-down menu and set a default scope.

    g. Click OK.

8. Verify that the search scopes work: open the start site, and verify that the scope drop-down menu contains File System and Team Site Only (it may take a minute before they show up the first time). Select either of these scopes, and do a search.

How It Works

By defining a search scope, you can limit the search results so that they only show items matching a scope rule; for example, only documents found in a given content source, or a subsite in the intranet, like a public archive.

The preceding was an example of basic search scope configurations. There is a lot more to know about search scope, so spend some time checking out the different options. The following are some things to test:

➤ **Scopes can be built upon keywords:** That is, you can create a scope that only shows results where the keyword *Security* is equal to *Public*.

➤ **Scopes can be local for a specific site collection:** To create such a scope, open the top site, and then click Site Actions ➪ Site Settings ➪ Site Scopes. Click New Scopes.

➤ **Scope rules can be negative:** That is, you can define a rule that says "All content except `http://srv1/teamsite`," and so on.

To understand what scopes are needed in your organization, you need to ask your users. A good way to start is to make an intelligent guess, and create some search scopes. Then ask users whether they are happy with these scopes, or whether something needs to be modified. Proper search scopes are especially important in large organizations or when a lot of objects are indexed. Be prepared for new scope requirements as time goes by and users learn more about how to use SharePoint for their daily work.

Customizing Search Features

You can customize the search and index feature in SharePoint Server 2010 in many ways. Some require just a web browser, whereas others require you to write code in Visual Studio 2010. The next section describes some of the most common customizations that you can do without coding.

Working with Managed Properties

When you search for a string, the result page shows a new feature introduced in SharePoint Server 2010: the *Refinements* area that shows up in the left pane on the result page. This refinement contains properties extracted from the result set. For example, if you search for "Abalon" and the result contains both Word and Excel files, then the refinement will allow the user to see either Word results, or Excel results, or both.

At the end of the refinement pane, tags are listed; these tags are found in the result set, but not all tags are visible. For example, any custom column created for a document library will not show up in that tag, even if the result contains objects that have that custom column set.

You can add your custom columns to the refinement list by making them a *managed property*. This is a configuration in the Search service application part, which you either configure with SharePoint Central Administration or with PowerShell. The following Try It Out describes how to create a new managed property for a custom column.

To prepare for creating a managed property you will first create a custom column named "Color" with three choices: Red, Yellow and Green, in a document library:

TRY IT OUT   Creating Custom Columns

1. Log on as a site owner, and open the team site `http://srv1/teamsite`.

2. Click on Shared Documents to open its page.

3. Switch to the Library tab on the ribbon, and click Create Column to open the "Create Column" form where you fill in the following fields:

    a. The Column name should be Color.

    b. The type of information in this column should be Choice.

    c. Type each choice on a separate line: Red, Yellow and Green (make sure to enter these choices on separate lines).

    d. The default value should be Green. Then click OK to create the column and close this form.

4. Now wait 10 minutes until the scheduled incremental index crawler runs, or force the indexer like this:

    a. Log on as a farm administrator to the SharePoint server.

    b. Start the SharePoint Central Administration tool.

    c. In the Application Management section, click Manage service application ➪ Search Service Application to open the "Search Administration" page.

d. Click Content Sources in the left pane to open the Manage Content Sources page.

e. Open the menu for the content source named "Local SharePoint sites," then select "Start Full Crawl."

f. Wait for this full crawl to be completed before you continue with the next Try It Out.

How It Works

A custom column must be created and indexed at least once before it can be used for creating managed properties.

TRY IT OUT   **Create Managed Properties**

In this example, you want to create a managed property for your custom column *Color*, which in this example is used in multiple document libraries. Note that this exercise requires that this custom column exist in a document library, and that the crawler has indexed this library at least once.

1. Log on as a farm administrator and start SharePoint Central Administration.

2. Click Manage Service Applications ⇨ Search Service Application to open the Search Administration page.

3. Click Metadata Properties in the left pane.

4. Click New Managed Property to open the New Managed Metadata page, and then continue as follows:

a. Set the Property name to Color.

b. Click Add Mapping, and the "Crawled property selection" form opens.

c. Type **Color** in the search field; that is, "Crawled property name," and click Find.

d. Select ows_Color (your custom columns begin with "ows_").

e. Select the ows_Color(Text) property, and click OK to return to the New Managed Property page.

f. Click OK again to save and close the New Managed Property page.

The managed property is now created.

How It Works

Managed properties are custom properties that you may use to add to search web parts.

Working with Federated Search

A *federated search* means that your search query is sent to external search engines, and the search results from both SharePoint Server 2010 search and external search engines are presented on one single page. This search is an enhanced version of the federated search feature that was added to MOSS 2007 search in the "Infrastructure update" patch that Microsoft released in 2008.

SharePoint Server 2010 comes with a ready-to-use web part for displaying federated search results; all you have to do is add the web part to the search result page, and enter the source; that is, which external search engine this web part will connect to, as described in next exercise.

> **NOTE** *If no results are found from a federated search, then the web part will be hidden.*

TRY IT OUT   Configure Federated Search

In this example, you add a federated search web part that connects to Bing.

1. Log on as a farm administrator, and open the top site.

2. Search for anything to display the search result page (`result.aspx`).

3. On the results page, click Site Actions ➪ Edit Page to open this web page in edit mode.

4. In the Right Zone click Add a Web Part.

5. Select the Search web part category, select Federated Results, and then click Add.

6. Edit the new web part (open its menu and select Edit Web Part), and then continue as follows:

    a. Set the Location menu option to Internet Search Results; this is Bing.

    b. Expand the Display Properties section and change the Results Per Page to 4 (just to understand how it works).

    c. Click OK to save and close.

7. Click Save and Close on the ribbon.

8. Search for any word, and see how the search result from Bing gets listed in the federated search web part.

How It Works

A federated search web parts takes the search query and sends it to an external search engine — for example, on the Internet. The result appears on the same page as the results from the SharePoint search.

SharePoint Server 2010 comes with several preconfigured federation sources, also known as *federated locations*. You can add new locations to SharePoint Server 2010 by downloading and importing FLD files from the following Microsoft site: www.microsoft.com/enterprisesearch/en/us/search-connectors.aspx. You can see how to do this in the following Try It Out.

TRY IT OUT **Add More Federated Locations**

In this example, you add the Google News search engine as a federated location.

1. Log on as a farm administrator and open SharePoint Central Administration.

2. Click Manage Service Applications ⇨ Search Service Application to open the Search Administration page.

3. Click Federated Locations in the left pane.

4. Click the link Online Gallery in the description for this page to open the Microsoft Enterprise Search site:

   a. On that Microsoft web page, Select the Federated Search Connectors page.

   b. Expand the News section in the right pane.

   c. Select Google News.

   d. Click Save and store the FDL file on your local file system; when the download is completed, click Close.

5. Now that you have the FDL file, import it to the SharePoint Server 2010 Search Service Application:

   a. Switch back to the Manage Federated Locations page in the Search Service Application.

   b. Click Import Location, browse to the FDL file, and open it. Click OK to start the import.

   c. The page that appears allows you to edit the properties for this FDL file, if necessary. In this example you don't need to do this. Click Done to complete the import of the federation location.

   d. Verify that Google News is now is listed among the other locations.

6. Now add Google News to a second federated search web part, using the steps in the earlier Try It Out, "Configure Federated Search." Note that the new web part you add will, by default, use the same federated location as the first one; that is, Bing. Change it to use Google News. Then test it by doing a search (see Figure 6-10).

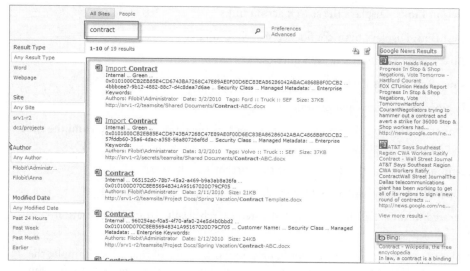

FIGURE 6-10

How It Works

Federated locations are FDL files that describe where to send the search query. You can add new locations by downloading them from the Microsoft Enterprise search page.

Managing and Customizing the Search Web Parts

SharePoint Server 2010 comes with a number of web parts related to search. In most cases, you can simply create a search site, using either the Enterprise Search Center or Basic Search Center site template. These two sites contain the typical web parts you need for searching and listing search results, including search refinements. The following is a list of all the search web parts in SharePoint Server 2010 Enterprise edition:

➤ **Advanced Search Box:** Open the "Advanced Search" tab on the Enterprise Search Site you created earlier in this chapter for an example of how this looks.

➤ **Federated Results:** Displays federated search results.

➤ **Find by Document ID:** Search a document with a specific ID.

➤ **People Refinement Panel:** Helps the user to refine people search.

➤ **People Search:** A query field for people search.

➤ **People Search Core Results:** Lists the people search results.

➤ **Refinement Panel:** Helps users to refine their search results.

➤ **Related Query:** Displays related search queries to the user query.

➤ **Search Action Links:** Displays the search action links.

➤ **Search Best Bets:** Displays high-confidence search results.

➤ **Search Box:** A field for general search queries.

➤ **Search Core Results:** Displays the search results.

➤ **Search Paging:** Displays navigation links on the search page.

➤ **Search Statistics:** Displays the search statistics, such as the number of results, and the time taken to complete the search.

➤ **Search Summary:** Displays suggestions for the current search query.

➤ **Search Visual Best Bet:** Displays high-confidence visual search results.

➤ **Top Federated Results:** Displays the top federated search results from the federation location.

All of these search web parts can or must be configured to work. Some of them, for example, the *Search Core Results,* can be configured to show more information than the default configuration does.

> **NOTE** *If you want the ranking value (that is, the stars) to be displayed in the search core results, see this Microsoft Technet blog article:* `http://tinyurl .com/SP2010-DisplayRanking.`

Most of the customizations of search web parts are performed by changing XML and XSLT code in the web part. This requires that the person doing this customization understands at least some XML code. You can also find many complete descriptions on Internet blogs, TechNet and MSDN articles, and many other sources that contain complete XML/XSLT code so you don't have to type in all code manually.

The following Try It Out describes a very simple example of how to customize a web part by modifying its XML settings; it shows how to change the advanced search page, so the user can specify that she wants Swedish search results only.

> **NOTE** *As organizations become more and more global, it is increasingly common for companies to support multiple languages, on both their external sites and their internal intranets.*

| TRY IT OUT | Customize Advanced Search Query Web Part |

In this example, you configure the web part to display the search scopes, and then you add an option to search for Swedish results only. (If Swedish isn't one of the languages included in your language pack, you can substitute whatever language is appropriate for this exercise.) You should use an XML editor for this exercise, to make viewing the code easier.

1. Log on as a site collection owner, and open the Search site.

2. Click the Advanced link to the right of the search field.

3. A page appears showing an option to select search results for a specific language; for example, English (see Figure 6-11).

4. Edit the web part to add Swedish as the second language option as follows:

a. Click Site Actions ➪ Edit Page to open this web page in edit mode.

b. Edit the Advanced Search Box web part (for example, select its checkbox and click Web Part Properties on the Web Part Tools tab).

FIGURE 6-11

c. In the web part property pane, expand the Search box and Scopes sections to see what configuration settings they contain. For example, in Scopes, set the "Show the scope picker" checkbox to display all scopes on the search page.

d. Expand the Properties section, and then select the Properties field. Click the square button that appears. A very simple text editor with all the properties for this web part opens (see Figure 6-12).

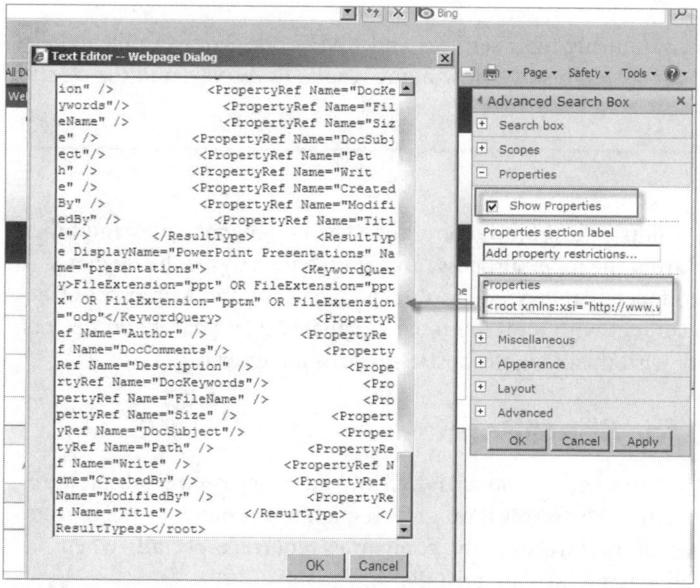

FIGURE 6-12

e. Copy all the content in this text editor (press Ctrl+A, then Ctrl+C) to your favorite XML editor. Then save a copy of the original settings, in case you need to restore them later.

f. Look for a line that looks like this; note that the `LangID = "sv"`:

```
<LangDef DisplayName="Swedish" LangID="sv" />
```

g. Scroll down to a section that begins with `<Languages>`, add a new line as the second language, and type `<Language LangRef="sv" />`. This section should now look like this:

```
<Languages>
    <Language LangRef="en" />
    <Language LangRef="sv" />
    <Language LangRef="fr" />
    <Language LangRef="de" />
    <Language LangRef="ja" />
    <Language LangRef="zh-cn" />
    <Language LangRef="es" />
    <Language LangRef="zh-tw" />
</Languages>
```

h. Copy all content in this XML editor and replace the content in the Text Editor in the web part, and then click OK.

i. Click OK again to save and close the web part configuration pane.

5. Click Save & Close on the ribbon to save this web page.

6. Open the Advanced Search page; verify that it now contains all scopes enabled for advanced search (see previous exercise about scopes) and Swedish as the second language option. Test it by first searching without a special language selection, and then with your added language.

How It Works

You can customize Search web parts by configuring their settings and XML code. For example, you can add more properties to be displayed for search results, how many results to display, and the selected search language.

One common question about search results is how SharePoint knows what language files and other objects contain. The answer is that during the index process, an algorithm analyzes the language for each object that is crawled. It is completely independent of language packs and Microsoft Office dictionaries. If a document contains content with more than one language, then SharePoint detects that and stores each language identity with the index properties for this document.

FAST Search Server 2010 for SharePoint

In April 2008, Microsoft acquired the Norwegian product *FAST* and has since been working hard to integrate it with SharePoint Server 2010. The result is an amazing add-on product to the search feature in SharePoint Server 2010 that offers features many companies require, especially when using SharePoint Server 2010 for public-facing Internet portals.

Preparing to Install FAST Search Server 2010

Installing FAST Search Server 2010 for SharePoint goes beyond the scope of this book, because it is an advanced task. However, this section describes the requirements to install FAST as well as what features and options it contains compared to standard search in SharePoint Server 2010.

This product is called *FAST Search Server 2010 for SharePoint* and its objective is to enhance, not replace, the standard search. It must be implemented as a separate server; that is, you need an extra server when adding FAST to the SharePoint farm. This requirement may change in future SharePoint releases, but the current version requires a separate server. The hardware and software requirements for the FAST server are listed in Table 6-2.

TABLE 6-2: FAST Search Server Requirements

DESCRIPTION	MINIMUM	RECOMMENDED
Operation system	Windows 2008 Server SP2 64-bit	Windows 2008 Server R2 64-bit
RAM memory	4	16
CPU cores	4	8
CPU GHz	2.0	2.0
Hard disk	50GB	1TB RAID with six spindles or more

Comparing FAST to SharePoint Search

FAST Search adds a completely new level of search functionality to SharePoint Server 2010. The following is a list of the most important features that FAST adds to the standard search features:

➤ **Content processing pipeline:** This feature makes it possible to write special search and result customizations using *FAST Enterprise Search Platform* (FAST ESP) — that is, the same type of development platform as in the original FAST product. This is important because many existing FAST customers have invested in customizations and linguistic features to meet their special needs.

➤ **Metadata extraction:** To improve the search results, FAST enables a much richer set of features to take advantage of indexed metadata to control faceted refinements, targeted queries, and relevance tuning.

➤ **Structured data search:** FAST enhances the capability to perform structured data search, compared to standard search in SharePoint Server 2010. This works with both internal SharePoint content and also external content that is connected to SharePoint by the SharePoint Business Data Connectivity service application.

➤ **Deep refinements:** The new search refinements in SharePoint Server 2010 Search are extended even further with the feature deep refinements of FAST. For example, FAST enables faceted search across any size, while retaining exact counts of the search results.

➤ **Visual search:** FAST adds document thumbnails and a preview of graphical files, including PowerPoint presentations. The user can scroll PowerPoint slides directly in the search results using a Silverlight application, without opening the file in PowerPoint.

➤ **Advanced linguistics:** FAST enhances the linguistic search features that come with SharePoint Server 2010 Search, including optimized processing for Chinese, Japanese, and Korean languages.

➤ **Visual Best Bets:** FAST enhances the search Best Bets that come with SharePoint Server 2010 to enable visual Best Bets, as well. Using a preview feature makes viewing images and videos directly in the search results possible.

➤ **Custom search experience:** This allows a customization of the search scope to adjust itself to the current user. For example, when a salesperson searches for *SharePoint*, he gets slightly different search results compared to when an IT administrator searches for the same word.

➤ **Extreme Scale and Performance:** Although the search and index performance in SharePoint Server 2010 is much improved compared to its predecessor, MOSS 2007, FAST increases it even further. For example, FAST manages a search index with billions of documents and thousands of search queries per second.

FAST Search Server 2010 for SharePoint is an advanced extension to SharePoint Server 2010, and you should plan very carefully before implementing this great search engine. It requires special FAST search administrators who analyze what and how users search in order to tune the search settings.

To conclude the comparison between all the search products that Microsoft offers, see Table 6-3, which compares all options, including the *Search Server Express 2010,* which is free, and its "bigger brother" *Search Server 2010,* which is not free.

TABLE 6-3: Comparing All Search Products that Relate to SharePoint 2010

SEARCH FEATURE	SHAREPOINT FOUNDATION 2010	SEARCH SERVER EXPRESS 2010	SEARCH SERVER 2010	SHAREPOINT SERVER 2010	FAST SEARCH SERVER 2010 FOR SHAREPOINT
Basic Search	Yes	Yes	Yes	Yes	Yes
Visual Best Bets	No	Limited	Limited	Limited	Yes
Search Scopes	No	Yes	Yes	Yes	Yes
Advanced Search Experience	No	No	No	No	Yes
Support for custom properties	No	Yes	Yes	Yes	Yes
Property extraction from unstructured text	No	Limited	Limited	Limited	Yes

SEARCH FEATURE	SHAREPOINT FOUNDATION 2010	SEARCH SERVER EXPRESS 2010	SEARCH SERVER 2010	SHAREPOINT SERVER 2010	FAST SEARCH SERVER 2010 FOR SHAREPOINT
Search Query Federation	No	Yes	Yes	Yes	Yes
Query suggestions	No	Yes	Yes	Yes	Yes
Similar results	No	Yes	Yes	Yes	Yes
Sort results based on managed properties or rank profiles	No	No	No	No	Yes
Relevance tuning by document or site promotion	No	Limited	Limited	Limited	Yes
Refine results using metadata from top results	No	Yes	Yes	Yes	Yes
Refine results using metadata from ALL results	No	No	No	No	Yes
Document thumbnails and preview	No	No	No	No	Yes
Search results available in Windows 7 desktop search	No	Yes	Yes	Yes	Yes
Social tagging and relation with people affect the ranking	No	No	No	Yes	Yes
User-generated tags and managed metadata affect the ranking	No	No	No	Yes	Yes
Multi-tenant hosting: data partitioning of crawled data based on tenants	No	No	No	Yes	No
Indexing of wide variety of web content, including JavaScript	No	No	No	No	Yes

MANAGING AUDIENCE TARGETING

One of the main problems with sharing information between many users is that a lot of information will always exist, but the average user is only interested in parts of that information. A common way of solving this problem is to create specific places for each type of information or interest group, such as local intranets for each department. However, this creates a new problem: now each user must know where to look, or even worse, information is stored multiple times, maybe in different versions. This is clearly something to avoid.

SharePoint Server 2010 has a solution: targeting. Almost every piece of information in a SharePoint site may be targeted for a specific audience. Note that SharePoint Foundation doesn't support targeting. You can use any of these groups for targeting: audience groups, SharePoint groups, AD distribution lists, and AD security groups. The following list shows the type of objects that you can control using targeting:

➤ **Wiki pages:** The content on these Wiki pages may be configured so that sales-related news items are only shown for the sales team, and IT will be the only group that sees IT related news, whereas other users may want to view both sales and IT news.

➤ **List and library items:** All lists and libraries can enable audience targeting; to display a filtered view you must display these lists and libraries using the Content Query web part. For example, you can make an Announcement item to be filtered for all but the Sales team.

➤ **Office links:** A link displayed in the Microsoft Office 2010 File Open dialog box can be filtered so it is available only to specific audiences.

➤ **Navigational links:** The links on the quick launch bar may also be targeted. The user will therefore only see the links that apply to his or her specific tasks.

➤ **Web parts:** Almost all web parts available to a SharePoint site have an option for targeting; it is usually in the web parts configuration pane, in the Advanced section.

Confusing audiences with security is easy. Let's make this very clear: audience filtering is not a security feature. It is a filter that displays or hides information based on membership in given groups. For example, if you know the URL to a news item that is hidden for you by this audience filtering, you may type it manually and still be able to view this news item.

> **NOTE** *The "Setting Up for Administration" section at the beginning of this chapter discussed some basic settings that can be helpful in following the Try It Outs for this chapter.*

TRY IT OUT **Use Target Filtering on a Web Part**

In this example, you want a specific web part in a team site to be visible only to the Start Members SharePoint group.

1. Log on as a site owner, and open the top site: `http://srv1`.

2. Add a new web part that you will configure so it's targeted only to Start Members:

  a. Click Site Actions ➪ Edit Page to open this web page in edit mode.

  b. Place the cursor where you want the new web part to be, and switch to the Insert tab on the ribbon.

  c. Click Web Part to open the Web Part form, select the Social Collaboration category, and then select Site Users. Click Add.

  d. Edit the new Site User web part.

  e. In the web part configuration pane, expand the Advanced section.

  f. In the Target Audiences section, enter **Start Members**.

  g. Click OK.

  h. Save this page.

3. Open this page as a user who is not a member of the Start Members group, and verify that this web part is not visible.

How It Works

You can target web parts and most other types of content to specific groups: SharePoint groups, security groups, distribution groups, and audience groups.

Planning Out Audience Groups

If you choose to implement audience groups, instead of using the other type of groups, you need to understand how to manage them. Audience groups are built upon rules that identify users based on properties or memberships. For example, you may have an audience group named Sales where all users with the property Department = Sales are members. A user may be a member of multiple audience groups; if so, this user will see all information targeted for any of these groups.

You may have as many audience groups as necessary, but when you get a lot of these groups getting confused is easy. Make sure you plan your audience groups, take a note of why you created these audiences, and make sure they are updated.

By default there is one audience group — *All site users*. As it says, it contains all users with access to SharePoint. You cannot remove or modify this audience.

Creating Audiences

The information in the user profile is often used for selecting members for an audience group. For example, suppose you want to create the audience mentioned earlier: Sales, based on the Department property. When you import the Department property from Active Directory into the SharePoint user profile, it is stored in two locations. The big question is which one of these locations will SharePoint use when compiling the audience group? The answer is the user profile. Actually, in most cases SharePoint uses the properties stored in the user profile database when compiling the rules that define audience groups. The exception is when the audience rule is based on memberships in AD groups; in this case, SharePoint must query the AD server to find out about group membership.

> **NOTE** *Before you start using audience groups, make sure you cannot use SharePoint groups, security groups, or distribution groups for targeting. For more details about creating audience groups, see Appendix C.*

Follow these steps to create the Sales audience group, based on the `Department` property setting in the user profile.

TRY IT OUT   **Create an Audience Group**

In this example, you create an audience group named Sales. To complete this exercise successfully, you must have the User Profile synchronization configured, and at least one user must have the AD property `Department` set to *Sales*.

1. Log on as a farm administrator, and open SharePoint Central Administration.

2. Click Manage Service Applications in the Application Management section.

3. Click User Profile Service Application.

4. Click Manage Audience in the People section.

5. Click New Audience, and then continue as follows:

     a. For Name enter **Sales**.

     b. Accept the other default settings and click OK.

     c. Select the Properties option, and select Department.

     d. Set the Operator to =.

     e. For Value, enter **Sales** (see Figure 6-13).

     f. Click OK.

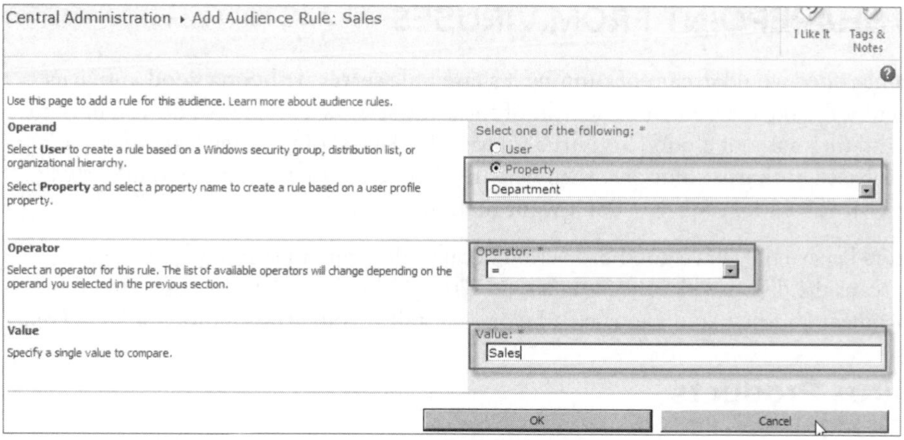

FIGURE 6-13

6. The new audience group Sales is now created. However, it does not contain any members until it has been compiled — a process that scans all users to find the ones that match this rule. Configure a compilation schedule as follows:

    a. Force a compilation for this new audience: click Compile Audience.

    b. Configure a schedule for this compilation. Go back to the User Profile management page again: click Application Management ⇨ Manage Service Applications ⇨ User Profile Service Application.

    c. Click Schedule Audience Compilation in the People section.

    d. Make sure to select Enable scheduling.

    e. Select "1:00 AM, every day," and then click OK.

7. This audience group is now created; verify that it has members. Click Manage Audience in the People section, then verify that Sales has at least one member.

8. Now test it. Go back to the page with the web part you inserted in the Try It Out "Use Target Filtering on a Web Part"; then change its Target Audience settings (in the Advanced section) to Sales. Click Check Names to verify that this audience group exists and click OK. Now log on as a user that is a member of the Sales department, and verify that you can see this web part; then log on as another user that is not a member of Sales and verify that this web part is hidden.

How It Works

Audience groups are a good choice if you cannot find matching SharePoint groups, security groups, or distribution groups. You create rules that define the membership for an audience group, typically based on user profile properties.

PROTECTING SHAREPOINT FROM VIRUSES

No network administrator would dream of running a shared file server without a good antivirus solution. SharePoint will take over much, if not all, of these file servers' content, so do you dare to store documents and files without a good antivirus solution for SharePoint, as well. If you say it's enough with client-based antivirus solutions, then you are also saying that it is okay to take away the file servers' antivirus solution. But you don't want that, do you?

Some administrators believe they have good protection because they run a file system antivirus solution that also scans the disk used by the SQL Server. Wrong! It will not detect viruses stored in the SharePoint document libraries. So do yourself a favor — install an antivirus solution for SharePoint.

Finding Antivirus Products

SharePoint does not include any type of antivirus protection; you must purchase this product separately. You can choose from several vendors, such as the following:

➤ **ForeFront Security for SharePoint** (www.microsoft.com/forefront): This very advanced antivirus solution for SharePoint is also integrated with several other security products from Microsoft, including a management application to configure and manage them all.

➤ **DocAve** (www.avepoint.com): AvePoint has supported SharePoint from its first release in 2001. Now AvePoint has teamed up with Trend Micro Partner to offer an outstanding antivirus solution for SharePoint.

➤ **Symantec Antivirus for Microsoft SharePoint** (www.symantec.com): A popular antivirus solution for SharePoint 2007 that also supports SharePoint 2010.

Make sure the antivirus solution you choose does not affect the general performance of SharePoint. It should also be easy to manage and work with; if possible, integrate it with your general IT management application.

Configuring the SharePoint Antivirus Feature

SharePoint Central Administration contains some configuration settings that relate to antivirus protection, but most of the configuration is usually done within the antivirus product you will choose. To see these configuration settings, start SharePoint Central Administration, click Security, and then click Manage antivirus settings. The settings on this page are as follows:

➤ **Antivirus Settings:** Specify when documents will be scanned and what to do with infected documents:

➤ Scan documents on upload

➤ Scan documents on download

➤ Allow users to download infected documents

➤ Attempt to clean infected documents

➤ **Antivirus Time Out:** Specify how long the virus scanner should run before timing out. Use this setting to control the load and performance hit on the server:

➤ Time out duration (in seconds): 300

➤ **Antivirus Threads:** Specify the number of execution threads that the antivirus engine may use. If the server performance goes down, then increase the number of threads:

➤ Number of threads: 5

Once again, these settings will not affect anything until you install an antivirus solution that is SharePoint integrated!

USING COMMAND-BASED MANAGEMENT TOOLS

Administrative tools with graphical user interfaces, like SharePoint Central Administration, are great to work with because you can easily see all the options and features available. But a graphical user interface can also be a problem in some cases; for example:

➤ **You need to repeat the same task:** For example, if you want to list all sites every week to learn about new sites.

➤ **You need to apply the same modification to a number of objects:** For example, if you need to apply a new site template to 250 team sites.

➤ **An inexperienced user in a remote office needs to do a customization:** For example, you want a sales manager to perform a modification on his local SharePoint Foundation server.

➤ **You need to document new settings:** For example, you want to document how to change the Search Service Application.

These are reasons why you need command-based management tools! SharePoint has from its start in 2001 used a tool named *STSADM*, which stands for *SharePoint Team Service Administration* (STS was the original name for WSS that today is SharePoint Foundation). Although STSADM has always offered powerful management operations, it lacked true support for scripting. SharePoint 2010 comes with the salvation: it is the first SharePoint release that fully supports the Microsoft general script language *PowerShell*. The following sections provide more details about these two command-based tools.

Performing Typical Administrative Tasks with STSADM

In SharePoint 2010, you will be able to manage and configure many SharePoint settings by using STSADM. However, its functionality is now reduced compared to STSADM for SharePoint 2007:

➤ STSADM 2010 supports 177 operations (that is, "commands")

➤ STSADM 2007 supports 198 operations

This reduction may look small, but it is a clear indication that STSADM will be replaced by PowerShell in the near future, maybe even in the next release of SharePoint. Table 6-4 lists all the operations that STSADM supports in SharePoint Server 2010.

TABLE 6-4: STSADM Operations in SharePoint Server 2010

OPERATION	OPERATION	OPERATION
activatefeature	enumdataconnection files	removeexemptuseragent
activateformtemplate	enumdeployments	removeformtemplate
addalternatedomain	enumexemptuseragents	removesolutiondeploymentlock
Addcontentdb	enumformtemplates	renameserver
adddataconnection file	enumgroups	renamesite
add-ecsfiletrusted location	enumroles	renameweb
add-ecssafedat aprovider	enumservices	restore
add-ecstrusteddata connection library	enumsites	retractsolution
add-ecsuserdefined function	enumsolutions	retractwppack
addexemptuseragent	enumsubwebs	runcontentdeploymentjob
Addpath	enumtemplates	scanforfeatures
addpermissionpolicy	enumusers	setadminport
Addsolution	enumwppacks	setapppassword
Addtemplate	enumzoneurls	setbulkworkflowtaskprocess ingschedule
Adduser	execadmsvcjobs	setconfigdb
Addwppack	export	setcontentdeployment jobschedule
Addzoneurl	exportipfsadminobjects	setdataconnectionfile property
allowuserformwebservi ceproxy	extendvs	set-ecsexternaldata
allowwebserviceproxy	extendvsinwebfarm	set-ecsloadbalancing
Authentication	forcedeletelist	set-ecsmemoryutilization
Backup	formtemplatequiesce status	set-ecssecurity

OPERATION	OPERATION	OPERATION
Backuphistory	getadminport	set-ecssessionmanagement
Binddrservice	getdataconnectionfile property	set-ecsworkbookcache
Blockedfilelist	getformtemplateproperty	setformsserviceproperty
canceldeployment	getproperty	setformtemplateproperty
changepermissionpolicy	getsitedirectory scanschedule	setholdschedule
copyappbincontent	getsitelock	setlogginglevel
createadminvs	getsiteuseraccount directorypath	setpolicyschedule
Creategroup	geturlzone	setproperty
Createsite	import	setrecordsrepositoryschedule
createsiteinnewdb	installfeature	setsearchandprocessschedule
Createweb	listlogginglevels	setsitedirectoryscanschedule
databaserepair	listregisteredsecurity trimmers	setsitelock
deactivatefeature	localupgradestatus	setsiteuseraccountdirectory path
deactivateformtemplate	managepermissionpolicylevel	setworkflowconfig
deleteadminvs	mergecontentdbs	siteowner
deletealternatedomain	migrategroup	spsearch
deleteconfigdb	migrateuser	spsearchdiacriticsensitive
deletecontentdb	monitordb	sync
Deletegroup	osearch	syncsolution
Deletepath	osearchdiacriticsensitive	unextendvs
deletepermissionpolicy	patchpostaction	uninstallfeature
Deletesite	profilechangelog	unquiescefarm
Deletesolution	profiledeletehandler	unquiesceformtemplate
deletetemplate	provisionservice	unregistersecuritytrimmer
Deleteuser	quiescefarm	unregisterwsswriter

continues

TABLE 6-4 *(continued)*

OPERATION	OPERATION	OPERATION
Deletewppack	quiescefarmstatus	updateaccountpassword
Deletezoneurl	quiesceformtemplate	updatealerttemplates
deploysolution	reconvertallformtemplates	updatefarmcredentials
deploywppack	refreshdms	upgrade
disablessc	refreshsitedms	upgradeformtemplate
displaysolution	registersecuritytrimmer	upgradesolution
editcontent deploymentpath	registerwsswriter	upgradetargetwebapplication
email	removedataconnectionfile	uploadformtemplate
enablessc	removedrservice	Userrole
enumallwebs	remove-ecsfiletrustedlocation	variationsfixuptool
enumalternatedomains	remove-ecssafedataprovider	verifyformtemplate
enumcontentdbs	remove-ecstrusteddata connectionlibrary	
enumdataconnectionfil edependants	remove-ecsuserdefinedfunction	

The following exercise illustrates how to perform a typical administrative task with STSADM, which in this case will be to list all sites and subsites in a site collection.

TRY IT OUT **List All Subsites for a Site Collection**

In this example you want to list all the subsites for the site collection `http://srv1`.

1. Log on as the farm administrator to the SharePoint server.

2. Open the preconfigured command shell that comes with your SharePoint installation: click Start ➪ All Programs ➪ Microsoft SharePoint 2010 Products ➪ SharePoint 2010 Management Shell.

3. This command shell is used for both PowerShell scripts and STSADM operations. To list all subsites for a site collection, type the following:

```
STSADM -O ENUMSUBWEBS -URL HTTP://SRV1
```

4. The result will look something like the following (in this example there are five subsites, all directly under the top site):

```
<Subwebs Count="5">
  <Subweb>http://srv1/customtrucks</Subweb>
```

```
    <Subweb>http://srv1/PublSite</Subweb>
    <Subweb>http://srv1/search</Subweb>
    <Subweb>http://srv1/secrets</Subweb>
    <Subweb>http://srv1/teamsite</Subweb>
</Subwebs>
```

5. However, this command only shows subsites in the first sublevel; it does not show whether deeper subsites exist. To see this, you can use the following command that will list all site collections and all their subsites in a given content database (in this example, WSS_Content):

```
STSADM -O EnumAllWebs -DATABASENAME WSS_CONTENT
```

6. The result is a complete list, too long to show here, so here is just part of the list where *all* the subsites for http://srv1 are listed:

```
    <Webs Count="9">
      <Web Id="84c1793d-9159-4138-9c30-57d8a41f9147" Url="/" LanguageId="1033"
TemplateName="ENTERWIKI#0" TemplateId="56" />
      <Web Id="628075d2-7c3d-4dbe-8e7a-b64634b96bfa" Url="/customtrucks"
LanguageId="1033" TemplateName="STS#0" TemplateId="1" />
      <Web Id="cc0414b4-c978-4f16-bdc6-db5886281153" Url="/PublSite" LanguageId=
"1033" TemplateName="CMSPUBLISHING#0" TemplateId="39" />
      <Web Id="3a85e216-86c4-4a12-a0b4-b6bcb97c610a" Url="/search" LanguageId="1033"
TemplateName="SRCHCEN#0" TemplateId="50" />
      <Web Id="160178a5-861c-454f-9f23-868a326abe2d" Url="/secrets" LanguageId="1033"
TemplateName="STS#1" TemplateId="1" />
      <Web Id="67155971-6a75-4c03-afba-38df84e895d7" Url="/secrets/teamsite"
LanguageId="1033" TemplateName="STS#0" TemplateId="1" />
      <Web Id="21a4e56f-2cd8-47c8-89fc-8a651b286a25" Url="/teamsite" LanguageId="1033"
TemplateName="STS#0" TemplateId="1" />
      <Web Id="b434da1d-7d6d-43ae-9d67-4029416ba03d" Url="/teamsite/abalon"
LanguageId="1033" TemplateName="STS#0" TemplateId="1" />
      <Web Id="e13529f3-d6b0-405b-b3c4-2b81fd90d847" Url="/teamsite/Sanjay"
LanguageId="1033" TemplateName="STS#0" TemplateId="1" />
    </Webs>
```

7. This list contains a lot of interesting information, and not only about the site tree structures. It also lists the language ID for each site (1033 is for US English) and the site template for each site (STS#0 is for Team Site and STS#1 is for Blank Site).

How It Works

STSADM is a command-based management tool for SharePoint 2010; it contains a large number of operations that you can use to list and manage most objects in SharePoint.

Using PowerShell with SharePoint 2010

PowerShell is a powerful script language from Microsoft, suitable for all kinds of applications that have an interface that allows PowerShell to read and write data to it. PowerShell 1.0 (code name "Monad") was released in 2006 for managing Windows XP, Windows Server 2003, and Windows

Vista. Version 2.0 of PowerShell was released in 2009 and supports Windows 7, Windows Server 2008 R2, and Exchange 2010.

SharePoint 2010 is the first release that fully supports PowerShell. It requires version 2.0 of PowerShell, and that is why you have to uninstall PowerShell 1.0 from Windows Server 2008 (see Appendixes A and C) before installing SharePoint.

The number of "cmdlets," that is, commands, in PowerShell 2.0 that relates to SharePoint 2010 is close to 500! It is safe to say that anything you can do with SharePoint Central Administration can also be done with PowerShell — and a lot more! If you invest time in learning how to use PowerShell for managing SharePoint, you will be greatly rewarded. At first, using it will feel a bit awkward, but after practicing just a day or two, you will begin to feel the true power a script language like PowerShell offers.

> **NOTE** *PowerShell 2.0 works both with SharePoint Foundation and SharePoint Server 2010. The only difference is that SharePoint Server supports more cmdlets and settings, because it contains many more features and service applications than SharePoint Foundation.*

This chapter cannot teach you all, or even half, of what you can do with PowerShell and SharePoint. You will find dedicated books for that purpose. But you can see a glimpse of its power and how easy it is to use. Start with seeing a listing all PowerShell cmdlets that relate to SharePoint 2010. Because there are so many, you will appreciate that you can paginate the listing — that is, show the list one page at a time.

Open the special command prompt window that allows you to work with PowerShell cmdlets on the SharePoint server: Click Start ➪ All Programs ➪ Microsoft SharePoint 2010 Products ➪ SharePoint 2010 Management Shell.

Then type this to list all SharePoint cmdlets:

```
Get-Command -pssnapin "Microsoft.SharePoint.PowerShell" | more
```

The first page begins with the following list:

```
CommandType     Name                            Definition
-----------     ----                            ----------
Cmdlet          Add-SPClaimTypeMapping          Add-SPClaimTypeMapping [-Ide...
Cmdlet          Add-SPDiagnosticsPerformance... Add-SPDiagnosticsPerformance...
Cmdlet          Add-SPInfoPathUserAgent         Add-SPInfoPathUserAgent [-Na...
Cmdlet          Add-SPPluggableSecurityTrimmer  Add-SPPluggableSecurityTrimm...
Cmdlet          Add-SPServiceApplicationProx... Add-SPServiceApplicationProx...
Cmdlet          Add-SPShellAdmin                Add-SPShellAdmin [-UserName]...
Cmdlet          Add-SPSiteSubscriptionFeatur... Add-SPSiteSubscriptionFeatur...
-- More   --
```

Press Enter or Space to display the next page; press Ctrl+C to stop the listing. This gives you an idea of how many of these cmdlets there are. Here are some tips that can help you when working with PowerShell:

➤ The Tab key works as a command-completion key. For example, if you type `Get-C` and press Tab, you will get `Get-Command`, which is the first cmdlet that begins with this string. Press Tab once more, and you will get the next matching cmdlet: `Get-ComputerRestorePoint`, and so on.

➤ Press Shift+Tab to go backwards to a previous matching cmdlet.

➤ Most cmdlets are not case-sensitive. For example, `Get-Command` is equal to `get-command`. If it does not work, then try to type exactly as the cmdlet or its arguments request.

➤ Many cmdlets have abbreviations. For example, instead of typing `Get-Command` you can type `gcm`.

➤ For help and information, type `Get-Help <cmdlet>`. For example, type `Get-Help Get-Command`.

➤ For more help, type `Get-Help <cmdlet> -full`. This gives you lots of information, including examples. Send the result to the command `more` to paginate it — for example, `Get-Help Get-SPSite -full | more`.

➤ The result given from a cmdlet can often be filtered. For example, if you list all service applications, you may want to see only their names and IDs. This is accomplished by piping (sending) the result to `Select` and defining what you want to see; see the following section.

Typical Administrative Tasks with PowerShell

PowerShell is hardly an application you can learn by reading about it. You must practice with it and see how it works. This section provides a number of examples on how to use PowerShell and its cmdlets to do typical administrative tasks with SharePoint 2010.

➤ You can list all site collections in a specific web application; in this example, `http://srv1` (the result is listed after the cmdlet):

```
Get-SPSite -WebApplication http://srv1

Url
---
http://srv1
http://srv1/my
http://srv1/my/personal/administrator
http://srv1/my/personal/anna
http://srv1/my/personal/johan
http://srv1/my/personal/malin
http://srv1/my/personal/marina
http://srv1/sites/abc
```

➤ You can list all service applications that are running, and you can filter the results so only their names and IDs are listed.

```
Get-SPServiceApplication | Select ID, Name
```

➤   If you copy one of the IDs from the filtered service applications, you can use it to show more information about that particular service application. A typical result is listed after the cmdlet:

```
Get-SPServiceApplication -identity <ID>
    Name                  : Search Service Application
    Id                    : 5b81b8ee-5fe3-478c-a9cc-b22ceeebe793
    ServiceName           : SearchQueryAndSiteSettingsService
    QueryTopologies       : {6b3fc446-cdd1-4cff-9cda-a1bfe5293f69}
    PropertyStores        : {Search_Service_Application_PropertyStoreDB_
                            55911ad46a1 64f92bae076962c263dc5}
    CrawlTopologies       : {ec52651b-ab37-4532-93d9-bac3f6ebb9ab}
    CrawlStores           : {Search_Service_Application_CrawlStoreDB_
                            9f0a81ec62a848 108d2935d6c1c2d19a}
    SearchAdminDatabase   : SearchAdminDatabase Name=Search_Service_Application_DB_
                            0c39595f829b4ed3b0c92f58947dff31
    Status                : Online
    SearchApplicationType : Regular
    DefaultSearchProvider : SharepointSearch
    Properties            : {Microsoft.Office.Server.Utilities.SPPartitionOptions}
```

➤   You can list all features that are enabled for a particular scope; for example, `http://srv1`:

```
Get-SPFeature -Site http://srv1
```

➤   The cmdlet `Set-SPSite` is used to manage settings for site collections. For example, if you want to add *filobit\marina* as a secondary site collection owner to `http://srv1`, then type:

```
Set-SPSite -Identity http://srv1-r2 -SecondaryOwnerAlias filobit\marina
```

➤   You can create a new site collection with `New-SPSite` — for example, `http://srv1/sites/test` — using the site template STS#0 (set to Team Site) and give it the name **Test Site**. Make Filobit\Johan the owner of this site:

```
New-SPSite -Url http://srv1/sites/test -OwnerAlias Filobit\johan -Name "Test Site" -Template STS#0
```

➤   You can also delete that site collection with `Remove-SPSite`; make sure this delete operation does not ask for confirmation:

```
Remove-SPSite http://srv1/sites/test -Confirm:$false
```

➤   You can combine cmdlets with a pipe (|) symbol, so the output from one cmdlet is used as input for a second cmdlet. For example, to list all subsites (in all levels) for `http://srv1`, type this:

```
Get-SPSite http://srv1 | Get-SPWeb
```

➤ You can use wildcard characters (*) with cmdlets. For example, if you want to list all site collections that start with the URL `http://srv1/sites/`, then type:

```
Get-SPSite http://srv1/sites/*
```

➤ A more interesting example is to add a setting to multiple objects with just one PowerShell line (try this with SharePoint Central Administration). For example, if you want to add Filobet/Malin as the secondary owner to all site collections that start with `http://srv1/sites/`, type this:

```
Get-SPSite http://srv1/sites/*| Set-SPSite -SecondaryOwnerAlias filobit\malin
```

➤ You can verify that the new settings are added correctly:

```
Get-SPSite http://srv1/sites/* Select Url, SecondaryContact
```

➤ Results from cmdlets can also be used as arguments in following cmdlets; this argument is often referred to as "$_". For example, if you want to list all site collections where filobit\ administrator is the owner, then enter:

```
Get-SPSite -Filter {$_.Owner -eq "filobit\administrator"}
```

You have now seen a few simple examples of what PowerShell can do. There are many more advanced things that you can do when you dive into the wonderful world of PowerShell.

 NOTE *One of many excellent sites that describes more about how to use PowerShell with SharePoint 2010 (and also 2007!) is* www.powershell.nu. *Another excellent site with general information about PowerShell is* www.powershell.com.

▶ WHAT YOU LEARNED IN THIS CHAPTER

TOPIC	KEY CONCEPTS
Different administrators	Farm administrator. Site collection administrator. Site owner.
Permission levels	Preconfigured permission roles. Based on individual permissions.
Permission groups	Security groups (AD and the local server). SharePoint groups.
Objects that can be granted permissions	Local users. AD users. Local security groups. AD security groups.
Adding permissions to external users	Claims security model. Forms-based authentication. Internal accounts.
Templates	Preconfigured settings for lists, libraries, or sites.
Search and indexing	SharePoint Foundation supports basic search only. SharePoint Server supports advanced search. FAST Search adds extended search capabilities.
Content source	A connection to a source that will be indexed by the crawler process; for example SharePoint, file servers, Exchange, Lotus Notes, and web applications.
Index scheduler	Not configured to run, by default; you must configure this manually. The best practice is to run incremental crawl only, because full crawl may take weeks for an organization with millions of objects.
Federated search	An external search engine that returns its results to the user's search query.
Copy lists	Use Microsoft Access or "Manage Content and Structure" in SharePoint Server.
Copy libraries	Export to library template with content, or use "Manage Content and Structure" in SharePoint Server.

TOPIC	KEY CONCEPTS
Audience targeting	A way to filter the content displayed, depending on the current user.
	Filter by SharePoint groups, security groups, distribution groups, or audience groups.
Antivirus for SharePoint	Must be purchased separately.
STSADM	The traditional command-based management tool that is likely to be replaced by PowerShell.
PowerShell	Microsoft general tool for powerful scripting and management of almost any server application, including SharePoint 2010.

7

Building Intranets and Internet Portals

WHAT YOU WILL LEARN IN THIS CHAPTER:

➤ How to Plan and Implement Intranets

➤ How to Plan and Implement Public Internet Sites

➤ How to Plan and Implement Extranets

➤ Differences Between Using SharePoint Foundation and SharePoint Server

➤ Customizing Web Pages

➤ Adding RSS and Twitter to the Web Site

➤ Managing Page Layouts

➤ Adding Multimedia Files to Web Sites

➤ Managing Accounts for External Users

➤ Protecting Web Connections

In previous chapters, you learned about creating sites and content and how to protect them using SharePoint's security features. This chapter presents the following three examples of SharePoint solutions:

➤ An intranet portal

➤ A public-facing Internet portal

➤ An extranet

When building these types of web applications, you are faced by multiple challenges. For example, who is the target group, and what is the budget for this project? This chapter shows you how to determine the answers to these questions. Each of the examples also describes how to build solutions using SharePoint Foundation versus SharePoint Server.

INTRANET PORTALS

An intranet is a web solution for presenting information to internal users in your organization. Intranets are the classical web application, and most organizations already have one. However, many existing intranets are no longer used as originally planned. The most common reasons for this are as follows:

➤ Information is updated too seldom.

➤ Information is targeted to specific users.

➤ The quality of the information is too low.

➤ Users cannot comment or rate information on the intranet.

➤ Finding the information you need is hard.

Before you start building an intranet, think hard about the preceding issues and how you plan to overcome them. If you don't, then your intranet project may end up being just a waste of time and money.

To get inspiration, look at successful implementations and analyze why they are successful. For example, try to visit other organizations and learn from their experience. Attend SharePoint conferences and learn more about the product. At such events, you will also often get in contact with other people who have the same interests as you. Another good way to get inspiration is to look at popular websites on the Internet. For example, look at a successful news site, such as the *New York Times* (www.nytimes.com), CNN (www.cnn.com), or BBC (http://news.bbc.co.uk). What makes such sites so interesting? You will probably notice some common factors such as the following:

➤ Constantly updated information

➤ Mix of global news and local news

➤ Lots of images and videos

➤ Capability for users to comment on articles

➤ Powerful search features

➤ Logical navigation

➤ Ease of use

Comparing your new intranet to a professional news site with lots of money and resources may feel unfair, but use the preceding list to inspire you and help you prioritize what features to focus on.

Analyzing the Needs

The objectives and expectations for the new intranet will define the technical needs for the server platform, such as how many servers you need, how much memory, and what SharePoint release is required to meet these needs.

When building a software solution, you need to know two things: the current situation and the objective. To determine these things, you must analyze what you have today as well as the users' needs, both today and tomorrow. The more time and energy you put into this analysis, the higher the chance that you will do the right thing and avoid costly mistakes. A golden rule when analyzing is to ask the right people, check the answers, if possible, and never accept a vague answer, such as "Our SQL Server will probably have capacity to support the new SharePoint server." If you are even the slightest bit unsure about some answers, make sure to start a thorough investigation to get the truth. This does not necessarily mean that you have to do everything yourself; delegating tasks to reliable people on your team is usually better.

Another golden rule when you start designing the SharePoint environment is KISS — *Keep It Simple, Stupid*! If you can make it with just one SharePoint server, then do it. If the intranet can work with just one site collection, then do it. If one document library is enough for storing all documents, then use one library. Every time you add more servers, more sites, and more document libraries, you also add to the complexity of this SharePoint solution. More complexity means more time for administration and management, plus a more complex environment to analyze if something goes wrong. So please, remember KISS — it can make your life easier, both when implementing the solution and managing it.

Your mission is to build the intranet, and you may start wondering what to do next. You should get some questions answered before you start, such as the following:

➤ Will SharePoint Foundation be sufficient as a platform for the intranet?

➤ If SharePoint Server is required, will the *Standard* edition meet the requirements, or do you need the *Enterprise* edition?

The answers to these questions will be driven by the requested intranet features. For example, if one requirement is to enable users to comment and rate information on the intranet, then you need SharePoint Server, because SharePoint Foundation does not support social tagging. Other chapters in this book compare different SharePoint editions in more detail, but Table 7-1 provides a quick summary.

TABLE 7-1: A Quick Comparison of Different SharePoint Editions

REQUESTED INTRANET FEATURE	REQUIRED SHAREPOINT EDITION
Easy web content management	SharePoint Foundation with its Wiki-based team sites
Support for basic document management and collaboration features	SharePoint Foundation
Advanced document management, with global Doc ID, document sets, and policies	SharePoint Server Standard
Advanced control of web content, such as approval workflows and scheduled publishing	SharePoint Server Standard
Support for audience targeting of web content	SharePoint Server Standard

continues

TABLE 7-1 *(continued)*

REQUESTED INTRANET FEATURE	REQUIRED SHAREPOINT EDITION
Search for content, both in SharePoint and in external content sources	SharePoint Foundation with Search Server Express 2010
Search for content, social tags, and people	SharePoint Server Standard
Advanced search with extended refinement features and preview of images, video, and PowerPoint slides	SharePoint Server Enterprise plus FAST Search Server 2010 for SharePoint
Support for social tagging; that is, users can tag, comment, and rate any type of object	SharePoint Server Standard
Support for integrating and displaying Microsoft Excel spreadsheets, Microsoft Access applications, and Microsoft Visio drawings directly in SharePoint	SharePoint Server Enterprise
Support for Business Intelligence, such as Key Performance Indicators, scorecards, and trend analysis	SharePoint Server Enterprise

Because SharePoint Foundation is a product that comes free with Windows Server 2008, and SharePoint Server is not free, you need to put a price tag on each feature on the "wish list" for the intranet. Maybe you can do fine with just SharePoint Foundation. Maybe SharePoint Server Standard will satisfy 80 percent of the needs. If so, is the remaining 20 percent so important that it is worth the extended price for SharePoint Server Enterprise?

Wishing is always free, but reality rules. Keep in mind that you can start with one edition and later upgrade; for example, if you start with SharePoint Server Standard and later want to upgrade to SharePoint Server Enterprise, the process is very easy. The real tipping point is whether you will start with SharePoint Foundation or SharePoint Server. Organizations that start with SharePoint Foundation often invest in solutions to overcome its limitations; if they later upgrade to SharePoint Server they may have to abandon these solutions if SharePoint Server has similar features built-in from start.

Building an Intranet Based on SharePoint Foundation

Once you've decided which SharePoint edition you're going to use, it is time to start implementing the intranet. This section describes how to implement an intranet based on SharePoint Foundation; later in this chapter, you'll learn how to build the same intranet with SharePoint Server 2010.

The Objective

Appendixes A and B describe how to install and configure SharePoint Foundation, so those processes are not described in this chapter. The following example assumes that SharePoint Foundation is installed, but nothing more; that is, no site collections are created yet. The main objective of this example is to create an intranet focused on displaying information targeted to the internal users in an organization called Filobit. To meet this objective, the intranet must include the following:

➤ A news list with text and pictures

➤ An RSS web part to display news items from an Internet news website

➤ A list of links to important locations inside SharePoint and other locations, including a file

➤ A Page Viewer web part that displays the content of a public Internet site

➤ Navigation lists for documents, contacts, and tasks related to specific projects or activities

➤ A list of employees, including e-mail addresses, phone numbers, and pictures

➤ A web part for displaying pictures

The Available Tools

Using SharePoint Foundation as the platform for the intranet offers the following tools and features:

➤ **Web Parts**

  ➤ *Relevant Documents*: Displays documents that are relevant to the current user

  ➤ *XML Viewer*: Displays XML information

  ➤ *HTML Form*: Connects a simple form to other web parts

  ➤ *Content Editor*: Displays rich text content, including pictures and links

  ➤ *Image Viewer*: Displays a specified picture

  ➤ *Page Viewer*: Displays another web page in an IFrame

  ➤ *Picture Library Slideshow*: Displays a slideshow based on images in a picture library

  ➤ *Silverlight*: Displays a Silverlight application

  ➤ *Site Users*: Displays a list of all users and groups with access to this site

  ➤ *User Tasks*: Displays tasks that are assigned to the current user

  ➤ *Farm Topology*: Displays the farm topology

➤ **Lists and Libraries**

  ➤ *Document Library*

  ➤ *Form Library*

  ➤ *Picture Library*

  ➤ *Wiki Page Library*

  ➤ *Announcement List*

  ➤ *Calendar List*

  ➤ *Contact List*

  ➤ *Custom List*

> ➤ *Discussion Board*

> ➤ *External List*

> ➤ *Issue Tracking List*

> ➤ *Links List*

> ➤ *Project Tasks List*

> ➤ *Survey List*

> ➤ *Task List*

➤ **Site Templates**

> ➤ *Team Site*

> ➤ *Blank Site*

> ➤ *Blog Site*

> ➤ *Document Workspace*

> ➤ *Meeting Workspace* (five different versions)

> ➤ *Group Work Site*

These are just some of the tools for building the intranet. You can also find third-party web parts on the Internet, some that are free (for example, see `www.codeplex.com`), and others that are commercial products. One problem in a pure SharePoint Foundation environment is that you cannot do target filtering on any information — either you see the list content, or you don't. The only way to control what users see in SharePoint Foundation is by using access permissions to sites and lists. SharePoint Foundation has no feature similar to the audience targeting that exists in SharePoint Server. So you must plan carefully on what to display, and how to navigate to other locations before you create an intranet for all users in your organization. One way to solve this problem is to create a top site that is the start of an intranet based on SharePoint Foundation, and that contains more general information, and from that site provide links to department intranets, team sites, and similar working areas.

Step 1 — Create a Site Collection

The first item you need to build for the intranet is a site collection. Because one requirement is to make it easy for web content managers to keep the content on the intranet updated, you will base the top site in this new site collection on the Team Site site template, as shown in the following Try It Out.

> **NOTE** *The following Try It Out will create a site collection on* `http://srv1/`
> `sites/home`*. The reason for this is to avoid a conflict in case you have created*
> `http://srv1` *for previous Try It Outs in this book. In order not to force you to
> delete* `http://srv1`*, this Try It Out will use a new URL. If you have not created
> a site collection on* `http://srv1`*, then you can use that URL instead of*
> `http://srv1/sites/home` *in the following two Try It Outs.*

TRY IT OUT   Create a Site Collection for the Intranet

In this example, you have a SharePoint Foundation server named srv1. You will create a new site collection called Home and base its top site on the Team Site template.

1.   Log on as a farm administrator, and open SharePoint Central Administration.

2.   In the Application Management section, click Create Site Collections to open the Create Site Collection page.

3.   In the new form, do the following to create the site collection:

   a.   Verify that the Web Application is set to `http://srv1`. If it's not, click on the URL and change it.

   b.   In the Title field, type **Home**.

   c.   Set the URL field to `http://srv1/sites/home`.

   d.   In the "Select a template" section, verify that the template is set to Team Site.

   e.   In the Primary site Collection Administrator User name field, enter **Filobit\Administrator**.

   f.   Click OK.

   When the process completes, a new page appears that states that the top level site was successfully created.

4.   Open a new web browser, and enter the URL `http://srv1/sites/home`. Verify that this site works as expected.

How It Works

In this exercise, you created a site collection that will be the start page of the intranet. By using the Team Site template for the top site, you will get a Wiki-based page layout, which is very easy to edit and manage for web content managers.

Step 2 — Customize the Intranet Start Page

The start page for this intranet needs to be customized. You will replace all its content with the following:

   ➤   An image at the top

   ➤   Static text below the image to greet the user

   ➤   One area with the latest news

   ➤   One area with links to other pages

   ➤   One search field

   ➤   Navigation tabs to departmental web pages

   ➤   A list with all users

To make the preceding changes, you need some pictures, some background areas, a list with links, and a list of users, as well as a list for news items.

TRY IT OUT   Customize the Intranet Home Page

In this example, you add one subsite each for HR, IT, and Sales in the same site collection you created in the previous Try It Out. You also add text to the intranet home page and create lists that will be displayed.

1.   Log on as the site collection owner and open `http://srv1/sites/home`.

2.   Create subsites for the HR, IT, and Sales departments as follows:

    a.   Click Site Actions ⇨ New Site to open the Silverlight-based Create form.

    b.   Select Team Site, and click More Options.

    c.   In the Title field, type **HR**.

    d.   In the URL Name field, type **hr**.

    e.   Accept the default user permissions.

    f.   Select Yes for the "Use the top link bar from the parent site?" option.

    g.   Click Create. The new HR site opens.

    h.   Click Home on the top navigation tabs to open the start page for this intranet (`http://srv1/sites/home`).

    i.   Repeat steps a–g to create the subsites for IT and Sales. Remember to go back to Home before creating a new department site.

3.   Create a list named Employees for all users in the organization as follows:

    a.   Click Site Actions ⇨ More Options ⇨ Contacts and in the Create page that appears, type **Employees** in the Name field. Click Create; this list will then open.

    b.   Click Add New Item, and add the name, e-mail address, and phone number of one employee in the organization. Click Save.

    c.   Repeat step 3b and add at least three people to the Employee list.

4.   Open `http://srv1/sites/home` again. You will now replace the current content on this page. Click Site Action ⇨ Edit Page to open this page in edit mode, and then do the following

    a.   Select all current content and delete it, including the picture and web part.

    b.   Switch to the Format Text tab on the ribbon. Click Text Layout and select "Two columns with header and footer."

    c.   Locate a wide and thin picture that you want to add to the top of this page. Add your picture to the header zone by choosing Insert ⇨ Picture ⇨ From Computer on the ribbon. Rescale it if necessary.

d. Set the cursor in the middle left zone, and then click Markup Style ➪ Callout 1. A colored box appears. In this box, type at least three news headlines that begin and end with double square brackets, like this: [[*The News Headline*]]. Note that you can resize the colored box.

e. Place the cursor directly to the right of the colored box, and add a second box based on the Callout 1 markup style. Type the headline **Employee of the week** and insert a picture of a person, then add some more descriptive text about this person. You can also change the style of the picture. For example, use the Picture Tools and change the Image Style to Light Border and the Position to Right. Then rescale both these boxes to make them equal in size.

f. Add the list of employees to the Footer zone at the bottom: Set the cursor in that zone, and click Insert ➪ Existing List in the ribbon to show all existing lists. Select Employees and click Add.

g. Add the list of links to the right middle zone: Place the cursor within that zone, and click Insert ➪ Existing Links ➪ Links.

h. Change the view for the link list to make it smaller: Open the menu on the web part for this list, and select Edit Web Part to open its configuration pane; then click "Edit the current view in the configuration pane." A message appears asking you to click OK to save your current work. Click OK. Deselect all columns except "URL (Url with edit menu)" and click OK. Click "Add new link" to add two or more links to any page; for example, to the HR Shared Documents library and to an external site. Make sure to add a short description, because this is the text that will be displayed in this list.

i. If necessary, align all web part objects on the web page to make the page look good, and then click Save & Close on the ribbon.

j. Remove the quick launch navigation bar on the left side of the web page: Click Site Actions ➪ Site Settings ➪ Tree View to open the Tree View page, and deselect both Enable Quick Launch and Enable Tree View.

k. The news headlines you created in step 4d have dotted underlines, which indicate they point to Wiki pages that are not yet created. Click on the first of these headlines, accept the option to create it, and enter the rich text, images, and web parts for this news article. Because this is the same type of Wiki page as the Home page, it supports the same type of rich editing features.

The picture should now look something like Figure 7-1 — a simple prototype made in 30 minutes with nothing more than SharePoint Foundation.

How It Works

Team sites are based on Wiki pages, and are therefore very easy to edit and customize. You can add web parts, pictures, and text blocks; change the page layout; and more. You can also add links to other pages (for example, news articles) by using Wiki links with square brackets, like this: [[*Link text*]].

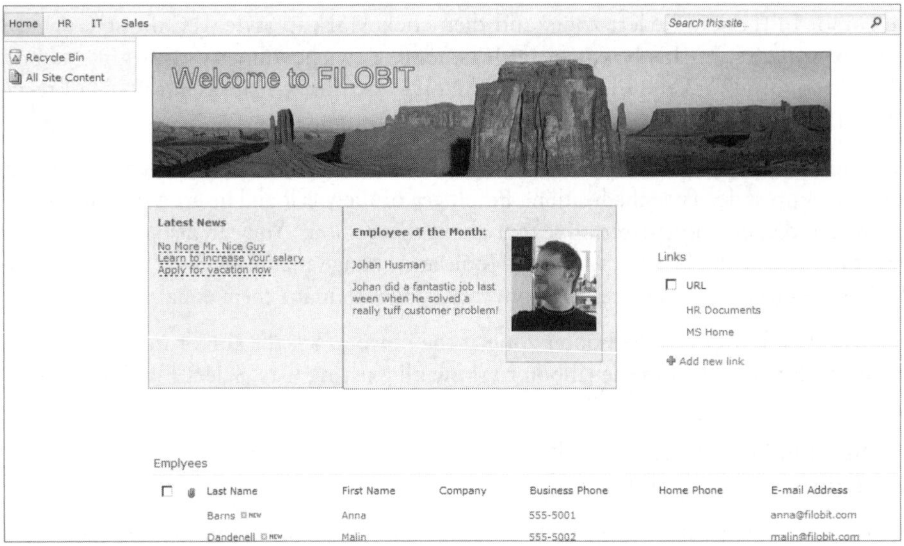

FIGURE 7-1

Creating a site collection is just the beginning. The next step is to add more text, web parts, and lists to the Home page and other pages. You could also customize these Wiki pages using SharePoint Designer 2010; for example, to add buttons and animated images and display content in external databases. For more information about SharePoint Designer, see Chapter 9.

Building an Intranet Based on SharePoint Server

Building intranets based on SharePoint Server 2010 offers so many options and features compared to SharePoint Foundation that describing them all in detail is hard, especially for SharePoint Server 2010 Enterprise edition. You should study Appendixes C and D as well as Chapters 1 through 6 to get the full picture of the available features. The best way of understanding how you can use this rich set of tools is, of course, to use them. The following sections describe building a similar type of intranet, as you did for SharePoint Foundation in the previous example, but now using SharePoint Server 2010.

The Objectives

Appendixes C and D describe how to install and configure SharePoint Server, so those process are not described in this chapter. The following examples assume that SharePoint Server is installed, but nothing more; that is, no site collections are created yet. The objective for this example is to create an intranet focused on displaying information targeted to the internal users in an organization called Filobit. Here is a list of what your intranet needs to include:

➤ A news list with text and pictures

➤ An RSS web part to display news items and weather forecasts from an Internet news website

➤ A document list that includes the latest modified documents in this site collection

➤ A Twitter client that shows a specific Twitter account

➤ Navigation lists for documents, contacts, and tasks related to specific projects or activities

➤ A web part for searching for people based on name, e-mail address, phone number, responsibilities, and more

➤ A web part that lists tasks for the current user

The Available Tools

It is safe to say that you have a very rich set of options to choose from. Table 7-2 presents the 68 web parts that come with SharePoint Server 2010 Enterprise.

TABLE 7-2: Web Parts in SharePoint Server 2010 Enterprise

Business Data Actions	Business Data Connectivity Filter	Business Data Item
Business Data Item Builder	Business Data list	Categories
Content Query	Relevant Documents	RSS Viewer
Site Aggregator	Sites in Category	Summary Links
Table of Contents	Web Analytics	WSRP Viewer
Document Set Contents	Document Set Properties	Choice Filter
Current User Filter	Data Filter	Filter Actions
Page Field Filter	Query String (URL) Filter	SharePoint List Filter
SQL Server Analysis Filter	Text Filter	HTML Form
InfoPath Form	Content Editor	Image Viewer
Media Web Part	Page Viewer	Picture Library Slideshow
My Calendar	My Contacts	My Inbox
My Mail Folder	My Tasks	PerformancePoint Filter
PerformancePoint Report	PerformancePoint Scorecard	PerformancePoint Stack Selector
Advanced Search Box	Dual Chinese Search	Federated Results
Find by Document ID	People Refinement Panel	People Search Box
People Search Core Results	Refinement Panel	Related Queries
Search Action Links	Search Best Bets	Search Box
Search Core Results	Search Paging	Search Statistics

continues

TABLE 7-2 *(continued)*

Search Summary	Search Visual Best Bet	Top Federated Results
XML Viewer	Silverlight Web Part	Contact Details
Note Board	Organization Browser	Site Users
Tag Cloud	User Tasks	

This is an impressive list of web parts. And it does not stop here — SharePoint Server 2010 also offers 19 types of lists and libraries and more than 20 types of site templates. It is obvious that the challenge is to know what tool or feature to use and when. That is a good challenge; it means that with SharePoint Server, you can build an intranet that meets all kinds of requirements, without needing to develop or purchase extra web parts or features. Still, there will be times when the user's expectation of the intranet requires added functionality. In this case, you will be happy to know that the Visual Studio 2010 development platform comes with really great support for building any kind of SharePoint solution.

Step 1 — Create a Site Collection

Start by creating a site collection for the intranet. Instead of using the Team Site template, as you did for SharePoint Foundation, you will use a more advanced Wiki template called Enterprise Wiki.

> **NOTE** *The following Try It Out will create a site collection on* `http://srv1/sites/sps`. *The reason for this is to avoid a conflict in case you have created* `http://srv1` *for any previous Try It Outs. If you have not created a site collection on* `http://srv1`, *then you can use that URL instead of* `http://srv1/sites/sps` *in the following two Try It Outs.*

TRY IT OUT   **Create a Site Collection for the Intranet**

In this example, you will create a new site collection called SharePoint Server and base its top site on the Enterprise Wiki template.

1. Log on as a farm administrator, and open SharePoint Central Administration.

2. In the Application Management section, click Create Site Collections to open the Create Site Collection page.

3. In the form that appears, enter these settings:

    a. Verify that the Web Application is set to `http://srv1`. If it's not, click on the URL and change it.

    b. In the Title field, type **SPS**.

    c. Set the URL field to `http://srv1/sites/sps`.

d. In the "Select a template" section, switch to the Publishing tab, and select Enterprise Wiki.

e. In the Primary Site Collection Administrator name field, enter **Filobit\Administrator**.

f. Click OK. When the site creation process is finished, a new page appears that states that the top-level site was successfully created.

4. Open a new web browser, and enter the URL **http://srv1/sites/sps**. Verify that this site works as expected.

How It Works

In this exercise, you created a site collection that will be the start page of the intranet. By using the Enterprise Wiki template for the top site, you will get a Wiki-based page layout, which is very easy for web content managers to edit and manage.

Step 2 — Customize the Intranet Start Page

You need to customize the start page for the intranet. You will replace all its content with the following:

- ➤ An image at the top
- ➤ A static text below the image to greet the user
- ➤ One area with the latest news
- ➤ One box to search for people
- ➤ One general search box
- ➤ RSS web parts to external RSS feeds
- ➤ Navigation tabs to departmental web pages
- ➤ A web part that lists the latest Twitter from a specific account

To do the preceding, you need some pictures, some background areas, a list with links, a list of users, and a list for news items. To test People Search, you must configure the User Profile Service Application; see Appendix D.

TRY IT OUT Customize the Intranet Home Page

In this example, you add one subsite each for HR, IT, and Sales. You also add text to the intranet home page and create a list that will be displayed.

1. Log on as the site collection owner and open http://srv1/sites/sps.

2. Enable all features for this site collection as follows:

a. Click Site Actions ➪ Site Settings to open the Site Settings page.

b. Click Site Collection Features in the Site Collection Administration section.

c.   Activate all features except SharePoint 2007 Workflows (this is only needed if you migrate from SharePoint 2007 and want old workflows to operate in SharePoint 2010).

d.   Go back to the start page at `http://srv1/sites/sps`.

3.   Create subsites for the HR, IT, and Sales departments as follows (these will be local intranets and will, in this example, do fine with a Team Site template, since it also is Wiki-based):

a.   Click Site Actions ⇨ New Site to open the Silverlight-based Create form.

b.   Select Team Site, and click More Options.

c.   In the Title field, enter **HR**.

d.   In the URL Name field, enter **hr**.

e.   Accept the defaults, including the Team Site template.

f.   Select Yes for the "Use the top link bar from the parent site?" option.

g.   Click Create. When the creation process is completed, the new HR site opens.

h.   Click SPS on the top navigation tab to open the start page for this intranet (`http://srv1/sites/sps`).

i.   Repeat steps a–g to create sites for IT and Sales; remember to go back to Home before creating the next department site.

4.   Next you customize the Home page as follows:

a.   On the Home page, click Edit Page to open this web page in edit mode.

b.   Select all current content (press Ctrl+A) and delete it.

c.   Add a picture the same way you did in the SharePoint Foundation intranet example — that is, set the cursor where you want the picture, and then on the ribbon's Insert tab, click Picture ⇨ From Computer. Rescale the picture if necessary.

d.   Insert a table under the picture with two columns and two rows.

e.   In the top-left cell, add a welcome heading and some text. You can use the formatting controls on the Format Text tab and the Styles and Markup Styles buttons to get the style you want. Also in this cell, add some Wiki links to news articles using double square brackets, like this: [[**Article_Headline 1**]], [[**Article_Headline 2**]], and so on.

f.   In the top-right cell, click the Insert tab on the ribbon to insert the People Search Box web part (in the Search category), and click OK. Then open its web part menu and select Edit Web Part to open the configuration page for this web part. In the Query Suggestion section, deselect "Show query suggestions," and in the Appearance section, change the title to **Search People**. Change the Width to 180 pixels, and then click OK to save.

g.   Directly under the People Search web part, in the same table cell, insert a picture of a user. Click on it and use the Picture Tools Design on the ribbon to set the Image Style to Light Border and the Position to Right. Add text in this column; for example, **Employee of the Week!** and some descriptive text.

h.   In the second line of the left table column, insert the Content Query web part, and then open its configuration pane (see step 4f). In the List Type section, set "Show items from this list type" to Document Library, "Content Type" to Document Content Type, and "Show items of this content type" to Document. In the Presentation section, set "Limit the number of items to display" to 5. In the Appearance section, change the Title to **5 Latest Documents**. Click OK to save this web part.

i. In the second row of the right table cell, insert the User Tasks web part, and then change its Title to **My Tasks** in the Appearance section. Click OK to save this web part.

j. Under the first table, create a new table with one row and three columns.

k. In the left table cell, insert the RSS Viewer web part. Open the configuration pane for this web part, and enter a URL to a RSS feed; for example, `http://eu.wiley.com/WileyCDA/feed/RSS_WILEY2_COMPUTING.xml`. In the Appearance section, change Chrome Type to None. Click OK.

l. In the center table cell, insert a second RSS Viewer. Open the configuration pane for that web part and enter the RSS feed URL to a weather channel; for example, `http://newsrss.bbc.co.uk/weather/forecast/9/Next3DaysRSS.xml`. In the Appearance section, change Crome Type to None. Click OK to save.

m. In the right table cell, insert an XML Viewer web part. Open its configuration pane to configure it to display your favorite Twitter account (see the Note that follows this Try It Out.).

n. Click Save & Close on the ribbon to save the new start page for this SharePoint Server–based intranet.

Your start page should look similar to the one shown in Figure 7-2.

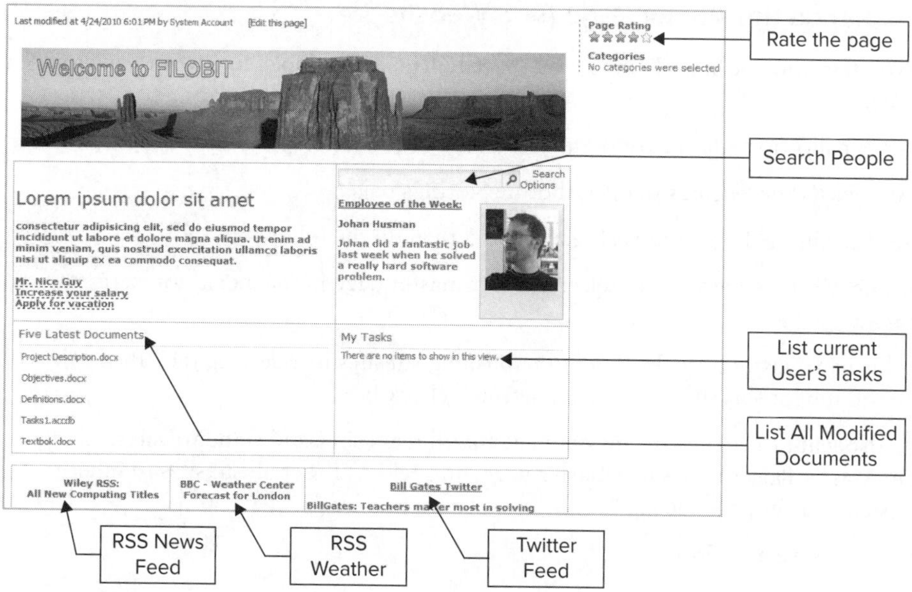

FIGURE 7-2

How It Works

The Enterprise Wiki site template in SharePoint Server supports many more features and web parts than the team site template in SharePoint Foundation, such as the Content Query web part that can present all new documents regardless of what site they belong to, and web parts for listing current user's information, displaying RSS feeds, searching for people, allowing the rating of content, and a lot more.

> **NOTE** To add a Twitter listing without code, see Randy Drisgill's great blog at http://blog.drisgill.com/2009/04/using-xml-web-part-to-show-your-twitter.html.

The intranet design in the preceding Try It Out was very simple and basic. The next step is to analyze what other features you could use to make it more interesting. For example, SharePoint Server supports audience targeting, so you should try it to see whether you can make a single web page that adjusts itself to the current user. Remember that users want to read about information that relates to them; seldom do they want to read information regarding other users and departments.

One quick way to change the overall layout of sites in an SharePoint Server–based environment, is to use another master page (Chapter 9 covers creating and managing master pages in more detail). The following exercise describes how to change to another master page to see how it looks. If you don't like the new design, simply reselect the original master page.

TRY IT OUT   Change the Master Page for a Website

In this example, you test how the SharePoint Server–based intranet site looks like when you change the current master page.

1. Log on as a site collection administrator, and open the intranet (http://srv1/sites/sps).

2. Click Site Actions ⇨ Site Settings to open the Site Settings page.

3. Click Master Page in the Look and Feel section, and then do the following:

   a. In the Site Master Page section, select another master page in the menu; for example, Nightandday.master.

   b. Push this new master page down to all publishing subsites by selecting the "Reset all subsites to inherit this site master page setting" check box.

   c. If you also want to change the master page for all team sites and standard sites, change System Master Page to the same master page, and select "Reset all subsites to inherit this system master page setting."

   d. Click OK to save and close.

4. Open the start page and view the result (see the example in Figure 7-3). Check other sites in this site collection. If you want to revert to the previous layout, change the master page settings back to the original master page, and make sure to select "Reset all subsites to inherit this system master page setting" if you used it in step 3b and/or 3c.

FIGURE 7-3

How It Works

A master page defines the navigation parts, page header, and style settings for fonts and colors. You can change the master page for any site, and push it down to subsites if necessary.

INTERNET PORTALS

When you're building an Internet-facing portal site, the same features are available to you as when you're building an intranet site. The main difference between these two types of sites has to do with protecting the Internet site and making sure that anonymous users don't see what you don't want them to. Note that an Internet site is not the same as an *extranet* site: the latter is used when external partners, customers, and other groups of known users access information on your website. For an administrator to be able to manage external users' access to SharePoint sites, these users must have user accounts in your IT environment that can be validated by SharePoint, or to be more exact, by the Internet Information Service (IIS) that governs the SharePoint application.

The Challenge of Public Websites

An Internet-facing portal (with a capital *I*, because it is a name!) is typically a site that people can access without any authentication process; that is, they log on automatically as anonymous users. SharePoint 2010 can offer anonymous access to the following:

➤ A separate *site collection* in an existing SharePoint environment configured as the public Internet site

➤ A single *subsite* in an existing site collection that hosts the public Internet site

➤ A separate *SharePoint Foundation or SharePoint Server 2010 server* dedicated for running the public Internet site

You face two important questions when planning a public Internet site: "How will users get access to this site?" and "Should the site be based on SharePoint Foundation or SharePoint Server 2010?" These questions and how to answer them are discussed later in this chapter.

Managing Web Content

Managing the content on a public Internet site is no different than managing it on an intranet portal. You use the same features and have the same tools for both types of sites. This is one of the great advantages of using SharePoint for both the intranet and the public Internet sites. They are both configured and managed the same way, and the content manager, authors, and users will know how to read, add, and search information and documents in both the intranet and Internet site. Reusing information is also easy. For example, PDF documents that are stored on the intranet can be replicated to the Internet site, and news on the Internet site can also be listed on the intranet, without any replication.

The typical tasks and issues that relate to content management on a public Internet site are as follows:

➤ Reusable content

➤ Look and feel

➤ Performance

➤ Search functionality

➤ Security

➤ Accessability

Later in this chapter, you find out more about security for both public Internet sites and extranet solutions. The following sections discuss the other listed items.

Reusable Content

If you want to publish information to 100,000 users instead of 100, you are probably more concerned about the quality of the content and that it is grammatically correct. Having some people who are responsible for approving web content before it gets published is very common. Chapter 4 covers content management, including workflows for approving new content.

One way to ensure the quality of the content is to use preconfigured text strings for text that will be used over and over again, such as copyright text and legal paragraphs. SharePoint Server supports a feature for this called *reusable content*. For example, you can use this feature to add predefined text blocks for the following types of content:

- ➤ Copyright text
- ➤ The byline (the author of an article)
- ➤ Quotes
- ➤ Legal statements
- ➤ Contact information, such as URL addresses and phone numbers

All reusable content is stored in a preconfigured list called Reusable Content in the top site of an SharePoint Server site collection. This is not just a list of predefined content that you can add to a web page; when you add reusable content, it will have a live link back to the appropriate item in this list of reusable content. For example, if you add copyright text to 1,000 web pages, and then later want to modify the text for the copyright, all existing copies of this copyright text will be replaced by the modified version. You can also configure a single item in the Reusable Content list to just copy the text to the website and then break the inheritance.

TRY IT OUT   **Manage Reusable Content**

In this example, you review and add items to the Reusable Content list.

1. Log on as a site collection owner, and open the Home site (`http://srv1/sites/sps`).

2. Click Site Actions ➪ View All Site Content to open the All Site Content page.

3. Click on the Reusable Content list.

4. This list contains some examples that you need to adjust to your organization's need. For example, to edit the byline, do the following:

   a. Click Byline.

   b. Click Edit Item.

   c. Change the Reusable HTML to **By Göran Husman** or any name you prefer.

   d. Click Save.

   e. Items in this list must be approved. Select the Byline check box and click Approve/Reject on the ribbon. Then select Approved and click OK.

5. Add a quote titled Quote-How_Hard to the Reusable Content list, as follows:

   a. Click Add New Item to open the Reusable Content - New Item form.

   b. In the Title field, type **Quote-How_Hard**.

   c. Select the "Show in drop-down menu" option.

    d. In the Reusable HTML section, click the Click here to add new content link and type **How hard can it be?**. Note that this text field supports full rich text formatting, including tables, links, and images.

    e. Click Save.

    f. Approve this item: Select the Quote-How_Hard check box, and click Approve/Reject on the ribbon. Select Approved and click OK.

6. Test these two reusable contents:

    a. Open the start page `http://srv1/sites/sps`, and click the Edit button on the ribbon to open this web page in edit mode.

    b. Place the cursor where you want the byline.

    c. Click the Insert tab on the ribbon, and then click Reusable Content.

    d. Hover your mouse over alternatives in the menu. Note the Select Byline preview function.

    e. Place the cursor where you want the new quote, click Reusable Content, and select Quote-How_Hard.

    f. Click Save & Close on the ribbon.

How It Works

Reusable content is a special type of list with strings that you can add to a publishing web page, but not team sites. Modifying an item in this list also updates all existing copies of that string on web pages.

Look and Feel

Another important issue regarding public Internet sites is the look and feel of the web pages. They must be nice and aesthetic to look at, but also easy, intuitive, and smooth to work with. Achieving this goal is harder than you may think. Many people with a technical background sometimes want to focus on functionality and then (if time permits) on graphical design. This method is so very wrong! It seems like end users can accept and forgive some functional flaws, as long as the site looks really nice.

Comparing the look of a public intranet site and an Internet site is a little like how people behave when the weekend comes: When you are going to a party, you want to look good; but after the weekend comes the plain working days — then you need to be dressed to work, not to party. It's the same concept with these sites: Internet sites are party time — put on the makeup, make it look good, and impress the public — whereas an intranet is the gray working day, so be careful with the makeup and forget about the tight dress.

If you are not a design specialist — that is, one part artist and one part technical designer — you should always look for assistance when designing a public Internet site. It will cost you money, but it will be worth it, because the whole idea of a public Internet site is to show your company at its best!

Performance

The subject of performance is related to the earlier discussion about look and feel. Looking good is not enough; a site must also be fast. What good does it do if you buy a $300 outfit and then your brain is not connected? Who will be impressed then? Make sure your site is both good-looking and fast.

With SharePoint, you can do the following to optimize the performance of your public Internet sites:

➤ Build a server farm that meets the expected workload. For example, you may need two or more web front-end servers and a fast SQL Server.

➤ Use the cache features that speed up access to websites with lots of content, such as large pictures and videos.

SharePoint Server 2010 is the first release that supports streaming video and audio. This means that you can add this type of multimedia to a public Internet site, and visitors will enjoy a quick start of the media file, regardless of how large it is. You insert media files to a publishing web page using the Video And Audio button on the ribbon. The streaming feature is automatically activated for these files.

> **NOTE** *For more information about streaming rich media and cache optimization in SharePoint 2010, see* `http://blogs.msdn.com/ecm/archive/2010/03/12/` `introducing-web-content-management-in-sharepoint-2010.aspx`.

Search Functionality

Previously you could have public Internet sites that did not support searching for internal content, but this is no longer true! If you build a nice-looking and fast site that does not support searching, then visitors to your public site will wonder why. To have a great Internet site, you need to support searching.

SharePoint Foundation supports a very basic search and index functionality. To get a decent search feature, you need to install the free Search Server Express 2010 on the SharePoint Foundation server.

SharePoint Server 2010 has a really great search feature! Public Internet sites that are based on SharePoint Server 2010 will be able to offer one of the absolute best search engines on the market. If you want to increase the search capability a lot more, then install a *FAST Search Server 2010 for SharePoint*. It is made for public sites, especially web shops and other types of sites that offer a lot of information to their visitors.

What about Bing, Google, and other web-oriented search products on the market? Well, many of them are fantastic search engines, but they all have the same problem: They do not understand SharePoint's structure and features; for example, custom metadata, managed keywords, tags, ratings, and notes. For example, if you use Google to search for the words *Volvo Custom Design*, you are satisfied if you find some good web pages that contain information about that query string. But a user in SharePoint who enters the same query string is most likely looking for a particular site or document and will not be happy with something that is close. They want a very specific object.

What License Does a Public Site Require?

Determining the answer to the question of what public site licensing is needed is similar to the process for determining whether to create an intranet or Internet site. It depends on the features you need, and how much money you are willing to spend on the solution. You have already seen that SharePoint Server 2010 contains great web content management (WCM) functionality, which is required for a serious Internet website. But for a small organization with simple needs, such as nice and easy-to-use content management features, the SharePoint Foundation with its Wiki-based team sites will do just fine. Some of the pros and cons of these versions are listed in Table 7-3.

TABLE 7-3: SharePoint Foundation or SharePoint Server for Internet Sites

FEATURE	SHAREPOINT FOUNDATION 2010	SHAREPOINT SERVER 2010
Web content management	Basic WCM is supported, including version history for web pages and check out/in.	There is full support for page layout files, version history, approval control, workflows, and more. You will not need any staging or test server.
Search	Yes, if you install Search Server Express 2010.	Supported in any source location that SharePoint has access to, and that is open for anonymous access.
Master pages	Partly supported	Full support
Excel services	No	Yes (Enterprise only)
Access service	No	Yes (Enterprise only)
Visio service	No	Yes (Enterprise only)
Form service	No	Yes (Enterprise only)
Price	Free server and client	Not free; requires server license and a special client license named *SharePoint Server 2010 for Internet*.

Installing a Public Website

SharePoint Server 2010 comes with a preconfigured site template especially for public Internet sites. Use it to get going quickly. For example, if you need to do a proof-of-concept (POC) installation to see whether SharePoint Server is the right product for your new public Internet site, install this site template and see what you can do with it; then change it or build a completely new site template from scratch.

Creating the Portal Site

To create a site collection for a public Internet site, you follow the same procedures you have done multiple times in this chapter, which is use the SharePoint Central Administration tool to create the site collection. However, you may choose to use a special site template for public sites named *Publishing Portal*, as described in the following exercise. To get better control of the access of this public site, you should use a separate IIS web application. This requires that the external DNS server publishes this name to the Internet and that the firewall is configured to accept incoming connections to this web application from the Internet.

TRY IT OUT Create a Public Internet Site

In this example, you create a new site collection in a new web application with a host header named Start. This example requires that you can add an entry to the DNS server for the new web application. You need to be a domain administrator to do this.

1. Log on as a domain administrator to a domain controller in your domain (which is `Filobit.com` in this example).

2. Start the DNS management tool: Click Start ➪ Administrative Tools ➪ DNS. Use this tool as follows:

   a. Expand the Forward Lookup Zones node and then the `Filobit.com` node (the domain name in this example).

   b. Right-click on the Filobit.com node name and select New Alias.

   c. In the form that appears, type in **Start** in the Alias Name field, and then type in **srv1.filobit .com** in the "Fully qualified domain name" field.

   d. Click OK. Now you have a registered alias name that you will use when you create the new web application in SharePoint.

3. Log on as the farm administrator to the SharePoint server, and start the SharePoint Central Administration tool.

4. In the Application Management section, click Manage Web Applications. On the Web Applications Management page, do the following:

   a. Click New on the ribbon.

   b. Select "Create a new IIS web site" and type **Start-Internet-Portal** in the Name field.

   c. Set the Port to **80**.

   d. Type **Start** in the Host Header field (this must match the name in step 2c).

   e. Set Allow Anonymous to Yes (this is required because it will be a public Internet site). The page should now look like Figure 7-4.

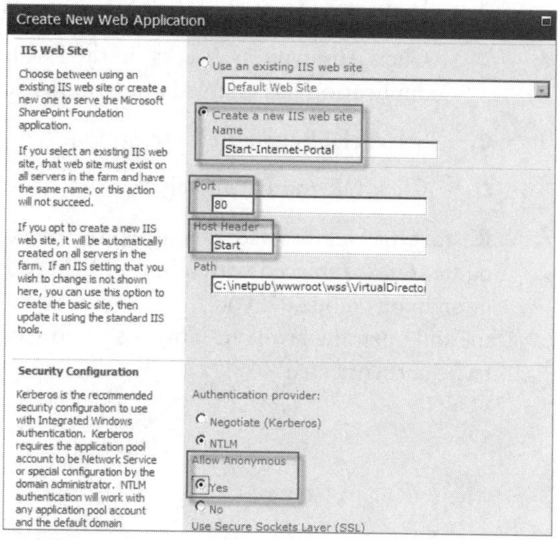

FIGURE 7-4

    f.   In the Application Pool section, select "Use existing application pool," and then select SharePoint - 80.

    g.   Change the Database Name to **Start_Content.**

    h.   Go to Service Applications. If you want to make all default service applications available in this new web application, then accept the default. If not, then change the "group of connections" to [Custom], and select the service applications you need in the Internet portal.

    i.   Click OK to save and close.

5.   Now you have a web application ready to host the new Start Internet portal site and accept anonymous access. Create the new site collection in this web application as follows:

    a.   Open the start page in SharePoint Central Administration.

    b.   Click Create Site Collections to open the Create Site Collection page.

    c.   Verify that the Web Application is set to `http://start`; if it's not, click on its name, and change the web application.

    d.   Type **Start** in the Title field.

    e.   In the Site Template section, click the Publish tab and select Publishing Portal.

    f.   Type **Filobit\Administrator** as the Primary Site Collection Administrator.

    g.   Click OK to save and close.

6.   When the new site collection is created, open it in a new web browser. Note that your name is listed in the top-right part of the page, which means you are authenticated. You configured this web application to accept anonymous access, but that is not enough. You need to configure each site to accept anonymous access as well, like this:

    a.   In the new Start site, click Site Actions ⇨ Site Permissions to open the Permissions page.

    b.   Click Anonymous Access on the ribbon (this button will only be displayed if the web application has enabled anonymous access).

    c.   Select the Entire Web site option.

    d.   Click OK to save and close.

7.   Restart the web browser, and open the Start site again (`http://start`). Note that your account name is now replaced with a link to Sign In (see Figure 7-5). You are now running this site in anonymous mode. (If you still see your account name, then it is cached. Log out and then in, and open the browser. Now it should work.) If you need to manage this site, click Sign In to be authenticated.

FIGURE 7-5

How It Works

Public Internet sites require that the web application that hosts the site collection is configured to accept anonymous access. If you use the same server for both the intranet and the public Internet site, you need two different web applications. Because both of them also use TCP port 80, you need to add a unique string as the Host Header name ("Start" in this example), and then create a matching DNS alias name pointing to the same server ("SRV1" in this example).

Creating Content

Creating content for public Internet sites is exactly the same process as for intranet sites. The easiest page layouts to work with are the Wiki-based sites; that is, Team Sites for SharePoint Foundation and Enterprise Wiki for SharePoint Server (see the section "Intranet Portals" in the beginning in this chapter, and Chapter 4). When you build a public Internet site based on the site template *publishing portal*, as in the previous Try It Out, it contains the basic libraries and workflows typical for a site that requires control over content management.

The old content management features in MOSS 2007 will still be supported, but they are enhanced with the new features for managing pictures and content in an easier way. For example, you can add news items by creating web pages based on the same page layouts as in MOSS 2007, and then publish them on a web page by using the Content Query web part.

TRY IT OUT   Create News Items in a Public Internet Site

In this example, you use an existing page library for storing news items and press releases, and then present these items by using the Content Query web part. To complete the following steps, you must complete the previous Try It Out, "Create a Public Internet Site."

1. Log on as a site collection owner, and open the Start site you created in the previous Try It Out exercise (http://start).

2. Click Sign In at the top right of this web page to authenticate. This is necessary to manage this site collection, which is configured to run anonymous access.

3. This top site already contains a subsite named Press Release; you can use it as an example of how to work with content in a public site. Click the Press Release link in the left pane.

4. Add a news article as follows:

a. Click Site Actions ⇨ New Page to open the New Page form.

b. Type in a page name (for example, **Article-1**) and then click OK.

c. The default page layout appears and is based on the Wiki standard. You can change to another layout, including the old news layouts from MOSS 2007, by clicking Page Layouts on the ribbon's Page tab, but in this example, keep the default page layout.

d. Change the title to **My First Article**.

e. Add some text and insert some pictures (click the arrow *under* the Picture button on the Insert tab if you want to upload pictures from the file system), as described in earlier Try It Out exercises in this chapter. You can also use the Wiki commands; for example, type [[and wait for the menu that appears with the existing pages, lists, and objects you can display. Use the keyboard arrows to select Lists in this menu, and then press Tab on the keyboard. Now you can see all available lists. Select Pages and then press Tab. Now you can see all objects in the Pages library. Select one of these objects, and press Enter on the keyboard. The two ending]] characters are automatically entered.

f. At the end of this page, locate Rollup Image. This is the image that will appear when the Content Query web part shows this news article as a summary. Click the "Click here to insert a picture from SharePoint" link and add a previously uploaded image, if possible in a small size (typically 100–200 pixels wide).

g. When this page is completed, click Save And Close on the Page tab ribbon.

h. Due to the preconfigured settings for sites based on the Publishing Portal template, you need to check in and then approve this article, using a content approval workflow. (You can later change these settings by configuring the Page library in this site.) Click the Publishing tab on the ribbon, and then click Submit to open the Submit For Approval form.

i. Type **My first article** in the Comments field, and click Continue.

j. The approval workflow starts, and you need to define some settings for this workflow. Enter **Pls approve my article.** in the Request field; set the "Due Date for All Tasks" to tomorrow; and set the "Duration Per Task" to 1 day (see Figure 7-6). Click Start.

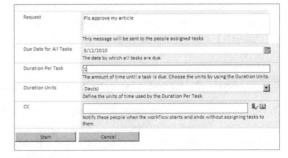

FIGURE 7-6

k. Your article appears, but it is not yet approved, so it is not public yet. The approver now needs to review and approve the article. Click Site Actions ⇨ View All Site Content to open the All Site Content page, and then click the Workflow Tasks list.

l. Note that only members of the Approvers group can approve this article. Since you are a site collection administrator, you can add your account to that group. In the Assigned To list column, click Approvers to open that group, and then click New to add your account.

m. Now you need to go back to the Workflow Tasks list (see step 4k). Click on the name of the workflow to open the Workflow Task form, and then click Approve (you can also open its properties and approve it).

5. The article is approved, but it is not displayed on any web page by default. You need to add a Content Query web part that displays news articles. To display the news articles on the Press Releases subsite, click the Press Releases link (`http://Start/PressReleases`). Then do this:

a. Click the Edit button on the ribbon, or click Site Actions ⇨ Edit Page to open this page in edit mode.

b. Scroll down this page to the Left Column zone, and then click Add a Web Part.

c. In the Content Rollup category, select Content Query and click Add.

d. In the new web part, click the "Open the tool pane" link.

e. Expand the Query section, and then select "Show items from the following list." Click the Browse button to open the "Select List or Library" form, and select the Pages library. Click OK to save.

f. Change the Content Type to Page Layout Content Type.

g. Expand the Appearance section and type **Latest News** in the Title field.

h. Click OK to save and close the web part configuration pane.

i. Click Save & Close on the ribbon to save the modified web page. You must also check in and approve the Press Release web page to make the new web part visible for all users: Click Site Actions ⇨ View All Site Content ⇨ Pages, select the check box for the "default" page file, and click Check In on the ribbon to open the Check In form. Select the Major Version (Publish) option, and click OK to start the Approval workflow. Click Start, and then approve the modified page.

6. Verify that the news article summary is listed on the page. The image you selected as the rollup image will be listed with the news title in the original size, so make sure to select rollup images in the correct size (see Figure 7-7).

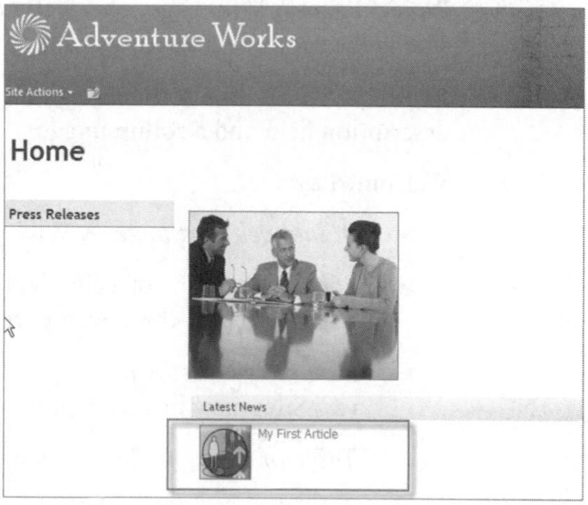

FIGURE 7-7

How It Works

News articles and similar articles are added as pages. You can select another page layout, if required. By default, the library that contains all news articles is configured to require approval, mandatory check out, and major and minor version history. All this is to prevent accidentally publishing content that is not approved. You can change these settings by configuring the Page library settings.

Working with Page Layouts

When creating news articles and similar content, you can choose between several page layouts; some of them are new for SharePoint Server 2010, and some are very similar to the page layouts in MOSS 2007. Creating new page layouts or editing existing ones is possible with SharePoint Designer, which you learn more about in Chapter 9.

SharePoint Server 2010 provides the following default layouts:

- ➤ **Article Pages** (all these contain one rollup image placeholder):
    - ➤ *Body only:* A Wiki page with no special image placeholder, but you can add pages to the Wiki pane
    - ➤ *Image on left:* A Wiki page with one image placeholder on the left side, and placeholders for an article date and byline
    - ➤ *Image on right:* A Wiki page with one image placeholder on the right side, and placeholders for an article date and byline
    - ➤ *Summary links:* A Wiki page, plus a web part for adding links, and placeholders for an article date and byline
- ➤ **Enterprise Wiki Page:** A Wiki page, plus web parts for page ratings and categories (tags)
- ➤ **Project Page:** A Wiki page, plus web parts for page ratings, categories, a URL to a project site, and a project status indicator
- ➤ **Redirect:** A URL link to the location this page will be redirected to; also includes a description field and a rollup image
- ➤ **Welcome Page:**
    - ➤ *Blank web part page:* A Wiki page, plus eight web part zones
    - ➤ *Splash:* Contains placeholders for a page image at the top center, two Summary link web parts, and three web part zones
    - ➤ *Summary links:* A placeholder for an image at the top-left position, a Wiki pane, two Summary link web parts, and three web part zones
    - ➤ *Table of Contents links:* Like the Summary links, plus a Table of Contents web part in the top web part zone

> **NOTE** You can change a page layout for an existing content page; for example, a news article.

To get to know these different page layouts, try them all, and see what they display and how they look. The Splash and Summary links are commonly used for the default page in a site. The Table of Contents has a special web part that is not available in other pages; it can display all the sites and pages in the current site collection (but not in other collections).

Using Multimedia for Public Sites

Multimedia files, such as audio and video, add a lot of value to any type of website, both intranets and public Internet sites. The problem has always been that SharePoint required the user to download the complete media file before it could start. You could also find third-party products or customized solutions that made streaming media in SharePoint possible.

Streaming is a technique where the media file starts as soon as a small part of it has been downloaded to the client; then during the presentation, the rest of the file is downloaded. The effect is that the user does not have to wait for a complete download, so the video or audio will start just a few seconds after the user selects the media file.

SharePoint Server supports streaming media with a special type of Silverlight web part, which works as a media player. This player supports files in WMA, WMV, and MP3 formats. The following Try It Out demonstrates how you can add multimedia to a Wiki-based web page.

TRY IT OUT Display Multimedia Files in SharePoint Server

In this example, you have a video file (.WMV) on your local file server that you want to display on a public Internet site. Note that this procedure will also work in an intranet portal. To complete this exercise you must have Silverlight installed on all computers that will open this page (see `www.microsoft.com/Silverlight` for download instructions).

1. Log on as a site owner, and open the top site (`http://start`).

2. Click the Edit button on the ribbon to open this page in edit mode.

3. Place the cursor on the web page where you want to add the media player.

4. Switch to the Insert tab on the ribbon, and then click Audio And Video.

5. Click on the Media Player web part and configure it as follows:

   a. Note that the Media tab on the ribbon is activated.

   b. Click the *text* Change Media to open its menu.

   c. Select From Computer.

   d. Browse to your media file (WMA, WMV, or MP3), and upload it to the Images library.

   e. Enter any properties you want for this file; for example, title, keywords, and comments.

f.   Test it: Click on the media player to start the film; click again to stop it.

g.   Note the different options on the Media tab: Start Media Automatically, Loop Until Stopped, and properties for Title, Size, and Styles.

h.   Instead of displaying the default image for the media player you can add your own preview picture: Click the *text* Change Image to open its menu, and then select From Computer to upload a picture (JPEG or PNG) and add it to the media player in one step.

6.   Switch to the Page tab on the ribbon, and click Save & Close. Because public sites have all the content control activated, you now have to continue as follows:

a.   Switch to the Publish tab on the ribbon.

b.   Click Submit to start the approval workflow (that you can remove if you don't want it).

c.   Enter a comment if you want, and click Continue.

d.   In the workflow form, click Start (you don't need to fill in these fields if you just want to do a test).

e.   Ask the approver to view their mailbox and follow the instructions to approve.

7.   The modified page with the Media Player web part is now published. Test it and verify that it works.

How It Works

You use the Silverlight-based Media Player web part in SharePoint Server 2010 to stream multimedia files. The WMA, WMV, and MP3 file formats are supported.

NOTE *Media files in other formats, such as AVI and MPG, must be converted before they can be used by SharePoint's media player. There are many free and commercial tools that can convert other file types to the supported WMA, WMV, and MP3.*

EXTRANET PORTALS

An *extranet* is a web part that is used by both internal users and external users, such as partners and customers. The only difference between a typical intranet and an extranet is that the latter is accessible from the Internet by people who do not belong to your organization.

So the main concerns when implementing an extranet are how to manage these external users and how to allow them access in a controlled and secure way.

Configuring an Extranet

The typical scenarios when implementing an extranet are as follows:

➤ **A few external people need access to a project site during its lifetime.** In this case, you probably don't need to set up a permanent extranet; simply create user accounts for these external users, grant them access to the project site (and nothing more!), and send them a link they can use from outside the organization. You must also configure the firewall to accept incoming connections to that project site.

➤ **Some external users need access for a long time.** For example, partners may need to find information about your products. In this case, you may need to configure a dedicated extranet solution, especially if many external people need access to it. If the information volume they need is limited, you can make one subsite (or possibly a separate site collection) the target site for these external users.

➤ **Many external users need constant access.** For example, if you have a member site for a user group community or a web shop with users who log on, you should build a separate SharePoint environment — either a separate farm, or a separate web application or site collection in your existing farm.

The first of these scenarios does not require any extra configuration, other than creating accounts for these external users, so it is not covered in this chapter. The third scenario (when using a separate farm) is also not covered, because this is no different from deploying any SharePoint server (see Appendixes A–D). However, it is instructive to explore how to enable a single site collection, or even a single subsite, for external users.

Granting external users access to SharePoint is the easy part; you do it exactly like you do any internal account. The big question is, "Where will you store the external user accounts?" You have these options:

➤ **Store them in the Active Directory (AD):** This option may be okay for a few accounts, but not more. The problems with such a solution are as follows:

   ➤ Your organization must purchase Windows licenses for these accounts.

   ➤ Your IT department is responsible for maintaining these accounts; for example, to reset passwords.

   ➤ AD accounts may have access to any type of resource on the internal network; for example, file, print, and mail servers. You really want to limit the access for these users to SharePoint alone.

➤ **Store them as local user accounts on the SharePoint server, with the following stipulations:**

   ➤ Your organization must purchase Windows licenses for these accounts.

   ➤ Your IT department is responsible for maintaining these accounts; for example, to reset passwords.

➤ **Store them using forms-based authentication (FBA):** This method requires that you configure a separate database that contains the account names and password. A web form is designed that users fill in to get authenticated when accessing SharePoint. Here are a few points about FBA:

➤ You don't need any license (besides SharePoint if the extranet is based on SharePoint Server instead of SharePoint Foundation).

➤ Your IT department is responsible for maintaining these accounts; for example, to reset passwords.

➤ You need to create and maintain the database and the login form.

➤ If users want to update documents on the extranet, they need to download them, update, and then upload them. FBA does not allow users to edit the document while it's stored in SharePoint.

➤ **Store them using claims-based authentication:** A new method introduced with SharePoint 2010 allows user accounts to be stored in the external system; for example, another organization's account system, Live ID accounts, and so on. Here are a couple of points about this method:

➤ It requires that you understand and can configure claims-based authentication, which is not so simple.

➤ With claims-based accounts, you simply grant the external users access to the extranet area (site, site collection, or server).

From an IT-management perspective, the claims-based method is the best, but it is also the most advanced to implement and configure. Whatever method you select, these external accounts will be granted access to the extranet just like you would any internal user. You can add these users to SharePoint groups and audience groups, or grant them direct access to SharePoint sites, lists, or objects.

MANAGING THE SECURITY OF PUBLIC WEBSITES

Technically, you could use an internal SharePoint server for the public Internet site, and then open the network firewall for anonymous access using port 80 — but this is a STUPID idea! Do not do this; it will only be a matter of hours before your entire network is invaded by nasty applications such as Trojan horses, viruses, and applications that use your internal mail server to send spam to the world. Doing this would result in all information on your network now being considered public, regardless of whether it is "secured" by file system permissions or not. There is a vast number of hacking tools, and they're free! Even a "script-kiddie" (a young computer nerd with no expertise in hacking and breaking applications) will be able to use these hacking tools as long as they can find a way into your internal network. So do you get the message? Do not open any anonymous connections from the Internet into your internal network. Period.

Avoiding Threats When Accessing Sites Over the Internet

A better idea, but still not good enough, is to place the SharePoint server directly on the *demilitarized zone* (DMZ), which is a network segment directly connected to your firewall, typically used for servers open for public access. The reason this is not a good idea is that the SharePoint server will be open for attacks — either *Denial-of-Service* (DoS) attacks or simply hacked using brute-force methods (that is, looking for known weaknesses in the server and its applications). Maybe you think this is not a serious problem? Then think again about all the public Internet sites where the content has been modified in a way that is not so flattering for the organization that owns the site.

The best idea is to use a firewall that works as an application proxy; that is, it can "pretend" to be an internal application, such as a SharePoint site. It works as follows (see also Figure 7-8):

1. The external user starts their browser and enters the URL to the SharePoint site. The connection will go to the network firewall.

2. The network firewall checks to see whether this URL is open for anonymous access; if so, a connection is established between the external user's web browser and the application proxy server that pretends to be a SharePoint server.

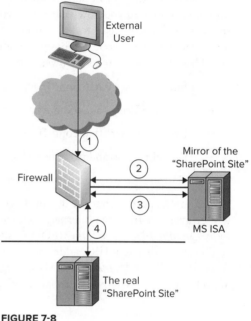

3. Whenever the external user requests content from the SharePoint server, such as a web page, the application server contacts the internal SharePoint server, retrieving that content.

4. The internal SharePoint server sends the requested information to the application server, which passes it back to the external user.

The important thing to understand is that under no circumstances will the external user get a direct connection to anything except the application proxy server when using this setup. All requests for content will be evaluated by that application proxy to ensure that public users can access only the web sites and content that are public.

FIGURE 7-8

Using Microsoft TMG Firewall

Microsoft has a great product for allowing external users access: *Microsoft Forefront Threat Management Gateway* (TMG), which replaces *Microsoft Internet Security and Acceleration Server* (ISA). It comes with configuration wizards that make configuring TMG to be a proxy server for SharePoint (and many other applications, such as an Exchange server) very easy. In fact, TMG is an excellent firewall as well as an application proxy, and you can most likely replace your current firewall solution with TMG.

The TMG server allows you to configure different security settings for different parts of the SharePoint farm. For example, you may have a single SharePoint server that is used for both the intranet and a public Internet site. With TMG, you can easily configure the connections to the intranet portal such that they require encrypted Secure Socket Layer (SSL) communication, whereas the public Internet part of the same server accepts anonymous connections over TCP port 80. TMG ensures that using the anonymous connection to access anything on the intranet is impossible.

> **NOTE** *Forefront TMG is a key component when exposing SharePoint to the Internet. Setting up a secure and safe connection that is fast and easy to manage is very easy with TMG. Read more about TMG at* www.microsoft.com/tmg.

Configuring Web Zones for Public Sites

Appendix A provides a detailed description on how web zones work in SharePoint. It is critical that you understand this before setting up access to SharePoint sites from the Internet. Here is a quick summary to remind you how web zones work in SharePoint: There are five zones, and the idea is to enable you, the administrator, to configure five different URLs to the same web application and its site collections. Each zone can have individual settings; for example, whether SSL should be used or not. These five zones are as follows:

➤ **Intranet:** Users that come from the internal network; that is, local users

➤ **Internet:** Users that come from outside the network, typically over the Internet

➤ **Extranet:** Users that come from either the local network or outside

➤ **Default:** The standard zone, which is set when you created the web application

➤ **Custom:** An extra zone, to be used if the other zones don't apply

For example, suppose that the default URL to the intranet portal site is http://srv1. If this intranet will be available from the Internet, then you cannot use a local address, that is, srv1. You need a *Fully Qualified Domain Name* (FQDN) address, such as http://intranet.filobit.com. How can you have two different URL addresses to the same intranet portal? You can do so easily by using the *Alternate Address Mapping* (AAM) settings in SharePoint Central Administration and configuring up to five different URLs for the same web application.

TRY IT OUT   **Add an FQDN Address to an Intranet**

In this example, you need to add a second URL to your intranet http://srv1 to enable access from the Intranet.

1. Log on as a farm administrator and start SharePoint Central Administration.

2. Select Application Management in the left pane, and click Configure Alternate Access Mappings to open the Alternate Access Mappings page.

3. Click Edit Public URLs to open the Edit Public Zone URLs page.

4. In the Alternate Address Mapping Collection box, select Change Alternate Address Mapping Collection, and then click the web application with the URL http://srv1. (By default this is SharePoint - 80.)

5. A single URL is listed: http://srv1. Click Edit Public URLs again. A form with all five web zones opens.

6. Add `http://intranet.filobit.com` in the Internet zone field (see Figure 7-9).

7. Click Save.

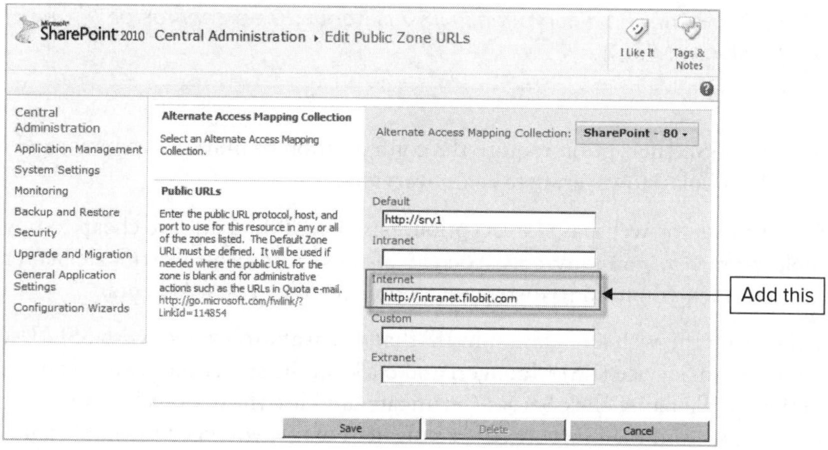

FIGURE 7-9

How It Works

AAM makes it possible to use up to five different URL addresses for a single web application and its site collections. The names are just labels; they don't mean anything special; for example, using the AAM zone *Custom* for Internet access is okay. What is important is to configure other applications so they match the AAM settings. The TMG rule, especially, must contain the same URL address as the AAM, and the external user must use that URL. Also, an Alias Record must exist in the public DNS with the same URL address that points to the TMG server.

Protecting the Extranet with SSL

Secure Socket Layer (SSL) is the most common encryption method for Internet connections. Setting it up is easy, ensuring that the data traffic between two computers is protected. SSL encryption is supported by SharePoint and is typically used when external web clients access SharePoint servers inside the organization. The easiest way to find out whether SSL is used for a connection is to look at the URL: If it starts with `https`, then it is protected by SSL.

An SSL connection is initiated at the very beginning of the connection. This means that when the user enters their account name and password, this traffic is also encrypted, and therefore protected. That is the reason it is okay to allow Basic Authentication, which is a method for authenticating a user that sends the user credentials unencrypted, including the password. Without SSL, this would be a very dangerous (and stupid) way to authenticate, but with SSL, *everything* is encrypted.

Why not use SSL every time — for example, both inside and outside the internal network? The answer is that it requires CPU resources and therefore reduces the overall performance. In plain English: If you want maximum speed and performance, avoid any type of encryption, including

SSL. If you need to protect the data traffic between the client and the server, then you don't have a choice: Use SSL!

> **NOTE** *In Windows 2008, the SSL encryption in IIS 7 is about 20 percent faster than in previous versions of IIS.*

The general steps for enabling SSL encryption require the configuration of multiple systems, and is not described in detail in this book. However, here is an overview:

1. Get an X.509 Certificate for web-based encryption, based on SSL. They are cheap to buy now; for example, from `www.godaddy.com`. You can also use Microsoft Certificate Server to create your own, but then you need to distribute its root certificate to all clients.

2. Install the certificate on the web application in IIS that you want to protect with SSL. Use the Internet Information Service (IIS) Manager, and click on the server name; for example SRV1. Then in the middle pane, click Server Certificate, and use the actions listed on the right pane to request and then import the certificate. Finally, you need to enable SSL encryption in the web application that hosts the SharePoint site that will be accessed over the Internet.

3. Configure your Forefront TMG server to accept SSL connections to the web application using an `https` URL address.

4. Configure an AAM address — for example, on the Internet zone — to use the same https URL address used in step 3. The previous "Configuring Web Zones for Public Sites" section described more about AAM zones.

In summary: SSL is very important to use for any connection between a client on the Internet and a SharePoint server (or any server, really) on the local network. If you are unsure of how to set up and configure SSL, ask for help. Setting up SSL correctly is too important to take a chance with; make sure it works 100 percent correctly the first time!

▶ WHAT YOU LEARNED IN THIS CHAPTER

TOPIC	KEY CONCEPTS
Needs analysis	Do this before anything else; it will guide you to the correct SharePoint edition.
	Engage your users early in the project, to ensure you get their input and impressions.
Intranet options	Using SharePoint Foundation or SharePoint Server depends on the features required by your users.
Public Internet sites	SharePoint Foundation offers basic functionality, but SharePoint Server is required if you need more advanced features.
Extranet sites	Same as intranet, but you must plan where to store external user accounts.
FBA	Forms-based authentication — a solution for extranet where the external user accounts are stored in a separate database, instead of AD.
Twitter feeds	You can configure an XML web part to show any Twitter account.
Web content management	WCM — very important for large intranets, and especially public Internet sites.
	SharePoint Foundation offers easy-to-use, Wiki-based editing of content pages with basic WCM features.
	SharePoint Server offers all the features in SharePoint Foundation, plus many more features, multimedia support. and content control.
Look and feel for websites	Very important for public Internet sites; make sure to have a designer professional help you with this.
Search	Important in all types of websites, including intranets as well as also public Internet sites.
SharePoint Server 2010 for Internet	A license form that is necessary when SharePoint Server 2010 servers are used for public Internet sites.
Multimedia support	SharePoint Server 2010 supports streaming of media files based on WMA, WMV, and MP3.
	Silverlight is required for the media player.

continues

(continued)

TOPIC	KEY CONCEPTS
Claims-based authentication	This is a new authentication mechanism introduced in SharePoint 2010 that makes it possible for IIS to authenticate user accounts stored in external systems.
	This is hard to configure but has very nice features.
ForeFront Threat Management Gateway	TMG — a very powerful, but easy-to-use firewall and proxy application server.
	Replaces MS ISA 2006.
Web zones	Used by AAM to allow up to five different URL addresses for a single web application.
Alternate address mapping	AAM — a feature configured with SharePoint Central Administration.
Fully qualified domain name	FQDN — the complete name, including domain, to a server; for example, `srv1.filobit.com`.
Secure Socket Layer	SSL — an encryption method for web connections.
	Recognizable by the `https://`.

8

Customizing SharePoint 2010

Creating new sites and lists in SharePoint 2010 by using only the browser is an easy task, but most organizations want to customize their look and feel; this is sometimes also referred to as *branding* or *design*.

Some of this customization is very easy to do, whereas other modifications require extensive knowledge of Hypertext Markup Language (HTML), Cascading Style Sheets (CSS), Extensible Stylesheet Language Transformations (XSLT), and general web design expertise to create a sophisticated design with a good portion of web standards and usability.

This chapter gives you the basic information needed to change the design of a SharePoint website. It also describes how to create no-code collaborative solutions in a broad spectrum of business scenarios, like using customized pages with in-built or custom SharePoint web parts, and managing client-side scripts. This chapter also gives you insight into developing a web part with Visual Studio 2010.

Chapter 9 teaches you more about composites, how to use SharePoint Designer 2010 to create a design, and how to customize a SharePoint site or a page.

MAKING DIFFERENT TYPES OF CUSTOMIZATIONS

A SharePoint 2010 site or a page out of the box is useful as it is and has a quite nice interface to start with, but it probably needs some customization to get the right look and feel and to get the dynamic information that will be displayed on the pages.

The following sections can help you understand the opportunities about customizations you can do with basic features such as changing a theme, managing the behavior of the navigation controls, or just changing the logo for your team site.

You will also learn how to use web parts to customize the information that displays in the SharePoint pages and how to determine when SharePoint Designer 2010 or Visual Studio 2010 is the best option for you when it comes to customizations. Let's get started with:

- ➤ Customizing look and feel with the browser
- ➤ Customizing pages with web parts
- ➤ Customizing with SharePoint Designer 2010

Customizing a Site's Look and Feel Using the Web Browser

You can customize the look and feel for the portal by applying a theme to a site or changing the logo type, the site name, the description of the site, and more. You can do this with the web browser on any computer, as long as you have the proper permission; you need to be a SharePoint administrator of the site or a member of the Designer site group to perform modifications of this type.

Here are some common things related to look and feel that you can easily customize through the browser:

- ➤ **Title and description of the website.** The title appears on each page of the site and the description appears on the home page.

- ➤ **Logo.** You can associate a custom logo — for example, your corporation's logo — to a site. Copy your logo to the front-end Web server; for example, `/_layouts/CustomImages/logo.png`. You can use Internet Information Services manager and browse to this virtual directory for the SharePoint web application. Using an image that's 60 × 60 pixels is recommended, if you are using the out-of-the-box look and feel.

➤ **Global navigation.** You can change the behavior of the global navigation (navigation across sites) quite a bit just by using the browser:

  ➤ Specify whether the navigation should display the same navigation items as the parent site — a setting that sometimes can be useful for an isolated site in the site collection.

  ➤ Specify whether the navigation should show subsites.

  ➤ Specify whether the navigation should show pages.

  ➤ Set the maximum number of dynamic items to show within a level in the navigation.

  ➤ Change the type of sorting (to either automatic or manual) for the items in the global navigation.

  ➤ Specify sort order, ascending order, or descending order.

  ➤ Specify whether to sort by Title, Created Date, or Last Modified Date.

  ➤ Navigation editing and sorting — you can reorder and modify the navigation items, and creating, deleting, and editing navigation links and headings is possible. You can also move navigation items under headings and choose to display or hide pages and subsites.

➤ **Quick Launch.** You can specify whether the Quick Launch (within a site) should be displayed to aid navigation.

➤ **Tree view.** You can specify whether the tree view should be displayed to aid navigation.

➤ **Theme.** You can specify a theme to change fonts and color scheme for your site. You select a SharePoint theme and use it as is, or fully customize such a theme. You can also create your own themes with Microsoft PowerPoint and upload them to the SharePoint Theme Gallery.

➤ **Welcome Page.** You can select which page to use as the welcome page for the site.

➤ **Master Page.** You can select which master page should be used by all publishing pages, form pages, and view pages in the site, and if you like, all the subsites.

➤ **CSS.** You can specify custom CSS to apply to a site and its subsites.

Customizing with Web Parts

To customize more than just the look and feel of SharePoint sites and pages, you can customize web content such as data, textual content, and images in a SharePoint page with web parts. A web part can be a prebuilt SharePoint module or a custom module developed with Visual Studio 2010 or SharePoint Designer 2010.

Web parts are simply the basic building blocks of a page in SharePoint and are server-side controls that run inside the context of special pages that consist of a title bar, a frame, and content. Web parts enable users to customize a page, such as specifying the ways in which information appears on the page. Web parts are configurable and reusable components, and they have several properties that can be customized through the browser.

To add a web part to a page through the browser, you just edit the page, click on the Insert tab in the ribbon, and then click the Web Part button. Then you can pick a web part to be inserted into the page from the list of available web parts in SharePoint.

Suppose that you are responsible for your team's website, and you need to change the homepage default layout to reflect the priorities of your team by specifying what information to display. To do this you can edit the page and remove, rearrange, or add web parts. Maybe you want to insert a Discussion Board web part, an embedded video related to your team's need of information, a Chart web part that displays your team's sales financial results, or a web part that integrates external data from a proprietary Line Of Business (LOB) system. These tasks are where web parts come in.

SharePoint comes with many out-of-the-box web parts that are ready to be used; the number of web parts that are included in SharePoint depends on which features are activated in the SharePoint environment and whether you are using SharePoint Server 2010 or SharePoint Foundation 2010.

Many SharePoint web parts do not appear in the global Web Part Gallery, but can be populated to the global gallery. But most of them have to be used in a very specific scenario; for example, the Blog Year Archive web part, which is only a function for blog sites.

As an administrator for a SharePoint site, you can upload and use web parts from vendors who sell web parts or open source communities such as CodePlex, or you can upload your own custom web parts that have been built in Visual Studio 2010 or SharePoint Designer 2010. Web parts can also be packed into one or more feature(s) and must be deployed on the SharePoint server.

Table 8-1 explains common customizations you can make to the page with the out-of-the-box web parts in SharePoint, using the browser.

TABLE 8-1: Examples of Some of the Common Web Parts

NAME	DESCRIPTION	FOUNDATION
Content Editor	Allows authors to enter rich text content or a client-side script	Y
Content Query	Used to display a dynamic view of content from sites	N
RSS Viewer	Used to display an RSS feed	Y
Media Web Part	Used to embed media clips (video and audio)	N
Excel Web Access	Used to interact with an Excel workbook	N
Chart Web Part	Used to visualize data on your sites	N
Silverlight Web Part	Used to display a Silverlight application	Y
Note Board	Used to enable users to leave short public notes on the page	Y
Site Users	Used to list the site users and their online status	Y
Picture Library Slide Show	Used to display a slideshow of images from a picture library	Y

Chapter 7 also provides a quick summary of all the web parts that come with SharePoint Server Enterprise.

Customizing Using SharePoint Designer 2010

You have now seen that you can customize the user interface of SharePoint a lot just by using the browser. But sometimes you need to make more modifications than what is possible with only the web browser, or you need to create advanced no-code collaborative solutions. This point is where SharePoint Designer 2010 comes in.

If you need to design in a customized way; create a web part that gets the information from an external data source such as an SQL database, an XML file, or a web service; set up an advanced workflow for a site; or if your task is to build an application for report processing — you will definitely need to use SharePoint Designer 2010.

SharePoint Designer 2010 is available as a free download and is a "What you see is what you get" (WYSIWYG) editor for SharePoint 2010, and it covers nearly every aspect you can think of when you need to design, modify, or enhance your SharePoint 2010 environment.

Chapter 9 provides more information about the SharePoint Designer 2010; here is a list of some things that are covered in that chapter:

➤ Creating the web design for the SharePoint site

➤ Managing a master page, page layouts, and CSS files

➤ Managing the Data View web part

➤ Managing the XSLT List View web part

➤ Customizing a SharePoint list form

➤ Using a web service

➤ Working with XSLT and Xpath

➤ Creating a workflow

CUSTOMIZING BASIC FEATURES

SharePoint has many smart and automated functions in regard to sites, pages, lists, or how you can provide the pages with various kinds of information in just a few clicks in the browser. However, to meet the users content and design needs, you will probably have to customize SharePoint in one way or another. Let's begin with the basic customizations you can make with the browser.

Customizing the Logo, Name, and Description

Examples of items you can customize and change after a site has been created are the site's title, description, and logo, as described in the following Try It Outs.

TRY IT OUT   Change the Title and Description

In this example, you learn how to change the title and the description for the team site.

1. Open a team site; for example, `http://srv1/teamsite`.

2. Click Site Actions ➪ Site Settings and click the Title, description, and icon link in the Look and Feel section.

3. Change the Title in the text box to **IT department**. Type a description for this website in the Description text box; for example, **Welcome to the IT department**.

4. Click OK.

5. Click IT in the breadcrumb to get to the homepage. You can now see that the site's title and description have changed.

How It Works

The title will appear on each page in the site as a part of the breadcrumb, in the global navigation, and at the top of the browser. The description only displays at the homepage of the site.

After you have changed the title for this site, go back and rename the site with its original name of Team Site; this book has several references to this sitename.

TRY IT OUT   Change the Logo in a Team Site

You can replace the site logo that appears at the top of the site with a custom image. In this Try It Out you replace the default image for the team site with another image.

1. Create or find a new logo in one of these formats: `.pgn`, `.gif`, or `.jpg`. The recommended size is 60 × 60 pixels.

2. Upload this image in the Site Assets library. Click Site Actions ➪ View All Site Content and click the Site Assets link under the Document Libraries section.

3. Click the Add document link. Browse to your image, select it, click Open, and then click OK.

4. Right-click the link for the name of the image. Select Copy Shortcut or the equivalent depending on which browser you use.

5. Click Site Actions ➪ Site Settings and click the Title, description, and icon link in the Look and Feel section.

6. Paste the URL into the text box. Delete the first part of the URL. Use a relative URL; for example, `/teamsite/SiteAssets/MyLogo.png`.

7. Click the "Click here to test" link below the URL field to make sure you got the correct URL, and then click OK. You can now see that the logo has changed.

How It Works

If you change the logo in the top site for the site collection, all the sites below it in the hierarchy will inherit this logo, but the change does not apply to subsites that have already been associated with a unique logo.

If you need to access a logo file in more site collections in the SharePoint web application, you can create a new subfolder under the `images` folder in the system files of the SharePoint server.

For example, assume you want to use the `My_Logo.png`. Create the new subfolder `Custom` and put `MyLogo.png` there. Set the location of the logo file to `/_layouts/images/custom/ MyLogo.png`.

Using an image with a transparent background gets you the best result because the ribbon has a colored background out of the box (see Figure 8-1).

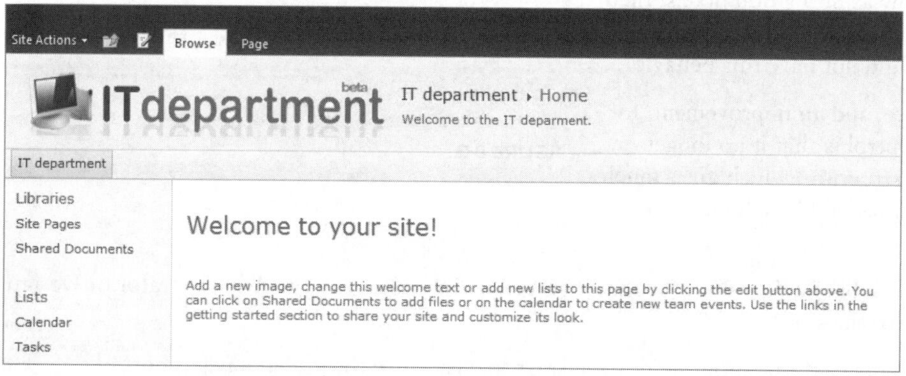

FIGURE 8-1

Managing Global Navigation

The global navigation, or the top navigation if you prefer, is an important part of the user interface in SharePoint in several aspects, and you can customize the navigation in several ways for your SharePoint sites.

You must consider several factors, such as the size of your site, the needs of the people, and who will use the site, when you choose to manage and organize the navigational structure for the SharePoint site.

Before you begin to customize the global navigation, I recommend you carefully plan the navigation first. Consider how the SharePoint sites are or should be structured, what type of information they contain, what type of information can be grouped and in what way, and the information structure in general. This is an important step in the site planning process.

This chapter does not get into information architecture and taxonomies in depth, but the way in which the content and the sites are organized and presented to the site's users — for example, in a hierarchical way or not — can influence your decision in regard to customizing the global navigation.

Global navigation is a key factor for orienting users of your SharePoint sites and enabling them to move among the sites and pages in the simplest possible way.

Quite a big difference exists between SharePoint 2010 and SharePoint 2007 in the way the global navigation renders. In SharePoint 2010, suppose that too many top-level sites display in the navigation, and the elements do not fit across the width of the page — the tabs in the global navigation will then be wrapped, and the tabs that go beyond the browser window to the right will appear in a new row. Even if the screen resolution is as low as 800 × 600 pixels, there will be no vertical scrollbar on the page. SharePoint 2007 did not have this behavior.

Another difference, and an improvement, for the navigation control is that it no longer produces a table structure, which gives much cleaner and well-formed HTML markup (see Figure 8-2).

FIGURE 8-2

To customize the global navigation for a SharePoint site, you must have the Administrator or Design permission level for the site.

Here are some points to think about before you start to customize the global navigation:

➤ Do you need to plan the information architecture before you can customize the global navigation?

➤ Should the site use Quick Launch? In what ways can it support the global navigation?

➤ Should the site have flyouts, and if so, in how many levels?

The following Try It Out shows how to start customizing global navigation.

TRY IT OUT   **Add and Edit Navigation Items**

In this example, you create a new tab in the global navigation and add a couple of links below this tab. You also learn how to edit items such as headings.

1. Open the home page of the portal: `http://srv1`.

2. Click Site Actions ➪ Site Settings and click the Navigation link under the Look and Feel section.

3. In the navigation settings page, click Add Heading in the Navigation Editing and Sorting section.

4. Type **Our Partners** in the Title field and click OK.

5. Click the new link with a folder icon that now appears under the global navigation, and then click the Add link in the Navigation Editing and Sorting section. Type **Microsoft** in the Title field and **http://www.microsoft.com** in the URL text field. Click the "Open link in new window" checkbox, and click OK.

6. Create at least two more links below the Our Partners heading using the preceding steps.

7. Click OK. Verify that these links are available in the global navigation.

8. Click Site Actions ⇨ Site Settings and click the Navigation link under the Look and Feel section.

9. Click the Our Partners heading, click the Edit link, change the title text to **External links**, and click OK.

10. Verify that these links are available in the global navigation.

How It Works

You can always customize the global navigation to meet your users' needs for information in conjunction with the automated and dynamic SharePoint links in the global navigation (see Figure 8-3).

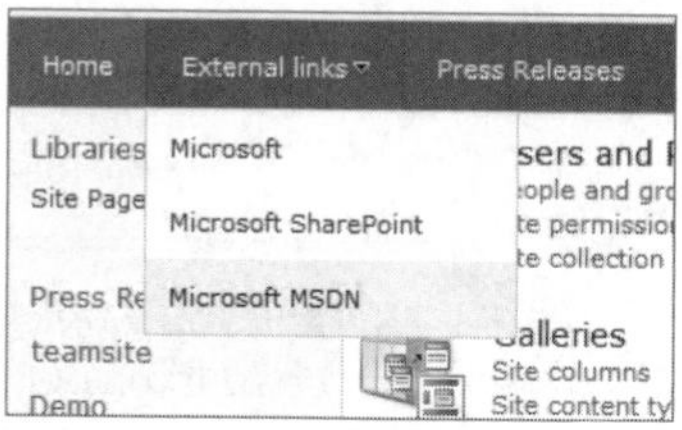

FIGURE 8-3

TRY IT OUT **Reorder Navigation Items**

In this example, you learn how to reorder and move link items in the global navigation.

1. Open the home page of the portal: `http://srv1`.

2. Click Site Actions ⇨ Site Settings and click the Navigation link under the Look and Feel section.

3. Click External link (the heading you just created in the preceding Try It Out).

4. Click Move Up. Move this heading all the way up to just below the top node, Global Navigation.

5. Select one of the SharePoint sites in the tree structure; for example, the team site. Move this site up to a position under the External links heading. Click OK.

6. Verify that these links are available and in the right position in the global navigation.

How It Works

The default sort setting in the global navigation is by title and in ascending order; however, you can always reorder and modify the navigation items.

If you set the sort order to "sort automatically," you will not be able to use the move commands.

TRY IT OUT **Hide a Navigation Item**

In this example, you learn how to hide and delete items in the navigation by using these steps:

1. Open the home page of the portal: `http://srv1`.

2. Click Site Actions ⇨ Site Settings and click the Navigation link under the Look and Feel section.

3. Click one of the sites in the tree structure, and click Hide. The icon for this site changes, and the text (Hidden) will appear after this site's name.

4.   Click OK.

5.   Verify that this link no longer is visible in the global navigation.

How It Works

Only SharePoint sites and pages can be set to hidden. Headings and links have to be deleted.

> *NOTE If you want to display the drop down in a tabbed navigation across the top, and need to display a two level deep structure, you need to customize this setting in the master page with SharePoint Designer 2010. You can read more about how to do this task in Chapter 9.*

Managing Quick Launch

You manage Quick Launch in approximately the same way you manage global navigation.

You can reorder and modify the navigation items, like the links to the Shared Documents or to the Calendar in the Quick Launch for a site. You can create, delete, and edit navigation links and headings. You can also move navigation items under headings and choose to display or hide pages and subsites.

TRY IT OUT   Enable the Tree View

The tree view displays site content in a physical manner. You can specify whether the tree view should be displayed to aid the navigation or not. The tree view displays the content of the sites — all the libraries, lists, discussion boards, surveys, and sites.

In this example, you activate the tree view.

1.   Open a team site; for example, `http://srv1/teamsite`.

2.   Click Site Actions ⇨ Site Settings and click the Tree view link under the Look and Feel section.

3.   Click the checkbox "Enable Tree View" to activate the Tree View. Click OK.

4.   Go back to the Tree view settings page and inactivate Quick Launch: Click Site Actions ⇨ Site Settings, and click the Tree view link under the Look and Feel section, deselect Enable Quick Launch, and click OK.

5.   Verify that only the tree view appears in the site.

How It Works

You can use a combination of Quick Launch and tree view, or display only one of them.

Hide the Quick Launch and the Tree View

There is no way out-of-the-box to hide the Quick Launch and tree view from the site settings or anywhere else in the SharePoint user interface. Suppose you have a team site and you want to use the full width for the home page of this site (see Figure 8-4).

FIGURE 8-4

To perform this task you can add the Content Editor web part to the home page and include just two CSS classes that override and hide the panel for the navigation controls.

You can read more about how to do it in this blog post: `http://chrisstahl.wordpress.com/2010/03/15/hide-the-quick-launch-in-sharepoint-2010/`.

CUSTOMIZING WITH THEMES

Using themes in SharePoint is an extremely quick and easy way to change font definitions, background colors, or hyperlink colors for a SharePoint site.

You can use a theme in a single site if you want it to have a unique appearance in the aspect of just color, or you can use a theme all over the site collection to comply with the corporate color standards. It can be used either with a custom master page or an out-of-the-box site template in SharePoint.

A theme in SharePoint 2010 is not the same as it was in previous versions of SharePoint; a theme is only for changing the colors. If you need a bit more advanced design, you have to do it with custom CSS and if necessary a custom master page.

To use and manage a theme, you no longer need to be a web designer or a developer. Any user with at least designer rights can apply a theme or make a basic color change to a site with one of the preinstalled themes. Themes are the simplest method for changing colors in SharePoint.

In previous versions of SharePoint, a theme had to be deployed to the file system on the front-end web server, which required time, access to the front-end web server, and last but not least, the skills of a developer. A theme in SharePoint 2010 is now much simpler to manage and deploy.

The theming engine is rebuilt; themes can still be found in the front-end web server, but are stored relative to the root under `14\Template\Global\Lists\Themes`. The themes are now the same as document themes for Office applications and have the same formatting capabilities. Themes are now packaged and based on Office Open XML format (OOXML) and use the .thmx file extension.

Another change and an improvement with themes in SharePoint 2010 is that a theme now can be used in symbiosis with a custom CSS file. For example, if you reference a custom CSS file in the master page and add the EnableCssTheming attribute with the value true, you can override the custom CSS with themes. Overriding one or more specific CSS classes in your custom CSS is even possible. This means that you can have a consistent look and feel all over the site collection using custom CSS, but at the same time, you can change the look and feel for a specific site, or just one or more parts of this site with a theme. To summarize:

➤ Themes in SharePoint 2010 are not the same as they were in previous versions of SharePoint.

➤ You can fully customize a preinstalled theme by selecting individual colors and fonts for a number of standard elements in a SharePoint site.

➤ Theme has inherited functionality. If you apply a theme to a top-level site you can choose to apply the theme to all the subsites.

➤ SharePoint offers 20 preinstalled themes.

➤ You can now upload a custom theme from a tool such as Microsoft PowerPoint or Microsoft Theme Creator.

➤ You can manage (for example, rename or delete) themes in the site settings for the top site.

➤ The preview function for a theme is enhanced.

You basically have three choices for how to accomplish your branding requirements:

➤ **Theme:** Use a theme when your requirements do not call for major look-and-feel changes, such as changing fonts and colors.

➤ **CSS:** Use CSS when you need to change more than just colors, such as changing the size of the user interface, changing positions of elements or spacing between elements, or changing background images.

➤ **Master page:** Use a master page when your requirements call for major changes that include customization of the page's structure.

In the following Try It Outs, you learn how to manage themes in SharePoint. You learn how to select and activate themes in SharePoint and how to upload a custom PowerPoint 2010 theme.

TRY IT OUT   Select a Theme

In this example, you select and customize a theme by selecting a color for some of the background elements. You also change the color scheme for your site to be pink.

1. Open a team site; for example, http://srv1/teamsite.

2. Click Site Actions ➪ Site Settings and click the Site theme link under the Look and Feel section.

3. Select Viewpoint, and click the Preview button. SharePoint generates a theme preview for you. Close this window.

4. Select the Modern Rose theme. Click the Apply button. Surf around on the site and see which elements have changed.

5. Go back and modify the color for some of the background elements: Click Site Actions ➪ Site Settings and click the Site theme link under the Look and Feel section.

6. Click the Select a color link for the Text/Background - Light 2. Type **#FEE8EC** and click OK.

7. Click the Apply button.

How It Works

To you don't want to use this color scheme, you can go back to the themes settings page and select Default (no theme). Figure 8-5 shows an example of a theme setting.

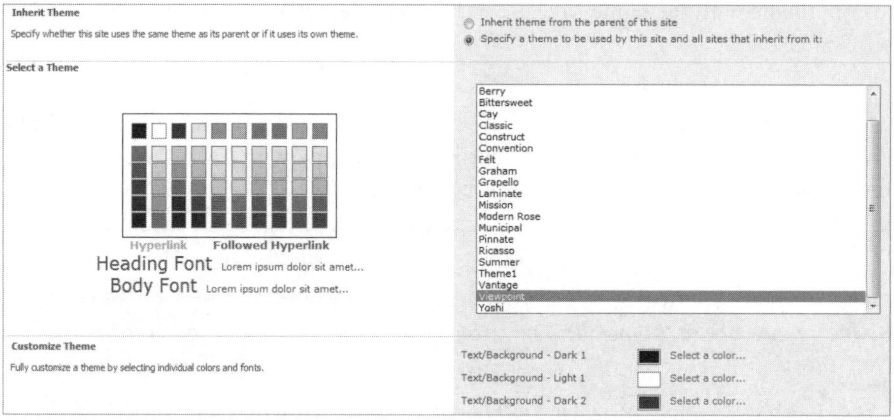

Inherit Theme
Specify whether this site uses the same theme as its parent or if it uses its own theme.

○ Inherit theme from the parent of this site
● Specify a theme to be used by this site and all sites that inherit from it:

Select a Theme

| Berry |
| Bittersweet |
| Cay |
| Classic |
| Construct |
| Convention |
| Felt |
| Graham |
| Grapello |
| Laminate |
| Mission |
| Modern Rose |
| Municipal |
| Pinnate |
| Ricasso |
| Summer |
| Theme1 |
| Vantage |
| Viewpoint |
| Yoshi |

Hyperlink   Followed Hyperlink
Heading Font   Lorem ipsum dolor sit amet...
Body Font   Lorem ipsum dolor sit amet...

Customize Theme
Fully customize a theme by selecting individual colors and fonts.

Text/Background - Dark 1   Select a color...
Text/Background - Light 1   Select a color...
Text/Background - Dark 2   Select a color...

FIGURE 8-5

TRY IT OUT   Upload a Custom Theme

In this example, you save a theme from Microsoft PowerPoint 2010 and upload it into SharePoint. Suppose your organization has a couple of PowerPoint slides that follow the graphical manuals — you can reuse these slides and convert them to SharePoint themes in less than a few minutes.

1. Open PowerPoint: Choose Start ➪ All Programs ➪ Microsoft Office ➪ Microsoft PowerPoint 2010.

2. On the Design tab in the Themes group, click the button next to the name of the theme color; for example, Perspective. Hold the mouse cursor over the preview images to see their names.

3. You can now create a custom color scheme for this theme if you like, but don't do this right now.

4. Save this theme without any modifications: Click the bottom arrow in the Themes dropdown and select Save Current Theme (see Figure 8-6).

FIGURE 8-6

5. Give the file the name **MyCustomTheme**, and save it (for example, on your desktop). Close PowerPoint 2010.

6. Open the home page of the portal: `http://srv1`.

7. Click Site Actions ⇨ Site Settings and click the Theme link under the Galleries section.

8. At the bottom of the page, click Add new item.

9. Click the Browse button and find the MyCustomTheme file; select the file and click the Open button.

10. Click OK in the upload dialog.

11. Give the file a description and click the Save button.

12. Open a team site; for example, `http://srv1/teamsite`.

13. Click Site Actions ⇨ Site Settings and click the Site theme link under the Look and Feel section.

14. Find your custom theme with the name MyCustomTheme. Select it and click Apply.

How It Works

PowerPoint 2010 does all the necessary package for you, so you don't need to deploy the theme in the server. You can now go on and customize this theme until you are happy with it, but after you have customized a theme in SharePoint, you cannot save this customization.

> **NOTE** *Read more about themes and how to plan on using them at the Microsoft TechNet library:*
>
> `http://technet.microsoft.com/en-us/library/ee424399(office.14).aspx`

> **NOTE** *As an alternative to creating themes with SharePoint or PowerPoint, you can use Microsoft Theme Builder. With this tool you can create themes for Word, Excel, and even Outlook. You can download the Theme Builder tool from this link:*
>
> `https://connect.microsoft.com/themebuilder?wa=wsignin1.0`

USING WEB PARTS

At this point you have learned about basic customizations for look and feel, such as how to customize global navigation and Quick Launch, and how to change a theme. Those elements are the cornerstones of the user interface, but if you want to customize the content — the ways in which information is presented — you can use web parts.

Web parts are the configurable building blocks that include textual content or data, which, among other components, present the content in a SharePoint page.

You can read more about all the web parts that come with SharePoint in Chapter 7.

Web parts offer a lot of possibilities for customizing content and data, and the challenge is knowing what tool or feature to use and when. As mentioned in the previous chapter, this is a good challenge; it means that with SharePoint Server you can build an intranet or public-facing website that meets all kinds of requirements, without needing to develop or purchase extra web parts or features.

Still, times will occur when the user's expectation of the websites requires added functionality. If so, you can either extend the out-of-the-box web parts with, for example, JavaScript, or use SharePoint Designer 2010 to create advanced no-code solutions; these are alternatives to downloading the solution you need from a third-party vendor or developing the solution with Visual Studio 2010.

SharePoint Web Parts

You can insert a web part onto the page by selecting the Web Part button on the Insert tab when you are editing a page.

In the following Try It Out, you insert and manage a few of the out-of-the-box web parts in SharePoint 2010.

TRY IT OUT   **Manage the Chart Web Part**

The Chart web part gives you the ability to create rapid out-of-the-box charts and dashboard solutions from SharePoint lists, web parts, or external data sources in a quite easy and highly configurable way.

Imagine that you want to display your team's first half year's expenses dynamically from a SharePoint list on the homepage of your team site using one or more charts.

In this example, you do this by creating a custom list with two columns that hold the amounts and the goal value; this list is going to be the data source for the Chart web part. The last step is setting up the Chart web part and making the necessary configurations until it meets your needs.

This web part is only available in SharePoint Server and comes as part of the Enterprise version of SharePoint.

1.   Open the home page of the portal: `http://srv1`.

2.   Click Site Actions ⇨ More Options.

3.   In the Create dialog, click the List link in the left navigation panel and select Custom List. Type the name **Amounts** in the field and click Create. Create two new columns for this list:

  a.   Click Create Column in the ribbon, give it the name **Expenses,** and click the Currency checkbox to set the type of information. Scroll down and click OK.

  b.   Click Create Column in the ribbon, give it the name **Target,** and click the Currency checkbox to set the type of information. Scroll down and click OK.

4. Add at least three items in this list; in the example that follows, the columns are in parentheses:

    a. Jan (Title), **4000** (Expenses), **3500** (Target)

    b. Feb (Title), **5000** (Expenses), **5200** (Target)

    c. Mar (Title), **5500** (Expenses), **4000** (Target)

5. Open a team site; for example, `http://srv1/webparts`.

6. Click Site Actions ⇨ Edit Page to get into Edit mode. As an alternative, you can click the Edit button at the site's top tab.

7. Click the standard image to the right side of the page and select Delete to delete this image. Click the Insert tab in the ribbon, and click the Web Part button. Select the Business Data category and click Chart Web Part. Click the Add button. A dummy chart appears on the page.

8. Click Data & Appearance and click OK. Click Connect Chart to Data, and click the Connect to a List checkbox. Click Next.

9. Select Root in the first dropdown and select Amounts in the next dropdown. Click Next. You can now filter the data, but don't do that right now. Click Next.

10. Expand Series Properties and change the name Default to **Expenses**. Select Spline in the dropdown for Series Type. Click the add icon [+] next to the Series dropdown, and change the name Series 2 to **Target**. Select Spline in the dropdown for Series Type. Select Target in the Y field dropdown.

11. Click the Finish button (see Figure 8-7).

FIGURE 8-7

How It Works

In this example, you connected to a SharePoint list; connecting to the following data sources is also possible using the following methods:

➤ You can use another web part. If you have another web part on the page that is capable providing data, you can use it as a data source.

➤ You can use an external content type that is defined in the Business Data Catalog. This could be an external SQL database table, view, or a stored procedure. You will read more about how to set up external content types in Chapter 9.

➤ You can use a workbook that has been defined in Excel services.

You can customize the look and feel of your chart in many different ways, and down to every single detail. For this task, the Chart web part has a wizard for all the customizations you can think of. Here are a few examples of settings that you can manipulate:

➤ Chart type — There are more than 100 variations of the types and of their subsequent variations; here are some of them:

  ➤ Bar

  ➤ Area

  ➤ Line

  ➤ Point/bubble

  ➤ Financial

  ➤ Pie

  ➤ Range

  ➤ Pyramid

➤ Theme

➤ Transparency

➤ Width and height

➤ 3D or 2D

➤ Rotation for the axes

➤ Perspective

➤ Analysis, such as setting a median value

➤ Showing or hiding legends and titles

➤ Font formats

➤ Showing or hiding the grid

➤ The use of tooltips or linked series, legends, and labels

TRY IT OUT Manage the Media Web Part

The Media web part as well as many other features in SharePoint 2010 uses the Silverlight 3 technology to present video and audio files in a web page.

In this example you manage the Media web part, and you embed a media (video) file (.wmv) onto a page. Before you follow this example be sure to have a video file ready to be uploaded in your environment.

To follow this example, you will create a new site for this web part, but of course, if you prefer to use another site that's okay.

1.   Open the home page of the portal: `http://srv1`.

2.   Click Site Actions ⇨ New Site and select Team Site.

3.   Type **Web Parts** as a title, and type **web parts** in the URL field. Click Create.

4.   Click Site Actions and Edit Page. You can as an alternative click the edit button on the site's top tab.

5.   Place the cursor just above the title of the Shared Documents web part, and click the Insert tab on the ribbon.

6.   Click the Video and Audio button. The Media web part appears. Click into the middle area of this web part, and click Change Media on the ribbon. Select From Computer.

7.   Click Browse and find your video file. Click Open, OK, and Save to upload the video in SharePoint.

8.   Click into the Media web part to verify that it can be loaded.

9.   Make a screen capture (press Prt Sc) that captures just the content in the movie when it is playing. Use your favorite picture manager application to create a preview image for the web part in the size of 300 × 200 pixels. Save the image (for example, on your desktop).

10.   Click the Change Image button on the ribbon and select From Computer. Click Browse, find your image, and select it. Click Open, OK, and Save to upload the image.

11.   Click the floppy disc icon at the top of the page to save and close. See Figure 8-8.

FIGURE 8-8

How It Works

Setting up a video in a SharePoint page is easy, and you can use some properties to ensure the best user experience, such as looping a video until the user stops it, starting a video automatically when the page loads, or like all other web parts, setting the appearance — for example, chrome type or width and height.

The most common supported media formats are:

➤ WMV

➤ MP4

➤ MP3

See MSDN for a full list of supported formats:

`http://msdn.microsoft.com/en-us/library/cc189080(VS.95).aspx`

If you have a video file with an unsupported media type, you can use an encoder such as Microsoft Expression Encoder to transform, for example, `.avi` to `.wmv`.

> **NOTE** *If you to need to show large, smooth-streaming videos in SharePoint, you can use, for example, Windows Azure to host your video files. You can also look at the possibilities with an extension to Internet Information Services 7, Internet Information Services smooth streaming, if you are interested in high-definition (HD 720p+) video playback through SharePoint.*

> **NOTE** *Microsoft Visual Studio 2010 and Microsoft Blend Expression (4) are the tools for you when you need to build custom web parts, rich Internet applications (RIAs) or powerful animations and graphics. With these tools you can, for example, create a Silverlight web part that reads and writes to a SharePoint list, using the client object model and REST.*

Web Parts with Visual Studio 2010

When it comes to creating your own web parts, you have Visual Studio for all kinds of solutions and SharePoint Designer for things like the Data View web parts.

With SharePoint 2010 and Visual Studio 2010 come Visual web parts, which enable developers to easily design a web part visually for SharePoint 2010 using the familiar method of dragging and dropping from the toolbox. Visual web parts can now be deployed to SharePoint with ease. You will no longer need to use the command-line tool STSADM to deploy your solution; Visual Studio 2010 will automatically do it for you, because your project from the start is associated with SharePoint and has a defined level of trust.

The STSADM.EXE utility has not completely gone; it's still there and you can use it as before in SharePoint 2007, but as an option you have now Windows Power Shell, which is the replacement for STSADM.

If you're new to SharePoint, Visual web parts are a great way to get started building custom applications for SharePoint 2010.

To follow this example, make sure you have Visual Studio 2010 and SharePoint 2010 installed on your Windows Server 2008 or Windows 7 environment.

> **TRY IT OUT** | **Create a Visual Web Part**

In this example, you develop a Visual web part with Visual Studio 2010, and deploy a web part to the site collection. This example is the first of three Try It Outs, and the purpose of these examples is that you will learn how to create a web part, manage it, and learn how to add code to it.

These examples end up in a finished web part that you can use in your environment or modify as you want.

Now, you'll create a form that lets you add announcements to, and remove them from, the SharePoint Lists Announcements box (see Figure 8-9).

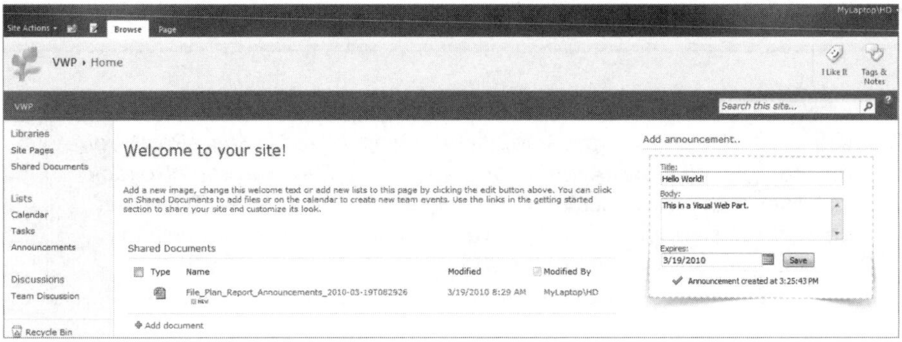

FIGURE 8-9

1.   Open Visual Studio 2010: Choose Start ⇨ All Programs ⇨ Microsoft Visual Studio 2010 ⇨ Microsoft Visual Studio 2010.

2.   In the start page of Visual Studio, click the New Project link. Select Visual C# and SharePoint in the left window under Installed Templates. You can, if you prefer, select Visual Basic as the language for your Visual web part.

3.   Select Visual Web Part and type **Add Announcement** in the Name textbox and click OK.

4.   Enter **http://srv1/** as the local site for debugging. Click the Finish button. Visual Studio now creates the project with all the files that Visual Studio 2010 needs for a Visual web part.

5.   Expand VisualWebpart1 and in the Solution Explorer double-click VisualWebpart1.webpart. Change the dummy text for the title and description like this:

```
<property name="Title" type="string">Add Announcement</property>
<property name="Desctiption" type="string">A Web Part that can add items to the
Announcement list in the site.</property>
```

6.   Expand Features in the Solution Explorer and double-click Feature1. Type **Add Announcement** in the Title field; type **Use this feature to activate the Add Announcement Web Part** into the Description field.

7.   Double-click `VisualWebpart1UserControl.ascx` in the Solution Explorer. Click the Split button below the page you have open. Place the cursor into the dotted box in the design view of the page. Type **Hello World! This is my first Visual Web Part.**

8. In the Solution Explorer, right-click Add Announcement and select Deploy. SharePoint now deploys this web part as a feature, and at the same time recycles the application pool for SharePoint. Shortly, you will be notified in the output window as to whether the build and deploy succeeded.

9. Use your browser and open a team site; for example, `http://srv1/teamsite`. Click Site Actions and Edit Page. Click the Insert tab on the ribbon, place the cursor in one of the zones, and click Web Part.

10. Click the Custom category, select your web part with the name Add Announcement, and click the Add button. Click the floppy disc icon at the top of the page to save and close the edit mode.

How It Works

You have now created a Visual web part that displays textual content, and you have also created and packed this web part into a feature (.wsp). A *feature* is a set of files containing the code and other elements such as images or CSS and more, that can be deployed to the SharePoint farm or site collection. A feature can be turned on or off by the SharePoint administrator in the user interface.

TRY IT OUT **Manage the Visual Web Part**

In this example, you update your web part and add a custom image icon for your feature. Before you begin, create a `.png` file in the size of 31 × 22 pixels. Name it **AddAnnouncement** and upload the image to this folder: `c:\Program Files\Common Files\Microsoft Shared\Web Server Extensions\14\template\images\`.

1. Open Visual Studio 2010 by choosing Start ➪ All Programs ➪ Microsoft Visual Studio 2010 ➪ Microsoft Visual Studio 2010.

2. In the start page of Visual Studio, click Add Announcement in Recent Projects at the start page.

3. Double-click `VisualWebpart1UserControl.ascx`. Change the text to only **Hello World!**.

4. In the Solution Explorer, double-click Features.

5. In the Properties window below the Solution Explorer, locate the Image URL textbox and type **AddAnnouncement.png**.

6. In the Solution Explorer, right-click Add Announcement and select Deploy. Wait a few seconds until the deploy has succeeded.

7. Use your browser and go back to the site where you first added your web part to verify the changes. Refresh the browser if nothing has happened.

8. Open the home page of the portal `http://srv1` and click Site Actions and Site Settings. Click the Site collection features link under Site Collection Administration.

9. Verify that you can see the icon, title, and description for your feature. See Figure 8-10.

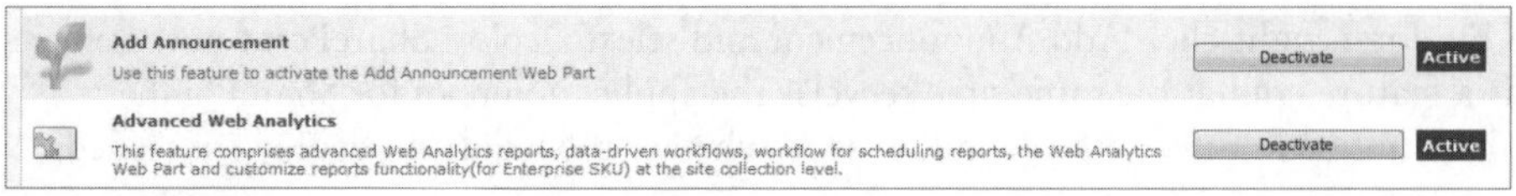

FIGURE 8-10

How It Works

As you can see, you can always go back to your project, make changes, and redeploy it. When you redeploy the project, Visual Studio reacts and deletes the existing solution, then adds and deploys a new version.

The web parts will be automatically stored in the Web Part Gallery for the site collections, and you can afterward change the properties for the web part, such as name, title, and description, or connect it to a group of web parts.

TRY IT OUT **Add Code in the Web Part**

In this next step, you add some controls and some code in your user control; this code will update your web part so it can communicate with the announcements list in the site.

1. Open Visual Studio 2010 by choosing Start ⇨ All Programs ⇨ Microsoft Visual Studio 2010 ⇨ Microsoft Visual Studio 2010.

2. In the start page of Visual Studio, click Add Announcement in Recent Projects.

3. Double-click `VisualWebpart1UserControl.ascx`. Click the Source button. You can close the Output window below the Source window.

4. Replace `<p> Hello World! </p>` with this code:

```
<div>
<div>
  <div>Title:</div>
  <div><asp:TextBox ID="TextBox1" runat="server"></asp:TextBox></div>
</div>

<div>
  <div>Body:</div>
  <div><asp:TextBox ID="TextBox2" runat="server" Rows="4"
  TextMode="MultiLine"></asp:TextBox></div>
</div>

<div>
  <div>Expires:</div>
  <div>
  <SharePoint:DateTimeControl ID="DateTimeControl1" runat="server" DateOnly="True" />
  <asp:Button ID="Button1" runat="server" Text="Save" onclick="Button1_Click" />
  </div>
</div>
```

```
<div>
  <div><asp:Label ID="Label1" runat="server" Text=""></asp:Label></div>
</div>
</div>
```

5. In the Solution Explorer, expand `VisualWebpart1UserControl.ascx` and double-click `VisualWebpart1UserControl.ascx.cs`.

6. Enter the following code below the last `using` (namespace) from the top.

```
using Microsoft.SharePoint;
using Microsoft.SharePoint.Security;
```

7. Enter the following code block, after the protected void code block (see Figure 8-11).

```
:

    protected void Button1_Click(object sender, EventArgs e)
    {
        using (SPSite site = new SPSite(SPContext.Current.Web.Url))
        {
            using (SPWeb web = site.OpenWeb())
            {

SPList Announcements = web.Lists["Announcements"];
SPListItem newAnnouncements = Announcements.Items.Add();

newAnnouncements["Title"] = TextBox1.Text;
newAnnouncements["Body"] = TextBox2.Text;
newAnnouncements["Expires"] = DateTimeControl1.SelectedDate;
Label1.Text = "Announcement created at " + DateTime.Now.ToString("T");
newAnnouncements.Update();
            }
        }
    }
```

```
using System;
using System.Web.UI;
using System.Web.UI.WebControls;
using System.Web.UI.WebControls.WebParts;
using Microsoft.SharePoint;
using Microsoft.SharePoint.Security;
namespace Add_Announcement.VisualWebPart1
{
    public partial class VisualWebPart1UserControl : UserControl
    {
        protected void Page_Load(object sender, EventArgs e)
        {
        }

        protected void Button1_Click(object sender, EventArgs e)
        {

            SPWeb web = SPContext.Current.Web;
            SPList Announcements = web.Lists["Announcements"];
            SPListItem newAnnouncements = Announcements.Items.Add();
            newAnnouncements["Title"] = TextBox1.Text;
            newAnnouncements["Body"] = TextBox2.Text;
            newAnnouncements["Expires"] = DateTimeControl1.SelectedDate;
            Label1.Text = "<div class='CustomWebPartLblImg'></div><div class='CustomWebPartLbl1'>" + "Announcement created at " + DateTime.Now.ToString("T") + "</div>";
            newAnnouncements.Update();

        }
    }
}
```

FIGURE 8-11

8. In the Solution Explorer, right-click Add Announcement and select Deploy.

9. Use your browser and go back to the site where you first added your web part to verify the changes. Refresh the browser if nothing has happened.

How It Works

The next step to improve this web part could be to complete the form with validation. ASP.NET provides a set of validation controls that you can use, such as the RequiredFieldValidator control in the user control (`ascx`), to ensure that the user fills in the title field.

You can also consider extending the web part with an open-source JavaScript library such as Ajax or jQuery, for things like performing asynchronous updates to reduce round-trips to the server. To create the look and feel for the web part, you can extend it with HTML, CSS, and icons.

I hope that you now have been inspired to go ahead and develop dynamic Visual web parts and other kinds of applications for SharePoint 2010. See Figure 8-12.

FIGURE 8-12

Finding Third-Party Web Parts

SharePoint is a great product in many ways, but sometimes you may need to extend it or customize it more. The alternatives are to build the solution yourself, find a consultant who can build it, find free source code from a community, or buy the solution from a vendor.

Buying a solution that has already been made for the purpose is often a smart money move. Solutions from an experienced SharePoint consultant or a well-known vendor are often good quality and are built with great expertise.

A big and growing worldwide, third-party market exists for SharePoint that helps you as an administrator, developer, or designer with all kinds of tools for design, implementation, migration, and management challenges.

The Internet is a great resource to find what you are looking for, such as add-ins, solutions, features, web parts, or code for SharePoint. Some solutions are free and some are commercial. A general bit of advice is to test it closely in your development environment before deploying it in the production environment.

CodePlex is the largest community for free SharePoint solutions and community-driven projects that exist alongside the official product releases from Microsoft. CodePlex is an open source forum hosted by Microsoft, but Microsoft doesn't control, review, revise, endorse, or distribute the third-party projects on CodePlex. Microsoft hosts the CodePlex site solely as a web storage site as a service to the developer community.

CodePlex is steadily growing and has at this moment more than 1,000 SharePoint 2007 and SharePoint 2010 projects and downloads. I'm sure you can find great value in many of them.

Take a look at all the SharePoint specific projects at `http://www.codeplex.com/site/search?projectSearchText=SharePoint`.

For more information, read the CodePlex Terms of Use at `http://www.codeplex.com/Legal/Terms.aspx`.

CLIENT-SIDE SCRIPTS IN SHAREPOINT

Server-side code is sometimes not the best option for creating applications. The IT department can disallow server-side code, or a SharePoint Designer no-code solution could be the optimal solution, or perhaps some lines of JavaScript or JScript are enough to accomplish what you need, as an alternative to creating a server-side code application.

Using ECMAScript — Client Object Model

ECMAScript is a standardized scripting language that is widely used on the web. It has several dialects such as JavaScript and Jscript.

With SharePoint 2010 comes a client object model based on the .NET framework. This allows developers to use Visual Studio 2010 to write applications that can access SharePoint from a client machine where SharePoint is not installed, without requiring the installation of any assembly code at the SharePoint server. For example, this enables you to consume and manipulate SharePoint data in a Windows Form application or a Silverlight application.

The client object model enables new kinds of applications and makes writing client-side code that interacts with SharePoint content easier.

With SharePoint 2010 come new application programming interfaces (APIs) for the client object model:

- ➤ ECMAScript — JavaScript and JScript
- ➤ Silverlight applications
- ➤ .NET-managed applications

Read more about how to use the client object model in SharePoint in the technical article "Using the SharePoint Foundation 2010 Managed Client Object Model" at the Microsoft MSDN library: `http://msdn.microsoft.com/en-us/library/ee857094(office.14).aspx#SP2010ClientOM_Overview`.

You can also use the ECMAScript through your own JavaScript files and to manipulate SharePoint 2010 objects with SharePoint Designer 2010 in, for example, an `.aspx` page or in a Data View web part.

The ECMAScript is a JavaScript file with the name `SP.js`, and you can find the file in the 14 hive: `C:\Program Files\Common Files\Microsoft Shared\Web Server Extensions\14\TEMPLATE\LAYOUTS\`.

Use ECMAScript

In this example, you use ECMAScript in an `.aspx` file to communicate with SharePoint. This script loads an alert that displays the logged-in user's name and login.

1. Open Notepad by choosing Start ⇨ Accessories ⇨ Notepad.

2. Type what follows:

```
<%@ Page Language="C#" %>
<%@ Register Tagprefix="SharePoint" Namespace="Microsoft.SharePoint.WebControls"
Assembly="Microsoft.SharePoint, Version=14.0.0.0, Culture=neutral,
PublicKeyToken=71e9bce111e9429c" %>
<!DOCTYPE html PUBLIC "-//W3C//DTD XHTML 1.0 Transitional//EN"
"http://www.w3.org/TR/xhtml1/DTD/xhtml1-transitional.dtd">
<html><head><title></title>
<SharePoint:ScriptLink runat="server" Name="sp.js" LoadAfterUI="true"
Localizable="false" ID="ScriptLink1" OnDemand="false" />

<script type="text/javascript">
ExecuteOrDelayUntilScriptLoaded(getWebUserData, "sp.js");
var context = null;
var web = null;
var currentUser = null;
    function getWebUserData() {
        context = new SP.ClientContext.get_current();
        web = context.get_web();
        currentUser = web.get_currentUser();
 currentUser.retrieve();
        context.load(web);
        context.executeQueryAsync(Function.createDelegate(this,
this.onSuccessMethod), Function.createDelegate(this, this.onFailureMethod));
    }
    function onSuccessMethod(sender, args) {
        var userObject = web.get_currentUser();
        alert('--Welcome--' + '\n User: ' + userObject.get_title() + '\n Login:
' + userObject.get_loginName());
    }
    function onFailureMethodl(sender, args) {
        alert('Request failed ' + args.get_message() + '\n' +
args.get_stackTrace());
    }
</script>
</head>
<body>
    <form id="form1" runat="server">
        <div>Example of ECMA</div>
        <SharePoint:FormDigest runat="server" />
    </form>
</body>
</html>
```

3. In Notepad, click File ⇨ Save As. Select Save as type and choose All Files. Type in the filename: **MyFirstEcma.aspx**.

4. Save the file in this location: **C:\Program Files\Common Files\Microsoft Shared\Web Server Extensions\14\TEMPLATE\LAYOUTS**.

5. Use your browser and go to `http://srv1/_layouts/MyFirstEcma.aspx`.

How It Works

ECMAScript will load "lazy"; that is, load a function only when it needs to be loaded. If you have a custom JavaScript that uses ECMAScript on page load, and ECMAScript has not loaded, your JavaScript will not get executed. To make sure your JavaScript code runs after `sp.js` finishes loading, you can put your JavaScript function into this:

```
ExecuteOrDelayUntilScriptLoaded(MyFunction, "sp.js");
```

Read more about ECMAScript and find a similar example at:

`http://praveenbattula.blogspot.com/2010/02/sharepoint-2010-client-object-model.html`

Using JavaScript in SharePoint

JavaScript is a popular object-oriented scripting language that can be used to enable programmatic access to objects in SharePoint on both the client side and the server side.

TRY IT OUT   Use JavaScript

In this example, you use JavaScript in a SharePoint page with help from the out-of-the-box SharePoint web part, Content Editor. The following script is simple to use and a typical example of using JavaScript in SharePoint for more than manipulating SharePoint objects. The script will calculate and display the time in days down to seconds left to a given target date.

1. Open Notepad by choosing Start ⇨ Accessories ⇨ Notepad.

2. Type what follows:

```
<script language="JavaScript">
TargetDate = "12/31/2020 9:00 AM";
CountActive = true;
CountStepper = -1;
LeadingZero = true;
DisplayFormat = "%%D%% Days, %%H%% Hours, %%M%% Minutes, %%S%% Seconds.";
FinishMessage = "The day is finally here!";
</script>
<script language="JavaScript"
src="http://scripts.hashemian.com/js/countdown.js"></script>
```

3. Replace the dates and time in the TargetDate to the date of your next birthday.

4. Save the file as the `.txt` type on your desktop, and name it **countdown**.

5. Open the home page of the portal: `http://srv1`.

6. Click Site Actions ➪ View All Site Content and click the Site Assets link to open this library. Click Add document, and click Browse to upload `countdown.txt` from your desktop. Click OK in the dialog that appears.

7. Open a site; for example, `http://srv1/teamsite`. Click Site Actions and Edit Page. Click the Insert tab on the ribbon and select Web Part.

8. Click the Media and Content category, and select Content Editor. Place the cursor somewhere in the page where you want to add the web part, and click Add.

9. Click the arrow in the header section of the web part and select Edit Web Part. See Figure 8-13.

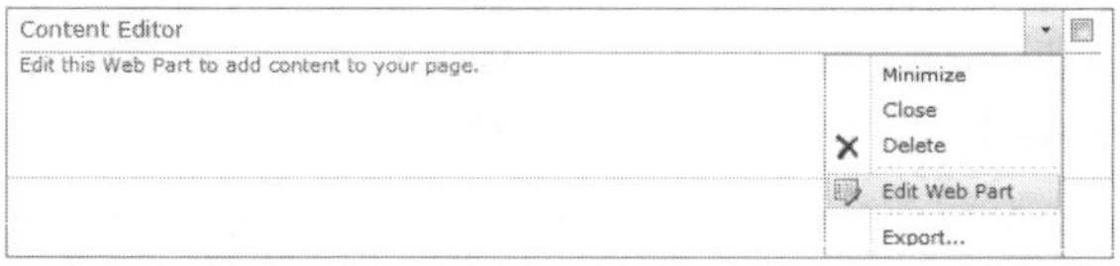

FIGURE 8-13

10. Link the countdown text file by typing **/SiteAssets/countdown.txt** in the Content Link field, in the Edit Web Part dialog.

11. Expand Appearance and enter **Countdown to my birthday.** In the bottom of the Appearance section, set Chrome Type to Title Only. Click OK. Click Save & Close on the ribbon.

How It Works

You can find many JavaScript examples on the Internet that can be used in SharePoint. The script in this exercise contains a reference to an external JavaScript file.

Using jQuery in SharePoint

jQuery is the most popular JavaScript library in use today. It's a part of Microsoft's official development platform and it is designed to change the way that you write JavaScript. A JavaScript library is a library of pre-written JavaScript controls that allow for easier development of JavaScript-based applications.

TRY IT OUT   **Use jQuery in SharePoint**

If you want to extend SharePoint functions, such as changing the behavior of a SharePoint list form or extending your SharePoint application or web design, jQuery could be of great value to you.

You can use jQuery in your SharePoint Designer or Visual Studio applications or even in a plain text file in a SharePoint library, and reference it from the Content Editor web part. You can use jQuery with ECMAScript without any conflict.

In the following example you create two links that can hide or show some content in the Content Editor. See Figure 8-14.

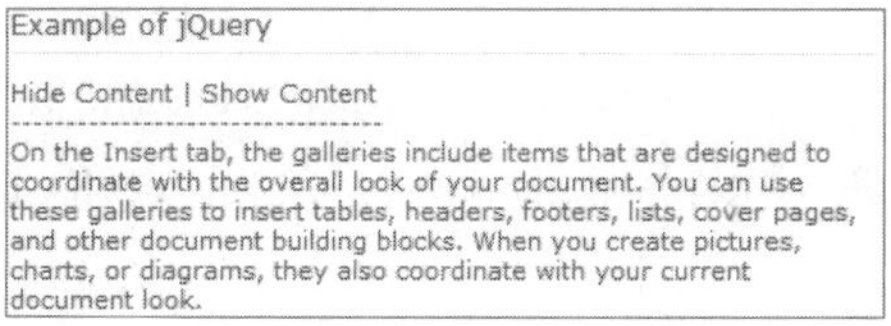

FIGURE 8-14

1. Open Notepad by choosing Start ➪ Accessories ➪ Notepad.

2. Type what follows:

```
<script src="http://ajax.microsoft.com/ajax/jquery/jquery-1.4.2.min.js"
type="text/javascript"></script>

<div>
<a href="#" id="hidr">Hide Content</a> |
<a href="#" id="showr">Show Content</a> <br />
---------------------------------
<div>
 <span class="TextBlock">
 Put some textual content here to be displayed or not
 </span>
</div>

<script type="text/javascript">
    $("#hidr").click(function () {
     $("span.TextBlock").hide(0);
    });
    $("#showr").click(function () {
      $("span.TextBlock").show(0);
    });
</script>
</div>
```

3. If you like, replace the textual content in the span tag "TextBlock" with your own content, such as text and an image.

4. Save the file as type .js on your desktop, and name it **jQueryExample**.

5. Open the home page of the portal: http://srv1.

6. Click Site Actions ➪ View All Site Content and click the Site Assets link to open this library. Click Add document, and click Browse to upload jqueryExample.js from your desktop. Click OK in the dialog.

7. Open a site; for example, http://srv1/teamsite. Click Site Actions and Edit Page. Click the Insert tab on the ribbon and select Web Part.

8. Click the Media and Content category, and select Content Editor. Place the cursor somewhere in the page where you want to add the web part, and click Add.

9. Click the arrow in the header section of the web part and select Edit Web Part.

10. Link the file jQueryExample by typing **/SiteAssets/jQueryExample.js** in the Content Link field.

11. Expand Appearance and enter **Example of jQuery**. In the bottom of the Appearance section, set Chrome Type to Title Only. Click OK. Click Save & Close on the ribbon. Try this script.

How It Works

jQuery has a large number of different extensions, widgets, and plug-ins that can be used in many scenarios for SharePoint development or branding, such as for creating accordions, auto complete form fields, sliders, or resizable objects. jQuery is not the only JavaScript library around. Prototype, script .aculo.us, and Dojo Toolkit are some other popular libraries.

In this example, you referenced the jQuery API from the Microsoft Ajax Content Delivery Network (CDN). The content in CDN is cached on servers around the world. As an alternative, you can store the jQuery API locally in a SharePoint library.

jQuery is available in two formats:

➤ Compressed, with a significantly smaller file size, for a production environment.

➤ Uncompressed, for debugging, for a development environment.

> **NOTE** *Find downloads, documentation, and tutorials about jQuery at:*
>
> `http://jquery.com/`
>
> *SPServices, a great jQuery library at CodePlex, abstracts SharePoint's Web Services and makes them easier to use. Right now it's early in the game — the latest release works for SharePoint 2010 but at the time of this writing is not yet supported, so stay tuned:*
>
> `http://spservices.codeplex.com/`
>
> *You can also check out 50+ Amazing jQuery examples:*
>
> `http://www.noupe.com/jquery/50-amazing-jquery-examples-part1.html`

▶ **WHAT YOU LEARNED IN THIS CHAPTER**

TOPIC	KEY CONCEPTS
Common terms	HTML — Hypertext Markup Language.
	CSS — Cascading Style Sheets.
	XSLT — Extensible Stylesheet Language Transformations.
	WYSIWYG — What you see is what you get.
	C# — A programming language.
	Aspx — The extension used for Microsoft ASP.NET web pages
	ASCX — User control. An .aspx page can contain a user control (code).
	API — Application Programming Interface.
	ECMAScript — A standard for JavaScript and JScript.
	JavaScript — A Netscape-developed scripting language.
	JScript — A Microsoft-developed scripting language.
	jQuery — Lightweight, cross-browser JavaScript library that emphasizes interaction between JavaScript and HTML.
	Ajax — Web development technique used on the client side to create interactive and asynchronous applications.
Visual Studio 2010	Microsoft tool for developing applications with different programming languages.
SharePoint Designer 2010	Editor for SharePoint 2010 that provides a set of powerful tools for branding, creation of non-code solutions, and a lot more.
Content Editor	Allows authors to enter rich text content or a client-side script.
Media Web Part	Use to embed media clips (video and audio).
Chart Web Part	Use to visualize data on SharePoint 2010 sites.
Silverlight Web Part	Displays Silverlight applications.
Visual Web Part	Enables developers to easily design a web part visually for SharePoint 2010, using the familiar method of dragging and dropping from the toolbox.
CodePlex	The largest community for free SharePoint solutions and community-driven projects that exists alongside the official product releases from Microsoft.

9

Using SharePoint Designer 2010

WHAT YOU WILL LEARN IN THIS CHAPTER:

- ➤ Customizing a Form
- ➤ Using XSL and XPath
- ➤ Working with the XSLT List View web part
- ➤ Working with the Data View
- ➤ Using a REST Web Service
- ➤ Managing Parameters
- ➤ Managing an External List
- ➤ Using InfoPath 2010
- ➤ Creating a Master Page
- ➤ Creating a Page Layout
- ➤ Creating a Custom CSS
- ➤ Creating a Workflow

In Chapter 8, you learned how to customize and extend SharePoint with the help of features and web parts such as the Silverlight web part, change a site's theme, and install custom web parts. As you've seen, you can do a lot of customization just by using the browser.

But if you need to brand SharePoint in the way that serves your needs best, or if you need to quickly build a web part that retrieves information from an external data source or sets up an advanced workflow for a site, you definitely need to use SharePoint Designer 2010 (SPD 2010). This chapter shows you how to do these things and more.

INTRODUCTION TO SHAREPOINT DESIGNER 2010

SharePoint Designer 2010 is like the previous version, SharePoint Designer 2007 — a free "what you see is what you get" (WYSIWYG) editor for SharePoint 2010 sites that provides a set of powerful tools for creating attractive sites, building no-code solutions, workflows, or an application for report processing. In fact, this editor covers nearly every job you can think of for modifying or enhancing your SharePoint 2010 environment. SharePoint Designer 2010 has excellent editorial support for underlying technologies such as ASP.NET, or established web standards such as XHTML.

SharePoint Designer 2010 allows you to work with advanced web design or no-code solutions by using toolbars in the ribbon similar to those in Microsoft Office applications.

SharePoint is built to allow an ordinary user with the proper permissions to easily change the layout of sites without any extra tool besides the web browser. This feature is very important because it makes it possible for non-developers to quickly adjust a site to their own needs. No web designer or administrator is required for this task.

> **WARNING** *SharePoint Designer is a powerful tool that should be used only by advanced and trained users, web designers, or developers. With SharePoint Designer, the administrator of the SharePoint environment can control where and how people use SharePoint Designer at all levels of their deployment, from server to site collection, and are able to preserve a consistent brand and layout across a site collection or web application by controlling the customization of pages, master pages, and page layouts.*

However, sometimes making more modifications than what is possible from the web browser is necessary; this is where SharePoint Designer 2010 comes in. This program was especially designed with SharePoint 2010 in mind, and has many features for enhancing the look and feel of SharePoint sites. No other design tools for websites have this functionality, so even if you prefer other design tools, you will need to use SharePoint Designer with SharePoint.

If you are serious about getting the most out of SharePoint 2010, then you need to understand SharePoint Designer. I'm sure you will appreciate SharePoint Designer 2010 a lot; it will be of great value when you need to build sophisticated solutions or work with branding and design for SharePoint.

Test it — it's available as a free download! Remember that SharePoint Designer is built just to help you build powerful applications on top of your SharePoint.

Is there a typical user of SharePoint Designer? Of course, it depends, but it's more a tool for the developer, web designer, or the administrator, rather than just a tool for everyone in the company.

This chapter can help you understand how to use this tool for customizing any type of SharePoint site.

SharePoint Designer 2007 Comparison

SharePoint Designer 2010 is in some parts a completely new product compared to its predecessor SPD 2007. The following list describes the most important changes you will find in SharePoint Designer 2010:

➤ The interface is completely redesigned and has the look and feel of the Office applications, with a ribbon, site summary, and Quick Launch.

➤ SharePoint Designer 2010 offers support for Business Connectivity Services (BCS), external content types, and lists.

➤ The XSLT List View web part (XLV) is available.

➤ Improved workflows are available, such as site workflows and reusable workflows, as well as Visio 2010 integration.

➤ You can create and attach content types.

➤ Configuring site, list, or object permissions is now possible.

➤ Code generation has been improved; you will from now on work in a more robust way in the design and the code view.

➤ Backup/restore and reports have been removed from SharePoint Designer.

➤ Features such as the built-in FTP, Contributor settings, and web package have been removed.

The History of SharePoint Designer

SharePoint Designer 2010 is the next generation of SharePoint Designer 2007, but is descended from previous generations of Microsoft FrontPage. Actually, it can be traced back to 1994 from the very first version of FrontPage.

FrontPage 1.1 was developed by Vermeer Technologies Incorporated (VTI), and was one of the first editing programs for the Web. A short time later Microsoft acquired Vermeer Technologies and the product, and from this very early version the resulting products would become FrontPage 97, FrontPage Express 2.0, FrontPage 98, FrontPage 2000, FrontPage 2002, FrontPage 2003, and SharePoint Designer 2007.

This first incarnation, however, still lives in the architecture of SharePoint 2010 — for example, _vti_bin, — that you will use when you connect to a web service from SharePoint Designer 2010.

What You Can Do with SharePoint Designer

As you've already seen in previous chapters, you can customize SharePoint 2010 through the web browser, such as by adding and managing web parts, but you can do these things and so much more with SharePoint Designer 2010.

Here is a quick list of things that SharePoint Designer allows you to do with SharePoint:

➤ Build composite SharePoint applications

➤ Manage data sources

  ➤ Lists and views

  ➤ Data views

  ➤ InfoPath-based forms

➤ Design advanced workflows

  ➤ For sites, lists, and content types

  ➤ Visio integration

  ➤ Manage tasks

➤ Brand SharePoint

  ➤ Manage master pages

  ➤ Manage page layouts

  ➤ Manage cascading style sheets (CSS)

➤ Administrate and configure components

  ➤ Manage site permissions

  ➤ Manage internal and external content types

  ➤ Manage site columns

Administrators can control where and how power users and web designers use SharePoint Designer at all levels, from server to site collection.

From a developer's view, SharePoint Designer 2010 is a companion and a friend. You can easily build prototypes with SharePoint Designer for a Visual Studio project; for example, you can do all the Business Connectivity Services (BCS) configurations in SharePoint Designer and then bring them into Visual Studio for further development.

No Code Required

SharePoint Designer 2010 allows you to build intuitive, attractive, and advanced solutions without code, using workflows tracking, reports or analysis, and Data Views. All you need to do is use templates, menus, and task panes. SharePoint Designer provides a fast and robust way to access a data source as an alternative to development with Visual Studio.

You can create custom data views and forms using ASP.NET, which allows you to integrate and manage many different types of external data into your site, including views that display data from one or multiple sources.

As a corporation, you may have a relational model SQL Server database and the need to view information from the database based on queries in a SharePoint site. To solve this issue you can create a page to read, edit, or delete information from this database.

SharePoint Designer 2010 provides an easy interface that lets you create views of data from a number of different data sources, and depending on your needs, use ASP.NET controls or the more SharePoint-specific XSLT List View web part (XLV).

A data source could be, for example, an XML file, RSS feed, server-side script, web service, or SharePoint list. From the flexible and powerful XSLT List View web part (XLV) follow tools for conditional formatting with XSLT; XPath formulas; parameters; and the possibility of filtering, sorting, or grouping that helps you create advanced data views.

SharePoint Designer contains many concepts and terms, so here is a short glossary with the common abbreviations. See Table 9-1.

TABLE 9-1: Technical Terms as Used in This Chapter

ABBREVIATION	FULL NAME	DESCRIPTION
ASP.NET	Microsoft ASP.NET	A free technology that allows programmers to create dynamic websites or applications.
XML	Extensible Markup Language	A language for the transportation and storage of data.
XSLT	Extensible Stylesheet Language Transformations	A language for formatting the presentation of XML data.
XPath	XML Path Language	A query language for selecting nodes from an XML document; designed to be used by XSLT.
RSS	Really Simple Syndication	An XML format for delivering regularly changing web content.
SOAP	Simple Object Access Protocol	A protocol for exchanging information between application components, in the implementation of a Web Service.
REST	Representational State Transfer	Like the SOAP protocol, but it is more simple and uses only HTTP and XML.

Branding

Branding is so much more than just images and background colors; many factors together create a good user experience. Clicking around in the sites and finding what you are looking for should be easy, and at the very least should match the corporation's graphic profile and reflect its identity and personality. The user experience should also be consistent, intuitive, and easy to understand.

With the help of master pages, page layouts, and cascading style sheets (CSS) you can create a consistent look and feel across all pages that you can easily update. SharePoint uses CSS, and it uses a lot of CSS. Modifying styles is important when you need to rebrand a SharePoint interface, just like any other web content management or collaboration tool. See Table 9-2.

TABLE 9-2: Glossary of Terms Regarding Branding

ABBREVIATION	FULL NAME	DESCRIPTION
	Master page	Defines the look, feel, and standard behavior for all the SharePoint pages.
	Page layout	A template that is used in conjunction with a master page to control the look, feel, and content of a page.
CSS	Cascading Style Sheets	Describes the presentation of a web page, and has a set of rules for fonts, colors, and more.

SHAREPOINT LISTS

SharePoint lists are a fundamental part of SharePoint, and the need to customize them is a common scenario. Sometimes you need to build a more intuitive and user-friendly form, or maybe create a report page that displays an average and summary of list items in a certain condition.

You can also extend list views or forms with client code; for example, if you need cascading dropdowns or if you want to prefill form fields based on parameters.

The following Try It Out shows how you can modify a lists form page.

TRY IT OUT **Customize a Form**

In this exercise, you create a custom form page that SharePoint can use to display data contained within a list. Suppose you want to make a condition that if the item in the form expires today, then the date should be highlighted.

1. Open SharePoint Designer 2010 (choose Start ⇨ All Programs ⇨ SharePoint ⇨ Microsoft SharePoint Designer 2010) and click the big Open Site button. Use the existing team site. Type **http://srv1/teamsite**.

2. Click Lists and Libraries in the left navigation panel, and click Announcements in the right window to get to the backstage page of the site.

3. Click New in the Forms section (the second box from the top at the right). The Create New List Form dialog will appear.

    a. Enter the filename **CustomDispForm** and select the type of form to create as "Display item form."

    b. Select the "Set as default form for the selected type" checkbox.

    c. Click OK.

    d. Click CustomDispForm.aspx; you can now edit this form page.

e. Preview this page in the browser — click on the Home tab and then Preview in Browser button (see Figure 9-1). You can add more browsers — for example, Firefox — to this list.

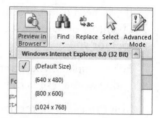

f. In the browser and in the ribbon, click Edit Item, change the Title and the Body text, set the date for Expires to the current date (today) and click Save. Close your browser.

FIGURE 9-1

g. Back in SharePoint Designer 2010, click the Split view at the bottom to control both the design and the code.

h. Select the value of Expires in the design mode to make it highlight in the code view.

i. The format of the date that is returned is in ISO format (YYYY-MM-DDTHH:MM:SSZ); to deal with this, you have to tweak the XSL code a little bit by replacing this tag:

```
<xsl:value-of select="@Expires"/>
```

with this tag:

```
<xsl:value-of select="ddwrt:FormatDate(string(@Expires) ,1033 ,1)" />
```

j. Select the value of Expires, and click Conditional Formatting from the Options tab in the ribbon. Select Format row.

k. In the Condition Criteria dialog, select Expires from the field name drop down. Set Comparison to Equals and the Value to [Current Date].

l. Click the Set Style button. In the Modify Style dialog, select background in the Category list and select a background color.

m. Select Font in the Category list, and set the font size to x-large and the color to red. Click OK.

n. Two Close buttons are on the page. Select the button at the top of the page, or select the whole row and delete it. Save the page.

o. Go to the browser and verify that everything went OK. See Figure 9-2.

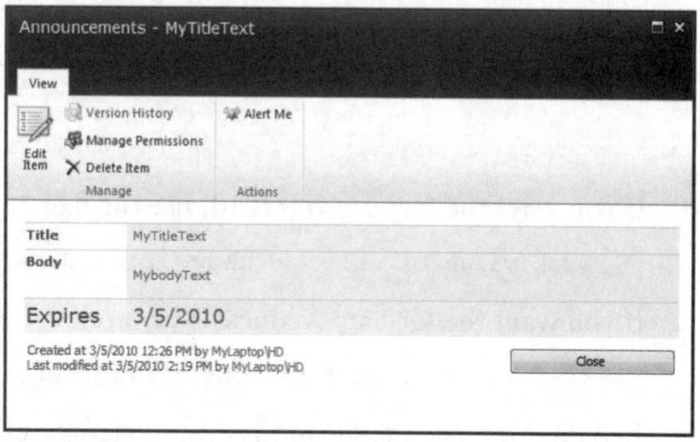

FIGURE 9-2

How It Works

In this example you created a new page, and SharePoint accepted this page to be the standard form page for view list items in the Announcement list.

If you need to work with a bit more advanced XSL formulas and functions such as mathematical operators or date functions (similar to formulas in Microsoft Excel), the XPath editor will be a useful tool for you.

For example, if you want more options for the date value output, you can use this tool to construct and view the results of your expressions as you type.

You can use eight format flags for the date value; notice the last part in this tag, the format flag (1):

```
<xsl:value-of select="ddwrt:FormatDate(string(@Expires) ,1033 ,1)" />
```

You can see all the flags that you can use and their results in Table 9-3.

TABLE 9-3: Format Flags

FORMAT FLAG	RESULTS
1	1/1/2010
3	Wednesday, March 03, 2010
4	4:37 PM
5	3/3/2010 4:37 PM
7	Wednesday, March 03, 2010 4:37 PM
12	4:37:52 PM
13	3/3/2010 4:37:52 PM
15	Wednesday, March 03, 2010 4:37:52 PM

If you want the format, 1/1/2010, use the flag 1.

```
<xsl:value-of select="ddwrt:FormatDate(string(@Expires) ,1033 ,1)" />
```

If you want the format, Wednesday, March 03, 2010, use the flag 3.

```
<xsl:value-of select="ddwrt:FormatDate(string(@Expires) ,1033 ,3)" />
```

Just double-click a *value* in the design view or click the *Formula button* on the Options tab in the ribbon to open the XPath Expression Builder. You can also open it from the Tag Properties task pane — click the Fx button. See Figure 9-3.

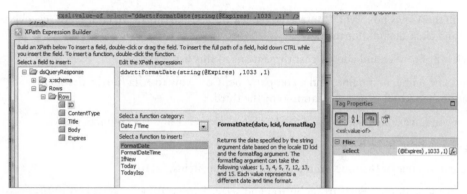

FIGURE 9-3

You can do a lot more with formulas; for example, you can do calculations of the sum of the data in two or more fields. Note that the 1033 stands for LCID, language code. You can change this to your language's code to make the date as it is used in your region.

For more information about XPath, go to the XPath tutorial at W3School:

```
http://www.w3schools.com/xpath/default.asp
```

THE XSLT LIST VIEW WEB PART

The XSLT List View web part (XLV) is a flexible component and a new powerful kid on the block in SharePoint Designer 2010 that replaces the predecessor List View web part (LVWP), which was a SharePoint Designer 2007 feature.

The XLV has several new benefits:

➤   The XLV supports both SharePoint Designer customization and in-browser modifications.

➤   It's more user friendly.

➤   It's developer friendly, using standard XSL instead of CAML.

The following Try It Out shows how to use the XSLT List View web part.

TRY IT OUT   **Use the XSLT List View Web Part**

In this example you customize a list view with the XLV. You create a contact list and use conditional formatting and inline editing to make some customizations for this view in both SharePoint Designer 2010 and the browser.

1.   Open SharePoint Designer 2010 (choose Start ➪ All Programs ➪ SharePoint ➪ Microsoft SharePoint Designer 2010) and click the big Open Site button. Use the existing team site. Type **http://srv1/teamsite**.

2.   Click the SharePoint Lists button in the ribbon and select Contacts. The Create list or document library dialog now appears. Enter **Customers** in the Name field, and click OK.

3. Click New in the Views box, type **Contacts** and click the "Make this the default view" checkbox. Click OK, and click the link for the new view.

4. Click Preview in Browser and add at least three items to this list.

    a. Type a last name, first name, and a company. Set Company to Alfa for the first item, Beta for the second item, and Gamma for the third.

    b. When you have done this, go back to SharePoint Designer and the contacts view.

    c. Press F5 to refresh the page.

5. Place the cursor in one of the rows where you can see your items.

    a. Click the Conditional Formatting button and select Format Row. See Figure 9-4.

    b. Set the condition criteria as follows: Field name to Company and Comparison to Equals, and type **Beta** in the Value field.

    c. Click the Set Style button.

    d. Select the Background category, and select a background. Click OK.

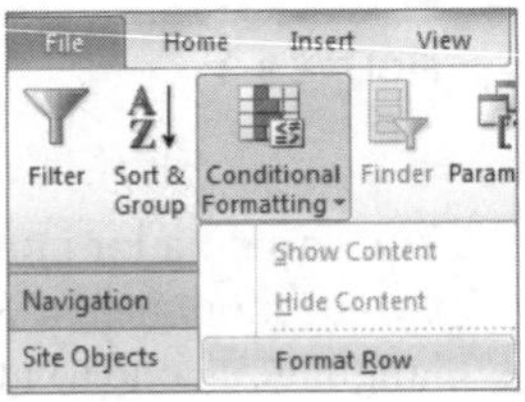

FIGURE 9-4

    e. In the ribbon and in the option tab, click Add/Remove Columns and select the displayed fields Business Phone and Home Phone. Use Ctrl to make multiple selections.

    f. Click the Remove button and click OK.

6. In the ribbon, click the Inline Editing button. This adds an edit link to every row so you can edit items directly in one place.

7. Click Sort & Group in the ribbon.

    a. Click Company and click the Add button.

    b. Click the Show group header checkbox and click OK.

    c. Try to delete the grouping header (Company) and do some other customization; the result could look similar to the image shown in Figure 9-5. Save the page.

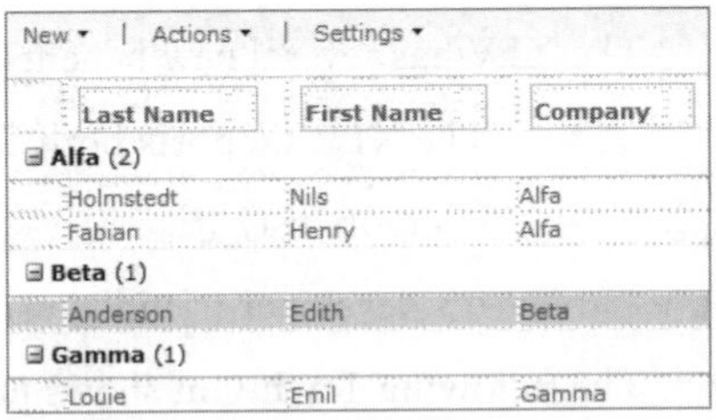

Last Name	First Name	Company
Alfa (2)		
Holmstedt	Nils	Alfa
Fabian	Henry	Alfa
Beta (1)		
Anderson	Edith	Beta
Gamma (1)		
Louie	Emil	Gamma

FIGURE 9-5

8. Go to the browser and look at the view.

    a. In the ribbon, click the List tab and click Modify View.

    b. Scroll down to the Group By section, expand it, and set the first group to None.

    c. Click OK. Notice that you can modify the view in SharePoint Designer, and in the browser. If you modified a view in SharePoint Designer 2007, you couldn't do any changes afterwards through the browser.

How It Works

This Try It Out was a quick overview of some of the new and improved functionalities that come with SharePoint Designer 2010. One of the new improvements in the XLV is that it can be customized both in the browser and in SharePoint Designer, which is a welcome feature!

THE DATA VIEW WEB PART

Now take a look at the wonderful Data View web part. This web part is one of the most powerful and flexible web parts in SharePoint and can be used to display and aggregate data from many kinds of data sources. You have probably heard people call it the "The Swiss army knife of SharePoint web parts;" it has been around as a part of SharePoint since SharePoint Portal Server 2003 and WSS 2.0. XSLT enables you to render the data in the data view however you want.

There is so much you can do with the data view in SharePoint Designer — here are a few examples:

➤ Pull data from any site in the site collection, and even aggregate data from more than one list

➤ Make a web part that shows all the sites in a site collection

➤ Build an employee directory web part

➤ Show the latest blog posts of mine

➤ Build a "What's up this week" web part based on one or more SharePoint calendars

You can connect a data view to the following data sources:

➤ SharePoint lists or libraries

➤ Databases

➤ Web services

➤ XML files

➤ Server-side scripts that return XML, like PHP, Cold Fusion, and more.

You can use a data view to build non-code applications in a simple way — you just select a data source and the fields to be displayed, and customize the rendering.

Some of the features for the data view:

➤ Filter, sort, and group

➤ Conditional formatting

➤ Parameters:

    ➤ Control

    ➤ Cookie

    ➤ Form

> ➤ Query string

> ➤ Server variable

➤ Formula

➤ Paging

➤ Asynchronous update (Ajax)

> ➤ Set refresh interval

➤ Inline editing

➤ Set chrome type and other web part properties

➤ Add connections (get or send information to another web part)

➤ Save a web part as a file or into the web part gallery

The following Try It Out shows how to build a web part using a REST Web service.

TRY IT OUT   Build a Web Part with REST

A Web service is an XML format that is based on the standard protocols SOAP or REST, and it can be used to send and receive information between websites.

In this example, you connect to an external source with the REST web service and create a client-side "gadget," a web part that displays the current weather condition in a given place. In this example, the web part will display the current weather in Stockholm, Sweden. You can change the location later. This does not require any assemblies to be deployed on the SharePoint server, as is usually the case when you build applications with SharePoint Designer.

1. Open SharePoint Designer 2010 (choose Start ➪ All Programs ➪ SharePoint ➪ Microsoft SharePoint Designer 2010) and click the big Open Site button. Use the top level site. Type **http://srv1/**.

2. Click Data Sources in the left navigation panel and click the REST Services Connection button. The Data Source Properties dialog now appears. See Figure 9-6.

FIGURE 9-6

3. In the field for the URL to the server-side script, enter this:

```
http://weather.yahooapis.com/forecastrss?w=906057&u=c
```

4. Click the General tab and give this data source a name — for example, **Weather now** — and click OK.

5. Click Site Page in the left navigation panel and then click the Page button in the ribbon. Select ASPX. Rename the file from Untitled_1.aspx to **WeatherConditions.aspx**.

6. Click the page to open it, click the little arrow inside the Edit File button, and select "Edit file in advanced mode."

7. In the ribbon and from the Insert tab, click the Data View button and select the recently created Data Source "Weather now."

8. Click the Paging button in the ribbon and select Display 1 item.

9. Save the page and preview it in the browser.

How It Works

You have created an fully functional web part that displays the weather right now in a given location, but it needs a bit more work to be useful as a web part in SharePoint. For example, see Figure 9-7. You can use a rich set of different web services with application programming interfaces (APIs) that expose data to create a mashup or a web part in SharePoint Designer — for example, applications like Microsoft Bing maps, Delicious, Flickr, and Twitter. These APIs have full documentation.

You can find the documentation that includes all the elements and their descriptions, and condition codes listed for the web service you just created at the following URL:

```
http://developer.yahoo.com/weather/
```

FIGURE 9-7

The following Try It Out shows how to use XSLT and to manage parameters in order to complete the weather web part.

TRY IT OUT   **Manage Parameters and Use XSLT**

In this example you change the location (WOEID), to a city by changing parameters in the web part; there is no need to change the location in the Data Source in this exercise.

A parameter can be used to pass (get or send) values of variables from a data source to an application. Take a close look at this end of this link:

```
/forecastrss?w=906057&u=c
```

w (WOEID) is the identifier for the location and could be a city or a zip code. u (unit) lets you get the value c (Celsius) or f (Fahrenheit).

Parameters are used by SharePoint in many different scenarios and can be used by a data view to pass form values or set a cookie, for example.

1.   To change your location, go to `http://weather.yahoo.com`.

2.   Enter a city or a zip code, and note the URL. The last part (the number) contains the parameters based off your selection. Copy this number.

3.   Go back to WeatherConditions.aspx. Click the Data Form web part in the Design mode.

 a.   Click the Parameters button.

 b.   Click the parameter w, and replace the Default value with that number you recently copy.

 c.   Change the Parameter u (unit), from c (Celsius) to f (Fahrenheit) if you prefer this unit. Click OK.

4.   Click Add/Remove Columns, select "high" and "low" to the right, and click Remove. Click OK.

5.   Select the "1-1" in the bottom row, and delete it. You can delete the whole table cell or table if you want.

6.   Delete the top row using the quick tag selector.

7.   Select the Data Form web part in the design mode and click Data Source Details in the ribbon. You can now access all the values that that can be used in your web part.

 a.   Select the code; you find this in the tree structure, in the Data Source Details task pane.

```
rss/channel/item/yweather:forecast/@code.
```

 b.   Drag the code, and place it just after the last text in the design mode.

 c.   Go to the code view and replace the condition code:

```
<xsl:value-of select="@code" />
```

 with this:

```
<xsl:choose>
  <xsl:when test="@code = 29"><img   src="http://l.yimg.com/a/i/us/we/52/29.gif"
alt="" /></xsl:when>
  <xsl:when test="@code = 30"><img src="http://l.yimg.com/a/i/us/we/52/30.gif"
alt="" /></xsl:when>

<xsl:otherwise>
<xsl:when test="@code = 3200"><img src="http://l.yimg.com/a/i/us/we/52/3200.gif"
alt="" /></xsl:when>
```

```
        </xsl:otherwise>

    </xsl:choose>
```

Suppose that the weather is sunny right now, and the condition code that describes the current conditions (@code) is shown as number 30. If you want to illustrate the weather with an image, you can use the xsl:choose for this task.

In this xsl that you just replaced, there are just two conditions (and an otherwise) in the statement and 48 conditions are available, from tornados and thunderstorms to hot and sunny weather.

In addition to these options, you can create and use your own animated images, and use colors that will fit on your corporate website. Why not be inspired from Microsoft desktop gadgets for Windows 7? See Figure 9-8.

FIGURE 9-8

How It Works

XSLT in data views transforms the XML that SharePoint retrieves from the data source into the page. You can edit the XSLT in the code view, and use conditional logics to style the data in different ways based on various conditions.

For more information about XSLT, go to the XSLT tutorial at W3School:

```
http://www.w3schools.com/xsl/default.asp
```

For more information about the XSL tags in data views, go to Marc D. Anderson's blog series, which contains 13 entries about the subject:

```
http://www.endusersharepoint.com/2010/01/19/unlocking-the-mysteries-of-data-view-
web-part-xsl-tags-part-1-overview/
```

EXTERNAL LISTS

Microsoft Business Connectivity Services (BCS) is significantly more useful and easy to use compared to the previous version, Business Data Catalogue (BDC) in MOSS.

BCS lets you easily define connections to a line of business data (LOB) or some other external data that you can access as a developer or designer. In addition, you can now use SharePoint Designer 2010 to create and configure BCS to pull data from external systems such as an SQL Server, .Net Assembly, or web service.

After you define and create BCS, you can create from within SharePoint Designer an external list that will show you the content of what the connections are attached to — for example, an SQL database table, view, or a stored procedure. The external list provides code generation for Create, Read, Update, and Delete (CRUD) functions in forms.

An external list acts just like any other SharePoint list and receives advantages such as the ability to create views and new SharePoint columns, sort, filter, and group. In SharePoint, your users can work with an external list just like they do a regular SharePoint list, which means that they can, for example, update or create new list items that go all the way back to the data source.

Integrating external data in SharePoint with external lists is easy, and SharePoint Designer provides an intuitive wizard for this task, as discussed in the following Try It Out.

TRY IT OUT   Create an External List

In this example you set up a link between BCS and a data source and then create an external list with SharePoint Designer 2010.

1.   Create some example data: either create your own database with a table in SQL server, or download an example database. For this example, use the AdventureWorksLT2008 (only the database). You can find it at CodePlex at `http://msftdbprodsamples.codeplex.com/ releases/view/37109`. Unzip the file and attach it to your SQL 2008 server.

2.   Open SharePoint Designer 2010 (choose Start ⇨ All Programs ⇨ SharePoint ⇨ Microsoft SharePoint Designer 2010) and click the big Open Site button. See Figure 9-9.

3.   Type, for example, **http://srv1/teamsite** and click Open. SharePoint Designer connects to the site and opens the relevant information.

FIGURE 9-9

a.   Click External Content Types, in the left navigation pane.

b.   In the ribbon, click External Content Type.

c.   Click the Name link (New External content type) and enter **Products**.

d.   Click the Display Name link (New External content type) and type **Products**.

e.   Connect to the database. Click the "Click here to discover external data sources and define operations" link.

f.   Click Add Connection, select SQL Server as the Data Source Type, and click OK.

g.   For Database Server, type *yourservername*, and for Database Name in this example, type **AdventureWorksLT2008**. Click OK.

h.   Expand the database and the tables, right-click Product, and select Create All Operations. See Figure 9-10.

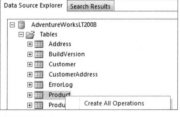

i.   In the All operations dialog, click Next and then Finish. You don't need to look at the warnings at this time. You have now set up your external content type. Save your external content type (press Ctrl+S).

FIGURE 9-10

4. Now create an external list in your team site. In SharePoint Designer on the ribbon, click Create Lists & Forms. Give the list a name — for example, **Adventure Works products**. Click OK.

5. Use your browser and go to the team site. You should see a link to the new Adventure Works products list. Click the link.

6. Edit one of the items in the list and save it. You can now work with this list by editing, adding, or deleting items. Try to create a view that filters only at the color silver, and set the descending sort order for ListPrice. See Figure 9-11.

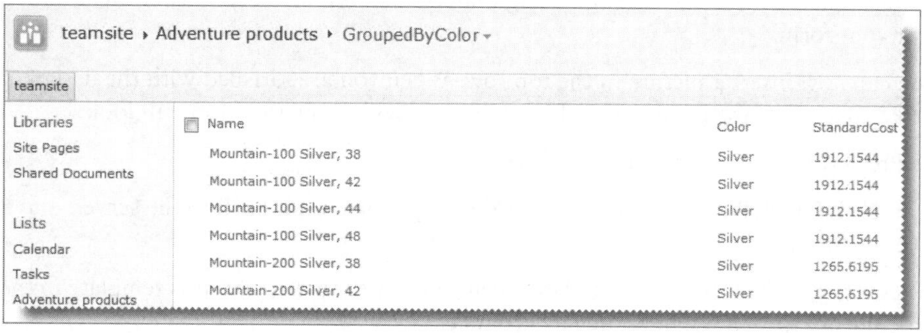

teamsite ▸ Adventure products ▸ GroupedByColor ▾			
teamsite			
	☐ Name	Color	StandardCost
Libraries			
Site Pages	Mountain-100 Silver, 38	Silver	1912.1544
Shared Documents	Mountain-100 Silver, 42	Silver	1912.1544
	Mountain-100 Silver, 44	Silver	1912.1544
Lists	Mountain-100 Silver, 48	Silver	1912.1544
Calendar	Mountain-200 Silver, 38	Silver	1265.6195
Tasks	Mountain-200 Silver, 42	Silver	1265.6195
Adventure products			

FIGURE 9-11

How It Works

As you now have seen, external content types and external lists are powerful functions in SharePoint Designer, and you create them with a few clicks. However, you can do a lot more than what you have tried up to this point — for example, you can use an SQL server stored procedure or a view to establish contact with a relational database.

After you have created an external content type from SharePoint Designer, it will be stored in the Service Application section in SharePoint Central Administration. From this place you can manage all external content types, such as set object permission. You can read more about external content types in the SharePoint 2010 SDK topic "What are External Content Types?" at `http://msdn .microsoft.com/en-us/library/ee556391(office.14).aspx`.

The following Try It Out shows how to use InfoPath 2010 to modify a list form.

TRY IT OUT Modify the External List Form with InfoPath 2010

InfoPath 2010 is a perfect tool when it comes to modifying list form pages. Using InfoPath, you can design the form in an attractive manner or, for example, create validations for the fields in the form. In this example, you learn how to use Info Path to create a custom design for a list form.

1. Click Lists and Libraries in the left navigation pane in SharePoint Designer and select the external list Adventure Works products you created in the preceding Try It Out.

2. On the ribbon, click Design Forms in InfoPath, and then click Item. InfoPath Designer 2010 opens.

3. At the very top of the form, in the first row, position the mouse cursor and type **Products Form**. See Figure 9-12.

4. On the ribbon, pick the Title format from the Font Styles selector.

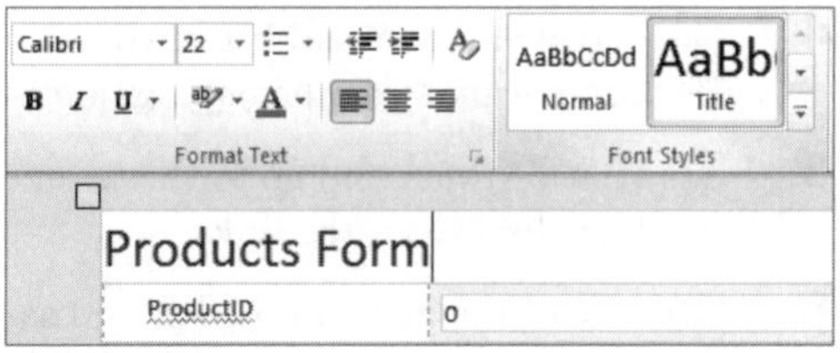

FIGURE 9-12

5. Point at the top-left square and select the Page Design tab on the ribbon. Select one of themes to set a color for your form.

6. If you want, you can now insert a picture in the top row. When you are satisfied with the design of the form, press F5 to preview the form in Info Path Filler to review how the form will look.

7. Click the Close Preview button when you are finished.

8. To save the form, click Quick Publish (or press Ctrl+Shift+Q) to submit it back to the server, and click OK to save the form.

9. Now choose where to save the Info Path Templates; you can, for example, save this template in the site's Shared Documents. Give it a name, such as **Products**.

10. Go to the Products list and edit the first object. See Figure 9-13.

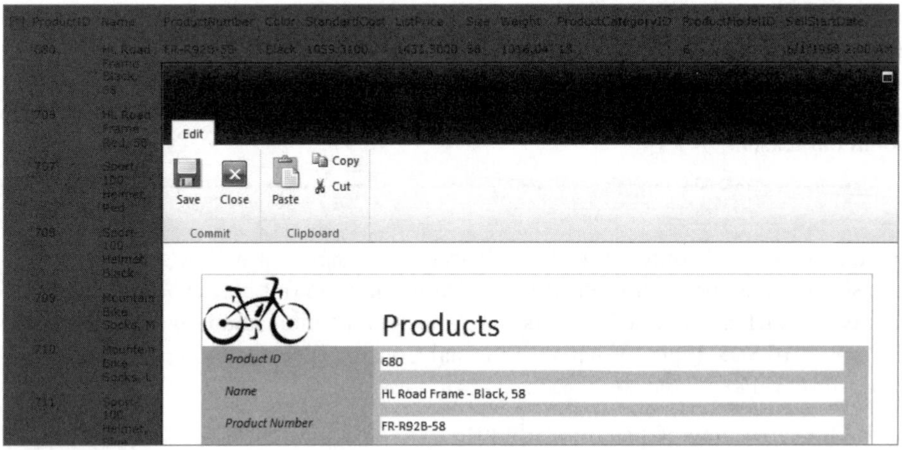

FIGURE 9-13

How It Works

This exercise was a quick walkthrough in InfoPath, a tool with great features that enable you to present your data in a high-quality way when you want to create smart and interactive form pages in SharePoint without any code. You can, for example, create validation, prepopulate form fields, execute rules and actions, or create tabbed navigation forms for a multiple-view form.

MANAGING MASTER PAGES

A master page provides a template-based consistent look and feel, and contains functions such as the top navigation, the Quick Launch, log on controls, or the search box for all the pages in your SharePoint sites. Together with content pages, they produce the output that combines content from the content page with the layout of the master page (see Figure 9-14).

All the elements that are common for all the pages in SharePoint can be defined in a master page, just like all the elements that are specific for a content page can be defined in a page layout. When you look at a SharePoint

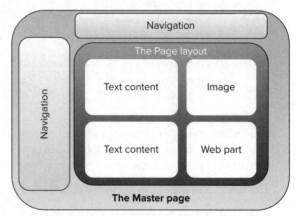

FIGURE 9-14

page in the browser, the content in this page is rendered by a combination of the master page and the page layout.

A master page contains several ASP.NET controls called *content placeholders* that connect to content controls in the attached SharePoint pages. The master page and the page layout work symbiotically to create the layout for a publishing page.

A master page includes a reference to one or more CSS files to use the CSS in all the pages that are attached to the master page. The master page can also include references to ECMAScript files — for example, a JavaScript file or a jQuery file.

Adding your own custom user controls in a master page, or even web parts, is possible. Depending on your needs, a SharePoint intranet or a SharePoint Internet site can use different master pages for one or all of the sites in the site hierarchy.

If you are planning to upgrade a master page from SharePoint 2007 to SharePoint 2010, and for the reason that SharePoint 2010 has new functionalities such as the ribbon, you must include two new placeholders in the upgraded master page (see Table 9-4). You also must delete three controls that now have moved into the new ribbon UI (see Table 9-5).

TABLE 9-4: New Placeholders in SharePoint 2010

PLACEHOLDER CONTROL	DESCRIPTION
`<asp:ContentPlaceHolder id="PlaceHolderQuickLaunchTop" runat="server">`	The top of the Quick Launch menu
`<asp:ContentPlaceHolder id="PlaceHolderQuickLaunchBottom" runat="server">`	The bottom of the Quick Launch menu

TABLE 9-5: Outgoing Controls in SharePoint 2007

CONTROL	DESCRIPTION
`<PublishingConsole:Console>`	Publishing console
`<PublishingSiteAction:SiteActionMenu>`	Site Actions menu
`Welcome`	Sign-in and log-in control

Read more about "How to upgrade an Existing Master Page to the SharePoint Foundation Master Page" at Microsoft MSDN at `http://msdn.microsoft.com/en-us/library/ ee539981(office.14).aspx`.

The benefits of master pages follow:

➤ It defines the design in one single file.

➤ An update in the master page affects all the SharePoint pages that are attached to this master page.

➤ It is a standard feature in ASP.NET.

The following Try It Out shows how to create a custom Master Page with SharePoint Designer 2010.

TRY IT OUT Create a Master Page

In this example, you create a customized master page based on one of the out-of-the-box master pages in SharePoint. You will change the behavior for the top navigation, and create a flyout menu in two levels.

1. Open SharePoint Designer 2010 (choose Start ➪ All Programs ➪ SharePoint ➪ Microsoft SharePoint Designer 2010) and click the big Open Site button.

2. Open the top level site: `http://srv1`.

3. Click Master Pages in the left navigation pane, right-click `v4.master`, and select Copy. Right-click again and select Paste.

4. Click `v4-copy(1).master`, and click the file name. Rename it to **v4_Custom.master**.

5. Click Edit file in the Customization box. Click Yes to check it out.

6. Using the split view, select the top navigation in the design view; on the ribbon, select the View tab. Now click the Zoom to Contents button. This function makes only the selected content visible on the page.

7. Click the Task Panes button in the ribbon to show task panes. Once the task panes appear to the right, click the arrow on the Task Panes button to activate the drop down menu. Select Tag Properties. Expand this task pane a bit to the left. You can see that a lot of properties can be set to SharePoint and ASP.NET controls, such as the top navigation.

8. Select the top navigation in the design mode. Under Behavior in the Tag Properties task pane, change the value for MaximumDynamicDisplayLevels from 1 to 2. See Figure 9-15.

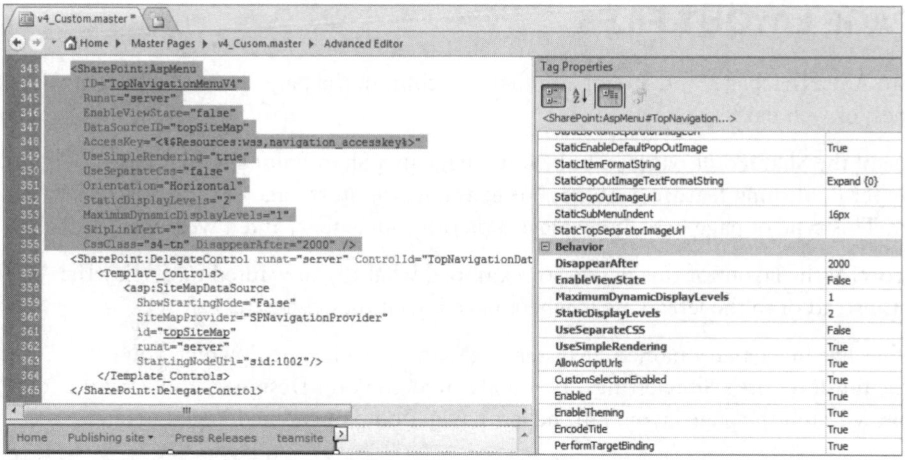

FIGURE 9-15

9. Save the page (Ctrl+S), and click Yes to save this page as a customized master page.

10. Use the browser to go to the top-level site, and select Site Actions ➪ Site Settings ➪ MasterPage under the Look and Feel section.

11. Specify the Site Master Page and the System Master Page, and select the v4_Custom .master in both drop-down menus. Select the "Reset all subsites to inherit this site master page setting" option for the site and the system master. Click OK. Use the browser to go to http://srv1 and verify that your custom master page affected the site. This example is based on a site structure with at least three levels of sites. See Figure 9-16.

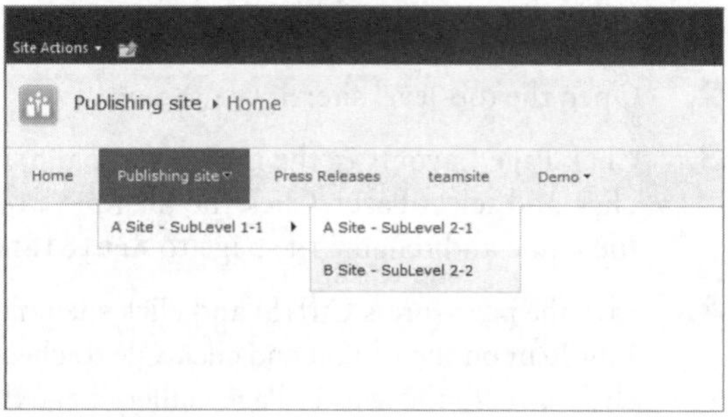

FIGURE 9-16

How It Works

As you can see, customizing a master page is easy. But you can, of course, do a lot more than this simple example demonstrates.

Compared to the default master page in SharePoint 2007, the master pages now have better code standards, and use strict XHTML as the default doc type declaration. This means that SharePoint is more cross-browser friendly and compliant for accessibility standards such as WCAG 2.

If you need to create your own branding, using the Starter Master Pages available from CodePlex as a starting point may be a good idea.

http://startermasterpages.codeplex.com/

Starter Master Pages were known previously as Minimal Master Pages in SharePoint 2007. These master pages contain only very minimal HTML styling to accommodate some of the specific needs of SharePoint 2010, and are commented throughout.

MANAGING PAGE LAYOUT FILES

A page layout is an ASP.NET page, and a template that can contain the page design, field controls, and web part zones, or web parts.

Take a look at one of the SharePoint pages, a publishing page in a SharePoint site that has the SharePoint Server Publishing feature enabled. For example, the start page of "Press Releases" in SharePoint Server. This type of page usually displays a picture, some text, and a web part.

But how do you control the layout of this page? For example, what if you wanted to display the image to the right instead of to the left? This is where page layout files come in.

The page layout files live in a gallery named "Master pages and page layouts," which you can browse to from the top-level site's Site Settings. If you are in SharePoint Designer, and have the top-level site open, you will find the page layouts in the left navigation pane named Page Layouts.

TRY IT OUT   Create a Page Layout

In this example, you create a new page layout and add a field control at the page, and create a new SharePoint site and a page.

1. Open SharePoint Designer 2010 (choose Start ⇨ All Programs ⇨ SharePoint ⇨ Microsoft SharePoint Designer 2010) and click the big Open Site button.

2. Open the top-level site: `http://srv1`.

3. Click Page Layouts in the navigation pane, right-click `ArticleLeft.aspx` and select Copy. Right-click and select Paste. Click the file `ArticleLeft_copy(1).aspx`. Click the link to the right of file name and rename the page to **ArticleLeft2.aspx**. Press Enter.

4. Save the page (press Ctrl+S) and click the link "Manage all file properties in the browser." Click Edit Item on the ribbon and click OK to check out the page. Change the Title to **Image on left 2** and click Save. In the Master Page Gallery page that appears, click the drop down next to `ArticleLeft2.aspx` and select Check In. Set the type of version to be a Major version. Click OK. Close the browser window.

5. In SharePoint Designer, back at the page, click Edit File, click Yes to check it out, and then confirm that you want to open the page in advanced mode by clicking Yes.

6. Click Article date in design view. In the View tab, click Task Panes and select Toolbox. Expand Page Fields, right-click Contact-Email Address and select Insert. Save the page (press Ctrl+S).

7. Browse to the top-level site and create a new site. Use the Publishing site template, and give it the name **Demo**. Click Site Actions, click Site Settings, and then click the "Page layouts and site templates" link.

8. Click the "Pages in this site can only use the following layouts" checkbox. Click the page layout that you just created, and click the Add button. Click OK.

9. Create a new page in this site: select Site actions and New Page. Type the name **Demo page** and click Create.

10. Click the Page tab in the ribbon and the Page Layout button. Select the page layout that you just created to change the page layout.

11. Click the link "Click here to insert a picture from SharePoint" in the Page Image field to upload an image. Type some text in the Page Content field, set the current date to the Article Date, and type an e-mail address in the Contact field.

12. Click the Publish tab, click the Publish button, click the Publish button, and then click Continue.

How It Works

You are now able to add your own field controls in a page layout, based on site columns and content types. You can read more about how to manage site columns and content types in Chapter 3.

MANAGING CSS

Cascading Style Sheets (CSS) is key in making SharePoint have a consistent look and feel; like most standard WCM systems, SharePoint uses CSS, and SharePoint uses it a lot! While the master page and the page layouts define the frame structure of the content and controls, CSS defines the look and feel — for example, with fonts, colors, and images. CSS can also be used to position and manipulate web page elements and objects.

If you want a design with a look and feel that ties in with your corporation's graphical profile, you need to learn how to use CSS and, of course, create a great web design that is more than just CSS, which requires a web or graphic designer's knowledge and skills.

SharePoint has references to CSS files from the master page — for example, if you look at the v4.master file in code view in SharePoint Designer, the reference to the CSS files looks like this:

```
<SharePoint:CssLink runat="server" Version="4"/>
```

If you perform a right-click on a SharePoint page that is attached to v4.master and select View Source, you will see that two CSS files actually are in use: the layout.css and the corev4.css. The core file, as its name suggests, is THE file for the look and feel of SharePoint, and is a huge file with about 7,000 rows. The core file defines the user interface (UI) in SharePoint, everything from the look and feel for the ribbon, to the current navigation or a single function in a document library.

If you open the core CSS, you will see that it contains many classes that have one or more properties and values. Take a closer look at one of the classes in this file:

```
.ms-siteactionsmenu{
display:inline-block;
vertical-align:top;
font-size:8pt;
}
```

You can see that the name of the class, the selector, is ms-siteactionmenu, and that the following declaration has three properties with values. This means that the content in an HTML element that is defined with this class will align to the top in the element.

Suppose you want to have some text in green, and that you have that text surrounded by a DIV tag:

```
<div class="MyClass">Some text goes here…</div>
```

The class, the selector, and the declaration in this example are defined as follows (see Figure 9-17):

```
.MyClass {
Color:green
}
```

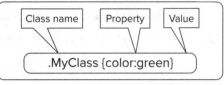

CSS in a nutshell:

FIGURE 9-17

➤   External style sheets are stored in CSS files.

➤   Styles define how to display HTML elements.

➤   Editing a single file CSS enables you to change the appearance and layout of all the pages in a website.

The following Try It Out shows how to create a custom CSS and how to attach this file to a master page.

TRY IT OUT   Create a Custom CSS File

In this example, you create a custom CSS file and make a reference to this file in a master page — the v4_Custom.master that you created in a previous example. You also learn how to override the SharePoint core CSS classes, the corev4.css, with your own CSS classes.

You also modify the look and feel of the top navigation and the top header.

1.   Using the browser, go to the top-level site and choose Site Actions ➪ Site Settings and click the Master page under the Look and Feel section.

2.   Specify the Site Master Page and the System Master Page: select the v4_Custom.master in both drop-down menus. Select the "Reset all subsites to inherit this site master page setting" option for the site and the system master. Click OK. Go back to the intranet's start page.

3.   Open SharePoint Designer 2010 (choose Start ➪ All Programs ➪ SharePoint ➪ Microsoft SharePoint Designer 2010) and click the big Open Site button.

4.   Open the top-level site: http://srv. Click All Files in the navigation pane. Click the Style Library folder. Click the Folder button on the ribbon. Type the name **CustomStyles**, and open this folder.

5.   Click the File button on the ribbon and select CSS. Right click on the file and select Rename; enter **CustomStyle.css**. You have now created an empty CSS file, and that is enough for the moment. Next you make a reference to this file from the master page.

6.   Click Master Pages in the navigation pane, click v4_Custom.master, and click Edit file.

7.   Use the code view and type a reference to the CustomStyle.css in the row below the SharePoint:CssLink tag:

```
<SharePoint:CssRegistration name="/Style Library/CustomStyles/CustomStyle.css"
After="corev4.css" runat="server"/>
```

8. Save the master page.

How It Works

No overrides or any changes to the UI have been made yet, so there is nothing to look at right now, and the custom CSS file is empty, but everything is set up for you to override the classes you want.

There's more than one way to reference a custom CSS in your master page. You can read about the most common ways to reference in this blog post:

http://erikswenson.blogspot.com/2010/01/sharepoint-2010-css-references-in.html

Because of the way that CSS cascades, the last referenced CSS file will always overwrite the one that comes before it. The CSSRegistration tag has a new property in SharePoint 2010 called After. This property enables you to have better control over the hierarchy for the classes and CSS files. The following Try It Out shows how to override classes in SharePoints Core CSS.

TRY IT OUT **Override the Core CSS**

In this example, you will learn how to override CSS classes in SharePoint by your own definitions of them. The goal is to customize the look and feel for global navigation.

To follow this example, you must first create a custom CSS file and a custom master page, and have a reference in the custom master page to this custom CSS file. See the preceding Try It Out for how to do this.

1. Open SharePoint Designer 2010 (choose Start ➪ All Programs ➪ SharePoint Microsoft SharePoint Designer 2010) and click the big Open Site button. Open the top-level site: http://srv.

2. Click Master Pages in the navigation page, click v4_Custom.master, and click Edit file to open the file in advanced mode.

3. Open corev4.css. To do this, in code view look for an HTML element that has a class name; for example, <td class="s4-titletext">. All names for classes in master pages are hyperlinked. Now click (Ctrl+click) s4-titletext and the corev4.css opens. Don't close corev4.css; switch back to the v4_Custom.master. This was just an example of how to find classes; now, on to the top navigation.

4. Use the split view and click the top navigation in the design view. Click Zoom to Contents in the View tab on the ribbon. You will now only see the control for the top navigation called SharePoint:AspMenu.

5. Look after the property for this control: CssClass. You will see that this property has the selector with the name s4-tn. Copy the name s4-tn (Ctrl+C). Go back to corev4.css and search (Ctrl+F) for s4-tn, and click the Find All button. You will now see that the search results find ten classes that have to do with the top navigation. Copy all these classes with their declarations; this should be about 52 rows, from row 2829 to 2880. See Figure 9-18.

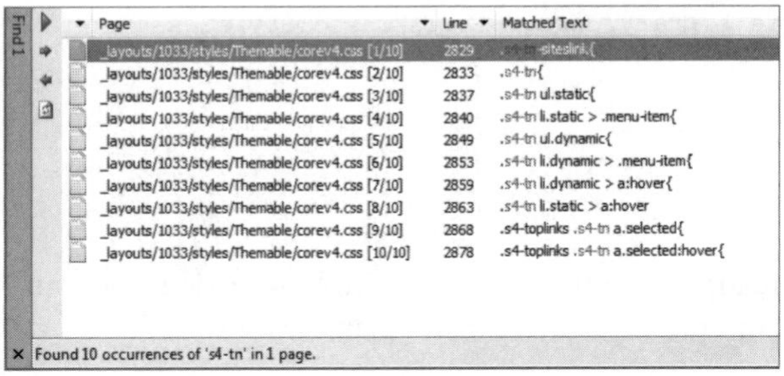

FIGURE 9-18

6. Paste what you have copied into the `CustomStyles.css`. Save the file and browse to `http://srv1` to verify that nothing has changed.

7. Go back to SharePoint Designer and to `CustomStyles.css` and do some changes to the classes. You can, for example, do this:

```
.s4-tn{
padding:0px;
margin:0px;
}
.s4-tn ul.static{
white-space:nowrap;
}
/*---modified---*/
.s4-tn li.static > .menu-item{
/* [ReplaceColor(themeColor:"Dark2")] */ color:#3b4f65;
white-space:nowrap;
border:10px solid transparent;
padding:4px 10px;
display:inline-block;
height:15px;
vertical-align:middle;
font-size:8pt;
color:#fff
}
.s4-tn ul.dynamic{
/* [ReplaceColor(themeColor:"Light2")] */ background-color:white;
/* [ReplaceColor(themeColor:"Dark2-Lighter")] */ border:1px solid #D9D9D9;
}
/*---modified---*/
.s4-tn li.dynamic > .menu-item{
display:block;
padding:10px 10px;
white-space:nowrap;
font-weight:normal;
color:#333
}
/*---modified---*/
.s4-tn li.dynamic > a:hover{
font-weight:normal;
/* [ReplaceColor(themeColor:"Light2-Lighter")] */ background-color:#f7f7f7;
color:#000
```

```
}
/*---modified---*/
.s4-tn li.static > a:hover{
/* [ReplaceColor(themeColor:"Accent1")] */ color:#fff;
text-decoration:none;
font-size:8pt;
}
/*---modified---*/
.s4-toplinks .s4-tn a.selected{
/* [ReplaceColor(themeColor:"Accent1-Medium")] */ border-color: #006E2E;
/* [ReplaceColor(themeColor:"Accent1-Lighter")] */border-bottom-color: #006E2E;
/* [ReplaceColor(themeColor:"Accent1-Lightest")] */border-top-color: #006E2E;
/* [RecolorImage(themeColor:"Light1")] */background: none;
/* [ReplaceColor(themeColor:"Accent1",themeTint:"0.35")] */
background-color: #006E2E;
/* [ReplaceColor(themeColor:"Accent1",themeShade:"0.20")] */color: #fff;
padding: 4px 5px;
margin: 0px 0px;
font-size:8pt;
}
.s4-tn {
/* [ReplaceColor(themeColor:"Accent1-Medium")] */ border-color: #fff;
/* [ReplaceColor(themeColor:"Accent1-Lighter")] */border-bottom-color: #fff;
/* [ReplaceColor(themeColor:"Accent1-Lightest")] */border-top-color: #fff;
/* [RecolorImage(themeColor:"Light1")] */background: none;
/* [ReplaceColor(themeColor:"Accent1",themeTint:"0.35")] */
background-color: #008000;
/* [ReplaceColor(themeColor:"Accent1",themeShade:"0.20")] */color: #fff;
padding: 0px 0px;
margin: 0px 0px;
font-size:8pt;
}
/*---modified---*/
.s4-toplinks .s4-tn a.selected:hover{
/* [ReplaceColor(themeColor:"Dark2")] */ color:#f7f7f7;
font-size:8pt;
}
```

8. Use the browser and verify that the global navigation now has changed.

How It Works

The purpose of this example is to give you a general overview about how to work with CSS. Hopefully you are now ready to create your design in SharePoint with SharePoint Designer and CSS.

As you can see in the preceding code, every CSS class that has been modified has inline comments. This is a best-practice recommendation; be sure to type a comment for your modifications or your own classes.

Remember that pages like the master page and the CSS are under version control; you can always revert to a previous version if your modifications go wrong in some part.

To learn more about CSS in general, go to http://www.w3schools.com/css.

USING WORKFLOWS

Workflows in SharePoint Designer are there to help you create automated business processes. Not so long ago this task was quite complicated for the developer, but with SharePoint Designer 2010 building sophisticated workflow logic without needing code is possible.

By using the embedded workflow designer in SharePoint Designer, you can create workflows with rules for conditions and actions that are associated with, for example, items in SharePoint lists or document libraries.

For example, suppose some people in your organization have the task to write, review, and approve contracts. They save them in a document library in their team website. To help them automate administration, you can use SharePoint Designer to create a route that sends an e-mail message to the reviewer when a new agreement has been added to the site. At the same time, a task can be created in the reviewer's task list. When the person reviewing this agreement specifies that the task is complete (approved or not), a variety of actions can be set through the route.

The changes and improvements of the workflow engine are relatively extensive. The following list compares the previous version of SharePoint Designer with the key changes and the new features of SharePoint Designer 2010:

➤ The workflow editors are now in full-screen mode and are integrated with contextual ribbons.

➤ Site workflows can be used, for example, if you need to execute a process on a document set.

➤ A workflow now can be defined as a global reusable template.

➤ With the parallel block feature, conditions, actions, and scopes can now run at the same time.

➤ You can import and export workflows to Visio 2010 in the Visio Workflow Interchange (VWI) format by using the graphical design workflow. This makes designing and structuring the workflow easier than before.

➤ The impersonation feature can temporarily elevate a non-privileged user so he can complete a task.

➤ A workflow can use an external list.

➤ Some of the new conditions include:

    ➤ If title field contains keywords

    ➤ If a person is a SharePoint user

    ➤ Check list item permission

➤ Some of the new actions include:

    ➤ Pause until date

    ➤ Send document to repository

> ➤ Find interval between dates

> ➤ Extract substrings

> ➤ Error message

> ➤ Look up manager of a user

> ➤ Delegate a task

If you are going to build advanced workflows, such as a workflow that initiates another workflow, watch out for looping; test it step by step before you deploy it. Logical errors are not that easy to prevent in a SharePoint Designer workflow, but you can add a log of history actions to see where the workflow is when it executes.

TRY IT OUT   **Create a Workflow**

In this example, you create a simple workflow that copies a document from one document library from another.

1. Open SharePoint Designer 2010 (choose Start ➪ All Programs ➪ SharePoint ➪ Microsoft SharePoint Designer 2010) and click the Team Site button. Specify the location as `http://srv1/workflowdemo`. Click OK.

2. Click the Document Library button on the ribbon and select Document Library. Enter the name **Archive** and click OK.

3. Click Lists and Libraries in the navigation pane, and then click Shared Documents. Click the Edit Columns button on the ribbon, and then click the Add New Column button. Select Choice.

4. Type these three choices, each choice on a separate line:

   > ➤ Yes

   > ➤ No

   > ➤ Maybe

5. Set the default value to No and click OK. Click the column name NewColumn1 and give it the name **Archive** and hit enter. Save it (press Ctrl+S).

6. Click Team Site in the navigation pane to get to the site's backstage view. Click the List Workflow button on the ribbon and select Shared Documents. In the Create List Workflow dialog, give it the name **Copy Items from Shared Documents to Archive**. Click OK.

   a. Click just above the colored line in the Step 1 box, click the Condition button on the ribbon, and select "If current item field equals value."

   b. Click the "field" hyperlink and select Archive.

   c. Click the "value" hyperlink and select Yes.

   d. Click just above the new colored line that appears in the box.

   e. Click the Action button on the ribbon and select Copy List Item.

    f.   Click the "this list" hyperlink and click OK to accept Current Item.

    g.   Click the "this list" hyperlink and select Archive.

7.   Click the Save button on the ribbon, and then click the name of your workflow in the left navigation pane under the workflow section to get to the backstage page for the workflow.

8.   Deselect the "Allow this workflow to be manually started" checkbox and select the "Start workflow automatically when an item is changed" option.

9.   Click the Publish button on the ribbon; this action also saves your workflow.

10.   Use the browser and go to `http://srv1/workflowdemo`. Click Shared Documents and click Add document. Upload a document; verify that the value is No for the Archive. Click Save.

11.   Use the drop down next to the document you uploaded and select Edit Properties.

12.   Set the Archive to Yes, and click Save.

13.   Click the Archive link in the Quick Launch and verify that the document has been copied to this library. If nothing happens, refresh the browser again.

How It Works

You can now go on and modify the workflow a bit more; maybe you want to delete the items in Shared Documents directly after an item has been copied, and send an e-mail to the person who is responsible for the shared document.

Maybe creating one more workflow, a *revert* workflow, is a good idea, in case you want to send an item back to Shared Documents if you perform a delete. I hope that you have gotten some ideas for how to manage a workflow from this simple example.

I recommend you try out the advantages that Visio 2010 has when working with SharePoint Designer 2010 to create workflows. This is a great way to visualize complex logic, or just to document the workflows. See Figure 9-19.

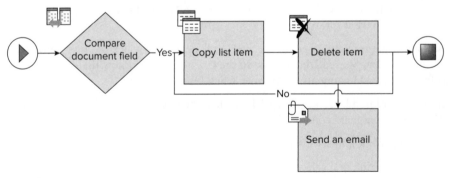

FIGURE 9-19

> **NOTE** *Learn more about SharePoint Designer 2010 at Microsoft:*
>
> `http://www.microsoft.com/sharepoint`
>
> *Ask a question or discuss SharePoint Designer 2010 and other customization issues at the SharePoint Developer Center Forum:*
>
> `http://social.msdn.microsoft.com/Forums/en-US/`
> `sharepoint2010customization/threads`
>
> *See SharePoint Designer videos by the author and MVP Asif Rehmani at SharePoint-Videos:*
>
> `http://www.sharepoint-videos.com/free-sharepoint-sharepoint-`
> `designer-and-infopath-2010-videos/`
>
> *Check out SharePoint Designers.Net, a small community for SharePoint Designer nerds:*
>
> `http://www.sharepointdesigners.net`

▶ WHAT YOU LEARNED IN THIS CHAPTER

TOPIC	KEY CONCEPTS
Common terms	WCM — Web Content Management
	WYSIWYG — What you see is what you get
	BCS — Business Connectivity Services
	XLV — The XSLT List View web part
	XPath — A query language for selecting nodes from an XML document, designed to be used by XSLT
	XML — Can transport and store data
	XSLT — A language for formatting the presentation of XML data
	RSS — An XML format for delivering regularly changing web content
	SOAP — A web service protocol
	REST — A web service protocol
Data View web part	A flexible web part and one of the most powerful SharePoint web parts. Can be used to display and aggregate data from many kinds of data sources.
XSLT List View web part	A flexible new component in SharePoint Designer 2010 that replaces the predecessor List View web part (LVWP), which was in SharePoint Designer 2007.
External list	An external list can read and update an external data source, and it acts just like any other SharePoint list. It receives advantages such as the ability to create views and new SharePoint columns, sort, filter, and group.
Master page	Defines the look, feel, and standard behavior for all the SharePoint pages.
Page layout	A page layout is a template that is used in conjunction with a master page to control the look, feel, and content of a page.
CSS	Describes the presentation of a web page and has a set of rules for fonts, colors, and more.
Workflow	Workflows in SharePoint Designer are a tool that lets you create business processes.

10
Backup and Restore

WHAT YOU WILL LEARN IN THIS CHAPTER:

➤ Planning a Backup of SharePoint

➤ Restoring SharePoint Objects

➤ Comparing Backup Tools

➤ Learning to Use PowerShell Backup and Restore Scripts

After reading this book, I am sure you will agree that SharePoint 2010 is a great product and a fantastic tool for managing information for your organization, regardless of what type of tasks or activities you may have. When a SharePoint project goes from being a test installation into a production environment it will rapidly contain important information that constantly grows every day. Sooner than you think, SharePoint will be a mission-critical application in your environment, so how can you protect it from a disaster scenario? By making backups, of course! An old geek joke goes: "What do you call a SharePoint administrator who does not do backups?" The answer: "Unemployed!"

This chapter tells you how to keep your job as a SharePoint administrator. It starts by describing what information you need to protect, and then lists all available options. You will learn how to perform backup and restore procedures and also read about other options, such as doing Microsoft SQL backups and using third-party backup tools.

PROTECTING SHAREPOINT CONTENT

Please remember this: You need to verify regularly that the backup and restore procedures work as expected; that is, that you can restore data. If you don't check regularly, you may be in a very painful situation when something needs to be recovered. The only way to ensure that the backup and restore procedures actually work is to test them live. During my 33 years in the computer business I have seen a large number of backup solutions that do not work when you actually need them! Many IT administrators seem to think that getting some sort of backup solution running (at least the first time) is enough, and then everyone can be happy. As a SharePoint consultant I am often hired by customers to help them in disaster situations, and all too often I discover that the customer's backup solution is useless. The most common reasons are:

➤ Wrongly configured backup procedures

➤ Hardware problems

➤ Backup media problems

In most cases these problems would be detected immediately when performing a test restore. So please make sure you don't join this group of surprised SharePoint administrators! By performing regular fire drills, you and your team will get the experience of how to perform a quick restore that actually works; this knowledge will help you all sleep well at night, and it will help you keep your job.

What Needs to be Protected?

Determining what needs to be protected is a good idea to start with — what data is it that you need to back up to ensure you can survive a catastrophic situation? The answer is both database content and files in the file system. If you only have a backup of the database content, you can restore all data, as long as you know exactly how the SharePoint servers were installed and configured; if you don't know this, then getting the system fully recovered may take you a long time. Having a backup of both content and binary files makes a restore much quicker.

The challenge when planning your backup strategy is that information related to SharePoint is stored in multiple locations, not just the databases, as one may believe. This section describes what you need to know to protect the SharePoint environment. There is one golden rule when it comes to SharePoint backup procedures (but not third-party products): What you back up is what you can restore!

In other words, if you make a backup of a site, you will be able to restore that site, and nothing but that site. For example, you will not be able to restore a list or a single document from the backup copy of that site. The consequence is that you will most likely develop a strategy consisting of several backup procedures that all work together to make possible the restoration of whatever data has been lost.

SharePoint Databases

All content in SharePoint sites is stored in a SQL Server database, including document and other data, configurations, and some, but not all, types of site customizations. SharePoint uses these types of databases, depending on whether it is SharePoint Server or SharePoint Foundation (see Table 10-1).

TABLE 10-1: SharePoint Database Types

DATABASE	CONTENT
Content Databases	For example, WSS_Content, which contains the typical site content, such as: All documents, news, links, contacts, and so on. All web parts and their settings. All local customizations done with SharePoint Designer.
Config Databases	For example, SharePoint_Config, which contains the global configuration settings shared among all SharePoint servers in the farm.
Service Application Databases	For example, Managed Metadata Service and User Profile Service Application. These databases contain configuration settings specific for their service applications.
Log Databases	For example, WSS_Logging, which contains logs of activities.

Many more databases are in SharePoint 2010 than were in its predecessor SharePoint 2007. A default configured SharePoint Server 2010 Enterprise edition has at least 19 different databases. The most important of all these databases are the content databases, because they contain the actual site content. If you have these databases, you can install a new farm, connect the content databases, and get all data back — at least all list content. If the new farm does not contain all features and web parts that the old farm had, you will probably not be able to restore the web pages that utilized these features and web parts. Still, you will be able to restore all list content in this recovered content database.

SharePoint Binary Files

If all databases are backed up, you will be able to restore all data and configurations, as listed in the earlier table. But in case of a total server disaster you will still lose SharePoint information, because some of it is stored in the file system on the SharePoint server. You may recall from Appendix C that different types of SharePoint servers exist with different roles:

➤ Front-end server — A SharePoint server responsible for one or more roles (see Table 10-2)

➤ Back-end server — The server running the Microsoft SQL database (SQL Express or Microsoft SQL Server)

If you are using separate front-end and back-end servers you have to back up both of them, because they both contain vital SharePoint information. The previous section described the information stored on the back-end server, in other words, all databases on the SQL server. The front-end server also contains information depending on what role it has in the SharePoint farm, as listed in Table 10-2.

TABLE 10-2: SharePoint Server Roles

SHAREPOINT ROLE	DATA IN THE LOCAL FILE SYSTEM
Web front end (WFE)	General SharePoint binary files
	Default site definitions, CSS files, and site themes
	Customized site definitions
	Customized CSS files
	Customized site themes
	Customized web part files
	Customized Solution/Feature files
Search	General SharePoint binary files
	Copy of index files (used by the search engine)
Index	General SharePoint binary files
	Index files generated by the crawler process
Service application, any type	General SharePoint binary files
	Customized application feature files

> **NOTE** *In a single server or small farm scenario all these roles run on the same SharePoint server.*

Later in this chapter you will see more about planning how to recover any of the server roles in Table 10-2.

Backup Options

As you learned from the previous sections, you should think carefully about how to design your backup plan. It may be more complicated than you expect, especially if you want to have multiple options for the restore process. Still, it is a very easy and manageable task when you know how to do it and what tools to use. SharePoint comes with several tools that you can use for backup of the most important SharePoint information:

➤ **SharePoint Central Administration tool:** Can do backup and restore of the complete SharePoint farm, service applications, web applications, databases and site collections, single sites, or export lists and libraries. Cannot be scheduled.

➤ **PowerShell:** Can do all that SharePoint Central Administration does, and can also be scheduled.

➤ **STSADM:** Can do backup and restore of complete farms, site collections, and single subsites. Can be scheduled.

You should learn to use these tools, because they focus on different backup scenarios. However, remember that they can only back up SharePoint data in the SQL database, and in the case of the full farm backup feature, also the index files, but no binary or customized files in the file system. Besides these tools that come with SharePoint, several commercial backup solutions are also available for both SharePoint Foundation and SharePoint Server; the end of this chapter offers more information about some of these.

Graphical Tools

Only one graphical backup tool is available, and that is the SharePoint Central Administration tool. It allows you to back up all, or just parts, of a SharePoint farm, and also to restore, but only from a full backup. This may sound strange, but it is, in fact, true. If you make a backup of a site collection with SharePoint Central Administration, it can only be restored by PowerShell or STSADM.

The backup procedures in SharePoint Central Administration are identical to those when using PowerShell or STSADM for backing up SharePoint content. This is the reason you can restore these backup sets with PowerShell and STSADM.

Note that no scheduling feature is available for backups in SharePoint Central Administration. Only manual backup and restore procedures are possible. If you want to schedule backups, then you have to use one of the two command shell tools that come with SharePoint 2010.

Command Shell Tools

In SharePoint 2010 you have two command shell tools: STSADM and PowerShell. The former has been around since the first release of SharePoint in 2001, and PowerShell is new for SharePoint 2010. The advantages of command shell tools follow:

➤   With just one line of text you can accomplish both simple and advanced backup and restore procedures.

➤   You can save the backup or restore procedure, which makes redoing it when needed easy.

➤   You can schedule backup and restore procedures by activating them with the Windows Scheduler tool.

➤   Save the procedure as a file and you will have documentation of how these procedures are managed.

PowerShell is the new kid on the block. STSADM will most likely go away in the near future, so make sure to focus on PowerShell; it contains about three times more SharePoint operations (known as *cmdlets* in PowerShell) than STSADM, aside from the fact that PowerShell is a great scripting language. Besides, all you learn about PowerShell can also be used on other Microsoft server applications, such as Microsoft Exchange and Microsoft SQL Server.

> **NOTE** *For a list of STSADM operations, and more general information about PowerShell, see Chapter 6.*

Moving and Copying Content

Sometimes you need to move or copy information, such as a list or a single document. For example, suppose that you have a document library in one site that you want to move to another site. Another example is when you need to copy a single document to another site collection. You can use several methods to move or copy a list or library, a list item, or a single document between two sites, but they all have drawbacks.

Copying or Moving a Single Document

A common procedure is to move or copy a single document to another location in SharePoint. The problem is that only the latest version of the document will be copied, and the Created and Modified dates and Created By and Modified By information will all be set to the time when you paste the document in the new location. The user who performed this operation will be listed for the Created By/Modified By property.

However, with SharePoint Server you can use the *Manage Content and Structure* feature, which retains the version history and values for the created and modified date information, but only within a single site collection. The four options are:

➤ Using the Windows Explorer view for a document library, you can right-click a document and select Copy (or Cut for move), then open the destination library (also in Windows Explorer view) and select Paste.

➤ Use Web Folders mapped to each library, then copy and paste between these folders like you do with standard file folders.

➤ Open the document in Microsoft Word, then save it in the destination library.

➤ Use the Manage Content and Structure feature (SharePoint Server only) if the source and destination library is within the same site collection.

Copying or Moving a Single List Item

List items, such as task items, links, or calendar events, cannot be copied like files in a document library. In this case, you need to use another technique. The following methods only move the latest version of the list item, including when you use the Manage Content and Structure feature. Here are three examples of how to copy a calendar event:

➤ Open the Contact list and select the Datasheet View. Right-click the contact row, select Copy, and then open the destination list in the Datasheet View. Right-click the first free row (marked with an asterisk [*]) and select Paste.

➤ Open the Contact list and click Open with Access. Open the destination list (also using Access), and copy and paste the item between these Access windows. Save and close Access.

➤ Use the Manage Content and Structure feature (SharePoint Server only) if the source and destination list is within the same site collection.

Copying or Moving a Complete List or Library

You can also copy or move lists and libraries; for example, a document library. In the following Try It Out, you will copy a complete library, including all of its settings and content, to another site in the same site collection.

Save the document library as a template, and make sure to select the Include Content checkbox. Open the destination site, and then create a new document library based on the template you just created.

Note that only the latest document versions will be copied, and they all will get today's date for Created/Modified; the Created By/Modified By property will be the user who performs this operation.

If the destination is in another site collection it will be a few more steps, as described in the following Try It Out. Begin as before: Save the document library as a template and make sure to select the Include Content checkbox. Then export this list template, and import it to the other site collection, as described next.

> **NOTE** *To complete the following exercise you need two site collections:* `http://srv1`, *which also has a subsite named IT, and* `http:/srv1/sites/start`. *Multiple chapters in this book, including Appendix A and C, describe how to create site collections. Chapter 7 describes how to create* `http://srv1/sites/start`.

TRY IT OUT | **Copy a Library to Another Site Collection**

In this example you have a document library in `http://srv1/it` that you want to copy to another site collection at `http://srv1/sites/start`.

1. Log on as a site collection administrator for both the source and destination site collections.
2. Open the source site: `http://srv1/it`.
3. Switch to the Library tab, and then click Library Settings.
4. Click Save Document Library as Template, and then enter these values in the resulting Save as Template page:
   a. Set Filename to **DocLib1**.
   b. Set Template name to **Doc Lib 1**.
   c. Set Template description to **Test of copying a library**.
   d. Select the Include Content checkbox.
   e. Click OK two times.
5. Open the top site in this site collection, `http://srv1`.
6. Click Site Actions ⇨ Site Settings to open the Site Settings page.

7. Click Lists templates, in the Galleries section, to open the All Templates page. Your new template will be listed here.

8. Click on its name, DocLib1, to open the File Download form and select Save. Enter a file name and note the file location, then click Save. The file type will be STP. Click Close in the dialog form that appears.

9. Open the top site in the destination site collection: http://srv1/sites/start.

10. Click Site Actions ⇨ Site Settings ⇨ List Templates.

11. Switch to the Documents tab on the ribbon, click Upload Document to open the Upload Template form, and continue as follows:

    a. Click Browse, and locate the STP file you saved in step 8.

    b. Click Open.

    c. Click OK to close the Upload Template form; now the List Template Gallery - <template_name> form appears.

    d. You can modify any template properties in this form, for example the template name or description. When ready, click Save.

    e. The List Template Gallery appears; verify that the uploaded template is now listed.

12. Open the destination site where you want to store the copy of the document library, for example http://srv1/sites/start in this site collection.

13. Click Site Action ⇨ More Options to open the Create form.

14. Select the Library category, and then click the template you uploaded in step 11. Enter a name for this library, and click Create.

15. Open the new library, and verify that it contains the same settings and content, except that no version history was retained.

How It Works

When copying or moving lists or libraries between site collections, you can save the list/library as a template, including its content. You then export the template to a file, and then import it to the destination site collection. Note that only the latest version of the document is stored in the template, and that the create and modify date is set to now, and the creator of all files will be you since you created this library.

For lists you can use the same method as you used in the preceding Try It Out, but you can also take advantage of the tight integration between SharePoint 2010 and Microsoft Access 2010, as described in Chapter 6.

Third-party tools can also help you move single documents and lists between site collections; see the end of this chapter for more information about these tools.

BACKUP PROCEDURES

In this section you will find a number of typical backup procedures, using either the SharePoint Central Administration tool, or one of the two command-line tools that comes with SharePoint 2010. Which one should you use? The answer is whichever one feels best and easiest for you; the important thing is that you do make backups. If none of these procedures feel right to you, then consider a third-party backup tool, which often is configured to run automatically.

Backing Up a Single Site

Several situations exist where it is necessary to back up a single site, such as when it contains very important content (for example, your boss's favorite site), or when you want to move a site to another farm (for example, from a test server to a production environment). The following sections show you how to back up a single site, using all backup tools that come with SharePoint 2010.

A backup of a single site is not really considered a backup. SharePoint refers to this as an export, which is also the term used in the backup tools.

> **NOTE** If the site you back up contains any subsites, they will also be included in the backup file.

Using SharePoint Central Administration

Use the steps in the following exercise to back up a single site using the SharePoint Central Administration graphical tool.

TRY IT OUT Back Up a Single Site with SharePoint Central Administration

In this example you back up the site on `http://srv1/it` to the following destination: `\\srv2\bkup\IT-Backup.bak`. You also retain the security settings for this site and all of its content, including version history.

1. Log on to the SharePoint server as a farm administrator.

2. Start the SharePoint Central Administration (Start ⇨ All Programs ⇨ Microsoft SharePoint 2010 Products ⇨ SharePoint 2010 Central Administration).

3. Select Backup and Restore in the left pane, then click Export a Site or List. On the resulting page, continue as follows:

  a. Click the field next to Site Collections, and change the site collection to `http://srv1` (because it is the top site, its URL will be "/"), and click OK.

  b. Change the site to **IT**, and click OK.

  c. Enter the filename: `\\srv2\bkup\IT-Backup.bak`.

    d. Select the Export Full Security checkbox.

    e. Set Export Versions to All Versions, which is the default setting.

    f. Click Start Export.

4. The Granular Backup Job Status page opens; it automatically refreshes the status every 30 seconds, but you can also click the Refresh link to see the current status of the backup job. On that page, in the Content Export section, you will see the status for this job (see Figure 10-1). When this status says "Succeeded" the backup job is complete.

5. Open the destination (\\srv2\bkup) and verify it contains the file IT-Backup.bak.

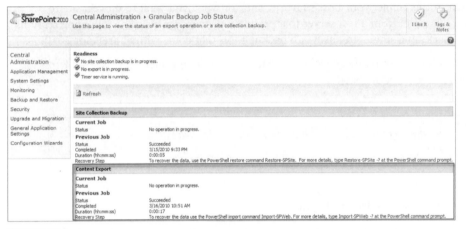

FIGURE 10-1

How It Works

A backup of a single site is regarded an export. You can choose to just export the site and its content, with or without security settings, and version history for its content. Note that any subsite to the exported site will also be backed up.

Using Command Shell Tools

Using a command shell tool to back up a single site is very easy, when you know the commands. You need to start the SharePoint 2010 Management Shell as follows: Click Start ➪ All Programs ➪ Microsoft SharePoint 2010 Products ➪ SharePoint 2010 Management Shell.

This tool gives you access to both STSADM and PowerShell 2.0. To back up a single site with STSADM in the same way you did earlier in SharePoint Central Administration, to the file IT-Backup_STSADM.bak, type this line in the command shell window, and press Enter:

```
Stsadm - o export -url http://srv1/it -includeusersecurity -versions 4 -filename
\\srv2\bkup\IT-Backup_STSADM.bak
```

The exact same command, but that exports to the IT-Backup_PS.bak file and is performed with PowerShell, looks like this:

```
Export-SPWeb http://srv1/it -includeusersecurity -includeversions All -path
\\srv2\bkup\IT-Backup_PS.bak
```

Now open the backup destination folder. Verify that it contains three files that all start with IT-Backup and end with .bak; note that they all have the same file size. This is a clear indication that all three methods for exporting a site generate the exact same result. This also means that whatever method you choose to perform the backup, you can later restore it with any of the three restore methods described later.

Backing Up a Site Collection

A site collection can contain any number of subsites, so the size of that site collection may be very large. Make sure to check its size before you back up a site collection to get prepared for the time needed to complete this process and the disk volume needed for the backup file.

If you back up a site collection you cannot restore a single site from that backup set. If you need to restore a single site from a site collection, you must first restore the site collection, export the site in question, and then import that site into the destination site collection.

Using SharePoint Central Administration

Follow these steps to back up a complete site collection, including all subsites, settings, and full version history for all content.

TRY IT OUT   Back Up a Site Collection with SharePoint Central Administration

In this example you back up the site collection http://srv1, including all subsites and all settings. You save the backup file as \\srv2\bkup\SRV1.bak.

1.   Log on to the SharePoint server as a farm administrator.

2.   Open the SharePoint Central Administration tool (Start ➪ All Programs ➪ Microsoft SharePoint 2010 Products ➪ SharePoint 2010 Central Administration).

3.   Select Backup and Restore in the left pane, and then click Perform a Site Collection Backup. On the resulting Site Collection Backup page, continue as follows:

    a.   Click on the field next to Site Collection, change the site collection to http://srv1, and then click OK.

    b.   Enter the filename: \\srv2\bkup\SRV1.bak.

    c.   Click Start Backup.

4.   The Granular Backup Job Status page opens, and in a few seconds it displays the current status for this backup job, under the Site Collection Backup heading. When the status indicates "Succeeded," the backup job is complete.

How It Works

A backup of a site collection will contain all subsites and all content, including permission settings, templates, and settings. This type of backup is also sometimes referred to as a *full-fidelity* backup.

Using Command Shell Tools

Start the SharePoint 2010 Management Shell by clicking Start ➪ All Programs ➪ Microsoft SharePoint 2010 Products ➪ SharePoint 2010 Management Shell.

To back up a site collection with STSADM in the same way you did earlier in SharePoint Central Administration, to the file SRV1_STSADM.bak, type this line in the command shell window, and press Enter:

```
Stsadm - o backup -url http://srv1 -filename \\srv2\bkup\SRV1_STSADM.bak
```

The exact same command in PowerShell, but that saves the backup file to SRV1_PS.bak, looks like this:

```
Backup-SPSite http://srv1 -path \\srv2\bkup\SRV1_PS.bak
```

Once again, open the backup destination folder, and verify that all .bak files that begin with SRV1 have the same size, because they all are identical, regardless of the backup tool used.

Backing Up a Complete Farm

The final scenario describes how to make a full backup of a complete SharePoint farm. This covers all SharePoint-related information in SQL Server, such as all site collections, including content, all configuration settings for the farm, and the service applications. A full backup also backs up the search index files. Still, some information is not backed up, such as:

➤ Binary files, or in other words, all application files for SharePoint

➤ Site definition files, created during SharePoint setup

➤ Images for icons, created during SharePoint setup

➤ All customized site definitions, images, and XML files

Do you need to back up the information in the preceding list? It depends. If you can accept reinstalling the server and reapplying customizations, then you don't need to back them up. This also assumes that you have documented all customizations and have the know-how to reinstall all third-party products, such as web parts and solutions. Most organizations would say they have complete documentation, but when the cruel reality comes, and you have to use this information, then all too often it shows that you missed some vital part. So, I recommend that you do a complete disk image backup of each SharePoint server, just to be on the safe side.

Using SharePoint Central Administration

Performing a complete farm backup is easy with SharePoint Central Administration, as described in the following Try It Out:

TRY IT OUT **Perform a Complete Farm Backup**

In this example you complete a full farm backup and save these backup files in \\srv2\bkup.

1. Log on to the SharePoint server as a farm administrator.

2. Start the SharePoint Central Administration tool (Start ➪ All Programs ➪ Microsoft SharePoint 2010 Products ➪ SharePoint 2010 Central Administration).

3. Select Backup and Restore in the left pane, then click Perform a Backup.

4. The Perform a Backup – Step 1 of 2: Select Component to Back Up page appears. It shows all the components you can back up, such as specific service applications and web applications, including content databases. In this example you want to do a complete backup, so select the Farm checkbox; note that all other check marks are automatically set. Click Next.

5. The Perform a Backup – Step 2 of 2: Select Backup Options page appears; continue as follows (see Figure 10-2):

a. Verify that the Backup Type is set to Full.

b. Verify that the Data to Back Up is set to Back Up Content and Configuration Settings. This ensures that configuration databases will also be backed up.

c. Enter the backup location: `\\srv2\bkup`.

d. Click Start Backup.

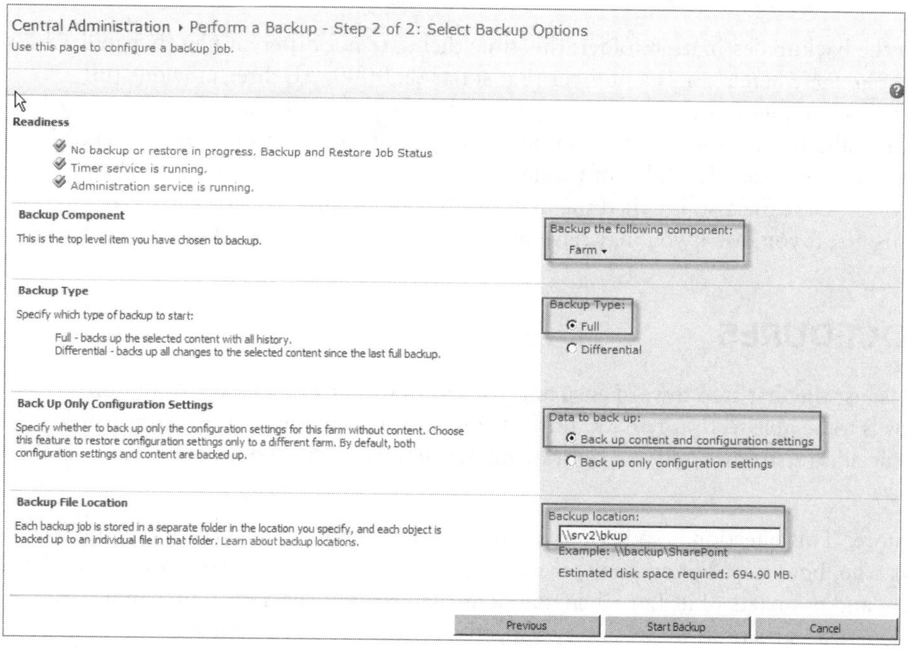

FIGURE 10-2

6. The page that appears shows the status for the backup process. The time needed to complete the backup depends on the data volume to back up, and how fast the backup file can be written to disk.

How It Works

A full backup of a SharePoint farm covers every SQL Server database related to SharePoint, as well as the search index files that are stored in the file system.

Using Command Shell Tools

Performing a full backup of a SharePoint farm using a command tool is as easy as all the previously discussed backup procedures. It is a single line that you can schedule to run regularly, for example, at 4:00 a.m. every day, by using the Task Scheduler tool that is included in Windows Server.

A full backup with STSADM is referred to as a *catastrophic backup.* It sure sounds like something very dangerous, but it is simply a backup that you can use in case there is a catastrophe. To run this type of backup you need the SharePoint 2010 Management Shell, as used in previous examples. Note that for a full backup you don't enter a filename, only the file location where the full backup will be stored — in this example \\srv2\bkup:

```
Stsadm - o backup -directory \\srv2\bkup\ backupmethod full -quiet
```

The last argument, `quiet`, ensures that this backup process does not list any progress messages, which is necessary when scheduling this command to run unattended with the Task Scheduler.

The exact same command in PowerShell looks like this:

```
Backup-SPfarm -Directory \\srv2\bkup -BackupMethod Full
```

Once again, open the backup destination folder; this time there are not different files, but folders that begin with `spbrnnnn` where *nnnn* is a number that starts on 0000. All three previous full backups store their backup files in their own `spbr` folder, and a separate file named `spbrtoc.xml` contains information about each folder — for example, the type of backup (full or incremental), date, and folder name. `toc` stands for Table of Contents, which is a good description of what it contains. This `spbrtoc.xml` file also is called the manifest file and is an XML-formatted text file. Be careful with this file; if you lose it you may have problems restoring data later!

RESTORE PROCEDURES

Making backups is just the first step toward ensuring you can restore data. The whole reason you make backups is to be able to restore data. It is, of course, very obvious, but it is sometimes forgotten, and some administrators only concentrate on making backups, and never bother to test whether they work.

What can you restore? This question is sometimes easily answered with "What you backed up!" This is not always true, but often. For example, if you back up a site collection, you can only restore that site collection, and not parts of it. But when you do a "catastrophic backup" you can use that backup set to restore just parts of it; for example, a specific content database or just global search settings.

The following sections cover more about restoring different types of content — from single items to complete farms.

Restoring Single Items and Lists

One of the best features when it comes to restoring content is the Recycle Bin in SharePoint. It was introduced in SharePoint Portal Server 2001, then disappeared in SharePoint Portal Server 2003, and then came back in 2007. In SharePoint 2010, both SharePoint Foundation and SharePoint Server, it works the same as it did in SharePoint 2007.

The absolute most common cause for a restore operation is that a user accidently deleted a document, and then wanted it back again. Now getting this document back is a breeze, because even the user can do this undelete operation of single items, thanks to the Recycle Bin feature available in all sites, both SharePoint Foundation and SharePoint Server. You do not have to activate anything to make this Recycle Bin work; it is enabled by default, and works like this:

➤ When a list item, such as a contact, or a library item, such as a document, is deleted it is copied to the site's Recycle Bin.

➤ If a complete list or library is deleted, it is copied to the Recycle Bin.

➤ A user can open the site's Recycle Bin and restore any of its deleted objects; users will only see the objects they deleted, not other users' deleted objects.

➤ The deleted object will stay in the Recycle Bin for 30 days by default.

➤ After 30 days, the object is moved from the site's Recycle Bin to a site collection Recycle Bin.

➤ Only the site administrator can restore objects from the site collection Recycle Bin.

> **NOTE** *Note that the Recycle Bin cannot restore deleted sites or site collections.*

You can configure how long SharePoint will store deleted items in the Recycle Bin; this setting is per web applications; that is, if multiple site collections use the same web application, they will all have the same Recycle Bin settings.

TRY IT OUT **Configure the Site Recycle Bin**

In this example, you extend the time information is stored in the site Recycle Bin from 30 days to 45, thereby giving users 15 days extra to recover any deleted item, such as a document or contact.

1. Log on to the SharePoint server as a farm administrator.

2. Start the SharePoint Central Administration tool (Start ➪ All Programs ➪ Microsoft SharePoint 2010 Products ➪ SharePoint 2010 Central Administration).

3. Select Application Management in the left pane, and then click Manage Web Applications.

4. On the Web Applications Management page, you will see all available web applications (see Appendixes A and B for more about web applications). Select the web application used for the intranet, typically SharePoint - 80, and then click General Settings on the Ribbon.

5. The Web Application General Settings form that appears contains many settings; scroll down to the end of this long form to the Recycle Bin section. Change the Delete Items in the Recycle Bin After field from 30 days to 45; see Figure 10-3.

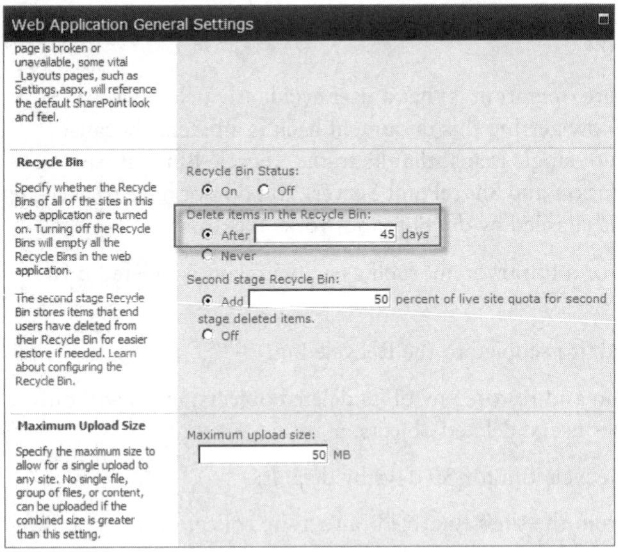

FIGURE 10-3

6. Verify that the Recycle Bin Status is on. If it's not, users cannot restore deleted items. Also note that the Second Stage Recycle Bin field is set to 50 percent of live site quota, which means that if a site collection has a space quota of 10 gigabytes, then the second stage Recycle Bin will be 5 gigabytes.

7. Click OK.

How It Works

Each web application has a setting for the Recycle Bin, both the one that the users can use (it stores deleted items for a default of 30 days), and the second stage Recycle Bin that only site collection administrators can use (it stores deleted items for a default of up to 50 percent of the site collection quota).

Restoring a Single Site

If you need to restore a single site, you will need a backup of that site. You cannot extract a single site from a site collection backup or a complete farm backup. Restoring a single site is referred to as *importing a site*. This job can only be performed by a command shell tool.

Restoring a Site with STSADM

For example, to import the site that you previously exported to the IT-Backup.bak file (you may remember that this particular file was exported using the SharePoint Central Administration — still, it can only be imported by STSADM or PowerShell), you open the SharePoint command shell and type:

```
Stsadm -o import -url http://start/it -filename \\srv2\bkup\IT-Backup.bak
-includeusersecurity
```

In this example the site will be imported to a new site collection with the URL `http://start/it`. Now, open this site and verify that it contains a copy of the IT site you backed up before.

> **NOTE** It is possible to restore the site collection to a separate recovery server. This is true even if that server belongs to a different Active Directory domain than the original SharePoint server. In that case, all user permissions in this site collection will be reset and the farm administrator will be the only account that can access the restored site collection.

Restoring a Site with PowerShell

The same procedure (which you did in the preceding section), but with PowerShell, looks a little different. The reason is that PowerShell requires that the site URL must exist before a site can be imported to that URL. If you want to overwrite an existing site with the backup content, then you enter:

```
Import-SPWeb http://srv1/it -path \\srv2\bkup\IT-Backup.bak -includeusersecurity
```

But if you want to restore the site to a new URL location, instead of overwriting, you must first create an empty site, and then import to that site. For example, suppose you want to import the `IT-Backup.bak` site as a subsite to the site collection `http://start`; then you enter:

```
New-SPWeb -url http://start/it | Import-SPWeb -path \\srv2\bkup\IT-Backup.bat
-IncludeUserSecurity
```

The first part, `New-SPWeb`, creates the empty subsite in `http://start/it`; the second part, `Import-SPWeb`, imports the backup file to that URL location and overwrites whatever was there.

Whatever method you use to import that backup file, it will immediately be available in SharePoint.

Restoring a Site Collection

The procedures for restoring a site collection greatly resemble the procedures for restoring single sites. The same limitation also exists: Only command shell tools can restore a site collection, not the SharePoint Central Administration tool, even though it can create site collection backups. The following sections show you how to use these command shell tools.

Restoring a Site Collection with STSADM

In a previous Try It Out, you backed up the `http://srv1` to the file `SRV1.bak`. If you need to restore that site collection to its original URL location, then enter this text in the command shell:

```
Stsadm -o restore -url http://srv1 -filename \\srv2\bkup\SRV1.bak -overwrite
```

> **WARNING** If you restore a site collection to its original location, you will overwrite all sites in that site collection. Make sure this is what you want to do.

The `-overwrite` parameter is needed to overwrite the existing site collection.

If you instead want to restore a single site, and all you have is a site collection backup, you can restore the site collection to a temporary URL, export the site as described earlier, and then import that site to the destination.

When restoring a site collection to another location, you can either use a separate SharePoint server, or restore the site collection to the production server, but to a different URL than the original.

For example, if you want to restore the backup of the site collection in `http://srv1` to the temporary URL `http://srv1/sites/temp`, you must first create a new content database because one site collection already exists with the URL `http://srv1` in the current database.

You must first create a placeholder for the new URL in this web application. You therefore have to run two STSADM operations, as described next.

1.   Create a placeholder for the new URL in a new content database named Temp_content — open the SharePoint command shell and type:

```
Stsadm -o createsiteinnewdb -url http://srv1/sites/temp -owneremail
administrator@filobit.com -ownerlogin filobit\administrator -databasename
Temp_Content
```

2.   Restore the `SRV1.bak` file to that new URL; you need to add the flag `-overwrite` to ensure that the restore process can overwrite the placeholder you created earlier.

```
Stsadm -o restore -url http://srv1 -filename \\srv2\bkup\SRV1.bak -overwrite
```

It may take a few minutes before SharePoint activates the restored site in the new Temp_content database; you can speed this up by resetting the IIS with this command:

```
IISReset
```

This IISReset command usually takes just a few seconds to complete; then open this site and verify that it contains a copy of the `http://srv1` site collection you backed up before. You can now use one of the procedures described in the "Moving and Copying Content" section earlier in this chapter to copy and move lists and libraries, or list items, if necessary.

> **NOTE**   *When running the* `IISRESET`, *all connections to the SharePoint server and other web applications on this server will shortly be disabled. If possible, prepare your users for a short break.*

Restoring a Site Collection with PowerShell

This section describes restoring a site collection, but with PowerShell. If you want to overwrite the existing site collection on `http://srv1` with the `SRV1.bak` file, then you enter:

```
Restore-SPSite http://srv1 -path \\srv2\bkup\SRV1.bak -Confirm:$False -Force
```

The `-Confirm:$False` parameter is needed to prohibit PowerShell from asking you for permission to complete the command; the `-Force` parameter is needed to overwrite the existing site collection.

> **WARNING** As described earlier, if you restore a site collection to its original location, you will overwrite all sites in that site collection. Make sure this is what you want to do.

When restoring a site collection to another location, you can either restore to a separate SharePoint server, or restore the site collection to the production server, but to a different URL than the original.

For example, if you want to restore the backup of the site collection in `http://srv1` to the temporary URL `http://srv1/sites/temp` you must first create a new content database because one site collection already exists with the URL `http://srv1` in the current database; then you can do a restore to that temporary URL, as follows:

1. Create a placeholder for the new URL in a new content database named Temp2_content. To do this, open the SharePoint command shell and type:

    ```
    New-SPContentDatabase -name Temp2_Content -WebApplication http://srv1
    ```

2. Restore the `SRV1.bak` file to that new content database, and give it the new URL:

    ```
    Restore-SPSite http://srv1 -path \\srv2\bkup\SRV1.bak -ContentDatabase
    Temp2_Content -Confirm:$False -Force
    ```

Unattached Content Database Data Recovery

A new feature in SharePoint 2010 makes restoring content from an unattached SharePoint content database possible. For example, you can recover a site collection, a site, or a list from that database. The term *unattached* means that the database is stored inside SQL Server, but not used by SharePoint or any other application. One way to get an unattached content database is to restore a database that was backed up previously by a backup solution such as the SQL Server Management tool.

For example, suppose you run a daily backup that also is used to back up SQL Server databases. Now one manager comes to you and says he deleted a site collection by mistake, and now you must restore it immediately (of course!). Because you don't have any specific SharePoint backups you cannot use any of the other methods described in this chapter. Luckily, you can use the new feature in SharePoint 2010 to recover data directly from an unattached database.

In the following Try It Out you learn how to recover data by using the SharePoint Central Administration tool. You can also use PowerShell to do this, but this time using a graphical user interface is nice, because you can browse between site collections, sites, and lists without having to know their names.

TRY IT OUT   Recover Data Using an Unattached Content Database

In this example, you make backups of SQL Server databases every night. Now you need to use yesterday's database backup to restore a single site named Finance that was stored in the site collection `http://srv1`. Your SQL Server administrator helps you restore that database from yesterday to the SQL Server that SharePoint uses, using a temporary name, Finance-Temp, in order not to overwrite the current version of the Finance database.

1. Log on to the SharePoint server as a farm administrator and start SharePoint Central Administration.

2. Select Backup and Restore in the left pane.

3. Click Recover Data from an Unattached Content Database. The Unattached Content Database Data Recovery form appears. Continue as follows:

    a. Verify that the SQL server name is correct; if it's not, change it.

    b. In the Database Name field, enter **Finance-Temp.**

    c. Verify that the option Choose Operation is set to Browse Content, and click Next.

4. The Browse Content page appears; continue as follows:

    a. Verify the correct site collection is listed; if it's not, click on the URL and change the site collection to the one that contains the Finance site.

    b. Click on No Selection, change the site, select Finance, and then click OK.

5. The Browse Content page appears again; select the Export Site or List option, and click Next. The Site Or List Export page opens. Continue as follows:

    a. Enter a location and filename where this backup of the Finance site will be exported; for example, `Finance-Backup.bak`.

    b. If you already have that file, you can choose to overwrite it by selecting the Overwrite Existing Files checkbox.

    c. If you also want to export the security permissions for this site, select the Export Full Security checkbox.

    d. The final option on this page is about version history for content; click on the Export Versions menu to select different levels of export; for this example, select All Versions.

    e. Click Start Export.

    f. The Granular Backup Job Status page opens. It shows the current status for this backup job. When the status is equal to "Succeeded," then you can switch to the destination file folder and verify that the file is actually there.

6. The final step is to restore, or really, import the Finance site, as described in the section "Restoring a Single Site" earlier in this chapter.

How It Works

SharePoint 2010 can temporarily mount a content database for restoring site collections, sites, and lists.

Restoring a Complete Farm

The ultimate restore process is to recover a complete SharePoint farm. It may sound tough, but doing it is as easy as doing any other type of restore. You can perform a complete farm restore with all three standard tools — SharePoint Central Administration, STSADM, and PowerShell. You see how to use all three methods in the following sections.

Using SharePoint Central Administration

Restoring a complete SharePoint farm is extremely easy, as long as your backup works as expected. Follow these Try It Out instructions to see how you do it.

> **NOTE** Before you can restore the SharePoint installation, you may need to reinstall your complete SharePoint server, depending on how big the damage is. Make sure to always document everything about your SharePoint and SQL Server so you can recover them in case something really bad happens. This documentation must describe Windows Server configuration, service pack levels, hot fixes, SharePoint configuration, added solutions, and web parts. Make sure to keep this documentation updated, and keep a copy of all binary files you will need in the event you need to recover a complete server.

TRY IT OUT   Restore a Complete SharePoint Farm

In this example you have a large problem: Your SharePoint server had a serious disk crash, so your only lifeline now is the backup, which you will use to complete this restore process. You have managed to reinstall the Windows 2008 Server, including SharePoint 2010. Now you need to restore all SharePoint content.

1. Log on to the SharePoint server and open SharePoint Central Administration (Start ➪ All Programs ➪ Microsoft SharePoint 2010 Products ➪ SharePoint 2010 Central Administration).

2. Select Backup and Restore in the left pane, and then click Restore from a Backup.

3. On the Restore from Backup - Step 1 of 3: Select Backup to Restore page, select the latest date for the backup you want to restore, and then click Next.

4. On the Restore from Backup - Step 2 of 3: Select Component page, you can select what to restore. In this example you want to restore everything from the latest backup, so select the Farm checkbox, and click Next.

5. On the last page, Restore from Backup - Step 3 of 3: Select Restore Options, you can select the backup options; for example, you can choose only configuration or data and configuration, change the user account names used as service accounts for service applications, change the database server name, and a lot more. In this example you want to do a complete backup to the same server as before, so follow these steps:

    a. Make sure to set the Type of Restore option in the Restore Option section to Same Configuration.

    b. Click OK to confirm you want to overwrite all selected components.

    c. Click Start Restore at the end of this page.

    d. The Backup and Restore Job Status page opens; click Refresh to see the latest status for this restore, or wait for the automatic refresh.

6. When the restore completes, open the start page of the intranet, and make sure everything has been restored to yesterday's status.

How It Works

SharePoint Central Administration is easy to work with when you are restoring a complete farm. It shows you all options and provides some guidance as to what to do.

Using Command Shell Tools

As expected, the two standard command shell tools can also do a complete restore. If you want to restore the complete farm, with the same configuration and SQL server, then either STSADM or PowerShell is very easy to use. However, if you want to restore to a new SQL Server, or change any of the service applications, then you may prefer the graphical SharePoint Central Administration tool, because using it is more intuitive.

If you prefer to restore the farm using STSADM, then open the command shell, and type:

```
Stsadm -o restore -directory \\srv2\bkup -Restoremethod overwrite
```

The `Restoremethod` parameter means that the backup will overwrite the existing configuration. Note that a restore of a farm may take many hours, or even days, depending on the data volume. A restore process is about three to five times slower than the corresponding backup, because a restore is much more CPU intensive; for example, when restoring data the process must add both content and then also update indexes and configuration files.

If you instead prefer to use PowerShell to do the same restore process, you enter this:

```
Restore-SPFarm -Directory \\srv2\bkup -RestoreMethod Overwrite
```

As with STSADM, you must also force PowerShell to overwrite the current configuration and content by entering the `RestoreMethod Overwrite` parameter.

Restoring a Specific Server Role

As described in Chapter 6, you can configure servers in a SharePoint farm to run different roles; for example, the web front end, search, index, and all service applications. Now assume you have four servers in your farm, running different roles. How should you plan for the possibility that one of these servers breaks down? This is the focus of the following sections.

The Web Front-End Role (WFE)

A SharePoint server running the web front-end role does not contain any local content that you need to back up, unless you have done customization of site definitions, images, XML, CSS, and template files, or if you have installed a language pack. Assume that this web front-end server crashes beyond repair — what would be the problem?

The answer depends on the customizations performed, and whether you can redo them or not:

➤ There are no customizations on the WFE server — just reinstall SharePoint, including service pack levels, and join the existing organization.

➤ Some customization has been performed, but everything is documented and you have access to the customized files — reinstall SharePoint, join the existing domain, and reapply the customizations.

➤ Some customization has been performed, but you don't have all the information about how it was done — you are in trouble, unless you have a full backup of the WFE server's SharePoint files.

The lesson is: If you have, or plan to have, any kind of customization, make sure to back up the WFE server and its SharePoint files.

The Search Server Role

If the Search server crashes, there is no real worry; just reinstall the SharePoint binaries, and the index files will be copied from the index server again.

The Index Server Role

For the index server, begin with reinstalling the SharePoint binary files on this server, and then initiate a full crawl of all content sources. This may take days, or in extreme cases, weeks to complete, depending on the data volume to be indexed. During this time users cannot trust that the search results they get are complete, because all data may not yet have been crawled.

If the index is configured to crawl any non-default type, for example, PDF files, these index filters (IFilters) must be reinstalled on the index server after the SharePoint binary files are installed.

Any Service Application Server Role

If the server running Excel Services or Central Administration crashes, just reinstall the SharePoint binaries; no specific data is stored on this server.

Recovering a SQL Server

You know from previous chapters and especially Appendixes A–D that all content is stored in a SQL Server. If this server crashes, then SharePoint stops — all of it, including SharePoint Central Administration. So getting the SQL Server up and running, including all of its content, is important.

A common practice in organizations is to run a specific backup procedure to protect all databases in the SQL Server, because this server may contain databases to more solutions than SharePoint. If you have such a backup, then all you need to do is reinstall the SQL Server binaries, including service packs, hotfixes, and any third-party add-ons, then restore all SQL Server databases from the latest backup set.

> **NOTE** *Remember that if the database you restore is, say, 12 hours old, then you will lose 12 hours of work when you restore that backup. SQL Server supports several smart backup procedures, including snapshot backups, which make doing a backup much more often than once per day possible, and thus make the data loss much less!*

But what do you do if the SQL Server doesn't run its own backup procedures? Then you must ensure that you have a complete farm backup, as described earlier in this chapter. With this complete backup you can at least restore all databases related to SharePoint. Once again, if you make backups once per day, you will lose all work after that time when you restore the backup set. You may need to design a more frequent backup procedure to reduce the data loss when doing a restore.

Making a Backup Plan

A backup plan is very important and something you should make before using SharePoint in a production environment. Exactly how this plan should look depends on many parameters, like:

➤ What SharePoint edition are you using — SharePoint Foundation or SharePoint Server?

➤ How important is the data stored in SharePoint?

➤ What sites will be most important to protect?

➤ How often are the sites updated?

➤ How much data is acceptable to lose?

The last bullet governs how frequently the backup needs to run; such as every hour or once every day. For example, if you back up at 5 a.m. every day and the server crashes at 2 p.m., you will lose everything that has been modified since 5 a.m. (nine hours) when you do the restore.

The descriptions you get here are just general guidelines that you can follow to make your own backup plan. And remember the initial statement in this chapter: If you don't regularly verify that the backups are working, you cannot be sure that your backup plan is working. Running fire drills now and then to see that you actually can restore data is important. I suggest that you do a test every month and verify that you and your fellow SharePoint administrators can do a restore of:

➤ A single document

➤ A single site

➤ A site collection

➤ The complete farm

A perfect environment for running fire drills is virtual computers, such as Windows 2008 Hyper-V virtual environments. They will allow you to test any restore procedures and redo them when necessary, without laborious reinstallation of the SharePoint environment. To perform these fire drills, you will need a backup plan. Use the following guidelines to write your own backup plan:

1. Document your SharePoint environment, such as:

   a. The name of the SharePoint server(s)

   b. The name of the Microsoft SQL Server

   c. The URL and Alternate Address Mappings for the SharePoint environment

   d. The IIS settings: all virtual server and application pool settings

   e. The search and index settings (if SharePoint Server)

   f. The Audience groups (if SharePoint Server)

   g. Any customization of the User Profile settings (if SharePoint Server)

   h. The security settings for the portal site areas (if SharePoint Server)

   i. All customization of portal sites (if SharePoint Server)

   j. A list of all web applications, site collections, and their owners

   k. Any non-default configuration settings of SharePoint

   l. A list of all added web parts, including where you found them

   m. A description of all modified SharePoint files, such as ASPX, CSS, and XML files

2. Decide if and when to run any of the three available export operations to protect important sites (like your boss's site) to make it very easy and fast to restore single sites and single items.

3. Decide if and when to back up site collections to make restoring site collections, sites, and single items easy.

4. Decide how often to run a complete farm backup, using any of the three tools (remember that only STSADM and PowerShell can be scheduled to run automatically).

5. Decide where to store the backup files, if you should overwrite them every time, or what to do with them.

6. Decide how often to run a file backup on the SharePoint server, including a System State backup that also covers the IIS metabase. This makes recovering from a complete disk crash possible.

7. Document the restore procedures, and who is responsible, including all contact information.

8. Document the fire drills: what to test, how often, and by whom.

I am sure you can think of more things to list in this backup plan. Just remember that this is a "living" document; it needs to be constantly updated — for example, when you add new web parts, change any configuration settings, or create new site collections. The perfect place to store this backup plan is, of course, in SharePoint, but this is not a good idea because you will need it in case of a SharePoint disaster. Make sure to have not one but at least two copies of this backup plan in different locations in case of fire, flooding, and similar disasters.

COMMERCIAL BACKUP TOOLS

Alternatives are available for the backup tools that come with SharePoint — both specific SharePoint backup utilities and SharePoint agents for general backup applications. They often make doing backups easier and in some cases make restoring things that SharePoint cannot do possible, such as restoring a specific version of a document.

The purpose of this section is to give you a general overview of these third-party tools to make you aware that they exist and how they can be an alternative to the SharePoint tools. This is not a complete list of everything that is available, so please do not get upset if I don't mention your favorite tool. As of this writing, only two backup tools are available for SharePoint 2010: Microsoft Data Protection Manager (DPM) 2010, and DocAve from AvePoint, but other backup vendors' tools will be released sometime during 2010. If you prefer another product, contact your vendor to see when it will support backup and restore of SharePoint 2010.

AvePoint Tools

One of the first vendors in 2001 that developed backup solutions specifically for SharePoint was AvePoint (www.avepoint.com) with its DocAve suite of products. It was also first with a backup solution for SharePoint 2010 and with migration tools for moving content from SharePoint 2007 and 2003 servers to SharePoint 2010. Its main product, DocAve, is today one of the most popular tools due to its very advanced restore options, while still being easy to manage. DocAve is a great product if you want to have all options available for a restore; this is what you are looking for. It also supports restoring data to another SharePoint server:

➤ Restore a single document, including all of its previous versions and properties

➤ Restore a specific version of a document instead of all versions

➤ Restore a single list item

➤ Restore a single list or library

➤ Restore a single site

➤ Restore a single My Site, or a part of it

➤ Restore a complete farm

Of course, DocAve also supports scheduled backup procedures, including multiple backup procedures running independently of each other. For example, you may want to do a full farm backup once every six hours and another backup for a specific site collection that runs once every hour.

Microsoft Data Protection Manager 2010

Microsoft has its own backup solution, called Data Protection Manager, or DPM (www.microsoft .com/dpm). It is a part of the bigger suite called System Center Data Protection Manager. This product can back up most, if not all, of the Microsoft server products, such as Windows Server,

SQL Server, Exchange Server, and SharePoint Server. This product is very interesting, because it can be used to back up all the Microsoft servers in a network. DPM 2010 offers the following restore features:

➤ Restore single documents

➤ Restore single lists and libraries

➤ Restore single sites

➤ Restore singe site collections

➤ Restore complete SharePoint environments

All these restore operations may be performed against the original SharePoint server or to another SharePoint server. DPM can also be used as a migration tool or when you need to create a test environment of your production server.

▶ **WHAT YOU LEARNED IN THIS CHAPTER**

TOPIC	KEY CONCEPTS
What data you should protect	All SQL databases related to SharePoint. All customized files, including XML and CSS. All custom-built site definitions.
SharePoint database types	Content databases: contain all user content. Config database: contains global configuration settings. Service Application Databases: specific databases for a given service application. Log databases: contain logs of activities.
Protecting specific server roles	Web front end: back up locally modified SharePoint files, site definitions, and images. Search role: none — the index server will copy ("propagate") a new index to the search server. Index role: reinstall all extra IFilters, then force a full indexing of all content sources. Specific Service Application roles: none.
Protecting SQL Server	If only SharePoint content is stored, then you can use a SharePoint backup for a complete farm backup. If there is more than SharePoint content in this SQL Server you will probably run a separate SQL Server backup procedure.
Standard SharePoint backup tools	SharePoint Central Administration. STSADM (command shell tool). PowerShell (command shell tool).
Copy and move list items	Use the Datasheet View and copy/paste. Export to Access, copy between Access databases, and then save. (SharePoint Server only): If source and content is within the same site collection, then use the Manage Content and Structure feature.
Copy and move library items	Use the Explorer view to copy and paste the files. (SharePoint Server only): If source and content is within the same site collection, then use the Manage Content and Structure feature.
Copy a list or library	Save the list or library as a template, including content, then create a new list/library in the destination based on this template.

TOPIC	KEY CONCEPTS
Back up single sites	Can be performed by SharePoint Central Administration tool, STSADM, and PowerShell.
	Use the Export site feature.
Back up a site collection	Can be performed by SharePoint Central Administration tool, STSADM, and PowerShell.
Back up a complete farm	Can be performed by SharePoint Central Administration tool, STSADM, and PowerShell.
Restore single items or complete lists	Use the built-in Recycle Bin feature.
	Stores deleted items for 30 days, then the administrator will have access to a second-stage Recycle Bin for each site collection (in the top site).
Restore a single site	Can be performed by STSADM and PowerShell.
Restore a site collection	Can be performed by STSADM and PowerShell.
Restore a complete farm	Can be performed by SharePoint Central Administration tool, STSADM, and PowerShell.
Restore data from an unattached content database	Mount the database in SQL Server, then use SharePoint Central Administration to restore a single list item, list, site, or site collection.
Content in a backup plan	Document all configuration settings.
	Document all service packs for SharePoint, Windows Server and SQL Server.
	Document all customizations.
	Document where backup files are stored.
	Document where all binary files are stored, including customizations and third-party add-ons.
	Document the SharePoint structure, such as server roles, site collections, security groups, and name standards.
	Document very important sites.
Third-party backup solutions	Are often easier and more convenient to do backup and restore procedures with.
	Microsoft DPM 2010 (www.microsoft.com/dpm).
Examples of third-party backup solutions	DocAve (www.avepoint.com).
	More products will be available.

A

Installing SharePoint Foundation 2010

In this appendix, you learn how to prepare and install *SharePoint Foundation 2010*, both with the Microsoft SQL Server Express that comes embedded with SharePoint Foundation, and using a full Microsoft SQL Server — in other words, both types of available database configurations. You also learn how to prepare for the installation and understand how SharePoint Foundation uses service accounts. After the installation is done, you learn how to check that everything is okay. You also learn basic troubleshooting techniques when the installation fails.

> **NOTE** SharePoint Foundation may be installed in either an Active Directory domain or a workgroup environment (for example, a stand-alone server). The instructions in this chapter describe how to use an Active Directory domain.

This appendix is organized by initial sections describing what you are about to do and why, then a step-by-step description on how to do it, and finally some more information on the steps involved, including any tips and tricks based on real-world scenarios. Appendix B offers more details about advanced configurations.

WHAT IS NEW IN THE ARCHITECTURE

SharePoint Foundation and its predecessor, WSS 3.0, share a lot of their architectural structure, but SharePoint Foundation also has several new features, which are important for the SharePoint administrator to understand. Many of these changes were only found in the previous Microsoft Office SharePoint Server (MOSS) 2007 version, and are much welcomed by most administrators. Here are some of the most important changes regarding the architecture:

➤ SharePoint Foundation now only runs on 64-bit Windows Server operating systems; that is, Windows Server 2008 and Windows Server 2008 R2. For software developer purposes, installing SharePoint Foundation on 64-bit Windows 7 is also supported, although this configuration is not supported for production environments.

➤ The new embedded Microsoft SQL Server 2008 Express is 64-bit only — and as in previous SharePoint versions you can configure SharePoint Foundation to use a separate Microsoft SQL Server 2005 or Microsoft SQL Server 2008 as long as they are 64-bit versions.

➤ SharePoint Foundation has a new user interface: the Fluent User interface, which is built on the same design as the "ribbon" introduced in Microsoft Office 2007, and is used for team sites, blogs, and workspaces, as well as for the SharePoint Central Administration tool.

➤ SharePoint Foundation now uses page files for its websites, such as the Team Site. These page files are stored in a local page library called "SitePages," very similar to how publishing pages were used in Microsoft SharePoint Office Server 2007 (MOSS 2007). Each page file may have its own permission setting, if you want to control who can see and use its content.

➤ The Team Site template in SharePoint Foundation is now based on Wiki page files, by default configured to use version history that allows you to revert to a previous page version.

➤ There are new types of site lists: Wiki Page Library (for web pages), Picture Library (for pictures), Forms Library (for XML-based forms), and External List (that connects to an external data source). There are also enhanced lists, such as Project Tasks and the Calendar.

➤ There are two new web parts: the Silverlight Web Part and the Relevant Documents.

➤ SharePoint 2010 introduces a new concept called *managed accounts*. These are service accounts used by services and features in the SharePoint environment. By using managed accounts, the SharePoint administrator no longer has to change the passwords of these service accounts by hand; SharePoint manages these accounts automatically.

> **NOTE** *The first version of SharePoint Services, released in 2001, was named SharePoint Team Services (STS). The STS acronym is still used even in today's version of SharePoint Foundation 2010. Whenever you see something that begins with "STS," such as* STSADM, *think "SharePoint Foundation."*

PREPARING FOR SHAREPOINT FOUNDATION

Before you install SharePoint Foundation, you must prepare several things; for example, you must prepare the Windows server and make sure it meets the requirements, then plan for the SQL Server, decide what type of installation to do, and then select the edition of SharePoint that meets your needs.

Hardware Requirements

SharePoint is an application that works best when it gets a lot of memory and CPU resources. SharePoint Foundation requires about twice as much memory as its predecessor, WSS 3.0; the reason is, of course, that the new SharePoint Foundation version has a large number of new features, as well as enhancements to existing features. A server with 4GB of memory can support up to several hundred SharePoint Foundation users, as long as you have the disk capacity to store all data needed; see the next section for more details.

You must understand several things when planning your SharePoint Foundation server:

➤ SharePoint is a web application! There is no permanent connection between the client browser and the SharePoint server. Every time a user opens a link or a document, the browser connects, downloads what is requested, and then closes the connection immediately after that, regardless of how long the user looks at that information.

➤ The number of users in the organization is not the same as the number of simultaneous users.

➤ Different activities in SharePoint require different resources; for example, displaying a project site normally generates a very light load on the server, whereas indexing the database generates a much higher load.

Calculating the Number of NOPS Required

A general, well-proven formula exists that you can use for calculating the load, or the *normalized operations per second* (NOPS), on the SharePoint server. From it you can estimate the number of supported users, given a certain hardware configuration. The formula requires you to find out or estimate a number of values:

$$\frac{A \times B \times C \times D}{360,000 \times E} = \text{Operations/second (NOPS)}$$

given the following estimated data that you must supply:

➤ A = The number of users

➤ B = The percentage of active users on a typical day

➤ C = The number of operations per active user per day

➤ D = The peak factor

➤ E = The number of working hours per day

Two of these estimated parameters need to be explained in more detail. The peak factor is a value between 1 and 10, which is used to indicate the peak hours during the work hours. For example, if the organization works from 9 a.m. to 5 p.m., it is a safe bet that most workers start their day by opening their SharePoint environment, because there is where all the information can be found; after that you will probably have an even load. Then directly after lunch, usage would peak again. A peak factor of 1 means "no peak load at all." A peak factor of 10 means "a peak load all day."

A typical organization would get a peak factor value of 5. If you want to be on the safe side, use a higher value than 7.

The other estimated parameter is the number of operations per active user per day, which has to do with how much your SharePoint environment will be utilized per day. This is also a value between 1 and 10, where 1 means your users access SharePoint for almost no time at all and 10 means your users work all day with SharePoint. A typical organization would get something close to 10 for this value.

Example 1: An Organization with 200 Very Active Users

Your organization has 200 employees (A). The percentage of active users in a typical day is 80 (B). The number of operations per active user is 10 (C). The number of working hours for the organization as a whole is 12 hours (E). You estimate the peak factor (D) to be 10, to be on the safe side. The formula for this organization will look like this:

$$\frac{200 \times 80 \times 10 \times 10}{360000 \times 12} = 0.37 \text{ NOPS}$$

Example 2: An Organization with 4,500 Normal Users

Your organization has 4,500 employees (A). The percentage of active users in a typical day is 50 (B). The number of operations per active user is 10 (C). The number of working hours for the organization as a whole is 12 hours (E). You estimate the peak factor (D) to be 5. The formula for this organization will look like this:

$$\frac{4500 \times 50 \times 10 \times 5}{360000 \times 12} = 2.60 \text{ NOPS}$$

Putting It into Practice

Now you have a good idea of the load your system will generate. The next step is to use this information to calculate the hardware you need. Several hardware vendors have excellent tools for analyzing how many users a given server may support; typically a single-server installation of SharePoint Foundation with a local SQL Server Express database, configured with 4GB memory, and 64-bit CPU will support more than 2 NOPS. Installing SharePoint Foundation and the full SQL Server 2005/2008 on separate servers with 4GB each will almost double the number of NOPS.

> **NOTE** *The hardware vendor HP has a nice SharePoint Size Tool that you can download for free. Go to* www.hp.com, *then search for "Activeanswers sizers"; in the result list, look for SharePoint to find the tool.*

From this information you can glean three important points:

➤ Make sure to have at least 4GB of memory on a SharePoint Foundation server.

➤ Multiple CPUs greatly enhance the number of supported users.

➤ For maximum performance, use a separate SQL Server; that is, build a small farm.

An important fact to remember here is that when a server has at least 4GB of memory, it will support several hundreds of light or medium users. Increasing that number to 8GB of memory and having two CPUs for the SharePoint Foundation server enables the support of several thousand users.

Microsoft's Recommended Hardware Requirements

Naturally, Microsoft has list of all the requirements for SharePoint Foundation. These numbers are a bit high, but "better safe than sorry." In other words, you can do it with less hardware, but why take the chance? You are about to build one of the most central information systems in your organization, so be sure it can handle the workload. These are the official *minimum* requirements from Microsoft:

➤ Processor: 64-bit, dual CPU, 3 GHz.

➤ Memory: 4GB for a stand-alone server (or a test server); or 8GB/server for any other installation scenario, such as a multiple server farm installation.

➤ 80GB free disk space: This only covers the SharePoint binary files plus a small local SQL Server installation.

➤ 100 Mbps network interface card (NIC).

Note that you may have to adjust these numbers for some organizations — especially the disk size, which does not take into account that a local SQL Server database will contain a lot of data. In fact, if you plan to store more than 25GB of data, you should go for the full SQL Server 2005 or 2008 and install it on a separate server. Microsoft's "Best Practice" recommendations for a SQL Server in a SharePoint environment are as follow:

➤ Disk subsystems: RAID-10 for all types of databases.

➤ Make sure the driver for the disk I/O subsystem and network cards (NICs) are all optimized for high performance; having something slow here affects the total performance of the SharePoint Foundation environment. Use Gigabyte NICs if possible, regardless of network load.

➤ Configure the disks that SQL Server uses so the NTFS "Allocation Unit Size" is set to be 64K (the default is 4K). This can result in a 30 percent performance increase.

➤ Place the Tempdb, content databases, and transaction log files on separate RAID-10 disks.

➤ Use multiple data files for each large content database and search databases, but keep the number of data files less than, or equal to, the number of CPU cores. Make sure to *not* use multiple data files for other database types!

➤ Try to keep the content databases less than 200GB. It will work even if you break this rule, but the time needed for database maintenance and repair tasks will increase, maybe by several days.

➤ A database with 50GB or more is considered a large database. If your site collection will store more than 50GB you should consider breaking up the site collection into two, with each having a separate content database.

➤ Recommended SQL Server memory size:

  ➤ Small (less than 50GB) environment: 8GB

  ➤ Medium (about 50GB) environment: 16GB

  ➤ Large (greater than 50GB) environment: 32GB

➤ CPU recommendations:

  ➤ Make sure to install a 64-bit SQL Server on 64-bit Windows Server 2008.

  ➤ If you have more than 20,000 users you should have two SharePoint Web Front-End (WFE) servers.

  ➤ Plan for two quad-core CPUs per 20,000 users.

  ➤ Use a maximum of 8 CPUs per server; if you need more power, install a second SQL Server.

Calculating the Disk Space Needed

The disk space that SharePoint Foundation itself requires is less than 600MB, and SQL Server binaries require about the same, so the important data volume to consider is the SQL databases where SharePoint will store all its information. Whether you use the SQL Server Express engine or the Microsoft SQL Server does not matter; you still need to follow this simple but important rule: You must always have at least 50 percent free space on your database disk!

If you do not, you will not be able to perform database maintenance and troubleshooting, because these activities may need to make a copy of the database to perform their tasks. So what will require the most space in the database? The answer is simple: your documents! They will not be compressed, so a 1MB Word file will require 1MB of database disk space (actually slightly more). If you activate version history for document libraries, then all document versions will also require disk space, since each version is stored as a complete document, not just the changes from previous versions. The other information stored in SharePoint will, of course, also require space, but it will most likely not require anything near as much as the documents. And a SharePoint site itself will require less than 200KB of database space.

> **NOTE** *The XML-based file format introduced in Microsoft Office 2007 generates files that are less than 50 percent of the size of previous Microsoft Office file formats! So just by using that file format or later, the SQL databases will be about half the size.*

So to estimate the disk space needed for your database, start by estimating the number of files it will contain. For example, assume you estimate that it will contain about 50,000 files and documents, with an average of 500KB; in total this will require 25GB. Add to that 5GB for the other type of information you will store and you get 30GB in total. Following the earlier rule, you must have at least a 60GB disk for the database alone.

Remember that implementing a *small farm* configuration, that is, one SharePoint Foundation server and one Microsoft SQL server, requires only the 60GB disk on the database server. The SharePoint Foundation server itself requires very little disk space.

Software Requirements

Because SharePoint Foundation runs on top of Internet Information Services (IIS) in Windows Server, you need to understand some more about IIS, virtual web servers, and application pools.

The IIS Virtual Server

In the good old days each web solution required its own physical web server, which was clearly not the most economical solution if you needed multiple websites. Microsoft solved this problem by enabling the IIS to create and manage virtual web servers — for example, the Default Web Site. Each web solution running on top of IIS 6 needs its own virtual web server. This will make running several web solutions on the same physical server possible. To make separating each virtual server possible, they must differ in at least one of the following: the IP number, the TCP port number, or the host header name.

But that solution created a new problem: If one web solution crashed, it also killed all other web solutions running in the same IIS. Microsoft solved this problem by creating something it called *application pools* inside IIS, which, simply put, defines a private virtual address space and security context for a web solution. Each web solution is linked to an application pool. However, each application pool can be linked to more than one web solution, thus sharing address space and security context, so if one of these web solutions crashes, then all may crash — but only in this application pool!

The terminology here is a bit confusing: IIS in general talks about *websites*, such as Default Web Site. SharePoint needed to extend these websites with more features to support its functionality. These extended websites are called web applications in SharePoint. But the term *web application* is also a common term for any web-based solution. However, when you see the term *web application* in this book, it always means "extended websites."

If you chose to perform a farm installation of SharePoint (see details later in this section), you must enter a user account that SharePoint's configuration wizard will set as the security *Identity* for the application pool that hosts the website running the *SharePoint Central Administration v4* tool. That account can be either a built-in account, like the *Network Service*, or a standard user account in Active Directory. SharePoint's configuration wizard automatically grants that account the following permissions to SQL Server and its databases: *Database Creators*, *Security Administrators*, and *Public*.

> **NOTE** *Running two or more web applications in the same application pool creates a potential security risk. It is technically possible for one web application to access the other web application and its content! Normally this access is acceptable, because you control the access to all sites and content using SharePoint's permission settings. However, for some organizations you need to avoid this type of access, maybe for legal reasons. If so, use a separate application pool with a unique security account for each web application.*

All other IIS websites used by SharePoint should use their own application pools, with an Identity account that is different from the one used by SharePoint Central Administration's application pool.

As mentioned earlier, before SharePoint can use a standard virtual IIS website, it must be extended with new functionality; such an extended virtual site in SharePoint is referred to as a *web application*. The administrator creates the web application in the SharePoint Central Administration tool by extending an existing virtual website in IIS (like the Default Web Site) or creating a new virtual website, which will then be extended. Each web application will then be used to host one or more *site collections*, as described in more detail later in this appendix.

Deciding Between SharePoint Foundation and SharePoint Server

Before you start installing SharePoint you have to answer an important question: What version of SharePoint do you need? Does the limited SharePoint Foundation offer enough features, or does your organization require the full SharePoint Server 2010?

Although SharePoint Foundation is a great product, you should really think twice before making the choice to install it instead of SharePoint Server 2010. The major benefit of SharePoint Foundation is the fact that it is free to download and run on any Windows 2008 Server, but it also has its shortcomings compared to SharePoint Server 2010. Analyze what problems you are trying to solve with SharePoint before choosing either version. If you choose SharePoint Foundation and later decide to upgrade to SharePoint Server 2010, it can be done, but you will have to complete several manual steps to make it work. The best course of action is to make sure you have the right version installed from the beginning.

To answer the question of which version to choose, think about what needs and issues you want to solve with your SharePoint installation. Most likely you cannot answer this question on your own; you need to have a talk with both the stakeholders and the end users, because they are the ones who will use SharePoint. Talk with people in your organization and ask questions like the ones in the following table to find out whether you need SharePoint Foundation or SharePoint Server.

QUESTION	PEOPLE TO ASK	COMMENT
Do you need an intranet for the whole organization?	Top management, people responsible for managing organization-wide information	For a small company with fewer than 50 users, SharePoint Foundation may be sufficient. But for organizations that deal with a large amount of information, SharePoint Server may better suit your needs.
Do you need a local intranet only for a single department or team?	Middle management, team leaders	SharePoint Foundation is a good choice if the department or team is working with the same type of information.
Is searching inside a specific SharePoint site enough for your needs?	All types of users	If the answer is yes, you may fulfill this need by using SharePoint Foundation search alone. Note that by installing the free Microsoft Search Server Express 2010 you can add a search functionality to SharePoint Foundation that is very close to what SharePoint Server 2010 Standard Edition offers.

QUESTION	PEOPLE TO ASK	COMMENT
Do you want to be able to search for information across any SharePoint sites and external data sources, such as the file servers and Microsoft Exchange?	All types of users	Only SharePoint Server offers global search functionality, but SharePoint Foundation will achieve the same functionality if you add Microsoft Search Server Express 2010.
Do groups of users need to share and update information, such as documents, contacts, and calendar items?	All types of users	If the answer is yes, this need is fulfilled with SharePoint Foundation.
Do you need a powerful way of presenting more information than just the e-mail address and phone number for some or all of your users?	Middle management, team leaders, project leaders	SharePoint Server has the User Profile feature, which contains a lot of information about each user that is also searchable.
Is it important to allow users to rate, comment, and use keyword tagging for document, page, and list contents?	Information management, middle management, team leaders, project leaders	Only SharePoint Server has this functionality.
Do you need a way to display Microsoft Excel spreadsheets and charts to users without requiring them to have Microsoft Excel?	Information management, middle management, team leaders, project leaders	SharePoint Server alone supports this with the Excel Service.
Do your users need to display and fill out intelligent forms with a web browser?	Information management, middle management, team leaders, project leaders	SharePoint Server alone supports this with the Forms Service.
Do you need powerful, yet easy web content management — for example, for public Internet portals?	Information management, middle management, team leaders, project leaders	SharePoint Server has this functionality built-in, which is greatly improved compared to MOSS 2007.
Do you have the budget to invest in SharePoint Server 2010?	Stakeholders, top management, CEO, CFO	SharePoint Server comes with a ton of features built-in, but it requires a server and user client access license.

If you get one or more answers that indicate a SharePoint Server solution is preferable, you must think carefully about what version to install. For some organizations the requested functionality offered by SharePoint Server only is not worth the financial investment that SharePoint Server requires, and for others it is. Always have a follow-up question ready when your users, especially the managers, tell you that they need a SharePoint Server-only feature — ask them, "Is this feature worth the investment of X amount of money?" It has happened more than once that these managers then say, "No! Let's start with SharePoint Foundation only." If so, let them know that an upgrade later on will require time and money, and starting with SharePoint Server is easiest if this is what they will need in the end — maybe this information will change their minds again.

Summary of Requirements

To summarize the requirements you can use this table, which lists Microsoft's minimum and recommended configuration. Remember that for a *pilot* installation you can actually get away with less than the minimum memory size listed in the following table, but for a production environment you should follow Microsoft's recommendations.

ITEM	MINIMUM REQUIREMENT	MICROSOFT RECOMMENDS
Operating system	Any edition of 64-bit Microsoft Windows Server 2008/2008 R2	Any edition of 64-bit Microsoft Windows Server 2008/2008 R2
CPU	One CPU (64-bit) running at 2.5 GHz	Two CPUs (64-bit) running at at least 3 GHz
RAM	4GB	8GB or more
Disk space	Minimum 6GB free disk space	Minimum 30GB free disk space
File system	NTFS	NTFS
IIS version	7.0 with ASP.NET (in Worker Process Isolation Mode)	7.0 with ASP.NET (in Worker Process Isolation Mode)
Database engine	64-bit SQL Server Express 2008	A separate 64-bit SQL Server 2008 R2
Internet browser	IE 7.0 with the latest service pack	IE 8 or later with the latest service pack

Preparing the Windows Server

Because SharePoint Foundation is a web application you must activate several Windows Server roles that are not configured by default. These are Internet Information Services (IIS) and .NET Framework 3.5.1; both of these two roles will automatically activate dependent roles that are required for these two main roles. By default, Windows 2008 will have PowerShell 1.0 installed, and that must be removed before running the prerequisite installation link in SharePoint 2010 setup. The following Try It Out provides the steps you need.

TRY IT OUT Prepare Windows Server 2008 for SharePoint Foundation

1. Log on as an administrator to the Windows 2008 server you will use for your SharePoint Foundation installation.

2. Start the Server Manager by choosing Start ⇨ Administration Tools ⇨ Server Manager.

3. Select Roles in the left navigation pane, then click Add Roles.

4. Select Application Server and Web Server (IIS), then click Next.

5. An information page about Web Server (IIS) appears. Click Next.

6. Another form appears asking whether you want to add role services required; that is, these are dependent roles that need to be activated. Click Add Required Role Services. The Installation Results page appears, as shown in Figure A-1. Then close the Server Manager.

7. Remove PowerShell 1.0 like this: Click Start ⇨ Run, enter cmd in the Open field, and then click OK to open the command shell window. Then type `C:\Windows\$NtUninstallKB926139$\Spuninst\Spuninst.Exe` and press Enter to remove PowerShell 1.0.

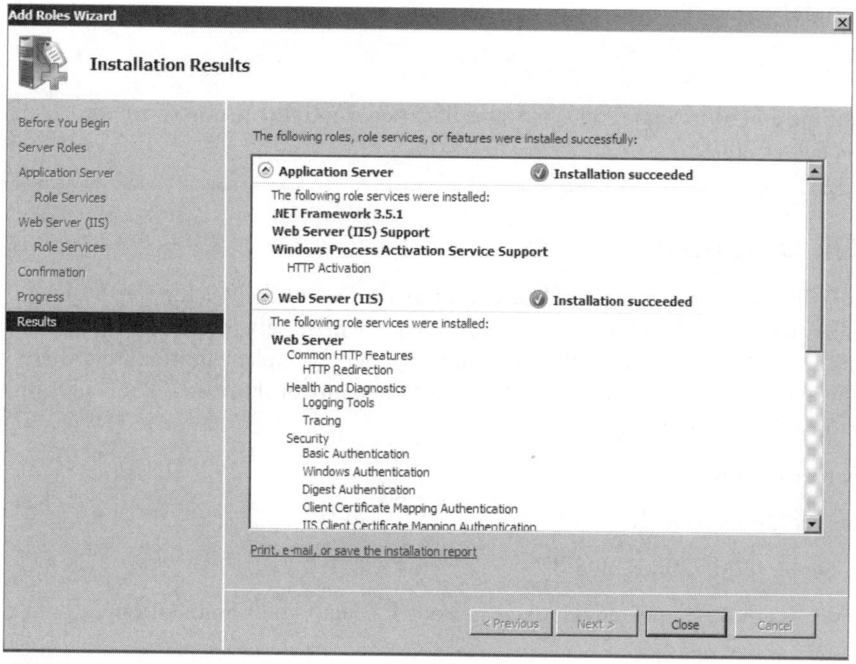

FIGURE A-1

How It Works

Windows Server 2008 must be prepared to enable installation of SharePoint Foundation. These steps accomplish that.

Now your Windows Server 2008 is prepared for the SharePoint Foundation installation. However, SharePoint Foundation has a feature that allows a list, such as a document library, to accept incoming e-mail using the SMTP standard. Note that to *send out* e-mail, SharePoint Foundation does not need any extra feature or role installed! If you need the feature that accepts incoming e-mail in SharePoint Foundation then you must first activate SMTP in Windows Server by using the steps in the following Try It Out.

TRY IT OUT Activate the SMTP Feature in Windows Server

1. Make sure you are logged on as a local server administrator and open the Server Manager.

2. Expand the Features node in the left pane.

3. Click Add Feature and select the SMTP option. The "Add role services and features required for SMTP Server" form appears.

4. Click Add Required Role Services, and then click Next three times.

5. On the Confirm Installation Selections form, verify that it lists SMTP Server, and click Install.

6. The Installation Results page appears; if it says the installation was successful, click Close. If not, correct the problem and try again.

How It Works

If you want to enable incoming e-mail to SharePoint lists and libraries, you must first activate the SMTP feature in Windows Server 2008.

Preparing the SQL Database

Four different database editions are supported by SharePoint 2010. One of them is the free SQL Server Express that comes with SharePoint and may be installed when SharePoint Server is installed. The other three options are basically the same; that is, a full SQL Server implementation, and there is nothing special to consider when configuring SharePoint Server to any of these three. So basically you have four different installation options:

➤ A local SQL Server Express

➤ A local SQL Server (2005/2008/2008 R2)

➤ A remote SQL Server (2005/2008/2008 R2)

The following table describes these supported database options for SharePoint Foundation.

DATABASE TYPE	LOCAL INSTALLATION	REMOTE INSTALLATION
SQL Server Express 2008	Yes	Not supported
Microsoft SQL 2005 Server x 64	Yes	Yes
Microsoft SQL 2008 Server x 64	Yes	Yes
Microsoft SQL 2008 R2 x 64	Yes	Yes

Remember that if you already have a 64-bit version of SQL Server 2005/2008/2008 R2 installed in your network, SharePoint can use it, if it has enough disk space and resources. (SharePoint Foundation will, in fact, work with a 32-bit remote SQL Server, but this configuration is not supported by Microsoft.)

> **NOTE** *Make sure to apply the latest service packs to SQL Server before using it with SharePoint.*

Single-Server Configuration with a Local SQL Server Express

This is an installation of both SharePoint Foundation and the free SQL Server Express on the same computer. Microsoft refers to this type of configuration as a *stand-alone* server. The typical scenario for this kind of configuration is when doing a pilot or evaluation of SharePoint. You should think twice before using this configuration in a production environment because of the 4GB size database limitation and the fact that you cannot upgrade to a full SQL Server.

Single-Server Configuration with a Local Microsoft SQL Server

This configuration is perfect for the small organization or department that wants a very good platform for building a basic intranet, for information sharing, and collaboration, as well as basic search capability. The cost is higher than the previous configuration because you need a Microsoft SQL Server license, but there is no size limit for the SQL databases. If you already have invested in the 64-bit Microsoft SQL Server 2005 or 2008, and it has the required disk, memory, and CPU capacity available, you could install SharePoint Foundation on that same server.

> **NOTE** *You need one Microsoft SQL Server Client Access License (CAL) for each SharePoint Foundation user, not just one for each service account. Make sure your current license agreement covers all the SharePoint Foundation users.*

A Small Farm: SharePoint Foundation Using a Remote Microsoft SQL 2005/2008/2008 R2 Server

The last configuration option is where you install SharePoint Foundation on one server and Microsoft SQL Server 2005/2008/2008 R2 on another server. Microsoft refers to this type of setup as a *small farm*. This type of configuration increases the number of supported users, plus you have all the functionality of the previously described configuration (using a local server). Once again, this type of installation would not be free because you need the Microsoft SQL Server, but if you have this server already installed in your IT environment, this SharePoint Foundation installation may have no extra cost involved. This depends on the type of license you have for the existing Microsoft SQL Server; for example, do you have a client access license for all users, including the SharePoint users, or (better still) do you have a CPU license that allows any number of users access to SQL Server?

This solution provides no additional SharePoint Foundation functionality, compared to a single-server configuration, besides the increased number of users supported. However, you could use this configuration with a clustered Microsoft SQL 2005/2008/2008 R2 Server environment, with up to eight nodes, thus giving you both fault tolerance and higher availability.

INSTALLING SHAREPOINT FOUNDATION

By now you have the necessary information to start the installation of SharePoint Foundation. The following section describes the exact steps required to install SharePoint Foundation in the three most common installation scenarios. Before you start following these steps, make sure nobody is using this server for anything else, at least not during the installation. If you have other applications installed on the same server, please make a backup before you start, in the unlikely case something goes wrong, and the server gets messed up beyond repair!

During the installation of SharePoint Foundation the setup program will create multiple new virtual IIS websites, which it will extend — that is, add more functionality to. This is referred to as creating a web application. This term means that the virtual IIS web server gets configured in such a way that SharePoint Foundation can use it. You cannot install SharePoint Foundation unless you have a web application. In simple scenarios, such as installing SharePoint Foundation and the embedded SQL Server Express together, the setup program for SharePoint Foundation will automatically create all the web applications required. In more complex scenarios, such as installing SharePoint Foundation and Microsoft SQL Server on separate servers (that is, a small farm), you will have to create some of the web applications manually. SharePoint will use these web applications for hosting site collections, which are collections of one or more SharePoint Foundation websites that belong to the same site tree.

> **NOTE** *The following sections provide three different installation scenarios. To help you avoid having to jump among these sections, each installation scenario offers complete instructions. So if you want to install a single server you only have to read that section.*

The Config and Content Databases

SharePoint Foundation uses two types of databases: the *configuration database* and the *content database*. During the installation of SharePoint Foundation you, or the setup program, will create these, depending on what type of installation you choose. These two database types contain the following information:

➤ **Configuration database:** This database maintains the entire configuration for SharePoint Foundation, such as the names of all SharePoint Foundation servers in the farm, their settings, and the SQL Server used. There is only one single configuration database for each SharePoint farm, regardless of the number of SharePoint Foundation and SQL databases. For SharePoint Foundation installations using the Microsoft SQL Server (that is, not SQL Server Express) you must name this configuration database; the default name is *SharePoint_Config*.

➤ **Content database:** This database contains all data and information that belongs to the SharePoint Foundation websites, such as news lists, document libraries, and the website itself. It also includes management data, such as usernames and permission settings. Initially you have one single content database, but if necessary you can create as many as you need. Large organizations may have more than 1,000 content databases. The first SharePoint Foundation content database gets the default name *SPF_Content*. You must name any new content database that you add.

The following sections discuss all three possible configurations of SharePoint Foundation. Each configuration is completely described, including detailed steps on how to perform this type of installation. Many of these steps are identical in two or sometimes all of the installation scenarios. I recommend that you focus on the type of installation that is most interesting to you at this moment. Later on, you can come back to this chapter when you need to perform another type of installation.

Installing a Stand-Alone SharePoint Foundation Server with the SQL Server Express

Installing an SharePoint Foundation using a Microsoft SQL Server Express database is very straightforward and easy. You can do it within 10 minutes, without much hassle. Use the steps in the following Try It Out to install both SharePoint Foundation and the SQL database on the same server. To download any updates, make sure the server has an Internet connection before you start.

TRY IT OUT   Install SharePoint Foundation and SQL Server Express on a Single Server

1. Log on as a domain administrator to the Windows 2008 server you will use for your SharePoint Foundation and SQL Server Express installation. This ensures that the domain administrator will be granted all permissions in the new SharePoint Foundation server.

2. Make sure the prerequisite steps for installing IIS and .NET Framework in Windows Server 2008/2008 R2 are completed; see the detailed instructions earlier in this chapter. Make sure Windows 2008 Server has the latest service packs and security patches installed by running Start ➪ All Programs ➪ Windows Update before you continue.

3. Download the latest version of SharePoint Foundation from Microsoft's website:

  a. Go to www.microsoft.com/downloads and enter **SharePoint Foundation** in the search field.

  b. Make sure to select the default language you need for your SharePoint Foundation installation, using the Change Language menu on this download page. This example shows the use of the English version! Then click Download to start the actual download (about 170MB).

4. Start the installation by running the SharePoint.exe file you downloaded:

  a. The start page for SharePoint Foundation 2010 installation opens. It displays a list of different options for preparing and installing SharePoint Foundation, plus links to more information. What you must do is to run a check that all prerequisites are installed and configured properly. In the Install section, click on the "Install software prerequisites" link.

  b. On the "Microsoft SharePoint Products and Technology 2010 Preparation Tool" page is a list of the products and updates that must be installed before SharePoint Foundation will install. Click Next to continue.

c. The next page that appears is the "License Terms for software products" that displays the license terms for the products and updates that are required to install SharePoint Foundation. If you accept their terms, select "I accept the terms of this agreement" and click Next to start the installation.

d. The Installation Complete page, which describes everything that was installed or updated, appears. Click Finish to close the Preparation Tool. The start page reappears. If there were any issues they will be listed, and you will see suggestions on how to solve them.

e. Click the Install SharePoint Foundation link to start the actual installation of SharePoint Foundation.

f. The license agreement for SharePoint Foundation appears. If you accept the terms, select "I accept the terms of this agreement" and click Continue.

g. The "Choose the installation you want" page that appears is important: Click Standalone to install SharePoint Foundation together with the SQL Server Express 2010 that is included in the SharePoint Foundation installation package. If you instead click Server Farm you will need a preinstalled Microsoft SQL Server, so for this scenario be sure to click Standalone; see Figure A-2.

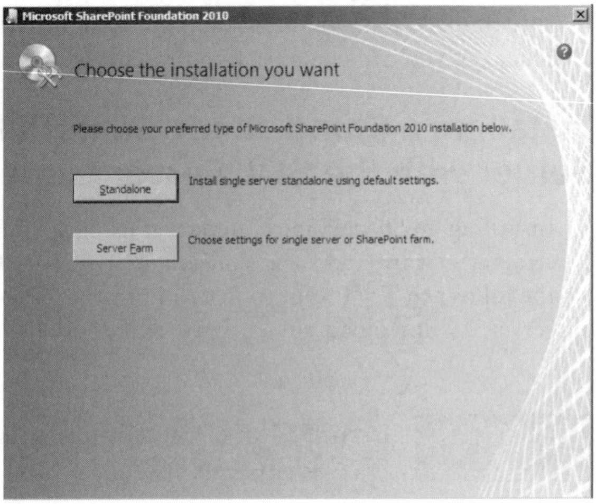

FIGURE A-2

h. The installation takes a few minutes; when it completes a page appears showing the option "Run the SharePoint Product and Technologies Configuration Wizard now" pre-selected. Click Close to close the setup program, and start the configuration wizard.

5. The configuration wizard sets up the necessary configurations needed to run SharePoint Foundation, such as creating the Central Administration tool and creating the web application needed to host the first site collection. You must complete this Configuration Wizard before you can use SharePoint Foundation. If you for some reason cannot do this now, this wizard is also available under Start ⇨ All Programs ⇨ Microsoft SharePoint 2010 Products. Make sure to answer the questions as follows:

a. On the Welcome to SharePoint Products and Technologies page, click Next.

b. A dialog box appears, informing you that the IIS and other related services will be started or reset during the configuration; click Yes to continue. The Configuration Wizard now starts and performs nine different tasks. This process takes 5–10 minutes to complete, depending on the server hardware.

c. When it completes, you should see the Configuration Successful page. Click Finish, and the Team Site created by the Configuration Wizard appears; see Figure A-3. This site is now ready to be used.

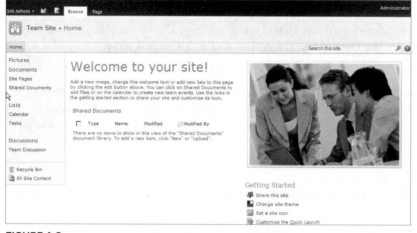

FIGURE A-3

How It Works

When installing SharePoint Foundation, you must first install the software prerequisite and then SharePoint Foundation 2010. You must also decide what type of configuration to install, such as a stand-alone server or a server farm. The installation guide can assist you with these steps.

Checking the Installation

Before going on, investigating what new things were installed on the server is a good idea. In short, you have a new SharePoint Central Administration tool, a team site, and corresponding web applications; that is, extended virtual IIS websites, plus a SQL Server Express with a number of databases. Start by checking the new web applications in IIS:

TRY IT OUT   Verify the Installation of SharePoint Foundation

1. Start by opening the IIS Manager: Start ➪ Administration Tools ➪ Internet Information Services (IIS) Manager.

2. Expand the server node, and then the Sites node. Note that you have four IIS virtual servers here:

- ➤ **Default Web Site:** This site is stopped, because another virtual server using TCP port 80 was created: SharePoint – 80. The reason is increased security; the files and locations for Default Web Site are well known, and therefore the target for malicious code, like viruses.

- ➤ **SharePoint – 80:** A new virtual server created by the Configuration Wizard that listens on TCP port 80. It is used by SharePoint for all user websites, such as project sites, team sites, and so on. This is where the autogenerated Team site is running.

- ➤ **SharePoint Central Administration:** Used by SharePoint for the administration website.

- ➤ **SharePoint Web Service:** This website makes it possible to use a technique called Web Services to read and write SharePoint data from external applications.

3. Select (click on) the SharePoint – 80 virtual server and select Advanced Settings in the right pane.

4. Note the name for the application pool this virtual server is using: SharePoint – 80; that is, the same name as for the site. Click OK to close the properties for this virtual server.

5. Select the Application Pools node in the left pane of the IIS Manager.

6. Select the application pool named SharePoint – 80 (used by the SharePoint – 80 virtual server), then scroll the page to the right to see the Identity column (you can also click on Advanced Settings). Note what security account this application pool is using. By default it is the predefined Network Service.

How It Works

After the installation of SharePoint Foundation is completed, you should always verify that SharePoint and its configuration are correct.

Now check the new applications on the virtual server used by the SharePoint Central Administration website:

TRY IT OUT Verify the Settings of the Web Application

1. Continue from the previous Try It Out: Under the Sites node, select SharePoint Central Administration v4 and click on Advanced Settings.

2. Note that this application pool is named SharePoint Central Administration v4. Close this dialog box.

3. Select that application pool and check the Identity account — it should also be Network Service, just like SharePoint – 80.

How It Works

The user account that SharePoint Foundation will use when communicating with SQL Server is listed as the application pool identity account.

> **NOTE** The identity account for this application pool is automatically granted access to the SQL Server Express database and is used by SharePoint Foundation whenever it needs to read or write to the databases.

To summarize, SharePoint Foundation primarily uses two virtual IIS servers: one for the websites used by the end users, and one for the Central Administration tool for SharePoint. These two virtual servers use separate application pools. But this type of installation has a number of issues that you must beware of before choosing it. The only real advantages of this installation option are that it is very fast and that it does not require a full SQL Server installed. The most important drawbacks with this installation option are as follow:

➤ Both these application pools use the same security account, which is normally considered not best practice, as you will see later on when you use the built-in Best Practice Analyzer tool.

➤ Upgrading the installation to a multiserver farm — for example, one SharePoint Foundation server and one SQL Server — will be hard. It will require a complete reinstallation of SharePoint Foundation, so in that case you would first need to back up your site collections, uninstall SharePoint Foundation, do either an installation with a local SQL Server or an installation with a remote SQL Server, and finally restore the site collections.

➤ No SQL Management tool is included with this type of database, so you cannot work with the databases in case you need to. All databases are stored in the same folder structure as the SharePoint Foundation files; see Figure A-4. There are also third party SQL management products available for SQL Server Express.

➤ The maximum amount of data you can store in this SharePoint environment is 4GB.

SharePoint Foundation is now installed in a stand-alone configuration; that is, using a local SQL Server Express. The next step is to adjust the settings in Central Administration so the installation suits the needs of your organization; for example, enabling SharePoint Foundation to send e-mail, and adding more intuitive URL addresses for the intranet. Appendix B describes these tasks in detail.

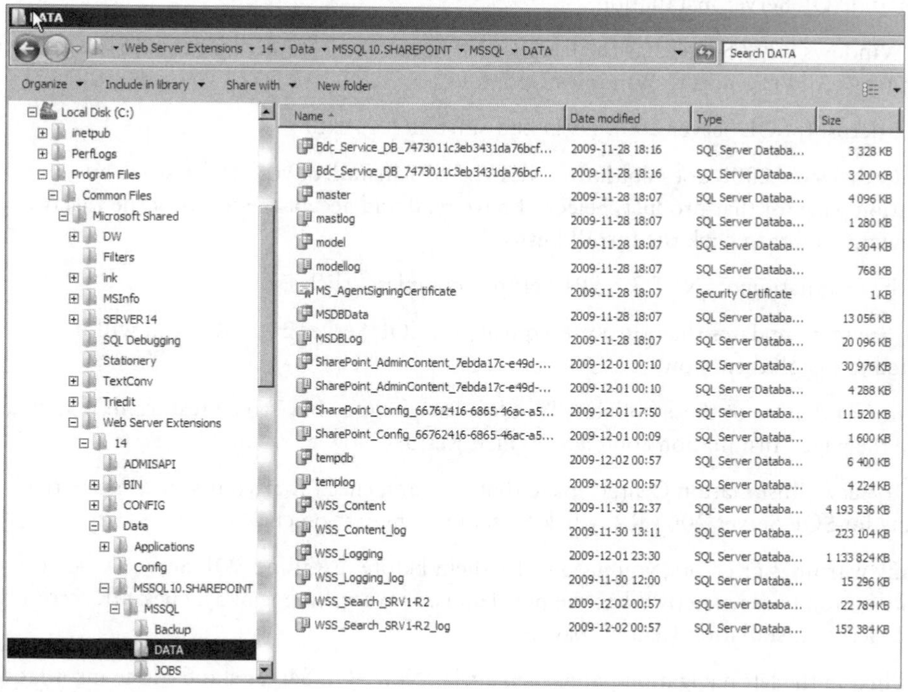

FIGURE A-4

Installing a Single Server with a Local Microsoft SQL Database

A single server with a local Microsoft SQL database installation is a much better option than the previously discussed stand-alone server installation, and it has no issues like the stand-alone server installation either. For example, it will allow you to later change the number of servers, such as for adding an extra SharePoint Foundation server, or move to separate SQL Server hardware. Maybe the strongest advantage with this installation option compared to the stand-alone option is that this installation has no size limitations. This is a strong reason for selecting the full Microsoft SQL Server instead of SQL Server Express. Because this type of setup requires a separate installation of SQL Server, as well as SharePoint Foundation, it takes more time to complete this operation.

The following Try It Outs describe how to install both Microsoft SQL Server 2008 and then SharePoint Foundation on the same server. Make sure to install the SQL Server before installing SharePoint Foundation!

> **NOTE** *To complete this procedure, you need an existing user account to use to run all SQL Server services.*

TRY IT OUT   Install Microsoft SQL Server 2008 R2

1. Log on as an administrator to the Windows 2008 server you will use for your SharePoint Foundation and SQL Server installation.

2. Make sure Windows 2008 Server has the latest service packs and security patches installed by choosing Start ➪ All Programs ➪ Windows Update.

3. Mount the Microsoft SQL Server 2008 DVD and start SETUP.EXE.

   a. If Windows Server 2008 does not have .NET 3.5 SP1 installed, you will first see an installation page for that product. Select "I have read and accept the terms of the License Agreement," and then click the Install button.

   b. When the installation of .NET 3.5 SP1 Setup is complete, click Exit.

   c. If there are more updates that are a prerequisite for SQL Server 2008 R2, you will be requested to install them now.

   d. After the installation of these updates, Windows Server may have to be restarted; if so you will see the page "Installation complete." Click Restart Now to restart the server.

4. On the "SQL Server Installation Center" page that appears, check that your server meets the requirements for SQL Server 2008 R2. Click System Configuration checker.

5. If you see any warnings or errors, you need to fix them before installing SQL Server. Click the Show details button to see exactly what the problem is. If everything is okay, click OK to return to the "SQL Server Installation Center" page.

6. Select Installing in the left navigation pane, then click "New SQL Server stand-alone installation or add features to an existing installation" to start the installation of SQL Server.

7. On the Setup Support Rules page that appears, you should see that there are no warnings or errors — this is actually the same type of test you performed earlier in step 5, so basically you can skip step 5. However, detecting problems before you try to install is usually better. Click OK to continue the installation. Be patient; several steps sometimes take minutes to complete.

8. The next page that appears is Product Key. If you are installing in a test environment you may choose between the Enterprise Evaluation or the full version. Note that for the full version, you need to enter any product key. If you choose the Enterprise Evaluation, be aware that this SQL Server will stop working after 180 days (6 months). Click Next to continue. The License Terms page appears.

9. Read the license and if you agree, select "I accept the license terms" and click Next. The Setup Support Files page appears.

10. These files are necessary for the SQL Server to operate properly. Click Install and wait several minutes for it to complete.

11. After installing the support files, the Setup Support Rules checker runs once again. This time you will see more than 10 different rules that are tested. They should all be okay, but if the Windows Firewall gets the Warning status you can click on its status link to see more details. Most likely, the checker will detect that your server has the Windows Firewall enabled, so the warning is safe to ignore unless you need to allow remote access. If so, disable Windows Firewall, or configure its port to allow remote access. See more about this topic on http://go.microsoft.com/fwlink/ ?LinkId=94001: "Configure the Windows Firewall to Allow SQL Server Access." Click Next to continue. The Configure Role page appears.

12. When preparing for an SharePoint Foundation installation you would most likely choose the SQL Server Feature Installation to install a complete SQL Server, including Reporting Services and Analysis Service. Click Next to continue.

13. In the Feature Selection page that appears, you choose what features to install. For an SharePoint Foundation installation you should install at least these options (see Figure A-5):

➤ Database Engine Service

➤ Management Tools – Complete (which also adds Management Tools – Basic)

Then choose carefully what file directories to use for SQL Server, using Shared feature directory and Shared feature directory (x86). As always, avoiding installing anything on the C drive is a good idea because it is heavily used by the Windows operating system. If you have another drive with enough disk space on this server, consider changing these two paths to that drive instead. Click Next to continue.

14. On the Installation Rules page that appears, check that there are no warnings or errors. If there are none, click Next to continue. If there are any issues, click Show details to see more about them. You must solve all errors before you can continue the installation.

15. The Instance Configuration page appears. If you want to use this SQL Server for other applications besides SharePoint Foundation, creating a named instance is a good idea. This will, in effect, create a private partition, or section, in SQL for all databases related to SharePoint Foundation (and there are a number of them; just wait and see). If this server will only be used by SharePoint Foundation, then it is okay to use the Default instance. Make your choice and click Next to continue.

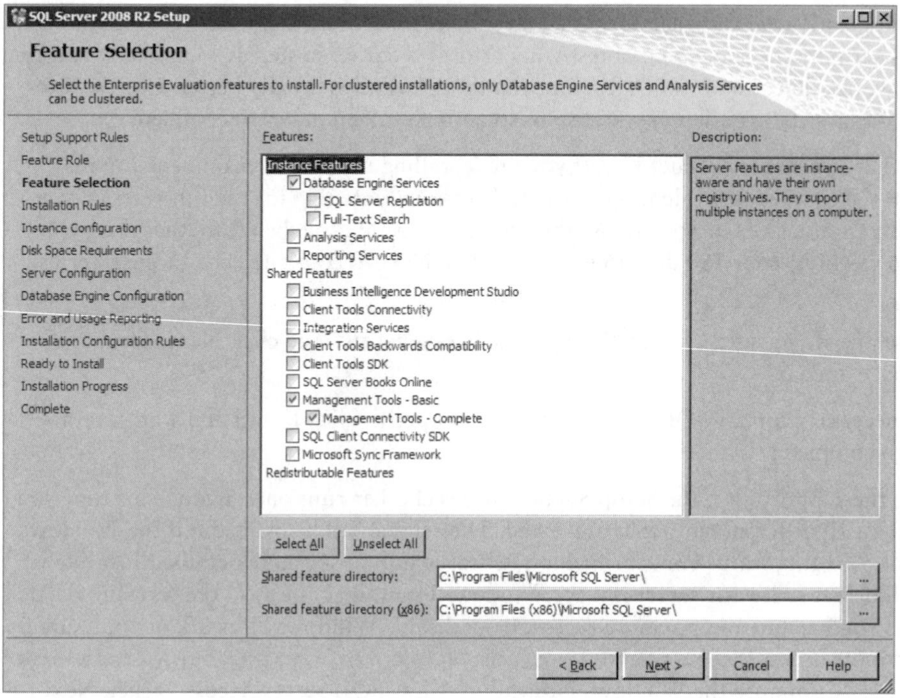

FIGURE A-5

16. The Disk Space Requirements page appears, informing you about the available disk space on the disk you selected earlier in step 13. If there is enough free space, click Next. If not, click Back until you get to step 13 again, and change the location.

17. On the Server Configuration page that appears, select an existing user account that will be associated with the SQL services. For a typical installation, using the same account is common practice; if this is okay, click "Use the same account for all SQL Server services" to enter the name and password for that account; if it is not okay, then enter each account individually. When ready, click Next to continue.

18. On the Database Engine Configuration page that appears, you define what type of authentication mechanism you want to use. The default is Windows authentication mode, which is also the best practice. Unless you have a good reason not to, go with that option.

    You must add the user account that will be the SQL Server Administration, typically the Domain Administrator account. To add the account you are logged on with, click Add Current User. To add another account, click Add and enter that account name.

    Also notice the Data Directories tab on this page — use it to view and possibly also change the file paths that SQL Server will use to store its databases, log files, and backup files. Change whatever you need, and then click Next to continue.

19. On the Error and Usage Reporting page that appears, you define whether SQL Server should send any error messages in SQL automatically to Microsoft, or to a specifically configured

report server in your organization. You can also choose to send feature usage data to Microsoft, including your hardware configuration and how you use SQL and its services. Microsoft will use this information to better understand how organizations all over the world use SQL Server, in order to enhance future releases, so using this option is a good thing. Make your choices and click Next to continue.

20. The Installation Configuration Rules page appears, which is yet another test, and if all is okay and no reports or warnings are listed, click Next to continue; otherwise, you must fix whatever problem is listed before you can go on.

21. The Ready to Install page finally appears, and it is a summary of all the options you made. If everything looks okay to you, then click Install to start the actual installation of SQL Server. If it's not okay, step back, do your changes, and make your way to this page again. When the installation starts, it is time to take a coffee break, because this may take time to complete — and you deserve a break after these steps!

22. The next page you see is Installation Progress, which lists all features as successfully installed. Click Next to continue.

23. The last page you see is Complete. In it you find information about the possible next steps after the installation. Click Close to complete the installation of this SQL Server 2008 R2. The SQL Server Installation Center reappears. Click "Search for product updates" and install the recommended updates, if any.

How It Works

You need to install SQL Server before installing SharePoint Foundation 2010 in a single server or a farm setup. The steps above describe a typical standard installation of SQL Server 2008 R2.

> **NOTE** If you installed the evaluation edition of SQL Server, and later decide you want to convert it to a full edition, you must first purchase the SQL Server license and run the SQL Server Installation Center again. Choose Maintenance in the left pane, click on Edition Upgrade, and select the full edition.

After this SQL Server installation, the next step is to install SharePoint Foundation. If you have not yet downloaded SharePoint Foundation, then go to the Microsoft Download Center at www.microsoft .com/download, and search for "SharePoint Foundation." Now use the steps in the following Try It Out to install SharePoint Foundation on this server to complete the single-server installation procedure.

> **NOTE** To complete this procedure, you need an existing user account for the communication between SharePoint Foundation and SQL Server, another user account for running all SharePoint services except the Central Administration tool, and a passphrase to be used as the farm passphrase. The server also will need an Internet connection.

TRY IT OUT   **Install SharePoint Foundation to Complete the Single-Server Installation**

1. Log on as a domain administrator to the Windows 2008 server you will use for your SharePoint Foundation and SQL Server Express installation. This ensures that the domain administrator will be granted all permissions in the new SharePoint Foundation server.

2. Make sure the prerequisite steps for installing IIS and .NET Framework in Windows Server 2008 R2 are completed; see the Try It Out "Prepare Windows Server 2008 for SharePoint Foundation" earlier in this chapter for detailed instructions. Make sure Windows 2008 Server has the latest service packs and security patches installed by running Start ⇨ All Programs ⇨ Windows Update before you continue.

3. Download the latest version of SharePoint Foundation from Microsoft's website:

    a. Go to www.microsoft.com/downloads and enter SharePoint Foundation in the search field.

    b. Make sure to select the default language you need for your SharePoint Foundation installation, using the Change Language menu on this page. This example shows the English version! Click Download to start the actual download (about 170MB).

4. Start the installation by running the SharePoint.exe file you downloaded:

    a. The start page for SharePoint Foundation 2010 installation opens. It shows a list of different options. What you must do is run a check that all prerequisites are installed and configured properly. In the Install section, click on the link Install software prerequisites.

    b. On the "Microsoft SharePoint Products and Technology 2010 Preparation Tool" page that appears is a list of the products and updates that must be installed before SharePoint Foundation will install. Click Next to continue.

    c. The license agreement for the products and updates that are required to install SharePoint Foundation appears. If you accept the terms, select "I accept the terms of this agreement" and click Next. The Microsoft SharePoint Products and Technologies 2010 Preparation Tool starts.

    d. When the installation is completed, the Installation Complete page appears, which describes everything that was installed or updated. Click Finish to close the Preparation Tool. The start page appears again, and it is time to install SharePoint Foundation.

    e. Click the Install SharePoint Foundation link to start the installation of SharePoint Foundation.

    f. The license agreement for SharePoint Foundation appears; if you accept the terms, select "I accept the terms of this agreement" and click Continue.

    g. In the "Choose the installation you want" page that appears, click Server Farm.

    h. The next page that appears is Server Type: You have two options, and choosing the right one is important. The default option is Standalone. Do not choose that option! It will actually do the same type of installation as the previously described installation; that is, using SQL Server Express, although you have a full SQL Server installed. Instead, make sure to *always* choose the Complete option. This option will allow you to connect this SharePoint Foundation to the full SQL Server you previously installed.

One more interesting tab is on this page: Data Location. Open it, and you will see that it allows you to choose the disk and folder to be used for storing SharePoint's index files. Because these index files may be several gigabytes in size, you should plan carefully where to store them. If you have another disk with enough available free space, it is a good candidate for this use.

When you are ready with the options on these two tabs (check again that you selected Complete installation), click Install Now. The installation of SharePoint Foundation begins; it is a good time for a quick coffee break.

i. When the installation completes, a page appears showing the option "Run the SharePoint Product and Technologies Configuration Wizard now" pre-selected. Click Close to close the setup program, and to start the configuration wizard.

5. The configuration wizard sets up the configurations needed to run SharePoint Foundation, such as creating the Central Administration tool, including the web application needed to host it. You must complete this Configuration Wizard before you can use SharePoint Foundation. Because you chose to install a complete SharePoint Foundation server, you get a few extra questions that you don't see when doing a stand-alone installation of SharePoint Foundation:

a. On the Welcome to SharePoint Products and Technologies page, click Next.

b. A dialog box appears informing you that the IIS and other related services will be started or reset during the configuration. Click Yes to continue. The Configuration Wizard now starts.

c. The Connect to a server farm page appears. Because this is the first server you install, select Create a new server farm. (If this were a server that should be added to an existing farm, you would instead choose Connect to an existing server farm.) Click Next.

d. Note that the Specify Configuration Database Settings page that appears is very important! Make sure to enter the correct information on it, because changing these values later is hard (but not impossible). See Figure A-6.

➤ **Database server:** Enter the name of your local Windows Server (because you run both SQL and SharePoint Foundation on the same server).

➤ **Database name:** Accept the default name, SharePoint_Config, unless you have a good reason to change it. Keeping the default name makes searching the Internet for information about this database easier (if you ever need to).

➤ **Username:** Enter the user account to be used by SharePoint Foundation when communicating with SQL Server. The best practice is to use a specific Active Directory account that is not used anywhere else in SharePoint Foundation.

➤ **Password:** Enter the password for this user account.

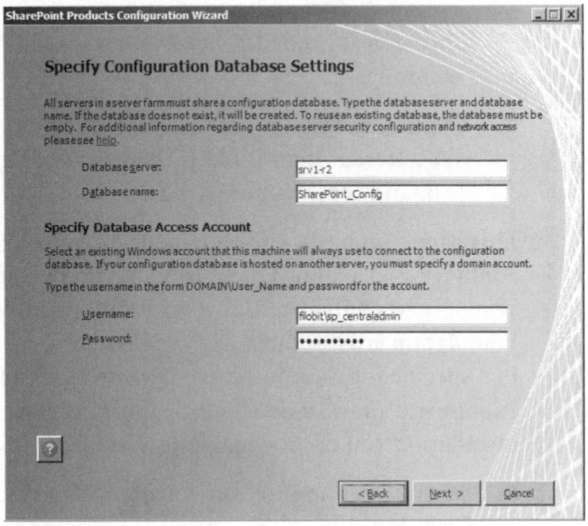

FIGURE A-6

Click Next to continue. The Configuration Wizard now checks these values, and if anything is wrong, such as the password, you will get informed and you can correct the error and click Next again.

e. The Specify Farm Security Settings page appears. This is a new type of protection that comes in SharePoint 2010: If you need to change important configuration settings in the farm, such as adding an extra SharePoint server to the farm, you need to enter this passphrase. Enter your farm passphrase and make sure to write it down and store it in a secure location. Click Next to continue.

f. The Configure SharePoint Central Administration Web Application page that appears contains two settings: port number and authentication mechanism, as shown in Figure A-7.

➤ **Specify port number:** You must add this TCP port number to the URL to SharePoint's Central Administration tool. By default it is a random number, but choosing your own port number

may be a good idea, because it will be easier to remember. Just make sure it is way above 1023 and less than 65535; for example, 5000.

➤ **Configure Security Settings:** The two authentication choices are NTLM or Negotiate (Kerberos). The default is NTLM, which is easiest to implement; however, Kerberos is more secure and faster in a large organization, but also requires more configuration and understanding to work. If you are uncertain about how to configure Kerberos, then go with the NTLM option. You can always change this later if needed. Click Next to continue.

FIGURE A-7

g. The summary page lists all settings you selected. If all is okay, then click Next to start the Configuration Wizard; otherwise, click Back and correct the settings.

This page also has a button named Advanced Settings. Click it to open a new page where you can configure SharePoint Foundation to run in Active Directory Account Creating Mode. This is a very special configuration, where you basically say that users who need access to your SharePoint Foundation environment can create their own accounts, which then will be automatically stored in a specific location in Active Directory. If you really want to do this, make sure to read the Administrators' Guide about this mode before continuing. For a typical SharePoint Foundation installation you do not enable this mode. Click Cancel to return to the previous page.

h. When the configuration wizard completes, you should see the Configuration Successful page. Click Finish.

> **NOTE** *If you need to rerun the Configuration Wizard, you will find it in Start ⇨ All Programs ⇨ Microsoft SharePoint 2010 Products. You can also run it as a command tool: PSCONFIG (stored in* `\Program Files\Common Files\Microsoft Shared\ Web Server Extensions\14\Bin`*). It has a number of options so make sure to read its help file before you run it:* `\Program Files\Common Files\Microsoft Shared\ web server extensions\14\Help\1033\PSCONFIG.CHM.`

How It Works

This procedure will install SharePoint Foundation 2010, using a local SQL Server. This type of installation has no size limitations for the content databases and will be suitable for organizations of up to 1000 users.

After the Installation

Before going on, investigating what new things were installed on the server is a good idea. In short, you have a new SharePoint Central Administration tool and some corresponding web applications; that is, extended virtual IIS websites and a number of new databases in SQL Server. Because the SharePoint Central Administration tool started automatically, continue with its settings to complete the basic configurations. Note that the URL to this tool contains the TCP port number you selected earlier in step 5f.

TRY IT OUT Run the Basic Configuration Settings in SharePoint Central Administration

1. The first time you open the Central Administration tool after an installation, you get a question about participating in Microsoft's Customer Experience Improvement Program. If you choose to participate in this program, all errors that you may later encounter in SharePoint Foundation will be sent automatically to Microsoft. This information will be used to enhance future versions of SharePoint Foundation, so participating is a good thing. Make your choice, and click OK to continue.

2. The next page that appears, "Configure your SharePoint farm," contains a question: "How do you want to configure your SharePoint Farm?" You have two options:

➤ **Yes, walk me through the configuration of my farm using this wizard:** This option is the easiest for the non-experienced SharePoint administrator, but you will get auto-generated names on databases and web applications and so on.

➤ **No, I will configure everything myself:** This option is the favorite for the experienced administrator who knows SharePoint and understands its options.

For this example, click the button "Start the Wizard."

3. The first page this wizard opens is where you configure your managed account. This is basically just a standard user account that SharePoint will associate with one or more SharePoint services (that is, background applications). You can create a new managed account (the user account must exist), or you can reuse the same account you entered in step 5d in the previous installation procedure. However, this is not the best practice — avoid reusing that particular account, and make sure to create a new managed account for these services!

The selected managed account will, by default, be associated with the two services listed on this page; that is, Business Data Connectivity and Usage and Health Data Collection; this is acceptable. Click Next to continue; this will add the selected user account as a managed account and complete the basic setup of SharePoint Foundation.

4. The second, and last, page the wizard displays is where you create a new (and first) Site Collection; that is, a top site that later can contain any number of subsites. Typically, this is the intranet start site. If you don't want to do this now, then click the Skip button. In this example, you will create a site named Start, using the Team Site template:

    ➤   **Title:** Start (you can change this name later).

    ➤   **Description:** Enter a description or leave it empty (you can change this description later).

    ➤   **URL:** This is the web URL that users enter in their web browsers to open this site. By default, it is always the same as the name of this Windows Server, but you can later add more URLs with better names. Accept the default here.

    ➤   **Select a template:** Select Team Site. You find out more about site templates in several sections in this book, but basically a template is a preconfigured site with a given design, lists, and information that you later can modify to your heart's desire. See Figure A-8.

    Click OK to create this site collection and its top site.

5. On the page that appears, click Finish to complete the wizard. The start page for SharePoint's Central Administration tool opens. Open a new web browser session, and enter the URL listed earlier in step 4. The new site collection will now appear.

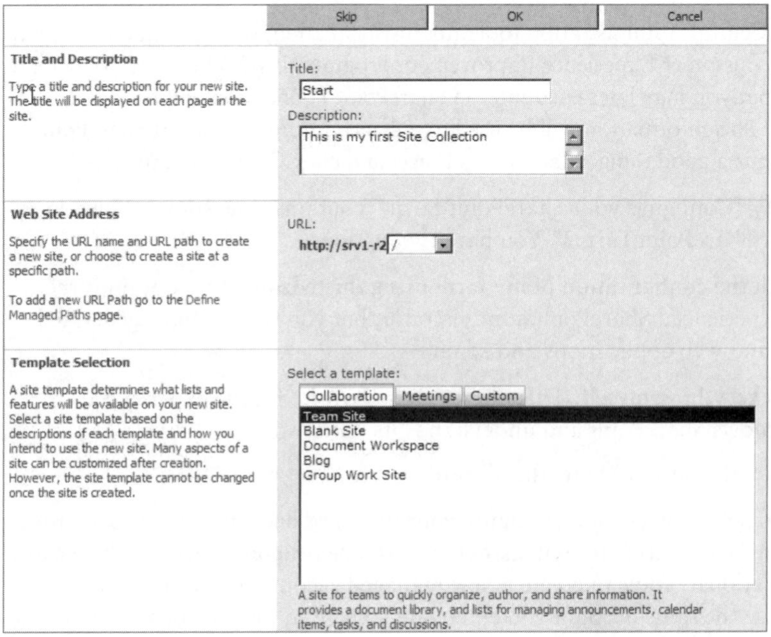

FIGURE A-8

How It Works

Run the Farm Configuration Wizard after an installation to enable and set up all standard configuration, including service applications. This wizard will also enable you to create your first site collection.

After that procedure it is time to check the new settings in IIS and the new databases in SQL Server.

TRY IT OUT   Check Out New IIS Settings and SQL Databases

1.   Open the IIS manager by choosing Start ➪ Administration Tools ➪ Internet Information Services (IIS) Manager.

2.   Expand the server node, and then the Sites node. Note that you have four IIS virtual servers here:

➤   **Default Web Site:** This site is stopped, because another virtual server using TCP port 80 was created: SharePoint – 80. The reason is increased security; the files and locations for Default Web Site are well known, and therefore the target for malicious code, like viruses.

➤   **SharePoint – 80:** A new virtual server created by the Configuration Wizard that listens on TCP port 80. It is used by SharePoint for all user websites, such as project sites, team sites, and so on. This is where the site collection Start is running.

➤   **SharePoint Central Administration:** Used by SharePoint for the administrative website.

➤   **SharePoint Web Service:** This service makes using a technique called Web Services to read and write SharePoint data from external applications possible.

3.   Select (click on) the SharePoint – 80 virtual server and select Advanced Settings in the right pane.

4.   Note the name for the application pool this virtual server is using: SharePoint – 80; that is, the same name as for the site. Click OK to close the properties for this virtual server.

5.   Select the Application Pools node in the left pane of the IIS Manager.

6.   Select the application pool named SharePoint – 80 (used by the virtual server SharePoint – 80), then scroll the page to the right to see the Identity column (you can also click on Advanced Settings). Note that the security account is the new managed account you just created. Never change this setting by using this form — you must always do changes using the Central Administration tool, or the script tools (STSADM or PowerShell). The reason is that if you change anything here, then SharePoint will be unaware of it, and therefore the change will not work.

Do the same checks with the virtual server used by the SharePoint Central Administration website:

7.   Under the Sites node, select SharePoint Central Administration v4 and click on Advanced Settings.

8.   Note that the application pool used by this web application is also named SharePoint Central Administration v4, just like its site; that is, web application. Close this dialog box.

9.   Open the Advanced Settings for this application pool and check the Identity account — it should be the account you entered when running the Configuration Wizard directly after the installation of SharePoint Foundation.

> **NOTE** *The application pool identity account is automatically granted access to the SQL Server database and is used by SharePoint Foundation whenever it needs to read or write to the databases; for example, when you create a new site collection or web application.*

10. The SQL Server also has been modified; there are new databases, and new user accounts have been granted access. Log on as an administrator to the server where SQL is installed, then start the SQL Server Management Studio (located in Start ➪ All Programs ➪ Microsoft SQL Server 2008 R2).

11. At the Connect to Server page, make sure the server type is Database Engine, the server name is (local), and the Authentication is Windows Authentication. Click Connect.

12. Expand the top node (local), then Databases. You should now see five new databases (where *xxxx* is a 32-bit globally unique identifier, or GUID):

➤ **Bdc_Service_DB_*xxxxx***: The database for the Business Connectivity Service

➤ **SharePoint_AdminContent_*xxxx***: The database for content in SharePoint Central Administration

➤ **SharePoint_Config**: The common configuration database for the farm

➤ **WSS_Content**: The database for the content in user site collections, e.g., the "Start" site you created

➤ **WSS_Logging**: The database for storing log information related to WSS_Content

13. Expand the Security node. Note that your two managed SharePoint accounts are listed here (added by SharePoint). Open the account used for the Central Administration application pool, and then select Server Roles. By default this account is granted the dbcreator, public, and securityadmin roles. Open the other managed user account, and it will only have the public role, because it does not need any more permissions to do its job.

14. Close the SQL Server Management Studio tool.

Hint: If the SQL Server Manager Studio tool does not display any detail in the right pane, then press F7 on your keyboard to activate the Object Explorer Details.

How It Works

When installing the SharePoint Central Administration tool and the first intranet, they will be associated with one separate web application each, which will be connected to an SQL content database each. These web applications will run within one application pool each.

To summarize, SharePoint Foundation primarily uses two virtual IIS servers: one for the websites used by the end users, and one for the Central Administration tool for SharePoint. These two virtual servers are referred to as web applications in SharePoint, and they use separate application pools and separate identity accounts. Now you have installed a SharePoint Foundation environment without any database size limitation, thanks to the fact that you used the full SQL Server. This SharePoint installation may be extended with more SharePoint Foundation servers to expand the number of users supported. In short, this is a very flexible SharePoint Foundation solution without compromises.

SharePoint Foundation is now installed as a single-server configuration; that is, using a locally installed SQL Server. The next step is to adjust the settings in Central Administration so the configuration suits the needs of your organization; for example, by enabling SharePoint Foundation to send e-mail, and adding more intuitive URL addresses for the intranet. Appendix B describes these tasks in detail.

Installing a Single Server Using a Remote Microsoft SQL Database

The third, and last, type of installation is known as a *small farm*: It consists of one server running SharePoint Foundation, and another server running SQL Server. Most of the steps in this configuration are identical to the previous configuration with a local Microsoft SQL Server, so the step-by-step instructions listed later in this section will be very short. The reasons for using a remote Microsoft SQL Server are as follow:

➤ **Increased performance:** The SharePoint Foundation server can handle many more users.

➤ **Fault-tolerance:** Connecting SharePoint Foundation to a Microsoft SQL cluster is possible.

➤ **Better economy:** You can use an existing Microsoft SQL Server that you already paid for.

Make sure you have the Microsoft SQL Server installed and running before performing the following steps:

TRY IT OUT **Install a Small SharePoint Farm**

1. Follow all the steps in the previous Try It Out, "Install SharePoint Foundation to Complete the Single-Server Installation," for installing SharePoint Foundation with a local SQL Server, except this one: In step 4h, when running the Configuration Wizard after installing SharePoint Foundation, you need to enter the remote server name where SQL Server is installed, then follow the rest of the steps as described.

2. Next, follow the steps in the earlier Try It Out, "Run the Basic Configuration Settings in SharePoint Central Administration."

3. Finally, follow the steps in the earlier Try It Out, "Check Out New IIS Settings and SQL Databases."

SharePoint Foundation is now installed in a Small Farm configuration; that is, using a remote SQL Server. The next step is to adjust the settings in Central Administration so the configuration suits the needs of your organization; for example, by enabling SharePoint Foundation to send e-mail, and adding more intuitive URL addresses for the intranet. Appendix B describes these tasks in detail.

MIGRATING FROM SQL SERVER EXPRESS TO MICROSOFT SQL SERVER

Many organizations start investigating what SharePoint Foundation can do by installing it using a local SQL Server 2008 Express database. The idea is often to run a pilot project. More often than not, this pilot project then turns into a production environment, with lots of important data that cannot be discarded. I am sure you don't belong to such an organization, but you probably know somebody else who does, right? In previous versions of SharePoint, that is, WSS 3, you could upgrade from SQL Server Express, but that is not the case anymore. Yep, that is the hard truth: There is no way to do an in-place upgrade of an existing SQL Server Express edition to a full SQL Server. The only thing you can do is to take a backup of all data, uninstall SharePoint Foundation, then reinstall it using a full SQL Server, and then restore the data. This section tells you about the only way to upgrade from SQL Server Express.

> **WARNING** *If you try an in-place upgrade of SQL Server 2008 Express, everything will look good at the beginning, but just before the actual upgrade process starts you will get an error stating, "The specified edition upgrade is not supported."*

Doing a File Backup of the SharePoint Foundation Databases

Because changing the database engine is a very sensitive operation, you must make sure to have an escape route, that is, a backup of all data. Either you make a full backup of the server, or you back up the data itself. Once again, you have two options for this. You can simply stop the SQL Server Express database and make a file copy of all the database files, or you can use the STSADM tool that comes along with SharePoint Foundation for backing up parts or the entire content database.

Before you do a backup, you need to know how data is stored in SharePoint. Every website you create in SharePoint Foundation is either a top site or a subsite. Top sites are the start of a site tree with any number of nested subsites, much like a top folder and its subfolders in a file system. SharePoint calls this a *site collection*. All site collections are stored in a SQL Server database. A database that stores site collections like intranets, document centers, and collaboration areas is called a *content database*. One content database can be shared by many thousands of site collections, or each site collection may have its own content database. But a site collection must always belong to a single content database; that is, spreading out data from one site collection over multiple content databases is not possible.

So when discussing how to make a SharePoint backup, you are usually most interested in understanding how to back up either a content database and all of its site collections, or a specific site collection. But several types of databases exist in SharePoint, storing information such as SharePoint farm configuration settings, the Central Administration tool itself, logging databases, and search and index databases. The following two Try It Outs provide steps on how to back up one or more content databases, and how to back up a single site collection. Start by backing up content databases.

TRY IT OUT   **Copy All SharePoint Foundation Database Files Manually**

To make a simple file copy of all SharePoint Foundation content databases in SQL Server Express, do this:

1.   Stop the SQL Server (SHAREPOINT) service (choose Start ⇨ Administrative Tools ⇨ Services) to be able to make a copy of the databases.

2.   Copy all the files in `C:\Program Files\Common Files\Microsoft Shared\Web Server Extensions\14\Data\MSSQL10.SHAREPOINT\MSSQL\DATA` to another file location.

> **NOTE** *To see what content database a site collection uses, open the Central Administration tool, select Manage content databases, and display the web application URL you are interested in. The first site collection is usually stored in WSS_Content. To back up that database, just copy WSS_Content.mdf.*

3. Start the SQL Server (SHAREPOINT) service again.

When later restoring these copies to another SQL Server, using the SQL Server Manager, make sure to "Attach" these databases, not "Restore," because that would require the files to be restored to the exact same file location as the original database files.

> **NOTE** *If the SQL Server upgrade procedure described later in this chapter fails for some reason, you need to restore the database files you just copied. Before that, make sure to have a working SharePoint Foundation and SQL Server Express installation, copy all files back to the original file location, and then restart the server.*

How It Works

You can copy and move complete SharePoint content databases without special third-party tools by stopping SQL Server (to unlock the databases) and the copying the physical SQL Server databases.

Backing Up a Site Collection

The second backup method describes how to back up a specific site collection; for example, the intranet site structure. If your SharePoint Foundation environment consists of multiple site collections, you must repeat the Try It Out "Use STSADM to Back Up a Site Structure" for all of them you want to back up. That is why making a backup of a complete content database is so popular, compared to this method. The result will be files that can be used to restore data into any SharePoint Foundation or SharePoint Server 2010 environment. The tool you use here is STSADM. EXE, although you can do it with PowerShell as well.

> **NOTE** *See Chapter 10 for details about using PowerShell for backup procedures.*

STSADM is stored deep down in the file system, or to be exact, in this folder:

```
C:\Program Files\Common Files\Microsoft Shared\web server extensions\14\BIN
```

STSADM is a command-based tool that you need to run in a command shell. Either you use the preconfigured command shell called the SharePoint 2010 Management Shell, which has the path to STSADM already defined, or you follow the steps in the later Try It Out to add the path to

STSADM so it works in any command shell, not only in the Management Shell. To use the first option:

1. Click Start ⇨ All Programs ⇨ Microsoft SharePoint 2010 Products ⇨ SharePoint 2010 Management Shell.

2. Run whatever STSADM or PowerShell commands you need.

STSADM is a command-based tool that you must run in a command shell. As a SharePoint administrator you will often need to access STSADM and other tools in this folder, and instead of entering the full path to these tools every time, configuring Windows to search in this folder directly is easier. If you are old enough to remember when MS-DOS ruled the PC world, you might remember a system variable named PATH. When you enter a program name in a command shell, Windows looks for that file in all folder paths defined in this variable. The following Try It Out shows you how to add the path to STSADM to this system variable.

TRY IT OUT   Update the PATH System Variable

1. Start Windows Explorer and open `C:\Program Files\Common Files\Microsoft Shared\web server extensions\14\BIN`. Right-click the file path in the Address field and select Copy.

2. Click the Start button to see the Windows start menu.

3. Right-click Computer and select Properties.

4. In the left pane of the dialog that appears, click Advanced system settings. A dialog box named System Properties with multiple tabs appears. Open the Advanced tab and click the Environment Variables button.

5. In the lower pane named System Variables, select PATH and click Edit.

6. In the Variable field, go to the end (use the End key or the right arrow on the keyboard). Type in a semicolon (;) as a separator, and then paste the path you copied in step 1. Then click OK three times to save this modification and close all the dialog boxes.

7. Test the modification by opening a command shell (choose Start ⇨ Run and type `Cmd`); then type `STSADM` in this command shell. If you get a long list of options, you did it right. If not, redo these steps, and make sure to do it right this time.

How It Works

Updating the system PATH parameter will make it possible to execute STSADM commands in any command shell window.

Now you have access to the STSADM command and all other tools in the same folder, regardless of where you are in the folder tree.

If you installed SharePoint Foundation using the Basic installation option, a site collection was automatically created, containing one top site. Appendix B provides more details about how to create new site collections. To make this example simple, suppose you only have a single site collection consisting of one top site with five subsites. The default URL address for the top site is based on the server name, so if the server is named SRV1, then the URL will be `http://srv1`. In the following Try It Out you back up this complete site structure to a file named `SPF-back.bak` in the folder `C:\Bkup`. To do this, follow these steps:

TRY IT OUT Use STSADM to Back Up a Site Structure

1. Log on to the SharePoint Foundation server as an administrator.

2. Open a command shell, type in the following text, and press the Enter key (remember to replace the `http://srv1` to match your own SharePoint environment):

```
Stsadm -o Backup -url http://srv1 -filename c:\bkup\SPF-back.bak
```

3. When the backup is done, you will see the `SPF-back.bak` file in the folder `C:\bkup`.

How It Works

You can back up a site collection to a single file. This site collection can be moved to another SharePoint farm, for example from a test farm to a production farm. See Chapter 10 for more information about backup and restore procedures.

MIGRATING FROM SQL SERVER EXPRESS TO SQL SERVER 2008

By now you should have your SharePoint Foundation environment backed up. It is time to upgrade the SQL Server Express database to the full Microsoft SQL Server 2008. As I said before, this process is complicated, because it requires a complete reinstallation of SharePoint Foundation, this time using a full SQL Server instead. The challenge is that only the content databases will be possible to restore, not the complete configuration (because that would take you back to the SQL Server Express scenario). That is what makes this such a risky and hard process.

Before you continue you must now manually document all configuration settings and customizations in SharePoint 2010 Central Administration, because you will have to redo them after the new installation of SharePoint Foundation:

➤ Note what language your site collections use. If you have multiple language packs, then you must apply the same language packs in the new SharePoint Foundation

➤ All the settings on the Application Management page

➤ All the settings on the System Settings page

➤ All the settings on the General Application Settings page

➤ Any third-party installed web parts, solutions, and features (make sure you know how to install them again)

➤ Any third-party index filters (iFilters), their icons, and modifications of the DOCICON.XML file

➤ Any customized files, like custom site definitions

When you are absolutely sure you have a backup that can restore the SharePoint Foundation in case the upgrade does not work, and that all non-default settings and customizations are documented, then, and only then, can you continue with the following steps.

> **WARNING** *Make sure you have a working backup in case this procedure for any reason does not work as expected! If you do not, you may lose data in SharePoint Foundation!*

TRY IT OUT   **Migrate from SQL Server Express to a Local SQL Server 2008**

1. Log on to the SharePoint Foundation server as an administrator.

2. Make sure no one is using the SharePoint Foundation system; for example, disconnect the SharePoint server from the internal network.

3. Uninstall SharePoint Foundation either by using the Control Panel ⇨ Uninstall a program, or running SharePoint Foundation Setup again and selecting the option to uninstall.

> **NOTE** *During the uninstallation you get a question asking whether the old SharePoint Foundation settings should be preserved or not. Select No.*

4. Delete the `\Program Files\Common Files\Microsoft Shared\Web Server Extensions\14` folder and everything under it.

5. Reboot the server to make sure nothing is stored in memory.

6. Follow all the instructions in the section "Installing a Single Server with a Local Microsoft SQL Database" — except step 4 (where you create the first site collection) in the Try It Out step-by-step instructions, "Run the Basic Configuration Settings in SharePoint Central Administration." The reason for this exception is that you will soon delete that web application.

7. Apply all the settings, customizations, and third-party add-ons you documented before starting this procedure, so the SharePoint Foundation configuration is restored.

8. When you have an SharePoint Foundation server with the same settings as before, it is time to restore the data. If you have a copy of the old content database, usually named WSS_Content, then do this:

    a. Start SQL Server Management Studio (click Start ⇨ All Programs ⇨ Microsoft SQL Server 2008 R2 ⇨ SQL Server Management Studio) and open the local server.

    b. Right-click on Databases in the left pane, and select Attach. The "Attach Database" form opens.

    c. In section "Databases to attach" click Add and select the copied MDF file; for example, `WSS_Content.mdf`, then click OK. The database is now listed among all other databases, but it is not yet used by SharePoint Foundation.

d. Because this database was created with a SQL Server Express, you must change its ownership before it can be used in the new SQL Server. Expand the Security node and then the Logins node and right-click on the account used by SharePoint Central Administration's application pool (as described earlier in this chapter), and select Properties. Then click User mapping and select the attached database (for example, WSS_Content), and set the database role membership to db_owner and public. Click OK to save and close.

9. In SharePoint's Central Administration tool, open the Application Management section, then click Web Applications.

a. Notice an object named SharePoint – 80. This is the one you will recreate and connect the attached database to. Select it and click Delete ➪ Delete Web Application (on the ribbon).

b. On the "Delete Web Application" form that appears, select "Delete content database = Yes," and "Delete II web site = No," then click Delete. A warning appears; click OK to continue.

c. On the ribbon, click New to open a new form. Select "Use an existing IIS web site," and select SharePoint – 80 from the drop-down menu. Further down on the same form, select "Use existing application pool," and then select SharePoint – 80. Finally, in the Database Name field, enter the name of the attached database; for example, WSS_Content, and click OK.

d. When the new web application is created, a status message appears; click OK.

10. Open a new web browser window, and enter the URL to this new web application. After a short delay all the site collections in this content database will be displayed, just like in the old SQL Server Express environment. If the collections do not show up, try this URL: `http://<servername>/_layouts/settings.aspx`. If this page shows up, then you missed restoring something that is used on this site, like a feature or third-party web part. Correct the problem and it will work.

How It Works

Databases from one SharePoint installation can be attached to a new SharePoint environment. This is an easy way of moving all SharePoint content to a new installation.

You can repeat this procedure anytime; it does not have to be directly after the reinstallation of SharePoint Foundation. If you have more content databases to move, just repeat the preceding steps, but in step 9a you need to create a new web application instead of deleting the existing SharePoint – 80. Appendix B shows you more about creating web applications.

> **NOTE** *The procedure for moving from SQL Server Express to a remote SQL Server is almost identical to the preceding procedure; the only steps that differ are that you enter the remote SQL server name when running the SharePoint 2010 Products Configuration Wizard, directly after the installation of SharePoint Foundation, and that you attach the copied MDF file to that remote SQL server.*

UPGRADING WSS 3.0 TO SHAREPOINT FOUNDATION

If you already have a WSS 3.0 environment installed and want to migrate to SharePoint Foundation 2010, then this section is for you. In SharePoint 2010 you have two ways to do an upgrade: an *in-place upgrade* (installing on top of the previous version) and a *content database attach*; that is, attaching the old database to a new SharePoint Foundation server. Throughout the generations of SharePoint, upgrading to a new version has sometimes been hard. Luckily, this is not true with SharePoint 2010. Migrating is a straightforward process, at least under certain conditions:

➤ **WSS 3.0 is a 64-bit version:** If it's not, you cannot do an in-place upgrade to SharePoint Foundation because that is 64-bit only. But you may be able to do the content database attach method.

➤ **WSS is connected to a local or remote 64-bit version of SQL Server 2005 or 2008:** Actually, it will work with a remote 32-bit SQL Server, but it is not supported. A local SQL Server must be 64-bit to be used for the in-place upgrade process; if it's not, try the content database attach method.

➤ **WSS is connected to a SQL Server Express with less than 4GB data per content database:** If not, the max limit of the SQL Server 2008 Express is exceeded and cannot be upgraded. Using the content database attach method should be possible.

➤ **The server meets the new hardware requirements:** At least 4GB of RAM is recommended; see more about the requirements earlier in this chapter.

➤ **WSS is running on a Windows Server 2008:** If it's not, you need to upgrade Windows Server if you want to do the in-place upgrade process.

➤ **Service Pack 2 for WSS is installed:** It is a requirement, and it also contains a new command to check whether the WSS server will be able to upgrade to SharePoint Foundation: STSADM -o preupgradecheck.

As you can see you must stay away from a number of "gotchas." If you can, then upgrading from WSS is easy. The following sections contain the steps for doing both the in-place upgrade and the content database attach method.

Upgrading WSS 3.0 Using the In-Place Method

Using the in-place method to do the upgrade is a very easy and straightforward process, assuming you meet the requirements listed in the previous section; that is, your WSS 3.0 is running on a 64-bit Windows Server 2008, and its SQL Server is either a SQL Server Express with less than 4GB content databases, or is using a full SQL Server 2005 or 2008.

Start by running the preupgradecheck command to find any issues before you start, as shown in the following Try It Out:

TRY IT OUT   Run the preupgradecheck in STSADM

1. Log on to the WSS server as an administrator.

2. Open a command window and run STSADM -o preupgradecheck (this assumes you added the BIN folder to the system PATH variable, as described earlier in this chapter).

This check may need some time to complete, especially if you have lots of data and features installed. When it's done, the result appears as a web page, as shown in Figure A-9.

If any issues are listed, you must first solve them before upgrading to SharePoint Foundation 2010. The result page contains links to more information.

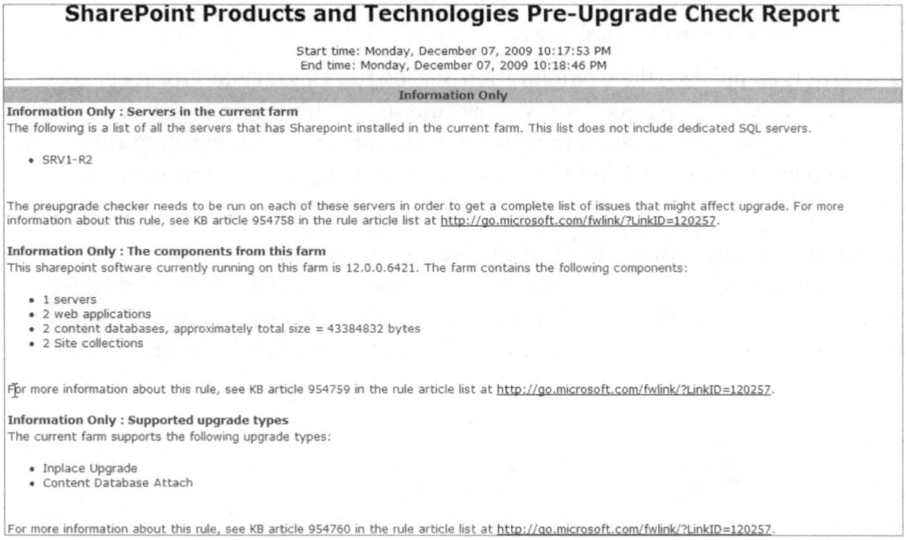

SharePoint Products and Technologies Pre-Upgrade Check Report

Start time: Monday, December 07, 2009 10:17:53 PM
End time: Monday, December 07, 2009 10:18:46 PM

Information Only

Information Only : Servers in the current farm
The following is a list of all the servers that has Sharepoint installed in the current farm. This list does not include dedicated SQL servers.

- SRV1-R2

The preupgrade checker needs to be run on each of these servers in order to get a complete list of issues that might affect upgrade. For more information about this rule, see KB article 954758 in the rule article list at http://go.microsoft.com/fwlink/?LinkID=120257.

Information Only : The components from this farm
This sharepoint software currently running on this farm is 12.0.0.6421. The farm contains the following components:

- 1 servers
- 2 web applications
- 2 content databases, approximately total size = 43384832 bytes
- 2 Site collections

For more information about this rule, see KB article 954759 in the rule article list at http://go.microsoft.com/fwlink/?LinkID=120257.

Information Only : Supported upgrade types
The current farm supports the following upgrade types:

- Inplace Upgrade
- Content Database Attach

For more information about this rule, see KB article 954760 in the rule article list at http://go.microsoft.com/fwlink/?LinkID=120257.

FIGURE A-9

How It Works

The Preupgradecheck operation will check an existing WSS 2007 installation and list any issues that may prohibit an upgrade to SharePoint Foundation 2010.

If no issues are reported, it is time to perform the actual in-place upgrade; here is a summary of how to install SharePoint Foundation (the detailed steps are described earlier in this appendix):

1. Download SharePoint Foundation with the same language as WSS 3.

2. Run the setup file for SharePoint Foundation.

3. Select the "Install software prerequisites" option and complete these steps. Note: Your server will reboot when completed.

4. Log on as the administrator again. This automatically starts a new process to complete the installation of the prerequisites. Click Finish to close the page that appears.

5. Run the setup program for SharePoint Foundation again. Select Install SharePoint Foundation.

6. After accepting the license agreement, the "Upgrade earlier versions" page appears, indicating that it found the WSS installation and that it will do an in-place upgrade. Click Install Now to continue. This step takes several minutes to complete, depending on the amount of data and the server hardware.

7. The next page, "Run Configuration Wizard," that appears is where you start the configuration wizard. Click Close.

8. The configuration wizard starts. Click Next.

9. When the wizard is completed, the Configuration Successful, Upgrade In Process page appears. It tells you that the upgrade process now runs as a timer job; that is, it is a background process, and you just have to wait for it to complete. Click Finish to close this page; this also opens the Central Administration tool and its Upgrade Status page (see Figure A-10).

For more details about the upgrade process: Look at the log file named `Upgrade-<date_and_time_and_number>.log` in this folder: `C:\Program Files\Common Files\Microsoft Shared\Web Server Extensions\14\LOGS`. When this log file contains the text "Upgrade session finished successfully" near the end of the file, the timer job is completed and the upgrade process is done.

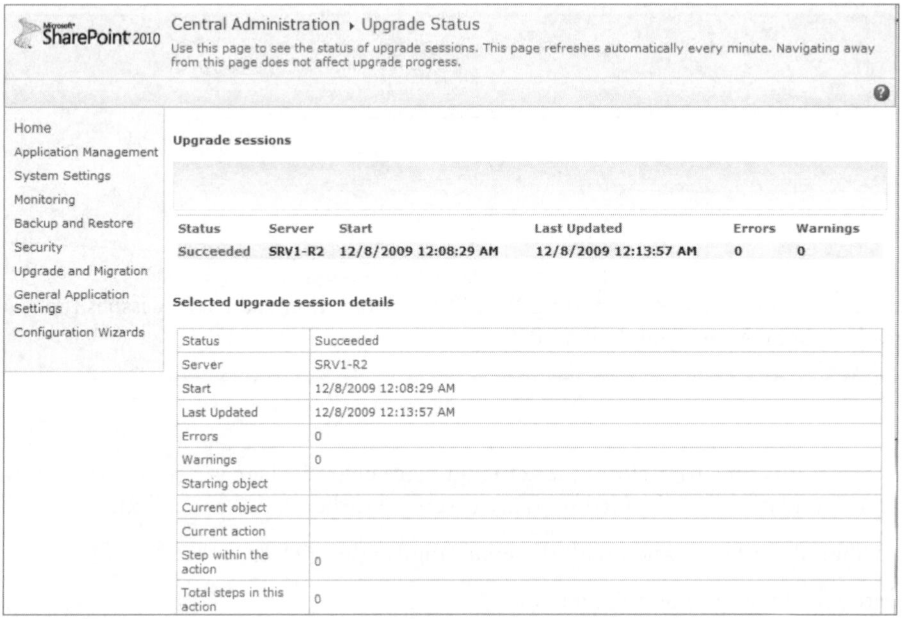

SharePoint 2010	Central Administration ▸ Upgrade Status					
	Use this page to see the status of upgrade sessions. This page refreshes automatically every minute. Navigating away from this page does not affect upgrade progress.					

Home	**Upgrade sessions**					
Application Management						
System Settings						
Monitoring						
Backup and Restore	**Status**	**Server**	**Start**	**Last Updated**	**Errors**	**Warnings**
Security	Succeeded	SRV1-R2	12/8/2009 12:08:29 AM	12/8/2009 12:13:57 AM	0	0
Upgrade and Migration						
General Application Settings	**Selected upgrade session details**					
Configuration Wizards	Status	Succeeded				
	Server	SRV1-R2				
	Start	12/8/2009 12:08:29 AM				
	Last Updated	12/8/2009 12:13:57 AM				
	Errors	0				
	Warnings	0				
	Starting object					
	Current object					
	Current action					
	Step within the action	0				
	Total steps in this action	0				

FIGURE A-10

If you open this site collection, you will find that it looks almost exactly as before, and this is no mistake. Your WSS is now converted to SharePoint Foundation "under the hood," but the user interface is still WSS. Some organizations will be very pleased with this, because their users can continue to use the sites just as they were in WSS. Other organizations want to take advantage of the new interface, with its ribbon and other new features. The great thing when upgrading to SharePoint Foundation is that you, the administrator, can test the new user interface and if you don't like it, you can return to the WSS interface; if you like it, then make it a permanent change.

Use the steps in the following Try It Out to test, and finally switch to, the new user interface.

TRY IT OUT   **Test the Visual Upgrade Feature**

1.   Log on as the farm administrator.

2.   Open the upgraded site in Internet Explorer and check out all sites; note how similar it is to the old WSS user interface.

3.   It's time to test the new interface. Select the start site, open the Site Action menu, and select Visual Upgrade. A web form opens where you can preview the new user interface, switch permanently, or display the old user interface. See Figure A-11.

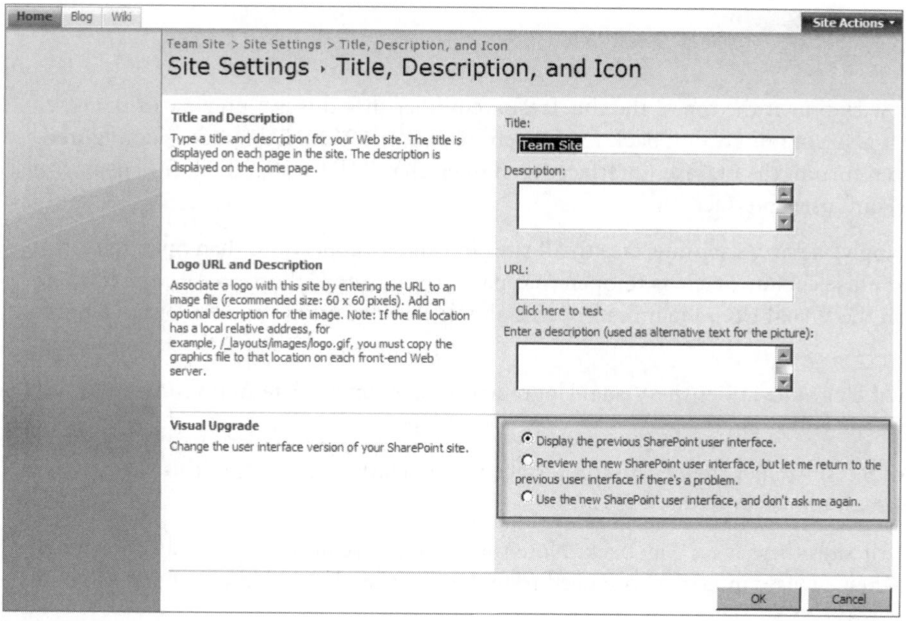

FIGURE A-11

4.   In the Visual Upgrade section, select the option "Preview the new SharePoint user interface, but let me return to the previous user interface if there's a problem" and click OK. The new user interface is applied to the current site; see Figure A-12.

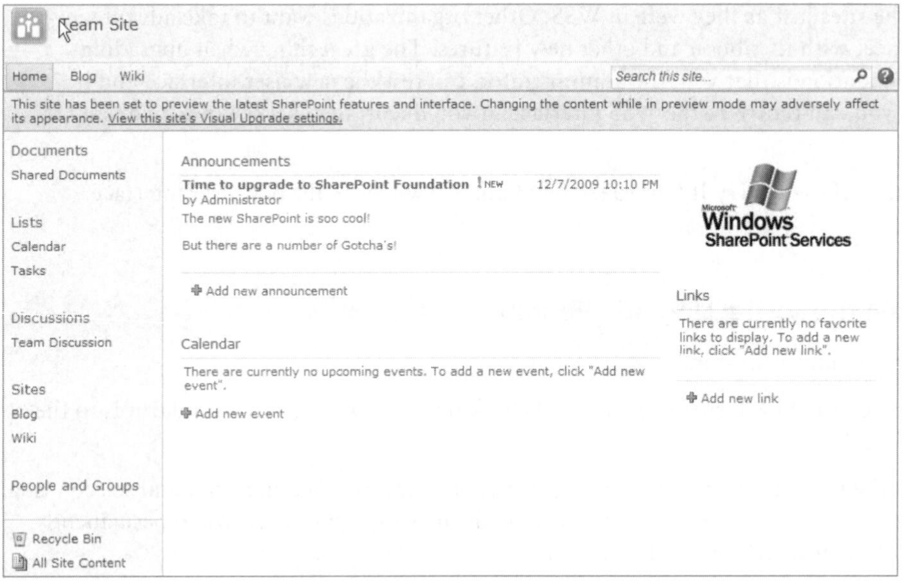

FIGURE A-12

5. Notice the yellow ribbon at the top of the site. It is a reminder that this is a preview of the new user interface; it also contains a link back to the web form where Visual Upgrade is configured. If you decide to return to the old user interface, then open that web form and select "Display the previous SharePoint user interface."

6. If you want to apply the new user interface to all sites in this site collection, then open the Site Actions menu, and select Site Settings to open that page. In the Site Collection Administration section, click on the Visual Upgrade link to open a simple configuration page for Visual Upgrade settings:

   ➤ **Hide Visual Upgrade:** Hides the Visual Upgrade option from the Site Actions menu for all sites in this site collection.

   ➤ **Update All Sites:** Applies the new user interface permanently in all sites in this site collection.

If you apply Update All Sites there is no way back. Note that if you have multiple site collections, and want them all to use the new user interface, you need to make this visual upgrade switch in each and every one of them.

How It Works

The Visual Upgrade feature makes it possible to test and finally apply the new graphical user interface to migrated WSS 3.0 sites.

Upgrading WSS 3.0 Using the Content Database Attach Method

Using the content database attach method to upgrade WSS 3.0 is also straightforward. Basically you take a copy of the WSS database, attach it to the new SQL Server 2008 in SharePoint Foundation, and then connect it to a web application. That is it. As described earlier, if the content database you move is larger than 4GB, then SharePoint Foundation must use a full SQL Server, not the SQL Server Express. As described in the section about in-place upgrade, make sure to run the preupgradecheck in STSADM before trying to upgrade them with the attach method.

Earlier, in the Try It Out "Copy All SharePoint Foundation Database Files Manually," you learned a very simple method of copying databases such as WSS_Content (both the MDF file and the LOG file), and then attaching the databases into the new SQL Server, described in steps 8a–8d, in the Try It Out "Migrate from SQL Server Express to a Local SQL Server 2008."

> **NOTE** *Note that the content database attach method previously described requires that WSS be disabled during the time it takes to copy the content databases. In some organizations, this is unacceptable. If so, you can set the database to be copied in read-only mode, and then copy it; this makes it possible for all users to continue to read all data in WSS, but not write or change anything. The detailed steps for this method are described in several websites; for example,* `http://technet.microsoft.com/en-us/sharepoint/ee517215.aspx`.

After attaching the content databases to the new SQL Server, then configure the upgrade of these databases using the steps in the following Try It Out.

TRY IT OUT Upgrade Databases Using the Database Attach Method

1. Log on to the WSS server as an administrator.

2. Open a command window and run STSADM -o preupgradecheck (this assumes you added the BIN folder to the system PATH variable, as described earlier in this chapter).

3. Stop the SQL Server (SHAREPOINT) service so you can make a copy of the databases.

4. Copy the MDF and corresponding LOG files in `C:\Program Files\Common Files\Microsoft Shared\Web Server Extensions\14\Data\MSSQL10.SHAREPOINT\MSSQL\DATA` that you want to upgrade to SharePoint Foundation. If the filenames do not conflict with existing databases, then you may store these files in the same folder as the other database files on the new SQL Server (usually `C:\Program Files\Microsoft SQL Server\MSSQL10_50.MSSQLSERVER\MSSQL\DATA`).

5. Start the SQL Server (SHAREPOINT) service again. But make sure users don't add any new information to the WSS sites, because it will not be copied to the SharePoint Foundation server.

6. Make sure the new SharePoint Foundation server has the same configuration settings and solutions in Central Administration as the old WSS server to make it possible to upgrade the databases. In this example, you attach a copied database named `WSS_Content.MDF`:

    a. Start SQL Server Management Studio and open the local server.

    b. Right-click on Databases in the left pane and select Attach. A form named "Attach Databases" opens.

    c. Click Add and select the file you copied; that is, `WSS_Content.MDF`. This will list the database in the top pane. Note that the current owner is the user account currently logged on (the administrator account). You must change it to the same user account used for the Central Administration application pool identity; click the Owner drop-down menu and this account should be listed. When ready, click OK. The database is now listed among all the other attached databases, but it is not yet used by SharePoint Foundation.

7. Before you can use this content database in SharePoint Foundation, you must upgrade it. In this example, you want to add the new database to an existing web application with the URL address `http://srv1`, but as a second site collection named "abc," so its URL will be `http://srv1/sites/abc`. You also want to preserve the old user interface initially (you can switch to the new user interface later on).

8. Open a command shell, and enter `STSADM -o addcontentdb -url http://srv1/sites/abc -databasename WSS_Content -preserveolduserexperience true`.

> **NOTE** *Note that you cannot move a content database created in MOSS 2007 to a SharePoint Foundation farm, because SharePoint Foundation is missing a lot of site definitions that MOSS uses.*

9. After the upgrade process of this content database is completed, you can open the site using the URL you entered earlier in step 7. As when you're doing an in-place upgrade, the result is a site collection that has preserved the old user interface. To upgrade it, use the Site Action menu and select Visual Upgrade, as described earlier in the "Upgrading WSS 3.0 Using the In-Place Method" section.

How It Works

A content database from WSS 3.0 can be copied and attached to the SQL server that SharePoint Foundation 2010 uses. This will then start the upgrade of this database to the new database structure used for SharePoint Foundation.

UNINSTALLING SHAREPOINT FOUNDATION

The final section of this chapter is about removing SharePoint Foundation. You can remove just a single site collection, for example, one used for your team sites; a web application, including its content databases; or a complete SharePoint Foundation installation and all of its databases. By default, all databases remain after SharePoint Foundation is uninstalled, so you can later reinstall SharePoint Foundation and reattach to these databases.

> **NOTE** *If you want to reinstall SharePoint Foundation on the same server, you need to remove all databases from the previous installation to avoid name conflict. SQL Server Express stores all databases in* `C:\Program Files\Common Files\Microsoft Shared\Web Server Extensions\14\Data\MSSQL10 .SHAREPOINT\MSSQL\DATA\`.

Removing a Single Site Collection

This process removes a given site collection in SharePoint Foundation from its web application, but it does not remove the binary files from the server, or its content database files. For example, you may have a test environment using one web application and a production SharePoint Foundation using another web application on the same physical Windows 2008 Server, and now you want to copy the site collection between these web applications.

To remove the test environment, follow these steps:

1. Start the SharePoint Central Administration tool.
2. Open the Application Management page.
3. Click "Delete site collection" in the Site Collections section.
4. Click the yellow menu No selection, and select Change Site Collection.
5. Verify that the web application is set to the one that contains the site collection you want to delete. If it's not, click on its menu, select "Change web application," and then select the correct web application.
6. Select the site collection to be removed. When you are absolutely sure it is the right one, click OK.
7. Details about the site collection to be removed appear; verify that this is the correct site collection. If it is, click Delete, and then OK to permanently delete this website.

The web application is still intact and may be used for new site collections. If you have other site collections in the same web application, they will not be affected, because the previous steps just deleted one specific site collection, not the complete web application.

Removing a Web Application

This process is very similar to removing a single site collection, but it has bigger consequences: If you remove an existing web application, all its site collections are also removed. Note that a web application may have any number of site collections, although the default limit is 15,000. To delete a specific web application, including its site collections, follow the steps below:

1. Start the SharePoint Central Administration tool.
2. Open the Application Management page.

3. Click Manage web applications in the Web Applications section. A list of all existing web applications appears.

4. Select the web application to be deleted — double-check that it is the right one! Click the Delete button in the ribbon.

5. A dialog form named "Delete Web Application" appears, where you can set whether to delete all content databases for this web application, as well, and whether you want to remove the IIS website used by this web application. If you are not sure what to delete, then say No to both of these options, because reactivating the web application and all of its site collections will be easy, by creating a new web application connecting it to the same IIS website and content database. Click Delete to complete this form, and then OK to confirm the delete operation.

Removing SharePoint Foundation Completely

A more drastic delete operation is to remove SharePoint Foundation completely from the Windows 2008 Server. This does not actually remove the database, be it the SQL Server Express or the full Microsoft SQL Server. If you also want to remove these databases, you must do this manually after SharePoint Foundation is uninstalled.

To remove SharePoint Foundation completely, follow these steps:

1. Choose Start ⇨ Control Panel ⇨ Uninstall a Program; this opens the "Programs and Features" form.

2. Select Microsoft SharePoint Foundation 2010 and then click the Uninstall button.

3. SharePoint's Setup dialog box opens and asks, "Are you sure you want to remove Microsoft SharePoint Foundation 2010 from your computer?" Click Yes to confirm you want to remove SharePoint Foundation. A warning appears: "Click OK to accept to delete SharePoint Foundation." After SharePoint Foundation is deleted, click OK to close the page that appears afterwards.

> **NOTE** *If this SharePoint Foundation installation was using SQL Server Express, it is also removed, but its database files (MDF and LOG) remain intact and can be attached to a new SQL Server. If the SharePoint Foundation installation was using a full SQL Server, it is not affected, and all SharePoint Foundation databases remain intact. Make sure to remove these databases if you want to clean up everything related to SharePoint Foundation.*

When you remove SharePoint Foundation, you also remove all virtual IIS websites used by SharePoint Foundation, along with its application pools. However, the Default Web Site remains after the installation, along with its application pool.

▶ **WHAT YOU LEARNED IN THIS CHAPTER**

TOPIC	KEY CONCEPTS
SharePoint Foundation Basics	Abbreviated SharePoint Foundation.
	STS was the first version of SharePoint Foundation. You will still today find several references to the acronym STS, although it actually refers to SharePoint Foundation.
	SharePoint Foundation can be installed as Stand-alone or Farm mode.
Installation Modes	Stand-alone means that SharePoint Foundation is installed on a server, including the integrated SQL Server Express edition.
	Farm mode means that SharePoint Foundation is configured to use a full SQL Server, either installed on the same server as SharePoint Foundation or a remote server.
SharePoint Foundation Requirements	SharePoint Foundation is 64-bit only.
	A 64-bit version of Windows Server 2008 or later is required.
	A 64-bit version of SQL Server (2005 or 2008) is required, even if it is a remote SQL server.
	Windows 2008 must be configured to run IIS and .NET Framework 3.51.
	For accepting incoming e-mail, Windows Server 2008 must be configured to run the SMTP role.
SQL Database options	SharePoint Foundation with an embedded version of SQL Server Express.
	SharePoint Foundation with a local SQL Server Express (Standard version).
	SharePoint Foundation with a local full SQL Server.
	SharePoint Foundation with a remote full SQL Server.
SharePoint Foundation Content	70 percent of all content in SharePoint Foundation is files and documents.
Application Pools	Virtual IIS storages for web applications.
	Each Application Pool is given a private memory area.
	Each application pool has one identity account – this account is used by SharePoint when accessing SQL Server.

continues

(continued)

TOPIC	KEY CONCEPTS
Web Applications	Hosts for web solutions, such as SharePoint Site Collections.
	One web application can host up to 15.000 site collections, by default – this value can be changed.
	Each Web application is connected to one or more SQL content databases.
	A web application is always associated with a specific application pool.
Database types	Configuration databases, such as Config_DB used by all SharePoint servers in a farm.
	Content databases, such as WSS_Content, that contain all content stored in SharePoint, such as files, documents, and list content.
Setup of SharePoint Foundation	The SharePoint.exe is the complete SharePoint Foundation installation package.
	Use the flag /Extract:<path> to extract all files and folders in this package.
	By default, SharePoint setup.exe will create a web application named "SharePoint – 80" that will store the first site collection.
SharePoint Foundation Configuration tools	STSADM: a command shell tool that will probably be replaced by PowerShell in the next release of SharePoint.
	PowerShell 2.0: an advanced, yet easy-to-use command shell tool that supports more than twice the number of operations, compared to STSADM.
Upgrading WSS to SharePoint Foundation	Run the STSADM -o preupgradecheck before trying to upgrade from WSS – it will report any issue that may prohibit the upgrade process.
	Content databases from WSS 3.0 can be attached to the SQL server used by SharePoint Foundation – They will then be upgraded to the new SharePoint Foundation database structure.
	Upgraded WSS sites will still have the same graphical user interface as in WSS – use the Visual Upgrade feature to first test the new interface, then do a permanent switch.
Delete and Uninstall SharePoint Foundation	A specific site collection can be deleted.
	A specific web application can be deleted, with its associated content databases, including all their site collections.
	A complete SharePoint Foundation installation can be deleted.

Configuring SharePoint Foundation 2010

WHAT YOU WILL LEARN IN THIS APPENDIX:

➤ SharePoint Administration

➤ Configuring Administrative Features

➤ Managing Security

➤ Managing Search and indexing

Appendix A covers the different installation scenarios available and how to set up SharePoint Foundation to work with either SQL Server Express or the full Microsoft SQL Server. This appendix covers more about configuring and managing an installed SharePoint Foundation, including how to activate and configure the search features. To successfully manage the SharePoint Foundation environment, you need to understand important concepts, such as websites, site collections, and the security model. The objective in this appendix is to give you the knowledge needed to set up the WSS environment so that it will match the needs of your users.

Before you start configuring SharePoint Foundation, check to see whether your server has the Internet Explorer Enhanced Security Configuration setting activated. If it is active, you will be prompted several times when opening web pages, including SharePoint's Central Administration tool, which may become annoying. You find this setting in the Server Manager (see Figure B-1), and its Configure IE ESC link in the Security Information section.

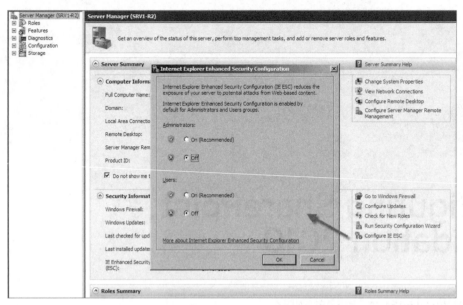

FIGURE B-1

If this setting is active, you may get problems performing some administrative tasks on the SharePoint server itself, depending on how your Internet Explorer is configured. If the URL used by SharePoint's Central Administration is something other than the Local Sites or Trusted Site zones, you may not be able to run scripts or execute code necessary for some parts of the SharePoint administration. You can solve this by disabling the Internet Explorer Enhanced Security Configuration (IE ESC) for the administrators, other users, or both:

1. Open the Server Manager (its button is by default added to the task bar on the desktop).

2. Select the Server Manager (*the_server_name*) node in the left pane.

3. Click Configure IE ESC.

4. On the page that appears, select whether you want to disable IS ESC for the administrators only, for users, or both. For a production server, you will probably just disable it for the administrators. Click OK to save and close.

5. Close the Server Manager.

IMPORTANT CONCEPTS FOR THE SHAREPOINT FOUNDATION ENVIRONMENT

SharePoint Foundation 2010 is a web application. It uses websites and web-related concepts to do its job. Some of these terms and functionality may be well known to you already. But some have very specific meanings in the SharePoint environment. You may recall from previous chapters that SharePoint Foundation is the basic foundation for SharePoint and that a big, but optional, package of extended services and functionality called SharePoint Server 2010 that you can add on top of

SharePoint Foundation, just as its name indicates. In other words, even if you implement SharePoint Server, you will still need the information in this appendix to understand how the SharePoint Foundation part works, because the basic structure and functionality in SharePoint 2010 is based on SharePoint Foundation, regardless of whether you have an SharePoint Foundation site or an SharePoint Server site.

The Architecture in SharePoint Foundation

Figure B-2 shows the relation between IIS, application pools, web applications, and site collections. Just like an onion, IIS consists of layers within layers. Let's start from the inside of this figure, that is, the site collection, and work towards the outer layer:

➤ A *site collection* is a top level site that acts as a container for zero or more *subsites*, also known as *subwebs*. In the figure, you see two site collections with two subsites each.

➤ Each site collection runs within a web application.

➤ A *web application* may host multiple site collections. In the figure you see three web applications, but only the first contains site collections.

➤ A web application is connected to one or more content databases. In the figure you see that each web application is connected to a content database (stored in SQL Server).

➤ Each web application is contained inside an application pool. In the figure you see two application pools, one with two web applications, and one more with one web application.

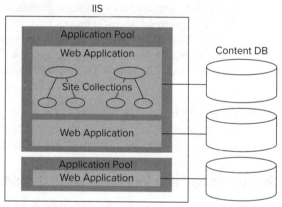

FIGURE B-2

➤ All application pools run within the Internet Information Services, IIS.

Another way to express the relations between these objects is to start from the outside and work toward the inner layer:

➤ The *IIS* is a service within Windows Server that allows any type of web-based program to run; for example, SharePoint.

➤ Inside IIS are one or more application pools, which are similar to virtual environments; for example, each application pool has its own memory space, CPU resources, and security ID (a user account).

➤ Inside each application pool are one or more web applications. A web application is an IIS website that has been extended by SharePoint.

➤ Each web application is connected to one or more SQL content databases. This means that all data that is put into a web application will therefore be stored in the connected content database.

➤ Web applications host one or more site collections. All the data in a site collection is stored in one single content database. Splitting a site collection between multiple content databases is not possible, but one single web application can host multiple site collections that use one content database each.

In plain English this means that all the documents, pictures, and other types of data that are stored in a site collection are therefore stored in the content database that is connected to the web application that hosts this site collection. So if you make a copy of all the content databases used by a web application, you will have a copy of all site collections that are hosted by that web application. If you stop a web application, you will make all its site collections unreachable, regardless of which content database they use.

> **NOTE** *An easy way to copy a site collection from one SharePoint server to another is to make a copy of its content database, attach it to another SQL server, and add it to a web application on that other SharePoint server — perfect for making a copy of a production environment to use in a test environment. If the original SharePoint server has extra add-ons installed, such as solutions or web parts, then the second server must also have the same add-ons installed.*

This is how SharePoint is designed. After an installation you will find multiple site collections stored in different web applications and all their data is stored in SQL Server content databases. The next section covers the two basic types of site collections used in SharePoint Foundation.

Administrative Websites and User Websites

SharePoint Foundation has two basic types of websites that are installed by default:

➤ The SharePoint Central Administration website is used for advanced configuration and management of SharePoint Foundation; for example, to create new web applications and site collections.

➤ The user website, typically based on the Team Site template, is also referred to as the intranet site (the project sites, meeting workspaces, and so on), and it contains the actual information that is shared between users, such as documents, lists, and images. There can be as many of these websites as needed.

One important distinction between these two types of websites is that only a SharePoint administrator has access to the administrative website, whereas everyone typically uses the user websites. As you may remember from Appendix A, the best practice is to use two different SharePoint web applications for these web applications; that is, they are using different virtual IIS web servers. See Figure B-3:

➤ **SharePoint Central Administration v4:** Used by the administrative website, it runs in its own application pool (default name: SharePoint Central Administration v3). By default this website uses a randomly selected TCP port, but you can set this number manually if you choose anything other than the Basic installation mode.

➤ **SharePoint – 80:** Used by the user website, it runs in a separate application pool (default name: SharePoint – 80). Note that the name for this virtual server may be different if you created a separate virtual server for this use; Default Web Site is also frequently used for this type of website. By default this website uses TCP port 80 to enable end users to easily use it.

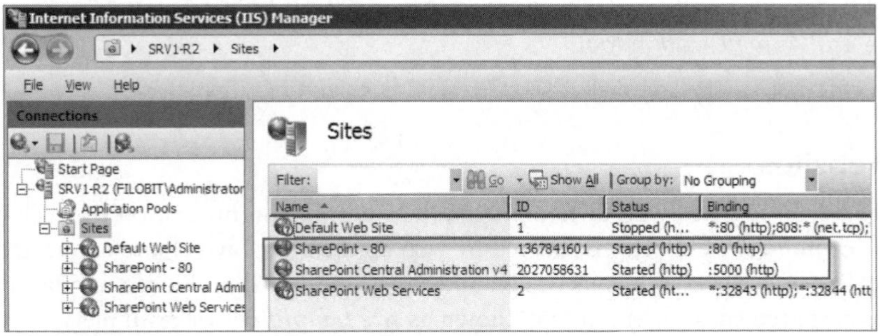

FIGURE B-3

If, for any reason, you need to stop all users from accessing the SharePoint Foundation environment, open the IIS Manager tool and right-click the SharePoint – 80 (or whatever virtual IIS server the user website uses) and select Manage Web Site ➪ Stop. To activate the same web application, right-click it, and select Manage Web Site ➪ Start.

Working with the SharePoint Central Administration Tool

You have already used the Central Administration website in Appendix A when installing SharePoint Foundation. This website allows the administrator to do more advanced administration and configuration of the SharePoint Foundation environment, such as create new web applications, create site collections, configure the content databases, and define what database server to use. In this appendix you learn more about all the important configuration settings available using this administration tool, and how to get the most out of your SharePoint Foundation environment.

SharePoint has its own security system that ensures only users with the proper permissions are able to access the Central Administration tool. By default, only the user account that you used when installing SharePoint Foundation will have access. To start this admin tool, click Start ➪ Microsoft SharePoint 2010 Products ➪ SharePoint 2010 Central Administration. If you know the TCP port number used by the web application that hosts this tool, you can also open a web browser on the server and enter the URL to the Central Administration tool, including its port number. For example, if the port number is 5000 you can open the admin tool using the URL address http://localhost:5000 — the string localhost will be replaced by the server name. The TCP port number was either randomly generated when you ran the configuration wizard after the installation of SharePoint Foundation, or if you installed a server farm with a Complete installation, you had the option of setting a specific port number, as described in Appendix A.

Be sure to protect this administrative website. If a malicious user can access it, that user can remove content or even remove SharePoint Foundation from the virtual IIS server. In other words, be very careful with the user account that is listed as SharePoint Farm Administrators (Central Administration ➪ Manage the Farm Administrators Group).

> **NOTE** *Use Secure Socket Layer (SSL) to protect the administrative site if you need to access it over insecure connections, like the Internet. If you don't need Internet access to this site, configure your firewall to prohibit access to the URL used by the Central Administration tool.*

Working with User Websites

Websites designed for end users are really no different from the Central Administration tool. The tool also consists of one or more site collections, hosted by web applications, which are connected to SQL content databases. The only difference is its design and functionality. SharePoint Foundation comes with several preconfigured sites for end users, known as *site templates*, for example:

➤ Team Site

➤ Blog Sites

➤ Meeting Workspaces (multiple templates)

To use them, you create a site collection and select one of these site templates. When you create subsites in this site collection, you also select a site template. As mentioned earlier, this site collection will, by default, be created in the web application SharePoint – 80, and its default content database is named WSS_Content. Later in this chapter you will learn more about site templates.

> **NOTE** *Only the farm administrator has the permission to create new site collections. New site collections are created by using the Central Administration tool, by STSADM, or by PowerShell scripts.*

USING THE CENTRAL ADMINISTRATION PAGE IN SHAREPOINT FOUNDATION

SharePoint Foundation offers a great number of configuration settings and features. If you want to learn them all, prepare to invest lots of time, especially if you also want to learn what you can do with the command tool STSADM and its new and smarter cousin, PowerShell. These command tools are important, because they offer some really great advantages compared to the graphical Central Administration tool:

➤ Enable more commands and functions, especially with PowerShell

➤ Enable you to easily rerun complex procedures by creating reusable scripts

➤ Can be used to document commands and procedures applied to SharePoint Foundation

STSADM has been around since the first version of SharePoint (2001), but will most likely be replaced by the new command script environment PowerShell that Microsoft uses for all server applications. SharePoint Foundation 2010 can still run them both, but I strongly advise you to learn PowerShell now: It is more flexible, and it supports more commands and functions than STSADM. In the following section you will learn about the commands in the Central Administration tool for SharePoint, but all of these could also be done with the command script tools.

Due to the large number of configuration settings, this tool is divided into eight different sections, plus one startup page named Central Administration (see Figure B-4) that shows a mix of the most common configuration links, regardless of what section they belong to, so don't be confused if you see the same links show up in multiple pages in this tool. The sections that follow focus on the most common and useful settings for a typical SharePoint Foundation environment.

> **NOTE** The Security section won't be discussed here because security is discussed in greater length later in this chapter in the "Security Settings in SharePoint Foundation" section.

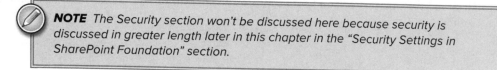

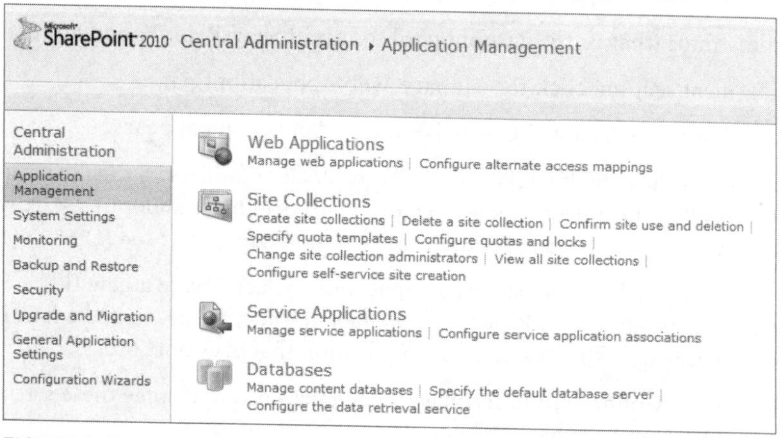

FIGURE B-4

Notice that the headings on this page are links, so you can choose to click on one, or click on the link in the left navigation pane, to open the corresponding page with all its settings. There is also a list named Resources that you can use to add links to the commands and settings you use most. In fact, you can add links to resources outside this tool, if you need to.

Application Management

Application Management consists of four sections: Web Applications, Site Collections, Service Applications, and Databases, each consisting of multiple links to configuration pages. The links and their settings on the Application Management page are used by the SharePoint administrator regularly; for example, when you need to create a new site collection in an existing web application, or when you want to manage a service application. The following sections contain more detailed descriptions of these settings.

Manage Web Applications

You use the Manage Web Applications settings (under Web Applications in Figure B-4) to manage existing web applications or create new ones. You may remember that web applications are used for hosting one or more site collections, and that every web application has at least one content database in the SQL Server.

In the following Try It Out you create a new web application called Projects (using port 80, which is already taken, so enter **Projects** as the Host Header name as well) that will use a new application pool called Projects (that is, the same name as the web application, which makes it easy to understand they are related), and connect this web application to a content database named Projects_Content.

TRY IT OUT   **Create a New Web Application**

1. Log on as the farm administrator (that is, the account used to install SharePoint Foundation).

2. In the Application Management section, click the Manage Web Applications page.

3. Click New on the Ribbon: A new form named Create New Web Application appears.

   a. For Authentication, accept the default Classic Mode Authentication, unless you really have a need for the new Claims Based Authentication mechanism. To read more about this start with the article found at `http://technet.microsoft.com/en-us/sharepoint/ee518670.aspx`.

   b. The IIS Web Site section is used for the new web application. Select Create a new IIS website, enter **Projects** as its name, and **Projects** as the Host Header name, to make it unique (otherwise, a conflict arises with the existing web application that uses port 80).

   c. Accept the default Security Configuration settings; if you later need to change these settings, then open this web application and change them.

   d. Note that the URL says `http://Projects:80`.

   e. In the Application Pool section, select Create new application pool, enter the name **Projects**, open the Configurable menu, and select the same account used for the SharePoint – 80 application pool (to see it, open IIS Manager, and check the Identity setting for SharePoint – 80).

   f. Make sure the Database Server is correct. Change the Database Name to **Projects_Content**.

   g. Accept the other default settings (unless you want to disable the Enable Customer Experience Improvement Program), and click OK at the end of this form to save and close it.

The new web application will now be created.

How It Works

You create a web application in SharePoint Central Administration when you need a container for one or more site collections. A web application will be connected to one or more content databases, stored in SQL Server.

After the new web application is created, you need to do one more thing before you create site collections in it: Add its Host Header name, Projects, to the Domain Name Server (DNS) in your network, and make sure it points to the SharePoint Foundation server. You have two options for this in DNS: Either create a canonical name (CNAME, which means an alias), or create an A-record (that is, the IP number) identical to the existing SharePoint Foundation server. In the following Try It Out, you add a CNAME in the FILOBIT.COM domain that will be an alias for the SharePoint Foundation server named SRV1:

TRY IT OUT Create a CNAME in DNS

1. Log on as the domain administrator on an Active Directory domain controller.
2. Open the DNS Manager (choose Start ⇨ Administrative Tools ⇨ DNS).
3. Expand the Forward Lookup Zones node in the left pane.
4. Right-click on your domain name, and select New Alias (CNAME):
   a. Alias name: **Projects** (that is, the Host Header name you entered in step 3b in the preceding Try It Out)
   b. Fully qualified domain name (FQDN) for target host: `srv1.filobit.com`
   c. Verify that the new alias name is listed and points to the SharePoint Foundation server.
5. Close the DNS Manager.

How It Works

When using Host Header names for SharePoint web parts, you must add a corresponding DNS entry, either an alias name (CNAME) or host name (A record) that points to the SharePoint server.

It may take a few minutes for the new DNS entry to be updated on all servers. If you want to force the update, open a command prompt, enter `IPCONFIG /FLUSHDNS`, and press Enter. The next logical step would typically be to create one or more site collections in the new Projects web application, but before you learn about this, some other settings for web applications are of interest.

Open the web application settings again (Application Management ⇨ Manage web applications). Select the web application you just created; that is, Projects (see Figure B-5). Notice that a number of buttons on the Ribbon get activated (in fact, all of them, if you have full access). Click on the text

General Settings right under the icon (not the icon, because it opens the default settings only); a list of the following options appears:

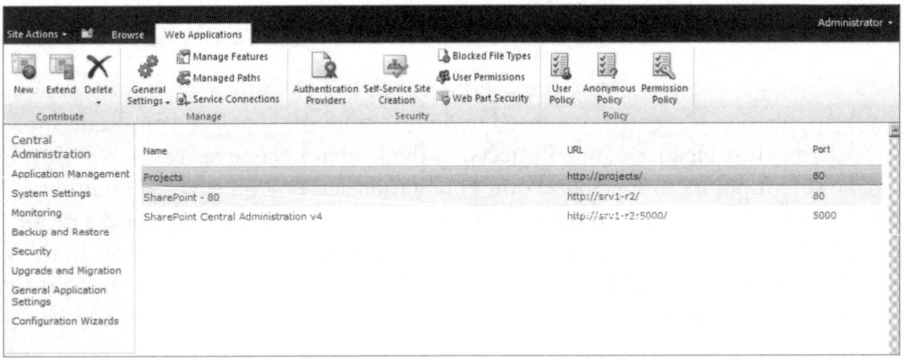

FIGURE B-5

➤ **General Settings:** Use this for setting a large number of options for the site collections stored in this web application:

    ➤ The default time zones (default: no zone selected)

    ➤ The default disk quota, that is, maximum data volume allowed (default: no quota)

    ➤ Whether the Enable Person Name smart tag and online status should be enabled or not (default: Yes)

    ➤ Whether alerts (that is, e-mail notifications) are on or off (default: On)

    ➤ The maximum number of alerts a user can create (default: 500)

    ➤ Whether RSS feeds are enabled or not (default: Yes)

    ➤ Whether the MetaWeblog API is enabled or not (default: Yes)

    ➤ Whether usernames and passwords from this API will be accepted (default: No)

    ➤ Whether web browser file handling is Permissive or Strict (default: Strict)

    ➤ Whether a time-out exists for security validation (default: On)

    ➤ How many minutes before the current security validation expires (default: 30)

    ➤ Whether sending a new user her name and password by e-mail is allowed (default: Yes)

    ➤ Whether the Application _Layouts page is allowed to reference the Master Pages (default: Yes)

    ➤ Whether the Recycle Bin is enabled or not (default: On)

    ➤ How many days deleted items will stay in the Recycle Bin (default: 30)

➤ What percentage of the site disk quota is used by the second stage recycle bin (default: 50)

➤ Whether website analytics are enabled or not (default: Yes)

➤ **Resource Throttling:** Use these settings to control the resource load by this web application and its site collections:

    ➤ Set the maximum number of items in a list that a database operation can involve at one time (default: 5000)

    ➤ Allow object model override by custom code (default: Yes)

    ➤ Set the max number of items for a database query (default: 20,000)

    ➤ Set the max number of list view lookups for a database query (default: 6)

    ➤ Enable a daily time window for large queries (default: No)

    ➤ If this daily time window is enabled, set the start time and the duration in hours (10 p.m., 0 hours)

    ➤ Set the max number of unique permissions for a list at one time (default: 50,000)

    ➤ Enable backward-compatible event handlers (default: Off)

    ➤ Enable HTTP request throttling to prohibit overload of web front-end servers (default: On)

    ➤ How many days entries will stay in the change log (default: 60)

➤ **Workflow Settings:** Controls whether workflows are enabled or not:

    ➤ Enable user-defined workflows for all sites in this web application (default: Yes)

    ➤ Alert internal users who do not have site access when assigned a workflow task (default: Yes)

    ➤ Allow external users to participate in workflows by sending them a copy of the document (default: No)

➤ **Outgoing E-Mail Settings:** These settings are normally inherited from the general e-mail settings for the farm, and therefore this form is empty. But you can specify settings for a given web application and its site collections:

    ➤ *Outbound SMTP server:* Enter the name for the SMTP server that SharePoint Foundation will send e-mail to.

    ➤ *From Address:* The mail address that SharePoint will use as the From address. Note that this address does not have to exist.

    ➤ *Reply-to Address:* If a user replies to an e-mail from SharePoint, it will be sent to this address (which must exist, unlike the From address).

    ➤ *Character set:* Keep its default setting of 65001 (Unicode UTF-8) unless there is an old receiving mail server.

➤ **Mobile Account:** Fill in these settings to enable SharePoint to send mobile text messages (SMS) instead of e-mail notifications to end users:

  ➤ *URL to SMS Service:* Enter the URL given by the SMS service provider.

  ➤ *User name:* Enter the account name registered at the SMS service provider.

  ➤ *Password:* Enter the password for the user name.

➤ **SharePoint Designer:** Use these settings to control whether and how SharePoint Designer 2010 will be enabled for sites in this web application:

  ➤ Enable SharePoint Designer: (default: Yes)

  ➤ Enable detaching pages from the site definition (default: Yes)

  ➤ Enable customizing Master Pages and Layout Pages (default: Yes)

  ➤ Enable managing of the website URL structure (default: Yes)

The preceding were just the settings for the General Settings button. A lot of other buttons are available for managing web applications. Instead of going into detail for every button, here is a general description of their settings, and how to use them (again, select the web application you want to manage before these buttons become active on the Ribbon):

➤ **Extend:** Use this button to create another web application that points to an existing web application. This feature is useful if you want to have two different configurations for the same site collections — for example, if you want to use anonymous access when accessing a site from outside, but authenticated access when accessing the same site from the internal network. In this case you need to add, or extend, an existing web application. This appears in the IIS Manager as a web application. You will learn more about this when discussing extranet and public websites in Chapter 7.

➤ **Delete:** Use this button when you want to delete a web application. Its menu has two choices:

  ➤ *Delete Web Application*: Also gives you options to delete or retain the associated content databases and IIS website

  ➤ *Remove SharePoint from IIS Web Site*: This deletes the web application, but you can choose to retain the associated IIS website or delete it.

➤ **Manage Features:** Allows you to manage the web application's features, if any.

➤ **Managed Path:** Add or delete URL paths to this web application. By default SharePoint Foundation has a path named sites that is used when you add more than one site collection to a web application. For example, if the URL to the web application is http://srv1 and it contains just one site collection, then http://srv1 is also the URL to this site collection. But when you add a second and third site collection, they cannot have this URL because it points to the first site collection. SharePoint solves this issue by adding the managed path sites to the URL and after that the name of the second site collection. For example, the URL to the second site collection, ABC, will have the URL http://srv1/sites/ABC. If you add more managed paths, make sure to select Type = *Wildcard inclusion* and they will be listed when you create new site collections in this web application. The term Wildcard inclusion means that this specific URL path can be used for multiple site collections; for example, "sites" can be used for http://srv1/sites/abc and http://srv1/sites/xyz. There is also another URL path type named Explicit inclusion that can only be used for one specific site collection, such as `http://srv1`, that is a root site.

➤ **Service Connections:** Use this setting to change the current web application's service associations. By default all web applications are associated with the service group *Default*, which usually runs all services. If you want to change that — for example, if the current web application doesn't use the Business Data Connectivity service — then you can switch to the group *Custom* and deselect that service, thus saving resources used by this web application.

➤ **Authentication Providers:** Use this setting to change the authentication settings for this web application, and a particular zone; for example, if you want to enable anonymous logon for a public website.

   ➤ *Authentication Type:* Choose between Windows, Forms, or Web single sign-on authentication (default: Windows)

   ➤ *Enable anonymous access:* (default: Disabled)

   ➤ *Require Use Remote Interfaces permission:* (default: Enabled)

   ➤ *IIS Authentication Settings:* Use these settings to define what authentication mechanism to use. The options are Integrated Windows Authentication with Negotiate (Kerberos) or NTLM, and Basic authentication (password is sent in clear text). Kerberos is a safer and faster authentication mechanism than NTLM, but Kerberos requires special preparation to work with SharePoint. The default setting is therefore NTLM, which does not require any extra steps and still offers a secure authentication that is acceptable to most organizations.

   ➤ *Enable Client Integration:* If this option is enabled, a user can open a document for editing and then save it back to SharePoint. If it's disabled, then the user must either use the Office Web Applications (if applicable) or download the document, edit it, and then upload it to SharePoint. The first option works fine when using Windows authentication, but not for users who authenticate using forms-based authentication. (default: Enabled)

➤ **Self-Service Site Creation:** Enable this option if users should be able to create new site collections without using the Central Administration tool. Use this setting with care: If enabled, you may end up with a large number of site collections, which may make SharePoint Foundation harder to manage. The user who created the site collection will also be its administrator; that is, have full control over it. You can require a secondary contact for the site collection, which will allow the user who creates a site collection to add more site collection administrators. Note that all users with access to SharePoint will be able to create site collections using the Self-Service site creation, as well as users with only read-access. (default: Disabled)

➤ **Blocked File Types:** This is a list of all file extensions and file types that are blocked; that is, they cannot be uploaded to SharePoint. Typically, these are executable files, scripts, and configuration files. The SharePoint administrator can add or remove file types in this list. If a user tries to upload a blocked file type, she will see a message that explains that this file type is blocked by the administrator.

➤ **User Permissions:** This page allows the administrator to control what permissions are enabled in this web application. For example, you can use it to disable the Add Items permission, thus blocking all users from adding a new document or list item in any site collections in this web application. (Default: all permissions are enabled.)

➤ **Web Part Security:** Use this form to control some settings related to web parts. For example, you can prohibit users from creating connections between web parts, and you can enable users with Contributor permission to edit scriptable web parts. (Default: web parts connections are enabled, and contributors are prevented from editing scriptable web parts.)

➤ **User Policy:** Lists the user accounts that can manage this web application. For example, if you want user Bill to manage a specific web application for the Default zone, click Add User, select the Default zone, and enter Bill's account in the Users field. Then choose what level of permission you want to grant Bill: Full Control, Full Read, Deny Write, or Deny All, and click Finish. Bill is now listed among the other user accounts. See also Permission Policy later.

➤ **Anonymous Policy:** Use this form to control what policy anonymous users will have. You can have different policies in different zones. The options are None — No Policy, Deny Write — Has No Write Access, and Deny All — Has No Access. Note that you must enable anonymous access before the options in this form get enabled.

➤ **Permission Policy:** Use this form to add, delete, or modify existing policy levels. These policies are listed in the User Policy form. For example, say that you want to prohibit the site collection administrator from having full control over all objects in the site collection `http://projects` .You would click on the policy level Full Control, make sure the Web Application is set to `http://projects`, and deselect the option Site Collection Administrator — Site Collection Administrators Have Full Control over the Entire Site Collection and Can Perform Any Action on Any Object.

Configure Alternate Address Mappings

The next configuration link in the Web Application section, on the Application Management page, is Configure Alternate Access Mappings. This important page needs to be correctly configured in order to allow users to get access to SharePoint, especially when the users access SharePoint sites from outside your network, such as from the Internet.

IIS can identify the URL a user types to open a SharePoint site. Sometimes you want to have different URLs depending on where the users are located when accessing the site. SharePoint lets you use five different labels, referred to as IIS *zones*, which match typical scenarios, like intranet users and Internet users. The names, in themselves, have no real significance, but they indicate their use and make understanding how to use them easier for the administrator. These five zones and their typical use are:

➤ **Intranet:** Users who come from the internal network; that is, a local user

➤ **Internet:** Users who come from outside the network, typically over the Internet

➤ **Extranet:** Users who come from either the local network or from outside

➤ **Default:** The standard zone, which was set when you created the web application

➤ **Custom:** An extra zone, to be used if the other zones don't apply

Some examples may help you understand these settings. Say that the standard URL you got when creating the web application was `http://srv1`, which is the name of the SharePoint server. You want a friendlier name, like `http://start`. But you also want to allow access to this site from the Internet, and that means you need a fully qualified domain name (FQDN) that users outside the corporate network enter to open this SharePoint site. You also want this URL to be `http://start .filobit.com`. Use the steps in the following Try It Out to configure the alternate address mapping to match these URLs:

TRY IT OUT   Configure Alternate Address Mapping

1. Log on as the farm administrator, and start the Central Administration tool (Start ⇨ All Programs ⇨ Microsoft SharePoint 2010 Products ⇨ SharePoint 2010 Central Administration).

2. Click on Application Management ⇨ Configure alternate address mapping to open the Alternate Address Mappings page.

3. Click Edit Public URLs to open the Edit Public Zone URLs page.

4. Check what web application is listed as the Alternate Access Mapping Collection. If it says No Selection or if it's not the one you want to edit, then click on its name, select Change Alternate Access Mapping Collection, and click on the right web application name (you will also see its URL).

5. You have five different zones. In this example you need to set three of them like this:

➤ **Default:** `http://srv1`

➤ **Intranet:** `http://start`

➤ **Internet:** `http://start.filobit.com`

Leave the other two zones (Custom and Extranet) empty; see Figure B-6. Click Save.

6. These URLs are activated immediately. But you need to add the name *Start* to the internal DNS, add *Start.filobit.com* to the external DNS, and configure the firewall to accept incoming traffic to `http://srv1.filobit.com`.

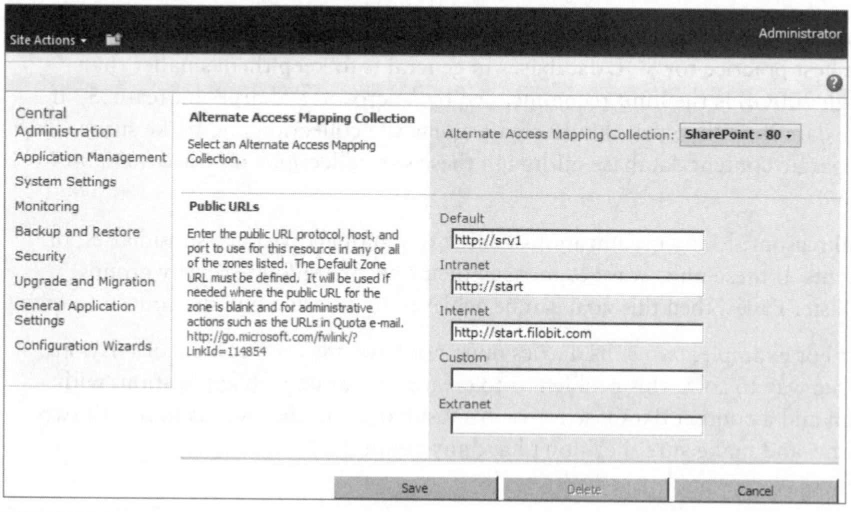

FIGURE B-6

How It Works

SharePoint allows five different URLs, known as zones, per web application. Each of these URLs may have a different configuration, for example `http://srv1` for internal use and `https://intranet.filobit.com` for access from the Internet. Ensure that the firewall accepts incoming connections that match the URL defined for one of these zones, typically the Internet Zone.

This is what happens now: If a user (regardless of location) opens the URL `http://start.filobit.com`, then SharePoint applies the configuration settings for the matching zone Internet. If the user opens `http://start`, SharePoint applies the configurations for the zone Intranet. You can define the configuration settings for a zone in several places; for example, using the web application's Authentication Providers, and the Anonymous Policy, which was described earlier in this appendix. You will learn more about these settings in Chapter 7, and see an example of how to use them in a real-life scenario.

Create Site Collections

SharePoint sites are based on site collections. Many organizations are satisfied with just a single site collection, whereas others require thousands to meet their needs. When you create a new site collection, you create a top site in a new site tree. Any subsites you need must be created from within that site collection; you cannot create subsites using the Central Administration tool.

Before you create a new site collection, ask yourself, "Why do we need a new site collection?" Multiple site collections increase the time it takes to manage your SharePoint environment; several features are bound to a specific site collection, such as SharePoint Groups, and if you want to have the same set of features in all site collections, you need to repeat the configuration for each site collection. (You can solve this issue by building PowerShell scripts, or developing custom code that sets the configuration in all site collections.) Still, some good arguments exist for creating new site collections. The following is a list of the most common reasons:

➤ **Large data volumes:** All content in a site collection must be stored in the same content database. The best practice for SQL databases in general is to keep them smaller than 50GB, although 200GB is the limit recommended by Microsoft's SharePoint team. So if you have more data than this, you should create a new site collection and make sure to store it in a separate content database (although these site collections may use the same web application).

➤ **Organizational reasons:** Many organizations consist of multiple divisions, subsidiaries, or large departments. If these units want to manage their own SharePoint security groups, layout, and Master Pages, then this goal can be achieved by creating one site collection each.

➤ **Legal reasons:** For example, two subsidiaries must not have any connections or relations, whatsoever. One way to solve this problem is to create a separate web application, with a site collection and a content database for each subsidiary. Another way is to install two SharePoint farms and make sure they don't have any connection.

In the following Try It Out, you create a new site collection in the same web application as the first site collection. This typically happens when the organization starts on a small scale, and later discovers that it needs more site collections, usually because the data volume has grown over the limits mentioned earlier. The URL to the first site collection is `http://start` and the new site collection will be named Research. The site collection administrator will be `Filobit\Anna` and `Filobit\Administrator`, described in the following steps.

TRY IT OUT   Create a Site Collection

This example assumes there is a user account named `filobit\anna`. You may need to replace that account to match your own domain setup.

1. Log on as a member of the Farm Administrators group and start the Central Administration tool (Start ➪ All Programs ➪ Microsoft SharePoint 2010 Products ➪ SharePoint 2010 Central Administration).

2. Click Application Management ➪ Create site collections to open the form where you define the settings for this new site collection. Enter the following values in this form:

   a. Title: Research (Keep this short, because it will be listed as a tab.)

   b. Description: Filobit Research Division

   c. URL: `http://start/sites/research` (You may remember that `sites` is a managed path.)

   d. Select a template: Team Site

   e. Primary Site Collection Administrator — User name: `Filobit\Anna`

   f. Secondary Site Collection Administrator — User name: `Filobit\Administrator`

   g. Select a quota template: No Quota

   h. Click OK to save and close this form; the site collection will now be created.

3. Click the `http://start/sites/research` link in the result page to open this Research site in a new web browser; after a short delay, it will show up.

How It Works

Create site collections for storing sites and their content. Set properties, such as title, description, site collection administrators, and what site template to use for the top site. All site collections must be created within a specific web application, which in turn is connected to a content database.

You may have some questions now, such as the following:

➤ Q: Why does the URL to the new site collection start with the same URL as the first site collection?

A: Because they share the same web application.

➤ Q: If I have two or more content databases for this web application, how can I force the new site collection to be stored in a specific database?

A: You can't! Not using the Central Administration tool. But using STSADM or a PowerShell script, you can. But you can do a trick; see the discussion after this list.

➤ Q: How do I get a URL like `http://research` instead of `http://start/sites/research`?

A: Create a new web application, and then create the Research site collection in that web application.

➤ Q: I want the top site in the new site collection to look exactly like the first one — is this possible?

A: Yes! Either you save the first top site as a site template (with or without its content) and use that template when creating the new site collection; or you create a site definition that is identical to the first top site and use that as a template.

The trick mentioned earlier is to set all content databases as Offline, except the one you want to use for the new site collection. The following Try It Out presents the steps to do this.

> **NOTE** *You will still be able to read and write to existing site collections, but no new site collection can be created as long as the database is offline.*

TRY IT OUT   Create a Site Collection in a Specific Content Database

1. Log on as a member of the Farm Administrators group and start the Central Administration tool (Start ➪ All Programs ➪ Microsoft SharePoint 2010 Products ➪ SharePoint 2010 Central Administration).

2. Click Application Management ➪ Manage Content Databases.

3. If you need to create the new content database, click Add a Content Database and fill in the form. (If you just want a new database with the default settings, enter the name for it and click OK.)

4. For each database you want to set offline, click on its name and change the Database status to Offline, and then click OK. When you are done, there should only be one database with the status Started; this is the one that the new site collection will be created in.

5. Click Application Management ➪ Create site collections to open the form where you define the settings for this new site collection. Enter the values for this site collection, as described in the previous Try It Out instructions. Click OK when done.

6. Wait until you see that the new site collection is successfully created. Now start the offline databases again: Open the Application Management ➪ Manage Content Databases Page. Note that the only database with Started status now has the Current Number of Site Collections set to 1.

7. For each database listed as Offline, click to open its configuration page and change the status to Started.

How It Works

In order to create a new site collection in a specific content database, you take all other databases offline in this web application, except the one that will be used for this site collection. Then set all databases online.

You will see a lot of examples of how to create site collections in this book. They will all follow the steps listed in the Try It Out "Create a Site Collection" earlier in this appendix. To create site collections using PowerShell scripts and STSADM, see Chapter 6.

Delete a Site Collection

If a site collection is no longer needed, you can delete it. This eases the amount of data to be backed up and cleans up the SharePoint site structure. But you must make sure to have a backup of this database in case you want it back! The To Do list before you delete a site collection is as follows:

➤ Make a backup of the site collection (using the Central Administration tool, STSADM, PowerShell, or a SharePoint-aware backup). It is also possible to back up using SharePoint Designer 2010.

➤ Make sure to update the documentation of the settings for this site collection:

 ➤ Its URL (which also shows its web application)

 ➤ Its content database

 ➤ Its site collection administrators

➤ Make sure no links in other site collections are pointing to the one that will be deleted.

➤ Test that the backup is possible to restore on another SharePoint server. (Chapter 10 describes how to make backups and do restores of site collections.)

➤ Make a second backup and store it in another location, just in case the impossible happens.

Then follow these steps to delete a site collection:

TRY IT OUT Delete a Site Collection

1. Log on as a member of the Farm Administrators group and start the Central Administration tool (Start ➪ All Programs ➪ Microsoft SharePoint 2010 Products ➪ SharePoint 2010 Central Administration).

2. Click Application Management ➪ Delete a Site Collection.

3. Notice that the Site Collection is listed as No Selection; click on this text and select Change Site Collection. This opens a list of all site collections for a specific web application. If this is not the correct web application, then click on its name and select Change Web Application. Then select the correct web application. Now you can see all the site collections for this web application.

4. Select the site collection to be deleted (notice that the first site collection is listed as "/"; this is also known as the root). Click OK.

5. A status page appears: Double-check to make sure that this is the site collection to be deleted. When you are sure, click Delete; otherwise, click Cancel to abort. There is a final check to see if you are really certain about this operation, because it cannot be undone, except by doing a restore. Click OK if you are sure.

How It Works

Delete a site collection you don't need anymore. There is no Undo for this operation, so make sure to create a backup of the site collection and document its settings before it is deleted. A site collection can be deleted by the SharePoint Central Administration tool, STSADM, or PowerShell.

You may have some questions now, such as:

➤ Q: What happens with other site collections in this web application when I delete a site collection?

A: Nothing, not even if you delete the root site collection.

➤ Q: Can I delete all site collections in one step?

A: No, but you can create a PowerShell script or STSADM command to delete multiple site collections. You can also delete the content database, if all site collections use a specific database.

➤ Q: I made a mistake — can I undo this delete operation?

A: No! The only way to get it back is to restore it using the backup you did before the delete. (You did a backup, right?)

Confirm Site Use and Deletion

You can configure SharePoint to monitor all site collections in a specific web application, and then send an e-mail to their site collection administrators asking whether the site collection is still active, in case it has not been used for a long time. SharePoint can also automatically delete the site collection, if a certain number of notifications are sent without receiving a reply. This feature is by default deactivated, but can be activated using the Site Use Confirmation and Deletion page, as shown in the following Try It Out.

TRY IT OUT Configure Site Use and Deletion

1. Log on as a member of the Farm Administrators group and start the Central Administration tool (Start ➪ All Programs ➪ Microsoft SharePoint 2010 Products ➪ SharePoint 2010 Central Administration).

2. Click Application Management ➪ Confirm Site Use and Deletion.

3. Verify that the correct web application is listed; if it's not, click on the name, then click Change Web Application, and select the correct web application. Fill in the form like this (values inside [ ] are default values):

a. **Send E-mail Notifications to Owners of Unused Site Collections:** Select this option if you want to enable monitoring of all site collections in this web application.

b. **Start Sending Notifications [90] Days:** Set the number of days a site collection can be unused before the first notification e-mail is sent to the site collection administrators.

c. **Check for Unused Site Collections and Send Notices [Daily] and Run the Check at [12 am] [00]:** Set how often SharePoint will check, and at what time.

d. **Automatically Delete the Site Collection if Use Is Not Confirmed:** Select this option if you want to activate the auto-delete feature. If so, then a second option is activated; see the following step.

e. **Delete the Site Collection after Sending [28] Notices:** Use this setting to configure how many unanswered notification e-mails will be sent before the site collection is auto-deleted.

How It Works

Unused site collections (but not individual subsites) can be detected and possibly even automatically deleted. Best practice is to configure this check to only send out an e-mail to the site collection owner to inform that this site collection has not been used for a given time.

If you activate all these settings it means the following: For a site collection that is unused for 90 days, SharePoint sends an e-mail daily at 12 a.m. asking whether the site collection should stay untouched or be deleted. After 28 unanswered e-mails, SharePoint will delete this site collection.

This feature may sound dangerous, but it could also be a benefit to a SharePoint administrator who has to manage a SharePoint server where site collections are constantly created, then used for a limited time, but no one cares to clean up these unused site collections. If you are uncertain of whether this feature is for your organization, then activate the e-mail notifications only, but not the auto-delete operation; you will get a good indication if there are, indeed, lots of unused site collections in your SharePoint farm.

Here are some common questions regarding this subject:

➤ Q: Is it possible to monitor a single subsite?

A: No.

➤ Q: Is it possible to monitor just one site collection?

A: No. This monitoring is only per web application, and all its site collections. But if you have only one site collection per web application, then it will work as you want.

➤ Q: Will SharePoint do a backup before deleting a site collection?

A: No. It is your responsibility to do backups.

➤ Q: Is it possible to send the notification e-mail to other people besides the site collection administrators; for example, to the Helpdesk?

A: No. But add the Helpdesk account to the list of site collection administrators, and they will get the notification.

➤ Q: Is it possible to send a notice if the site collection has not been used for just a week?

A: No. The number of days of inactivity must be between 30 and 365.

Specify Quota Templates

A quota template is a preconfigured size limit that can be applied to a site collection. You can define a hard limit; that is, no more data can be added when this limit is reached. You can also define a warning limit. If any of these two limits are exceeded, an e-mail will be sent to the site collection administrators.

Configuring these quote templates does not activate them. The next step is to apply these templates to new and existing site collections. See Figure B-7 for an example of a template called *Projects* that has a maximum limit of 1000MB and a warning limit at 800MB. To find out how to apply these quota templates, see the next section.

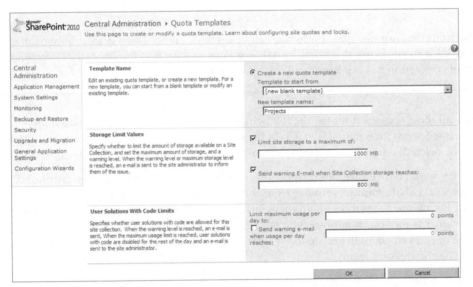

FIGURE B-7

Configure Quotas and Locks

The Configure Quotas and Locks page is used to apply quota templates to site collections. You can also use it to partly or completely lock a site collection, apply a quota template, and set a maximum limit on how many "points" a custom code is allowed to generate.

Before making any changes on the Configuration Quotas and Locks page, make sure you have the correct site collection listed at the top-right part of this page; if the site is not correct, click on it and select Change Site Collection. Click on the site collection for which you want to configure quotas and locks. If you don't see that site collection now, you are probably looking at the wrong web application; if so, click on the link next to the Web Application and change it.

When you are sure the correct site collection is listed, look at the Site Lock section: The site collection owner is listed here (but cannot be modified). Below the owner is the Lock Status for This Site. There are four status options:

➤ **Not Locked:** This is the default.

➤ **Adding Content Prevented:** No new data can be added to this site collection, regardless of whether it is the top site or any of its subsites.

➤ **Read-only** (blocks additions, updates, and deletions)

➤ **No Access**

For example, if you want to copy a site collection to another SharePoint farm (such as a test farm), select the Read-only status for that site collection; that way, you can be sure no one is adding new information during this copy phase, but users are still able to read from this site collection.

In the Current Quota Template section on this page you can apply any of the existing quota templates (see the description for Specify Quota Templates earlier in this chapter). You can also apply custom limits in megabytes for this site collection, instead of applying a quota template. Note that the current data volume for this site collection is listed here.

At the end of this Site Collection Quotas and Locks page you see User Solutions Resource Quota. This is a way for the SharePoint administrator to control custom-developed code that runs in a "sandbox solution" to prohibit it from taking too many resources and affecting the overall performance of the SharePoint server. The points for a sandbox solution are based on 14 different metrics, such as CPU resources and number of critical exceptions. If the solution exceeds a daily limit (default: 300 points) it will be shut down. By default, an e-mail notification will be sent to the site collection administrator when the number of points exceeds 100. At the end of this page you will find the average usage of points for today and for the last 14 days.

> **NOTE** This article explains more about sandbox solutions and how the points are calculated: http://msdn.microsoft.com/en-us/magazine/ee335711.aspx.

Change Site Collection Administrators

The Change Site Collection Administrators page allows you to define the two main administrators for this site collection, sometimes referred to as the *site collection owners*. These are the ones who will receive the e-mail notifications generated by SharePoint when limits are exceeded, such as the maximum number of daily points mentioned earlier.

There are two types of administrators: the Primary Site Collection Administrator and the Secondary Site Collection Administrator. Note that you must enter user accounts only; security groups or SharePoint groups are not supported.

Before you change these two administrators, make sure that you are configuring the correct site collection. (See its name in the top-right part of the page; if you don't see it, change it as described earlier.)

Here is an example of usage: Suppose that you, as the farm administrator, need to take control over a site collection to solve an issue. You could use this page to replace either of these two accounts with your account, fix the issue, and then restore the previous administrator account.

Another typical example is when a user who is listed as a site collection administrator leaves the organization, and a new user will replace her.

> **NOTE** *One way to avoid the issues when a site collection administrator leaves the company is to use role-based user accounts for these site collection administrators, such as* `Filobit\SiteCollection-A-Admin` *and* `Filobit\ Site Collection-B-Admin`.

View All Site Collections

When you need a view of all the site collections in a given web application, then this page is what you want. As described several times before, you must first check, and possibly change, the web application listed at the top-right part of this page.

If more than 10 site collections exist, you can click to scroll forward to the next 10 site collections. Click on a site collection to see more information about it, such as:

➤ **URL:** The URL address of this site collection

➤ **Title:** The title of the top site

➤ **Description:** The description of the top site

➤ **Primary administrator:** The user account listed as the primary site collection administrator

➤ **E-mail Address:** The e-mail address of the primary site collection administrator

➤ **Database Name:** The name of the content database that stores all data for this site collection

In other words, this page is a very good way to find out a lot of information about site collections, not the least of which is the name of its content database in case you have multiple databases connected to a web application.

Configure Self-Service Site Creation

In some implementations of SharePoint 2010, you may want all users to be able to create new site collections. The problem is that they need access to the Central Administration tool to do that. SharePoint solves this problem by offering a self-service site-creating feature that works for a given web application. By default, this feature is disabled, but enabling it is easy (some would say too easy).

When this feature is enabled, a news item is created in the Announcement list for the top site of the first site collection created in this particular web application. This news item contains the following text:

> Self-Service Site Creation has been enabled for this Web application. Go to `http://projects/ _layouts/scsignup.aspx` to create a new root Web site.

Note the URL: `http://projects/_layouts/scsignup.aspx`; it is the link to the form where you define the values for the new site collection. If you want to make finding this link easy for the users, then add it to the page as a navigation link or create a button with SharePoint Designer and associate it with this link.

> **NOTE** *If you lose this news item, or its link, recreating it is easy: The URL is always* `/_layouts/scsignup.aspx` *added to the URL of the top site. For example, if the top site URL is* `http://intranet` *then the self-service site-creating page is* `http://intranet/_layouts/scsignup.aspx`.

In the following Try It Out, you enable the self-service site creation for the web application `http://srv1`, then test it, and finally copy its URL to a navigation link.

TRY IT OUT   Configure Self-Service Site Creation

1. Log on as a member of the Farm Administrators group and start the Central Administration tool (Start ➪ All Programs ➪ Microsoft SharePoint 2010 Products ➪ SharePoint 2010 Central Administration).

2. Click Application Management ➪ Configure self-service site creation to open the Self-Service Site Collection Management page.

3. Make sure the correct web application (`http://srv1` in this example) is selected; if it's not, click on the current URL and change it.

4. To enable self-service site creation, select the option On in the section Enable Self-Service Site Creation.

5. If you want the creator of this site collection to be the sole site collection administrator, leave the Require second contacts option unchecked. If you want to force the creator to enter both a primary and a secondary site collection owner, select that option. Best practice is to require two contacts and make the second contact a role-based user, such as `Filobit\HelpDesk` and similar.

6. Click OK to save and close this page; this feature is activated immediately.

7. Start a web browser and open the top site for the first site collection in this web application. Look at the Announcements list — you should see a news item with the title Self-Service Site Creation; open that news item and click its link. The New SharePoint Site page opens, where you define the settings for the new site collection. Cancel this form, and return to the top site.

8. To make finding this link easier for users, open the news item again, right-click on the link, and select Copy Shortcut. Then close the news item.

9. On the top site, click Site Actions ➪ Site Settings, then click Quick Launch in the Look and Feel section to open the Quick Launch page.

10. You want to create a new navigation heading, so click *New Heading*. In the URL field, enter a / (a front slash indicates the top site), and then enter **Self-Service** as the description. Click OK to reopen the Quick Launch page.

11. Click New Navigation Link. Paste the URL into the Type the Web Address field; enter the description **Site Creation**, change the Heading to **Self-Service**, and click OK.

12. Test it: Click on the Self-Service heading in the left pane (the Quick Launch), and the top site should appear. Then click on Site Creation under the Self-Service heading, and the form for creating a new site collection should appear (that is, the same form that appeared earlier in step 7).

> **NOTE** In step 11, you can also enter the relative URL `/_layouts/scsignup.aspx`.

How It Works

Use the Self-Service Site Creation feature in SharePoint 2010 to enable any user to create new site collections in a specific web application. The user will be the site collection administrator for this new site collection. To make it easy for users to create new site collections, create a link to the page where the new site collection is defined.

If self-service site creation feature is enabled, a big risk exists that there will be more site collections than you, the administrator, wish for. A good way to keep track of site collections that are created, but then never used, is to activate the Confirm Site Use and Deletion feature, described earlier in this chapter. If you enable it, then you should also force the users to enter two site collection owners, and one of them should be you, or the Helpdesk, or a similar managing account. This way, you will know whether site collections are no longer in use.

Manage Service Applications

The concept of service applications is new for SharePoint 2010 and will give you, as an administrator, much better control of the resources applied to each web application. Previously, in SharePoint 2007, one big collection of services, named Shared Service Provider, was applied to all web applications, regardless of whether these services were used or not.

The predecessor, WSS 3.0, did not have a Shared Service Provider, so controlling individual services for a given web application was not possible, but SharePoint Foundation 2010 has a number of service applications:

➤ **Application Discovery and Load Balancer:** This service allows multiple SharePoint Foundation servers to run as a web cluster, with load balancing and failover — if one SharePoint Foundation goes down, the remaining SharePoint Foundation servers in the cluster take its load. This general service is not applied to a specific web application!

➤ **Business Data Connectivity (BDC):** This is a new service for SharePoint Foundation that previously only existed in MOSS 2007. With this service, you can configure SharePoint Foundation to read and write to external data sources, such as Oracle databases, Microsoft SQL Server, and Excel files.

➤ **Security Token:** This service assists the BDC service when connecting to external sources that require authentication.

➤ **Usage and Health Data Collection:** This is used by SharePoint 2010 to write data to the logging folder (`C:\Program Files\Common Files\Microsoft Shared\Web Server Extensions\14\LOGS`) and the logging database in SQL Server (WSS_Logging). This general service is not applied to a specific web application!

In SharePoint Central Administration, click Application Management ➪ Manage service applications to open the Manage Service Application page. This page shows the status of these service applications; you can manage some, but not all, of them. Note that this page says nothing about which web application uses what service. To see this information use the Service Connection button on the Manage web application page, as described earlier in this chapter. The buttons on the Ribbon (see Figure B-8) are used for the following actions:

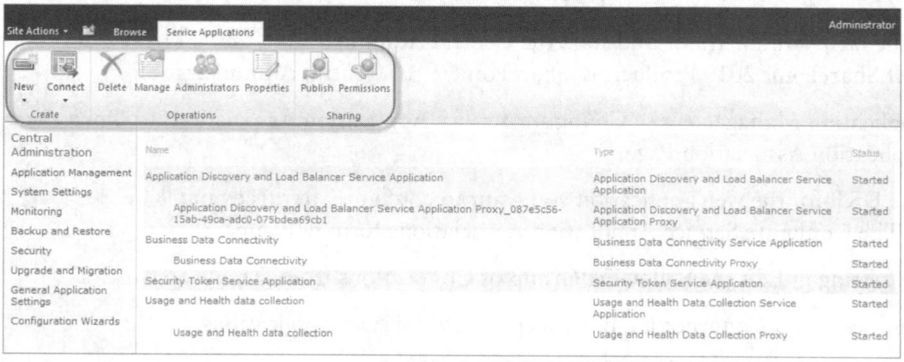

FIGURE B-8

➤ **New:** Create a new service application. For example, you can create multiple BDC service applications, or you can create a service application that did not previously exist.

➤ **Connect:** Use this button to connect to a BDC service application, which is created and published in another SharePoint Foundation farm.

➤ **Delete:** Remove the current service application, and possibly also its associated databases.

➤ **Manage:** Configure the current service application. For example, select the BDC service and click this button to manage its existing external content types; that is, definition of connections to external data sources.

➤ **Administrators:** Specify the users who can manage the current service application. If you add a user who is not a SharePoint farm administrator, he will automatically be granted access to Central Administration and can manage all settings related to this service application.

➤ **Properties:** Configure the properties of the current service application. For example, select the Business Data Connectivity service application (make sure to select this service by clicking on its type, not its name!), and you can configure the SQL Server name and database name used by this service.

➤ **Publish:** Make the current service application available to other SharePoint Foundation farms. This will also create the unique connection URL that the remote farm must enter to connect to this service.

➤ **Permissions:** Specify the user accounts, or other security principal object, that can invoke the current service application from a remote SharePoint farm.

Configure Service Application Associations

The Configure Service Application Associations page allows the administrator to enable or disable service applications for a specific web application. In other words, this is an alternative to using the Service Connection button on the Manage web application page, as described earlier in this chapter. For example, if you have a web application with the URL `http://projects` and you want to disable the BDC service application for that web application, use the steps in the following Try It Out:

TRY IT OUT   **Configure Service Application Associations**

1. Log on as the farm administrator and start the Central Administration tool (Start ➪ All Programs ➪ Microsoft SharePoint 2010 Products ➪ SharePoint 2010 Central Administration).

2. Choose Application Management ➪ Configure Service Application Associations to Open the Service Application Association Page.

3. Click on the URL for the web application you want to configure, in this example `http://projects`. The Configure Service Application Associations form will appear.

4. Change the setting in Edit the Following Group of Connections from Default to Custom.

5. Deselect Business Data Connectivity, but select all other service applications.

6. Click OK to save and close this form. The Service Application Association page reappears; notice that `http://projects` now has Custom listed as the Application Proxy Group.

How It Works

In SharePoint 2010 it is possible to control exactly what service applications are used in a specific web application. By default, all service applications are activated for all web applications.

Later in this chapter you will learn how to create new application proxy groups, with preconfigured service applications, instead of using the Custom proxy group.

Manage Content Databases

This page lists all content databases for a given web application; you can also add new content databases and modify or delete existing databases. For an existing database you will see its current number of site collections, its status (Started or Stopped), whether it is read-only or not, the site collection warning level (default: 9000), and the maximum number of site collections (default: 15,000).

To modify an existing database, make sure you are using the correct web application (look at the upper-right corner), then click on the database name to open its configuration page:

➤ **Database Status:** If Ready, then you can access and create new site collections in this database. If Offline, then no new site collections can be created, but users can read and write to existing site collections.

➤ **Database Schema Versions:** This is for information only. It lists the current version of the database schema.

➤ **Failover Database Server:** If you have a replica of the production SQL Server, then enter its name here, and SharePoint will automatically fail-over to that replica in case the production SQL server is unreachable.

➤ **Number of Sites before a Warning Event Is Generated:** The default value is 9,000 site collections.

➤ **Maximum Number of Sites That Can Be Created in This Database:** The default is 15,000 site collections.

➤ **Select Microsoft SharePoint Foundation Search Server:** If you run two or more SharePoint Foundation servers, one of them will run the search service. Select that SharePoint Foundation server in this menu to enable search and index features for this content database.

➤ **Remove Content Database:** Delete the current database from this web application, but this database will still not be deleted from the SQL Server. In other words, adding this content database again and revoking all its site collections is possible.

➤ **Preferred Server for Timer Jobs:** If multiple SharePoint Foundation servers are in your farm you can select one of them to be the preferred server for running timer jobs; for example, workflows that are waiting for a specific time to start or continue.

To add a new content database to an existing web application, use the steps in the following Try It Out:

TRY IT OUT Add a New Content Database

1. Log on as the farm administrator, and start the Central Administration tool.

2. Choose Application Management ➪ Manage content databases.

3. Make sure the correct web application is open; if it's not, click on the current URL in the top-right corner, then click Change Web Application and select the correct web application.

4. Click Add a Content Database, then enter these values in the form:

a. **Database Server:** Enter the name of the SQL server that will store this database. Most often, it will be the same SQL Server as for all other SharePoint databases, but using a second database server is possible, if needed.

b. **Database Name:** Enter a name that is easy to understand, both for you and for other administrators, including SQL Server administrators who need to understand what the databases are used for. By default, SharePoint will suggest WSS_Content for all new content databases; if that name is already taken, it will add a global unique identifier (GUID), which is a string of 32 hexadecimal (0 – F) characters, to its name. Be nice to yourself and others; change this name to something more reader-friendly.

c. **Database Authentication:** Accept the default, that is, Windows Authentication, unless you have a good reason not to.

d. **Failover Database Server:** If you have a replica of the production SQL Server, then enter its name here, and SharePoint will automatically fail-over to that replica in case the production SQL server is unreachable.

e.   **Select Microsoft SharePoint Foundation Search Server:** If you run two or more SharePoint Foundation servers, one of them will run the search service. Select that SharePoint Foundation server in this menu to enable search and index features for this content database.

f.   **Number of Sites Before a Warning Event Is Generated:** The default is 9,000 site collections. This number is very high for most SharePoint implementations, so you may need to set a lower limit.

g.   **Maximum Number of Sites That Can Be Created in This Dataset:** The default is 15,000 site collections. This, too, might need to be set to a lower limit.

5.   Click OK to save and close this form. The new database is now created and associated with the current web application.

How It Works

A web application can have multiple content databases associated with it. Typically each database has a limited number of site collections in order to keep the size of the database within the best practice limits (200 GB).

Specify the Default Database Server

Use the simple Specify the Default Database Server form to set the default database server and, in case it uses SQL Server authentication, its user account and password. The values you enter here will be used when configuring other settings that relate to SQL Server; for example, when adding a new content database.

Configure the Data Retrieval Service

You use the Configure the Data Retrieval Service form to configure the data retrieval service globally, or for a specific web application. These settings apply to data connections; for example, custom code that reads external data sources. The settings on this form are:

➤ **Web Application:** If this is set to Global Settings then the following settings on the Configure the Data Retrieval Service page are the default settings for all web applications. If you want to change a specific web application, click on Global Settings, and select the web application.

➤ **Customize Web Application:** (Only visible if you configure a specific web application.) Select this box if this web application should inherit the global settings for the Configure Data Retrieval Service, or if it should be customized. If the web application inherits the settings, then no other settings on this form can be set (Default: Inherit the Global Settings).

➤ **Enable Data Retrieval Service:** This service must be enabled in order to allow query requests to be processed. This setting affects these data retrieval services: Microsoft SharePoint Foundation, OLEDB, SOAP Passthrough, and XML-URL (Default: Enabled).

➤ **Limit Response Size:** This setting controls the size of the Simple Object Access Protocol (SOAP) response when retrieving data from a data source (Default: 10,000KB).

➤ **Update Support:** Support for update queries can be controlled with this setting, and this applies to the OLEDB data retrieving services (Default: Disabled).

➤ **Data Source Time-out:** The data retrieval service will time out if the data source does not respond within the duration set by this parameter. The affected data retrieval services are OLEDB, SOAP Passthrough, XML-URL, SoapDataSource, and XmlUrlDataSource (Default: 30 seconds).

➤ **Enable Data Source Control:** This setting affects the following data source controls: SPXmlDataSource, XmlUrlDataSource, SoapDataSource, and AggregatedDataSource (Default: Enabled).

System Settings

The System Settings section in SharePoint Central Administration contains links to manage servers, e-mail settings, and farm management. Use the System Settings when you need to do any of the following:

➤ Manage servers in this farm

➤ Manage services on servers

➤ Configure outgoing e-mail settings

➤ Configure incoming e-mail settings

➤ Configure mobile accounts

➤ Configure alternate address mappings

➤ Manage farm features

➤ Manage farm solutions

➤ Manage user solutions

➤ Configure privacy options

➤ Configure cross-firewall access zones

All of these links are described in the following sections. To open any of these links, click System Settings in the left pane of the SharePoint Central Administration tool.

Manage Servers in This Farm

The Manage Servers in This Farm page displays general information about this SharePoint farm, such as the configuration database version, the configuration SQL server name, and the configuration database name. It also lists all the servers in this farm, including the SQL Server and e-mail server, and the following information about them:

➤ **Server Name:** Its NetBIOS name only, not the fully qualified domain name (FQDN)

➤ **SharePoint Products Installed:** What is installed on this server; for example, Microsoft SharePoint Foundation 2010

➤ **Services Running:** A list of all the activated services running on this server. For a single server you should see at least the following services listed, possibly more:

   ➤ Business Data Connectivity

   ➤ Central Administration

   ➤ Microsoft SharePoint Foundation Database

   ➤ Microsoft SharePoint Foundation Web Application

   ➤ Microsoft SharePoint Foundation Workflow Timer

➤ **Status:** Lists any actions that need to be taken

➤ **Remove Server:** This is a link to remove this server from the list. However, if this is a SharePoint server, you should uninstall the program using SharePoint's Setup application (which will detect that this server is already installed and give you an option to uninstall it) or Control Panel ➪ Uninstall a Program.

> **NOTE** *Non-SharePoint servers, such as a SQL Server or e-mail server, may display "Not Configured" in the Services Running column — this is normal. Don't try to change it.*

Manage Services on Server

The Manage Services on Server page displays a list of all available services for the server listed in the Server field. You may start or stop these services listed on this form, and some of them, like the SharePoint Foundation Search service, are configurable. These services are typically listed in a newly installed single-server installation of SharePoint Foundation:

➤ Business Data Connectivity (Started)

➤ Central Administration (Started)

➤ Microsoft SharePoint Foundation Incoming E-mail (Started)

➤ Microsoft SharePoint Foundation Subscription Settings Service (Stopped)

➤ Microsoft SharePoint Foundation User Code Services

➤ Microsoft SharePoint Foundation Web Application (Started)

➤ Microsoft SharePoint Foundation Workflow Timer Service (Started)

➤ SharePoint Foundation Search (Stopped)

> **NOTE** *The search service is stopped; you need to configure that to activate the search and index feature in SharePoint Foundation. You learn more about that in Chapter 6.*

If you have multiple SharePoint servers in the farm, then click the Server link at the top of this form to switch to the other servers. You don't need to be connected physically to these servers, because all configuration data is stored in the single configuration database, and that database is shared among all SharePoint servers in a farm.

Configure Outgoing E-Mail Settings

Use the Configure Outgoing E-Mail Settings page to enter the parameters that SharePoint requires to send e-mail, using the SMTP mail standard:

➤ **Outbound SMTP server:** Enter the server name or the full FQDN name for the SMTP server that SharePoint will send all e-mail messages, notifications, warnings, and other types of messages to. It does not need to be a Microsoft Exchange server (although I lift my hat to you if it is), but it must apply to the SMTP standard.

➤ **From Address:** This is the address that the mail recipient will see as the sender. Note that this is just a display address, and does not need to exist. All mail that SharePoint sends will come from this address, so think about a good name that will not make your users worried. Assume, for example, that you enter Administrator@filobit.com as the From address — then probably several users will wonder why they receive mail from the administrator. Choose a more neutral address, maybe sharepoint@filobit.com, intranet@filobit.com, or something similar.

➤ **Reply-to Address:** In case the recipients of these mails reply, the messages will go to this address. In other words, this address must exist and be monitored. Good candidates for this option are administrator@filobit.com or helpdesk@filobit.com.

➤ **Character Set:** Don't change the default setting: 65001 (Unicode UTF-8). Seriously, if the server listed as the outbound SMTP server does not understand this character set, then it is time to replace it with something modern, such as Exchange 2010!

Configure Incoming E-Mail Settings

SharePoint Foundation can accept incoming e-mail and store it, including attachments, in a SharePoint list. This means that SharePoint Foundation will work as an SMTP e-mail server. A number of configuration options exist for this feature, and you set these on the Configure Incoming E-Mail Settings page.

> **NOTE** *Before incoming e-mail settings can be activated, the Windows server needs to activate the SMTP feature. Appendix A provides the steps for doing this.*

The options on this page are:

➤ **Enable Sites on This Server to Receive E-mail?** Select Yes to activate this SharePoint feature (Default: No).

➤ **Settings Mode:** Choose Automatic if you want to use Windows Server's SMTP feature. If you want to use another e-mail application on this server, then select Advanced and define the e-mail drop folder where SharePoint will look for incoming e-mail.

➤ **Use the SharePoint Directory Management Service to Create Distribution Groups and Contacts?**

  ➤ No: Mail-enabled lists will not be listed in Active Directory as mail-enabled contacts. You can still send e-mail to that list if you know its mail address.

> **NOTE** *You can manually add mail-enabled contacts to Active Directory for the mail-enabled lists. Make sure the contacts have the same primary SMTP address as the mail-enabled list. This contact can also have a reader-friendly secondary SMTP address, plus a display name that complies with your organization's naming standard.*

  ➤ Yes: Choose this option if you want to create a corresponding mail-enabled contact in Active Directory when you mail-enable a SharePoint list. If you select this option, you must also enter the Active Directory container where these contacts will be created. This may sound like a good idea, but note that this address may not follow the name standard for e-mail addresses in your company, and it may look strange for Outlook users to find these types of addresses listed in Outlook's Global Address List. Test this feature before you implement it in a production environment.

  ➤ Use Remote: If you have configured a remote SharePoint Directory Management Web Service, select this option, and then enter the Directory Management Service URL.

> **NOTE** *If you select the Yes option, make sure the Central Administration application pool account has write access to Active Directory.*

➤ **E-mail Server Display Address:** Enter the mail domain address for all of SharePoint's mail-enabled lists. The default value is a combination of the server name plus the domain name; for example, if the server name is srv1, and the domain is filobit.com, then the mail domain for mail-enabled lists will be srv1.filobit.com. So if you give a list the mail address Invoices, then its complete mail address will be Invoices@srv1.filobit.com.

> **NOTE** *If you want to use another domain address, you must configure the SMTP stack in Windows Server to accept incoming mail for that domain, plus add a Mail Exchanger (MX) record in the DNS for that domain that points to this server.*

➤ **Safe E-Mail Servers:** This has two options: Accept Mail from All E-mail Servers (the default) and Accept Mail from These Safe E-mail Servers. Use the second option if you need to control what servers can send e-mail to SharePoint, and enter the IP address to the safe server.

TRY IT OUT Configure a Library for Incoming E-mail

In this example you want to activate the incoming e-mail settings in SharePoint Central Administration and then e-mail-enable the Shared Documents library in the team site `http://srv1/teamsite`. This library will then be able to save incoming e-mail, both the message body and any attachments. In order to complete this example, the SMTP service must be activated in Windows Server.

1. Logon as a farm administrator and open SharePoint Central Administration (Start ⇨ All Programs ⇨ Microsoft SharePoint 2010 Products ⇨ SharePoint 2010 Central Administration).

2. Select System Settings and then click Configure Incoming E-mail Settings to open its configuration page. Note: If you now get a message that the SMTP service is not started, follow the instructions in the Appendix A Try It Out "Activate the SMTP Feature in Windows Server" and then restart this exercise.

3. In the section Enable Sites in This Server to Accept E-mail, select the option Yes. Accept the default settings in the other sections. Make sure to take a note of the the E-mail Server Display Address in the Incoming E-Mail Server Display Address section; in this example it will be `@srv1.filobit.com`. Click OK to save and close this page. SharePoint is now configured to accept incoming e-mail, but you must also configure each list or library to accept e-mail, as described next.

4. Log on as a site collection owner and open the site with the document library you want to e-mail-enable; in this example `http://srv1/teamsite`.

5. Click on Shared Documents to open its page.

6. In the Library tab on the Ribbon, click Library Settings to open the Document Library Settings page, then click to open the Incoming E-mail Settings page. Continue with:

  a. Set the option Allow This Document Library to Receive E-mail? to Yes.

  b. Set the E-mail address to DocLib1 to set the complete e-mail address to this library to `DocLib1@srv1.filobit.com`. Make a note of this address.

  c. Set the option Save Original E-mail? to Yes. This will ensure that the mail message is stored in this library, but only the text body in the e-mail.

  d. Accept remaining default settings, for example, that all mail attachments will be stored in the root folder of this document library. Click OK to save and close this page.

7. The library is now ready to accept incoming e-mail. Test it by sending an e-mail including an attachment:

  a. Start your local mail client. It must be connected to a local mail server in your network — for example, Microsoft Outlook, which is connected to your local Exchange server.

b. Compose a new e-mail, including a subject and an attachment, for example, a Word file, and send it to `DocLib1@srv1.filobit.com`.

c. Within a minute this mail message will show up in the Shared Document library in `http://srv1/teamsite`; note that the message is stored as one file, and the attachment (the Word file in this example) is stored as a separate file.

How It works

Enabling incoming e-mail is a three-step process; first you must install the SMTP Service in Windows Server, then SharePoint server must be configured to enable incoming e-mail, and then each library or list must enable incoming e-mail.

> **NOTE** *If no mail message shows up in the document library, check that the sender of the mail message is allowed to create content in this library (for example Contributors), and that the mail server your mail client uses has access to the srv1.filobit.com server.*

Configure Mobile Account

SharePoint Foundation can send text messages using the *Short Message Service* (SMS) standard. To enable that feature, you must configure these parameters on the Mobile Account page:

➤ **The URL of Text Message (SMS) Service:** Enter the URL to the SMS service to be used by SharePoint for sending notifications and alerts. Note that you most likely will need to register with an SMS provider first. On this page is a link named *Microsoft Office Online* that takes you to a web page at Microsoft where you can choose a local SMS provider.

➤ **User Name:** Enter the user account name, as registered at the SMS provider.

➤ **Password:** Enter the password for this User Name.

Configure Alternate Address Mappings

Earlier in this chapter you saw how to use and configure alternate address mappings, often referred to as AAM. Their purpose is to enable the use of multiple URL addresses to a web application and its site collections, using different zones for each URL. For example, you can allow users on the internal network to enter `http://start` to open the intranet, whereas users connecting over the Internet must enter `https://start.filobit.com`.

When you open the Configure Alternate Address Mappings page, you see all available URLs to all web applications, including their zones. The three buttons for configuring AAM URLs are:

➤ **Edit Public URLs:** Opens a form where you can enter the public URL addresses that users will use to open this web application and its site collections. Open the menu next to Alternate Access Mapping Collection and select the web application you want to configure. Then you can see all its existing public URL zones; see Figure B-9, which shows two zones defined. Enter the new URL in a proper zone; for example, if you want to add an extranet URL, then use the zone Extranet. Note that when you create a new public URL, a matching internal URL will automatically be created.

➤ **Add Internal URL:** Use this option if you need to add extra internal URLs to the public URLs. However, this task is usually not required for a typical SharePoint configuration. To configure internal URLs, open this form, select the proper Alternate Access Mapping Collection, and add the extra URL you need for a public URL.

➤ **Map to External Resource:** Use this button to add a URL mapping to an external resource. The effect is that you create a new alternate access mapping collection. This is also a rare configuration setting. For more information about this option, see the Microsoft blog article at `http://tinyurl.com/external-resource-mapping` that is written for SharePoint 2007, but still is valid for SharePoint 2010.

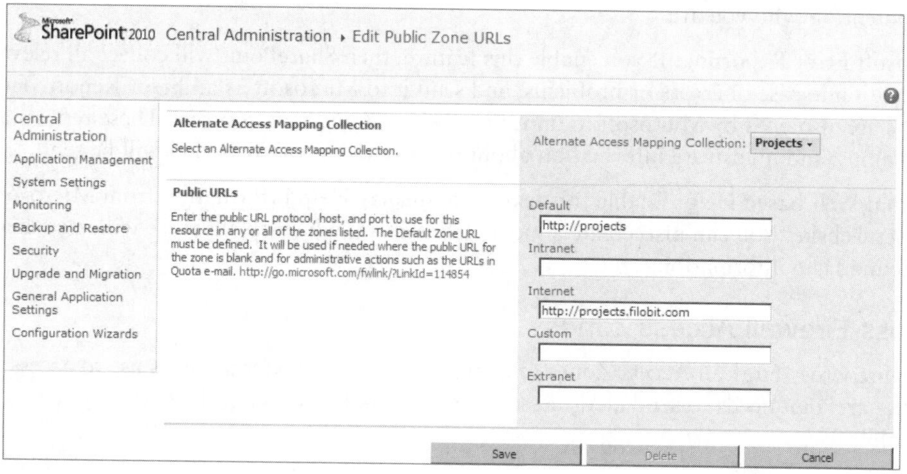

FIGURE B-9

Manage Farm Features

In SharePoint Foundation 2010 the Manage Farm Features page contains just one feature: Office.com Entry Points from SharePoint. It is active by default, but you can deactivate it, if necessary. This feature enables entry points from the SharePoint user interface that allow users to browse SharePoint solutions from Office.com.

Manage Farm Solutions

Solutions are custom applications that extend the functionality in SharePoint. You can develop SharePoint Solutions, using Visual Studio .NET, or purchase solutions from third-party vendors. The Manage Farm Solutions page, also known as the Solution Management page, lists all deployed solutions and their statuses. By default no solutions are in a newly installed SharePoint server.

Manage User Solutions

The Manage User Solutions page is also known as the User Solution Management page. Use this page to block deployed farm solutions from running in SharePoint sites. You can also configure how the solution will run, either on the SharePoint server that is used to access this solution (if there are multiple SharePoint front-end servers, you will have a load-balancing of this solution) or on a particular SharePoint server.

Configure Privacy Options

Use the Configure Privacy Options page to configure the following privacy options:

➤ **Customer Experience Improvement Program:** If you accept to participate, then SharePoint will send information to Microsoft about the server hardware and how SharePoint is used. This information is used by Microsoft to understand what they need to do better in the next release of SharePoint. This feature will not send any personal information, such as files or list content, or who you are.

➤ **Microsoft Error Reporting:** If you enable this feature, then SharePoint will collect all relevant information in case of errors or problems, and send it to Microsoft as an Error Report. These reports are also used by Microsoft to understand what it needs to improve. These reports are anonymous, and no private information about the user or the organization will be sent.

➤ **External Web-based Help:** Enable this feature to display Help information from Microsoft's support website. You can also create a local Help system, which this feature will use when displaying Help information.

Configure Cross-Firewall Access Zones

Use the Configure Cross-Firewall Access Zones to define the URL that external users use to access SharePoint. If SharePoint needs to send alert messages to their mobile phones, the URLs will be adjusted to mobile use.

Monitoring

The Monitoring section in SharePoint Central Administration contains links to health analyses, definitions of timer jobs, and multiple reports. Use the Monitoring section when you need to configure and manage any of the following:

➤ Review Problems and Solutions

➤ Review Rule Definitions

➤ Review Job Definitions

➤ Check Job Status

➤ Configure Diagnostic Logging

➤ View Health Reports

➤ Configure Usage and Health Data Collection

These features are described in detail in the following sections. To access these features, start the SharePoint Central Administration and click Monitoring.

Review Problems and Solutions

The Review Problems and Solutions page lists all errors and issues with the current solution. These problems are usually discovered by the new Best Practice Analyzer that is built into SharePoint 2010, both SharePoint Foundation and SharePoint Server. It divides the reports into four categories: Performance, Security, Configuration, and Availability. See Figure B-10 for an example with multiple issues listed under three of these categories.

> **NOTE** *If there are issues discovered by the Best Practice Analyzer, a notification will be listed on the information bar on the start page of the SharePoint Central Administration tool.*

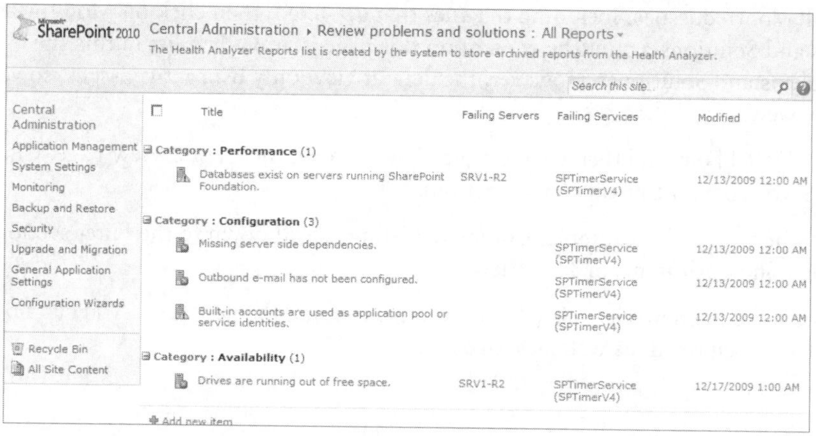

FIGURE B-10

The icons for the reported issues indicate whether this problem is serious or not. In Figure B-10 you can see that three issues are listed with red marks. These are things you need to fix; the other two have yellow warning signs, which indicate that this item is not following best practice, but it will still work. To see more about the reported issue, click on the issue to open a new form. For example, if you click the issue "Outbound e-mail has not been configured," you can see all the information SharePoint has about this issue; see Figure B-11. The problem is that the outbound e-mail server is not yet configured. If you fix this (choose System Settings ⇨ Configure outgoing e-mail settings), then click on the Reanalyze Now button (shown in Figure B-11), this issue should be resolved. You may have to refresh the web page before the issue is removed from this list.

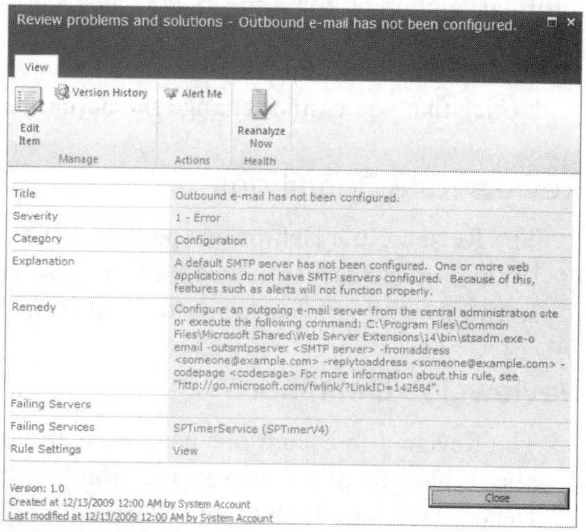

FIGURE B-11

All issues and reports are based on rules defined by Microsoft. To see all the rules, use the steps in the following Try It Out:

TRY IT OUT   **Manage the Best Practice Analyzer settings**

1. Choose Monitoring ⇨ Review problems and solutions to open the Review Problems and Solutions: All Reports page.

2. On the Ribbon, click Site Actions ⇨ View All Site Content ⇨ Health Analyzer Rule Definitions to open the list with all the rules, grouped into the four categories.

3. Click on the rule "Outbound e-mail has not been configured" to view its settings. It is configured to run weekly and check all servers in the farm. Say you want to check this every month instead — click Edit Item, change the Schedule to Monthly, and click Save; the All Rules page reopens.

4. If you want to see all reported issues, including the ones that are fixed, then click on Monitoring ⇨ Review Problems and Solutions again (the content on this page is actually a list in this site named Review Problems and Solutions). However, the default view only lists active issues, so you need to create a new view.

5. Click the List tab in the Ribbon, and then click Create View to open the Create View page. Click All Reports (in the Start from an Existing View section).

6. Enter a name for this new view; for example, **Complete Listing**, scroll down to the Filter section, and select the option "Show All Items in This View."

7. Click OK to save and close the new view. The list now appears using the new view. You can now see all reports that have been fixed, as well as active issues.

How It Works

SharePoint 2010 comes with an intelligent monitoring module known as the Best Practice Analyzer. It will continuously monitor a number of parameters and settings that are defined in the list Review Problems and Solutions. Any issues found will be listed on the Review problems and solutions page, including information on how to fix the issue.

Notice that you cannot change the actual rules, just configure it and enable or disable it.

Review Rule Definitions

The Review Rule Definitions page is actually a shortcut to the Health Analyzer Rule Definition list mentioned earlier in step 2 of the preceding Try It Out, "Manage the Best Practice Analyzer settings," so if you just want to see these rules, this page is the easiest way.

Review Job Definitions

The Review Job Definitions page lists all job definitions in this SharePoint farm. In total there are about 30 of them per web application, possibly more. For example, you will see Audit Log Trimming, Dead Site Delete, Disk Quota Warning, and Recycle Bin listed on this page. For each job in this list you will see its name, its associated web application, and schedule type (Minute, Hourly, Daily, Weekly, and Monthly). In the left pane are links to filter these job definitions:

➤ **Timer Job Status:** Lists jobs that wait to start (10 jobs per page), and the time they will start. At the bottom of this page is a status page showing the status from the last run, and when it was performed.

➤ **Scheduled Jobs:** Lists all jobs that wait to start, including when they will run.

➤ **Running Jobs:** Lists all jobs that currently are running, and when they started. Normally you do not see any jobs here, unless they take some time to complete.

➤ **Job History:** Lists all jobs that have completed, including when they started and their duration.

➤ **Job Definition:** The default list view that lists all defined jobs.

Click one of these jobs to edit its settings; for example, Audit Log Trimming (see Figure B-12). Notice that you can change the time it is scheduled to run. At the bottom are buttons for Run Now and Disable.

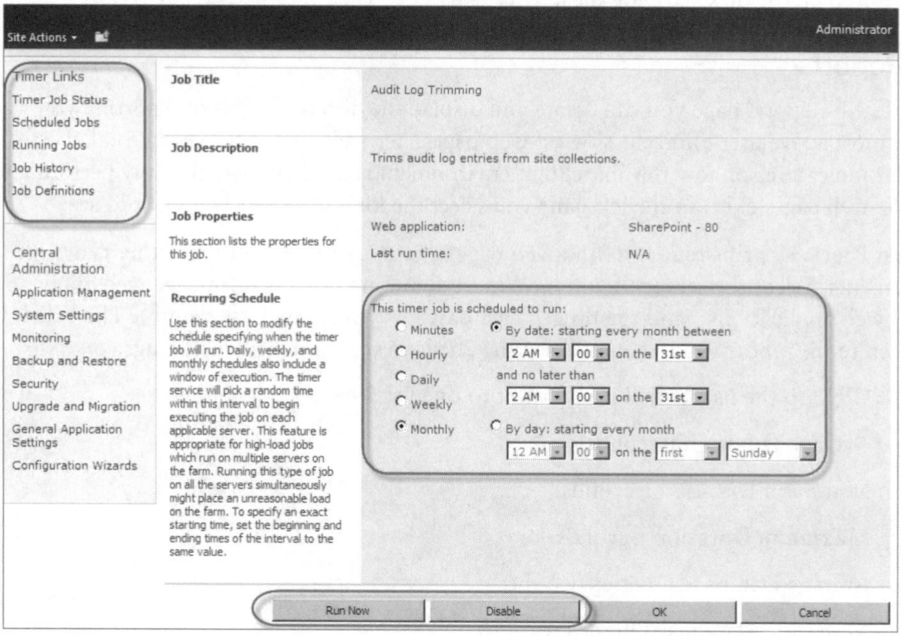

FIGURE B-12

Check Job Status

Check Job Status is just a quick link to open the Timer Job Status view, as described earlier in the Monitoring — Review Job Definitions section.

Configure Diagnostic Logging

On the Configure Diagnostic Logging page you can define exactly what type of logging you want, and to what level of detail:

➤ **Event Throttling:** Select one or more main categories, or their subcategories: Business Connectivity Service, SharePoint Foundation, WSS Search Diagnostics, or All Categories. Then select the Least Critical Event to Report to the Event Log: None, Critical, Error, Warning, Information, and Verbose). Then select the Least Critical Event to Report to the Trace Log, and set it to one of the same. If you want different log levels for different categories, then select the first one, set its level, then select the second category and set its level and so on.

➤ **Event Log Flood Protection:** Enable this setting to avoid filling the log files with repeating events.

➤ **Trace Log:** Set the path to the log file (by default, it is `\Program Files\Common Files\\ Microsoft Shared\Web Server Extensions\14\LOGS\`), how many days to store log files, and possibly set a maximum disk space available for the log files (Default: Not enabled), to avoid filling up the disk with log files.

View Health Reports

On the View Health Reports page you can create and display the different types of reporting you want, such as for the most active users, and the slowest web pages, per web application or in total. These reports are clear indications of how the SharePoint environment is used and whether any performance issues in specific web pages exist. In the left pane you select the kind of report you want to see:

➤ **Slowest Pages:** Use this report to find web pages that may need tuning or other types of adjustments. Select the server (if you have more than one in your farm), the web application (or all web applications), and the range (Last day, Last week, or Last month). Then click Go to generate the report where you will see the 25 slowest web pages, including:

   ➤ URL (to the page; click if you want to open that page)

   ➤ Average Duration (seconds)

   ➤ Minimum Duration (seconds)

   ➤ Maximum Duration (seconds)

   ➤ Average Database Queries (Count)

   ➤ Minimum Database Queries (Count)

   ➤ Maximum Database Queries (Count)

   ➤ Number of Requests

➤ **Top Active Users:** Use this report to identify the most active users (and least active users); this may help you understand how SharePoint is used, and whether it has been accepted by your users or not. You can select a specific SharePoint server (if you have more than one), web application, and time range (Last day, Last week, or Last month). Click Go to generate the report, and a list of users appears, including:

> ➤ *User logon names:* Including the domain name; for example, *filobit\administrator.*

> ➤ *Number of requests:* Meaning how many web pages this user has opened.

> ➤ *Last Access Time:* Displays the date and time this user requested a web page.

> ➤ *Percentage of Successful Requests:* Should be 100 percent. If it's not, there may be some issues regarding access to some web pages.

Configure Usage and Health Data Collection

On the Configure Usage and Health Data Collection page you configure whether you want to enable usage data collection, and what type of events you want to record in the log files. By default, all types of events are logged. This log information is then used by the analysis and reporting features (see previous sections), but they also require system resources and disk space, so it is a tradeoff between interesting information and server performance.

This page contains the following options and settings:

> ➤ **Enable Usage Data Collection:** You may turn this log collection on or off (Default: Enabled).

> ➤ **Events to Log:** Choose from the following list what events to log:

>> ➤ Content Import Usage

>> ➤ Content Export Usage

>> ➤ Page Requests

>> ➤ Feature Use

>> ➤ Search Query Usage

>> ➤ Site Inventory Usage

>> ➤ Timer Jobs

>> ➤ Rating Usage

> ➤ **Log File Location:** (Default: `C:\Program Files\Common Files\Microsoft Shared\Web Server Extensions\14\LOGS\`)

> ➤ **Maximum Log File Size:** (Default: 5GB)

> ➤ **Enable Health Data Collection:** (Default: Enabled)

> ➤ **Health Logging Schedule:** Click the link to open the job and set its schedule.

> ➤ **Log Collection Schedule:** Click the link to open the job and set its schedule.

> ➤ **Database Server:** Set the logging database server (Default: the same SQL used by SharePoint Foundation).

> ➤ **Database Name:** The name of the logging database (Default: WSS_Logging).

> ➤ **Database Authentication:** Choose between Windows authentication or SQL authentication (Default: Windows authentication).

Backup and Restore Features

Chapter 10 covers all the configuration settings in this section, but here is a quick overview of the Backup and Restore features:

➤ **Perform a Backup:** Select what to back up (from a complete farm to a single content database) and where to store the backup files, and then start the backup process. Note that this process cannot be scheduled using this feature; use PowerShell or STSADM to schedule backups.

➤ **Restore from a Backup:** Select what to restore (from a complete farm to a single content database) and from what file location, and then start the restore.

➤ **Configure Backup Settings:** Set the number of backup and restore threads, plus the backup location.

➤ **View Backup and Restore History:** Use this to see all the available backup sets.

➤ **Check Backup and Restore Job Status:** Use this to see the status of current jobs.

➤ **Perform a Site Collection Backup:** Back up a single site collection.

➤ **Export a Site or List:** Back up (export) a single website or list to a file.

➤ **Recover Data from an Unattached Content Database:** This works with databases that exist in the SQL Server, but is not used by any SharePoint web applications.

➤ **Check Granular Backup Job Status:** Lists all current and previous backup jobs, including exports of sites and lists, and their status.

Upgrade and Migration

The Upgrade and Migration section in SharePoint Central Administration contains links to view the product and patch status and upgrade status. Use the Upgrade and Migration section when you need to configure and manage any of the following:

➤ Check Product and Patch Installation Status

➤ Review Database Status

➤ Check Upgrade Status

These features are described in the following sections. To access these features, start the SharePoint Central Administration and click Upgrade and Migration.

Check Product and Patch Installation Status

Use the Check Product and Patch Installation Status page to view a list of all the servers in the farm, version of SharePoint, and their installation status. For example, Figure B-13 shows the list for a single server installation on a server named SRV1-R2. Note that this list will grow when you apply service packs or upgrades to newer versions. This feature is new for SharePoint 2010, and will be invaluable when you need to find out what SharePoint versions and service packs are installed.

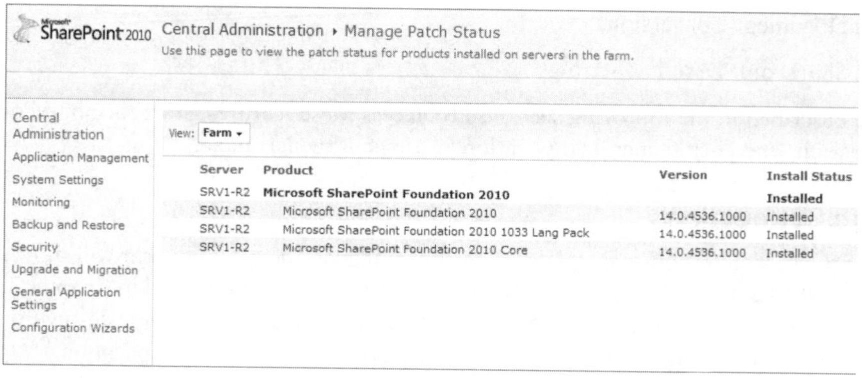

FIGURE B-13

Review Database Status

Review Database Status is also a great new feature in SharePoint 2010 — it lists all the content databases, their names, and what SQL instance names they belong to, plus the type of database and its status; if you need to do anything with a specific database, it will be listed on this page. See Figure B-14.

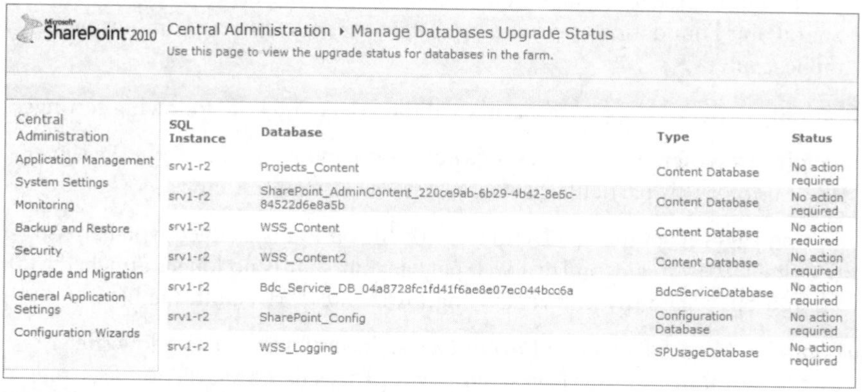

FIGURE B-14

Check Upgrade Status

The Check Upgrade Status page displays the status of ongoing upgrades and their details. This list will be empty if there are no current upgrades. If you are performing an upgrade, use this page to see whether you need to take some actions.

General Application Settings

The General Application Settings section in SharePoint Central Administration contains links to configure external connections, conversions, and SharePoint Designer settings. Use the General Application Settings section when you need to configure and manage any of the following:

➤   Configure Send to Connections

➤ Configure Document Conversions

➤ Configure SharePoint Designer Settings

These features are described in the following sections. To access these features, start the SharePoint Central Administration, and click General Application Settings in the left pane.

Configure Send to Connections

Use the Configure Send to Connections page to define the preconfigured destinations that will show up when a user selects to send a document to another location, as described in more detail in Chapter 3. By default there is no preconfigured destination, but you can add as many as required. These destinations are called Send To Connections and are global for all site collections in a given web application.

Configure Document Conversions

Document conversions are a very handy feature when you need automatic conversion from one file type to another; for example, from an Office .docx file to an .aspx web page file. However, SharePoint Foundation does not support document conversions.

Configure SharePoint Designer Settings

Use the Configure SharePoint Designer Settings page to control how SharePoint Designer 2010 may be used within the SharePoint Foundation environment. There are four different options, which you configure per web application:

➤ **Web Application:** Set the web application that will be affected by the following settings.

➤ **Enable SharePoint Designer:** This is a main switch — do you want SharePoint Designer 2010 enabled or not for this particular web application? (Default: Enabled)

➤ **Enable Detaching Pages from the Site Definition:** If this option is enabled, you can use SharePoint Designer 2010 to customize a web page layout so it is no longer attached to the general site definition, previously known as "unghosted sites." (Default: Enabled)

➤ **Enable Customizing Master Pages and Layout Pages:** Specify whether to allow site administrators to customize Master Pages and Layout Pages using SharePoint Designer. (Default: Enabled)

➤ **Enable Managing of the Web Site URL Structure:** If this option is enabled, you can use SharePoint Designer 2010 to modify the URL site structure. (Default: Enabled)

Configuration Wizards — Launch the Farm Configuration Wizard

The Configuration Wizards section in SharePoint Central Administration contains a link to Launch the Farm Configuration Wizard. Use this wizard when you want to configure service applications and managed service accounts for the SharePoint farm.

These service applications will be set up and configured with default settings for a typical organization. You can later change these settings or manually create new service applications, if needed. The following Try It Out describes how to run this configuration wizard.

TRY IT OUT | Run the Configuration Wizard

1. Log on as the administrator, start the Central Administration tool, and choose Configuration Wizard ⇨ Launch the Farm Configuration Wizard.

2. Select the option Walk Me through the Settings Using This Wizard. I Will Select the Services to Use in This Farm and the Type of Site to Create. Click Next.

3. Select the Service Account to be used for the service applications listed below. You can either use existing accounts or enter a user account that SharePoint will register as a managed account. Select the services you want to create. Click Next. This procedure may take a few minutes.

4. The final step is to create a site collection. If you don't want it, click Cancel; otherwise, create it (see previously in this appendix how to create site collections).

How It Works

This wizard will ask you a few simple questions and then automatically install and configure the service applications you selected. You can also install these service applications manually, instead of running the wizard, but that will require more knowledge about how to configure SharePoint Foundation 2010.

You can also configure everything manually. This is harder and takes more time, but it will give you much more control over the installation. Typically, this is the preferred option for an experienced SharePoint administrator. If you select this option, you actually return to the start page for Central Administration; that is, no wizard, or guide, will help you.

SECURITY SETTINGS IN SHAREPOINT FOUNDATION

Central Administration has a specific section for security settings where you will find a large number of links to different security related settings, as listed below:

➤ **Manage the Farm Administrator groups:** Define users and groups that will have full access to the SharePoint farm.

➤ **Approve or reject distribution groups:** SharePoint can suggest that a distribution group should be created; with this link you can view and approve these suggested distribution groups.

➤ **Specify web application user policy:** Manage permissions for specific service accounts in SharePoint, such as the Search Crawling account.

➤ **Configure managed accounts:** Configure all managed accounts, for example whether passwords should be automatically changed.

➤ **Configure service accounts:** Change service accounts for service applications.

➤ **Configure password change settings:** Manage automatic password changes and who will be notified about these changes.

➤ **Specify authentication providers:** Manage security settings for the zones for each web application. For example, enable anonymous access and Kerberos authentication.

➤ **Manage trust:** Add and manage trust relationships between SharePoint farms.

➤ **Manage antivirus settings:** Configure settings related to antivirus scanners; for example, whether documents should be scanned during upload to a library and whether infected documents should be blocked from download to the client computer.

➤ **Define blocked file types:** Control what file types SharePoint will prohibit to upload to libraries. For example, by default you cannot upload .EXE files.

➤ **Manage web part security:** Define the global settings for web parts for a given web application; for example, whether web parts should be allowed to be connected and whether the Web Part Gallery will be available.

➤ **Configure self-service site creating:** Define whether end users will be able to configure site collections. By default this is enabled for the web application that hosts My Sites.

➤ **Configure information rights management:** IRM helps protect sensitive documents stored in SharePoint from being misused; for example, it ensures that no one except the intended user can read a specific Office document, regardless of whether they manage to get a copy of that document. IRM depends on the Windows Rights Management Services (RMS); use this configuration page to define the location of the Windows server that runs the RMS service.

> **NOTE** *SharePoint Server also has a page called Configure Information Management Policy, which is different than Configure Information Rights Management. Knowing this difference can be helpful if you are working in SharePoint Foundation and a colleague tells you about some configuration settings and you can't seem to find them on the Configure Information Rights Management page.*

Security is an important topic in SharePoint, and instead of just listing all these security settings, the following sections will describe important security concepts and let you test them using a number of Try It Out exercises. You will also find security-related topics discussed in almost all chapters in this book, from creating site collections and sites to managing lists and documents. This will help you understand when and how to use these security options.

SharePoint Foundation is secure by design and by default. To do anything at all in a SharePoint Foundation environment, you need to be granted permission. In SharePoint there are three types of user accounts:

➤ **Managed Accounts:** Also known as *service accounts*, they are used by SharePoint itself to run services and connections to external sources. The accounts are, in fact, ordinary user accounts, typically created in Active Directory, but they are granted special permissions when the administrator defines them as managed accounts.

➤ **Administrators:** Sometimes known as *owners*, they have full access to some objects in SharePoint; see more about administrators in the next section of this appendix.

➤ **Users:** Users have at least read access to some objects in SharePoint; for example, a site or a document. Typically these are ordinary Active Directory user accounts. A special type of user, known as *Anonymous User*, is typically used when you allow anonymous access to a site or list. You learn more about anonymous access later in this appendix. Chapter 7 shows you examples of how to use anonymous access.

Comparing SharePoint Administrators

SharePoint has three main types of administrators, which are granted access and permissions to manage different objects in SharePoint:

➤ **Farm administrators:** A user or security group that can manage the complete farm using SharePoint Central Administration tool, STSADM, or PowerShell. The user account used to install the first SharePoint Foundation server was automatically added to the Farm Administrators group. This user can add and remove any user account to this group, using Central Administration ➪ Security ➪ Manage the Farm Administrators group, or with a PowerShell script.

➤ **Site collection administrators:** A user (but not security group) who is granted full access to a specific site collection. When you create a new site collection you must define a primary site collection administrator, and optionally a secondary site collection administrator. If more administrators are required, then open the top site in this site collection and choose Site Actions ➪ Site Settings ➪ Site Collection Administrators (there is also another path to this page: Site Actions ➪ Site Permissions, then click Site Collection Administrators in the Ribbon).

➤ **Site owner:** A user or security group that is granted full access to a site (usually a subsite). If you create a subsite, you will be its owner; that is, its administrator. To add more users, or security groups, as site owners, open the site, click Site Actions ➪ Site Permissions and click on the link *<site name>* Owners.

An easy way to see the difference between these three types of administrators is to compare what they can and cannot do. The following table lists some common operations.

OPERATION	FARM ADMINISTRATOR	SITE COLLECTION ADMINISTRATOR	SITE OWNER
Manage SharePoint using its Central Administration tool	Yes	No	No
Create and delete site collections	Yes	No	No
Add and remove site collection administrators	Yes	Yes	No
Take ownership of sites and subsites	No	Yes	No
Manage access to a specific site or subsite	No	No	Yes
Run STSADM	Yes	Partly*	Partly*
Run PowerShell script	Yes	Partly*	Partly*
Configure site collection features, such as master pages, content types, and SharePoint groups	No	Yes	No
Create subsites in an existing site collection	No	Yes	Yes

continues

(continued)

OPERATION	FARM ADMINISTRATOR	SITE COLLECTION ADMINISTRATOR	SITE OWNER
Configure local settings in a subsite, such as customize the page layout, create new lists, delete lists, and delete this subsite	No	No	Yes
Allow security groups (local or AD) as members	Yes	No	Yes

*The site collection administrator and the site owner can perform actions that relate to their own site collections or sites, respectively, if they have access to the SharePoint server itself — for example, they can make backups.

Setting User Permission Levels

User permissions are used to grant the typical end user access to SharePoint; for example, a site. To protect the SharePoint environment, there are more than 30 different detailed permissions, such as Read Item, Create Item, and so on. To make applying a combination of permissions easier, SharePoint allows you to create preconfigured security roles, known as *permission levels*. These levels may be applied to a user, a security group, or a SharePoint group (more about these in the next section).

Let's dive a bit deeper into creating permission levels — the complete list of permissions available appears in the following table.

PERMISSION	DESCRIPTION
Manage Lists	Create and delete lists, add or remove columns in a list, and add or remove public views of a list.
Override Check-Out	Discard or check in a document that is checked out to another user.
Add Items	Add items to lists and add documents to document libraries.
Edit Items	Edit items in lists, edit documents in document libraries, and customize web part pages in document libraries.
Delete Items	Delete items from a list and documents from a document library.
View Items	View items in lists and view documents in document libraries.
Approve Items	Approve a minor version of a list item or document.
Open Items	View the source of documents with server-side file handlers.
View Versions	View past versions of a list item or document.
Delete Versions	Delete past versions of a list item or document.
Create Alerts	Create e-mail alerts.
View Application Pages	View forms, views, and application pages. Enumerate lists.

PERMISSION	DESCRIPTION
Manage Permissions	Create and change permission levels on the website and assign permissions to users and groups.
View Web Analytics Data	View reports on website usage.
Create Subsites	Create subsites such as team sites, Meeting Workspace sites, and Document Workspace sites.
Manage Web Site	Grants the ability to perform all administration tasks for the website as well as manage content.
Add and Customize Pages	Add, change, or delete HTML pages or web part pages, and edit the website using a Windows SharePoint Foundation–compatible editor.
Apply Themes and Borders	Apply a theme or borders to the entire website.
Apply Style Sheets	Apply a style sheet (.CSS file) to the website.
Create Groups	Create a group of users that can be used anywhere within the site collection.
Browse Directories	Enumerate files and folders in a website using SharePoint Designer and Web DAV interfaces.
Use Self-Service Site Creation	Create a website using Self-Service Site Creation.
View Pages	View pages in a website.
Enumerate Permissions	Enumerate permissions on the website, list, folder, document, or list item.
Browse User Information	View information about users of the website.
Manage Alerts	Manage alerts for all users of the website.
Use Remote Interfaces	Use SOAP, Web DAV, the Client Object Model, or SharePoint Designer interfaces to access the website.
Use Client Integration Features	Use features that launch client applications. Without this permission, users will have to work on documents locally and upload their changes.
Open	Allows users to open a website, list, or folder in order to access items inside that container.
Edit Personal User Information	Allows a user to change his or her own user information, such as adding a picture.
Manage Personal Views	Create, change, and delete personal views of lists.
Add/Remove Personal Web Parts	Add or remove personal web parts on a web part page.
Update Personal Web Parts	Update web parts to display personalized information.

These permissions cannot be granted directly to a user; instead you must create permission levels, that is, permission roles, to a user. SharePoint comes with a number of preconfigured permission levels, which will typically cover the most common needs of security roles. These permission levels are listed next, and their corresponding permissions are listed in the tables that follow:

➤ **Read:** Can view pages and list items and download documents.

➤ **Contribute:** Can view specific lists, document libraries, list items, folders, or documents when given permissions.

➤ **Design:** Can view, add, update, delete, approve, and customize.

➤ **Full Control:** Has full control.

➤ **Limited Access:** Can view specific lists, document libraries, list items, folders, or documents when given permissions.

> **NOTE** *Limited Access is a special type of permission role used by SharePoint to indicate that a user or group is granted direct access to specific objects; for example, a list or a single document. Don't let the term* Limited *fool you — such a user may have full control over a single object. A better term would be* Specific Access.

To better understand the difference between Read and Contribute, look at the following tables where all the detailed permissions are listed for each default permission level, except Limited Access and Full Control because that covers exactly what its name implies: all permissions, as described in the previous table.

READ	DESCRIPTION
View Items	View items in lists and view documents in document libraries.
Open Items	View the source of documents with server-side file handlers.
View Versions	View past versions of a list item or document.
Create Alerts	Create alerts.
View Application Pages	View forms, views, and application pages. Enumerate lists.
Use Self-Service Site Creation	Create a site collection using Self-Service Site Creation. Note that this feature must first be turned on!
View Pages	View pages in the current website.
Browse User Information	View information about users of the website.
Use Remote Interfaces	Use SOAP, WebDAV, the Client Object Model, or SharePoint Designer interfaces to access the website.

READ	DESCRIPTION
Use Client Integration Features	Use features that launch client applications. Without this permission, users will have to work on documents locally and upload their changes.
Open	Allows users to open a website, list, or folder in order to access items inside that container.

CONTRIBUTE	DESCRIPTION
Add Items	Add items to lists and documents to document libraries.
Edit Items	Edit items in lists, edit documents in document libraries, and customize web part pages in document libraries.
Delete Items	Delete items from a list and documents from a document library.
View Items	View items in lists and view documents in document libraries.
Open Items	View the source of documents with server-side file handlers.
View Versions	View past versions of a list item or document.
Delete Versions	Delete past versions of a list item or document.
Create Alerts	Create e-mail alerts.
View Application Pages	View forms, views, and application pages. Enumerate lists.
Browse Directories	Enumerate files and folders in a website using SharePoint Designer and Web DAV interfaces.
Use Self-Service Site Creation	Create a site collection using Self-Service Site Creation. Note that this feature must first be turned on!
View Pages	View pages in a website.
Browse User Information	View information about users of the website.
Use Remote Interfaces	Use SOAP, WebDAV, the Client Object Model, or SharePoint Designer interfaces to access the website.
Use Client Integration Features	Use features that launch client applications. Without this permission, users will have to work on documents locally and upload their changes.
Open	Allows users to open a website, list, or folder in order to access items inside that container.
Edit Personal User Information	Allows a user to change his or her own user information, such as adding a picture.

continues

(continued)

CONTRIBUTE	DESCRIPTION
Manage Personal Views	Create, change, and delete personal views of lists.
Add/Remove Personal Web Parts	Add or remove personal web parts on a web part page.
Update Personal Web Parts	Update web parts to display personalized information.

DESIGN	DESCRIPTION
Manage Lists	Create and delete lists, add or remove columns in a list, and add or remove public views of a list.
Override Check-Out	Discard or check in a document that is checked out to another user.
Add Items	Add items to lists and documents to document libraries.
Edit Items	Edit items in lists, edit documents in document libraries, and customize web part pages in document libraries.
Delete Items	Delete items from a list and documents from a document library.
View Items	View items in lists and view documents in document libraries.
Approve Items	Approve a minor version of a list item or document.
Open Items	View the source of documents with server-side file handlers.
View Versions	View past versions of a list item or document.
Delete Versions	Delete past versions of a list item or document.
Create Alerts	Create e-mail alerts.
View Application Pages	View forms, views, and application pages. Enumerate lists.
Add and Customize Pages	Add, change, or delete HTML pages or web part pages, and edit the website using a Microsoft SharePoint Foundation–compatible editor.
Apply Themes and Borders	Apply a theme or borders to the entire website.
Apply Style Sheets	Apply a style sheet (.CSS file) to the website.
Browse Directories	Enumerate files and folders in a website using SharePoint Designer and Web DAV interfaces.
View Pages	View pages in a website.
Browse User Information	View information about users of the website.
Use Remote Interfaces	Use SOAP, WebDAV, the Client Object Model or SharePoint Designer interfaces to access the website.

DESIGN	DESCRIPTION
Use Client Integration Features	Use features that launch client applications. Without this permission, users will have to work on documents locally and upload their changes.
Open	Allows users to open a website, list, or folder in order to access items inside that container.
Edit Personal User Information	Allows a user to change his or her own user information, such as adding a picture.
Manage Personal Views	Create, change, and delete personal views of lists.
Add/Remove Personal Web Parts	Add or remove personal web parts on a web part page.
Update Personal Web Parts	Update web parts to display personalized information.

If these default permission levels are not what are needed, you have two options: Either modify an existing default permission level, or create a new one. If you only need a minor modification of a default permission level, doing just that is very tempting. But wait! This practice is risky, because all other administrators, today and tomorrow, will "know" what default permission each level has. For example, I had an organization contact me about a strange issue: Users with Contribute level could create subsites, although the default setting is that only users with Full Control, that is, owners, have that permission. The reason was that one previous administrator was asked to enable users with Contribute level permission to create subsites, so he simply added that permission to the Contribute level, but he forgot to mention that to the new administrator and to document the installation.

The right way to create a group with both Contribute level permission and Create Subsite ability is to create a new permission level, using the default Contribute as a template. Remember that permission levels are defined per site collection; that is, you cannot create or modify these levels using the Central Administration tool. The steps in the following Try It Out describe how to do that.

TRY IT OUT Create a New Permission Level

1. Open the top site in the site collection where you want to create the new permission level. You must be logged on as a site collection administrator.

2. Click Site Actions ⇨ Site Permissions and click Permission Levels on the Ribbon.

3. Because you will use Contribute as a template, click on it to open its detailed permissions.

4. Scroll to the end of this form and click Copy Permission Level. This gives you a new, unnamed form with the exact same permissions as Contribute.

5. Enter a name for this new level; for example, **Enhanced Contributor**, and a description: **Same as Contributor plus can create subsites.**

6. Select the required permission, Create Subsites, and then click Create.

7. Verify that the new permission level is listed among the others.

How It Works

Think of permission levels as security roles for a specific site collection; these permission levels consist of a number of detailed permissions. SharePoint Foundation comes with four standard levels, including Full Control, Design, Contribute, and Read. Permission levels can be defined per site; any permission role defined on the top site level will be inherited by all subsites unless they have a specific permission level setting.

Using SharePoint Groups

Previously, you learned that a user must be associated with a permission level role before she can access anything in SharePoint; for example, to open a website the user must have at least Read level permissions. You grant the permission level directly to a user, or to a security group:

TRY IT OUT Grant a User Read-Level Access

1. Open the site (top site or subsite) as a site owner.

2. Click Site Actions ⇨ Site Permissions and click Grant Permissions on the Ribbon.

3. In the Grant Permission form that appears, enter the user account (or security group) in the Users/Groups box, then select Grant Users Permissions Directly, and select Read — Can View Pages and List Items and Download Documents.

4. Click OK to save and close.

How It Works

Control user access by granting their accounts direct permission, using any of the existing permission roles. Best practice is to make the user a member of a group that has been granted a permission role, as described next.

Most organizations don't want to grant permissions to individual user accounts, because managing a lot of accounts over time is hard. But the preceding steps also work for security groups (local or AD groups). But sometimes you need to group people in SharePoint, but no matching security group exists — what do you do? This is where the SharePoint groups come in and save you from creating new security groups. A SharePoint group is like a security group, but it only works in the SharePoint environment. You cannot see these groups outside SharePoint, for example, in Active Directory. Only user accounts and security groups can be members of a SharePoint group; nested groups are not allowed. That is, a SharePoint group cannot be member of another SharePoint group.

When you create a new site, for example, the top site in a new site collection, you will automatically create three SharePoint groups. The names of these SharePoint groups are based upon the name of the site. For example, if the site name is "ABC" you will get these SharePoint groups:

> **NOTE** *When creating a subsite, you are given an option of inheriting its parent permissions or using unique permissions. Only when selecting unique permissions will this site get its own SharePoint groups, as described later.*

> ➤ **ABC Visitors:** This SharePoint group is associated with the permission level Read. Any member of this group can view, copy, and print content in lists and libraries, including previous versions, if any.

> ➤ **ABC Members:** This SharePoint group is associated with the permission level Contribute. Members of this group can also add, modify, and delete lists and library content.

> ➤ **ABC Owners:** This SharePoint group is associated with the permission level Full Control. Members of this group have full access to this site and all its content.

> **NOTE** *Not only are these SharePoint groups convenient for granting users access, they also have some functionality when used in SharePoint Server 2010 (the My Profile link). You can find out more about that in Appendix D.*

When necessary you can create new SharePoint groups; for example, if you need a group of users who can add content but also create subsites; only members of the Owner group can do that. But before you start creating this new group, you need a new permission level role that matches the permission you need; that is, Contribute plus the Create Subsite permission in this example. To create a new SharePoint group and grant this new permission level, see the following steps:

TRY IT OUT   Create a New SharePoint Group

1. Log on as site owner and open the site where you want to create the new SharePoint groups; for example, the site ABC.

2. The first action is to create the group: Click Site Actions ⇨ Site Permissions and then click on Create Group in the Ribbon.

3. On the web page Create Group that appears, enter these settings:

    a. Name: Enter the name for this group; for example, **ABC Contributor Plus**. Try to use a descriptive name; a good idea is to use the same prefix (ABC in this example) as the default groups.

    b. About Me: Enter a description of this group.

    c.   **Group Owner:** Define who can change the settings for this group, including its membership. By default, it will be the user who created the group.

    d.   **Group Settings:** This section allows you to define who can view the membership of this group, and who can edit its membership.

    e.   **Membership Request:** This section allows you to define whether users can request to join and leave this group. The default is No. If you set this option to Yes, you can auto-accept the request, or send an e-mail with this request to the address you enter in the field "Send membership requests to the following e-mail address." This could also be a mail group, such as `Support@filobit.com`.

4.   Click Create. This new SharePoint group appears, with all of its current members; that is, the user account defined in step 4c. If required, add new members to this group now by clicking New and entering user accounts and/or security groups. Click OK when done.

5.   Add this group to the site, and grant it the required permission level. Click Site Actions ⇨ Site Permissions and then click on Grant Permissions.

6.   In the Users/Groups field, enter the new SharePoint group name, and click Grant Users Permission Directly to display all available permission levels. For this example, select the new permission level, ABC Contributor Plus, and click OK.

> **NOTE** *If a name you enter is underlined in red, then SharePoint cannot identify it with certainty. Right-click on it to see a list of candidates, if any. Select the one you want. You can also click on the browse icon (a book) to search for user accounts, security groups, and SharePoint groups.*

How It Works

SharePoint groups are a complement to ordinary security groups, but they can only be used to grant permissions to SharePoint objects. A SharePoint group can contain user accounts and ordinary security groups, but not other SharePoint groups. You grant permissions to a SharePoint group by selecting a permission level for it.

    All objects with access to this site are now listed on this page; that is, user accounts, security groups, and SharePoint groups. If you want to remove one, select its checkbox, and click Remove User Permissions on the Ribbon. If you need to change the permission, select the object's checkbox and click Edit User Permissions.

Granting Anonymous Access

    In some situations, you need to allow anonymous users access to a website. You should think hard about this before you open up SharePoint — or anything else, for that matter — to everyone. Or perhaps what you really want is to open SharePoint Foundation for all users in your organization, which is different from opening it up to anonymous users. The following section presents the steps on how to perform both of these configurations.

Opening SharePoint Foundation Sites for Every User in Your Organization

When users log on to a network, such as an Active Directory domain, they get authenticated. Windows automatically adds these authenticated users to two special groups: One is called Everyone, and the other is called Authenticated Users. You can grant either of these two groups access to SharePoint; for example, by making the group a member of a SharePoint group such as Visitor.

The difference between Everyone and Authenticated Users is that the Authenticated Users group contains only members who actually have logged on, using an ordinary user account, whereas the group Everyone also contains any type of connected session that does not require explicit logon, also known as a *NULL session*. In other words, granting the Authenticated Users group access to SharePoint is safer. To add the Authenticated Users group access, follow these instructions:

TRY IT OUT Open SharePoint Foundation for Read Access to All Authenticated Users

1. Log on as a site owner.

2. Open the website you want to open for all authenticated users. Note that this setting only affects the current site (and all subsites that inherit permission settings from it). This setting can be used on every website that has unique permission settings, not just the top site.

3. Click Site Actions ⇨ Site Permissions and click Grant Permissions. The Grant Permissions dialog appears; see Figure B-15.

4. Enter **Authenticated Users** in the Users/Groups field, and click the Check Names icon; the name will now be replaced with NT AUTHORITY\authenticated users.

5. Select the permission required: Use the drop-down menu for Grant Permissions and select the SharePoint group with Read access (usually the Visitors group); you can also grant Read access directly by choosing the Grant User Permission Directly option and selecting the Read permission level.

6. Click OK to save and close this page.

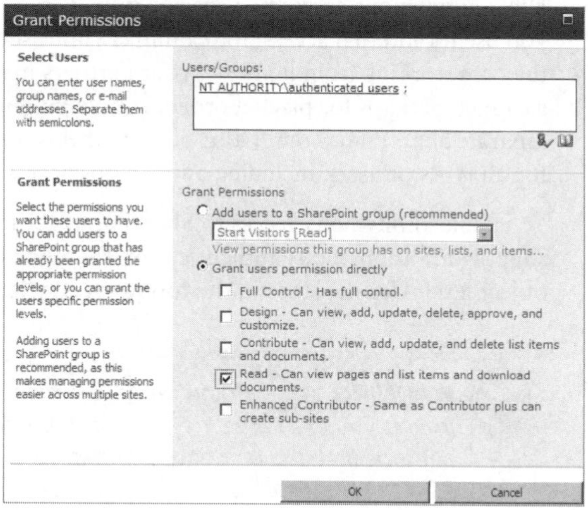

How It works

Enabling read access to the built-in domain group Authenticated Users will ensure that all users that can log on to the domain will have Read access to the SharePoint environment.

FIGURE B-15

Once again, this method is an easy and safe way to open a SharePoint Foundation site to everyone with a user account in your organization; you can be sure no one outside the organization will be able to access this site.

Opening SharePoint Foundation Sites for Anonymous Access

If you want to give everyone access, regardless of whether they are internal or external users, the previous method will not work, because external uses don't have user accounts in your domain. A typical example is when you want to open a website to everyone on the Internet. Most likely, such a SharePoint Foundation environment will not contain sensitive information or anything not meant for public access. There are three common scenarios when exposing a SharePoint Foundation server to the Internet:

➤ **Connect the SharePoint Foundation server directly to the Internet:** Bad idea! It will not survive for long before someone hacks it. Do not connect any server directly to the Internet!

➤ **Protect the WSS server behind a firewall:** Better idea. Many organizations find this an acceptable solution — if the firewall is properly configured. Typically such a SharePoint Foundation server will be connected to the Demilitarized Zone (DMZ) network segment.

➤ **Protect the WSS behind a ForeFront TMG server, which in turn may be protected by the ordinary firewall:** This is a very good solution that will satisfy even very high security requirements. Users on the Internet will never access the SharePoint Server directly; instead they will be directed to the ForeFront TMG server, which in turn connects to the SharePoint Foundation server, grabs the information the user requests, and sends it back to the user.

The SharePoint Foundation server in the last scenario is so well protected that you may choose to allow anonymous access to a specific website that resides on the same SharePoint Foundation server you use for internal access; for example, your users could access the SharePoint Foundation site when they are working from home; or your partners may access a specific SharePoint Foundation site as an extranet, perhaps for placing orders and looking up internal prices. It is up to you whether you want a separate SharePoint Foundation server for this, or whether you want to run a single SharePoint farm for all types of users, including anonymous access, internal users, and extranet users.

To enable anonymous access to SharePoint, for example, a single site, you first need to activate the support for anonymous authentication for a given web application, then enable it on the site or object level. Use the steps in the following Try It Out to do it.

> ⊗ **WARNING** *Avoid doing the following Try It Out on your production environment, unless you are very sure you want to enable it for anonymous access. Try these settings first in a test environment.*

TRY IT OUT Open a SharePoint Foundation Site for Anonymous Access

1. Begin by activating anonymous authentication: Log on as a farm administrator and open the Central Administration tool.

2. Click Application Management ➪ Manage Web Applications to open the Web Application Management page.

3. Select the web application that contains the site you want to enable for anonymous access, and then click the Authentication Providers button on the Ribbon.

4. A new form, Authentication Providers, appears, listing all the zones for this web application; click the zone that you want to use for anonymous access, for example, Default.

5. Set the Enable Anonymous Access checkbox, and click Save.

The action you just took was to activate anonymous authentication for a specific zone belonging to a specific web application. Behind the scenes, SharePoint configured the corresponding IIS website (for example, the Default Web Site) to allow anonymous access. Never change the IIS website manually; it must be modified by SharePoint to work properly. If you want to check the new settings in the virtual IIS website, then do this:

6. Open the Internet Information Services (IIS) Manager, then:

a. Expand the server node in the left navigation pane, and click on the Sites node.

b. Select the virtual IIS server used by SharePoint Foundation (for example, Default Web Site), then scroll down the center pane until you see an icon named Authentication. Double-click that icon to display the current settings.

c. Note that the status for Anonymous Authentication is enabled. Right-click on this line and select Edit. This will show that IIS will use the account IUSR whenever someone tries to access anything in this virtual IIS server. If you prefer, you can use the Set button and set another account instead.

d. Click Cancel unless you changed the account and want to save it.

e. Close the IIS Manager. You do not need to reset IIS to activate any modification.

So far only authenticated users will be able to get access! It is time to activate Anonymous Access to a specific SharePoint site:

7. Log on as the site owner and open the SharePoint Foundation website you want to enable for Anonymous Access. Note that it can be any type of site; it does not have to be a top site.

8. Click Site Actions ⇨ Site Permissions. Notice the new button, Anonymous Access. Click on it to open the Anonymous Access web form like the one shown in Figure B-16.

9. Select what rights the anonymous users will have on this site. In this example, select Entire Web Site. The options on this page are:

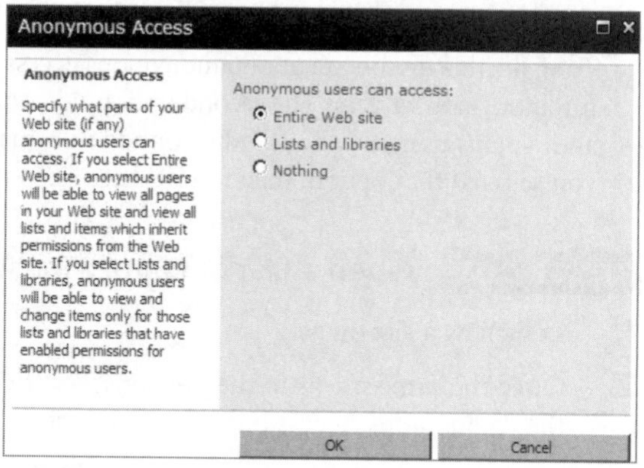

Anonymous Access

Anonymous Access

Specify what parts of your Web site (if any) anonymous users can access. If you select Entire Web site, anonymous users will be able to view all pages in your Web site and view all lists and items which inherit permissions from the Web site. If you select Lists and libraries, anonymous users will be able to view and change items only for those lists and libraries that have enabled permissions for anonymous users.

Anonymous users can access:

- ⦿ Entire Web site
- ⭕ Lists and libraries
- ⭕ Nothing

OK   Cancel

FIGURE B-16

> **Entire Web Site:** Anyone can read every part of this particular SharePoint Foundation site, including all lists and libraries and their contents. Warning: This will also allow anonymous access to any subsite that inherits its permissions from this site!

➤ **Lists and Libraries:** Anyone that has explicitly enabled anonymous access can access the list or library on this SharePoint Foundation site (see the next Try It Out for how to do that). Because the anonymous users cannot view the start page for this website, they must be given a direct URL link to the list or library they are allowed to view. For example, this link could be implemented as a button on the public start site.

➤ **Nothing:** The default choice. Nothing is accessible to anonymous users.

10. Click OK to save and close this web folder. Note that the following list now states clearly that anonymous users have access to the entire website. If there are users with explicit permission to any object here, it will be listed on an information bar that will show up. This setting will immediately be active.

How It Works

First you need to enable anonymous access to a web application, which will automatically configure the corresponding IIS website settings to enable anonymous access. Then you enable anonymous access to either a site or list/library. Note that if you enable access to a site and then a subsite inherits these security settings, it will also be open for anonymous access.

To test that it works, start a new web browser to avoid cached logon credentials. You may even have to log out and log in again to see this in action. Open the anonymous site by entering the full URL to that site (you cannot browse to it from another site, because then you would already be authenticated). Notice that you will be able to view any part of this SharePoint Foundation site now, but you cannot add or change any settings because you are accessing the site anonymously, and therefore SharePoint cannot see what permission your user account normally would have. But there is a new link named Sign In showing up in the upper-right corner of the home page for this site; click on it to log on, and then your normal permission will be active.

To make this discussion about anonymous access complete, you must know how to open specific lists for anonymous access. The second option, Lists and Libraries, in step 9 in the previous Try It Out allows anonymous users to view, modify, or add information in any list that you open for anonymous access. If you selected that option, then follow these steps to open a list or library for anonymous access:

TRY IT OUT   **Open a List or Library for Anonymous Access**

1. Log on as a site owner.

2. Open the same site as in the previous Try It Out. Click Site Actions ➪ Site Permissions and click the Anonymous Access button. Change the option to Lists and libraries, and click OK.

3. Open the list or library you want to enable for anonymous users; for example, the Shared Documents library.

4. Select the Library tab, and then click the Library Permissions icon at the far right on the Ribbon.

5. You must now first stop the inheriting of the parent permissions before this list can be opened for anonymous access. Click Stop Inheriting Permissions. Click OK.

6. Click on the new button that showed up: Anonymous Access.

7. Set the type of access anonymous users will have in this particular list or library:

➤ **Libraries:** Anonymous users can be granted View Items access only.

➤ **Lists:** Anonymous users can be granted one or more of these permissions: View, Add, Modify, and Delete Items.

8. Select View Items and click OK to save and close this page. This setting will be effective immediately.

How It Works

Instead of enabling anonymous access to a complete site, you can enable anonymous access to a specific list or library in this site. Note that this requires that the user have a URL that points directly to that list or library, since they cannot open the site and browse for the list or library.

Test this new access by starting a new browser session, and then typing the URL directly to that document library. You will be able to view and copy these documents, but not modify or delete them. If you try to open another part of this website, for example, its home page, you will be prompted because that is not open for anonymous access any longer — only this library.

> **NOTE** Do not forget to restore these settings, unless you actually want to enable anonymous access. The easiest way is to configure the same web application and its zone again, to disable anonymous access. This immediately removes all settings related to anonymous access in all site collections.

SEARCH AND INDEXING IN SHAREPOINT FOUNDATION

A newly installed SharePoint Foundation farm does not have search activated, unless specifically configured to do so. This section in this appendix explains how to activate and manage search and indexing in SharePoint Foundation.

Before searching is possible at all, SharePoint must index the information. Only then will searching be possible. Indexing uses a module often called a *crawler* to look in all locations for information that can be indexed, such as documents, list content, and picture properties. This index is by default stored in the same SQL Server as the other SharePoint content.

By default, only specific file types can be indexed; for example, Microsoft Office files, web files, and text files. One very common file type is missing: PDF. Is that because Microsoft wants to make it harder to work with PDF files? No! Microsoft is not allowed to add any proprietary file format, and the PDF type is owned by Adobe, so that is why it's not indexed by default. In this section you learn how to configure SharePoint's crawler to index PDF files.

> **NOTE** Important: SharePoint is security-aware, and the search results will only list items that the current user has at least Read access to.

Activating the SharePoint Foundation Search Service

Activating search is a two-step process, and if you fail to complete both steps, search will not work in SharePoint Foundation. The first step is to configure and start the search service, and the second is to configure the web applications and their content databases to use this search service.

Step 1 — Configure the Search Service

Step 1 is enabling the search service in SharePoint Foundation, and by that also enabling the indexer and its crawler. You need to be a farm administrator to perform the steps in the following Try It Out.

TRY IT OUT   Configure SharePoint Foundation Search Service

1. Log on as a farm administrator and start the Central Administration tool.

2. Choose System Settings ➪ Manage services on server to open the Services on Server page.

3. Note that the SharePoint Foundation Search is not started; click on Start next to this service.

4. On the web page Configure Microsoft SharePoint Foundation Search Service Settings on Server that appears, enter these values:

   a. **Service Account:** Enter a user account that will run the search service. It could be the same search account used for other SharePoint services, but do not use the account used for running the Central Administration application pool account, because that does not follow best practices.

   b. **Content Access Account:** Enter the account that the search service will use when crawling content. Avoid accounts with administrative permissions, because then also non-published information will be indexed and may show up as a search result. On a single-server configured SharePoint Foundation, the default user account is NT AUTHORITY\LOCAL SERVICE. You can accept that account, or change it to a user account (no administrative permissions required).

   c. **Search Database:** This section has multiple settings. Enter the name for the SQL Server (the default is the same server as used by SharePoint Foundation) and the database name (the default is WSS_Search_Srv1 for a server named Srv1). The last option is what type of database authentication you want; the default is Windows authentication, which is also the recommended option.

   d. **Failover Server:** If you have configured a mirrored SQL Server environment, then enter the name for that mirror server. In case the primary SQL Server stops, the mirror will automatically be used instead, until the primary is up again.

   e. **Indexing Schedule:** Set how often the indexer will run its crawler process. The default is once per hour, which means that it takes one hour before newly added information will be available to search for. You can change this schedule, for example, to every 10 minutes, but be aware that the demand on the CPU resources will increase some.

5. Click OK to save and close this page.

How It Works

You must manually start the search service for SharePoint Foundation in order to activate the index and search feature. Then you need to configure the index settings, such as the indexing schedule, what SQL server database to use for the index, and what service accounts to use when crawling content.

Step 2 — Configure Web Applications to Use the Search Services

The exact steps for doing this depend on whether you are creating a new web application after the search service is activated, or whether the web application already existed. If you create a new web application, you must configure its content databases instead. You need to be a farm administrator to perform the steps in the following Try It Out, which describes creating a new web application after the search is activated.

TRY IT OUT	Create a New Web Application and Configure It to Use the Search Service

1. Log on as a farm administrator and start the Central Administration tool.

2. Choose Application Management ⇨ Manage web applications to open the Web Applications Management page.

3. Click New on the Ribbon: The form Create New Web Application appears. Note that these steps are described in more detail in the Try It Out "Create a New Web Application" earlier in this appendix.

   a. For Authentication, accept the default Classic Mode Authentication, unless you really have a need for the new Claims Based Authentication mechanism.

   b. The IIS Web Site section is about the IIS Web Site to be used for the new web application: Select the option Create a New IIS Web Site, then enter its name and a host header name, if necessary, to make it unique: otherwise, a conflict arises with the existing web application that uses port 80. Remember to add this host header name to the DNS as an Alias record for the server name, as described earlier in this appendix.

   c. Accept the default Security Configuration settings.

   d. Notice that the URL is `http://<Your_Host_Header_Name>:80`.

   e. In the Application Pool section, select either to use an existing pool, or create a new one.

    f.   Make sure the Database Server is correct. Enter a name for this database.

    g.   If you have a mirror of the production SQL Server, enter the name for this mirror server.

    h.   The Search Server is important for the search functionality; use its menu and select the server that runs the search service (most likely this server).

    i.   Accept the other default settings (unless you want to disable Enable Customer Experience Improvement Program), and click OK at the end of this form to save and close it.

The new web application will now be created.

How It Works

After the Search Service for SharePoint Foundation is enabled, you must configure new content databases to use that service in order to make the content in this database indexed and, therefore, searchable.

To activate the search feature for web applications that already existed before the search service was started, you must configure the content databases associated with these web applications, as described in the following Try It Out:

TRY IT OUT   **Configure Existing Web Applications to Enable the Search Feature**

1.   Log on as a farm administrator and start the Central Administration tool.

2.   Choose Application Management ➪ Manage content databases to open the Manage Content Database page.

3.   Make sure the correct web application is selected; if it's not, click on the current URL (upper-right corner) and change the web application.

4.   The associated content databases for this web application now appear. Click on the first database name to open its configuration form.

5.   Scroll down to Search Server; use the menu for Select Microsoft SharePoint Foundation Search Server and select the server that runs the search service.

6.   Click OK to save and close.

How It Works

All content databases that existed before you activated the search service for SharePoint Foundation need to be configured to use this service in order to get its content indexed and therefore searchable.

After completing the preceding Try It Outs, just wait for the indexer to crawl all content in SharePoint. Remember that it will take at least as long as you have configured the search service scheduler to run before you will find any search results. To test the search feature, open a top site, and enter a word that you know for sure exists in this site, be it a document, a list content, or a web page; see an example of a search result in Figure B-17.

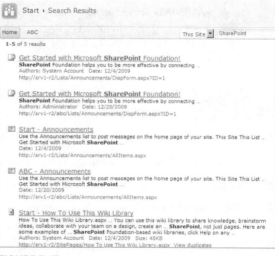

FIGURE B-17

Managing the Search Service

The search service in SharePoint Foundation is simple but effective in smaller implementations. If you later upgrade to SharePoint Server 2010, you will get a very intelligent search engine. However, that also means that you need to purchase a server license and client access licenses. If you want a much smarter search engine for your SharePoint Foundation, without paying any extra money, then you must look at Microsoft Search Server Express 2010, which is free. This search engine is actually the same as the one used by SharePoint Server 2010, except that some features are not available for SharePoint Foundation, such as user-defined keywords and managed metadata structures and people-search. You can find more information on these features in Chapter 5, Chapter 6, and Appendix D.

Understanding the Default Search Features in SharePoint Foundation

The search feature in SharePoint Foundation has some limitations that you should be aware of:

➤ A search query returns results from the current site and subsites, if any. Sites above, and other site collections, are not queried.

➤ Only SharePoint content is indexed, and therefore searchable. You cannot index content outside SharePoint Foundation, such as the file server or other web servers.

➤ No graphical user interface exists for managing search settings, except to configure the Search Service (but PowerShell and, to some extent, STSADM has commands for configuring the search feature).

➤ You cannot create customized search scopes to limit the search results to a specific content source or type.

This means that the SharePoint Foundation administrator must know how to manage the search feature. For example, in case the search queries don't give the expected results, you need to rebuild the index. This can happen when you do a restore of SharePoint content, or in case of a power outage. You have two options for resetting the index: Use the Central Administration tool and restart the search service, or run a STSADM or PowerShell command; both procedures are described next.

> ⓧ **WARNING** *Resetting the index using the Central Administration tool requires a complete reinstallation of the search service and reconfiguring of all content databases. If possible, use the STSADM or PowerShell method instead.*

TRY IT OUT **Reset the Search Index in SharePoint Foundation Using Central Administration**

1. Log on as the farm administrator and start the Central Administration tool.

2. Click System Settings ➪ Manage services on server to open the Services on Server page.

3. Stop the SharePoint Foundation Search service; click OK to accept to stop it.

4. Wait until the Search service has completely stopped, then start this service again; note that you need to configure all settings for the search service again.

5. Open all existing content databases and add the Search Server, as described earlier.

How It Works

When resetting the index you need to reconfigure both the search server settings and the search settings for all content databases.

The only advantage of this method is that it is performed using the graphical Central Administration tool. A much better and faster way is to use the steps in the following Try It Out:

TRY IT OUT **Reset the Search Index in SharePoint Foundation Using STSADM**

1. Log on as the farm administrator and Choose Start ➪ All Programs ➪ Microsoft SharePoint 2010 Products ➪ SharePoint 2010 Management Shell to open the PowerShell command shell window.

2. Type this command in the command shell window to reset the search index in SharePoint Foundation: `stsadm -o spsearch -action fullcrawlstart`.

How It Works

You can use STSADM to reset the search index instead of using SharePoint Central Administration.

This procedure doesn't require any reconfiguration of the search service or content databases. If you want to see more information about the search service, type `stsadm -o spsearch -action list`. This command lists the name of the search database, the current status of the search service (Online / Offline), and what content databases are indexed.

> **NOTE** *SharePoint does not differ between localized characters, like "a" and "ä," which is very important in many languages, such as Swedish, French, and German. To enable this differentiation, type the following command (note that this will also reset the index):* `stsadm -o spsearchdiacriticsensitive -setstatus True -force.`

Indexing Proprietary File Types

As mentioned previously, Microsoft is not allowed to add the features for indexing proprietary file formats, such as PDF and most CAD file formats. To open such a file, the indexer needs an *index filter*, more commonly known as an *iFilter*. This small application understands how to read the content for a given file. SharePoint Foundation comes with iFilters for indexing all common Microsoft Office file formats, plus a number of standard formats such as TXT and HTML.

To teach SharePoint Foundation to index PDF files, you need an iFilter for PDF. The two sources for this particular iFilter are Adobe's public website and a third-party developer named Foxit that is very popular due to its speed compared to Adobe's iFilter. Next you must reconfigure the registry on the SharePoint Foundation server to define that PDF files should be indexed. The final step is optional, which is to add the PDF icon to SharePoint so users will see this well-known icon whenever there is a PDF file. The following Try It Out presents the exact steps.

> **NOTE** *Chapter 6 shows you how to configure SharePoint Server 2010 to index PDF files; the following steps are only for SharePoint Foundation.*

TRY IT OUT   Prepare SharePoint Foundation to Index PDF Files

1. Log on to the SharePoint Foundation server as an administrator.

2. Download the PDF iFilter from either of these sources (note that it must be a 64-bit version):

> ➤ Go to `http://www.adobe.com/download` and search for the latest iFilter, then download it to the SharePoint Foundation server. Notice that this iFilter is free, but is a bit slower than the product below.

> ➤ Go to `http://www.foxitsoftware.com/pdf/ifilter/` and download the iFilter to the SharePoint Foundation Server. This iFilter is not free, but it is several times faster than the iFilter from Adobe.

3. Install the downloaded iFilter, using the default settings.

4. Start the Registry Editor: Click Start ➪ Run, type **Regedit**, and then click OK.

> **a.** Open the following registry key: `HKEY_LOCAL_MACHINE\SOFTWARE\Microsoft\Shared Tools\Web Server Extensions\14.0\Search\Applications\<GUID>\Gather\Search\Extensions\ExtensionList`.

> **b.** Open the Edit menu, select New ➪ String Value, type in **47**, and press Enter to save this new string value.

c. Right-click the new registry entry, and click Modify.

d. In the Value data section, type in **pdf**, and then click OK.

5. Use the fact that the STSADM operation `spsearchdiacriticsensitive` resets the index; this is necessary to make SharePoint discover and index all existing PDF files.

a. Choose Start ⇨ All Programs ⇨ Microsoft SharePoint 2010 Products ⇨ SharePoint 2010 Management Shell to open the PowerShell command shell window.

b. If the current `spsearchdiacriticsensitive` setting is False (that is, the default), then type **stsadm -o spsearchdiacriticsensitive -setstatus False -force**. If the status is True, then type **stsadm -o spsearchdiacriticsensitive -setstatus True -force**.

6. Start to rebuild the index now, instead of waiting for the scheduled index process: type **stsadm -o spsearch -action fullcrawlsearch**.

How It Works

Enabling the Search Service in SharePoint Foundation to index PDF files requires modifications in the Registry of the SharePoint server, and the installation of a 64-bit iFilter for PDF. By enabling the spsearchdiacriticsensitive flag, the crawler will understand the difference between o and ö and other non-English characters, which is very important in our increasingly diverse global community.

Test to search for words you know exist in one of the PDF files stored in SharePoint; if all is correctly configured, then this file will show up in the search result.

▶ **WHAT YOU LEARNED IN THIS APPENDIX**

TOPIC	KEY CONCEPTS
Sites and Site Collections	All sites are members of a site collection.
	Each site collection has one top site.
	All site collections are hosted by a specific web application.
	A site collection stores all its data in one specific content database.
	Site collections are created with the Central Administration tool, STSADM, or PowerShell.
	Moving a site collection from one content database to another is possible.
	A number of settings are exclusive for one site collection and will not be replicated to other site collections; for example, SharePoint Groups, Master Pages, and Page Layouts. So think carefully before you decide to create a new site collection, because it will increase the management burden.
Web Applications and Content Databases	One web application can host many thousands of site collections.
	The web application is associated with one, or possibly more, SQL content databases.
	You can have multiple web applications in one server.
	Each web application runs within an application pool.
	One application pool can host multiple web applications.
	If you copy one content database to another SharePoint Foundation farm, you will copy all site collections in this database.
	The best practice is to keep the content databases below 200GB.
Administrative Tools	The main administration tool is the SharePoint 2010 Central Administration website.
	STSADM is a command-based configuration tool that has been with SharePoint since its first release; this version is reduced in functionality, compared to previous STSADM versions.
	PowerShell is the new and much richer command-based configuration tool; it runs in a special command window that you activate by choosing Start⇨ All Programs⇨ Microsoft SharePoint 2010 Products⇨ SharePoint 2010 Management Shell.

continues

(continued)

TOPIC	KEY CONCEPTS
SharePoint Central Administration	SharePoint Central Administration is divided into a number of pages: **Central Administration:** The start page that contains the most frequently used commands. **Application Management:** For managing web applications, site collections, service applications, and databases. **System Settings:** For managing servers and services, e-mail and SMS, and farm features. **Monitoring:** For viewing the health analyzer, timer jobs, and different reports. **Backup and Restore:** For performing backup and restore procedures. **Security:** For managing administrators and users, plus general security settings. **Upgrade and Migration:** For performing upgrade actions and patch management. **General Application Settings:** For configuring external service connections and SharePoint Designer settings. **Configuration Wizards:** For starting the configuration wizard.
Service Applications	Service applications are new to SharePoint 2010 and replace the Shared Service Provider (SSP) in SharePoint 2007. Service applications are associated with one or more web applications. SharePoint Foundation now supports the Business Data Connectivity service, which allows easy access to external data sources (previously available only in MOSS 2007).
Backup and Security Features	SharePoint Foundation allows you to back up a farm, web application, content database, site collection, list, or library. Backup tools are SharePoint Central Administration, STSADM, and PowerShell. Restore data with the Central Administration tool, STSADM, or PowerShell. The three types of administrators are farm administrator, site collection administrator, and site owner. SharePoint groups are similar to security groups in AD; use them to grant permissions to users and security groups to SharePoint objects such as sites, lists, and list items. Permission levels are preconfigured permission roles: Read, Contribute, Visitor, and Full Control. Anonymous access can be granted to individual sites or to lists and libraries.

TOPIC	KEY CONCEPTS
Search Feature	SharePoint Foundation's search feature is similar to its predecessor in WSS 3.0. Install Microsoft Search Server Express 2010 to get an advanced search feature in SharePoint Foundation.
	The search feature must be managed by STSADM or PowerShell (better) if you want to do something more than start the search service.
	Teaching the search service to index proprietary file formats, such as PDF, is possible — you need a 64-bit iFilter for that file type, plus some Registry settings.

C

Installing Microsoft SharePoint Server 2010

This appendix shows you how to install Microsoft SharePoint Server 2010. You learn the differences between the database options for the two available types, how to prepare the server for the installation, and to understand the system user accounts involved in this action. After the installation is complete, you learn how to check that everything is okay as well as some basic troubleshooting tips.

> **NOTE** *If you plan to install SharePoint Server 2010, then you do not need to read Appendix A about installing SharePoint Foundation 2010. All you need to know to install SharePoint Server 2010 is covered in this appendix!*

This appendix starts by describing what to do before starting the installation, followed by the step-by-step instructions on how to install, followed by the initial configuration that will complete the installation. Appendix D covers the details about managing and configuring an installed SharePoint Server 2010.

PREPARING FOR SHAREPOINT SERVER 2010

SharePoint Server 2010 is basically a superset of SharePoint Foundation. In other words, when installing SharePoint Server, you really install SharePoint Foundation plus a great number of new or enhanced features. The information in Appendix B is valid also for a SharePoint Server 2010 server, but there are more features to configure and manage, which you learn about in Appendix D.

When running a SharePoint Server environment, you will create both SharePoint Foundation sites and SharePoint Server sites; they differ in functionality and purpose. Typically SharePoint Foundation sites are called *team sites*, whereas the more advanced SharePoint Server sites are *publishing sites* or sites with special functionality, like advanced search and document centers. The procedure to install SharePoint Server is very similar to SharePoint Foundation, but several important differences exist. For example, SharePoint Server has the following:

➤ More system user accounts to define and plan for

➤ More databases will be created in the SQL Server

➤ New SharePoint service roles

➤ More features to learn and manage

Therefore you must plan more carefully when installing SharePoint Server, compared to SharePoint Foundation. But you also gain many new and enhanced features that enable you to build better solutions for sharing information between users in teams, departments, and complete organizations, and for more effective personal use.

Preparing the Windows Server

The preparation before installing SharePoint Server is very similar to the preparations to install SharePoint Foundation. You must prepare the Windows Server operation systems by activating and configuring some of its services and features. There are changes in the SharePoint 2010 architecture, compared to its predecessor SharePoint 2007, that affect the requirements for both hardware and software configurations. The following is a list of the most important changes:

➤ SharePoint Server now requires 64-bit Windows Server 2008 operating systems; that is, Windows Server 2008 or Windows Server 2008 R2. For software developer purposes, installing SharePoint Server on 64-bit Windows 7 is also supported, although this configuration is not supported for production environments.

➤ The new embedded Microsoft SQL Server 2008 Express is 64-bit only, but as in previous SharePoint versions you can configure SharePoint Server to use a separate 64-bit version of Microsoft SQL Server 2005 or Microsoft SQL Server 2008.

➤ A new user interface — the Fluent User Interface — is built on the same design as the "ribbon" introduced in Microsoft Office 2007 and is used for team sites, blogs, and workspaces, as well as for the SharePoint 2010 Central Administration tool.

➤ There are new types of site lists: *Wiki Page Library* (for web pages), *Asset Library* (for multimedia files), and *External List* (that connects to an external data source). There are also enhanced lists, such as the Project Tasks and the Calendar.

➤ There are several new web parts: for example, the *Silverlight Web Part, Media Web Part,* and the *Chart Web Part.*

➤ The search and index feature is greatly enhanced; for example, now it is possible to do refinements in the search results, based on file types, authors, and tags, just to mention a few.

➤ SharePoint 2010 introduces a new concept: *Managed Accounts*. These are service accounts used by services and features in the SharePoint environment. By using managed accounts, the SharePoint administrator no longer has to change the passwords of these service accounts by hand; SharePoint manages these accounts automatically.

> **NOTE** *The first version of SharePoint Services, released in 2001, was named SharePoint Team Services (STS). The STS acronym is still used even in today's version of SharePoint 2010. Whenever you see something that begins with STS, such as STSADM, think SharePoint 2010.*

Because SharePoint Server is a web application you must activate several Windows Server roles that are not configured by default. These are Internet Information Services (IIS) and .NET Framework 3.5.1; both of these roles will automatically activate dependent roles that they require. By default, Windows 2008 will have PowerShell 1.0 installed, and that must be removed before running the prerequisite installation link in the SharePoint 2010 setup. The following Try It Out contains the steps you need to follow:

TRY IT OUT ▌ Prepare Windows Server 2008 for SharePoint Server

1. Log on as an administrator to the Windows 2008 server you will use for your SharePoint Server installation.

2. Start the Server Manager by choosing Start ➪ Administration Tools ➪ Server Manager.

3. Select Roles in the left navigation pane, then click Add Roles.

4. Select Application Server and Web Server (IIS), then click Next.

5. An information page about Web Server (IIS) appears; click Next.

6. A form appears asking whether you want to "Add role services required" — these are the dependent roles that need to be activated. Click Add Required Role Services.

7. The Installation Results page appears (see Figure C-1). Click OK to close this page.

8. Remove PowerShell 1.0 like this: Click Start ➪ Run, enter cmd in the Open field, and then click OK to open the command shell window. Then type C:\Windows\$NtUninstallKB926139$\ Spuninst\Spuninst.Exe and press Enter to remove PowerShell 1.0

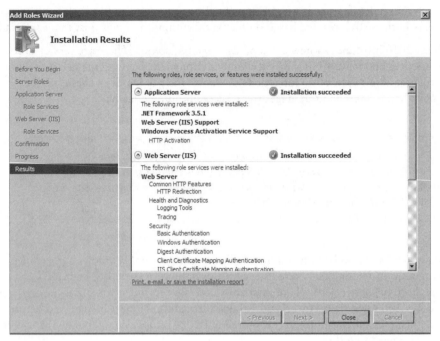

FIGURE C-1

How It works

Windows Server 2008 must be prepared to enable installation of SharePoint Server 2010. These steps accomplish that.

Now your Windows Server 2008 is prepared for the SharePoint Server installation. However, SharePoint Server has a feature that allows a list, such as a document library, to accept incoming e-mail using the SMTP standard. Note that in order to *send out* e-mail, SharePoint Server does not need any extra feature or role installed! If you need the feature that accepts incoming e-mail in SharePoint Server using SMTP, you must first activate it in Windows Server via the following steps:

> **NOTE** *Chapter 6 will describe how to configure SharePoint lists to accept incoming e-mail.*

TRY IT OUT Activate the SMTP Feature in Windows Server

1. Make sure you are logged on as a local server administrator and open the Server Manager.

2. Expand the Features node in the left pane.

3. Click Add Feature and check the SMTP option.

4. The "Add role services and features required for SMTP Server" form appears. Click Add Required Role Services, and then Next three times.

5. On the Confirm Installation Selections form, verify that it lists SMTP Server. Click Install.

6. After the installation is done, the Installation Results page appears. If it says the installation was successful, click Close. If not, correct the problem and try again.

How It works

If you want to enable incoming e-mail to SharePoint lists and libraries you must first activate the SMTP feature in Windows Server 2008.

Hardware Requirements

SharePoint is an application that works best when it gets lots of memory and CPU resources. SharePoint Server requires about twice as much memory as its predecessor, MOSS 2007; the reason is, of course, that the new SharePoint Server version has a lot of new functionality, as well as enhancements to existing features. A server with 4GB of memory will support up to several hundred SharePoint Server users, as long as you have a SQL Server with enough disk capacity to store all data needed; see the next section for more details.

You must understand several things when planning your SharePoint Server hardware:

➤ SharePoint is a web application! There is no permanent connection between the client browser and the SharePoint server. Every time you open a link or a document, the browser connects, downloads the requested information, and then closes the connection immediately after that, regardless of how long the user looks at that information.

➤ The *total number* of users in the organization is not the same as the number of *simultaneous users*.

➤ Different activities in SharePoint require different resources; for example, displaying a project site normally generates a very light load on the server, whereas running the index crawler generates a much higher CPU load.

Calculating the Number of NOPS Required

You can use a general, well-proven formula for calculating the load, or the *normalized operations per second* (NOPS), on the SharePoint server. From that you can estimate the number of supported users, given a certain hardware configuration. The formula requires you to find out or estimate a number of values:

$$\frac{A \times B \times C \times D}{360,000 \times E} = \text{Operations/second (NOPS)}$$

This is the estimated data that you must supply:

➤ A = The number of users

➤ B = The percentage of active users on a typical day

➤ C = The number of operations per active user per day

➤ D = The peak factor

➤ E = The number of working hours per day

Two of these estimated parameters need to be explained in more detail. The peak factor is a value between 1 and 10, which is used to indicate the peak hours during the work hours. For example, if the organization works from 9 a.m. to 5 p.m., you can safely bet that most workers start their day by opening their SharePoint environment, because that is where all the information can be found; after that you will probably have an even load. Then directly after lunch, another peak would occur. A peak factor of 1 means "no peak load at all." A factor of 10 means "a peak load all day." A typical organization would get a peak factor value of 5. If you want to be on the safe side, use a higher value of 7.

The other estimated parameter is the number of operations per active user per day, which has to do with how much your SharePoint environment will be utilized per day. This is also a value between 1 and 10, where 1 means your users access SharePoint for almost no time at all and 10 means your users work all day with SharePoint. For a typical organization you would get something close to 10 for this value.

Example 1: An Organization with 200 Very Active Users

Your organization has 200 employees (A). The percentage of active users in a typical day is 80 (B). The number of operations per active user is 10 (C). The number of working hours for the organization as a whole is 12 hours (E). You estimate the peak factor (D) to be 10, to be on the safe side. The formula for this organization will look like this:

$$\frac{200 \times 80 \times 10 \times 10}{360,000 \times 12} = 0.37 \text{ NOPS}$$

Example 2: An Organization with 4,500 Normal Users

Your organization has 4,500 employees (A). The percentage of active users in a typical day is 50 (B). The number of operations per active user is 10 (C). The number of working hours for the organization as a whole is 12 hours (E). You estimate the peak factor (D) to be 5. The formula for this organization will look like this:

$$\frac{4,500 \times 50 \times 10 \times 5}{360,000 \times 12} = 2.60 \text{ NOPS}$$

Putting It into Practice

Now you have a good idea of the load your system will generate. The next step is to use this information to calculate the hardware you need. Several hardware vendors have excellent tools for analyzing how many users a given server may support; typically a single-server installation of SharePoint Server with a local SQL Server database, configured with 8GB memory and a 64-bit dual CPU, will support up to 2 NOPS. Installing SharePoint Server and the full SQL Server 2005/2008 on separate servers with 8GB each doubles the number of NOPS.

> **NOTE** *The hardware vendor HP has a nice SharePoint Size Tool that you can download for free. Go to* www.hp.com, *then search for "Activeanswers sizers"; in the result list, look for SharePoint to find the tool.*

From this information you can learn three important things:

➤ Make sure to have at least 4GB of memory on a SharePoint Server.

➤ Multiple CPUs greatly enhance the number of supported users.

➤ For maximum performance, use a separate SQL Server; that is, build a farm.

The important fact to remember here is that when a SharePoint server has at least 4GB of memory and a separate SQL Server, it can support several hundreds of light or medium users. If you increase that to 8GB of memory and two CPUs for the SharePoint Server, it can support several thousands of users.

Microsoft's Recommended Hardware Requirements

Naturally Microsoft has list of all the requirements for SharePoint Server. These numbers tend to be a bit high, but "better safe than sorry." In other words, you can do it with less hardware, but why take the chance? You are about to build one of the most central information systems in your organization, so make sure it can handle the workload. These are the official numbers from Microsoft for a *minimum* requirement:

➤ Processor: 64-bit, dual CPU, 3 GHz.

➤ Memory: 4GB for a stand-alone server (or a test server); or 8GB/server for any other installation scenario, such as a multiple server farm installation.

➤ 80GB free disk space; this only covers the SharePoint binary files plus a small local SQL Server installation.

➤ 100 Mbps network interface card (NIC).

Note that these numbers may have to be adjusted for some organizations. The disk size, especially, does not take into account that a local SQL server database will contain a lot of data. In fact, if you plan to store more than 25GB of data, you should install SQL Server 2005 or 2008 on a separate server. Here are Microsoft's "best practice" recommendations for a SQL Server in a SharePoint environment:

➤ Disk subsystems: RAID 10 for all types of databases.

➤ Make sure the driver for the disk I/O subsystem and network cards (NICs) are all optimized for high performance. Something being slow here affects the total performance of the SharePoint Server environment. Use gigabyte NICs if possible, regardless of size.

➤ Configure the disks that SQL uses so the NTFS Allocation Unit Size option is set to be 64K (default is 4K). This setting can result in a 30 percent performance increase.

➤ Place the Tempdb, content databases, and transaction log files on separate RAID 10 disks.

➤ Use multiple data files for each large content database and search databases, but keep the number of data files less than, or equal to, the number of CPU cores. Make sure to *not* use multiple data files for other database types!

➤ Try to keep the content databases less than 200GB; SharePoint Server will work even if you break this rule, but the time you need for database maintenance and repair tasks will be longer by up to several days.

➤ A database with 50GB or more is considered a large database. If your site collection will store more than 50GB in its content database, consider breaking up the site collection into two, each with a content database.

➤ Recommended SQL Server memory size (but it will still work with much less memory):

  ➤ Small (less than 50GB) environment: 8GB

  ➤ Medium (about 50GB) environment: 16GB

  ➤ Large (greater than 50GB) environment: 32GB

➤ CPU recommendations:

  ➤ Make sure to install a 64-bit SQL Server on the 64-bit Windows Server 2008.

  ➤ If you have more than 20,000 users you should have two SharePoint Web Front-End (WFE) servers.

  ➤ Plan for two quad-core CPUs per 20,000 users.

  ➤ Use a maximum of 8 CPUs per server; if you need more power, install a second SQL Server.

As you can see, these numbers that Microsoft recommends are in the high end, but if you want the best performance in a production environment and you have the budget, then by all means follow these recommendations. If you just want to test SharePoint Server, 4GB will work fine for a single-server installation; that is, both SharePoint Server and SQL Server installed on the same hardware.

Calculating the Disk Space Needed

The disk space that SharePoint Server itself requires is less than 1GB, so the important thing to plan for is the database where SharePoint will store all its information. In other words, the data disk used by the SQL Server application (the SQL Server itself requires only a few hundred MB of disk space for its binary files). It does not matter if you are using the SQL Server Express engine or the Microsoft SQL Server; you still need to follow this simple but important rule: You must always have at least 50 percent free space on your database disk!

Otherwise, you will not be able to perform database maintenance and troubleshooting, because these activities may need to make a copy of the database to perform their tasks. So what will require the most space in the database? The answer is simple: your documents! They will not be compressed, so a 1MB Word file will require slightly more than 1MB of database disk space. If you activate version history for document libraries, then all document versions will also require disk space, since each version is stored as a complete document, not just the changes from previous versions. The other things you store, like list items and calendar bookings, will, of course, also require disk space, but not nearly as much. A SharePoint site itself requires less than 200KB of database space.

> **NOTE** *Note that the XML-based file format first introduced in Microsoft Office 2007 generates files that are less than 50 percent of the size of previous Microsoft Office file formats!*

So to estimate the disk space needed for your database, start by estimating the number of files it will contain. For example, assume you estimate that it will contain about 50,000 files and documents, with an average of 500KB; in total this will require 25GB. Add to that 5GB for the other type of information you will store and you get 30GB in total. Following the earlier rule, you must have at least a 60GB disk for the content database alone. A good indication of how much disk space will be required is to look at the current file system. Although it probably contains a lot of multiple copies of the same file and historic data, it will give you an estimate of how much data SharePoint will store after some time.

Summary of Requirements

To summarize the requirements you can use this table where Microsoft lists its minimum and recommended configurations. Remember that for a *pilot* installation you can actually get away with less than the given minimum memory size listed in the following table, but for a production environment you should follow Microsoft's recommendations:

ITEM	MINIMUM REQUIREMENT	MICROSOFT RECOMMENDS
Operating system	Any edition of 64-bit Microsoft Windows Server 2008 and 2008 R2	Any edition of 64-bit Microsoft Windows Server 2008 and 2008 R2
CPU	1 CPU (64-bit) running at 2.5 GHz	Two CPUs (64-bit) running at at least 3 GHz
RAM	4GB	8GB or more
Disk space	Minimum 6GB free disk space	Minimum 30GB free disk space
File system	NTFS	NTFS
IIS version	7.0 with ASP.NET (in Worker Process Isolation Mode)	7.0 with ASP.NET (in Worker Process Isolation Mode)
Database engine	64-bit SQL Server Express 2008	A separate 64-bit SQL Server 2008 R2
Internet browser	IE 7.0 with the latest service pack	IE 8 or later with the latest Service Pack

Software Requirements

As mentioned earlier, SharePoint Server requires a 64-bit Windows Server 2008 or 2008 R2, for a production environment. (Installing SharePoint Server on a 64-bit Windows 7 for developing purposes is possible.) SharePoint Server is a web-based application and will run within Internet Information Services (IIS) in Windows Server. Therefore you need to understand some more IIS concepts, like virtual web servers and application pools.

The IIS Virtual Server

In the good old days, each web solution required its own physical web server. This was clearly not the most economical solution if you needed multiple websites. Microsoft solved this problem by enabling the IIS to create and manage virtual web servers; for example, the *Default Web Site*. Each web solution running on top of IIS 6 needs its own *virtual web server*. This makes running several web solutions on the same physical server possible. To make it possible to separate these virtual servers, they must differ in at least one of the following: the IP number, the TCP port number, or the host header name.

But that solution created a new problem: If one web solution crashed, it also killed all other web solutions running in the same IIS. Microsoft solved this issue by creating something it called *application pools* inside IIS, which; simply put; defines a private virtual address space and security context for a web solution. Each web solution is linked to an application pool. However, each application pool can be linked to more than one web solution, thus sharing address space and security context; if one of these web solutions crashes, then all may crash — but only in this application pool!

The terminology here is a bit confusing: IIS in general talks about "websites," like the Default Web Site. SharePoint needs to extend these websites with more features to support SharePoint functionality. These *extended* websites are called *web applications* in SharePoint. But the term *web application* is also a common term for any web-based solution. However, when you see the term *web application* in this book, it always means "extended websites."

If you chose to perform a farm installation of SharePoint (see later in this section), you must enter a user account that SharePoint's configuration wizard will set as the security identity for the application pool that hosts the website running the SharePoint Central Administration v4 tool. That account can be either a built-in account, like the *Network Service*, or a standard user account in Active Directory. SharePoint's configuration wizard will automatically grant that account the following permissions to SQL Server and its databases: Database Creators, Security Administrators, and Public.

> **NOTE** *Running two or more web applications in the same application pool creates a potential security risk. It is technically possible for one web application to access the other web application and its content! Normally this access is acceptable, because you control the access to all sites and content using SharePoint's permission settings. However, for some organizations you need to avoid this type of access, maybe for legal reasons. If so, use a separate application pool with a unique security account for each web application.*

All other IIS websites used by SharePoint should use their own application pools, with an Identity account that is different from the one used by the SharePoint Central Administration application pool.

As mentioned earlier, before SharePoint can use a standard virtual IIS website, it must be extended with new functionality; such an extended virtual site in SharePoint is referred to as a *web application*. The administrator creates the web application in the Central Administration tool by extending an existing virtual website in IIS (like the Default Web Site) or creating a new virtual website, which will then be extended. Each web application can then be used to host one or more *site collections*, as described in more detail later in this appendix.

Determining When You Need SharePoint Server

Because SharePoint Foundation 2010 is free to use with Windows 2008 Server, and SharePoint Server 2010 requires both a server license and user licenses (known as *client access licenses*, or CALs), you should carefully analyze the needs of your organization. Appendix B contains a more complete list of questions, but the following table lists some of the more common arguments for using SharePoint Server. If the analysis shows that your organization requires one or more of the following features, then you need SharePoint Server. These questions should most likely be answered by multiple groups of users and stakeholders in your organization.

QUESTION	PEOPLE TO ASK	COMMENT
Do you need an intranet that allows you to target information to certain groups?	Top management, people responsible for managing organization-wide information	Only SharePoint Server allows audience targeting of web parts, news items, and lists of information.
Do you want to be able to search for information stored both inside and outside SharePoint?	All types of users	Only SharePoint Server offers global search functionality built into the product.
Do you need an easy way of managing and presenting more information about your users than just their e-mail addresses and phone numbers?	Middle-management, team leaders, project leaders	SharePoint Server has the User Profile database, which handles any number of properties about users. Use it to search for people with specific properties or build an enhanced "Employee List."
Does a need exist to be compliant with special regulations such as SOX or HIPAA?	Top management, legal department, information managers	SharePoint Server has support for compliance, policies, and auditing of documents and other types of information.
Does a need exist to let users fill in intelligent forms using a web browser?	Top management, people responsible for managing organization-wide information	SharePoint Server Enterprise edition has the Forms Services that will meet this need.

continues

(continued)

QUESTION	PEOPLE TO ASK	COMMENT
Does a need exist to share Excel spreadsheets among users without disclosing the formulas, and use these spreadsheets with a web browser?	Top management, people responsible for managing organization-wide information	SharePoint Server Enterprise edition has the Excel Services that meet this need.
Does a need exist to integrate Visio drawings into SharePoint; for example, to process maps?	Top management, legal department, information managers	SharePoint Server has support for Visio Services. Define automatic actions for each part of the Visio drawing with SharePoint Designer 2010.
Does a need exist to integrate Microsoft Access databases and applications into SharePoint?	Top management, people responsible for managing organization-wide information	SharePoint Server supports Microsoft Access by its Access Services.
Does a need exist to connect SharePoint to external data; for example, an Oracle database or SAP system.	Top management; sales managers, HR managers	SharePoint Server Enterprise edition has the Business Data Catalog feature that will meet this need.

The license model for SharePoint Server is based on the SharePoint Server edition, the number of SharePoint Server servers, and the number of SharePoint Server users; that is, client access licenses (CALs). If a user is just reading information, she still needs one SharePoint Server CAL. The exact cost for SharePoint Server installation depends on your type of software agreement with Microsoft and the number of users. If you have many users, you will pay less per user license, compared to a few users. You need to contact your license distributor to get the exact price.

SharePoint Server allows you to choose between the free, but limited, SQL Express 2008 database and the full and unlimited Microsoft SQL 2005 or 2008 server. Because the SQL Express size limit of 4GB is so low, in practice, you must choose the full Microsoft SQL Server for a production environment. Note that it does not have to be an exclusive Microsoft SQL Server for SharePoint Server; if you have an existing Microsoft SQL Server and it has available capacity, you can use it.

Choosing Between SharePoint Server Standard and Enterprise Edition

Before you install SharePoint you have to answer two important questions, because their answers affect the installation procedure, which is hard to change later on. The first question is determining what version of SharePoint you need: Is the limited SharePoint Foundation enough, or does your organization require the full SharePoint Server 2010? The second question is what type of SQL Server SharePoint will use: the SQL Server Express that comes with SharePoint Server, or the full SQL Server 2005 or 2008 that must be purchased separately and installed before you start the installation of SharePoint Server.

SharePoint Server 2010 is a great product, but SharePoint Foundation is also very good; you need to analyze the needs of your users before deciding which one of these to install. The major benefit of SharePoint Foundation is the fact that it is free to download and run on any Windows 2008 Server, but it also has its shortcomings compared to SharePoint Server 2010. The major benefit of SharePoint Server is that it has so many features, but the cost is higher because SharePoint Server requires a server license and each user needs a client access license (CAL). You should analyze what problems you are trying to solve with SharePoint before choosing either version. If you choose SharePoint Foundation and later decide to upgrade to SharePoint Server 2010, you can do so, but you will have to complete several manual steps to make it work. So the best course of action is to make sure you have the right version installed from the beginning.

There are two editions of SharePoint Server: Standard and Enterprise. They differ in both functionality and price. You can upgrade from Standard edition to Enterprise, but not the other way around. Some of the most important features that are unique to SharePoint Server compared to SharePoint Foundation, plus differences between Standard and Enterprise editions, are listed in the following table:

FEATURE/FUNCTION	DESCRIPTION	STANDARD	ENTERPRISE
Manage Content and Structure	A feature that gives a hierarchical view of each site collection. The users can do anything their permissions allow them to do, like create new subsites, including lists and libraries, list all documents awaiting approval, plus a lot more.	Yes	Yes
My Profile	A personal site for each user, where he can store personal files, images, and so on plus enter public information about himself, such as pictures, interests, current projects, and so on.	Yes	Yes
Social Networking Web Part	Used in personal sites (My Profile) to show other people with whom you have something in common, such as members of the same group. You can also see the tags and notes created by a specific user.	Yes	Yes
User Profile Database	Stores properties about users; can synchronize user properties in Active Directory and any other LDAP source.	Yes	Yes
Audit Targeting	Allows the content author to target information to a specific group of people; for example, show IT-related information only to computer nerds.	Yes	Yes
Enterprise Site Templates	Used to build portal sites based on Wiki sites and publishing pages, also known as Web Content Management–controlled web pages.	Yes	Yes

continues

(continued)

FEATURE/FUNCTION	DESCRIPTION	STANDARD	ENTERPRISE
Roll-up Web Parts	Show information stored in other locations that is related to the current user, such as tasks assigned to me.	Yes	Yes
Organizational view	Shows the organizational tree structure, including information about their current status.	Yes	Yes
Enterprise Search	Allows the user to search in more than 200 file types in almost any content source, and search for properties.	Yes	Yes
People Search	Search for people based on properties such as names, department, company, skills, title, and more.	Yes	Yes
Business Data Search	Allows the user to search in external data sources connected to SharePoint using the Business Data Catalog, such as databases, SAP, Line-of-Business systems, and so on.	No	Yes
FAST Advanced Search	Client license to run FAST search engine to enhance the Enterprise Search engine.	No	Yes
Retention and Audit Policy	Control documents and information retention and auditing.	Yes	Yes
Policies, Audit, and Compliance	Makes it possible to support compliance of SOX, ISO, and HIPAA.	Yes	Yes
Slide Libraries	Stores single PPT pages individually, regardless of what PPT presentation they belong to; then selects the pages needed to create a new presentation.	Yes	Yes
Digital Assets Library	Stores image, audio, and video files, including previews.	Yes	Yes
Site Variations	Makes creating a website that adjusts its language for content, depending on the current user, possible.	Yes	Yes
Browser-based XML forms	Allows the user to open and use InfoPath forms in a web browser.	No	Yes

FEATURE/FUNCTION	DESCRIPTION	STANDARD	ENTERPRISE
Browser-based Excel sheets	Allows the user to open and use Excel spreadsheets and diagrams in a web browser.	No	Yes
Share Excel sheets	Stores Excel spreadsheets and diagrams in SharePoint's Excel Services.	No	Yes
Data Connection Libraries	A defined connection to an external data source that allows Microsoft Office 2007 applications to share and use these data sources.	No	Yes
Business Data Connectivity (BDC)	Configures connections to external data sources, then uses that data in SharePoint lists and Web Parts.	No	Yes
Business Data Web Parts	Specially designed Web Parts for displaying external data retrieved by the BDC.	No	Yes
Report Center	A special website for managing Report Libraries, Data Connection Libraries, and spreadsheets typically used for business intelligence.	No	Yes
PerformancePoint Services	A business intelligence solution that enables users to communicate goals and status to drive results, using Key Performance Indicators (KPIs) with drill-down, history, and trend analysis.	No	Yes
Visio Services	Connects and displays interactive Visio files.	No	Yes
Access Services	Connects and displays Microsoft Access database applications.	No	Yes

Understanding the Database Combinations

Four different database editions are supported by SharePoint 2010. One of them is the free SQL Server Express that comes with SharePoint and may be installed when SharePoint Server is installed. With a full SQL Server implementation, there are no special considerations when configuring SharePoint Server and you have three different installation options:

➤ A local 64-bit SQL Server Express

➤ A local 64-bit SQL Server (2005/2008/2008 R2)

➤ A remote 64-bit SQL Server (2005/2008/2008 R2)

The following table describes the supported database options for SharePoint Server in more detail:

DATABASE TYPE	LOCAL INSTALLATION	REMOTE INSTALLATION
SQL Server Express 2008	Yes	Not supported
Microsoft SQL 2005 Server x64	Yes	Yes
Microsoft SQL 2008 Server x64	Yes	Yes
Microsoft SQL 2008 R2 x64	Yes	Yes

Remember that if you already have a 64-bit SQL Server 2005/2008/2008 R2 installed in your network, SharePoint can use it, if it has enough disk space and resources. SharePoint can, in fact, work with a 32-bit remote SQL Server, but it is not supported by Microsoft.

> **NOTE** *Make sure to apply the latest service packs to SQL Server before using it with SharePoint.*

Single-Server Configuration with a Local SQL Server Express

This is an installation of both SharePoint Server (including SharePoint Foundation) and the free SQL Server Express on the same computer. Microsoft refers to this type of configuration as a *stand-alone* server. The typical scenario for this kind of configuration is when doing a pilot or evaluation of SharePoint. Think twice before using this configuration in a production environment, because of the 4GB size database limitation and the fact that you cannot upgrade to a full SQL Server.

Single-Server Configuration with a Local Microsoft SQL Server

This configuration is perfect for the small organization or department that wants a very good platform for building a basic intranet for information sharing and collaboration, as well as basic search capability. The cost is higher than for the previous configuration because you need a Microsoft SQL Server license, but there is no size limit for the SQL databases. If you already have invested in the 64-bit Microsoft SQL Server 2005 or 2008, and it has the required disk, memory, and CPU capacity available, you could install SharePoint Server on that same server.

> **NOTE** *You need one Microsoft SQL Server client access license (CAL) for each SharePoint Server user, not just one for each service account. Make sure your current license agreement covers all the SharePoint Server users.*

A Small Farm: SharePoint Server with a Remote Microsoft SQL 2005/2008/2008 R2 Server

The last configuration option is where you install SharePoint Server on one server and Microsoft SQL Server 2005/2008 on another server. Microsoft refers to this setup as a *small farm*. This type of configuration increases the number of supported users, and you have all the functionality of the previously described configuration. Once again, this installation would not be free because you need the Microsoft SQL Server, but if you have this server already installed in your IT environment, SharePoint Server may be free. This depends on the type of license you have for the existing Microsoft SQL Server; for example, do you have a client access license for all users, including the SharePoint users, or (better still) a CPU license that allows any number of users access to SQL Server?

This solution provides no additional SharePoint Server functionality compared to a single-server configuration, besides the increased number of users supported. However, you could use this configuration with a clustered Microsoft SQL 2005/2008 Server environment with up to eight nodes, thus giving you both fault tolerance and higher availability.

The Front-End and Back-End Roles

SharePoint Server has a lot more built-in functionality than SharePoint Foundation. To provide this functionality, SharePoint Server is divided into multiple services, known as *front-end* roles. These roles are:

- ➤ Web Service
- ➤ Search Service
- ➤ Index Service
- ➤ Help Search Service
- ➤ Excel Calculation Service
- ➤ Visio Services (new for SharePoint Server 2010)
- ➤ Access Services (new for SharePoint Server 2010)
- ➤ Document Conversion Services

All these service roles can be configured to run on a single SharePoint Server server or be distributed over several servers. Besides these front-end service roles, you also hear the term *back-end* server, which simply means the server that runs SQL Server, which can be the same physical server as the front-end server. In this case, you have a single-server configuration.

By dividing the SharePoint Server functionality into different roles, you can build solutions that match your requirements. For example, one organization with 10,000 users may be satisfied with a small farm consisting of one front-end server running all SharePoint Server roles and one back-end server running Microsoft SQL Server. Another organization with 500 users may require fault-tolerance and build a solution with multiple front-end servers running the Web and Search services; one more front-end server running the Index, Excel, and Conversion services; plus a clustered SQL environment as the back-end server. It all depends on the requirements and on the budget for this SharePoint project.

> **NOTE** *If you are uncertain about which type of SharePoint Server installation to do, start with a small farm and expand it if you find that it does not match your needs. You will also be surprised by the performance a small installation will have — maybe you don't need all the servers you planned for?*

In the earliest versions of SharePoint, only a limited number of configurations were supported, usually referred to as small, medium, and large farms. This is no longer the case in SharePoint 2010; you have the freedom now to configure whatever combination of front-end and back-end servers you want for your SharePoint environment. SharePoint Server 2010 offers a number of services; the most commonly used are described in the following sections.

The Web Service Role

This front-end role actually runs on both SharePoint Server and stand-alone SharePoint Foundation installations. It is responsible for answering any requests from users who connect to the SharePoint server. In other words, this role shows the user the website pages and content. This Web role constantly reads and writes to the back-end server to do whatever the user requests.

The basic action in any web application is very simple: A web client requests a web page by entering a URL address or clicking a link. This is known as a GET request and results in a connection to the web server, asking the web server to find the requested content and send it back using the HTML format. After that, the session between the client and the server is disconnected. When the user clicks another link or button, a new connection is established. After the new content is sent back to the client, the session is disconnected again. There is no requirement that the exact same web server be used for all the connected sessions from a web client. If you have two or more web servers with access to the same information, another web server may accept the next connection from this web client. This is known as a *stateless connection*.

SharePoint's Web front-end (WFE) role uses stateless connections. If you install the WFE role on several servers, distributing the client load between them is possible. But you must solve two problems first. One is to make sure all WFE servers have access to the same information. You do this by using a common back-end database for all of them. The second problem to solve is that all of these web servers must look like a single SharePoint server; otherwise, the web clients must select a particular web server to communicate with. Using the Windows 2008 Network Load Balancing (NLB) service solves the second issue. The NLB service is a feature in Windows 2008 and 2008 R2 Server that allows up to 32 physical web servers to share a virtual server name. The web clients only see one virtual WFE server, regardless of how many there are. This is known as a *web cluster*. SharePoint supports a web cluster with up to eight servers running the WFE role.

To summarize: Use the NLB service when you need to create a web cluster with two or more SharePoint servers running the Web front-end role. The web cluster will automatically direct a new client session to the WFE server with the least load. If a WFE server becomes unreachable, all clients, both current and new, will automatically be directed to another WFE server. The result is both load balancing and fault tolerance.

The Search Service Role

The Search Service SharePoint role exists only on SharePoint Server installations; SharePoint Foundation alone does not have it. This role is also referred to as the Query role. The responsibility of this role is to answer search queries entered by the client. For example, when a user searches for the word *Viking*, this happens:

1. The user enters the word or phrase in the search field in SharePoint Server.

2. This request is received by the Web front-end service.

3. The Web front-end service sends the request to the Search service.

4. The Search service looks for this phrase in its index files.

5. The results ("No match," or a list of matching documents, files, and pages) are returned in XML format to the Web front-end service.

6. The Web front-end service converts the result to HTML format and sends this information back to the client.

This raises several questions: What are index files, where do they come from, and where are they stored? The answers are: An *index file* is a list that may consist of many thousands of words with a pointer to all the content sources — that is, files, documents, list items, and pages — where these words will be found. Also metadata and tags are included in the index. These index files are created by the Index service and replicated to each server running the Search service. The actual index consists of multiple physical files, but there is only one master index, regardless of the number of content sources. These index files are stored locally on the server running the Search service, in the folder you select during the installation. The default folder is `C:\Program Files\Microsoft Office Servers\14.0\Data\Office Server\Applications`.

> **NOTE** *Storing an index file on the C: drive may be unwise, since that disk is often limited in size, and index files can require many gigabytes of disk space. Use the command* `stsadm -o spsearch -indexlocation <path>` *to change the location for the index files.*

You can install more than one SharePoint Server server running the Search service. Because this service uses local index files, it is not dependent on other servers or roles to do its job. Combining the Search service with other services, such as the Web and Index services, is possible. This makes it possible to use the Search role on the same server that is running the Web Front-End role, even in web farm scenarios, as long as each Search role server has identical copies of the index files. This would result in load balancing and fault-tolerance for the search feature in SharePoint Server.

The Index Service Role

This SharePoint service is also exclusive for SharePoint Server installations only. The index service is responsible for building the index files by crawling content sources. The SharePoint administrator configures what content sources this service will index, and how often. The index files created by the crawling process are automatically copied by the index service to all search servers, in case you have a configuration with a separate index and search servers. You can configure this role to index the following content sources:

➤   The complete SharePoint farm

➤   Any file server in your network

➤   Your Microsoft Exchange server (including public folders)

➤   Any Lotus Notes database

➤   Any other web application internally

➤   Any external website on the Internet

➤   External data sources, using the Business Data Connectivity service

For example, you can configure the Index service to scan and index all files and documents on your file server, all public folders in your Microsoft Exchange server, your partner's public websites, and your Oracle database. When the users later search for information, they will find it, as long as it is stored in any of these content sources, including any part of the SharePoint database.

The Index service is very resource intensive, especially regarding CPU and disk access. By installing a separate SharePoint Server server with this service, many more users will be supported in the SharePoint environment. SharePoint 2010 introduced a new architecture that allows multiple index servers working in parallel, thus creating a fault-tolerance environment. In other words, if one index server goes down, another index server will take over the indexing crawling. You can also load balance by dividing the content sources to be indexed between the index servers.

The SharePoint Foundation Search Service

The SharePoint Foundation Search service is available for both SharePoint Foundation and SharePoint Server installations. When you install SharePoint Server, this service is mainly responsible for indexing SharePoint's help files, thus making them searchable. Note that this service will not index the user content of an SharePoint Foundation server, only the help content!

The Excel Calculation Service

(SharePoint Server Enterprise) The Excel Calculation Service is classified as an application service in SharePoint, and its purpose is to give users access to Microsoft Excel spreadsheets — data, charts, and formulas — from within SharePoint sites. These spreadsheets may be stored in document libraries or outside SharePoint. You can install this service on multiple SharePoint servers to achieve fault tolerance and load-balancing.

The Document Conversion Service

(SharePoint Server Enterprise) The purpose of the Document Conversion service is to make possible the conversion of documents from one file format to another; for example, from InfoPath forms to HTML, or an Microsoft Word .docx file to HTML format. One common use of this service is to convert news articles created in Word to web pages (ASPX files), which is called *Smart Client Authoring*.

 NOTE *Learn more about Smart Client Authoring in Chapter 4.*

The Access Service

(SharePoint Server Enterprise) The Access service makes hosting and facilitating Microsoft Access 2010 applications in SharePoint possible. For example, you can create a database application that hosts helpdesk events (including rules for sending mail), escalates unsolved issues, and creates reports of activities. This service is new for SharePoint Server 2010, compared to its predecessor, MOSS 2007.

The Business Data Connectivity Service

(SharePoint Foundation and SharePoint Server) The Business Data Connectivity service, also known as BDC, allows SharePoint to establish a communication channel with data sources outside SharePoint, like Microsoft SQL Server, Oracle database, or an Excel spreadsheet stored in a file server. Using BDC you can read, write, and search in these external data sources using SharePoint tables and BDC Web Parts. This service in SharePoint Server 2010 is an enhanced version of the BDC in MOSS 2007.

The Managed Metadata Service

(SharePoint Server Enterprise) The Managed Metadata service enables global metadata taxonomy and folksonomy, available to all SharePoint sites or just a specific site collection. Use this service to manage hierarchical metadata structures that will be used by SharePoint authors when tagging documents, images, and other types of items. This service is new for SharePoint Server 2010, compared to its predecessor, MOSS 2007.

The PerformancePoint Service

(SharePoint Server Enterprise) Use the PerformancePoint service to manage the PerformancePoint (PP) feature built into SharePoint Server 2010. With PP a user can define a number of objectives, such as a minimum sales figure per day or a maximum number of helpdesk issues per day, then see a graphical indicator of how well she meets these objectives. For example, if today's sales result is too low at lunchtime, a yellow traffic light may appear on the SharePoint site, which can indicate that something has to be done quickly. This service is new for SharePoint Server 2010, compared to its predecessor, MOSS 2007.

The PowerPoint Service

(SharePoint Server Enterprise) The PowerPoint service enables the PowerPoint Broadcast Site feature; you use it to publish PowerPoint presentations in real time to any user with access to that site, without requiring the user to have PowerPoint installed. To publish a presentation you need PowerPoint 2010. This service is new for SharePoint Server 2010, compared to its predecessor, MOSS 2007.

The Usage and Health Service

(SharePoint Server Enterprise) The Usage and Health service is responsible for collecting data about SharePoint usage for analysis and reporting. This data collection also includes messages sent to the Event Viewer as well as IIS logs. This service is new for SharePoint Server 2010, compared to its predecessor, MOSS 2007.

The User Profile Service

(SharePoint Server Standard and Enterprise) The User Profile service manages the user profile database, its properties, and the synchronization between the database and Active Directory. It is also involved in My Profile sites, previously known as "My Sites." This service in SharePoint Server 2010 is enhanced compared to the User Profile service in MOSS 2007.

The Secure Store Service

(SharePoint Server Enterprise) The Secure Store service replaces the Single Sign-on database in MOSS 2007. Its purpose is to store and manage accounts and passwords for external data sources. Typically it is used to build a web part that displays information stored in an external data source that requires authentication. Instead of requiring the user to enter the account and password, the web part will fetch them from the Secure Store and use it to authenticate, completely transparently to the user.

The Visio Graphics Service

(SharePoint Server Enterprise) The Visio Graphics service allows the user to display and manipulate Visio diagrams and objects on a SharePoint site, without requiring users to have Visio installed. These Visio diagrams can also be connected to workflows by means of SharePoint Designer 2010; for example, when a user selects an object on the diagram, some action takes place, such as a Word template opening. This service is new for SharePoint Server 2010, compared to its predecessor, MOSS 2007.

The Word Automation Service

(SharePoint Server Enterprise) The Word Automation service enables an automatic conversion from one Word file format to another, for example, from DOCX to PDF, or DOC to XPS. To do the actual conversion you need to write code. This service is new for SharePoint Server 2010, compared to its predecessor, MOSS 2007.

> **NOTE** Read more about the Word Automation Service on `http://tinyurl` `.com/word-as`.

The Word Viewing Service

(Requires both SharePoint Server 2010 Standard or Enterprise and Office Web Apps) Use this service to manage the settings for the Word web application. This service is new for SharePoint Server 2010, compared to its predecessor, MOSS 2007.

INSTALLING SHAREPOINT SERVER

By now you have the necessary information to start the installation of SharePoint Server. The following section describes the exact steps required to install SharePoint Server 2010. If you have other web applications installed on the same server, please make a backup before you start to be prepared for the unlikely possibility that something goes wrong and the server gets messed up beyond repair!

> **NOTE** *You can also install SharePoint in a virtual server, like Hyper-V, and make snapshot backups before you start, to make it easy to go back to a previous point in time in case something goes wrong and you need to redo some action.*

When installing SharePoint Server in Server farm mode, you have a choice of which web application to use for the portal and team sites. When you select the virtual IIS server for this web application, it is automatically extended, and you do not need to do this manually.

> **NOTE** *In the following sections are three complete step-by-step instructions on how to install SharePoint Server. You only have to read the description for the particular type of installation you are about to do.*

Installing a Stand-Alone SharePoint Server with the SQL Server Express

Installing SharePoint Server using its embedded Microsoft SQL Server Express database is very straightforward and easy. You can do it within 10 minutes, without much hassle. Follow these steps to install both SharePoint Server and the SQL database on the same server:

> **NOTE** *To complete this procedure you need the installation files for SharePoint Server 2010 and the product key for the edition of SharePoint Server you are about to install. The server must have Internet access in order to download any software prerequisites for SharePoint Server, and the server must also have a connection to its Active Directory domain controller.*

TRY IT OUT   Install SharePoint Server and SQL Server Express on a Stand-alone Server

1. Log on as a domain administrator to the Windows 2008 server you will use for your SharePoint Server and SQL Server Express installation. This ensures that the domain administrator will be granted all permissions in the new SharePoint Server server.

2. Make sure the prerequisite steps for installing IIS and .NET Framework in Windows Server 2008/2008 R2 are completed; detailed instructions appear earlier in this appendix. Make sure Windows 2008 Server has the latest service packs and security patches installed by running Start ⇨ All Programs ⇨ Windows Update before you continue.

3. Mount the installation file or media with SharePoint Server 2010.

4. Start the setup file for SharePoint Server 2010:

   a. The first dialog page is a menu of different options. What you must do is run a check that all prerequisites are installed and configured properly. In the Install section, click on the "Install software prerequisites" link.

   b. The page "Microsoft SharePoint Products and Technology 2010 Preparation Tool" that appears lists the products and updates that you must install before SharePoint Server will install. Click Next to continue.

   c. The license agreement for the products and updates that are required to install SharePoint Server appears. If you accept the terms, select "I accept the terms of this agreement" and click Next to start the installation.

   d. The Installation Complete page appears, describing everything that was installed or updated. Click Finish to close the Preparation Tool. The start page reappears. If there were any issues they will be listed, and you will see suggestions on how to solve them.

   e. Click the Install SharePoint Server link to start the actual installation of SharePoint Server.

   f. On the first page that appears, you see Enter your Product key:. Enter your key and click Continue.

   g. The license agreement for SharePoint Server appears. If you accept the terms, select "I accept the terms of this agreement" and click Continue.

   h. The "Choose the installation you want" page that appears next is important. Click Standalone to install SharePoint Server together with the SQL Server Express 2010 that is included in the SharePoint Server installation package. If you instead click Server Farm you will need a preinstalled Microsoft SQL Server. For this scenario be sure to click Standalone; see Figure C-2.

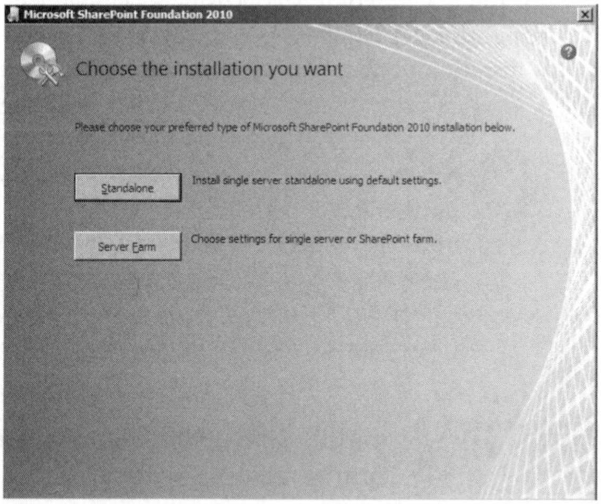

FIGURE C-2

   i. The installation takes a few minutes; when it completes a page appears with the option "Run the SharePoint Product and Technologies Configuration Wizard now" pre-selected. Click Close to close the setup program; this will start the configuration wizard automatically.

5. The configuration wizard sets up the configuration needed to run SharePoint Server, such as the Central Administration tool, and creates the web application needed to host the first site collection. You must complete this configuration wizard before you can use SharePoint Server. If you for some reason cannot do the wizard now, it is also available under Start ➪ All Programs ➪ Microsoft SharePoint 2010 Products. Make sure to answer the questions as follows:

> **NOTE** *This server needs to have contact with its domain controller to create the configuration database. If you install SharePoint Server on a virtual server, make sure the DC is also running.*

a. On the Welcome to SharePoint Products and Technologies page, click Next.

b. A dialog box appears informing you that the IIS and other related services will be started or reset during the configuration: Click Yes to continue. The configuration wizard now continues, and performs nine different tasks; it takes 5–10 minutes to complete, depending on the server hardware.

c. When it has completed, the Configuration Successful page should appear. Click Finish.

d. The configuration wizard creates an empty site collection and opens the page where you select its site template, as shown in Figure C-3. Choose the site template you want to use for the top site of this site collection. For example, under the Publishing tab you find the Enterprise Wiki, which is commonly used as a start site for intranets. Click OK when you have selected the site template.

e. The Set up Groups for this Site page then appears, which is where you define access permissions to this top site. Unless you have special requirements, accept the default settings and click OK.

The new top site appears, and you can start using it immediately.

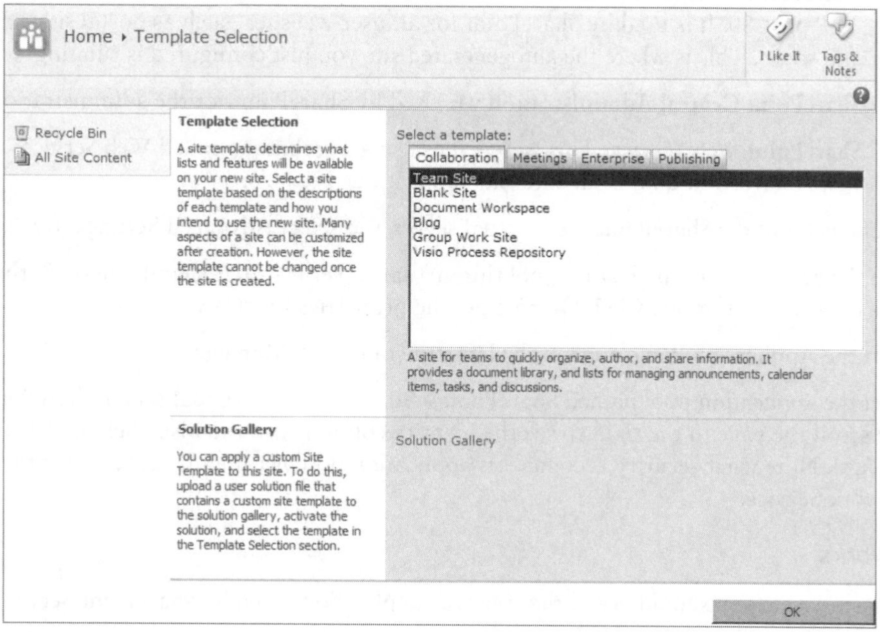

FIGURE C-3

How It Works

When installing SharePoint Server 2010 in stand-alone mode, it will first install the embedded SQL Server Express, then all SharePoint Server binary files, and then run a configuration wizard that will create the SharePoint Configuration Wizard tool and the connection to the SQL Server Express.

Checking the Stand-Alone Installation of SharePoint Server

Before going on, investigating what new things were installed on the server is a good idea. In short, you have a new SharePoint Central Administration tool, a team site, and corresponding web applications; that is, extended virtual IIS websites, plus a SQL Server Express with a number of databases. Start by checking the new web applications in IIS:

TRY IT OUT   Checking the Stand-Alone Installation

1. Start by opening the IIS manager: choose Start ➪ Administration Tools ➪ Internet Information Service (IIS) Manager.

2. Expand the server node, and then the Sites node. Note that you have four IIS virtual servers here:

➤ **Default Web Site:** This site is stopped because another virtual IIS web server using TCP port 80 was created: SharePoint – 80. The reason is increased security because the files and locations for Default Web Site are well known, and therefore the target for malicious code, like viruses.

➤ **SharePoint – 80:** A new virtual server created by the configuration wizard, which listens on TCP port 80. It is used by SharePoint for all user websites, such as portal sites, team sites, and so on. This is where the autogenerated site you just configured is running.

➤ **SharePoint Central Administration v4:** Used by SharePoint for the administration website.

➤ **SharePoint Web Service:** This web makes using a technique called Web Services to read and write SharePoint data from external applications possible.

3. Select (click on) the SharePoint – 80 virtual server and select Advanced Settings in the right pane.

4. Note the name for the application pool this virtual server is using: SharePoint – 80, that is, the same name as for the site. Click OK to close the properties for this virtual server.

5. Select the Application Pools node in the left pane of the IIS Manager.

6. Select the application pool named SharePoint – 80 (used by the virtual server SharePoint – 80), then scroll the page to the right to see the Identity column (you can also click on Advanced Settings). Note what security account this application pool is using. By default it is the predefined Network Service.

How It Works

After the installation you should verify that the web applications used by SharePoint Server are set up correctly.

You should also check that the web application for the SharePoint Central Administration tool is created and that it is properly configured.

TRY IT OUT   Check the SharePoint Central Administration tool

1.   Continue from the previous Try It Out: Under the Sites node in the IIS Manager, select SharePoint Central Administration v4 and click on Advanced Settings.

2.   Note that the application pool is also named SharePoint Central Administration v4. Close this dialog box.

3.   Select that application pool and check the Identity account — it should also be Network Service, just like SharePoint – 80.

How It Works

The SharePoint Central Administration tool is installed as a web application, associated with its own application pool.

NOTE *This Identity account is automatically granted access to the SQL Server Express database and is used by SharePoint Server whenever it needs to read or write to the databases.*

Summarizing the Stand-Alone Installation of SharePoint Server

SharePoint Server primarily uses two virtual IIS servers: one for the websites used by the end users, and one for the Central Administration tool for SharePoint. These two virtual servers use separate application pools. But this type of installation, that is, the stand-alone server, has a number of issues that you must beware of before choosing it for a production environment. The only real advantages of this installation option are that it is very fast and that it does not require a full SQL Server version installed. The most important drawbacks with this installation option are as follows:

➤   Both these application pools use the same security account, which is normally considered not the best practice, as you discover later on when you use the built-in Best Practice Analyzer tool.

➤   Upgrading it to a multiserver farm — for example, one SharePoint Server server and one SQL Server — is hard. It requires a complete reinstallation of SharePoint Server, in which case you would first need to back up your site collections, then uninstall SharePoint Server, do either an installation with a local SQL Server or an installation with a remote SQL Server, and finally restore the site collections.

➤   No SQL Management tool is included with this type of database, so you cannot work with the databases in case you need to. However, there are third-party SQL management products available for SQL Server Express. All databases are, by default, stored in the `C:\ Program Files\Microsoft Office Servers\14.0\Data\MSSQL10.SHAREPOINT\MSSQL\ DATA` folder, unless you selected another installation location.

> **NOTE** *This is not the same folder location as used by SQL Server Express with SharePoint Foundation 2010. See Appendix A for more details.*

➤ The maximum amount of data you can store in this SharePoint environment is 4GB.

SharePoint Server 2010 is now installed in a stand-alone configuration; that is, using a local SQL Server Express. The next step is to adjust the settings in Central Administration so the configuration suits the needs of your organization; for example, enabling SharePoint Server to send e-mail and adding more intuitive URL addresses for the intranet. Appendix D describes this process in detail.

> **NOTE** *If you follow the instructions above, you should succeed in installing SharePoint Server. The most common reason for an unsuccessful installation is that the software prerequisites are not fulfilled.*

The following section describes how to install SharePoint Server using the Microsoft SQL Server database instead of the SQL Express database. You can skip that section if it does not match your required installation procedure. However, if you want to know how to install SharePoint Server in advanced mode using the full SQL Server product, be sure to read the following section.

Installing SharePoint Server Using the Microsoft SQL Database

The most common installation scenario for small- and medium-sized organizations is SharePoint Server that uses a Microsoft SQL Server; this SQL server may be installed on the same server as SharePoint Server, referred to as a single-server, or a remote server, referred to as a small farm. Many of the following steps are identical to the previous installation scenario using a local SQL Express database, except for these important things:

➤ You must install the Microsoft SQL Server before the installation of SharePoint Server. If you install SQL Server 2005, then you must also install Service Pack 3 and its cumulative update 3, or later. If you install SQL Server 2008 then install the latest Service Pack 1 plus its cumulative update 2, or later. If you install SQL Server 2008 R2 make sure to install its latest service pack and cumulative updates.

➤ You need to define at least four service accounts:

  ➤ One account to run all SQL services (for example, filobit\sql_service)

  ➤ One account to be used as the application pool identity for the SharePoint Central Administration tool (for example, filobit\sp_centraladmin)

  ➤ One account to run general SharePoint services (for example, filobit\sp_service)

  ➤ One account to be used by the SharePoint Search feature (for example, filobit\sp_search)

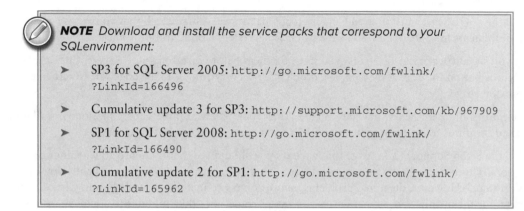

NOTE *Download and install the service packs that correspond to your SQLenvironment:*

➤ SP3 for SQL Server 2005: `http://go.microsoft.com/fwlink/?LinkId=166496`

➤ Cumulative update 3 for SP3: `http://support.microsoft.com/kb/967909`

➤ SP1 for SQL Server 2008: `http://go.microsoft.com/fwlink/?LinkId=166490`

➤ Cumulative update 2 for SP1: `http://go.microsoft.com/fwlink/?LinkId=165962`

This type of installation is a much better option than the previously discussed stand-alone server option, and it has no issues like the ones mentioned in the previous section. For example, it allows you to later change the number of servers, such as when adding an extra SharePoint Foundation server, or move to a separate SQL Server hardware. Maybe the strongest advantage of this installation option compared to the previous one is that it has no size limitations. This is a strong reason for selecting the full Microsoft SQL Server. Because it requires a separate installation of SQL Server, as well as SharePoint Server, completing this operation takes more time, up to an hour, depending on your hardware.

The following sections describe how to install both SharePoint Server and Microsoft SQL Server 2008 on the same server. Make sure to install the SQL Server before installing SharePoint Server!

NOTE *To complete this procedure you need an existing user account to be used to run all SQL Server services.*

TRY IT OUT   **Install Microsoft SQL Server 2008 R2**

1. Log on as a local administrator to the Windows 2008 server you will use for your SharePoint Server and SQL Server installation.

2. Make sure Windows 2008 Server has the latest service packs and security patches installed by choosing Start ➪ All Programs ➪ Windows Update.

3. Mount the Microsoft SQL Server 2008 DVD and start SETUP.EXE.

    a. If Windows Server 2008 does not have .NET 3.5 SP1 installed, you will first see an installation page for that product. Select "I have read and accept the terms of the License Agreement," and then click the Install button.

    b. When the installation of .NET 3.5 SP1 Setup is complete, click Exit.

    c. If there are more updates that are a prerequisite for SQL Server 2008 R2, you will be prompted to install them now.

    d. After the installation of these updates, Windows Server may have to be restarted; if so you will see the page "Installation complete." Click Restart Now to restart the server.

4. On the "SQL Server Installation Center" page that appears, first check that your server meets the requirements for SQL Server 2008 R2 by clicking System Configuration Checker.

5. If you see any warnings or errors, you must fix them before installing SQL Server. Click the Show Details button to see exactly what the problem is. If everything is okay, click OK to return to the previous page.

6. Select Installing in the left navigation pane, then click "New SQL Server stand-alone installation or add features to an existing installation" to start the installation of SQL Server.

7. On the Setup Support Rules page that appears you should see that there are no warnings or errors. This is actually the same type of test as was done earlier in step 5, so basically you can skip step 5. However, detecting problems before you try to install is usually better. Click OK to continue the installation. Be patient; several steps sometimes take minutes to complete, so just wait for their completion.

8. Then the Product Key page appears. If this is a test environment you may choose between the Enterprise Evaluation version and the full version. If you choose the Enterprise Evaluation, you must be aware that this SQL Server will stop working after 180 days (6 months). Click Next to continue.

9. The License Terms page appears. Read the license and if you agree, select "I accept the license terms" and click Next.

10. The Setup Support Files page appears; these are files necessary for the SQL Server to operate properly. Click Install and wait several minutes for the installation to complete.

11. After installing the support files, the installation program once again runs the Setup Support Rules checker — this time you will see more than 10 different rules that are tested. They should all be okay, but if the Windows Firewall gets the *Warning* status you can click on its status link and see more details. Most likely, you will detect that your server has the Windows Firewall enabled, which is safe to ignore unless you need to allow remote access. If so, disable Windows Firewall, or configure its port to allow remote access. See more about this on `http://go.microsoft.com/fwlink/?LinkId=94001`: "Configure the Windows Firewall to Allow SQL Server Access." Click Next to continue.

12. The Configure Role page appears. When preparing for a SharePoint Server installation you would most likely choose the SQL Server Feature Installation to install a complete SQL Server, including Reporting Services and Analysis Service. Click Next to continue.

13. The Feature Selection page appears. This is where you choose what features to install. For a SharePoint Server installation you should install at least these options (see Figure A-5):

➤ Database Engine Service

➤ Management Tools – Complete (which also adds Management Tools – Basic)

Then choose carefully what file directories to use for SQL Server, using Shared feature directory and Shared feature directory (x86). As always, a good practice is to avoid installing anything on the C: drive because it is heavily used by the Windows operating system. If you have another drive with enough disk space on this server, consider changing these two paths to that drive instead. Click Next to continue.

14. The Installation Rules page appears again (do you start to see a pattern here?). If there are no warnings or errors, click Next to continue. If there are any issues, click Show Details to see more about them. You must resolve all errors before you can continue the installation.

15. The Instance Configuration page appears next. If you want to use this SQL Server for other applications besides SharePoint Server, creating a named instance is a good idea. This will, in effect, create a private partition, or section, in SQL for all SharePoint Server-related databases (and there are a number of them; just wait and see). If this server will only be used by SharePoint Server, then using the default instance is okay. Make your choice and click Next to continue.

16. The Disk Space Requirements page appears, giving you information about the available space on the disk you selected in step 13 earlier. If enough free space exists, click Next. If not, click Back until you get to step 13 again, and change the location.

17. The Server Configuration page appears. Select an existing user account that will be associated with the SQL services. For a typical installation, using the same account is common ; if this okay with you, click "Use the same account for all SQL Server services" to enter the name and password for that account. If it is not okay, then enter each account individually. When ready, click Next to continue.

18. The Database Engine Configuration page appears. On this page you define what type of authentication mechanism you want to use. The default is Windows authentication mode; using it is also a best practice. Unless you have a good reason not to, go with that option. You must add the user account that will be the SQL Server Administration. To add the account you are logged on with, click Add Current User. To add another account, click Add and enter that account name.

Also notice a tab named Data Directories on this page. Use it to view, and possibly also change, the file paths that SQL Server will use to store its databases, log files, and backup files. Change whatever you need to change, and then click Next to continue.

19. The Error and Usage Reporting page appears. Here you can define whether SQL Server should send any error messages in SQL automatically to Microsoft or a specifically configured report server in your organization. You can also choose to send feature usage data to Microsoft, including your hardware configuration and how you use SQL and its services. Microsoft will use this information to better understand how organizations all over the world use SQL Server, in order to enhance future releases, so this is a good thing. Make your choices and click Next to continue.

20. Once again, the Installation Configuration Rules page appears, performing yet another test; if all is okay and no reports or warnings are listed, click Next to continue; otherwise, fix whatever problem is listed before you can go on.

21. The Ready to Install page appears; it is a summary of all the options you made. If the summary looks okay to you, then click Install to start the actual installation of SQL Server. If it doesn't, go back through the steps, make your changes, and go on to this page again. When the installation starts, it is time to take a coffee break, because this may take time to complete — and you deserve it after these steps!

22. The Installation Progress page appears. It should list all features as successfully installed. Click Next to continue.

23. The last page to appear is Complete. Here you find information about possible next steps after the installation. Click Close to complete the installation of this SQL Server 2008 R2. The SQL Server Installation Center reappears. Click "Search for product updates" and install the recommended updates, if any.

> **NOTE** *If you install the evaluation edition of SQL Server, and later decide you want to convert it to a full edition, you must first purchase a SQL Server license, run the SQL Server Installation Center again, choose Maintenance in the left pane, click on Edition Upgrade, and select the full edition.*

How It Works

You need to install SQL Server before installing SharePoint Server 2010 in a single server or a farm setup. The steps above describe a typical standard installation of SQL Server 2008 R2.

After this SQL Server installation, you must next install SharePoint Server 2010. If you want to do a test installation and have not yet downloaded SharePoint Server, then open Microsoft Download Center, that is, `www.microsoft.com/download`, and search for SharePoint Server 2010. Use the steps in the following Try It Out to install SharePoint Server on this server to complete the single-server installation procedure.

> **NOTE** *To complete this procedure you need the product key for SharePoint Server, the installation media for SharePoint Server 2010 (make sure it is the right language), an existing user account for the communication between SharePoint Server and SQL Server, another user account for running all SharePoint services except the Central Administration tool, and a passphrase to be used as the farm passphrase. Note that the evaluation copy of SharePoint Server will require an evaluation product key, which will be listed on the download page for SharePoint Server.*

TRY IT OUT | **Install SharePoint Server 2010 to Complete the Single-Server Installation**

1. Log on as a domain administrator to the Windows 2008 server you will use for the SharePoint Server and SQL Server installation. This will ensure that the domain administrator will be granted all permissions in the new SharePoint Server server.

2. Make sure the prerequisite steps for installing IIS and .NET Framework in Windows Server 2008 R2 are completed; see the Try It Out "Prepare Windows Server 2008 for SharePoint Server" earlier in this appendix for detailed instructions. Make sure Windows 2008 Server has the latest service packs and security patches installed by running Start ⇨ All Programs ⇨ Windows Update before you continue.

3. Mount the SharePoint Server 2010 installation media.

4. Start the installation by running the setup file:

    a. The start page for SharePoint Server 2010 Installation opens; it shows a list of different options. What you must do is to run a check that all prerequisites are installed and configured properly. In the Install section, click on the link "Install software prerequisites."

    b. On the "Microsoft SharePoint Products and Technology 2010 Preparation Tool" page that appears is a list of the products and updates that must be installed before SharePoint Server will install. Click Next to continue.

    c. The license agreement for the products and updates that are required to install SharePoint Server appears. If you accept the terms, select "I accept the terms of this agreement" and click Next. The Microsoft SharePoint Products and Technologies 2010 Preparation Tool starts.

    d. When the installation is completed the Installation Complete page appears, which describes everything that was installed or updated. Click Finish to close the preparation tool. Now you are returned to the start page again, and it is time to install SharePoint Server.

    e. Click the Install SharePoint Server link to start the installation of SharePoint Server.

    f. Enter the Product Key for SharePoint Server 2010, then click Continue.

    g. The license agreement for SharePoint Server appears. If you accept the terms, select "I accept the terms of this agreement" and click Continue.

    h. The "Choose the installation you want" page appears. Click Server Farm.

    i. The next page that appears is the *Server Type*. You have two options, and choosing the right one is important. The default option is the stand-alone. Do not choose that option! It will do a stand-alone type of installation — that is, using a SQL Server Express — and ignore the fact that you have a full SQL Server installed. Instead, make sure to *always* choose the Complete option. That option allows you to connect this SharePoint Server to your pre-installed full SQL Server.

        One more interesting tab on this page is Data Location. Open it, and you will see that it allows you to choose the disk and folder to be used for storing SharePoint's index files. Because these index files may be several gigabytes in size, you should plan carefully where to store them. If you have another disk with enough available free space, it is a good candidate for this use. When you finish with the options on these two tabs, check again that you selected Complete installation, and click Install Now, which starts the installation of SharePoint Server. This is a good time for a quick coffee break.

    j. When the installation completes a page appears with the "Run the SharePoint Product and Technologies Configuration Wizard now" option pre-selected. Click Close to close the setup program; this will also start the configuration wizard.

5. The configuration wizard sets up the necessary configuration needed to run SharePoint Server, such as creating the Central Administration tool, including the web application needed to host it. You must complete this configuration wizard before you can use SharePoint Server. Because you selected to install a complete SharePoint Server server, you now get a few extra questions that you don't see when doing a stand-alone installation of SharePoint Server:

    a. On the Welcome to SharePoint Products and Technologies page, click Next.

    b. A dialog box appears informing you that the IIS and other related services will be started or reset during the configuration. Click Yes to continue. The configuration wizard now continues.

c. The "Connect to a server farm" page appears. Because this is the first server you install, select "Create a new server farm." (If this were a server that should be added to an existing farm, you would instead choose "Connect to an existing server farm.") Click Next.

d. The next page that appears is Specify Configuration Database Settings — this is a very important page! Make sure to enter the correct information here, because changing these values later is hard (but not impossible). See Figure C-4.

> ➤ **Database server:** Enter the name of your local Windows Server (because you run both SQL and SharePoint Server on the same server).

> ➤ **Database name:** Accept the default name SharePoint_Config, unless you have a good reason to change it. This name makes searching the Internet for information about this database easier (if you ever need to).

> ➤ **Username:** Enter the user account to be used by SharePoint Server when communicating with SQL Server. Make sure to enter this account as <domain>\<account>; for example Filobit\ sp_centraladmin. The best practice is to use a specific AD domain account for this that is dedicated for this role, that is not used anywhere else in SharePoint Server.

> ➤ **Password:** Enter the password for this user account.

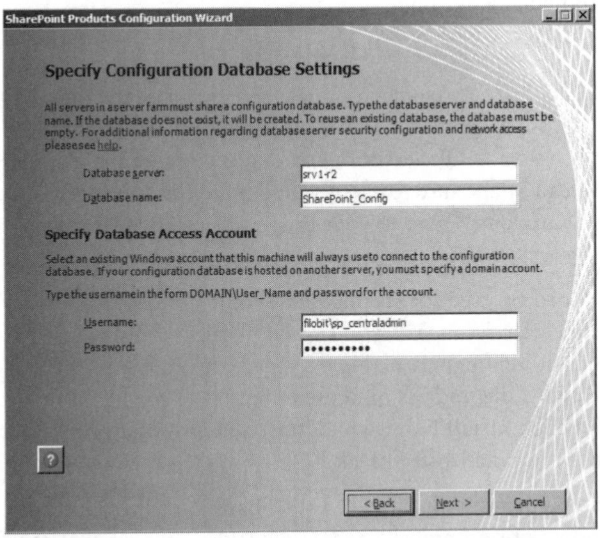

FIGURE C-4

Click Next to continue. The configuration wizard now checks these values, and if anything is wrong, such as the password, you will get informed and you can correct the error and click Next again.

e. The Specify Farm Security Settings page appears. These settings are a new type of protection that comes in SharePoint 2010. If you need to change important configuration settings in the farm, such as adding an extra SharePoint server to the farm, you need to enter this passphrase. Enter your farm passphrase and make sure to write it down and store it in a secure location. Click Next to continue.

f. The Configure SharePoint Central Administration Web Application page appears, containing two settings — port number and authentication mechanism (see Figure C-5):

➤ **Specify port number:** You must add this TCP port number to the URL to SharePoint's Central Administration tool. By default it is a random number, but choosing your own port number may be a good idea, because it will be easier to remember. Just make sure it is way above 1023 and less than 65535; for example, 5000.

➤ **Configure Security Settings:** The two authentication choices are NTLM or Negotiate (Kerberos). The default is NTLM, which is easiest to implement; Kerberos is more secure and faster in a large organization, but also requires more configuration and understanding to work. If you are uncertain about how to configure Kerberos, then go with the NTLM option. You can always change it later if needed. Click Next to continue.

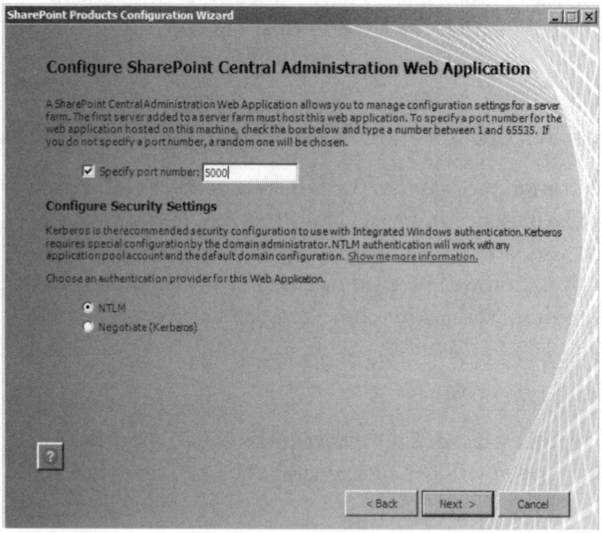

FIGURE C-5

g. The last page before the configuration wizard starts working is a summary of the settings you selected. If all is okay, then click Next to start; otherwise, click Back and correct the settings. This procedure consists of 10 configuration tasks; now may also be a good time for a coffee break.

h. When the wizard completes, you should see the Configuration Successful page. Click Finish to complete the configuration wizard. Then continue with the configuration listed in the next Try It Out section.

> **NOTE** If you need to rerun the configuration wizard, you can find it in Start ➪ All Programs ➪ Microsoft SharePoint 2010 Products. You can also run it as a command tool: PSCONFIG (stored in \Program Files\Common Files\Microsoft Shared\ Web Server Extensions\14\Bin). It has a number of options so make sure to read its Help file before you run it: \Program Files\Common Files\Microsoft Shared\web server extensions\14\Help\1033\PSCONFIG.CHM.

How It Works

Installing SharePoint Server 2010 in a single-server mode requires that the full SQL Server is already installed. You will need an Active Directory account that SharePoint Server will use when communicating with the SQL Server. The configuration wizard will automatically add this account to SQL Server with the correct permissions.

After the Installation

Before continuing, investigating what new things were installed on the server is a good idea. In short, you have a new SharePoint Central Administration tool and some corresponding web applications; that is, IIS websites that have been extended by SharePoint, plus a number of new databases in SQL Server. Because the SharePoint Central Administration tool started automatically, continue with its settings and complete the basic configurations. Note that the URL to this tool contains the TCP port number you selected earlier in step 5f.

TRY IT OUT   Run the Basic Configuration Wizard in SharePoint Central Administration

1. The first time you open the Central Administration tool after an installation you get a question about participating in Microsoft's Customer Experience Improvement Program. If you choose to participate in this program, all errors that you later may encounter in SharePoint Server will be sent automatically to Microsoft. This information will be used to enhance future versions of SharePoint Server, so participating is a good thing. Make your choice, and click OK to continue.

2. The next page is Configure your SharePoint farm, and it contains a question: "How do you want to configure your SharePoint Farm?" You have two options:

➤ **Yes, walk me through the settings using this wizard:** This option is the easiest for the non-experienced SharePoint administrator, but you will get autogenerated names on databases, web applications, and so on.

➤ **No, I will configure everything myself:** This option is the favorite for the experienced administrator who knows SharePoint and understands its options.

In this example, use the option "Yes, walk me through the settings using this wizard" (which is the default) and click Next.

3. The first page this wizard opens is where you select the *managed account*: This is a standard user account that SharePoint will associate with one or more SharePoint services (that is, background applications). You can create a new managed account (the user account must exist), or you can reuse the same account as you entered in step 5d of the previous installation procedure. However, this practice is not recommended by Microsoft. Avoid reusing that particular account, and make sure to create a new managed account for these services!

The selected managed account will, by default, be associated with all the available services listed on this page (15 services for SharePoint Server Enterprise edition, whereas SharePoint Foundation only has 2); for example, Access Service, Application Registry Service, and Business Data Connectivity. Click Next to continue; this adds the selected user account as a managed account for the selected services and completes the basic setup of SharePoint Server.

4. On the second, and last, page the wizard displays the form where you create the first site collection and its top site. Typically, this is the intranet start site. If you don't want to do this task now, then click the Skip button. In this example you will create a site named "Start" using the Enterprise Wiki site template. Here are the options:

➤ **Title:** Start (you can change this name later).

➤ **Description:** Enter a description or leave it empty (you can also change this later).

➤ **URL:** This is the web URL that users enter in their web browsers to open this site. By default it is always the same as the name of this Windows Server, but you can later add more URLs with better names. Accept the default here.

➤ **Select a template:** Open the Publishing tab and select Enterprise Wiki (see Figure C-6). You learn more about site templates in several sections in this book, but basically a template is a preconfigured site with a given design, lists, and information that you later can modify to your heart's desire.

Click OK to create this site collection and its top site.

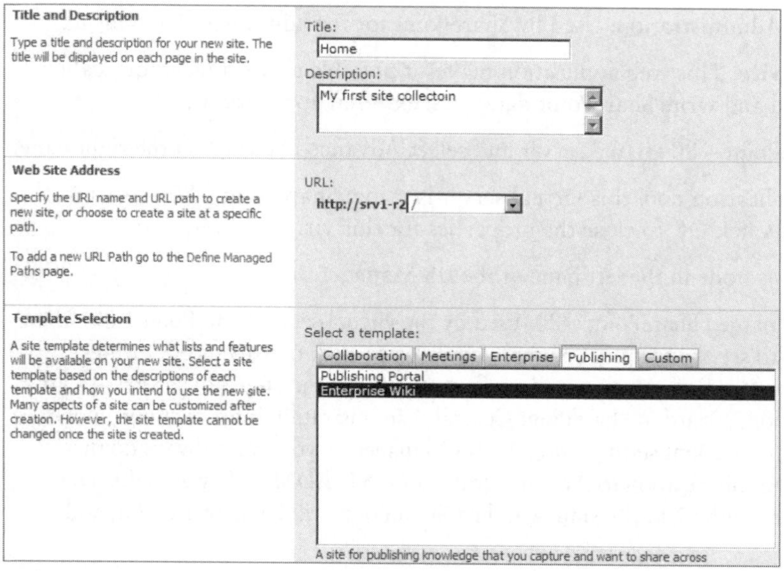

FIGURE C-6

5. On the page that appears, click Finish to complete the wizard. The start page for SharePoint's Central Administration tool opens. Open a new web browser session and enter the URL listed earlier in step 4 — the new site collection now appears.

How It Works

Run the Farm Configuration Wizard after an installation to enable and set up all standard configurations, including service applications. This wizard will also enable you to create your first site collection.

Now you have an SharePoint Server installed using a local SQL Server, and your first site collection is created. After all these steps it is time to check the new settings in IIS and the new databases in SQL Server, using the steps in the following Try It Out.

TRY IT OUT **Check Out New IIS Settings and SQL Databases**

1. Open the IIS manager by choosing Start ⇨ Administration Tools ⇨ Internet Information Service (IIS) Manager.

2. Expand the server node, and then the Sites node. Note that you have four IIS virtual servers here:

   ➤ **Default Web Site:** This site is stopped, because another virtual server using TCP port 80 was created during the installation of SharePoint Server: SharePoint – 80. The reason Default Web Site is not used is to increase the security; the files and locations for this website are well known, and it is therefore a primary target for malicious code, such as viruses.

   ➤ **SharePoint – 80:** This is a new virtual server created by the configuration wizard that listens on TCP port 80. It is, by default, used by SharePoint for all user websites, such as Enterprise Wiki, team sites, and so on. This is where your new site collection is running.

   ➤ **SharePoint Central Administration:** Used by SharePoint for the administrative website.

   ➤ **SharePoint Web Service:** This web application makes it possible to use a technique called Web Services to read and write SharePoint data from external applications.

3. Select (click on) the SharePoint – 80 virtual server and select Advanced Settings in the right pane.

4. Note the name for the application pool this virtual server is using: SharePoint – 80 — that is, the same name as for the site. Click OK to close the properties for this virtual server.

5. Select the Application Pools node in the left pane of the IIS Manager.

6. Select the application pool named SharePoint – 80 (used by the virtual server SharePoint – 80), then scroll the page to the right to see the Identity column (you can also click on Advanced Settings). Note that the security account is the new managed account you defined in step 3 of the Try It Out "Run the Basic Configuration Wizard in SharePoint Central Administration"; for example, filobit\ sp_service. Never change this account setting using the IIS Manager — you must always do these changes using the Central Administration tool or the script tools (STSADM or PowerShell). The reason is that if you change anything in IIS Manager, then SharePoint will be unaware of it, and therefore it will not work.

   Make the same checks with the virtual server used by the SharePoint Central Administration website:

   a. In the IIS Manager, under the Sites node, select SharePoint Central Administration v4 and click on Advanced Settings.

   b. Note that its application pool is also named SharePoint Central Administration v4, just like the site. Close this dialog box.

   c. Open the Advanced settings for this application pool and check the Identity account — it should be the account you entered when running the configuration wizard directly after the installation of SharePoint Server; for example, filobit\sp_centraladmin.

> **NOTE** This user account is automatically granted access to the SQL Server database and is used whenever SharePoint Server needs to read or write to the databases; for example, when you create a new site collection or web application.

7. The SQL Server also has been modified — there are new databases, and new user accounts have been granted access. Log on as an administrator to the server where SQL is installed, then start the SQL Server Management Studio (located in Start ➪ All Programs ➪ Microsoft SQL Server 2008 R2).

a. At the Connect to Server dialog that appears, make sure the server type is Database Engine, the server name is (local), and the Authentication is Windows Authentication. Click Connect.

b. Expand the top node (local), then Databases. You should now see about 20 new databases, where some of the names end in a 32-bit globally unique identifier, or GUID; see Figure C-7.

```
Object Explorer                                          ▾ ₽ ×
Connect ▾ 🛂 🛂 ∎ 🔻 🔁 🔏
□ 🐻 (local) (SQL Server 10.50.1092 - FILOBIT\administrator)
  □ 📁 Databases
    ⊞ 📁 System Databases
    ⊞ 📁 Database Snapshots
    ⊞ 🗊 Application_Registry_Service_DB_3fa0946c125149c2aba1f33e2b188fe2
    ⊞ 🗊 Bdc_Service_DB_3baede2b65774cf3bf76fd33ed82270c
    ⊞ 🗊 Managed Metadata Service_92ac387f983b4d92bf010c9418ec0226
    ⊞ 🗊 PerformancePoint Service Application_87f6a4d9107944469ac536a49f8fc320
    ⊞ 🗊 Search_Service_Application_CrawlStoreDB_1d9eaf2918994244b49ed55e1e0c3b8d
    ⊞ 🗊 Search_Service_Application_DB_4a0df253763e4ed08a9accc239130fa7
    ⊞ 🗊 Search_Service_Application_PropertyStoreDB_34c4b0ee49bd4c9db2548301ce9fd270
    ⊞ 🗊 Secure_Store_Service_DB_5b162c3fd13d43ec83613bd39c0f32f1
    ⊞ 🗊 SharePoint_AdminContent_248808c7-ff31-4529-9358-e7213168ebb7
    ⊞ 🗊 SharePoint_Config
    ⊞ 🗊 StateService_413f3ab6ff6f44ea96a1097713dbf3a7
    ⊞ 🗊 User Profile Service Application_ProfileDB_5eec36d94855409e90750fb75cc13a8e
    ⊞ 🗊 User Profile Service Application_SocialDB_7b404787baaa44eb8a6e708f997b5cfa
    ⊞ 🗊 User Profile Service Application_SyncDB_817520036f7d483bab346824732edd80
    ⊞ 🗊 WebAnalyticsServiceApplication_ReportingDB_3ee5166b-6617-41d8-abe8-fe064377d8cf
    ⊞ 🗊 WebAnalyticsServiceApplication_StagingDB_3e93381b-f0bc-41da-8c78-52a264e38207
    ⊞ 🗊 Word Automation Services_37832e75d0ec41ecb599e6fffe8389e1
    ⊞ 🗊 WSS_Content
    ⊞ 🗊 WSS_Logging
  ⊞ 📁 Security
  ⊞ 📁 Server Objects
  ⊞ 📁 Replication
  ⊞ 📁 Management
```

FIGURE C-7

c. Expand the Security node. Note that your two managed SharePoint accounts are listed here (added by SharePoint); see Figure C-8. Double-click on the account used for the Central Administration application pool (for example, filobit\sp_centraladmin), and then select Server Roles. By default this account is granted the dbcreator, public, and securityadmin roles. Open the other managed user account (for example, filobit\sp_service); it will only have the public role, because it does not need any more permissions to do its job.

d. Close the SQL Server Management Studio tool.

> **NOTE** *If the SQL Server Manager Studio tool does not display any detail in the right pane, then press F7 on your keyboard to activate the Object Explorer Details.*

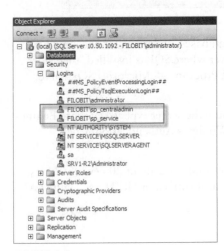

FIGURE C-8

How It Works

When installing the SharePoint Central Administration tool and the first intranet, they will each be associated with a separate web application and be connected to a separate SQL content database. These web applications will run within one application pool each.

Summarizing the SharePoint Server Single Server Installation

SharePoint Server primarily uses two virtual IIS websites: one for the SharePoint sites used by the end users (for example, the intranet), and one for the SharePoint Central Administration tool. These two virtual websites use separate application pools and separate identity accounts. Now you have a SharePoint Server 2010 environment without any database size limitation. It may be extended with more SharePoint Server servers that join this SharePoint farm. In short, this is a very flexible SharePoint Server solution without any compromises.

SharePoint Server is now installed as a single-server configuration; that is, using a locally installed SQL Server. The next step is to adjust the settings in Central Administration so the configuration suits the needs of your organization; for example, enabling SharePoint Server to send e-mail and adding more intuitive URL addresses for the intranet. Appendix D describes these tasks in detail.

Installing SharePoint Server 2010 Using a Remote SQL Server

The third, and last, type of installation is known as a *small farm* — it consists of one server running SharePoint Server, and a separate server running SQL Server. Most of the steps in this configuration are identical to those for the previous configuration with a local Microsoft SQL Server, so the step-by-step instructions listed next will be very short. The advantages of using a remote Microsoft SQL Server are as follows:

➤ **Increased performance:** The SharePoint Server server can handle many more users.

➤ **Fault-tolerance:** Connecting SharePoint Server to a Microsoft SQL cluster is possible, thus achieving a fault-tolerant database environment.

➤ **Better economy:** You can use an existing Microsoft SQL Server that you already paid for, as long as it meets the requirements listed earlier and has the resources available that are needed for the SharePoint environment.

Make sure you have the Microsoft SQL Server installed and running before performing the following steps:

TRY IT OUT   Install SharePoint Server 2010 Using a Remote SQL Server

1. Follow all the steps in the previous Try It Out "Install SharePoint Server to Complete the Single-Server Installation" for installing SharePoint Server with a local SQL Server, *except this*: In step 5f, when running the configuration wizard after installing SharePoint Server, you need to enter the remote server name where SQL Server is installed, then follow the rest of the steps as described.

2. Follow the steps in the earlier Try It Out "Run the Basic Configuration Settings in SharePoint Central Administration."

3. Follow the steps in the earlier Try It Out "Check Out New IIS Settings and SQL Databases."

SharePoint Server 2010 is now installed in a small farm configuration; that is, using a remote SQL Server. The next step is to adjust the settings in Central Administration so the configuration suits the needs of your organization; for example, enabling SharePoint Server to send e-mail and adding more intuitive URL addresses for the intranet. Appendix D describes these tasks in detail.

How It Works

Installing SharePoint Server 2010 using a remote SQL Server is almost identical to install SharePoint Server using a local SQL Server. This type of installation is usually referred to as a small farm.

MIGRATING FROM SQL SERVER EXPRESS TO MICROSOFT SQL SERVER

Many organizations start investigating what SharePoint can do for them by installing SharePoint Server using a local SQL Server Express database. The idea is often to run a pilot project. More often than not, this pilot project then turns into a production environment, with lots of important data that cannot be discarded. I am sure you don't belong to such an organization, but you probably know somebody else who does, right? In the previous versions of SharePoint Server, that is, MOSS 2007, you could upgrade from SQL Server Express, but that is not the case anymore. Yep, that is the hard truth — there is no way to do an in-place upgrade of an existing SQL Server Express edition to a full SQL Server; the only thing you can do is to make a backup of all data, uninstall SharePoint Server, reinstall it using a full SQL Server, and then restore the data. This section tells you about the only way to upgrade from SQL Server Express.

> **WARNING** *If you try an in-place upgrade of SQL Server 2008 Express, everything will look good at the beginning, but just before the actual upgrade process starts an error appears stating, "The specified edition upgrade is not supported."*

Doing a File Backup of the SharePoint Server Databases

Before you do a backup, you need to understand how data is stored in SharePoint. Every website you create in SharePoint Server is either a top site or a subsite. Top sites are the start of a site tree with any number of nested subsites, much like a top folder and its subfolders in a file system. SharePoint calls this a *site collection*. All site collections are stored in a SQL Server database. A database that stores site collections like intranets, document centers, and collaboration areas is called a *content database*. One content database can be shared by many thousands of site collections, or each site collection may have its own content database. But a site collection must always belong to a single content database; that is, spreading out data from one site collection over multiple content databases is not possible.

So when discussing how to make a SharePoint backup, you are usually most interested in understanding how to back up either a content database and all its site collections, or a specific site collection. But several types of databases exist in SharePoint, storing information such as SharePoint farm configuration settings, the Central Administration tool itself, log databases, and search and index databases. These types of databases will not be upgraded, only content databases.

> **NOTE** *To see what content database a site collection uses, open the Central Administration tool, select Manage content databases, and display the web application URL you are interested in. The first site collection is usually stored in WSS_Content. To back up that database, just copy* `WSS_Content.mdf`*.*

Because changing the database engine is a very sensitive operation, you must make sure to have an escape route; that is, a backup of all data, in case something goes wrong. Either you make a full backup of the server, or you back up only the data itself; once again, you have two options to make a backup of data only. You can simply stop the SQL Server Express database and make a file copy of all the content database files, or you can use the STSADM tool that comes with SharePoint for backing up the content databases.

> **NOTE** *If you want to copy single content databases, make sure to copy both the MDF and its corresponding LDF file. Otherwise, you may not be able to attach this database to the new SQL Server later on.*

TRY IT OUT   Copy All SharePoint Server Database Files Manually

To make a simple file copy of all SharePoint Server databases and their log files in SQL Server Express, follow these steps:

1. Stop the SQL Server (SHAREPOINT) service (choose Start ➪ Administrative Tools ➪ Services) so you can make a copy of the databases.

2. Copy all the files in C:\Program Files\Microsoft Office Servers\14.0\Data\MSSQL10. SHAREPOINT\MSSQL\DATA to another file location.

3. Start the SQL Server (SHAREPOINT) service again.

When later restoring these copies to another SQL Server using the SQL Server Manager, make sure to "Attach" these databases, not "Restore," because that would require the files to be restored to the exact same file location as the original database files.

> **NOTE** *If the SQL Server upgrades procedure described later fail for some reason, you need to restore the database files you just copied. Before that, make sure to have a working SharePoint Server and SQL Server Express installation, stop its services, copy all files back to the original file location, and then restart the server.*

How It Works

It is possible to copy SharePoint's database files manually. You must first stop SharePoint to unlock these databases. Then you can move the database files to a new SQL Server.

Backing Up a Site Collection

The second backup method describes how to back up a specific site collection; for example, the intranet site structure. If your SharePoint Server environment consists of multiple site collections, you must repeat the steps for all site collections you want to back up. That is why making a backup of a complete content database is so popular, instead of individual site collections. The result will be backup files that you can use to restore data into any SharePoint Server 2010 environment. The tool you use here is STSADM.EXE, although you can do it with PowerShell as well. STSADM is stored deep down in the file system, or to be exact, in this folder:

```
C:\Program Files\Common Files\Microsoft Shared\web server extensions\14\BIN
```

STSADM is a command-based tool that you must run in a command shell. Either you use the preconfigured command shell called the SharePoint 2010 Management Shell, which has the path to STSADM already defined, or you follow the steps in the following Try It Out to add the path to STSADM so it works in any command shell, not just in the Management Shell.

To use the STSADM in the Management Shell, click Start ➪ All Programs ➪ Microsoft SharePoint 2010 Products ➪ SharePoint 2010 Management Shell. Run whatever STSADM or PowerShell commands you need.

To use the second option, that is, adding the path to STSADM, use the steps in the following Try It Out. If you have multiple SharePoint Servers, you need to do this on each server. As a SharePoint administrator you will sometimes need to run STSADM, and instead of entering the full path to this tool every time, configuring Windows to search in this folder directly is easier. If you are old enough to remember when MS-DOS ruled the PC world, you might remember there was a system variable named PATH, which still is valid today. When you enter a program name in a command prompt window, Windows looks for that filename in all folder paths defined in the PATH variable. This is how to add the path to STSADM to this system variable:

TRY IT OUT   Update the PATH System Variable

1. Start Windows Explorer and open `C:\Program Files\Common Files\Microsoft Shared\web server extensions\14\BIN`. Right-click the file path in the Address field and select Copy.

2. Click the Start button to see the Windows start menu.

3. Right-click Computer and select Properties.

4. In the left pane, click Advanced System Settings. A dialog box with multiple tabs opens. Open the Advanced tab and click the Environment Variables button.

5. In the lower pane named System Variables, select PATH and click Edit.

6. In the Variable field, go to the end (use the End key or the right arrow on the keyboard). Type in a semicolon (;) as a separator, and then paste the path you copied in step 1. Click OK three times to save this modification and close all dialog boxes.

7. Test your change by opening a command shell (choose Start ➪ Run and type **Cmd**); then type **STSADM** in this command shell window. If you get a long list of options, you did it right. If not, redo these steps, and make sure to do it right this time.

How It Works

Standard command shell windows do not include a path to the STSADM utility. You can add that path manually to the system variable PATH.

Now you have access to the STSADM command and all other tools in the same folder, regardless of where you are in the folder tree.

If you installed SharePoint Server using the Basic installation option, a site collection was automatically created, containing one top site. In Appendix B you learn more about how to create new site collections. To make a simple example, say you only have one site collection consisting of one top site, with five subsites. The default URL address for the top site is based on the server name, so if the server is named SRV1, then the URL will be `http://srv1`. In the following Try It Out you back up this complete site collection to a file named `SPS-back.bak` in the folder `C:\Bkup`. To do this, follow these steps:

TRY IT OUT **Use STSADM to Back Up a Site Collection**

1. Log on to the SharePoint Server server as an administrator.

2. Open a command shell, type in the following text, and press the Enter key (remember to replace the `http://srv1` to match your own SharePoint environment):

```
Stsadm -o Backup -url http://srv1 -filename c:\bkup\SPS-back.bak
```

3. When the backup is done, you will see the filename `SPS-back.bak` in the `C:\bkup` folder.

How It Works

Backing up a site collection with a command utility like STSADM is very easy. In Chapter 10 you will learn how to perform the same type of backup, using the new command utility PowerShell.

Migrating from SQL Server Express to SQL Server 2008

By now you should have your SharePoint Server environment backed up. It is time to upgrade the SQL Server Express database to the full Microsoft SQL Server 2008. As mentioned before, this process is complicated, because it requires a complete reinstallation of SharePoint Server, this time using a full SQL Server. The challenge is that only the content databases will be possible to restore, not the complete configuration (because that would take you back to the SQL Server Express scenario). That is what makes this such a risky and hard process.

Before you continue you must now manually document all configuration settings and customizations in SharePoint 2010 Central Administration, because you will have to redo them after the new installation of SharePoint Server. This is something you should always do, to ensure you know how SharePoint is configured, in case something happens. The system documentation should contain the following information:

➤ Any language packs installed; these must be installed in the new SharePoint Server server

➤ All the settings on the Application Management page

➤ All the settings on the System Settings page

➤ All the settings on the General Application Settings page

➤ Any third-party installed web parts, solutions, and features. (Make sure you know how to install them again.)

➤ Any third-party index filters (iFilters), their icons, and modifications of the DOCICON.XML file

➤ Any customized files, like custom site definitions

When you are absolutely sure you have a backup that can restore the SharePoint Server in case the upgrade does not work, and that all non-default settings and customizations are documented, then, and only then, can you continue with the steps in the following Try It Out:

> **WARNING** *Make sure you have a working backup in case this procedure for any reason does not work as expected! If you don't, you may lose data in SharePoint Server!*

TRY IT OUT **Migrate from SQL Server Express to a Local SQL Server 2008**

1. Log on to the SharePoint Server server as an administrator.

2. Make sure to inform all users that they will be unable to work with SharePoint during this migration. One way of ensuring no one is using the SharePoint Server system is to disconnect the server from the internal network before you start migrating.

3. Uninstall SharePoint Server, either using the Control Panel ⇨ Uninstall a program command, or running SharePoint Server Setup again and selecting the option to uninstall.

> **NOTE** *During the uninstallation you get a question asking whether the old SharePoint Server settings should be preserved or not — select No.*

4. Delete this folder and everything under it: `\Program Files\Common Files\Microsoft Shared\ Web Server Extensions\14`.

5. Reboot the server to make sure nothing is stored in memory.

6. Follow all the instructions in the previous section "Installing SharePoint Server Using the Microsoft SQL Database" — except for step 4 (that is, where you create the first site collection) in the step-by-step Try It Out instructions "Run the Basic Configuration Settings in SharePoint Central Administration." The reason for this exception is that you will soon delete that web application.

7. Apply all the settings, customizations, and third-party add-ons you documented before starting this procedure, so the SharePoint Server configuration is restored.

8. When you have a SharePoint Server server with the same settings as before, it is time to restore the data. For example, if the database to restore is named WSS_Content, then do this:

   a. Start SQL Server Management Studio and open the local server.

   b. Right-click on Databases and select Attach. A form named Attach Databases opens.

   c. Click Add and select the copied MDF file; for example, `WSS_Content.mdf`, then click OK. The database is now listed among all other databases, but it is not yet used by SharePoint Server.

   d. Because this database was created with a SQL Server Express, you must change its ownership before you can use it in the new SQL Server. Expand the node Security in the left pane, and then select Logins and right-click on the account used by the SharePoint Central Administrations application pool (as described earlier in this appendix) and select Properties to open the Login Properties page. Click User mapping in the left pane and select the attached database (in this example WSS_Content), plus set the database role membership to db_owner and public. Click OK to save and close.

9. Start SharePoint's Central Administration tool, Click the Application Management section in the left pane, and then click Web Applications in the right pane.

a. You will see an object named SharePoint – 80. This is the one you want to connect the newly attached database to. Select it and click Delete ⇨ Delete Web Application (on the ribbon).

b. On the form that appears, select Yes for Delete content database, and No for Delete IIS website, then click Delete. A warning appears; click OK to continue.

c. On the ribbon, click New and a new form opens. Select "Use an existing IIS website," and select SharePoint – 80 from the drop-down menu. Further down on the same form, select "Use existing application pool," and then select SharePoint – 80. Finally, in the Database Name field, enter the name of the attached database; for example WSS_Content, and click OK.

d. When the new web application is created, a status message appears; click OK.

10. Open a new web browser and enter the URL to this new web application; after a short delay all the site collections in this content database will appear, just like in the old SQL Server Express environment. If they do not show up, try this URL: `http://<servername>/_layouts/ settings.aspx`. If this page shows up, but not the start page for the migrated content database, then you missed restoring something that is used on this site, like a feature or third-party web part. Correct the problem and the start page will work.

How It Works

This is a technique to make a copy of the database, then reinstall a new SQL Server, and then attach the copied databases to the new SQL Server.

This procedure can be repeated anytime — it does not have to be directly after the reinstallation of SharePoint Server. If you have more content databases to move, just repeat the preceding steps, but in step 9a you need to create a new web application instead of deleting the existing SharePoint – 80. Appendix B shows you more about creating web applications.

> **NOTE** The procedure for moving from SQL Server Express to a remote SQL Server is almost identical to the preceding procedure; the only things that differ are that you enter the remote SQL server name when running the SharePoint 2010 Products configuration wizard, directly after the installation of SharePoint Server, and that you attach the copied MDF file to that remote SQL server.

UPGRADING MOSS 2007 TO SHAREPOINT SERVER 2010

If you already have a MOSS 2007 environment installed, and want to migrate to SharePoint Server 2010, then this section is for you. In SharePoint 2010 you have two ways to upgrade: *in-place upgrade* (installing on top of the previous version) and *content database attach*; that is, attach the old databases to a new SharePoint Server server. Throughout the generations of SharePoint, upgrading to a new version has sometimes been hard. Luckily, this is not true in this version: Migrating is a straightforward process, at least under certain conditions:

➤ **MOSS 2007 is a 64-bit version:** If it's not, you cannot do an in-place upgrade to SharePoint Server because that is 64-bit only. But you may be able to do the content database attach method.

➤ **MOSS 2007 is connected to a local or remote 64-bit version of SQL Server 2005 or 2008:** Actually, this type of migration will work with a remote 32-bit SQL Server, but it is not supported. A local SQL Server must be 64-bit to be used for the in-place upgrade process; if it's not, try the content database attach method.

➤ **MOSS 2007 is connected to a SQL Server Express with less than 4GB data per content database:** If it's not, the max limit of the SQL Server 2008 Express is exceeded, and cannot be upgraded. Using the content database attach method should be possible.

➤ **The server meets the new hardware requirements:** At least 4GB of RAM is recommended; see more about the requirements earlier in this appendix.

➤ **MOSS 2007 is running on a Windows Server 2008:** If it's not, you first need to upgrade Windows Server if you want to do the in-place upgrade process.

➤ **Service Pack 2 for MOSS 2007 is installed:** It is a requirement, and it also contains a new command to check whether the MOSS server will be able to upgrade to SharePoint Server: `STSADM -o preupgradecheck`.

So you must stay away from a number of "gotchas." If you can do that, then upgrading from MOSS 2007 is easy. The following section lists the steps for doing both the in-place upgrade and the content database attach method.

Upgrading MOSS 2007 Using the In-Place Method

This process is very easy and straightforward, assuming you meet the requirements listed in the previous section; that is, your MOSS is running on a 64-bit Windows Server 2008, and its SQL Server is either a SQL Server Express with less than 4GB of content databases or is using a full SQL Server 2005 or 2008.

Begin by running the `preupgradecheck` to find any issues before you start the upgrade process:

TRY IT OUT Run the `preupgradecheck` in STSADM

1. Log on to the MOSS 2007 server as an administrator.

2. Open a command shell and run `STSADM -o preupgradecheck` (assuming you added the `BIN` folder to the system `PATH` variable, as described earlier in this appendix).

This check may need some time to complete, especially if you have lots of data and features installed. When it's done, the result appears as a web page; see parts of that page in Figure C-9.

If any issues are listed, you must resolve them. The result page contains links to more information.

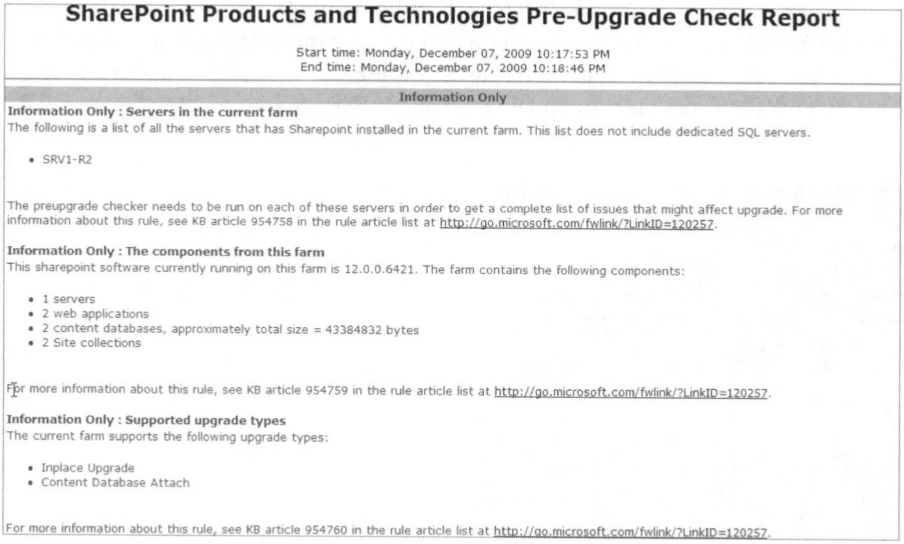

SharePoint Products and Technologies Pre-Upgrade Check Report

Start time: Monday, December 07, 2009 10:17:53 PM
End time: Monday, December 07, 2009 10:18:46 PM

Information Only

Information Only : Servers in the current farm
The following is a list of all the servers that has Sharepoint installed in the current farm. This list does not include dedicated SQL servers.

- SRV1-R2

The preupgrade checker needs to be run on each of these servers in order to get a complete list of issues that might affect upgrade. For more information about this rule, see KB article 954758 in the rule article list at http://go.microsoft.com/fwlink/?LinkID=120257.

Information Only : The components from this farm
This sharepoint software currently running on this farm is 12.0.0.6421. The farm contains the following components:

- 1 servers
- 2 web applications
- 2 content databases, approximately total size = 43384832 bytes
- 2 Site collections

For more information about this rule, see KB article 954759 in the rule article list at http://go.microsoft.com/fwlink/?LinkID=120257.

Information Only : Supported upgrade types
The current farm supports the following upgrade types:

- Inplace Upgrade
- Content Database Attach

For more information about this rule, see KB article 954760 in the rule article list at http://go.microsoft.com/fwlink/?LinkID=120257.

FIGURE C-9

How It Works

The preupgradecheck operation in STSADM checks a number of settings and features in MOSS 2007, looking for anything that would prohibit an upgrade to SharePoint Server 2010.

When no issues are reported it is time to perform the actual in-place upgrade; the following steps are just a summary of how to install SharePoint Server, because the detailed steps were described earlier in this appendix:

1. Logon to the MOSS server as the farm administrator for MOSS 2007.

2. Mount the SharePoint Server media with the same language as MOSS 2007.

3. Run the setup file for SharePoint Server.

4. Select Install software prerequisites and complete all the steps.

5. Select Install SharePoint Server and enter the Production Key.

6. After accepting the license agreement, you get the Upgrade earlier versions page. It says that it has found a previous version of this product, and that it will do an in-place upgrade. Click Install Now to continue. This step may take several minutes to complete; however, the actual migration has not yet started.

7. After the installation is completed, make sure to check that the "Run the SharePoint Products and Technologies Configuration Wizard now" option is set, and then click Close.

8. The configuration wizard starts; click Next.

9. Enter the passphrase for this farm.

10. The next page is the Visual Upgrade, which lets you configure the Visual Upgrade settings for the upgraded MOSS sites. If you are uncertain about switching to the new user interface in SharePoint 2010, then accept the default setting — "Preserve the look and feel of existing SharePoint sites, and allow end users to update their sites' user experience." See Figure C-10.

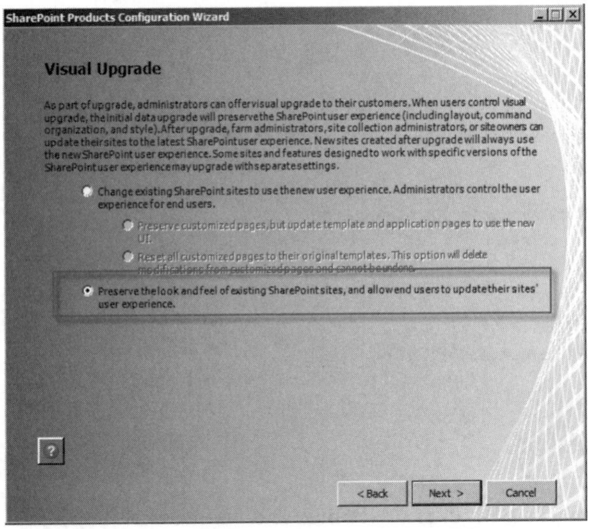

FIGURE C-10

11. On the "Completing the SharePoint Products Configuration Wizards" page, verify that the information is correct, and click Next. Then wait for all 10 configuration tasks to complete.

12. When the wizard completes, the Configuration Successful, Upgrade In Process page appears (see Figure C-11). It tells you that the upgrade process now runs as a timer job; that is, it is a background process, and you just have to wait for it to complete. Click Finish to close this page; this also opens the Central Administration tool and its Upgrade Status page that updates every minute; see Figure C-12.

For more details about the upgrade process: Look at the log file named `Upgrade-<date_and_time_and_number>.log` in this folder: `C:\Program Files\Common Files\Microsoft Shared\Web Server Extensions\14\LOGS`. When this log file contains the text "Upgrade session finished successfully" near the end of the file, the timer job is completed and the upgrade process is done.

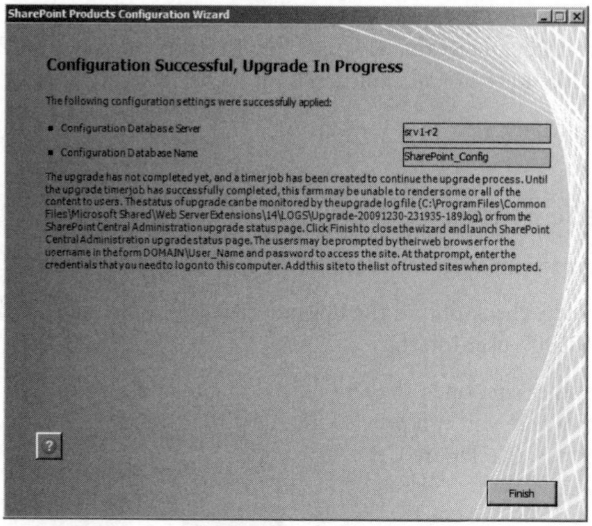

FIGURE C-11

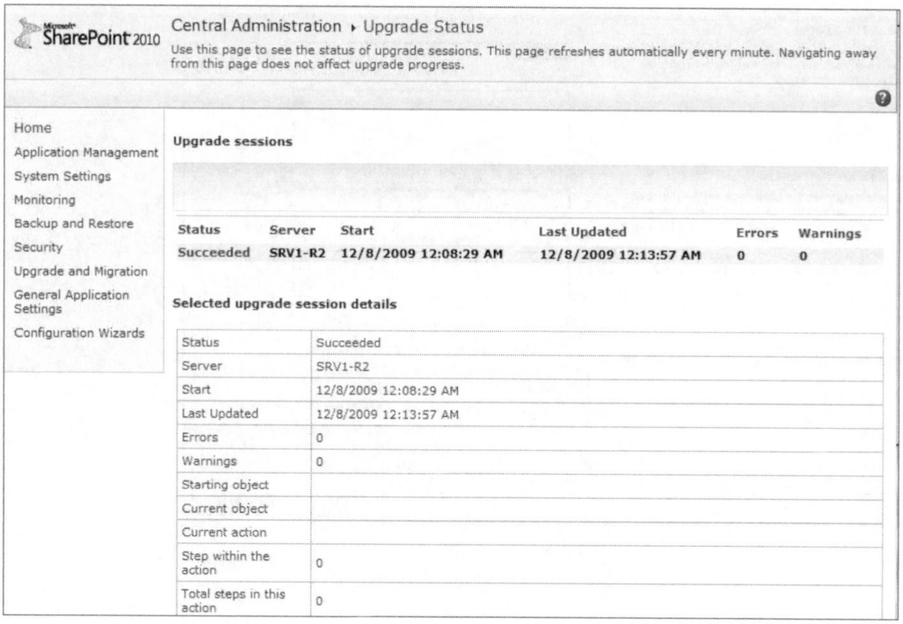

FIGURE C-12

If you open this site collection, you will find that it looks almost exactly as before, and this is no mistake. Your MOSS sites are now converted to SharePoint Server "under the hood," but the user interface is still MOSS 2007. Some organizations will be very pleased with this, because their users can continue to use the sites just as they were in MOSS. Other organizations want to take advantage of the new interface, with its ribbon and other new features. The great thing when upgrading to SharePoint Server is that you, the administrator, can test the new user interface; if you don't like it, you can return to the WSS interface. If you like it, then you can turn it into a permanent change.

Follow these steps to test, and finally switch to, the new user interface:

TRY IT OUT Using the Visual Upgrade Feature

1. Log on as the site collection administrator for the upgraded website.

2. Open the upgraded site in your web browser, check out all the upgraded sites — note how similar their graphical layout is to the old MOSS 2007 user interface.

3. Time to test the new interface: Select the start site, open the Site Action menu, and select Visual Upgrade, which opens a web form where you can preview the new user interface, switch permanently, or display the old user interface. See Figure C-13.

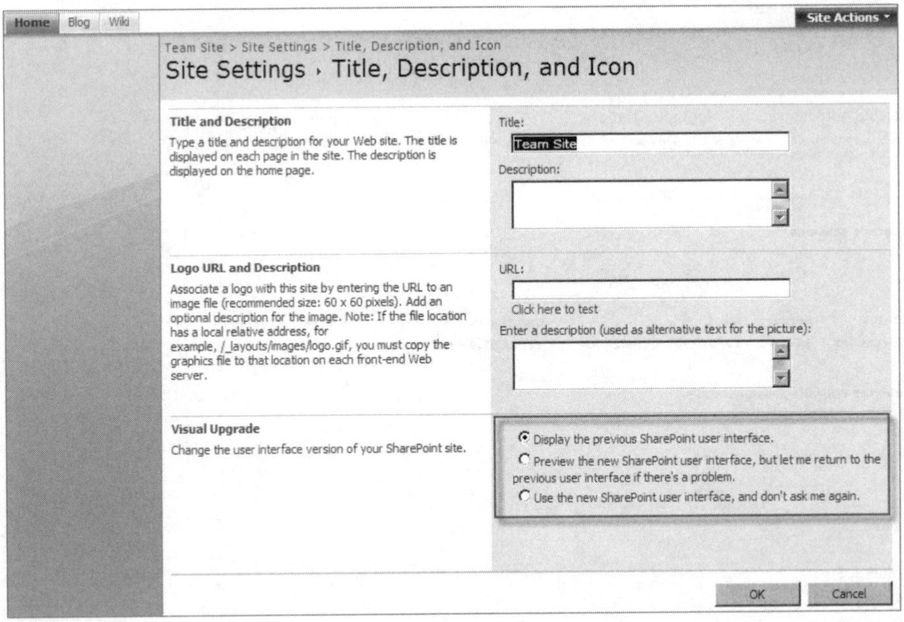

FIGURE C-13

4. In the Visual Upgrade section, select the option "Preview the new SharePoint user interface, but let me return to the previous user interface if there's a problem" and click OK. The new user interface is applied to the current site.

5. Notice the yellow ribbon at the top of the site; it is a reminder that this is a preview of the new user interface; it also contains a link back to the web form where Visual Upgrade is configured. If you decide to return to the old user interface, then open that web form and select Display the previous SharePoint user interface.

6. If you want to apply the new user interface to all sites in this site collection, then open the Site Actions menu and select Site Settings to open that page. In the Site Collection Administration section, click on the Visual Upgrade link to open a simple configuration page for Visual Upgrade settings:

➤ **Hide Visual Upgrade:** This hides the Visual Upgrade option from the Site Actions menu for all sites in this site collection.

➤ **Update All Sites:** Use to permanently apply the new user interface in all sites in this site collection.

7. If you apply the Update All Sites option, there is no way back. Note that if you have multiple site collections, and want them all to use the new user interface, you need to make this switch in each and every one of them.

How It Works

Visual Upgrade makes it easy to temporarily switch to the new graphical user interface in SharePoint Server 2010 on upgraded MOSS sites. It is also possible to switch permanently to the new graphical user interface

Upgrading MOSS 2007 Using the Content Database Attach Method

The content database attach method is a straightforward upgrade method. Basically you take a copy of the MOSS content database, attach it to the new SQL Server 2008 in SharePoint Server, and then connect it to a web application. That is it. As described earlier, if the content database you move is larger than 4GB, then the SharePoint Server must use a full SQL Server, not the SQL Server Express. As described in the section about in-place upgrade, make sure to run the `preupgradecheck` in STSADM before trying to upgrade the databases with the attach method.

In the earlier Try It Out, "Copy All SharePoint Server Database Files Manually," you learned a very simple method of copying databases, such as WSS_Content (both the MDF file and the LDF file) and then attaching the databases to the new SQL Server, described in steps 8a–8d, in the Try It Out "Migrate from SQL Server Express to a Local SQL Server 2008."

> **NOTE** Note that the inplace upgrade method described earlier requires that MOSS is disabled during the time it takes to copy the content databases. In some organizations, this downtime is unacceptable. If this is the case, you can set the database in read-only mode, and then copy it; this makes it possible for all users to continue reading all data in MOSS, but not write or change anything. The detailed steps for making this change are described on several websites, for example: http://technet.microsoft.com/en-us/sharepoint/ee517215.aspx.

After attaching the content databases to the new SQL Server, configure the upgrade of these databases by using the steps in the following Try It Out:

TRY IT OUT Upgrade Databases Using the Database Attach Method

1. Log on to the MOSS server as an administrator.

2. Open a command window and run *STSADM –o preupgradecheck*. This assumes you added the BIN folder to the system PATH variable, as described earlier in this appendix.

3. Stop the service *"SQL Server (SHAREPOINT)"*, in order to be able to make a copy of the databases.

4. Copy the MDF and corresponding LDF-files in *C:\Program Files\Common Files\Microsoft Shared\ Web Server Extensions\14\Data\MSSQL10.SHAREPOINT\MSSQL\DATA* you want to upgrade to SharePoint Server — If the file names does not conflict with existing databases, then you may store these files in the same folder as the other database files on the new SQL Server (usually *C:\Program Files\Microsoft SQL Server\MSSQL10_50.MSSQLSERVER\MSSQL\DATA*).

5. Start the *"SQL Server (SHAREPOINT)"* service again. But make sure users don't add any new information to the WSS sites, since that will not be copied to the SharePoint Server server.

6. Make sure the new SharePoint Server server has the same configuration settings and solutions in Central Administration as the old MOSS server to make it possible to upgrade the databases. In this example, you attach a copied database named *WSS_Content.MDF*.

    a. Start SQL Server Management Studio and open the local server.

    b. Right-click on Databases and select Attach. A form named "Attach Databases" opens.

    c. Click Add and select the file you copied, that is, `WSS_Content.MDF` — this lists the database in the top pane. Note that the current owner is the user account currently logged on (the administrator account). You *must* change that to the same user account used for the Central Administration application pool identity. Click the menu for the Owner field, and this application pool account should be listed. Select that account, and click OK. The database is now listed among all other attached databases, and it has the correct owner, but it is not yet used by SharePoint Server.

7. Before this content database can be used in SharePoint Server, it must be upgraded, which you will do with the help of STSADM (PowerShell can also do this). In this example, you want to add the new content database to an existing web application that has the URL address `http://srv1`. You want the attached content database and its site collection to use the URL `http://srv1/sites/abc`. You also want to preserve the old user interface initially (the site collection owner can switch to the new user interface later on). Open a command shell, and enter **STSADM –o addcontentdb –url http:// srv1/sites/abc -databasename WSS_Content -preserveolduserexperience true**.

8. After the upgrade process of this content database completes, you can open the site using the URL you entered earlier in step 7. As when you perform an in-place upgrade, the result will be a site collection that has preserved the old user interface. To upgrade it, use the Site Action menu,

and select Visual Upgrade as described in the earlier section "Upgrading MOSS 2007 Using the In-Place Method."

How It Works

The Database Attach upgrade method requires that you copy the MOSS databases to the SQL Server used by SharePoint Server, and then attach these databases to SharePoint Server. Then you start the actual upgrade of these databases using STSADM or PowerShell.

UNINSTALLING SHAREPOINT SERVER

The final section of this appendix is about removing SharePoint Server. You can select to remove just a single site collection; a web application, including its content databases; or a complete SharePoint Server installation and all its databases. By default, all databases remain after SharePoint Server is uninstalled, so you can later reinstall SharePoint Server and reattach it to these databases.

> **NOTE** *If you want to reinstall SharePoint Server on the same server, you need to remove or rename all existing databases from the previous installation to avoid name conflict. SQL Server Express that comes with SharePoint Server 2010 stores all databases in* `C:\Program Files\Microsoft Office Servers\14.0\Data\MSSQL10.SHAREPOINT\MSSQL\DATA\.`

Removing a Single Site Collection

This process removes a given site collection in SharePoint Server from its web application, but it does not remove the binary files or its content database files from the server. For example, you may have a test environment using one web application and a production SharePoint Server using another web application on the same physical Windows 2008 Server, and now you want to copy the site collection between these web applications.

To remove the test site collection, follow these steps:

TRY IT OUT   **Remove a Site Collection**

1.   Log on as the farm administrator and start the SharePoint Central Administration tool.

2.   Click on Application Management in the left pane.

3.   Click "Delete site collection" in the Site Collections section.

4.   Click the yellow menu "No selection," and select Change Site Collection.

5. Verify that the Web Application is set to the one that contains the site collection you want to delete. If it's not, click on its menu, select Change web application, and then select the correct web application.

6. Select the site collection to be removed; when you are absolutely sure it is the right one, click OK.

7. Details about the site collection to be removed appear; verify that the information is correct. If it is, click Delete, and then OK to permanently delete this website.

How It works

A farm administrator can remove any site collection by using the SharePoint Central Administration tool or the command shell tools STSADM and PowerShell.

> **WARNING** *There is no undeleting feature when you are deleting a site collection. If you made a mistake, then you must restore the site collection. See Chapter 10 for more information.*

The web application is still intact, and may be used for new site collections. If you have other site collections in the same web application, they will not be affected, because the previous steps just deleted one specific site collection, not the complete web application.

Removing a Web Application

Sometimes you may need to remove a complete web application, including all its site collections — for example, if you set up a web application for a text environment that no longer is needed. This process for removing a web application is very similar to the process for removing a site collection, but it has bigger consequences: If you remove an existing web application, all its site collections will also be removed. Note that a web application may have any number of site collections, although the default limit is 15,000. To delete a specific web application in the test environment, follow these steps:

TRY IT OUT Remove a Web Application

1. Log on as a farm administrator and start the SharePoint Central Administration tool.

2. Click on Application Management in the left pane.

3. Click "Manage web applications" in the Web Applications section — this shows you a list of all existing web applications.

4. Select the web application to be deleted; double-check that it is the right one! Click the Delete button in the ribbon.

5. A dialog form named Delete Web Application appears, where you can set whether all content databases for this web application will be deleted as well, and whether you want to remove the IIS website used by this web application. If you are not sure what to delete, then say No to both of these options, because then reactivating the web application and all its site collections will be easy, by creating a new web application, connecting it to the same IIS website, and attaching the old content database. Click Delete to complete this form, and then OK to confirm the delete operation.

How It works

A farm administrator can remove any existing web application. This operation will remove all site collections in that web application. There is no way to undo this operation, except restoring it from a previous backup.

Removing SharePoint Server Completely

A more drastic operation than the previous remove procedures is to remove SharePoint Server completely from the Windows 2008 Server. This does not actually remove the database, be it the SQL Server Express or the full Microsoft SQL Server. If you also want to remove these databases, you must do it manually after SharePoint Server is uninstalled.

To remove SharePoint Server completely, follow these steps:

TRY IT OUT   Removing SharePoint Server Completely

1. Log on as a domain administrator with full control of this SharePoint Server 2010 server and its SQL Server.

2. Select Start ⇨ Control Panel ⇨ Uninstall a Program, which will list all installed programs.

3. Select Microsoft SharePoint Server 2010 and then click the Uninstall button.

4. Click Yes to confirm you want to remove SharePoint Server. A warning message appears. Click OK to accept to delete SharePoint Server. After SharePoint Server is deleted, click OK to close the page that shows up afterward.

> **NOTE** *If this SharePoint Server installation was using SQL Server Express, it will also be removed, but its database files (MDF and LDF) will remain intact in the file system and can be attached to a new SQL Server. If the SharePoint Server installation was using a full SQL Server version, it will not be affected, and all SharePoint Server databases will remain intact in SQL Server. Make sure to remove these databases if you want to clean up everything related to SharePoint Server, which is especially important if you want to do a clean reinstallation of SharePoint Server 2010.*

When you remove SharePoint Server, you also remove all virtual IIS websites used by the SharePoint Server, along with its application pools. However, the *Default Web Site* remains after the installation, along with its application pool.

▶ WHAT YOU LEARNED IN THIS CHAPTER

TOPIC	KEY CONCEPTS
Background of SharePoint	SharePoint Team Service was the first version, later renamed WSS and now SharePoint Foundation 2010.
	The abbreviation STS is still used in SharePoint Server 2010, for example in STSADM.
Different SharePoint configurations	Stand-alone — SharePoint Server 2010 + the embedded SQL Server Express, both installed on the same server
	Single-Server — SharePoint Server 2010 and a full SQL Server version installed on the same server
	Farm configuration — One or more SharePoint Server 2010 servers and one or more remote SQL Servers
Hardware Requirements	Minimum 4 GB of memory, 8 GB recommended for small and medium size SharePoint Server installations
	One 64-bit 2.5 GHz CPU minimum, but two or more recommended
	100 Mbps Network Interface Card (NIC)
	80 GB free disk space
Software Requirements	64-bit Windows Server 2008 or later
	64-bit SQL Server 2005 / 2008 / 2008 R2
	IIS 7.0 with ASP.NET and .NET Framework 3.51
Content Databases	Stores all the content in SharePoint.
	About 70 percent of the size is related to documents.
Config databases	Stores configuration settings in SharePoint.
	SharePoint_Config contains all global settings that are shared among all SharePoint servers in a farm.
Configuration Tools	Graphical User Interface: SharePoint Central Administration
	Command Shell: STSADM (which eventually will be removed in future versions of SharePoint)
	Command Shell: PowerShell, the new and very powerful script language that has more than 500 applets related to SharePoint administration
Upgrade procedures for SQL	There is no automatic upgrade available from SQL Server Express used in MOSS 2007, but it can be done manually.
	It is possible to migrate from SQL Server Express to a full SQL Server by using manual steps.

TOPIC	KEY CONCEPTS
Upgrade procedures for SharePoint	Always run the STSADM operation PreUpgradeCheck before attempting to upgrade MOSS 2007 to SharePoint Server 2010.
	Inplace Upgrade method: Will upgrade an existing MOSS 2007 to SharePoint Server 2010, if all hardware and software requirements are met.
	Content Database Attach method: Copy the MOSS content databases to the new SharePoint Server 2010 environment, attach them, and start the upgrade using STSADM.
Remove a Site Collection	Use SharePoint Central Administration for this procedure.
	STSADM and PowerShell also support operations to remove site collections.
	Note that there is no undelete feature for this procedure. The only way to get the site collection back is to restore it from a previous backup.
Remove a Web Application	Use SharePoint Central Administration for this procedure.
	STSADM and PowerShell also support operations to remove web applications.
	Note that there is no undelete feature for this procedure. The only way to get the web application back is to restore it from a previous backup.
Remove a complete SharePoint Server Server	Run the Control Panel and its Uninstall a program to delete a complete server.
	If this was the last SharePoint Server server in this farm, then the farm is also removed.
	Content databases will be retained when uninstalling a SharePoint Server server. Remember to also delete these files in case you want to do a clean reinstallation.

D
Configuring SharePoint Server 2010

WHAT YOU WILL LEARN IN THIS APPENDIX:

➤ SharePoint Administration

➤ Configuring Administrative Features

➤ Managing Security

➤ Working with Site Templates

➤ Configuring Search and indexing

➤ Managing User Profiles

In Appendix C you learned how to install SharePoint Server, including SQL database options, and how to upgrade from the previous version, MOSS 2007. As mentioned in Chapter 1, SharePoint Server is based on SharePoint Foundation but has an extensive set of extra features, such as advanced search and indexing, Excel services, and business intelligence web parts built-in. To fully understand SharePoint Server and get the most out of its rich feature set you need to understand important concepts about how to manage SharePoint Server.

Appendix B covers all the configuration settings for SharePoint Foundation, and all of this information is also applicable when managing a SharePoint Server environment. This appendix focuses on concepts, features, and configuration settings that are specific for SharePoint Server — therefore you need to read Appendix B before you read this appendix. Just to make it easier for you, some important concepts described in Appendix B are also repeated in this appendix.

IMPORTANT CONCEPTS FOR THE SHAREPOINT SERVER ENVIRONMENT

SharePoint Server is a web application that leverages Internet Information Services (IIS) in Windows Server to operate. SharePoint Server uses IIS websites for its web applications and stores all content such as documents and news items in a Microsoft SQL Server database. In this section you learn more about the SharePoint Server architecture and how to manage SharePoint Server using the *SharePoint Central Administration* tool.

The Architecture in SharePoint Server

The following is a quick recap of the section about SharePoint Foundation architecture in Appendix B to explain the relationship between IIS and SharePoint Server concepts. For more details, see the section, "The Architecture in SharePoint Foundation" and its figures in Appendix B:

➤ A *site collection* is a top website with zero or more subsites, also known as *subwebs*. You can also say that a top level site is a container for subsites.

➤ Each site collection runs within a *web application*.

➤ A web application may host multiple site collections.

➤ A web application is connected to one or more *content databases* that are stored in a SQL Server.

➤ Each web application is contained inside an *application pool*.

➤ One application pool can host multiple web applications.

➤ All application pools run within Internet Information Services.

In plain English this means that all the documents, pictures, and other types of data that belongs to a site collection are stored in a content database, which is connected to the web application that hosts this site collection. So if you make a copy of a content database, you will have a copy of all site collections that are hosted by the web application connected to that particular content database. If you stop a web application, you will make all its site collections unreachable.

After installing SharePoint Server 2010 and completing the SharePoint Products and Technology Configuration Wizard, as described in Appendix C, you will have three IIS websites (or "web applications" in SharePoint terminology):

➤ SharePoint Central Administration v4

➤ SharePoint Web Services

➤ SharePoint - 80

The first web application is used by SharePoint's administrative tool. The second is for enabling web services for both SharePoint itself and other applications that need to read or write to SharePoint. The third web application, SharePoint - 80, is typically running the SharePoint sites used by ordinary users, for example, the intranet and collaboration sites.

TRY IT OUT **Disable a Web Application and its Site Collections**

1. Log on to the SharePoint server as an administrator.

2. Open the IIS Manager: Choose Start ⇨ Administrative Tools ⇨ Internet Information Services (IIS) Manager.

3. Expand the server node in the Connections pane.

4. Expand the Sites node.

5. Right-click the web application SharePoint - 80 (or whatever virtual IIS server the user website uses).

6. Select Manage Web Sites ⇨ Stop.

How It Works

By stopping the IIS website that SharePoint uses as a web application you will also prohibit all types of access to the SharePoint sites within that web application. This can be handy if you need to stop all users from accessing SharePoint sites while you do some maintenance on the server or the SQL server. To enable the web application, repeat steps 1–5 in the preceding Try It Out, and then select Manage Web Sites ⇨ Start.

Working with the Central Administration Tool

One of the most important tools for the SharePoint Server administrator is SharePoint Central Administration (choose Start ⇨ All Programs ⇨ Microsoft SharePoint 2010 Products ⇨ SharePoint 2010 Central Administration). This tool allows the administrator to configure and manage all common tasks related to SharePoint. However, some tasks are better executed with or only available using the command-based tools — STSADM and PowerShell. This section focuses on how to use SharePoint Central Administration. As described in more detail in Appendix B, only a very few users will have the permissions to run any of these three administrative tools; by default it is these users:

➤ The account used to install SharePoint Server, typically the Domain Administrator account

➤ The account set to be the security "Identity" for the application pool used by SharePoint Central Administration v4

➤ All members of the Administrators local group on the SharePoint Server

These two accounts, and the local group, are automatically added to a special SharePoint group named *Farm Administrators* (see Figure D-1). If you are a member of this group, you can add and delete any user account (local or AD account) or security groups (local or AD security groups).

> ⊗ **WARNING** *Make sure that the Administrators local group on the SharePoint server only contains members who should have full administrative access to the SharePoint farm!*

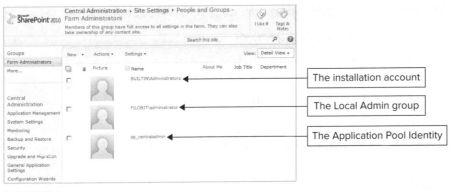

FIGURE D-1

Using Service Applications

SharePoint Server 2010 comes with a lot of features and functionality built into the product. A lot of these are implemented as *service applications*, and to make using these applications easier, SharePoint groups them into *application proxy groups*. Each web application in SharePoint will be associated with one of these application proxy groups, thus enabling its service applications for all site collections in that particular web application.

This technique gives the administrator much better control over what service applications a specific web application has access to, compared to the *Shared Service Provider* module in the previous version of SharePoint (that is, MOSS 2007). Because every service application requires resources, such as memory and CPU, it is important that only required service applications are enabled.

The number of service applications depends on what edition of SharePoint Server 2010 you are using, as shown in the following table. For comparison this table also lists what service applications SharePoint Foundation supports.

Comparing Service Applications in SharePoint 2010 Editions

SERVICE APPLICATION	SHAREPOINT FOUNDATION	SHAREPOINT SERVER STANDARD	SHAREPOINT SERVER ENTERPRISE
Access Service	No	No	Yes
Application Discovery and Load Balancer Service Application	Yes	Yes	Yes
Application Registry Service	No	Yes	Yes
Business Data Connectivity	Yes	Yes	Yes
Excel Services	No	No	Yes

SERVICE APPLICATION	SHAREPOINT FOUNDATION	SHAREPOINT SERVER STANDARD	SHAREPOINT SERVER ENTERPRISE
Managed Metadata Service	No	Yes	Yes
PerformancePoint Service Application	No	No	Yes
Search Service Application	No	Yes	Yes
Secure Store Service	No	Yes	Yes
Security Token Service Application	Yes	Yes	Yes
State Service	No	Yes	Yes
Usage and Health Data collection	Yes	Yes	Yes
User Profile Service Application	No	Yes	Yes
Visio Graphics Service	No	No	Yes
Web Analytics Service Application	No	No	Yes
Word Automation Services	No	No	Yes
Lotus Notes Connector Service	No	No	Yes

The following sections cover how to manage and configure these service applications and the application proxy groups.

UNDERSTANDING THE CENTRAL ADMINISTRATION PAGE IN SHAREPOINT SERVER

This section offers a closer look at the features and service applications in SharePoint Server 2010, by using the SharePoint Central Administration tool. Once again, be sure to read Appendix B first, because the following sections only describe what is unique for SharePoint Server.

Log on as an administrator, and start the SharePoint Central Administration tool. It consists of eight different sections, plus one start page. Each section contains a number of links to new configuration pages. The following is an overview of all these sections and the options they contain when you select them; later on you will learn more details about each section:

➤ **Central Administration** is the start page, containing links to the most commonly used configuration pages.

➤ **Application Management** contains links to four subsections that group related topics:

    ➤ *Web Applications:* Create and manage web applications plus alternate access mappings (AAMs)

    ➤ *Site Collections:* Create and manage site collections

> ➤ *Service Applications:* Manage service applications and application proxy groups

> ➤ *Databases:* Create and manage content databases and configure the data retrieval service

➤ **System Settings** contains the following three subsections:

> ➤ *Servers:* Manage services and servers in the farm

> ➤ *E-mail and Text Messages (SMS):* configure in- and outgoing e-mail settings as well as SMS and mobile account settings

> ➤ *Farm Management:* Configure farm features and solutions, alternate address mappings, and privacy options

➤ **Monitoring** contains the following three subsections:

> ➤ *Health Analyzer:* Review problems and solutions

> ➤ *Timer Jobs:* Review and check job status

> ➤ *Reporting:* View reports and diagnostic loggings, Information Management Policy reports, Health reports, and Web Analytics reports

➤ **Backup and Restore** contains two subsections:

> ➤ *Farm Backup and Restore:* View, configure, and execute backup and restore jobs

> ➤ *Granular Backup:* Configure and execute backup jobs on specific objects, such as a site collection or a list

➤ **Security** contains three subsections:

> ➤ *Users:* Manage farm administrators, distribution groups, and application user policies

> ➤ *General Security:* Configure managed accounts, service accounts, authentication providers, antivirus settings, blocked file types, web part security, and self-service site creation

> ➤ *Information Policy:* Configure Information Rights Management and its policy settings

➤ **Upgrade and Migration** contains only one subsection:

> ➤ *Upgrade and Patch Management:* Configure license type enterprise features, check product and patch installation status, upgrade status and database status

➤ **General Application Settings** contains six subsections:

> ➤ *External Service Connections:* Configure and manage "send to" connections and document conversions

> ➤ *InfoPath Forms Services:* Manage and configure InfoPath templates, services, and data connections the web services provide for InfoPath Forms Services

> ➤ *Site Directory:* Configure a farm global site directory and scan for broken links

➤ *SharePoint Designer:* Configure what features in SharePoint Designer 2010 are allowed to be used

➤ *Search:* Configure and manage farm-wide administration and crawler impact rules

➤ *Content Deployment:* Configure and manage content deployment paths and jobs

➤ **Configuration Wizards** contains just one subsection:

➤ *Farm Configuration:* Use this to start the configuration wizard that will assist you in creating and configuring services and features in SharePoint Server 2010.

As you can see, a great number of configuration pages exist, and each of these pages contains even more settings. In the following sections you will learn more about these and how to use them. Please note that the descriptions in the following sections only cover the settings that are exclusive for SharePoint Server 2010; be sure to check Appendix B for the settings that are common for both SharePoint Foundation and SharePoint Server to get a complete description!

NOTE *The following sections describe all features in SharePoint Server 2010 Enterprise Edition. Some of these are only available in the Enterprise Edition of SharePoint Server 2010; refer to the table earlier in this appendix that compares the different SharePoint editions.*

Application Management

Application Management consists of four sections: Web Applications, Site Collections, Service Applications, and Databases, each consisting of multiple links to configuration pages. The links and their settings on the Application Management page are used by the SharePoint administrator regularly; for example, when you need to create a new site collection in an existing web application, or when you want to manage a service application. The following sections contain more detailed descriptions of these settings.

The following configuration pages are the same as those found in SharePoint Foundation and are discussed in Appendix B:

➤ **Configure Alternate Access Mappings:** Use the Configure Alternate Access Mappings page to configure alternative URL addresses to SharePoint site collections. For example, the default URL to the intranet start page is based on the SharePoint Server server name, such as http://srv1, but most organizations want to change that to something more meaningful for their users, such as http://intranet.

➤ **Delete a Site Collection:** Use the Delete a Site Collection page to delete existing site collections, when needed.

➤ **Confirm Site Use and Deletion:** Use the Confirm Site Use and Deletion page to configure automatic deletion of unused site collections.

➤ **Specify Quota Templates:** Use the Specify Quota Templates page to configure quota templates, that is, size limits, that you can apply to site collections (but not individual subsites, unfortunately).

➤ **Configure Quotas and Locks:** Use the Configure Quotas and Locks page to apply quota templates to sites and to apply locks (read-only, write, and no access) to site collections.

➤ **View All Site Collections:** Use the View All Site Collections page to list all site collections for a given web application. You will also see more information about each site collection, such as its title, URL, description, primary site collection administrator, and what content database this collection uses.

➤ **Configure Self-Service Site Creation:** Use the Configure Self-Service Site Collection page to enable any user to create a site collection without using the SharePoint Central Administration tool. If you configure SharePoint Server to use a separate site collection for users' "My Profile" sites, then you may need to enable self-service site creation for that site collection.

➤ **Configure Service Application Associations:** Use the Configure Service Application Associations page to manage application proxy groups. The only difference between this page in SharePoint Server and SharePoint Foundation is that there are more service applications in SharePoint Server.

➤ **Manage Content Databases:** Use the Manage Content Databases page to manage content databases associated with each web application.

➤ **Configure the Data Retrieval Service:** Use the Configure the Data Retrieval Service page to manage settings for data retrieval service.

The following sections discuss the other configuration pages in a more SharePoint Server-specific context.

Manage Web Applications

The settings on the *Manage Web Applications* page are used by the SharePoint administrator regularly; for example, if you need to create a new web application, or if you want to manage an existing web application.

To create a new web application, or extend an existing one, follow the steps in Appendix B. There are no specific settings for SharePoint Server compared to SharePoint Foundation.

When managing existing web applications, be aware that some new settings exist for SharePoint Server. In the following list, those settings that are identical to those found in SharePoint Foundation are marked "Same as SharePoint Foundation." Read Appendix B for more information about these settings. To see and manage the new settings in SharePoint Server 2010 listed on this page, select an existing web application and then click the following buttons on the ribbon:

➤ **Extend:** Same as SharePoint Foundation

➤ **Delete:** Same as SharePoint Foundation

➤ **General Settings:** Same as SharePoint Foundation

- ➤ **Manage Features** in SharePoint Server has several features not available in SharePoint Foundation:

  - ➤ *Document Sets metadata synchronization* (Default: Active): This feature enables synchronization of metadata in Document Sets.

  - ➤ *Office Server Enterprise Search* (Default: Active): Enables the search (that is, not the FAST search engine) in SharePoint Server 2010, with features like People Search, search using the Business Data Connector, and external content search.

  - ➤ *Office Server Site Search* (Default: Active): Enables searching in websites and lists.

  - ➤ *SharePoint Server Enterprise Web application features* (Default: Active): Enables features that come with SharePoint Server 2010 Enterprise Edition, such as Visio Services, Access Services, and Excel Services.

  - ➤ *SharePoint Server Standard Web application features* (Default: Active): Enables the features that come in SharePoint Server Standard Edition, such as User Profiles and Search for Users.

- ➤ **Managed Paths** has two new default managed path items that relate to the feature "My Profile":

  - ➤ *my* (Type: Explicit inclusion): The URL path to the public part of a user's "My Profile" site

  - ➤ *my/personal* (Type: Wildcard inclusion): The URL path prefix for each user's personal "My Profile" site

- ➤ **Service Connections** lists all available service applications for this particular web application. The following is a list of all service applications for a SharePoint Server Enterprise edition. If you want to change any of these settings, use the top menu on this Form and switch to *[Custom]*:

  - ➤ *Access Service*

  - ➤ *Application Registry Service* (Also on SharePoint Foundation)

  - ➤ *Business Data Connectivity* (Also on SharePoint Foundation)

  - ➤ *Excel Services*

  - ➤ *Managed Metadata Service*

  - ➤ *PerformancePoint Service Application*

  - ➤ *Search Service Application*

  - ➤ *Secure Store Service*

  - ➤ *State Service*

  - ➤ *Usage and Health Data Collection*

  - ➤ *User Profile Service Application*

  - ➤ *Visio Graphics Service*

  - ➤ *Web Analytics Service Application*

  - ➤ *Word Automation Services*

➤ **Authentication Provider:** Same as SharePoint Foundation

➤ **Self-Service Site Creation:** Same as SharePoint Foundation

➤ **Blocked File Types:** Same as SharePoint Foundation

➤ **User Permissions:** Same as SharePoint Foundation

➤ **User Policy:** Same as SharePoint Foundation

➤ **Anonymous Policy:** Same as SharePoint Foundation

➤ **Permission Policy:** Same as SharePoint Foundation

As you can see, several features and settings are exclusive for SharePoint Server, and it is important to know and understand how to use to utilize the rich feature sets in SharePoint Server. This book provides several examples on how and when to use these settings.

Create Site Collections

Use the Create Site Collections page to configure new site collections, when needed. All settings on this page are identical to those in SharePoint Foundation, except that more site templates are available, as described next. For more details about these settings, please see Appendix B.

A *site template* is a preconfigured website with a specific design, layout, and possibly also a number of lists pre-created. In SharePoint Server the following site templates are default:

➤ **Collaboration tab (SharePoint Foundation and SharePoint Server)**

    ➤ *Team Site*

    ➤ *Blank Site*

    ➤ *Document Workspace*

    ➤ *Blog*

    ➤ *Group Work Site*

    ➤ *Visio Process Repository*

➤ **Meetings tab**

    ➤ *Basic Meeting Workspace*

    ➤ *Blank Meeting Workspace*

    ➤ *Decision Meeting Workspace*

    ➤ *Social Meeting Workspace*

    ➤ *Multipage Meeting Workspace*

➤ **Enterprise tab (SharePoint Server only)**

    ➤ *Enterprise Center*

    ➤ *Records Center*

- ➤ *Business Intelligence Center*

- ➤ *Enterprise Search Center*

- ➤ *My Site Host*

- ➤ *Basic Search Center*

- ➤ **Publishing tab (SharePoint Server only)**

  - ➤ *Publishing Portal*

  - ➤ *Enterprise Wiki*

- ➤ Custom tab (SharePoint Foundation and SharePoint Server)

  - ➤ *< Select template later. . . >*

For more details about these settings, please see Appendix B.

Change Site Collection Administrators

Use the Change Site Collection Administrators page to set the primary and secondary site collection administrator for any site collection. This feature may be handy if one of these two administrators is replaced by a new person, or if you need to temporarily grant yourself access to a site collection for support reasons. If you need more than two administrators in a specific site collection, open its top site and change its "Site collection administrators" (see Chapter 2). All settings on this page are identical to those in SharePoint Foundation. For more details about these settings, please see Appendix B.

Manage Service Applications

Use the Manage Service Applications page to manage all service applications in SharePoint Server. Depending on what edition of SharePoint server you use, there will be close to 20 default service applications, compared to four in SharePoint Foundation; see the complete list in the "Service Applications" section earlier in this appendix.

Each service application has different configuration settings, and some of the service applications consist of multiple pages with lots of settings, such as for the Search service application. The following is a list with more details about each of these SharePoint Server Enterprise service applications:

- ➤ **Access Services** enables you to run Microsoft Access 2010 applications from within SharePoint, making it possible for end users to access these applications using only a web browser. Click on this service application to manage a number of settings to control the load and resources this service requires:

  - ➤ *Maximum Columns Per Query* (Default: 32): Set the maximum number of columns that can be referenced in a query.

  - ➤ *Maximum Rows Per Query* (Default: 50,000): Set the maximum number of rows in a list that can be used in a query.

  - ➤ *Maximum Sources Per Query* (Default: 8): Set the maximum number of lists that can be used in a query.

➤ *Maximum Calculated Columns Per Query* (Default: 10): Set the maximum number of calculated columns that can be included in a query.

➤ *Maximum Order by Clauses per Query* (Default: 4): Set the maximum number of Order by clauses in a query.

➤ *Allow Outer Joins* (Default: Yes): Select if Left and Right Outer Joins are permitted in a query (Note: Inner joins are always permitted.)

➤ *Allow Non Remotable Queries* (Default: Yes): Allow queries that cannot be remoted to the database tier to run.

➤ *Maximum Records per Table* (Default: 500,000): Set the maximum number of records for any table in an application.

➤ *Maximum Application Log Size* (Default 3,000): Set the maximum number of records for an Microsoft Access Service Application Log list. Note that −1 means "No limit."

➤ *Maximum Request Duration* (Default: 30): Set the maximum duration in seconds allowed for a request from an application. Note that −1 means "No limit."

➤ *Maximum Sessions per User* (Default: 10): Set the maximum number of sessions allowed per user. If the user exceeds this number by starting a new session, the oldest session will be deleted. Note that −1 means "No limit."

➤ *Maximum Sessions per Anonymous User* (Default: 25): Set the maximum number of sessions for an anonymous user. If this number is exceeded, then the oldest session will be deleted. Note that −1 means "No limit."

➤ *Cache Timeout* (Default: 300): Set the maximum time in seconds for the data cache. Note that −1 means "No limit." Valid values: 1 to 2,073,600 seconds (24 days).

➤ *Maximum Session Memory* (Default: 64): Set the maximum amount of memory in MB that a single user can use. Valid values: 0 (disabled) to 4,095.

➤ *Maximum Private Bytes* (Default: −1): Set the maximum number of private bytes in MB that the Microsoft Access Database Service process can allocate. Note that −1 means "50 percent of the physical memory."

➤ *Maximum Template Size* (Default: 30): Set the maximum size in MB for Access templates. Note that −1 means "No limit."

➤ **Excel Services** enables you to run Microsoft Excel spreadsheets from within SharePoint, and to present parts of all content in a given spreadsheet using the Excel web part. It contains five subforms, all with multiple settings. The following list describes the subforms, but not all of their detailed settings:

➤ *Global Settings:* Use this page to define load balancing, memory, and throttling thresholds. You can also set the unattended service account and the data connections time-out values.

➤ *Trusted File Locations:* Set the file locations that are trusted to host Excel files that can be used by Excel Services and its Excel web parts.

➤ *Trusted Data Providers:* Set the data providers that can be used by the data connections.

➤ *Trusted Data Connection Libraries:* Set the document libraries in SharePoint that can store data connection files.

➤ *User Defined Function Assemblies:* Define the managed code assemblies that may be used by the Excel spreadsheets.

➤ **Managed Metadata Service** enables you to define and manage metadata in SharePoint; that is, both hierarchical metadata trees and the flat structured list of keywords (often referred to as "tags"). Managed Metadata Service also enables the use of farm global content types — that is, content types that can be used in any site collection. You learn more about how to use these managed metadata in Chapters 3 and 6 (see Figure D-2).

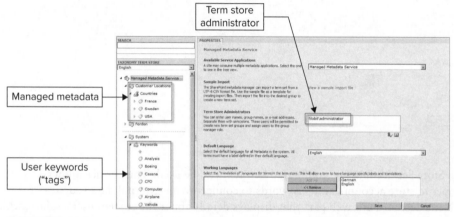

FIGURE D-2

➤ **PerformancePoint Service** enables a number of features and web parts related to business intelligence (BI), such as key performance indicators (KPIs), trend analysis, and corresponding web parts. This service has four subforms, all with multiple settings each. Chapter 4 shows you how to use this rich set of BI features. The four subforms are as follow:

➤ *PerformancePoint Service Application Settings:* Use this to configure cache settings, filters, and query time-outs.

➤ *Trusted Data Source Location:* Use this to define the trusted locations for data sources.

➤ *Trusted Content Location:* Set the locations that can store dashboards and scorecards.

➤ *Import PerformancePoint Service 2007 Content:* Use this form to manage the import of data from the previous edition of PerformancePoint Server 2007.

➤ **Search Service Application** is the main search administration page with many settings and configuration forms. You can find more details about search settings in Chapter 6 (see Figure D-3).

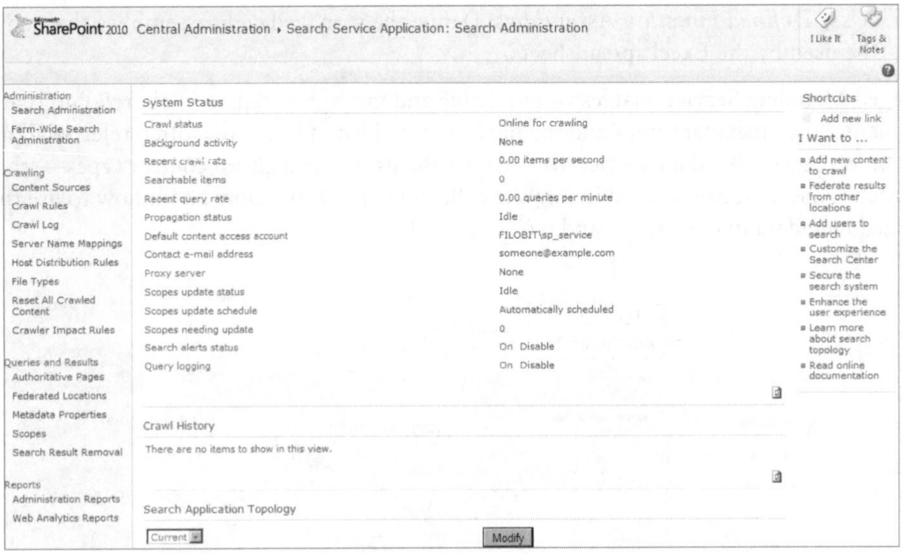

FIGURE D-3

➤ **Secure Store Service** must be configured before it can be used. This service allows a developer to store accounts and passwords to connect to an external data source — for example, a custom-built web part that displays details about the current user's salary, which is retrieved from a human resource application using an Oracle database. This service replaces the Single Sign-On service in MOSS 2007 and is beyond the scope of this book.

➤ **User Profile Service Application** offers access to the 20 different configuration forms that are related to user profiles. The following is a list of these configuration forms, grouped in four sections. Chapter 5 covers more about My Profiles; Chapter 6 covers managing User Profiles.

   ➤ *People*

      ➤ Manage User Properties

      ➤ Manage User Profiles

      ➤ Manage User Sub-types

      ➤ Manage Audiences

      ➤ Schedule Audience Compilation

      ➤ Manage User Permissions

      ➤ Compile Audiences

      ➤ Profile Services Policies

- ➤ *Synchronization*

  - ➤ Configure Synchronization Connections

  - ➤ Configure Synchronization Timer Jobs

  - ➤ Configure Synchronization Settings

  - ➤ Start Profile Synchronization

- ➤ *Organizations*

  - ➤ Manage Organization Properties

  - ➤ Manage Organization Profiles

  - ➤ Manage Organization Sub-types

- ➤ *My Site Settings*

  - ➤ Set up My Site

  - ➤ Configure Trusted Host Locations

  - ➤ Configure Personalization Site

  - ➤ Publish Links to Office Client Applications

  - ➤ Manage Social Tags and Notes

➤ The **Visio Graphics Service** enables you to manage and display Microsoft Visio 2010 drawings in SharePoint using a specific web part. To find out more about how to use Visio in SharePoint 2010, see Chapter 9. Here are the two subforms for this service:

  - ➤ *Global Settings:* Use these settings to manage security, performance, and data connections.

  - ➤ *Trusted Data Providers:* Use these settings to manage data providers used by data connections.

➤ The **Web Analytics Service Application** enables statistics and analysis of user behavior, such as what sites are most used, who is the most active user, and what type of web browser is most popular. This service does not have any particular settings, except the following.

  - ➤ *Data Retention Period* (Default: 25 months): This setting defines how long data will be stored in the web analytics database. To set this value, open the *Properties* for this service, not the *Manage* settings!

➤ **Word Automation Services** enables a custom-developed application to convert Office documents to other formats; for example, from DOCX to PDF or XPF. Because this is a developer-oriented service, it is not described in this book, but a good start to understand how to use it is this article: http://blogs.msdn.com/microsoft_office_word/archive/2009/12/16/Word-Automation-Services_3A00_-What-It-Does.aspx.

To summarize: SharePoint Server 2010 has many services that need to be managed and configured in order to enable the incredibly rich set of features in SharePoint Server. The preceding list gives you a short presentation of each service, but to really understand how to use them you need to read all the chapters in this book. An important improvement in SharePoint Server 2010 is that each web application now can choose only the service applications that are required, while MOSS 2007 required that each web application connect to a group of service applications, known as the Shared Service Provider.

Specify the Default Database Server

Use the Specify the Default Database Server page to define the default SQL Server for storing content databases. If the server is configured to use SQL Server authentication, then use this page to set the user account and password that will be used when SharePoint connects to SQL Server.

System Settings

The System Settings section in SharePoint Central Administration contains a number of links related to server services, e-mail settings, and global farm settings and features. All the links in SharePoint Foundation's System Settings page are the same as in SharePoint Server 2010; the difference is the configuration settings available in these links.

The following configuration pages are exactly the same as those found in SharePoint Foundation and are discussed in Appendix B:

➤ Manage Services in this farm

➤ Configure outgoing e-mail settings

➤ Configure incoming e-mail settings

➤ Configure mobile account

➤ Configure alternate access mappings

➤ Manage farm solutions

➤ Manage user solutions

➤ Configure privacy options

➤ Configure cross-firewall access zone

The following configuration pages have more settings in SharePoint Server 2010 than the corresponding page in SharePoint Foundation and will be described in more detail in the following sections:

➤ Manage services on server

➤ Manage farm features

Manage Services on Server

Use the Manage Services on Server page to start, stop, and manage services. This page is described in more detail in Appendix B, but SharePoint Server contains a lot more services. The following is a list of these services and their settings:

➤ **Access Database Service:** No settings available

➤ **Application Registry Service:** No settings available

- **Business Data Connectivity:** No settings available

- **Central Administration:** No settings available

- **Document Conversion Load Balancing Service:**

  - Select the server to run the load balancing service.

  - Set the communication scheme (Default: HTTP): Choose between HTTP and HTTPS.

  - Set the TCP port that the load balancer service will use for communication (Default: 8093).

- **Document Conversions Launcher Service:**

  - Select the server to run the launcher service.

  - Select the load balancer service to be associated with this launcher.

  - Set the TCP port number to be used by the launcher for communication (Default: 8082).

- **Excel Calculation Service:** No settings available

- **Lotus Notes Connector:** No settings available

- **Managed Metadata Web Service:** No settings available

- **Microsoft SharePoint Foundation Incoming E-Mail:** No settings available

- **Microsoft SharePoint Foundation Subscription Settings Service:** No settings available

- **Microsoft SharePoint Foundation User Code Service:** No settings available

- **Microsoft SharePoint Foundation Web Application:** No settings available

- **Microsoft SharePoint Foundation Workflow Timer Service:**

  - Set the *Workflow Timer Batch Size*, that is, the number of workflow events processed during every time interval on this server (Default: 100).

- **PerformancePoint Service:** No settings available

- **Search Query and Site Settings Service:** No settings available

- **Secure Store Service:** No settings available

- **SharePoint Foundation Search:** Use this service to define the following settings. Note that this service is, by default, not used in an SharePoint Server environment:

  - *Service Account:* Username and password

  - *Content Access Account:* Username and password

  - *Database Server*

  - *Database Name*

  - *Database Authentication:* Choose *Windows Authentication* or *SQL Authentication*

➤ *Failover Server:* The failover database server name

➤ *Indexing Schedule:* Configure how often to run this indexing service (Default: Every hour)

➤ **SharePoint Server Search:** Use this page to define farm-wide settings regarding search and indexing. See also Chapter 6 for more information about configuring this service:

➤ *Proxy Server* (Default: None)

➤ *Time-out (seconds):* The Default is 60 seconds for connection time and 60 seconds for request acknowledgement time.

➤ *Ignore SSL warnings* (Default: No)

➤ *Modify Topology:* Of the Search service application

➤ **User Profile Service:** No settings available

➤ **User Profile Synchronization Service:** No settings available

➤ **Visio Graphics Service:** No settings available

➤ **Web Analytics Data Processing Service:** No settings available

➤ **Web Analytics Web Service:** No settings available

➤ **Word Automation Service:** No settings available

Manage Farm Features

Use the Manage Farm Features page to manage all features for this farm. This list depends on the installed SharePoint Server edition; Enterprise has more features than Standard edition. The following list describes the features in SharePoint Server Enterprise edition:

➤ **"Connect to Office" Ribbon Controls:** Activate this feature to display buttons on the ribbon for creating library shortcuts. Note that this requires Office 2010. If this option is enabled Office will periodically cache templates available in those libraries on the user's local machine.

➤ **Access Service Farm Feature:** Activate Access Services for this farm.

➤ **Data Connection Library:** Activate the Data Connection Library feature.

➤ **Excel Services Farm Feature:** Activate Excel Services for this farm.

➤ **FAST Search for SharePoint Master Job Provisioning:** Activate FAST Search for the SharePoint Master Job.

➤ **Global Web Parts:** Activate additional web parts that can be used in all types of sites.

➤ **Office.com Entry Points from SharePoint:** This feature allows users to browse SharePoint solutions from www.office.com from a SharePoint site.

➤ **Office Synchronization for External Lists:** Activate this feature to enable offline synchronization for external lists with Microsoft Outlook and SharePoint Workspace clients.

➤ **Social Tags and Note Board Ribbon Controls:** Activate this feature to enable entry points for social tagging and note board commenting to the ribbon.

➤ **Spell Checking:** Activate spell checking when editing list items.

➤ **Visio Process Repository:** Activate the Visio Process Repository feature in document libraries

➤ **Visio Web Access:** Enable web-based presentations of Visio drawings.

Manage Farm Solutions

Solutions are custom applications that extend the functionality in SharePoint. You can develop SharePoint Solutions using Visual Studio .NET or purchase solutions from third-party vendors. The Manage Farm Solutions page, also known as the *Solution Management* page, lists all deployed solutions and their status. By default, no solutions are in a newly installed SharePoint server.

Manage User Solutions

The Manage User Solutions page is also known as the *User Solution Management* page. Use this page to block deployed farm solutions from running in SharePoint sites. You can also configure how the solution will run, either on the SharePoint server that is used to access this solution (if there are multiple SharePoint front-end servers, you will have a load-balancing of this solution) or on a particular SharePoint server.

Configure Cross-Firewall Access Zones

Use the Configure Cross-Firewall Access Zones to define the URL that external users use to access SharePoint. If SharePoint needs to send alert messages to their mobile phone, the URLs will be adjusted for mobile use.

Monitoring

The Monitoring section in SharePoint Central Administration contains links to health analyses, definition of timer jobs, and multiple reports. Almost all of the links point to configuration pages that are exactly the same in SharePoint Foundation and SharePoint Server, except these three pages, which contain more configuration settings in SharePoint Server 2010:

➤ View Administrative Reports

➤ Review Information Management Policy Usage Reports

➤ View Web Analytics Reports

The following configuration pages are the same as those found in SharePoint Foundation and are discussed in Appendix B:

➤ Review problems and solutions

➤ Review rule definitions

➤ Review job definitions

➤ Check job status

➤ Configure diagnostic logging

➤ View health reports

The following sections discuss the other configuration pages in a more SharePoint Server-specific context.

View Administrative Reports

Use the View Administrative Reports page to display search administrative reports. SharePoint Server comes with several predefined reports, as listed below, but you can also create your own reports:

- CrawlRatePerContentSource
- CrawlratePerType
- QueryLatency
- QueryLatencyTrend
- SharePointBackendQueryLatency
- CrawlProcessingPerActivity
- CrawlProcessingPerComponent
- CrawlQueue

To use these reports, just click on them and SharePoint will create the report with the most current information, either in a graphical presentation or in a table form. For most of these reports, you can select specific filters, for example, specific dates.

Review Information Management Policy Usage Reports

Use the Review Information Management Policy Usage Reports page to configure and generate reports about information management policy usage. This page contains the following settings, per web application:

- **Schedule Recurring Reports** (Default: Daily at 1:00 a.m.): Define when to run and generate these reports.
- **Report File Location** (Default: none): Set where these reports will be stored.
- **Report Template** (Default: "Use the default report template"): Set what report template to use — the default or a custom template.

Configure Usage and Health Data Collection

Use the Configure Usage and Health Data Collection page to enable and configure the usage and health logs. This page contains the following settings:

- **Usage data collection** (Default: Enabled): Use this setting to enable or disable the data collection.
- **Event Selection** (Default: All events selected). Use this setting to select what events to log:
  - *Content Import Usage*
  - *Content Export Usage*
  - *Page Requests*
  - *Feature Use*

> ➤ *Search Query Usage*

> ➤ *Site Inventory Usage*

> ➤ *Timer Jobs*

> ➤ *Rating Usage*

➤ **Usage data collection settings** (Default: 5GB maximum, stored in `C:\Program Files\ Common Files\Microsoft Shared\Web Server Extensions\14\Logs`): Use this setting to define where to store the log files and their maximum size in GB. You may want to move these log files to another disk, to avoid filling the boot partition disk with log files.

➤ **Health Data Collection** (Default: Enabled): Use this setting to enable or disable the health data collection. Click on Health Logging Schedule to see and manage the health logging schedule.

➤ **Log Collection Schedule:** Click on Log Collection Schedule to list and manage the log collection schedule.

➤ **Logging Database Server:** Use this page to set the database server name, the database name, and how to authenticate.

➤ **View Web Analytics reports:** Use this page to view the web analytics reports for each web application used for end user sites.

Backup and Restore Features

Chapter 10 covers all the configuration settings in this section, but here is a quick overview of the Backup and Restore features:

➤ **Perform a backup:** Select what to back up (from a complete farm to a single content database) and where to store the backup files, and then start the backup process. Note that this process cannot be scheduled using this feature; use PowerShell or STSADM to schedule backups.

➤ **Restore from a backup:** Select what to restore (from a complete farm to a single content database) and from what file location, and then start the restore.

➤ **Configure backup settings:** Set the number of backup and restore threads, plus the backup location.

➤ **View backup and restore history:** Use this to see all the available backup sets.

➤ **Check backup and restore job status:** Use this to see the status of current jobs.

➤ **Perform a site collection backup:** Back up a single site collection.

➤ **Export a site or list:** Back up ("export") a single website or list to a file.

➤ **Recover data from an unattached content database:** This works with databases that exist in the SQL Server, but is not used by any SharePoint web applications.

➤ **Check granular backup job status:** Lists all current and previous backup jobs, including exports of sites and lists, and their status.

Security

SharePoint Central Administration has a specific section for security settings where you will find a large number of links to different security-related settings, as listed below:

➤ **Manage the farm administrator groups:** Define users and groups that will have full access to the SharePoint farm.

➤ **Approve or reject distribution groups:** SharePoint can suggest that a distribution group should be created; with this link you can view and approve these suggested distribution groups.

➤ **Specify web application user policy:** Manage permissions for specific service accounts in SharePoint, such as the Search Crawling account.

➤ **Configure managed accounts:** Configure all managed accounts; for example, whether passwords should be automatically changed.

➤ **Configure service accounts:** Change service accounts for service applications.

➤ **Configure password change settings:** Manage automatic password changes and who will be notified about these changes.

➤ **Specify authentication providers:** Manage security settings for the zones for each web application; for example, enable anonymous access and Kerberos authentication.

➤ **Manage trust:** Add and manage trust relationships between SharePoint farms.

➤ **Manage antivirus settings:** Configure settings related to antivirus scanners; for example, whether documents should be scanned during upload to a library and whether infected documents should be blocked from download to the client computer.

➤ **Define blocked file types:** Control what file types SharePoint will prohibit from uploading to libraries. For example, by default you cannot upload .EXE files.

➤ **Manage web part security:** Define the global settings for web parts for a given web application; for example, whether web parts should be allowed to be connected and whether the Web Part Gallery will be available.

➤ **Configure self-service site creating:** Define whether end users will be able to configure site collections. By default this is enabled for the web application that hosts My Sites.

➤ **Configure information rights management:** IRM helps protect sensitive documents stored in SharePoint from being misused; for example, it ensures that no one except the intended user can read a specific Office document, regardless of whether someone manages to get a copy of that document. IRM depends on the Windows Rights Management Services (RMS); use this configuration page to define the location of the Windows server that runs the RMS service.

➤ **Configure Information Management Policy:** This page is unique for SharePoint Server and is described in more detail later in this appendix.

Security is an important topic in SharePoint that is the same in both SharePoint Foundation and SharePoint Server 2010. Appendix B describes security-related features in detail, including a number of Try It Out exercises that will help you understand how security works. You will also find security-related topics discussed in almost all chapters in this book, from creating site collections and sites to managing lists and documents, that will help you understand when and how to use these security options. The following section describes some SharePoint Server-specific security settings.

Configure Information Rights Management Policy

Use the settings on the Configure Information Rights Management Policy page to manage and configure policies for these features:

➤ **Labels:** Define labels that can be inserted into Microsoft Office documents to ensure that important properties are included when the document is printed. You can also search for documents with specific labels.

➤ **Barcodes:** Create unique barcode identities to be inserted into Microsoft Office documents. You can also search for documents with specific barcodes.

➤ **Auditing:** Enable or disable the audit feature for user actions, such as opening a list item in read-only mode or copying a document. These audits will be written to the audit log.

➤ **Retention:** Enable or disable the retention feature; that is, specify when a retention action will start — for example, 12 months after the document was created.

Upgrade and Migration

The Upgrade and Migration section in SharePoint Central Administration contains links to view the product and patch status and upgrade status. Some of these links are identical in SharePoint Server and SharePoint Foundation, but others are unique for SharePoint Server. Use the Upgrade and Migration section when you need to configure and manage any of the following:

➤ Convert farm license type (SharePoint Server only)

➤ Enable Enterprise features (SharePoint Server only)

➤ Enable Features on existing sites (SharePoint Server only)

➤ Check product and patch installation status (SharePoint Foundation and SharePoint Server)

➤ Review database status (SharePoint Foundation and SharePoint Server)

➤ Check upgrade status (SharePoint Foundation and SharePoint Server)

The links that are unique for SharePoint Server are described in the following sections. (The other links are discussed in Appendix B.) To access these features, start the SharePoint Central Administration, and click Upgrade and Migration.

Convert Farm License Type

Use the Convert Farm License Type page to enter a new license key; for example, if you want to convert a trial version of SharePoint Server 2010 to a full version. All content, sites, and features in the trial version will be retained when you enter the new license key; the only thing that happens is that the time limitation of 180 days will be removed. You don't even have to reboot the SharePoint Server server. You can just as easily use this configuration page to upgrade from SharePoint Server Standard to SharePoint Server Enterprise, but to enable the enterprise features in SharePoint Server Enterprise you must also activate these features; see the following configuration link.

Enable Enterprise Features

Use the Enable Enterprise Features page to convert a SharePoint Server Standard edition to an Enterprise edition. You must first enter the SharePoint Server Enterprise license key; see the previous configuration link about Farm License Type.

General Application Settings

The General Application Settings section in SharePoint Central Administration contains links to configure several SharePoint features; some of them are identical to the General Application Settings page in SharePoint Foundation, such as Configure SharePoint Designer settings, but most of these links are unique for SharePoint Server:

- **Configure send to connections:** (SharePoint Foundation and SharePoint Server) See Appendix B for more information.

- **Configure SharePoint Designer Settings:** (SharePoint Foundation and SharePoint Server) See Appendix B for more information.

- **Configure document conversions:** (SharePoint Foundation and SharePoint Server, but only SharePoint Server comes with predefined converters installed.)

- **Manage form templates:** (SharePoint Server) Manage and upload InfoPath forms.

- **Configure InfoPath Forms Services:** (SharePoint Server) Configure features related to InfoPath forms; for example, whether forms are browser-enabled; and maximum time for user sessions.

- **Upload form template:** (SharePoint Server) Upload forms from the file system.

- **Manage Data Connection Files:** (SharePoint Server) Upload and manage existing connection files, which describe how to connect SharePoint to an external data source.

- **Configure InfoPath Forms Services Web Service Proxy:** (SharePoint Server) Enable an InfoPath proxy to enhance the performance of InfoPath forms.

- **Configure the Site Directory:** (SharePoint Server) Define the location for the Site Directory site.

- **Scan Site Directory Links:** (SharePoint Server) Open existing URL links in the Site Directory and see whether they still are valid.

- **Farm Search Administration:** (SharePoint Server) Configure settings for proxy server, time-outs, and whether SSL warnings should be ignored.

- **Crawler Impact Rules:** (SharePoint Server) Use this page to manage crawler impact rules, to control the load placed by the crawler on a data source.

- **Configure content deployment paths and jobs:** (SharePoint Server) Manage the paths (source and destination site) used to deploy (replicate) content; for example, between an internal SharePoint server to a public Internet site.

- **Configure content deployment:** (SharePoint Server) Manage the settings for the content deployment, such as the import and export servers.

- **Check deployment of specific content:** (SharePoint Server) List the result of the content deployment; for example, see what content has been deployed to a remote site and when.

These features are described in the following sections. To access these features, start the SharePoint Central Administration and click General Application Settings in the left pane.

InfoPath Forms Service

Use the InfoPath Forms Service configuration pages to manage settings related to the InfoPath Forms Service:

➤ **Manage form templates:** Display properties for current templates, activate or deactivate the form to site collections, and upload new form templates.

➤ **Configure InfoPath Forms Services** contains many settings:

  ➤ *User Browser-enabled Form Templates*: The default is "Allow users to browser-enable form templates" and "Render form templates that are browser-enabled by users."

  ➤ *Data Connection Timeouts*: The default is 10,000 milliseconds for data connection timeouts and 20,000 milliseconds for maximum data connection timeouts.

  ➤ *Data Connection Response Size:* The default is 1,500 KB as the maximum size.

  ➤ *HTTP data connections:* The default is "Require SSL for HTTP authentication to data sources."

  ➤ *Embedded SQL Authentication:* The default is "Allow embedded SQL authentication" is not enabled.

  ➤ *Authentication to data sources*: The default is "Allow user form templates to use authentication information contained in data connection files" is not enabled.

  ➤ *Cross-Domain Access for User Form Templates*: The default is "Allow cross-domain data access for user form templates that use connection settings in a data connection file" is not enabled

  ➤ *Thresholds:* The default is "Number of postbacks per session: 75" and "Number of actions per postback: 200."

  ➤ *User Sessions*: The default is "Active sessions should be terminated after 1,440 minutes (24 hours)" and "Maximum size of user session data: 4,096 KB."

Site Directory

Use the Site Directory page settings to configure the use of a Site Directory — that is, a list of all sites and subsites in a farm. There are two configuration pages:

➤ **Configure the Site Directory:** Set the URL to the master site directory in this farm. You can also force all new sites and subsites to be listed in the directory and configure whether site categories are mandatory or not.

➤ **Scan Site Directory Links:** Enter the URL to site directory views you want to check for broken links. You can also force site titles and descriptions in the site directory to match the actual site title and description.

Search

Use the links in the Search page to configure the following settings:

➤ **Farm Search Administration:** This configuration page is identical to the one found when you manage the Services on servers and the Search Service settings; see the section "Services on Server" earlier in this appendix.

➤ **Crawler Impact Rules:** Define new rules and manage old crawler rules; see Chapter 6 for more details about the search feature.

Configure Content Deployment Paths and Jobs

Use the Configure Content Deployment Paths and Jobs settings to define new deployment paths and jobs — for example, if you have an internal subsite that you want to replicate to an external Internet-facing SharePoint site.

Configure Content Deployment

Use the Configure Content Deployment page to configure these settings:

➤ **Accept Content Deployment Jobs:** Define whether this server will receive content deployment jobs from another farm (Default: "Reject incoming content deployment jobs.")

➤ **Import Server:** Define what SharePoint Server server will accept incoming deployment jobs.

➤ **Export server:** Define what SharePoint Server server will send outgoing deployment jobs.

> **NOTE** *Both the import server and the export server need to be running an administration web application for the farm!*

➤ **Connection Security:** Default: "Require encryption." In plain English, the default setting is that all content deployment data traffic must use an HTTPS encrypted tunnel, which will protect user account names and passwords that are used to authenticate to the import server.

➤ **Temporary Files:** Define where to store temporary content deployment jobs. These files will then be deleted when the deployment is completed. The default path is `C:\ProgramData\ContentDeployment`.

➤ **Reporting:** Set the number of reports to be stored for each content deployment job (Default: 20).

Check Deployment of Specific Content

Use the Check Deployment of Specific Content page to list the status for a specific content deployment job. You must enter the URL for the object, and then click Check Status.

Configuration Wizards — Launch the Farm Configuration Wizard

The Configuration Wizards section in SharePoint Central Administration contains a link to "Launch the Farm Configuration Wizard." Use this wizard when you want a really quick way to configure service applications with their managed service accounts for the SharePoint farm.

These service applications will be set up and configured with default settings for a typical organization. You can later change these settings or manually create new service applications, if needed. The following Try It Out describes how to run this configuration wizard.

TRY IT OUT Run the Configuration Wizard

1. Log on as the administrator, start the Central Administration tool, and choose Configuration Wizard ⇨ Launch the Farm Configuration Wizard.

2. Select the option "Walk me through the settings using this wizard. I will select the services to use in this farm and the type of site to create." Click Next.

3. Select the Service Account to be used for the service applications listed below. You can either use existing accounts or enter a user account that SharePoint will register as a managed account. Select the service applications you want to create and configure. Click Next. This procedure may take a few minutes.

4. The final step is to create a site collection. If you don't want it, click Cancel; otherwise, create it (see previously in this chapter how to create site collections).

How It Works

This wizard will ask you a few simple questions and then automatically install and configure the service applications you selected. You can also install these service applications manually, instead of running the wizard, but that will require more knowledge about how to configure SharePoint Foundation 2010.

COMPLETING THE BASIC SHAREPOINT SERVER CONFIGURATION

As described earlier in this appendix, SharePoint uses extended versions of IIS websites for hosting collection of sites; these extended websites are referred to as *web applications*. Each web application can host multiple site collections. Each web application is connected to one or more SQL databases, known as *content databases*, that store all data in the site collections.

SharePoint Server 2010 uses web applications exactly the same way that SharePoint Foundation does, and Appendix B describes these concepts in detail. This section focuses on what you typically do after installing your first SharePoint Server to prepare it for start creating site collections.

Configuring Outgoing E-mail Settings

After installing SharePoint Server and activating all required service applications (for example, the Managed Metadata and Business Data Connectivity Services), you must do some things before you start building your SharePoint sites. The first is typically to enable SharePoint to send e-mail, then configure the search and indexing feature. If you want specific features, such as Excel Services, you also need to configure these before you can use them. Throughout the book you will see lots of examples and scenarios describing how to configure and use these features and services, and therefore the following instructions are a brief description of what most administrators want to do immediately after the installation of SharePoint Server.

TRY IT OUT **Configure General Settings for Outgoing E-mail**

In SharePoint, end users may request e-mail status messages — for example, if a specific document is modified, or when a new contact is added to a contact list. SharePoint also sends mail to site owners and the administrator to inform them about warnings and errors.

1. Log on as the farm administrator, and start the SharePoint Central Administration tool.

2. Switch to the System Settings page, and click "Configure outgoing e-mail settings."

3. In the Outbound SMTP server field, enter the server name that runs an SMTP mail service, like Microsoft Exchange. Note that you may need to configure this SMTP server to accept incoming e-mail from the SharePoint Server server.

4. In the "From address" field, enter the mail address that you want SharePoint to use when sending e-mail. Note that this mail address does not have to exist! It will only be used as a From address; that is, the recipients of these e-mails will see this address as the sender. Choosing a neutral address, such as intranet@filobit.com or sharepoint@filobit.com, is wise. You can surely imagine that if end users receive mail from administrator@filobit.com, they will wonder why you are sending them e-mail regarding information in SharePoint, so make sure it is a good name.

5. In the "Reply-to address" field, enter an existing mail account that will receive the mail, in the unlikely case that the recipient of these e-mails will reply. Common mail accounts for this field are administrator@filobit.com and helpdesk@filobit.com.

6. The default value for "Character set" should be fine in most situations. Only change this value when needed, typically when the SMTP server is not fully compliant to the SMTP standard. If this value is wrong, then typically non-US characters, such as é and ö, in the e-mail will be removed or replaced with other characters.

How It Works

These steps describe how to configure the general settings for outgoing e-mail from SharePoint and will apply to all web applications in the farm, including SharePoint Central Administration. If needed, you can configure specific settings for each web application, as described in the next Try It Out steps.

TRY IT OUT   Configure Outgoing E-mail Settings for a Specific Web Application

The general settings for outgoing e-mail will apply to all current and future web applications. Sometimes you need to configure e-mail from a specific web application to use a specific SMTP server, or set a specific From address. The following example describes how to configure specific settings for a web application named SharePoint - 80.

1. Log on as the farm administrator and start SharePoint Central Administration.

2. Switch to Application Management ⇨ Manage web applications.

3. Select the web application to be configured: in this example, SharePoint - 80.

4. On the ribbon, click the *text* General Settings to open its menu, and select Outgoing E-mail. (If you click on the button, the General Settings page will open, which is not what you want this time.)

5. Change the setting you need to be specific for this web application, for example, the From address, and click OK.

How It Works

By configuring the settings for a specific web application, you can define different outgoing e-mail settings for any web application without affecting the other web applications.

Configuring the Search and Index Feature

Another setting you typically want to configure before you start creating site collections is the search and indexing feature. Chapter 6 describes this feature in more detail, so this section covers only the basic configuration.

First you must create the Search Service Application, either manually (choose SharePoint Central Administration ⇨ Manage service applications ⇨ New ⇨ Search Service Application), or by running the configuration wizard (choose SharePoint Central Administration ⇨ Configuration Wizards ⇨ Launch the Farm Configuration Wizard). Then you configure the schedule for running the crawler process that builds the search index, as described in the following Try It Out.

TRY IT OUT   Configure the Index Crawler Schedule

1. Log on as the farm administrator and start SharePoint Central Administration.

2. Open Administration Management ⇨ Manage applications.

3. Select Search Service Application and click the Manage button (or click on the name of this service to open its Manage page directly). See Figure D-4.

New	Connect	Delete	Manage	Administrators	Properties	Publish Permissions
	Create			Operations		Sharing

Settings	Application Registry Service	Application Registry Proxy	Started
Configuration Wizards	Business Data Connectivity	Business Data Connectivity Service Application	Started
	Business Data Connectivity	Business Data Connectivity Proxy	Started
	Excel Services	Excel Services Web Service Application	Started
	Excel Services	Excel Services Web Service Application Proxy	Started
	Managed Metadata Service	Managed Metadata Service	Started
	Managed Metadata Service	Managed Metadata Service Connection	Started
	PerformancePoint Service Application	PerformancePoint Service Application	Started
	PerformancePoint Service Application	PerformancePoint Service Application Proxy	Started
	Search Administration Web Service for Search Service Application	Search Administration Web Service Application	Started
	Search Service Application	Search Service Application	Started
	Search Service Application	Search Service Application Proxy	Started
	Secure Store Service	Secure Store Service Application	Started
	Secure Store Service	Secure Store Service Application Proxy	Started

FIGURE D-4

4.   In the left pane, click Content Sources.

5.   Click on Local SharePoint Sites. This opens the default content source that all current and future site collections will automatically be added to.

6.   Scroll down in this page to the Crawl Schedule section. Click Create schedule, but only for the Incremental Crawl field. The form "Manage Schedules" opens where you set the schedule.

7.   Make sure the Type option is set to Daily, select "Repeat within the day" and set the Every field to 10 minutes.

8.   Click OK to save and close this form. The Edit Content Source page reappears. Notice that the Incremental Crawl field now says "Every 10 minute(s) from 00:00 for 24 hour(s) every day" (see Figure D-5).

Manage Schedules	□ ✕

Manage Schedules

* Indicates a required field

Type Select the type of schedule.	⦿ Daily ○ Weekly ○ Monthly		
Settings Type the schedule settings.	Run every: *	1	days
	Starting time:	12:00 AM ▾	
	☑ Repeat within the day		
	Every:	10	minutes
	For:	1440	minutes

OK	Cancel

FIGURE D-5

9. Select the "Start full crawl of this content source" option. Then click OK to close the settings for this content source. This forces the crawler process to start immediately.

How It Works

By setting a recurring schedule for the crawler process, you make sure that all current and future content in any SharePoint site will be searchable. In this example you set the crawler to run every 10 minutes, and the consequence is that it will take a maximum of 10 minutes before a new piece of information is searchable. You may be tempted to run it more frequently, like once every minute, but the crawler process is very CPU intensive and will affect the overall performance of the SharePoint server, unless you match its load with its hardware capacity.

When you have completed the appendix to this point, you have a SharePoint environment with all the basic features and configurations needed to start creating the sites for the end users. If you are in a hurry, then refer to Chapter 2 to learn how to build team sites. But I suggest that you read the rest of this appendix to learn other important features and concepts in SharePoint Server that will help you get the most out of SharePoint Server.

CONFIGURING LOG OPTIONS

Every time an issue or problem occurs in SharePoint, it will be registered in a log file. These log files can be very helpful if you need to understand why something does not work as expected. SharePoint has a default setting for what to log, but you can adjust these settings to match your requirements.

SharePoint has a specific service for managing these log files: *Unified Logging Service*, or ULS. This service is greatly enhanced compared to the one in the previous version of SharePoint:

➤ Event throttling gives you more granular control over what is logged.

➤ Correlation ID tracking makes it easier to see log events related to the same issue.

➤ Event Log Flood Protection (EVFP) prohibits the log files from being filled with repeating log events for the same issue. Instead there will be one event registered that also mentions how many of these events have occurred.

➤ ULS now stores all application log events, instead of using multiple log files as previous SharePoint versions did.

➤ Third-party products can be used to create log events and analyze logs in ULS. For example, in www.codeplex.com you can download "SharePoint LogViewer" and "SharePoint 2007 Features," which are free ULS viewers that also work with SharePoint 2010.

➤ PowerShell has specific commands (*cmdlets*) for managing log events.

➤ By using the file compression feature in the NTFS file system, log files are reduced in size by more than 50 percent, compared to SharePoint 2007.

Besides the ULS feature, SharePoint now also logs usage and performance information, which makes it possible for the administrator to create reports about how SharePoint is used. For example, you can create a report to see not only the most popular sites and most active users, but also how the index crawler performs and what features are used. This last feature is also very handy if you want to see how many users you have who use SharePoint Enterprise features, and compare them to the number of SharePoint Enterprise client access licenses (CALs).

All this information is first stored in log files on each SharePoint server in the farm, then the content of these log files is copied to a specific SQL database for as long as you need it; this makes comparing different time periods and seeing how features and behavior changes over time possible. The following Try It Out has the steps for managing and configuring one of these log options.

TRY IT OUT　**Manage the Usage and Health Feature**

Use these steps to view and manage the settings for the Usage and Health feature — for example, what events to log and the name of the database. In this example you change the schedule for how often the content in the log files is copied into the database to once per day.

1.　Log on as the farm administrator and start SharePoint Central Administration.

2.　Choose Monitoring ➪ Configure usage and health data collection to open the "Configure web analytics and health data collection" page.

3.　In the section "Usage Data Collection," you can see that this data collection feature is enabled by default. In the section "Event Selection" you see what events to log. By default all features are logged. Change any of these settings, if required.

4.　There are two schedule settings — one for health logging and one for log collection. In this example click Log Collection Schedule to change how often log files are imported to the database. The Job Definitions page appears, in which you define the timer jobs, and where the jobs related to log collections are listed.

5.　Click on Microsoft SharePoint Foundation Usage Data Import.

6.　You can see that the default import schedule is once every 30 minutes. Change this setting to Daily and set the start time to 12:00 a.m. and the end time to 3:00 a.m.

7.　Click OK to save and close.

The modification is now completed.

How It Works

By configuring the usage and health data collection, you can control what events to load and how often. These settings are important since they affect the performance of the server.

The following steps describe how to configure the level of detail of the information you want to log and for what features. This is especially useful when you need to investigate a reocurring error or issue. For example, say you see multiple events in the log about Visio, and you need more information to understand what to do. In this case you can increase the details about Visio Services that will be logged.

Configure the Log Details

In this example you increase the logging details for the Visio Graphics service. This can be very valuable when you are looking for information about an issue related to the Visio Graphics service. When you have solved the issue, you should restore the logging details back to the default settings.

1. Log on as the farm administrator and start SharePoint Central Administration.

2. Choose Monitoring ➪ Configure diagnostic logging to open the Diagnostic Logging page.

3. Take a moment and look at all the default settings; you will see that no specific details are logged. You can also see that the Event Flood Log Protection is enabled, as well as where the log files are stored and for how many days. Currently, no limit is set on how much disk space log files can use (that is, if you have a small disk, then it can be filled up by log files).

4. In the Event Throttling section, all available categories are listed; expand the Visio Graphics Service, and you will see six sub-categories. Select Visio Graphics Service and all sub-categories will also be selected.

5. Open the menu for the "Least critical event to report to the event log"; if you want the log to display everything, that is, events that work as well as warnings and errors, then select Verbose.

6. Select the same log level for "Least critical event to report to the trace log."

7. Click OK to save the new settings and close this page.

8. Now let the system run for some time, then investigate the log events (choose Start ➪ Administrative Tools ➪ Event Viewer) to see all the events that relate to Visio Graphics.

9. When you want to set the log level back to the default, repeat step 2, select Visio Graphics Services, and change both "Least critical event to report to the event log" and "Least critical event to report to the trace log" to the value "Reset to default." Click OK.

How It Works

Use the diagnostic logging settings to configure what level of details you need to log. Remember that increased logging also increases the CPU load and the size of log files, so stick to default levels unless you really need more information.

When you need information on how SharePoint is used by users, then look at the reports built into SharePoint Server. Note that these reports need some data to be interesting. There is not much point in creating a report if you just installed SharePoint. The following steps describe how to create and view these reports.

Create Usage Reports

1. Log on as the farm administrator and start SharePoint Central Administration.

2. Choose Monitoring ⇨ View health reports to open the "View Health Report" page, and by default the "Slowest Pages" report is displayed.

3. In the left pane you see the two types of reports you can create: Slowest Pages and Top Active Users. Select one of them, then select the server, web application, and date range, and click OK.

4. View the result: You will see different values, depending on the type of report. For example, Top Active Users lists the user names, number of requests, last access time, and percentage of successful requests.

5. Test the Slowest Pages report. It shows you a lot of information about these pages, such as average duration, maximum duration, average database queries, and number of requests. This gives you important information about your SharePoint farm, and indicates whether some web pages need to be made to load faster.

How It Works

Usage reports are created when you request them; the data comes from the log database, not the log files in the file system.

If you need more detailed reports of specific features in SharePoint, then you need the Web Analytics reports. Note that this feature is only available for the Enterprise edition of SharePoint Server 2010. These reports can be exported to Excel, and you can create custom reports. To generate a report you must first select the web application you want to analyze; then Web Analytics will provide you with a list of available reports in the left pane, divided into multiple sections. See also the following Try It Out.

➤ **Summary:** A summary of all the following sections

➤ **Traffic**

    ➤ *Number of Page Views*

    ➤ *Number of Daily Unique Visitors*

    ➤ *Number of Referrers*

    ➤ *Top Pages*

    ➤ *Top Visitors*

    ➤ *Top Referrers*

    ➤ *Top Destinations*

    ➤ *Top Browsers*

➤ Search

    ➤ *Number of Queries*

➤ Inventory

    ➤ *Number of Site Collections*

    ➤ *Top Site Collection Templates*

➤ **Customized Reports**

    ➤ *CrawlRatePerContentSource*

    ➤ *CrawlRatePerType*

    ➤ *QueryLatency*

    ➤ *QueryLatencyTrend*

    ➤ *SharePointBackendQueryLatency*

    ➤ *CrawlProcessingPerActivity (in Advanced Reports)*

    ➤ *CrawlProcessingPerComponent (in Advanced Reports)*

    ➤ *CrawlQueue (in Advanced Reports)*

> **NOTE** *Clicking on the Customized Reports link opens a new window that lists all the search administrative reports. This is the same page you see when clicking Monitoring ➪ Search administration reports, described earlier in this appendix.*

TRY IT OUT   **View Web Analytics Reports**

The following steps describe how to create the reports listed earlier.

1. Log on as the farm administrator and start SharePoint Central Administration.

2. Choose Monitoring ➪ View Web Analytics reports to open the "Web Analytics Reports — Summary" page.

3. Click on the web application you want view the reports for.

4. In the left pane of this page, select the report you want.

5. In the menu bar of the report screen, you will see the default date interval; to change it click Change Settings to display the ribbon.

6. The ribbon contains buttons for changing the date interval. To export the current report to Excel click Export to Spreadsheet.

7. You can customize some, but not all, of these reports. For example, select the report Number of Page Views, click on Change Settings, and then click the Customize Report button. This customized report requires that Excel Services is created and configured.

How It Works

Web Analytics reports are a feature only available in the Enterprise edition of SharePoint Server, because the reports are dependent on Excel Services. These reports use the same log database as for the Usage Reports.

SECURITY SETTINGS IN SHAREPOINT SERVER

The security settings for SharePoint Server are based on SharePoint Foundation. Therefore you will see a very little difference between the two versions; for example, the same type of administrator exists in SharePoint Foundation and SharePoint Server, such as farm administrators, site collection administrators, and site owners. Information about these administrators is described in Appendix B and will not be repeated here. All permission settings in SharePoint Server regarding sites, lists, and libraries are also identical to those in SharePoint Foundation.

The differences between SharePoint Foundation and SharePoint Server are really very small, and everything you can do in SharePoint Foundation you can also do in SharePoint Server. For example, all permission settings, such as *Add Items* and *Create Subsite*, are identical, except for one: *View Web Analytics Data*, which is only available in SharePoint Server Enterprise edition. To learn more about security settings in SharePoint, read Appendix B, which describes all you need to know about permissions and how you manage them.

SharePoint Groups in SharePoint Server

The only important difference between SharePoint Server and SharePoint Foundation is that SharePoint Server has more default SharePoint groups than SharePoint Foundation, because of the fact that it has more features, such as Approvers, who can approve a modified web page before it gets public — for example, a news article on the intranet. The following table compares the default SharePoint groups for SharePoint Server and SharePoint Foundation:

Default SharePoint Groups in SharePoint Server and SharePoint Foundation

SHAREPOINT GROUP	SHAREPOINT FOUNDATION	SHAREPOINT SERVER	DEFAULT PERMISSIONS
Visitors	Yes	Yes	Can read and copy information
Members	Yes	Yes	Can create and modify list items
Owners	Yes	Yes	Has full control of the site and its content
Viewers	Yes	No	Can view pages and list items, but not download documents
Approvers	No	Yes	Can edit and approve pages, list items, and documents

SHAREPOINT GROUP	SHAREPOINT FOUNDATION	SHAREPOINT SERVER	DEFAULT PERMISSIONS
Designers	No	Yes	Can edit lists, libraries, and pages. Can create Master Pages and Page Layouts, and the look and feel of the site, including CSS files
Hierarchy Managers	No	Yes	Can create sites, lists, list items, and documents
Quick Deploy Users	No	Yes	Can schedule Quick Deploy jobs
Restricted Readers	No	Yes	Can view pages and documents, but not previous versions or review user rights
Style Resource Readers	No	Yes	Can read the Master Page gallery and the Restricted read permission to the Style Library

> ⊗ **WARNING** Do Not Change the Style Resource Readers Group! *By default, all authenticated users are members of the Style Resource Readers group, which is necessary to open a site page, including its master page. Do not remove the membership of this group, nor delete this SharePoint group, unless you fully understand the consequences!*

Showing Permissions for a Specific User

"Check Permissions" is a new security-related feature in SharePoint Server, not found in MOSS 2007. It allows a site owner to view what permissions a user or group has in a particular site. This feature is also available in SharePoint Foundation and works the same way. Use it to expand a security group in Active Directory to find out about its members. This way, you can find out what permissions a given user has; the user inherits these permissions through membership in a security group.

For example, suppose that Anna is a member of the SharePoint group Intranet Visitors and of the Active Directory security group _Editors. Now assume that Intranet Visitors is granted Read access to the ABC site, and _Editors is granted Approve permissions to the same site. If you run the Check Permissions feature you will see something like Figure D-6.

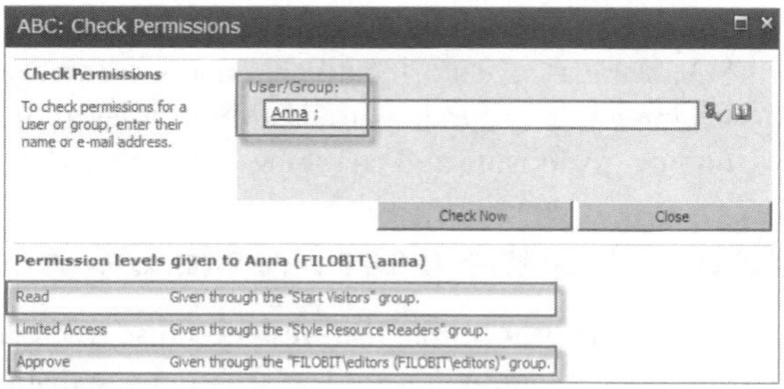

FIGURE D-6

> ✎ **NOTE** *To follow the next Try It Out you need a subsite where at least one user account is granted any type of access.*

TRY IT OUT   Show Permissions for a Specific User

This feature only works per site or subsite. You must be the site owner to check these permissions. In this example you open a subsite and see what permissions a specific user is granted.

1. Log on as a site owner and open the subsite.

2. Click Site Actions ⇨ Site Settings to open the Site Settings page.

3. Click Site permissions (in the Users and Permissions section).

4. Click Check Permissions in the ribbon.

5. Enter the name of the user — and click Check Now.

6. All permissions granted to this user appear. Close the windows when done.

How It Works

SharePoint lists all permissions granted to a specific user in a specific site. Membership in SharePoint groups and Active Directory security groups are automatically expanded, and will be listed on the result list.

MANAGING USER PROFILES

Collaboration platforms are really not that useful if they cannot manage information about their users. SharePoint 2010 is taking this issue very seriously, so one of its cornerstones is to manage all kinds of information about users, not only common properties like e-mail address, department, and who they report to, but also their expertise, responsibilities, and interests. And it does not stop there; SharePoint Server also keeps track of what keywords and tags a user adds to files and list items, plus what files he has modified, and more. All or part of this information is available to other users, depending on their permissions, either by viewing it on a specific web page named My Profile or when searching for a person.

SharePoint Server uses multiple SQL databases for storing these user properties, and then another SQL database for storing all personal information, such as documents, pictures, and blog posts. Chapter 5 describes how to use My Profiles and user properties in more detail. This section focuses on how to activate and configure the service that enables the management of user profiles.

Activating the User Profile Service Application

To activate user profile features you must create and configure the *User Profile* service application. If you ran the Configuration Wizard after the installation, you will most likely have this server up and running already. If not, see the following steps for how to create this service application. As you can see, these instructions are rather complicated, so consider running the Configuration Wizard now to create this service application.

TRY IT OUT   **Create the User Profile Service Application**

1.   Log in as a farm administrator and open SharePoint Central Administration.

2.   Later in this instruction you will need a dedicated site collection to be used by My Site, and you will need two managed paths. If you don't have them, then you must first create them using the following steps:

    a.   Click Application Management ➪ Manage web applications to open the Web Applications Management page.

    b.   Select the web application to be used by My Sites. For example, in a small organization you could use the same web application as for the intranet. Click Managed Paths on the ribbon; the Define Managed Paths appears.

    c.   Look at the Included Paths section. If it already contains the "my" and "my/personal" paths, you can go to step 2e. Otherwise, continue with the In the Path field; enter the URL path to the public part of My Site — for example, **my** — and set the Type to Explicit inclusion, then click the Add Path button. This new path now appears.

    d.   In the Path field, enter the second URL path, this time for all users' personal My Sites — for example, **my/personal** — set the Type to Wildcard inclusion, and then click Add Path. Both these new paths are now listed. Make sure they have the correct type set.

    e.   Click OK to close this form.

    f.   Continue by creating the new site collection for My Site: Click Application Management ➪ Create site collections. A new form opens.

    g.   Make sure the listed web application (at the top of this form, in yellow) is the same as the one you created the managed path for in step 2c; if it's not, click on the web application name and change it.

    h.   Fill in the title; for example, **My Site**.

    i.   Open the URL menu and set the explicit inclusion managed path created in step 2c; for example, **/my**.

    j.   In the section Template Selection, select the My Site Host template on the Enterprise tab.

    k.   In the Primary Site Collection Administrator field, enter the Farm Administrator account name.

    l.   Click OK to create this site collection. Now you have the site collection and managed path that you will need later in steps 4p and 4q.

3.   Click Application Management ➪ Manage service applications to open the Manage Service Applications page.

4.   In the ribbon, click New ➪ User Profile Service Application. The "Create New User Profile Service Application" form opens where you define the properties for this service from top to bottom:

    a.   Enter a descriptive name; for example, **User Profile Service Application**.

    b.   Select "Use existing application pool," and from its menu choose SharePoint Web Services Default. Creating a new application pool is also possible, but this is the one the Configuration Wizard would choose.

c. In the Profile Database section, enter the database server name. Typically you use the default database server.

d. Enter the SQL database name; for example, **User Profile Service Application ProfileDB**.

e. Make sure to use Windows authentication for the database authentication mechanism.

f. Enter the failover database server name, if you have one.

g. In the Synchronization Database section, enter the database server name; typically you will use the default database server.

h. Enter the name for this synchronization database; for example, **User Profile Service Application_SyncDB**.

i. Make sure to use Windows authentication for the database authentication mechanism.

j. Enter the failover database server name, if you have one.

k. In the Social Tagging section, enter the database server name; typically you will use the default database server.

l. Enter the database name; for example, **User Profile Service Application_SocialDB**.

m. Make sure to use Windows authentication for the database authentication mechanism.

n. Enter the failover database server name, if you have one.

o. In the Profile Synchronization Instance section, enter the SharePoint server in the farm you want to run the synchronization process.

p. In the My Site Host URL section, enter the URL to an existing site collection that will host users' My Sites. Note that this site collection must be built using the My Site Host site template or no site template at all — for example, `http://srv1:80/my/`.

q. In the My Site Managed Path section, enter the managed URL path to each user's personal My Site — for example, **my/personal**.

r. In the Site Naming Format section, select what type of naming standard to use for users' personal sites; the default is "User name (do not resolve conflict)," which works fine in a single Active Directory domain environment, because each user's site URL would be based on his or her account name. For example, a user with the logon name "anna" would get `http://srv1/my/personal/anna`. If there are multiple AD domains you should consider one of the other two naming options: "User name (resolve conflicts by using domain_username)" or "Domain and user name (will not have conflicts)."

s. Click OK to save and close this form.

How It Works

SharePoint uses three different databases for storing all information related to users. These three databases are associated with the User Profile service application. Two specific site collections are used for enabling the My Site feature: one for the public site that shows the user's public information and properties, and one for the user's private My Site.

Configuring User Profile Synchronization

All user properties must come from somewhere, either from the user herself who enters these properties by using her My Site, or from the farm administrator who enters these properties by using SharePoint Central Administration. But you can also configure SharePoint to synchronize these properties with external systems, such as Active Directory, and other databases that understand the Lightweight Directory Access Protocol (LDAP) standard, such as Microsoft SQL, Oracle, and Novell eDirectory. The first Try It Out in this section describes how the farm administrator can configure what properties exist and how to enter their values. The second part of this section describes how to configure SharePoint Server to synchronize with AD.

Managing User Profile Properties

Before you can manage user profile properties, you need the User Profile service application running. You also need the proper permission to manage these properties; by default, this is only granted to the farm administrator.

Take a look at the default settings for these user profile properties: Open the SharePoint Central Administration tool, then click Application Management ➪ Manage service applications and click on User Profile Service Application to open a new configuration page with links to all the features related to user profiles (see Figure D-7).

People Manage User Properties | Manage User Profiles | Manage User Sub-types | Manage Audiences | Schedule Audience Compilation | Manage User Permissions | Compile Audiences | Profile services policies	**Profiles** Number of User Profiles — 1 Number of User Properties — 67 Number of Organization Profiles — 1 Number of Organization Properties 15 **Audiences**
Synchronization Configure Synchronization Connections | Configure Synchronization Timer Job | Configure Synchronization Settings | Start Profile Synchronization	Number of Audiences — 1 Uncompiled Audiences — 0 Audience Compilation Status — Idle Audience Compilation Schedule — Every Saturday at 01:00 AM
Organizations Manage Organization Properties | Manage Organization Profiles | Manage Organization Sub-types	Last Compilation Time — Not compiled **Profile Import Settings** Profile Import Status — Idle Membership and BDC Import Status Idle
My Site Settings Setup My Sites | Configure Trusted Host Locations | Configure Personalization Site | Publish Links to Office Client Applications | Manage Social Tags and Notes	Current Import Stage — None Import Schedule(Incremental) — No schedule set

FIGURE D-7

By default, SharePoint keeps track of 58 properties for each user and 11 properties related to the users' organization, as listed in the following table.

User Profile Properties

PROPERTY NAME	PROPERTY TYPE
Id	Unique identifier
SID	Binary
Active Directory Id	Binary

continues

(continued)

PROPERTY NAME	PROPERTY TYPE
Account name	Person
First name	String (Single Value)
Phonetic First Name	String (Single Value)
Last name	String (Single Value)
Phonetic Last Name	String (Single Value)
Name	String (Single Value)
Phonetic Display Name	String (Single Value)
Work phone	String (Single Value)
Department	String (Single Value)
Title	String (Single Value)
About me	HTML
Personal site	URL
Picture	URL
User name	String (Single Value)
Quick links	String (Single Value)
Web site	URL
Public site redirect	URL
Data source	String (Single Value)
MemberOf	String (Multi Value)
Dotted-line Manager	Person
Peers	String (Single Value)
Ask Me About	String (Multi Value)
Skills	String (Multi Value)
Interests	String (Multi Value)
SIP Address	String (Single Value)
My Site Upgrade	Boolean
Don't Suggest List	Person
Proxy address	String (Multi Value)
Hire date	Date
Display Order	Integer
Claim User Identifier	String (Single Value)

PROPERTY NAME	PROPERTY TYPE
Claim Provider Identifier	String (Single Value)
Claim Provider Type	String (Single Value)
Last Colleague Added	Date
Outlook Web Access URL	URL
Saved Account Name	String (Single Value)
Saved SID	Binary
Resource Forest SID	Binary
Object Exists	String (Single Value)
Office Location	String (Single Value)
Time Zone	Time zone
Distinguished Name	String (Single Value)
Source Object Distinguished Name	String (Multi Value)
Last Keyword Added	Date
Work e-mail	E-mail
Mobile phone	String (Single Value)
Fax	String (Single Value)
Home phone	String (Single Value)
Office	String (Single Value)
Past projects	String (Multi Value)
Schools	String (Multi Value)
Birthday	Date no year
Assistant	Person
Status Message	String (Single Value)
E-mail Notifications	Integer

As an administrator you can add, modify, or delete these properties by clicking on the property name, then selecting Edit in the menu that appears. For example, one company may need to keep track of each user's shoe size, golf handicap, or how many times she has been married. Just add the properties you need, configure whether the user herself is allowed to enter the value, then configure who will see this information; for example, everyone, or just the user's manager. Follow these steps to view and manage user profile properties.

TRY IT OUT   Add User Profile Properties

In this example you add a new property for storing the user's golf handicap. Users should be able to enter this value themselves. Its value should be visible to everyone.

1. Log on as the farm administrator and open SharePoint Central Administration.

2. Click Application Management ➪ Manage service applications to open the "Manage Service Application" page.

3. Locate the user profile service, by default named User Profile Service Application, and click on its name to open its management page (or select it and click Manage on the ribbon).

4. Click Manage User Properties. This displays all current properties.

5. Click the New Property button and enter these values in the new form:

    a. Name: **GolfHandicap**

    b. Display Name: **Golf Handicap**

    c. Type: Integer

    d. Default User Profile Subtype: Yes

    e. Description: **Enter your current Golf Handicap**

    f. Policy Setting: Optional

    g. Default Privacy Setting: Everyone

    h. Select the "Allow users to edit values for this property" option.

    i. Select the "Show on the Edit Details page" option.

    j. Click OK to save and close this new property.

6. Verify that the new property is listed under the Custom Properties section header.

How It Works

Each user property is stored in a SQL database, managed by the User Profile service application. The administrator can add, delete, and modify user properties. The administrator can configure the value for a user property to be set manually by the user (using My Site), set by the administrator (using SharePoint Central Administration), or imported from external data sources, such as Active Directory.

This new property is now visible on each user's My Profile page; the user can set its value by clicking Edit My Profile on the Overview tab in his or her personal My Profile site.

Other user properties may be synchronized with an external data source, typically Active Directory, as described in the next section.

Importing User Properties

When adding user properties it quickly becomes obvious that neither the users themselves nor an administrator should enter the values of user properties. The reason for this is typically that these properties already exist in another data source, for example Active Directory, and you want to avoid entering the same properties in more than one place. This is where user profile synchronization gets interesting. This feature allows SharePoint to read most external data sources and import their values into a corresponding user property in SharePoint's User Profile database. By default, SharePoint can import values from these sources:

- ➤ Active Directory
- ➤ Any source available through Business Data Connectivity
- ➤ IBM Directory (LDAP)
- ➤ Novel eDirectory (LDAP)
- ➤ Sun ONE Directory (LDAP)

The most common import source is Active Directory, for properties such as e-mail address, department, phone number, and title. To configure this import, you follow these steps:

1. Configure the synchronization connection.
2. Configure synchronization timer jobs.
3. Define what properties to import.

The last step is, by default, automatically configured for a number of properties when the data source is Active Directory. Still, you may want to change these values or configure more properties to be imported. These steps are covered in the following Try It Out.

TRY IT OUT Configure Synchronization Connections

In this example, you configure a synchronization connection to an Active Directory domain named filobit.com and import properties for all user accounts. You will use the account filobit\sp_centraladmin, which must be a member of the Domain Admin group to have the permissions needed to manage Active Directory. Be sure to replace these example values to match your own setup when configuring your production environment!

1. Log on as a farm administrator, then open SharePoint Central Administration.
2. Click Application Management ➪ Manage service applications.
3. Click User Profile Service Application to open its Manage page.
4. In the Synchronization section, click Configure Synchronization Connection to open the Synchronization Connections page.
5. Click Create New Connection and set the following values (see also Figure D-8). Remember to replace these values with your own:
   a. Connection Name: Filobit
   b. Type: Active Directory
   c. Forest Name: filobit.com
   d. Accept the default option "Auto discover domain controller."
   e. Accept Windows Authentication as the authentication provider type.

f.   Account Name: filobit\sp_centraladmin

g.   Password: Enter the password twice for this account.

h.   Accept the default Port number 389.

i.   Click Populate Containers to display a tree view of all AD containers. If you don't see any containers, verify that the forest name is correct and that the account in step f is allowed to read AD.

j.   Select the top container FILOBIT; this automatically selects all subcontainers as well.

k.   Click OK to save and close this page; the Synchronization Connections page reappears, and the new connection is listed.

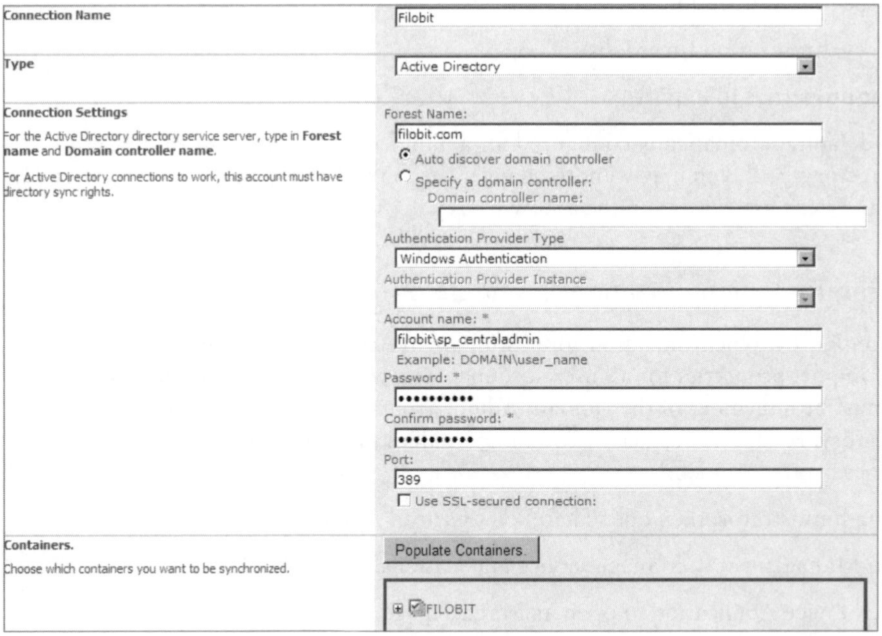

Connection Name	Filobit
Type	Active Directory
Connection Settings For the Active Directory directory service server, type in **Forest name** and **Domain controller name**. For Active Directory connections to work, this account must have directory sync rights.	Forest Name: filobit.com ◉ Auto discover domain controller ○ Specify a domain controller: Domain controller name: Authentication Provider Type Windows Authentication Authentication Provider Instance Account name: * filobit\sp_centraladmin Example: DOMAIN\user_name Password: * •••••••••• Confirm password: * •••••••••• Port: 389 ☐ Use SSL-secured connection:
Containers. Choose which containers you want to be synchronized.	Populate Containers ⊞ ☑FILOBIT

FIGURE D-8

How It Works

SharePoint Server can import properties from external data sources, such as Active Directory. Writing back from SharePoint's user profile settings to that external data source is also possible, but is not described here since it is beyond the scope of this book.

TRY IT OUT   Configure a Synchronization Timer Job

This is the second step when configuring a user profile import. In this example, you configure the import to run between 3:00 and 4:00 a.m. every day.

1.   Open the User Profile Service Application management page again (see steps 1–3 in the previous Try It Out).

2.   Click Configure Synchronization Timer Jobs to open the "Edit Timer Job" page, and then fill in the following values:

   a.   In the Recurring Schedule section, select the option Daily and set the start time to 3:00 a.m. and stop time to 4:00 a.m.

   b.   Click Enable to save these settings and start this timer job.

3.   The Timer Job Definitions page opens. Verify that you can find the User Profile Service Application — User Profile Incremental Import Job listed; click on this job to verify that it is running. Click Run Now to start the import now (see Figure D-9).

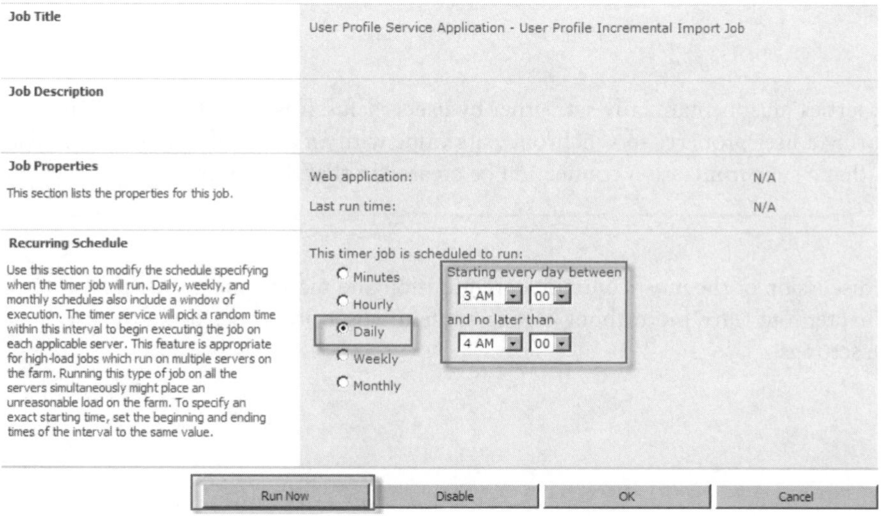

Job Title	User Profile Service Application - User Profile Incremental Import Job
Job Description	
Job Properties	Web application: N/A
This section lists the properties for this job.	Last run time: N/A

Recurring Schedule

Use this section to modify the schedule specifying when the timer job will run. Daily, weekly, and monthly schedules also include a window of execution. The timer service will pick a random time within this interval to begin executing the job on each applicable server. This feature is appropriate for high-load jobs which run on multiple servers on the farm. Running this type of job on all the servers simultaneously might place an unreasonable load on the farm. To specify an exact starting time, set the beginning and ending times of the interval to the same value.

This timer job is scheduled to run:

- Minutes
- Hourly
- Daily
- Weekly
- Monthly

Starting every day between 3 AM : 00
and no later than 4 AM : 00

[Run Now]   [Disable]   [OK]   [Cancel]

FIGURE D-9

4.   Open the User Profile Service Application management page again. Verify that the information in the Profile Import Settings section (in the right pane of this page) matches your settings; you should also see that the Number of User Profiles increases as the import process proceeds.

How It Works

The synchronization timer job enables the farm administrator to define the schedule for importing (and exporting, if enabled) user properties, using the synchronization connection.

> **TRY IT OUT**   Configure an Existing Property to Synchronize with AD
>
> This final step is optional. Use it if you want to enable the import of a user property in SharePoint from an existing property in Active Directory. In this example you import the AD property "mobile" to the SharePoint user property "Mobile phone."
>
> **1.**   Continue on the User Profile Service Application management page.
>
> **2.**   Click on Manage User Properties.
>
> **3.**   Click on Mobile phone, then select Edit and fill in these values:
>
>   **a.**   Scroll down this page to the Add New Mapping section.
>
>   **b.**   Set Source Data Connection to Filobit (that is, the connection you defined earlier).
>
>   **c.**   Set the Attribute to Mobile.
>
>   **d.**   Set the Direction to Import.
>
>   **e.**   Click OK to save and close.
>
> **4.**   Verify that the property now is listed as importing from AD.
>
> ### How It Works
>
> By default, all user properties must be manually set, either by users themselves or by the SharePoint administrator. Configuring a user property to synchronize its value with an external data source is also possible. This requires that a synchronization connection be created to that data source.

This concludes the discussion of the most common configuration and management settings for user profiles. See Chapter 5 to learn more about how to configure user properties using the user's personal My Profile settings.

▶ WHAT YOU LEARNED IN THIS APPENDIX

TOPIC	KEY CONCEPTS
General SharePoint Server configurations	SharePoint Server is based on SharePoint Foundation, so you need to understand how to configure SharePoint Foundation before configuring SharePoint Server. Make sure to read Appendix B before reading this Appendix D.
	SharePoint Server uses the same default web applications and application pools as SharePoint Foundation.
Installation of SharePoint Server 2010	Hardware minimum requirements: 4GB memory
	Software requirements: Windows Server 2008 or 2008 R2, 64-bit
	SQL Server 2005, 2008, or 2008 R2 is required (all 64 bits).
	The included SQL Server is limited to 4GB per database.
Web applications ("web app")	A web app is an extended IIS website.
	A web app hosts one or more site collections.
	A web app is always associated with one or more SQL Server databases.
	A web app is contained inside an application pool.
Service applications	Replaces the SSP in MOSS 2007.
	Several of these service applications are enhanced versions of the services in SSP in MOSS 2007; for example, Search and Excel Services.
	SharePoint Server Standard comes with 10 default service applications.
	SharePoint Server Enterprise comes with 17 default service applications.
	Most service applications have one or more SQL databases. Some have three databases.
	A default installation of SharePoint Server Enterprise edition creates close to 20 SQL databases.
Managed metadata	To enable tags, keywords, and structured metadata, you need to create a Managed Metadata service application.
	The Managed Metadata service application is also used for creating a "master" site content type; that is, a content type that can be utilized in any site collection in a farm.
SharePoint Server administration	Very similar to SharePoint Foundation administration, except that it has a lot more configuration settings.
	A user can be granted administrative permission to a farm or to a specific part; for example, a service application.

continues

(continued)

TOPIC	KEY CONCEPTS
Security settings in SharePoint Server	Uses the same settings as in SharePoint Foundation. One difference between SharePoint Server and SharePoint Foundation is that SharePoint Server has more SharePoint groups than SharePoint Foundation. You can list all permissions granted to a user for a specific site, but not for a complete farm or site collection.
User profiles	Create a User Profile service application to enable management of user properties, personal My Sites, and organizational tree views. By default, 67 user profiles are created per user; 58 of these are configurable using the User Profile service application in SharePoint Central Administration. User properties can be synchronized with external data sources, such as Active Directory and LDAP-compatible data sources. You can create new user properties when needed, either for manual update or for synchronization with external data sources.

INDEX